# British Politics

## Second Edition

ROBERT LEACH
BILL COXALL
LYNTON ROBINS

palgrave
macmillan

First published as *Contemporary British Politics* in 1989
Second edition 1994
Third edition 1998
Fourth edition 2003

First published as *British Politics* in 2006

Second edition published 2011 by
PALGRAVE MACMILLAN

Palgrave Macmillan in the UK is an imprint of Macmillan Publishers Limited,
registered in England, company number 785998, of Houndmills, Basingstoke,
Hampshire RG21 6XS.

Palgrave Macmillan in the US is a division of St Martin's Press LLC,
175 Fifth Avenue, New York, NY 10010.

Palgrave Macmillan is the global academic imprint of the above companies
and has companies and representatives throughout the world.

Palgrave® and Macmillan® are registered trademarks in the United States,
the United Kingdom, Europe and other countries

ISBN  978-0-230-27233-0    hardback
ISBN  978-0-230-27234-7    paperback

This book is printed on paper suitable for recycling and made from fully
managed and sustained forest sources. Logging, pulping and manufacturing
processes are expected to conform to the environmental regulations of the
country of origin.

A catalogue record for this book is available from the British Library.

Library of Congress Cataloging-in-Publication Data
Leach, Robert, 1941–
British politics / Robert Leach, Bill Coxall, Lynton Robins. —2nd ed.
p. cm.
Includes index.
ISBN 978–0–230–27234–7 (alk. paper)
1. Great Britain—Politics and government.  I. Coxall, W. N.
II. Robins, L. J. (Lynton J. )  III. Title.
JN318.L43 2011
320.441—dc22                                        2011008508

10  9  8  7  6  5  4  3  2  1
20  19  18  17  16  15  14  13  12  11

Printed and bound in China

British Politics

## Palgrave Foundations

*A series of introductory texts across a wide range of subject areas to meet the needs of today's lecturers and students*

*Foundations* texts provide complete yet concise coverage of core topics and skills based on detailed research of course requirements suitable for both independent study and class use – the firm foundations for future study.

Published

*A History of English Literature (second edition)*
*Biology*
*British Politics (second edition)*
*Chemistry (fourth edition)*
*Communication Studies*
*Contemporary Europe (third edition)*
*Economics*
*Economics for Business*
*European Union Politics*
*Foundations of Marketing*
*Global Politics*
*Modern British History*
*Nineteenth-Century Britain*
*Philosophy*
*Physics (third edition)*
*Politics (third edition)*
*Theatre Studies*

# Contents

# List of Illustrative Material

## Key Thinkers

## Images

# Preface

The 2010 UK general election marked the end of thirteen years of Labour rule, by far the longest continuous period that party had enjoyed in office. It also produced the first hung Parliament since 1974, and subsequently the first British coalition government since 1945. The Conservative–Liberal Democrat coalition has already marked out much of its programme for a whole parliament, and has changed the style of British politics. How far it will eventually transform its substance remains to be seen. There is never an ideal time to produce a new book on British politics – authors and publishers always risk being overtaken by events. Yet this seems a good time to re-examine British government and politics, to review what appears novel and reappraise its more familiar principles and practices.

The content of this new edition is now almost wholly my personal responsibility. I had no part in the first three editions of this book's predecessor, *Contemporary British Politics* (1989, 1994, 1998). It was Bill Coxall and Lynton Robins who deserve the credit for establishing this successful textbook. I was initially drafted in to work with Lynton after the sad death of Bill Coxall in 1999, and took the lead in preparing the fourth and final edition of *Contemporary British Politics* (2003). Lynton then decided to withdraw from active participation, while the publishers Palgrave Macmillan thought this was an appropriate time for a more comprehensive rewrite and redesign. The first edition of *British Politics* appeared as part of their Foundations series in 2006.

That book, only a few years old, now seems a record of a past political age. Then Blair was still Prime Minister, and Brown as Chancellor presided over a booming economy. Ken Livingstone remained Mayor of London and Labour the dominant partner of a coalition government in Scotland, while the impasse in Northern Ireland persisted. The remarkable DUP–Sinn Fein power-sharing agreement, the SNP minority government in Edinburgh, the whole Brown premiership, the global financial crisis and economic recession, and the spending cuts of the Cameron-led coalition that emerged from the 2010 election still lay in the future. However, while it is now all change at the top in terms of party, personnel and policy, some other aspects of British and global politics have shown a more depressing continuity. These include the persistent threat of terrorism, the enduring quagmire of Iraq and Afghanistan, and the lack of progress in tackling the linked problems of climate change and world poverty. This new edition has to cover all this, and much else besides. It has necessarily involved not just extensive updating of every chapter, but substantial restructuring of material, and some radical revision of analysis.

The original expectation was to publish earlier in 2011. However a decision was taken to delay publication until after the results of the Alternative Vote referendum and elections in May 2011. There is never an ideal time to publish a new book on British politics – one always risks being overtaken by events. Yet in retrospect the delay was more than justified, as the conduct of the AV campaign and its outcome, combined with election results, have considerable implications for the future of the coalition government. Moreover, the remarkable elections for the Scottish Parliament have finally alerted those living south of Hadrian's Wall that the break up of the United Kingdom is now a real possibility. The delay has also allowed some coverage of dramatic developments in the wider world and UK foreign policy.

The design and presentation has also been substantially transformed along with much of the content. This should make the book not only more attractive in appearance, but more user-friendly. However, older readers will still find that most of the features of the previous edition have been retained and in many cases extended and improved. These features include chapter summaries and questions for further discussions, as well as extensive boxed material on comparative politics, key thinkers, and academic controversy.

There are also copious highlighted definitions, as well as numerous maps, timelines, charts, figures, tables and photos to illustrate the text.

As always, I owe many debts. Some of those to other academic sources will be obvious from the bibliography. I also owe a considerable debt of gratitude to an anonymous reviewer of an earlier draft whose warm and enthusiastic support was encouraging, but whose perceptive comments on some chapters led to some restructuring of material as well as correction of a few embarrassing 'typing errors'. I would also like to thank Stephen Wenham and Helen Caunce of Palgrave Macmillan for their encouragement and help throughout, and Keith Povey and Ian Wileman for their extremely thorough and professional editing and presentation of my text. However, my greatest debt is, as ever, to my wife Judith.

ROBERT LEACH

The author and publishers would like to thank the following who have kindly given permission for the use of pictorial copyright material:

Press Association, pp. 6, 22, 86, 101, 122, 123, 130, 134, 149, 150, 162, 182, 221, 232, 254, 278, 318, 433; Getty, pp. 120, 315; Judith Leach, p. 292; Robert Dahl, p. 152; Photofusion, p. 406; European Union, p. 182; Library of Congress, p. 177; Maria Novak, p. 129. The image on p. 203 is reproduced under terms of the Open Government Licence v1.0.

Every effort has been made to contact all the copyright-holders, but if any have been inadvertently omitted the publisher will be pleased to make the necessary arrangement at the earliest opportunity.

# CHAPTER 1

# Politics, Democracy and Power

Politics has engaged some of the greatest human minds, from Plato and Aristotle in the fourth century BCE onwards. It continues to fascinate, to judge simply from the increasing numbers studying the subject. Yet the fascination is far from universal. *Why We Hate Politics* is the title of one recent book by a British academic (Hay, 2007), written in response to evidence of increasing political disillusionment and apathy, and before the parliamentary expenses scandal of 2009 powerfully reinforced public alienation in Britain from politicians and political parties. This alienation is disturbing, not least because the United Kingdom, along with most other countries in the world, claims to be a democracy, a system of government that requires some public political interest and involvement. Indeed another prominent political scientist has found it necessary to explain *Why Politics Matters* (Stoker, 2006).

Perhaps we should not be surprised that the subject inspires such contradictory feelings. Politics is bound up with controversy, which is one reason why it both attracts and repels. Some of this controversy surrounds burning current political issues, including contrasting approaches to reducing the budget deficit and regulating the banking system in the wake of the financial crisis, or tackling climate change or global poverty. Some of it concerns the mechanics of government and the political process, such as reforming the electoral system and parliament or re-examining the rela-

tionship between the constituent nations of the United Kingdom. Some of it relates to deeper questions that have long exercised philosophers and political scientists over ideas and values, the distribution of political power, and the nature of politics itself, which is the subject of this chapter.

## What is politics?

Various answers have been given to the simple question 'What is politics?'

- 'The science and art of government'
  (Shorter Oxford English Dictionary)
- 'Who gets what, when, how'
  (H. Lasswell, American political scientist)
- 'The authoritative allocation of value'
  (David Easton, American political scientist)
- 'The art of the possible'
  (R. A. Butler, British Conservative politician)

The first definition links politics and government in a common-sense way. B. Guy Peters (in Leftwich, 2004, p. 23) similarly proclaims: 'The ultimate and defining purpose of politics is governing and making public policy.' Clearly politics is about government, and this book analyses at some length the institutions of government. Yet this definition implies that politics is a rather remote activity, not for ordinary people. How far does politics include the governed as well as those doing the governing?

And does it just involve the government of states? Some definitions of politics suggest not only that it is a universal human activity, as the ancient Greek philosopher Aristotle argued, but that it can take place at very different levels and in different spheres. Thus some talk of the politics of the golf club, or the boardroom, or the university. However, the study of politics does in practice focus largely on states rather than what is sometimes called 'micro-politics'.

The two crisp American definitions suggest (in rather different language) that politics is about choosing between alternatives. Individuals, communities and governments cannot have everything they want, but must determine their priorities. Butler hints at the constraints involved in the political process. Compromise is often necessary because different sections of the community want different and often conflicting things. It is not possible to please everyone all the time. Thus political decisions commonly produce winners and losers.

Some have seen disagreement and conflict as the very essence of politics, and emphasize its violent and coercive side, which may appear only too obvious in the modern world. Thus the Chinese Communist leader Mao Zedong, asserted 'Political power grows out of the barrel of a gun', while the German military strategist Von Clausewitz claimed 'War is nothing but a continuation of politics by other means.' Often, 'might' seems to matter more than 'right'. Indeed, those who have physical force on their side may determine what is right. Justice appears to be merely 'what is in the interests of the stronger party' (as the sophist Thrasymachus declared in Plato's *Republic*, one of the earliest and most celebrated analyses of politics).

Yet such interpretations of politics do not tell the whole story. Politics may arise out of disagreement and conflict, which can sometimes take a violent form, but it also involves the search for a peaceful resolution of conflict through compromise. Political power may be used for constructive as well destructive purposes. Indeed a 'political solution' is commonly seen as an alternative to violence. Winston Churchill, famous largely as a great war leader, once observed 'Jaw jaw is better than war war', while a noted French political scien-

tist, Maurice Duverger (1972, p. 221), defined politics as 'a continual effort to eliminate physical violence'. Politics, he claimed, 'tends to replace fists, knives, clubs and rifles with other types of weapons', although he added sadly, 'it is not always successful in doing so.'

## The scope of politics: the role of the state

The study of politics from earliest times has focused largely on a unit of government called the **state**. States have differed considerably in geographical extent and population size over space and time, from the small 'city states' of ancient Greece, through more recent nation states and colonial empires to the considerable variation in size and wealth of modern independent sovereign states. The state which is the focus of this book is the United Kingdom of Great Britain and Northern Ireland, which is just one of 192 independent sovereign states who today are members of the United Nations.

The term 'independent sovereign state' is commonly used to stress that the state has supreme (or sovereign) power within its own borders, and no external power can interfere in its internal affairs. No particular system of government is implied. A state can be an hereditary monarchy, a military dictatorship or a representative democracy. The state is (substantially) a 'compulsory' association for those who live within its borders (see Weber's definition below). Membership is not voluntary as it is (normally) for political parties, or groups promoting an interest or cause. Compulsion suggests an element of coercion, sometimes involving physical force. Many states were first established by conquest or revolution, although some grew through the dynastic alliances of their rulers. More recently states have sometimes combined or split following the votes of their citizens in plebiscites.

---

● A **state** is a political and governmental unit – a compulsory association that is sovereign over a particular territory.
'The state is a human community that (successfully) claims the monopoly of the legitimate use of physical force within a given territory (Max Weber, German sociologist).

Weber's standard definition also recognizes that the authority of the state rests ultimately on force, but his emphasis is different. The state has a *monopoly* of the use of *legitimate* force within a given territory. Without such a monopoly, individuals and groups can take the law into their own hands with impunity, and there is lawless chaos, as in some modern 'failed states'. Weber also stresses that the force is legitimate (or lawful). This may mean simply that the state is widely accepted as legitimate and acts within the law that it has itself established. In practice states established through violent usurpation or conquest often acquire legitimacy over time, through the acquiescence or willing acceptance of their subjects and through their acceptance by the governments of other states.

There are wide disagreements over the role of the state and the scope of politics. Some liberals and conservatives would draw a clear distinction between the state and **civil society**, between a public or political sphere and a private sphere of life from which politics should be excluded – for example, the family and other voluntary associations.

Champions of the free market would seek to exclude the state (and politics) from much economic activity, and place firm limits on government intervention. By contrast, many socialists have sought to establish a political system in which the state controlled the economy (see Chapter 7). Fascism was associated with a totalitarian theory of the state, under which the state was all-embracing and excluded from no sphere of activity.

While some of these approaches to politics have become less fashionable, other contemporary political ideologies have involved a radical reinterpretation of the scope and the legitimate sphere of politics. Thus feminists insist 'the personal is political'. They are not just concerned with formal legal equality in the public sphere, but with gender relations in the family, home and bedroom, because these are seen as central to the injustice and oppression suffered by women. Consequently, interpersonal relations, sexual relations and the division of labour within the home are not purely

private matters but a legitimate sphere for political engagement. At another level Green ideas have politicized a whole range of issues relating to the environment which at one time were seen as having not much, if anything, to do with politics (see Chapter 7).

## Authority, power and influence

Politics is clearly about **power**, but this key concept is difficult to define. Power suggests a capacity to achieve desired results, and compel obedience. It may be lawful or unlawful. An armed criminal may force his victims to do things that they would not choose. He is clearly exercising power, although unlawfully. Others, such as a government minister or a judge, may also wield effective power, but power which is generally recognized as lawful. The term **authority** is widely used to describe the rightful use of political power, or legitimate power. Power may compel obedience, while authority is widely accepted by those over whom it is exercised. We voluntarily obey those in authority because we accept the legitimacy of their power.

Why do we obey them? The German sociologist Max Weber distinguished between three main types or sources of authority: traditional, charismatic and legal-rational. Traditional authority rests on long-established custom – the authority of a tribal chief or hereditary monarch, for example. Charismatic authority derives from the compelling personal qualities of an individual – the authority exercised by a Napoleon, Hitler or (more positively) Nelson Mandela. They are obeyed because of *who* they are, rather than because of *what* they are. Legal-rational authority is authority based on formal rules. An elected politician or appointed government official may be obeyed, not because of custom, nor because of their personal qualities, but because it is acknowledged that they legitimately hold their office under accepted rules and procedures. It is the office or post rather than the person occupying it whose authority is obeyed. Weber considered that legal-rational authority is the characteristic form of authority in the modern world. Both modern

---

● **Civil society** refers to the part of social life which is (or some consider should be) outside the control of the state, e.g. clubs, groups and associations, private business, the family.

---

● **Power** is the capacity to achieve desired goals.

---

● **Authority** is the rightful or legitimate use of power.

bureaucracy and representative democracy involve legal-rational authority.

Power is sometimes also distinguished from **influence**. While power implies a capacity to determine outcomes directly, influence suggests the ability to shape outcomes indirectly, to exert pressure on those who are taking the decisions, persuading them to change their opinion and behaviour. The study of politics involves examining not just the formal institutions and offices directly involved in government, but also the influences on government and the policy process, the role, for example, of business organizations and trade unions, religious sects, voluntary bodies and cause groups. Many political decisions taken by politicians or civil servants may have their origin and explanation in the successful influence of groups outside government (see Chapter 8).

## Democracy – power to the people?

Britain, along with most states in the modern western world, and many others elsewhere, claims to be a **democracy**. This near universal approval of democracy as a system of government is relatively recent. A form of democracy flourished in ancient Athens nearly two and a half thousand years ago, but from then until at least the late eighteenth century democracy scarcely existed anywhere, and was regarded as a remote and essentially impractical system of government. While direct rule by all the people themselves was just about possible in a small city state like ancient Athens, it was impractical for the extensive empires and large nation states which have flourished subsequently.

Democracy became more feasible with the development in the nineteenth century of **representative democracy**, government by the elected

---

● **Influence** involves the ability to shape a decision or outcome through various forms of pressure.

---

● **Democracy** is a term derived from ancient Greek to mean the rule or power of the people.
'Our constitution is called a democracy because power is in the hands not of a minority but of the whole people.'
    (Pericles of Athens, 431 BCE, as reported in Thucydides' *History of the Peloponnesian War* (tr. Warner), p, 145)
The former US President Abraham Lincoln defined democracy as 'government of the people, by the people, for the people'
    (1863, Gettysburg address).

---

representatives of the people, rather than **direct democracy,** or government by the people themselves. It is representative democracy rather than direct democracy that has become the approved system of government over much of the modern world, although some advocate extending direct citizen participation in the political process beyond voting, infusing representative democracy with elements of direct democracy.

Democracy may have become widely approved (at least in theory) but it has often been accorded only faint praise by some influential modern thinkers and politicians. Whether modern representative democracy does ensure real government by the people, as Abraham Lincoln asserted, is far from clear. Indeed it does not even invariably result in a government chosen by the majority of the people (see Chapter 5). Yet at a minimum in mature democratic systems it does offer an element of real choice between rival parties and

---

● **Representative democracy** involves indirect government by the people through representatives elected by the people.

---

● **Direct democracy** involves the direct and continuous participation of citizens in government.

programmes, it does render opposition respectable rather than treasonable, and it does provide for the peaceful transfer of power between governments. These are very considerable benefits which should not be under-rated, particularly when the alternatives are considered.

While the British like to think they invented modern representative democracy, the Americans and the French have a rather better claim. The American rebels against the British state and crown, through their successful Declaration of Independence of 1776, and the constitution they devised for the United States of America soon afterwards, effectively created what was to become the first modern democracy. The French revolution of 1789 substituted the ideas of popular sovereignty and liberty, equality and fraternity (initially only briefly) for the autocracy of the old French monarchy.

Britain only came to terms with democracy rather later. Although England boasts an ancient Parliament with over seven hundred years of near continuous existence since it was established in 1265, even the lower house of that Parliament, the House of Commons, was not democratically elected until recently. Only a small proportion of adult males could participate in elections until a series of Reform Acts extended the vote to most men in the course of the nineteenth century. Women could not vote until 1918, and they only obtained the vote on the same terms as men in 1928. Even today it is questionable how far Britain satisfies all the conditions to qualify as a full and fair system of representative democracy (see Box 1.2).

How far and fully Britain satisfies these conditions will be discussed in more detail later in this book (particularly in Chapter 5), although it would be generally conceded that British elections do involve a real choice and that they are not patently rigged (as they are in some countries). Yet regardless of the extent of the right to vote and the mechanics of the electoral system, there are many who would question whether 'government of the people, by the people, for the people' is a reality in Britain. Are the elected representatives of the people the real rulers of Britain? Do these elected representatives really serve the interests of the people, or simply their own interests? (This was a

## BOX 1.2

# Conditions for representative democracy

- Full adult franchise – all adults have the right to vote
- A secret ballot – helps ensure voting without intimidation or bribery
- Regular elections – governments and parliaments must not be able to postpone elections
- Fair elections – each vote should count equally
- An effective choice of candidates and parties for voters
- A level playing field between rival parties and candidates contesting elections
- A free and diverse media enabling a wide expression of views

question many asked after the UK parliamentary expenses scandal of 2009.) If Britain is a democracy that in theory gives power to the many, not the few, how far do ordinary people have any real control or influence over those who govern them?

Voting offers only a limited choice. Those who bother to use their vote may determine which of two or three rival teams of politicians occupy government posts for the next four or five years, but does this give voters significant influence over key government decisions and policies? What other opportunities do citizens have to participate in the political process? How far can 'ordinary people' hope to have a real voice in the many decisions that affect them? Indeed, perhaps the greatest threat to democracy today comes not from the threat of a military coup and the imposition of dictatorship but from growing political apathy and declining popular participation in the political process. These questions will be addressed throughout this book but particularly in Chapters 4 to 9.

## Power in Britain

Do elected politicians make the real decisions that affect the British people? Perhaps the real decision-makers are not the politicians who tend to dominate the news but relatively faceless civil servants or advisers. Alternatively, more real power and influ-

**Image 1.1 Representative democracy in action!**

A man with his dog votes at an improvised polling station in a temporary hut at Coven Heath in the constituency of South Staffordshire in the General Election of 5 May 2005. A healthy democracy is widely held to require a high participation in the electoral process. In response to declining turnout in UK elections, more accessible, voter-friendly locations for polling stations in supermarkets, pubs and even fish and chip shops have been provided. To make voting easier still there have also been trials with other means of registering votes, including telephone and internet voting. However, only easier postal voting has had much effect on turnout. (For more on voter turnout, see Chapter 4.)

ence may be exercised by individuals who are not part of the formal political process at all – businessmen (and they are usually still men!), bankers, or owners of newspapers, television companies and other media, some of whom may not even be British. Newspapers and magazines sometimes attempt to compile lists of the most powerful people in Britain. These may generally be headed by the Prime Minister, as one might expect, but often include prominent businessmen, media magnates, appointed officials, and even sports personalities and pop idols, interspersed among some other elected politicians. Such lists are hardly scientific and may reflect little more than the highly subjective views of the journalists who compose them. However, they do suggest that power is not just confined to those who hold some formal position in government, and that business tycoons such as Rupert Murdoch or Sir Richard Branson may have more power than some Cabinet Ministers.

One cynical conclusion might be that 'money talks'; those with substantial wealth and income can use it to buy (sometimes literally) political influence. Yet there is no simple correlation between wealth and power. Newspapers also sometimes list the wealthiest people in Britain, but some of the names near the top of such lists, such as the Duke of Westminster or the Queen, do not figure prominently, if at all, in the lists of those with power. There are others, such as leading footballers or pop stars, who avoid any formal association with politics

and lack significant economic power, but may have enormous influence as role models for behaviour, and perhaps contribute more to changing political attitudes on key issues than professional politicians. Yet again, it is possible that real power and influence is exercised by many who are not celebrities – 'faceless bureaucrats', or sinister anonymous figures pulling strings behind the scenes.

However, this whole approach may make too much of the power of particular individuals. Ministers and company chairs come and go, but the organizations they head generally last much longer. Perhaps we should be looking at the power of institutions or corporate power. Perhaps the civil service, or the City of London, or multi-national corporations exercise far more effective power and influence in the British political process than any single personality. Alternatively, power may not lie with particular institutions but with more amorphous interests or **elites**, such as '**the ruling class**' or '**the establishment**', or 'big business' or 'the

---

● **The establishment** is a term sometimes used to describe the British elite, an unaccountable dominant social group largely educated at leading private schools and ancient universities.

● An **elite** is a small dominant group. Elite theorists argue that power is inevitably exercised by the few (or by an elite or elites), even in nominally democratic organizations or states.

● **The ruling class** is a term used particularly by Marxists to describe those who own and control capital, and whose economic power gives them political power.

military-industrial complex' or 'global capitalism.' Those who hold formal positions of power, such as elected politicians, are perhaps driven by interests outside their control.

Alternatively we can seek to identify those who are effectively excluded from power. Thus it is often suggested that certain groups or interests might be marginalized in the political system – the unemployed, or ethnic minorities, or teenagers, or women, or those who live and work in the countryside. There may be sub-cultures, an underclass, or possibly a whole gender largely excluded from the political process.

All this implies that power may be rather or very unevenly distributed. Some, perhaps a small minority, appear to have a great deal of power, others relatively little influence, while others again may be virtually excluded from any effective participation in the decisions which affect their lives. Yet while **elitism** suggests that political power is narrowly concentrated, **pluralism** implies that ordinary people do have the capacity to influence and even determine key outcomes, in accordance with notions of democracy.

The distribution of power may also change over time. The journalist Anthony Sampson wrote a series of books examining power in Britain, the first in 1962, the last in 2005. He suggested that over that period some institutions, such as the trade unions and the universities, had lost influence, while the media had become more important than ever. He thought power had become more centralized, and the Prime Minister and the Treasury more dominant, while the Cabinet and the civil service were less influential. Looking back with a more sceptical eye Sampson had become

---

● **Elitism**, suggests power is substantially concentrated in the hands of an elite or ruling class.

● **Pluralism** involves the belief that power is widely dispersed through society.

● **Neo-pluralism** is a modified version of pluralism which still emphasizes the dispersal of power while acknowledging the influence of key interests (e.g. business).

● **Democratic elitism** is a modified form of elitism which still emphasizes the importance of elites or leadership in politics, while acknowledging that competition between elites (e.g. through elections) encourages them to be responsive and accountable to the masses.

'more impatient and intolerant of the humbug and deceptions of democracy' (Sampson, 2005, p. xii), which is, of course, only one person's view, and not necessarily right. Moreover, he died before the financial and economic crises of 2007 onwards and the 2010 coalition government that might have suggested further changes in the distribution of power and influence in Britain.

## Perspectives on power

Who then rules Britain? It is a simple question, to which a variety of simple answers may be given. Britain has Cabinet or Prime Ministerial government; parliamentary sovereignty; an elected dictatorship; government by bureaucracy; business or corporate power; the dominance of an 'establishment' or 'ruling class'. All these answers, and others besides, have some plausibility and are worth serious consideration. Yet although it is certainly possible to provide a wealth of relevant information and analysis which should help towards an appreciation of who rules Britain, it should be acknowledged right away that it is impossible ultimately to give an authoritative and definitive answer to the question. Those answers that are given inevitably reflect different interpretations of the facts, contrasting perspectives on politics, and varied underlying ideological assumptions.

The term 'model' is often used in social science to describe a simplified version of reality. We try to make sense of a wide range of possibly relevant information by constructing simple hypotheses about the relationship between key variables, and see how far the real world fits the resulting models. Some simple models of the possible distribution of power in society are shown as Academic Controversy 1.1. The crucial question is how far power is dispersed or concentrated in the political system, but the different models also provide alternative explanations of the institutions and mechanisms involved.

They are not the only possible models, and indeed, different names or versions of these models may be encountered elsewhere. Moreover, not all the models are mutually exclusive. 'Pluralism', 'liberal capitalism' or 'liberal democracy' are the names often given to a composite

*Academic controversy 1.1*
# Competing models of the possible distribution of power

| Name of model | Key players | Power | Evidence | Thinkers |
|---|---|---|---|---|
| Representative democracy model | Individual voters through the ballot box | Dispersed | Formal political mechanisms, electoral system, written constitutions | Bentham, J S Mill |
| Market model | Individual consumers and producers through the free market | Dispersed | Classical economic assumptions – evidence of working of market | Adam Smith, Hayek, Friedman |
| Pluralist model | Pressure groups and parties | Relatively dispersed | Influence of groups in case studies of decision making | Bentley, Truman, Robert Dahl, neo-pluralists (e.g. Lindblom) |
| Elitist model | Elites (e.g. social, business, military, or bureaucratic) | Concentrated | Reputation of key figures and their inter-relations | Pareto, Mosca, Michels, Wright Mills |
| Marxist model | Ruling class ('bourgeoisie' in a capitalist society) | Highly concentrated | Distribution of income and wealth – working of capitalist system | Marx, Lenin, Trotsky, Gramsci, Ralph Miliband |

version of the first three models listed here, suggesting a model where power is dispersed through a mixture of the ballot box, the free market and the influence of group interests on the policy process. Certainly these institutions and processes can be seen as playing a mutually reinforcing role. Yet they also reflect different and sometimes competing perspectives. Some old fashioned liberals (or those on the modern New Right) place far more emphasis on the free market than the verdict of the ballot box, particularly if that leads to interference with free market forces. Similarly, they may fear that group influences represent selfish sectional interests and illegitimate power that may distort the market. While pluralists assume a role for elections and representative institutions, they regard these as only

providing a very limited, occasional and blunt instrument for popular political participation, and place more emphasis on the continuous influence of countless pressure groups on the policy process. How persuasive are these models? Which is the most convincing? The obvious answer is to look at the evidence, but the problem here is that each model begins from rather different assumptions, employs different methodologies and looks at different sorts of evidence. The representative government model largely assumes that political power lies where the constitution, laws and other official documents say it does, so here it is important to examine the theory and practice of the key institutions. The market model derives its key assumptions from classical economics. It is countless individual producers and consumers operating through the market who determine the crucial questions of 'who gets what, when, how'. The role of politics in this economic process is (and, they argue, should be) strictly limited, as government intervention can only distort the operation of the free market and lead to a less efficient allocation of resources. Evidence in support of these assumptions comes from analysis of market forces and government intervention in practice. Pluralists cite case studies in decision-making to demonstrate the role of large numbers of different groups in the political process. Elitists by contrast identify key individuals or groups who dominate decision-making in their communities. Marxists infer political power from economic power. They document the massive inequalities in income and wealth in modern capitalist society and assume that it is those who control the means of production who will also control the political process.

At this point an intelligent reader coming to the study of politics for the first time might think 'Hold on! Is this description or prescription? Political science or ideology?' The answer is, inevitably, both. While writers on politics may conscientiously strive to provide an accurate picture of the way in which the political process actually operates, they are inevitably influenced by their own fundamental assumptions, and sometimes also by their ideals. Marx believed he was providing a dispassionate analysis of the underlying forces within capitalism, but it is difficult to divorce this analysis entirely from his condemnation of capitalism and hopes for a future socialist revolution. He wrote: 'Philosophers have only interpreted the world, the point however is to change it.' (*Theses on Feuerbach*). There is a similar mixture of analysis and prescription among modern free marketeers. Like Marx, they too want to change the world, although in a quite different direction. Moreover, while much of the debate between pluralists and elitists apparently involves dispassionate social scientific research into the distribution of power, most of those involved are also defending or advancing theories of democracy, and implicitly or explicitly criticizing or defending the processes they describe.

## Ideas and interests

The study of politics, from Plato onwards, assumed the importance of political ideas. It has been said that there is nothing so important as an idea whose time has come. Democracy, national self-determination, socialism, the free market, are all examples of powerful ideas that have, at one time or another, appeared to change the world. A new idea, or perhaps more commonly, the revival of an old idea, may still today seem to drive political change. It is often suggested that political parties, or potential political leaders, need a 'big idea' if they are to succeed.

Yet at various levels the importance of ideas in politics has been questioned. One objection is that much modern politics seems to be more about presentation (see Chapter 9) than values, principles and ideas. Image is more important than substance. Voters judge politicians by their physical appearance and mannerisms, their hair, clothes, voice and accent, rather than their principles. Politicians and parties increasingly seem to communicate with the wider public through slogans and soundbites rather than carefully argued manifestos and reasoned speeches. Politics is reduced to manipulation and marketing, like the sale of soap powder or cornflakes.

Ideas, however, require communication, and this can take place at various levels. Soundbites are not new, but have been cogently expressed by some of the greatest political philosophers and practising politicians the world has known. Lincoln's definition of democracy, or Churchill's observations on the same subject (see p. 4, Box 1.1) are particularly memorable soundbites, regularly quoted to convey important truths – although of course such terse statements commonly require further examination, elaboration and qualification. Similarly, politicians may be coached to improve their image and presentation, remodelling their clothes, hair, voice and posture (as for example was Margaret Thatcher), but this does not necessarily mean they have nothing of substance to say. Margaret Thatcher had an important message to communicate (whether one agrees with it or not).

At another level, it may be argued that the ideas we hold and express are conditioned by our background and circumstances. We conveniently assume that what is to our benefit is fair and just. Thus our core beliefs may simply involve a rationalization of our own self-interest. From a Marxist perspective, political ideas are essentially a rationalization of the interests of different economic classes.

However, Marx also argued that 'the ruling ideas in every age are the ideas of the ruling class'. Plausibly, the dominant class, (capitalists in a capitalist society), are in a strong position to influence or condition the thinking of subordinate classes, through for example the education system and the mass media. Thus the manual working class may come to hold views that are not in their objective interests. Consequently, they may reject socialism (very much in their objective interests from a Marxist perspective). By contrast, liberals and modern neo-liberals assume that individuals act in their own rational self-interest (as voters and consumers). If they reject socialism it is because they have concluded it is not in their interest or unworkable (correctly, from a neo-liberal perspective).

Both Marxists and neo-liberals thus in their different ways suggest that it is interests (individual or class) that drive political behaviour. Yet both paradoxically illustrate the power of ideas. Marx's ideas inspired political movements around the world and revolutions in Russia, China and elsewhere which did much to shape the issues and conflicts of the twentieth century. The revival of free market ideas by modern neo-liberals similarly transformed the government and politics of the western world, before going on to affect (with varying success) the economies and societies of the Communist world, most of which spectacularly imploded after the collapse of the Berlin Wall in 1989. Ideas can still exert a powerful grip on our collective consciousness.

## Ideologies

Much modern political differences arise from rival political perspectives or **ideologies**, reflecting distinctive assumptions, and involving different political prescriptions. Most British political controversy, and much in the western world more generally, has long seemed to focus on the arguments between and within the mainstream ideologies of liberalism, conservatism and socialism (see Chapter 7)

Typically, a political ideology provides a description and interpretation of contemporary society, explaining why and how it has come to be as it is, and how far it might be changed. Thus conservatism involves suspicion of change which may reflect broad satisfaction with the current social, economic and political system, or pessimism over the chances of securing any improvement. Socialism, by contrast, combines radical criticism of the existing social and political order with the hope and expectation that a fairer and better alternative is possible. However, some of the deepest ideological divisions are over strategy, the means to achieve desired ends. Thus socialists differ more over the means to achieve socialism than ends, Greens are split between fundamentalists and realists over how far they are prepared to compromise their principles, while conservatives disagree over the best way of preserving social and political stability.

Ideologies are neither uniform nor static. While they transcend national boundaries, the particular form they take is influenced strongly by the historical context and the prevailing culture of a country. Thus the British interpretation of liberalism, conservatism and socialism is distinctive, reflecting British political circumstances (see Chapter 7). Ideologies also adapt to changing conditions, frequently reinterpreting old values and principles. All mainstream British ideologies have evolved and changed over time, although this has often involved bitter debate between modernisers and their opponents over the real meaning of conservatism, liberalism and socialism.

---

● A **political ideology** involves any connected set of political beliefs with implications for political behaviour. This is the neutral understanding of the term as it is most commonly used today (Seliger, 1976; McLellan, 1995; Leach, 2009). On this definition, conservatism, liberalism, socialism, fascism, nationalism and feminism are all ideologies. However, the term 'ideology' has often been used – and is still sometimes employed – in a pejorative (hostile or negative) sense, and equated with rigid adherence to political dogma, which critics have sometimes associated with Marxism. Marxists, by contrast, have interpreted ideology as the rationalization of material interests, particularly the interests of the ruling class.

## *Academic controversy 1.2*
## Left and right

The labels 'left' and 'right' are still widely used to clas-sify ideologies and political parties, and to describe the position of individual thinkers and politicians. The terms derive from the seating positions in the National Assembly following the 1789 French revolution, when the most revolutionary members sat on the left and the more conservative members on the right. Today on the conventional left–right political spectrum communists are placed on the far left, socialists on the left, conser-vatives on the right and fascists on the far right. Liberals (including the British Liberal Democrats) might be located somewhere in the centre, although the term 'liberal' today covers a wide range.

*Left–right, conventional scale*

| Far left | Left | Centre | Right | Far right |
|----------|------|--------|-------|-----------|
| Communists | Socialists | Liberals | Conservatives | Fascists |

Other ideologies are more difficult to place. Nationalism is today more commonly associated with the right, although in different times and places it has been linked with ideas and parties from across the ideo-logical spectrum. Many members of Plaid Cymru (the Welsh nationalist party) and the Scottish National Party would place themselves on the left. Greens are generally linked with the left, although Greens them-selves often claim to be off the scale – 'not left, not right but forward'.

Indeed, if degrees of 'left' and 'right' can be marked on a scale it is by no means clear what that scale is measuring. Attitudes to change? Attitudes to authority? Attitudes to capitalism and the free market? None of these seems to fit closely the way in which the terms 'left' and 'right' are actually used (see Leach, 2009, pp. 10–13). Consequently, some argue the terms are confusing and should be abandoned (Brittan, 1968). Others have suggested a more complex two-dimen-sional system of classifying political ideas, with atti-tudes to authority on the vertical axis and attitudes to change on the horizontal axis (Eysenck, 1957). Whatever the merits of such more complex systems of classification of political attitudes, it is unlikely that they will ever displace the more familiar language of left and right.

## Policies – who gets what, when, how?

Older books on politics concentrated on political ideas, institutions and processes, but often neglected the decisions, policies and outcomes that are the product of the political system. Yet it is through policies that politicians try to implement their values and priorities. Thus it is almost impos-sible to understand British conservatism without examining some of the policies that Conservative politicians have pursued. How policies are made tells us much about the political system in action (see Chapter 19). Where did the initiative come from? Who influenced the policy process and affected the outcome? How far did wider public opinion play a part? How was the policy imple-mented? How far did the policy meet its proclaimed objectives? What explanations can be offered for its apparent success or failure? Who ultimately gained and who lost? Some of the answers to these questions may provide suggestive clues to the distribution of political power and influence.

Yet some of the most important areas of policy may be subject to forces partially or substantially outside the control of domestic politics. Commonly, governments are judged by how they manage the economy. While they claim credit for the good times, they often blame economic disas-ters on global circumstances outside their control, as with the 2008 banking crisis. Opposition politi-cians naturally take a different view, condemning the government for their mismanagement.

Apportioning responsibility is not easy. Apparent success may be due as much to good luck as good judgement, with the converse applying to failure. Yet even in an increasingly globalized economy, governments by their actions or inactions can help or hinder national prosperity (see Chapter 20).

Public services such as health and education are now at the centre of political debate in Britain. Upon the quality of these services depends an important element of the quality of life of individuals and communities. Poor education in schools, colleges and universities ultimately affects everyone, not just the unfortunate recipients. Thus it has long been recognized that such services cannot be left to the free market. Yet how far the state should intervene, the level of service, and the method of control, delivery and finance of services remain acutely controversial (see Chapter 21).

Can governments eradicate poverty? If the rich are getting richer, is that necessarily a bad thing? How far is it the role of government to promote equality and social justice? Such questions are at the centre of debate between socialists, liberals and conservatives, and the answers depend inevitably on ideological assumptions as well as economic analysis. Yet the relative poverty of some can affect people generally, obviously from the payment of taxes to fund social security benefits, less directly from the possible knock-on effects on national economic prosperity, health, education and crime. Child poverty, the problems of low income and one-parent families, run-down housing estates and deprived urban areas are problems which successive British governments have tried to tackle in different ways.

Moreover, issues of equality and social justice are not just related to economic deprivation. but to the treatment of categories or communities within the general population. Whole categories of people, including women, ethnic minorities, faith groups, the disabled, gays and others, may be more systematically excluded from power and a share of general prosperity as a result of blatant or more subtle forms of discrimination, injustice and prejudice. The proposed remedies often reflect not only alternative values but different perspectives on the nature of the problem (see Chapter 22).

Foreign policy manifestly has causes and consequences beyond national boundaries. While Britain has not been involved in a major war since 1945, British troops have been engaged in active combat in (among other places) Korea, the South Atlantic, the Persian Gulf, Kosovo, Afghanistan and Iraq. Britain's membership of the North Atlantic Treaty Organization (NATO), a military alliance initially covering the leading states of North America and western Europe, has determined much of its foreign policy. There has also been a tension between the 'special relationship' with the USA on the one hand, and ties with nearer neighbours in the European Union on the other. Yet a more fundamental problem for Britain and other advanced capitalist countries are the gross and intensifying differences in living standards across the world, which could now threaten a political explosion (see Chapter 24).

However, it is no longer only the threat of violent conflict between the 'haves' and the 'have-nots' which now endangers the future of the planet. The relationship of humankind with its environment has only been widely recognized as a serious issue in relatively recent times, but for some this has become the supreme political problem facing this country and the world generally. Finite resources are being used up, and various forms of environmental pollution threaten irreversible changes to soil and climate. At best, future generations may suffer a heavy burden from our extravagance. At worst, 'spaceship earth' could be heading for catastrophe. The politics of the environment has added a new dimension to ethical and political debate (see Chapter 23).

## British politics?

This is a book that focuses primarily on British politics. This may appear unduly narrow and insular, particularly in the light of discussion in the previous section, which raises some questions about the whole future of **independent sovereign states** in circumstances of increasing **globalization**. If many of the problems facing us are

---

● An **independent sovereign state** is a state which has a monopoly of supreme (or sovereign) power within its borders, not subject to interference in its internal affairs by any outside power.

● **Globalization** is a term that emphasizes the increasing interdependence of people, organizations and states in the modern world and the growing influence of global economic, cultural and political forces or trends. It implies limits to state sovereignty.

substantially global, surely we should be focusing our attention on global politics, rather than the institutions, processes and policies of a single state.

Even so, there is still much to be said for the in-depth study of a particular political system, either in parallel or prior to other studies. This helps to explain the special characteristics of British politics, and the interdependence of features of the British political system as a whole. Moreover, a close study of British politics does not preclude the study of comparative politics, nor international relations and global politics. Thus while this book, as the title suggests, focuses on British politics, it is not wholly confined to Britain, partly because much of politics in Britain is influenced by wider forces, such as European integration and globalization.

Specific aspects of British government and politics can only be appreciated in comparison with practices elsewhere. Both the similarities and the differences with other states can be instructive. It is, for example, virtually impossible to discuss the system of voting in Britain, its advantages and disadvantages, and proposals for reform, without some reference to voting systems in other countries (see Chapter 5). In this book there will be frequent references to politics and government in other countries, some in special Comparative Politics boxes. Of course, none of this can be a substitute for a systematic analysis of comparative politics, but it may perhaps help foster an interest in other political systems, as well as setting British political institutions and practices in a broader context.

Needless to say, the level at which decisions should be taken is often an acutely controversial political question. Some fear British national sover-eignty is being eroded and British citizens are losing control of decisions that affect them, while others seek to devolve power downwards to the nations, regions and localities within the United Kingdom. If these hopes or fears are fully realized, this could even mark the end of British politics.

Britain's membership of what is now the European Union has been acutely controversial since the British government first applied to join in 1961, and more particularly from 1973, when the Heath government signed the treaty of accession (Young, 1998). Some see the European Union as providing Britain with an opportunity to exert more political and economic influence, in co-opera-tion with other member states, over decisions that affect all Britons. Others fear the absorption of Britain into a European superstate, which they see as a threat to British independence and identity. Whatever view is taken it is clear that the institu-tions and processes of the European Union are now an important element of the politics which affect us all. Indeed, the impact of Europe on British govern-ment and politics will be a running thread through-out this book (but see especially Chapter 15).

Yet the future of British politics is not just affected by the threat (real or exaggerated) of a European superstate. The very term 'Britain' and the notion of 'British politics' is itself increasingly contested (Davies, 2000, pp. 853–86). The official name of the state (since 1922) is The United Kingdom of Great Britain and Northern Ireland, often described more simply as The United Kingdom or by the acronym UK. Northern Ireland remains part of the United Kingdom, although its inhabitants remain fiercely divided in their political allegiance. The majority insist they are 'British', rather more passionately than most people who live across the Irish Sea in Great Britain. A large minor-ity consider themselves Irish rather than British, and wish to belong to the Irish Republic rather than remain within the UK or British state. The political future of Northern Ireland remains acutely controversial, although the remarkable 2007 power-sharing agreement between republican Sinn Fein and the Democratic Unionist Party provides grounds for cautious optimism that whatever tran-spires need not involve further bloodshed and violence.

Even without the long-running problem of Northern Ireland, the future of Britain and the British state is an increasingly open question. England is the largest of the constituent parts of Britain in territory and by far the largest in popula-tion. Many of those who live in England describe themselves almost interchangeably as 'English' or 'British', a confusion which can infuriate those who live in Scotland or Wales. Wales was absorbed by the English crown in the Middle Ages and was formally politically united with England in 1536. Scotland was an independent state until King James VI of Scotland became also James I of England in 1603 although this union of the crowns did not involve full political union until 1707. The notion of a British state and the image of 'Britannia' effectively date from then. Some inhabitants of Scotland and Wales consider themselves to be both Scots or Welsh and British. Others consider themselves primarily or exclusively Scots or Welsh, and a significant minority would prefer to be part of an independent Scotland or Wales (see Chapters 3 and 16). Indeed, some have long forecast the imminent 'break-up of Britain' (Nairn, 1981, 2000).

The 'break-up of Britain' has become rather more likely since the Scottish National Party won the 2007 Scottish Parliament election in Scotland and went on form a minority administration, and made substantial further gains in 2011 to win the majority of seats, and promise a referendum on independence. Meanwhile Plaid Cymru, the Welsh nationalist party did well enough to enter coalition with Labour after the 2007 elections for the Welsh Assembly, but lost votes and seats in 2011, with Labour gaining just enough seats to govern alone in 2011. If the majority of those in Scotland and/or Wales clearly wished to be part of a separate state it would be impossible to maintain the union. 'Britain' would no longer exist as a meaningful political entity (although it would probably survive as a

useful geographical term to describe the island). 'British politics' would be confined to the history books, to be replaced by the study of English (or Scottish or Welsh) politics (see Chapter 16).

Yet for the present 'British politics' remains a convenient shorthand term to describe politics and government at various levels inside the United Kingdom, and the growing two-way influences between UK and other levels of government, European and international. This is sometimes described as multi-level governance. While many of the crucial decisions that affect British citizens are still resolved within Britain's central government around Whitehall and Westminster, others are effectively taken elsewhere. Some decisions are made above the level of the British state – for example, by the United Nations, the International Monetary Fund, the World Trade Organization, the North Atlantic Treaty Organization or (especially) the European Union. Other decisions are taken below the level of the central United Kingdom government based in Whitehall and Westminster, by devolved parliaments and assemblies (see Chapter 16) or local councils (see Chapter 17). British politics is thus increasingly multi-layered.

## SUMMARY

- Politics involves far more than government and party politics. It is about power and decision-making which affect all our lives, and determines how scarce resources are allocated – 'who gets what, when, how'.

- There are disagreements over the legitimate scope of politics. Some distinguish between a public or political sphere and a private sphere, between the state and 'civil society'. Others would deny that politics can or should be excluded from many areas previously considered private.

- Although politics is clearly about power, this is difficult to define and measure. A distinction can be drawn between power and authority (or legitimate power). Those without formal power may still have influence over decisions that affect them.

- Britain is called a representative democracy, implying that the people or the majority have effective influence over government and over decisions that affect them. Britain satisfies most of the conditions commonly laid down for representative democracy.

- Yet there is disagreement over the distribution in power in Britain. Some argue that it is effectively concentrated in the hands of the few, others that it is widely dispersed. Theories or 'models' of power reflect conflicting underlying assumptions and look at different kinds of evidence.

- Although politics is about the conflicting interests of different social or ethnic groups, it is also about ideas. Political differences commonly reflect contrasting underlying ideological assumptions.

- Many crucial political decisions that affect people in Britain are made both above and below the level of the British state, for example by international institutions, the European Union, devolved governments in Scotland, Wales and Northern Ireland, local councils and other public bodies. There is no longer a single British government, but rather a complex system of multi-level governance. However, most British citizens are still principally affected by political decisions made in Westminster and Whitehall.

- Even so the very future of British government and politics is now uncertain, particularly as a result of increased support for Scottish, Welsh and Irish nationalism within the United Kingdom that could lead either to a quasi-federal or fully federal system of government, or the end of the Union.

## QUESTIONS FOR DISCUSSION

- What is politics? Why do many people seem to show a distaste for politics?

- Is it possible, or desirable, to take such issues as education, health, defence or law and order out of politics?

- Should we distinguish between a political (or public) sphere and a private sphere from which politics should be excluded?

- What do you understand by democracy? How far is Britain a democracy?

- Who governs Britain? Where does power lie in Britain? Is power highly concentrated in the hands of the few, or relatively widely dispersed?

- Is political change driven by ideas and principles, or by economic and social change?

- What do you understand by the terms 'left' and 'right'? How far are these terms still relevant to the analysis of contemporary British politics?

- Does it still make sense to study British politics, particularly when the British state is apparently in process of being eroded from both above and below?

- Would Northern Ireland, Scotland, Wales (and perhaps England) be better served by independence, rather than the continuation of the Union?

## FURTHER READING

The first chapter of Andrew Heywood's *Politics* (3rd edition, 2007) addresses the question 'What is Politics?' It includes a particularly useful brief discussion of power. There is also a brief discussion of alternative views on the nature of politics in Leach, *The Politics Companion*, (2008, pp. 7–17). The same subject is treated in more depth from different perspectives by several authors in Leftwich (2004). Older classic texts include Harold Lasswell (1935), and Bernard Crick's *In Defence of Politics* (1964, 4th edition 1993) which is thought-provoking, if a little idiosyncratic. The French political scientist Maurice Duverger's *The Study of Politics* (translated by R. Wagoner, 1972) is still worth reading. Anthony Arblaster (1987) provides a readable short introduction to *Democracy*. C. B. Macpherson's almost as brief *The Life and Times of Liberal Democracy* (1977) might also be consulted. Fuller and more ambitious is David Held (1987), *Models of Democracy*.

The distribution of power in Britain is, inevitably, a controversial subject. One readable personal view is provided by the journalist Anthony Sampson (2005), *Who Runs This Place?*, the last of a series of studies of the 'Anatomy of Britain' which he began in 1962. For a more theoretical discussion of power see Lukes (1974).

Dunleavy and O'Leary (1987), *Theories of the State* provide a clear account of most of the models of power (pluralism, eltitism, Marxism, etc.) briefly described in this chapter.

On the issues around the widespread current disillusionment with politics and democracy there are two provocative prize-winning books: Gerry Stoker (2006), *Why Politics Matters,* and Colin Hay (2007), *Why We Hate Politics.*

# CHAPTER 2

# The Shadow of the Past: British Politics since 1945

Much of British politics can only be understood in the light of history, including distant episodes beyond living memory, and more recent developments which generations still alive today experienced, and which helped to shaped their own political ideas. Thus in early twenty-first-century Britain there remain millions of older pensioners who lived through the Second World War – some who fought in it, many more who experienced the bombing and wartime shortages and privations of the civilian population. Others grew up in the early post-war years, when the welfare state was established and Britain still appeared to rule an extensive empire abroad. These subsequently experienced the rapid, sometimes painful, disengagement from empire and partial engagement with Europe, as well as the sexual revolution of the Sixties, and the economic and industrial problems of the seventies. A later generation, sometimes dubbed 'Thatcher's children', reached maturity in the long period of Conservative rule from 1979 to 1997. Young adults in Britain today, voting for the first time in 2010, grew up under New Labour, with no personal memory of previous Conservative governments. They may, however, pick up impressions of periods

they have not lived through, from family, school and the media: the 'spirit of the Blitz', wartime and post-war rationing and controls, the Irish troubles, the miners' strike.

As these examples may suggest, some perceptions of the past involve a widely shared vision, part of 'being British' while others may be far more divisive. This is particularly obvious in Northern Ireland, where the unionist and nationalist communities have their own highly distinctive interpretation of historical events. Yet elsewhere in Britain perceptions of past events may also be strongly coloured by distinctive class, religious or ethnic backgrounds.

If the past shapes everyone's political attitudes and behaviour, it also influences ministers, civil servants and others actively involved in making policy and taking critical political decisions. British economic and social policies in the early post-war period were strongly shaped by experience of the inter-war years, particularly mass unemployment. Post-war foreign policy was conditioned by the failure of the 'appeasement' of dictators in the1930s. The economic policies of the Thatcher government were shaped by the perceived economic problems of the previous decades. Each new political crisis evokes parallels with the past. The Brown government's handling of the 2008 banking and economic crisis was partly conditioned by, and inevitably compared with, the handling of the Depression in 1931.

Sometimes, of course, the lessons of the past may mislead. Circumstances change. Politicians, like generals, may be trying to 'fight the last war' rather than confront altered conditions. Yet as the philosopher George Santayana (1863–1952) once observed, 'Those who cannot remember the past are condemned to repeat it.'

## Britain after the Second World War – the end of empire and the Cold War

Britain emerged from the Second World War as a victor, escaping the defeat and occupation that was the fate of much of continental Europe, and still apparently a great power, one of the 'big three' (along with the USA and USSR) determining the shape of the post-war world. Yet Britain's great power status was largely illusory. The British economy, already for half a century or more in relative decline, was further damaged by the war, and British manufacturing industry was ill-equipped to compete effectively with the United States, and subsequently with the fast-recovering economies of western Europe and Japan. The British Empire was to be substantially liquidated within twenty years, although it continued to influence political attitudes, and was a factor in Britain's failure to engage more positively with continental Europe.

The conversion of the former British Empire into a Commonwealth of independent states proceeded rapidly. The white settler dominated former colonies of Canada, Australia, New Zealand and South Africa had long gained 'dominion' status and effective independence. Although they actively supported Britain in two world wars, they otherwise looked after their own economic and political interests, resisting pressure from Conservative-led British governments to pursue 'imperial preference' in trade. India and Pakistan became independent in 1947; Burma and Ceylon (now Sri Lanka) followed in 1948. Elsewhere British governments tried for a

time to preserve colonial rule, sometimes in the face of nationalist revolts (e.g. Kenya and Cyprus), but ultimately lacked the will and means to resist the anti-colonial tide. With the granting of independence to most former colonies in Asia and Africa in the 1960s, only a few trouble spots remained. These included Rhodesia (where a white minority government made a unilateral declaration of independence in 1965, the new black majority state of Zimbabwe not emerging until 1980), and Hong Kong, transferred to Chinese sovereignty in 1997. Only a few scattered remnants of empire survive (for example, the Falkland Islands and Gibraltar).

Loss of empire was regretted by many in Britain, particularly on the right of the Conservative Party, although it was celebrated by others active in organizations such as the Movement for Colonial Freedom. However, transition from empire to Commonwealth, while it involved some violence and bloodshed, was largely achieved peacefully, without the traumatic consequences for domestic politics of the French disengagements from Indo-China and Algeria. Even so, there was a painful process of adjustment. As a former American Secretary of State, Dean Rusk, famously observed, 'Great Britain has lost an empire and not yet found a role.'

Britain's post-war foreign policy was largely shaped by the **Cold War** between the two superpowers of the United States and the Soviet Union. Although both had been wartime allies, there was never any doubt that Britain would side with the USA, becoming one of the founding members of the North Atlantic Treaty Organization (NATO), established in 1949, and America's most reliable ally. However, the 'special relationship' with the United States was always an unequal one, with the United Kingdom very much a junior partner.

---

● The term '**Cold War**' describes the long conflict from the end of the Second World War to the fall of the Berlin Wall (1989) between the Union of Soviet Socialist Republics (USSR) and its allies on the one hand, and the United States and its allies on the other. It was a 'cold' war because it never involved direct armed conflict between the two major powers, despite periodic crises when the Cold War threatened to become a hot war. Some argue this was only prevented by the fear of mutually assured destruction (MAD) in such a war between the two major nuclear powers.

## COMPARATIVE POLITICS  2.1
# Continuity and change in Britain and other countries

British politics appears a model of stability and continuity when compared with the politics of many other states. France, for example, has experienced a succession of revolutions and regime changes over little more than two centuries, including several forms of monarchy, two periods of empire and five republics. Italy and Germany, which only became nation states in the late nineteenth century, went through similar upheavals, culminating in the fascist and Nazi dictatorships, before the restoration of parliamentary democracy following the military defeat of those regimes in 1945. Spain, Portugal and Greece have only more recently re-established democracy after periods of dictatorship. Eastern European countries only escaped from communist dictatorship with the fall of the Berlin Wall in 1989. Most states now represented at the United Nations did not even exist in 1945; many were former colonies that have since gained their independence, while other new countries have emerged from the partition of larger states.

Britain experienced religious upheavals in the sixteenth century and violent civil war and political revolutions in the seventeenth, but since then its politics has evolved largely peacefully. The bullet has not generally been a feature of the politics of mainland Britain (although Ireland is another matter). Violence has rarely erupted, with the bombing of the Conservative party conference in 1984 and of London in July 2005 as disturbing exceptions. While revolution has very occasionally been feared or threatened, political crises were invariably resolved peacefully. Even so, the appearance of stability and continuity is in some respects illusory. Britain retains a monarchy, a Prime Minister and Cabinet, and two Houses of Parliament, but none of these operate in remotely the same way as they did in the eighteenth or nineteenth centuries. Power has shifted, and the substance of British politics has profoundly changed (and not just as a result of coalition government). In many ways Britain is not the same country it was a hundred, fifty or even twenty-five years ago.

---

Although Britain became a nuclear power, its independent nuclear deterrent became in practice increasingly dependent on American rockets and submarines. The one occasion when a British government engaged in a foreign policy adventure opposed by the United States, the Anglo-French attack on the Suez Canal in 1956, they were forced into a humiliating climb-down entailing the resignation of Eden, the Prime Minister responsible.

The illusion of world power status, the 'special relationship' with the USA, and the continuing concern with the empire and commonwealth effectively deterred British governments from closer engagement with continental Europe. Neither Labour nor the Conservatives were interested in joining the European Coal and Steel Community, set up by the 1951 Treaty of Paris, or the European Economic Community, established by the 1957 Treaty of Rome. Britain thus missed the opportunity to help shape the new Europe.

## Post-war Britain: the welfare state and the mixed economy

The end of war and Labour's unexpected landslide election victory in 1945 seemed to mark a decisive break with the politics of the past. Attlee's government promised a new dawn, particularly for the less affluent majority. Yet the new government both built on and was constrained by the legacy of the past. All parties were determined to turn their backs on the policies of the inter-war years that had failed to deal with unemployment at home or the rise of the fascist dictators abroad. It was no accident that it was first Labour and then former Conservative rebels such as Churchill, Eden and Macmillan who dominated the politics of the early post-war years. At the same time many of the policies they pursued had their roots in the past, and in the experience of war and the wartime coalition government.

## TIMELINE 2.1

# The end of empire *(dates when former British colonies became independent)*

| | | | | |
|---|---|---|---|---|
| **1947** | India, Pakistan | | **1965** | Singapore, Gambia |
| **1948** | Burma (Myanmar), Ceylon (Sri Lanka) | | **1966** | Guyana, Barbados |
| **1957** | Malaysia | | **1967** | Aden and Yemen |
| **1960** | Cyprus, Nigeria, Ghana, Lesotho | | **1970** | Fiji |
| **1961** | Sierra Leone, Tanzania | | **1971** | Gulf states |
| **1962** | Jamaica, Uganda | | **1980** | Zimbabwe* |
| **1963** | Kenya | | **1997** | Hong Kong (transferred to China after lease expired) |
| **1964** | Malta, Malawi, Tanzania, Zambia | | | |

\* Date when independence was recognized. The white settler government of Ian Smith had earlier made a unilateral declaration of independence in 1965.

It has been claimed that there was indeed a substantial **consensus** between the major parties on economic and social policies in the post-war period, based on widespread acceptance of the economic ideas of the economist, John Maynard **Keynes** and the social reformer William **Beveridge** (see p. 22). Hence it is sometime described as the 'Keynes-Beveridge consensus'. Key elements of agreement included the system of government, the welfare state, the mixed economy, Keynesian full employment policy, and, in most respects, foreign and defence policy. However, the extent and even the reality of the post-war consensus has been questioned.

In 1946 the Labour government substantially implemented the 1942 Beveridge Report, establishing the welfare state and providing social security funded by national insurance contributions (Dutton, 1997, pp. 17–20). It also created in 1948

● **Consensus** means agreement. The term '**consensus politics**' implies a fundamental agreement among the governing elite, the major parties and (more questionably) the wider public over assumptions, ideas and policies.

the new National Health Service (NHS) providing universal free healthcare paid for largely by national taxation. Labour also expanded education, social services, housing and town and country planning. Later Conservative governments embraced the welfare state, including the NHS, which they had earlier opposed. Indeed, by the 1950s the welfare state was almost universally approved (Coxall and Robins, 1998, Chapter 10).

Ironically, it was Attlee's Labour government which was responsible for the first significant exception to free healthcare. Charges for teeth and spectacles were introduced by the Chancellor of the Exchequer, Hugh Gaitskell, to help pay for the Korean war in 1951. This provoked the resignation of the left-wing socialist Aneurin Bevan, the architect of the NHS, together with Harold Wilson, a future Labour leader, and initiated the split between Bevanites and Gaitskellites which continued to affect the party long after its leading figures died (Bevan in 1960, Gaitskell in 1963). The new health service charges, however, foreshadowed later concerns over the escalating cost of the NHS in particular and the welfare state in general, and the

## TIMELINE 2.2

# British governments and Prime Ministers from Churchill to Cameron

|           | Prime Minister        | Governing party or parties            |
|-----------|-----------------------|---------------------------------------|
| 1940–1945 | Winston Churchill     | Coalition                             |
| 1945–1951 | Clement Attlee        | Labour                                |
| 1951–1955 | Winston Churchill     | Conservative                          |
| 1955–1957 | Sir Anthony Eden      | Conservative                          |
| 1957–1963 | Harold Macmillan      | Conservative                          |
| 1963–1964 | Sir Alec Douglas-Home | Conservative                          |
| 1964–1970 | Harold Wilson         | Labour                                |
| 1970–1974 | Edward Heath          | Conservative                          |
| 1974–1976 | Harold Wilson         | Labour                                |
| 1976–1979 | James Callaghan       | Labour                                |
| 1979–1990 | Margaret Thatcher     | Conservative                          |
| 1990–1997 | John Major            | Conservative                          |
| 1997–2007 | Tony Blair            | Labour                                |
| 2007–2010 | Gordon Brown          | Labour                                |
| 2010–     | David Cameron         | Conservative–Liberal Democrat coalition |

implications for the burden of taxation. The post-war decades involved a growth in both state spending and taxation that was unprecedented in peacetime.

Labour's policy of nationalization involved a more contentious extension of state intervention. Attlee's Labour government brought into public ownership the Bank of England (1946), coal (1947), electricity, gas and rail (all 1948), and finally steel and road haulage (1949), thus establishing a mixed economy with a substantial state sector. Yet this fell well short of the wholesale intro-duction of 'common ownership of the means of production, distribution and exchange' to which Labour was apparently committed in Clause Four of its own constitution. Moreover, of these measures only steel and road haulage was acutely controversial. The other industries which were nationalized were either already substantially municipally owned (electicity, gas) or declining (railways, coal). The Conservatives, on coming to power in 1951, partially denationalized steel and road haulage, but otherwise maintained the mixed economy with a substantial state sector.

## Key thinker: William Beveridge

William Beveridge (1879–1963) was a leading academic and social reformer who chaired the Committee on Social Insurance and Allied Service (1942). The Beveridge Report proposed a system of national insurance 'from the cradle to the grave'. Churchill's wartime government was initially reluctant to endorse such radical reform, but was effectively bounced into its acceptance by public enthusiasm. Beveridge became briefly a Liberal MP from 1944–5 and subsequently a Liberal peer. His name is closely associated with that of **Keynes** as the cost of Beveridge's scheme for national insurance could only be kept within reasonable bounds by the pursuit of Keynesian full employment economic policies.

Although continuing some rationing in the face of post-war shortages, Labour did not attempt detailed controls of production or workforce. Attlee's government adopted Keynesian economic management, and this was maintained by their Conservative successors. Indeed, there appeared so little difference between the economic policies pursued by the Labour Chancellor Hugh Gaitskell, and the Conservative Chancellor R. A. Butler that *The Economist* in 1954 coined the term 'Butskellism'

to describe their approach (Dutton, 1997, p. 57). Commonly, this involved increasing demand in the economy whenever unemployment appeared to be rising above politically acceptable levels by reducing taxation and/or increasing government spending (if necessary running a budget deficit). However, these policies apparently succeeded in maintaining close to full employment, in marked contrast to the inter-war period (Coxall and Robins, 1998, Chapter 9).

## Key thinker: John Maynard Keynes

John Maynard Keynes (1883–1946) had been a brilliant critic of inter-war government policy, notably in his damning indictment of the post-First World War peace settlement, *The Economic Consequences of the Peace,* and of Chancellor Winston Churchill's return to the gold standard in 1925. His great contribution to economics came in 1936 with the publication of *The General Theory of Employment, Interest and Money.* Keynes believed in government management of the economy to achieve desirable economic objectives, including full employment, stable prices, steady economic growth and a healthy balance of payments. This was to be done by influencing total (or aggregate) demand for goods and services, through fiscal and monetary policy, without requiring direct intervention or controls on particular firms or industries. In the Second World War Keynes joined the Treasury, and his economics became the new orthodoxy. His 'managed capitalism' was attractive to leading post-war politicians across the political spectrum, including Conservatives such as Harold Macmillan and 'Rab' Butler, and Labour's Hugh Gaitskell and Tony Crosland. Thus both Labour and Conservative governments pursued Keynesian demand management policies to secure full employment. Subsequently, from the 1970s on, Keynesian policies were blamed by the Conservative New Right for increasing government spending and fuelling inflation. However, the 2008 banking and subsequent economic crisis briefly assisted a revival of the ideas and prescriptions of Keynes, at least until the emergence of the coalition government under Cameron in 2010.

## TIMELINE 2.3

# The welfare state: key developments

| | |
|---|---|
| **1942** | Report on Social Insurance and Allied Services (the Beveridge Report) |
| **1944** | Education Act |
| **1944** | White Paper on employment policy (high and stable level of employment) |
| **1945** | Family Allowances Act |
| **1946** | National Insurance Act (implemented Beveridge Report) |
| **1948** | Establishment of the National Health Service |

## The under-performing economy, 'stagflation' and crisis: 1964–79

Despite continuing political stability coupled with the establishment and maintenance of full employment, a mixed economy and the welfare state, all did not seem well with the British economic and political system in the 1960s and 1970s. Britain's economic growth, admittedly higher than in the past, was only modest in comparison with that of major competitors in North America, western Europe and Japan. Low growth was blamed on 'stop-go' policies, under which expansion led to inflation and a balance of payments crisis, followed by cuts in public spending, recession and increased unemployment, sparking reflation and a recurrence of excess demand and rising prices (see Figure 2.1). Thus governments seemed incapable of pursuing steady growth. Britain's competitiveness also appeared to be undermined by relatively low labour productivity, exacerbated by strikes and other problems with industrial relations, and outdated management.

After thirteen years of Conservative rule a new Labour government under Harold Wilson was elected in 1964, pledged to modernize the economy and secure an annual rate of economic growth of 4 per cent to pay for further social reform and increased spending on public services. Yet the government was handicapped by a deteriorating balance of payments and increasing pressure on the exchange rate of the pound sterling, which eventually forced devaluation in 1967, an event from which Wilson's reputation never quite recovered. Both his government and the following Conservative government under Heath (1970–4) attempted to reform trade unions and industrial relations, but failed. Increasing numbers of days were lost to industrial action, culminating in the miners' strike of 1973–4 that effectively brought down the Heath government.

The Keynes-Beveridge consensus was increasingly challenged. Some criticized the rising cost of the welfare state while others questioned its effectiveness. Problems such as homelessness, failing schools, child poverty and inner-city decline showed that the system was not providing effective social security 'from the cradle to the grave'. Moreover, although Keynesian theory recommended contrasting policy remedies to cope with inflation on the one hand or economic stagnation with rising unemployment on the other, by the 1970s governments were confronted with rising prices *and* rising unemployment. Journalists coined the term '**stagflation**' to describe this apparently new phenomenon.

● '**Stagflation**' was a term coined in the 1970s to describe simultaneous inflation and economic stagnation, a combination previously considered almost impossible from Keynesian assumptions.

# *Academic controversy 2.1*
# Consensus politics

There has been a long-running debate about the nature and extent of Britain's post-war consensus, a term suggesting considerable common agreement within the British political establishment on ideas and policies. Even before the term consensus was much used, the Canadian Robert McKenzie (1955) claimed there were minimal differences between the major British parties, while British observers saw much in common between the social democracy of Gaitskell and Crosland and the One Nation Conservatism of Macmillan and Butler. Two Americans provide some explanation why this should be so. Anthony Downs (1957) argued that, within a two-party system, parties seek to maximize their vote by competing for the support of the median voter in the middle ground. Daniel Bell (1960) suggested that the west was witnessing the 'end of ideology'; policy makers used modern social science to find practical solutions to problems, rather than relying on old ideological assumptions. Marxists, however, argued that apparent consensus values reflected the inevitable dominance of business values in a capitalist system.

While some critics (Pimlott, 1994, Jones and Kandiah, 1996) have denied the existence of consensus politics, others have assumed that it did exist, and have gone on to explain how and why the consensus ended with a widening gulf between free market conservatism and a revived left-wing socialism (Kavanagh, 1990). Still others have pointed to the re-establishment of a new, or 'Blairite' consensus (Fielding, 2003). (For a historical overview see Dutton, 1995, and Coxall and Robins, 1998.)

---

Politicians from both parties concluded that unreasonable wage increases were pushing up prices. Thus governments from Macmillan's to Callaghan's tried to restrain inflationary pressures through various forms of incomes policy. This entailed making deals with the leaders of business and organized labour. Some observers discerned a new system of making policy involving government, the Confederation of British Industry (CBI) and the Trades Union Congress (TUC), a process described as '**tripartism**' or '**corporatism**.'

The terms described who was involved but said little about the power relationships between them. While some saw corporatism as a new political system involving partnership with business and labour, others saw it as an essentially top-down process, bypassing Parliament and people. Some socialist critics thought the apparent participation of the unions in policy-making was essentially cosmetic; the reality involved restraints on workers' wages in the interest of business profits. By contrast, critics on the right thought the unions had been given too much power, and that incomes policies interfered with free market forces, further damaging Britain's competitiveness. In practice, incomes policies appeared to restrain wage rises in the short term, but were difficult to maintain on a longer-term basis.

The Heath government's attempts to control inflation were not helped by the 1973 energy crisis which saw a quadrupling of oil prices. This underlined the continued importance of Britain's coal industry and the industrial muscle of the miners, who began a national strike in 1973. Heath responded by imposing a three-day working week to save energy costs. The crisis provoked an early election in February 1974 which the government narrowly lost, allowing Wilson to return as the Prime Minister of a minority Labour government, which acquired a slim majority in a second election the same year.

● **Corporatism** in Britain is taken to mean a process of policy-making involving government and the major economic interests, capital and labour.

● **Tripartism** is a term with a similar usage to describe decision-making by three major partners: the government, the Confederation of British Industry (representing employers) and the Trades Union Congress (representing workers).

**Figure 2.1**  The 'stop–go' cycle

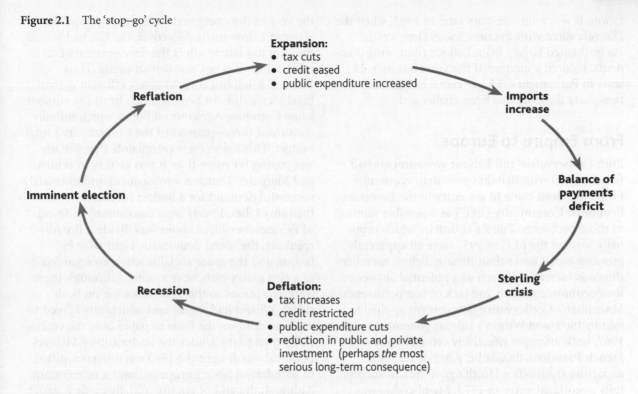

Sources: Derived from Thomas, 1992, p. 55; Coxall and Robins, 1998, p. 217.

Inflation continued to rise steeply to 27 percent in the Labour government's first year (Dutton, 1997, p. 102). The government initially sought to maintain its spending plans by borrowing. In 1976, after Callaghan had replaced Wilson as Prime Minister, mounting debts forced the government to seek a massive loan from the International Monetary Fund (IMF) under conditions which required major cuts in public spending. Confidence in Keynesian solutions was undermined, as Callaghan mournfully acknowledged to the Labour Party Conference in 1976:

> We used to think that you could just spend your way out of recession and increase employment by cutting taxes and boosting government spending. I tell you, in all candour, that that option no longer exists, and that in so far as it ever did exist, it only worked . . . by injecting a bigger dose of inflation into the economy, followed by a higher level of unemployment as the next step. (Callaghan, 1987, p. 426)

Savage deflationary policies eventually enabled the Labour government to control spending and reduce inflation but at considerable political cost, alienating voters and many in the unions, and dividing the Labour Party. The last version of incomes policy introduced by the Callaghan government culminated in strikes by key public sector workers, a 'winter of discontent' leading to Labour's defeat at the polls in 1979.

The apparent failure of governments of both parties to solve Britain's economic problems was a factor in the decline of their support. The combined two-party vote which had reached 97 per cent in 1951 fell to 75 per cent in two elections in 1974. An immediate beneficiary of this loss of confidence in the two major parties was the old Liberal Party, which had been one of two main parties until the First World War but had been reduced to a mere six seats in Parliament in the 1950s. A Liberal revival culminated in the party winning close to a fifth of the votes in 1974, but because of Britain's electoral system this only secured a doubling of their parliamentary representation. It was a similar story later in 1983, when the Liberals allied with the new Social Democratic Party, formed largely from Labour right-wing dissidents, secured a quarter of the votes but only 23 seats in Parliament ( 3.5 per cent). Even so, the two-party duopoly had been challenged.

## From Empire to Europe

Both Conservative and Labour governments had failed to deal with Britain's persistent economic problems. Both came to see entry to the European Economic Community (EEC) as a possible solution to those problems. The six countries which originally formed the EEC in 1957 were all apparently growing much faster than Britain. British membership was increasingly seen as a potential answer to slow economic growth and lack of competitiveness. Macmillan's Conservative government applied to join in 1963, and Wilson's Labour government in 1967, both attempts effectively vetoed by the French President, de Gaulle. After de Gaulle's departure from office Heath's government successfully negotiated entry in 1973. Membership was subsequently endorsed by two-thirds of British voters in a referendum in 1975, after some minor renegotiation of the terms of entry by the incoming 1974 Labour government.

The time finally seemed ripe for Britain to engage with Europe. Earlier obstacles to membership, including ties with the British Empire, Commonwealth and wider world, no longer seemed so important. Most former colonies had achieved or would very soon achieve, full independence. British forces had been withdrawn from east of Suez, in line with a scaling-down of defence commitments, and sterling was no longer an important reserve currency. The leaders of all three parties had supported entry, and those politicians who had opposed it largely accepted that the 1975 referendum had settled the issue for the immediate future.

However, the British commitment to Europe was less than wholehearted and entry into the European Community (EC) provided no instant answer to Britain's economic problems. The timing was unfortunate; the UK missed out on the years of growth and rising living standards that the original six member states had experienced, and joined in

the year of the energy crisis that precipitated an economic downturn. Moreover, the UK had joined the club too late to affect the development of its rules, which did not suit British needs. Thus Britain's small but comparatively efficient agricultural sector did not benefit much from the cumbersome Common Agricultural Policy which initially consumed three-quarters of the Community's total budget. This led to early complaints that Britain was paying far more than it was getting in return, and Margaret Thatcher's subsequent and ultimately successful demand for a budget rebate. Only the then tiny Liberal Party were consistently in favour of EC membership. Labour was divided. Broadly speaking, the social democratic right were in favour, and the more socialist left, who regarded it as a rich man's club, were against, (although there were exceptions to this generalization on both sides). Wilson had finally and reluctantly agreed to a referendum on the issue to paper over the cracks in his own party. Under the leadership of Michael Foot, Labour fought the 1983 election committed to withdrawal from Europe without a referendum. Although the end of empire initially made it easier for many Conservatives to accept Europe as a practical alternative, a significant minority remained opposed to the implications for Britain's national sovereignty, their number growing from the early 1990s, until the Conservatives became a largely eurosceptic party. Ironically, over the same period the majority of the Labour Party became more positive towards Europe (see also Chapter 15).

## Northern Ireland, Scotland and Wales

To other observers in the 1970s the main threat to the integrity and sovereignty of the United Kingdom came not from Europe but within, from the resurgence of separatist nationalism in Northern Ireland, Scotland and Wales. This may have been linked with the relative political and economic decline of Britain, now neither a world power, nor the centre of an extensive overseas empire. Some Scots and Welsh felt they were no longer partners in a great imperial enterprise, but neglected second-class citizens of a shrunken British state. Economic problems hit the more peripheral areas of the United Kingdom particularly hard – Northern Ireland shipbuilding, the coal and steel industries of South Wales, and the industrial belt of central Scotland. Those nationalists who had always questioned union with England now had additional economic arguments to support their case.

Northern Ireland posed the first and most immediate threat to the British state. Following persistent Irish nationalist pressure in the nineteenth and early twentieth centuries Ireland had been partitioned, substantially on religious lines, in 1922, with the majority of the country becoming an independent Irish state. The predominantly Protestant six counties of the province of Northern Ireland remained part of the British state. It had its own devolved government and parliament, but also sent MPs to the Westminster parliament. While the Protestant majority maintained a fierce allegiance to the British crown, most Catholics were nationalists who sought unification of the six counties with the Irish Republic. Even so, despite periodic disturbances the province had been fairly quiet since the war. The Ulster Unionist Party, then affiliated to the Conservatives, dominated both the Stormont parliament and Northern Ireland representation at Westminster. The nationalist party Sinn Fein won odd seats in predominantly Catholic areas, but declined to take them up, as they did not recognize British rule. Unionist (and Protestant) domination of the province seemed complete, while Catholics were a disadvantaged minority.

From the mid-1960s, Catholics dissatisfied with their second-class status demanded civil and political rights. This led to political disturbances. Concessions announced by the unionist government upset many 'loyalist' Protestants without winning support from Catholics. The two communities became increasingly polarized. Sectarian riots led to the rise of a new hard-line Protestant unionism, in which Ian Paisley was to become a key figure. Troops sent in by the British government to restore order in 1969 were at first welcomed by the Catholics, who had suffered attacks by loyalists. However, perhaps inevitably, these troops soon became targets for nationalists who saw them as representatives of an alien occupying force. The Provisional Irish Republican Army (IRA) began a violent campaign to secure, firstly, the withdrawal

of British troops and, ultimately, a united Ireland. In 1972, the events of 'Bloody Sunday', when British troops fired on demonstrators, killing thirteen civilians, led to the suspension of the Stormont government and the imposition of direct rule from Westminster. Violence, involving sectarian murders, revenge attacks and bombings, was to remain a feature of Ulster life for a quarter of a century, and was periodically exported to the mainland of Britain. A series of political initiatives failed to end the cycle of violence.

The Irish nationalist challenge to the Union was paralleled by a resurgence of Scottish and Welsh nationalism, although these have been almost entirely non-violent. Parliamentary by-election victories for nationalists led to a more marked advance for the Scottish National Party and (to a lesser extent) Plaid Cymru in the two general elections of 1974. Disturbed by the threat to its support in Scotland and Wales, Labour promised a new elected Scottish Parliament and Welsh Assembly, involving some devolution of power rather than the independence pursued by nationalists. This first attempt at devolution foundered with the failure to secure sufficient votes in referendums in 1979, an outcome that precipitated the fall of Callaghan's Labour government. The Conservatives had long been the party of the Union, and the governments of Thatcher and Major made no concessions to nationalist pressures that seemed to recede for a time in Scotland and Wales, although not in Northern Ireland.

## Social change and the politics of protest: the Sixties and after

Prime Minister Harold Macmillan (1957–63) once famously boasted, 'You've never had it so good.' Despite Britain's relatively low growth and other economic problems, living standards rose continuously in the post-war decades. Following the end of rationing and wartime shortages there was a greater range of goods on which to spend money, including durable consumer goods such as cars, washing machines and television sets, increasingly within the range of ordinary working people. Some argued that increased prosperity was affecting political allegiances. Workers in the then flourishing car industry acquired middle-class lifestyles, and perhaps attitudes, for the middle-class vote was then overwhelmingly Conservative. A 1959 election slogan 'Life's better under the Conservatives. Don't let Labour ruin it.' was accompanied by pictures showing a happy middle-class family with father, mother and two children enjoying their new home and car.

Yet increasing prosperity was accompanied by other social change, less consistent with traditional family values. It was becoming easier for both men and women to choose alternative lifestyles. The Sixties have been associated with increased sexual liberation. Contraceptive pills enabled couples to plan or avoid parenthood. More couples lived openly together unmarried. Illegitimacy lost much of its earlier stigma. Abortion was legalized in 1967. Divorce law was reformed, making divorce easier and cheaper. Homosexual acts, previously punishable by law, were legalized between consenting adults, although it is taking much longer for public attitudes to homosexuality to change.

Some critics deplored increased social and sexual permissiveness and the effects it had on the traditional family, and particularly on the children of casual unions and broken marriages. While easier divorce enabled some men to abandon middle-aged wives for younger partners, it also allowed some women to escape from bad marriages. Women's increased earning power gave them more freedom to choose and control their own lives.

The families portrayed in election posters, in commercial advertising, and in the media generally, remained overwhelmingly white until the last years of the twentieth century. Yet one largely unintended consequence of empire had been substantial immigration into Britain from its former colonies, particularly from the West Indies, the Indian subcontinent and parts of Africa. The growing black and Asian population faced considerable prejudice and discrimination, and in the largely inner urban areas where most of them settled there were ethnic tensions and sometimes serious riots. It was only gradually that sports stars, comedians, professionals and politicians from ethnic minorities obtained acceptance by the majority: but, over a period, Britain has clearly become a multicultural society, accommodating a range of different religions, languages and lifestyles. Ethnic minorities

have undoubtedly brought a new dimension to British politics, yet there is still tension and conflict. The children and grandchildren of immigrants, while often assimilating much of British culture, have been less prepared to accept the casual discrimination and prejudice their elders ignored.

Social change provoked political change. Largely outside the parties, the politics of protest grew in the 1960s and the 1970s. The Campaign for Nuclear Disarmament (CND) organized a series of massive marches against the bomb, while they and other groups demonstrated against the American war in Vietnam, as part of a growing peace movement. Others became active participants in the developing green movement. The continuing economic, social, legal and political inequality suffered by women inspired a powerful feminist movement, which helped secure significant changes in the law and some real advances in employment opportunities, childcare and political representation. In response to the racist agitation stimulated by some far right groups, and tacitly endorsed by a few mainstream politicians, the Anti-Nazi League and ethnic minority groups sought to counter racial prejudice and discrimination, and champion the rights of minorities. Much of this politics of protest involved a reaction against the political mainstream and the established traditional parties, and cut across old class divisions. The relative homogeneity of British society and culture, proclaimed by some earlier British and foreign observers, seemed to be breaking down.

## Conservative dominance: Thatcherism and the free market

However, the impact of the new politics can be exaggerated. In some respects, the Conservative election victory in 1979, which inaugurated eighteen years of Conservative rule, can be seen as a reaction against much of the social and political change outlined above. Britain's new Prime Minister, Margaret Thatcher, spoke the language and reflected the values of the white English middle classes. She was to prove the most controversial figure in British post-war politics. Her legacy is still hotly contested. To her admirers she was a great leader who restored the British economy, confronted and defeated enemies at home, while resolutely defending and advancing Britain's interests abroad. To her critics, including not only Labour and the trade unions but some Conservatives (see, for example, Gilmour, 1992), her government was harsh and divisive, with disastrous implications for Britain's social harmony, its manufacturing industry and its public services.

The 1979 election was not the only nor the principal cause of the changes in the British state, economy and society which took place in the last decades of the twentieth century. The Labour government had already largely abandoned Keynesianism and introduced public spending cuts. Both the Wilson and Heath governments had attempted to reform industrial relations, anticipating some of the Thatcher curbs on trade unions. To an extent, what came to be called Thatcherism was a response to changing economic conditions in Britain and the wider world. Western governments of various political colours pursued similar policies. Yet despite these reservations, it is worth recording the verdict of Nigel Lawson, Thatcher's former Chancellor and once close ally, who resigned after quarrelling with his chief over exchange rate policy. She had, he said, 'transformed the politics of Britain – indeed Britain itself – to an extent that no other Government has achieved since the Attlee Government of 1945–51'.

Mrs Thatcher broke decisively from consensus politics. She declared in 1979 'I am a conviction politician. The Old Testament prophets did not say, Brothers I want a consensus' (quoted in Dutton, 1997, p. 110). She rejected Keynesian economics because she was a convinced supporter of the free market economics of Hayek, Friedman, and the founder of classical economics, Adam Smith (see discussion of Thatcherism and the New Right in Chapter 7). Like Friedman, she saw control of the money supply as the key to controlling inflation, and early on the term '**monetarism**' was used to describe her philosophy.

---

● **Monetarism** involves controlling inflation by controlling the money supply. More broadly, monetarists rejected interventionist Keynesian policies and increased government spending, which fuelled inflation, particularly if financed by budget deficits and borrowing, in favour of 'rolling back the state' and reducing government spending to promote free enterprise and a healthy economy.

In practice, her government was not particularly effective in controlling the money supply; high interest rates damaged manufacturing industry and substantially increased unemployment. Nor was it particularly successful in cutting total state spending, partly because the rise in unemployment increased the cost of welfare benefits. Yet her free market views did inspire the policy with which she became most associated: privatization.

Privatization involves the transfer of ownership of assets from the public sector to the private sector. The major nationalized industries – British Telecom, British Gas, British Airways, the British Steel Corporation, the Water Authorities and the electricity industry – were sold off under the Thatcher government, British Rail following under her successor, John Major (see Timeline 2.4). Although advocates of privatization claimed significant gains in economic efficiency, critics suggested these public assets were undervalued and sold at a loss. However, privatization produced political dividends for the Conservatives, by extending a 'property-owning democracy' and promoting 'popular capitalism.' Another massive transfer of property ownership from public to private sector was secured by legislation obliging local authorities to sell council houses at substantial discounts to tenants; in ten years 1.3 million council houses were sold under the 'right to buy.'

While there were some real cuts in public services, the welfare state was not substantially reduced. Mrs Thatcher declared 'the NHS is safe in our hands', and spending on education per pupil slightly increased. However, these services were exposed to increased competition through the introduction of an internal market in the health service and similar developments in education. Moreover, some ancillary health and local government services were subjected to Compulsory Competitive Tendering (CCT) whereby services such as cleaning, catering, laundry, refuse collection and ground maintenance were put out to tender to the lowest bidder, which was often a private sector firm.

The Thatcher government also took on the trade unions. Strikes by public sector workers during the 1979 'winter of discontent' were thought by many to be harming British industry and hurting the public and had been a significant factor

## TIMELINE 2.4

### The main privatizations involving former public enterprise

| | | | | |
|---|---|---|---|---|
| **1981** onwards | British Aerospace | | **1989** | Water authorities |
| **1984** onwards | British Telecom | | **1990** | Electricity distribution |
| **1986** | British Gas | | **1991** | Electricity generation |
| **1987** | British Airways | | **1995** | British Rail |
| **1988** | British Steel Corporation | | | |

in the Conservative election victory. Curbs on union powers, such as compulsory strike ballots and restrictions on picketing, were initially popular, while rising unemployment weakened effective trade union resistance. Yet, when the government's fight with the unions reached its climax with the miners' strike of 1984–5, public sympathy began to switch to the coal miners, who suffered increasing hardship the longer the strike lasted. This sympathy increased when it appeared that Thatcher's government was determined to secure the miners' total defeat, perhaps in revenge for the humiliation the NUM had inflicted on a previous Conservative government in 1974.

It was however, Thatcher's image and record in foreign affairs that earned her the nickname Iron Lady. She secured a rebate in the British contribution to the European Community budget, establishing a reputation for standing up for British interests abroad. Her style of diplomacy hardly endeared her to the UK's European partners, although she had earlier supported Britain's entry to the EC, and later signed the Single European Act, even, near the end of her premiership, allowing British entry into the Exchange Rate Mechanism (ERM). More to her taste was the special relationship with the United States and with her political soul-mate, President Ronald Reagan, to whom she was a reliable ally in the last years of the Cold War. The end of the Cold War appeared as a victory for their joint vision of free market capitalism over communism.

Without Reagan's strong tacit support it is unlikely that Britain could have recovered the Falkland Islands. The Argentine invasion of the remote British south Atlantic colony in early 1982, could have brought down her government, caught totally unprepared; the entire Foreign Office team of ministers accepted responsibility and resigned. A substantial task force sailed to the Falklands to recapture the islands. What began as a political disaster became a personal triumph for the Prime Minister, if an expensive and divisive one, and Thatcher went on to win the 1983 election by a landslide.

The Falklands and the miners' strike typify Thatcher's leadership style as warrior rather than healer. She was reluctant to compromise at home or abroad. She was also essentially an English politician, who showed little sympathy or understanding for Scottish and Welsh interests and susceptibilities. Thus she opposed devolution, while support for her party steadily declined in Scotland and Wales. She also took on local government, which was largely in the hands of opposition parties, abolishing the Greater London Council led by Ken Livingstone. The disastrous poll tax, which provoked riots and substantial electoral reverses, was the culmination of a succession of curbs on local government spending which were a major factor in Thatcher's eventual fall in 1990.

By then she had won three elections and served as premier for over 11 years, a longer continuous term than any of her predecessors since Lord

Liverpool in the early nineteenth century. She might have lasted longer still had she not succeeded in antagonizing not only the political opposition, but a substantial section of her own party, including some former leading allies, especially Michael Heseltine, Nigel Lawson and Geoffrey Howe. It was Howe's devastating resignation speech that precipitated Heseltine's challenge to her leadership.

Her successor, John Major, had a difficult act to follow, his six-and-a-half-year premiership seeming in retrospect little more than a prolonged coda to Thatcherism, although his style was more consensual. Although the Major government replaced the poll tax with the council tax, it otherwise maintained and extended Thatcher's competition and privatization policy. Major inherited the American-led first Gulf War, launched in response to Saddam Hussein's invasion of Kuwait, and in Europe, reflecting growing Conservative euroscepticism, he negotiated opt-outs for Britain from the Single European Currency and the Social Chapter at the Maastricht Treaty.

Britain's role in Europe had been a Conservative achievement, yet opinion in the party increasingly moved against the European Union at the very time when the previously divided and hostile Labour Party was moving in the other direction. The dramatic events of 'Black Wednesday', with Britain's forced exit from the ERM and the effective devaluation of the pound, which occurred in 1992 shortly after Major had secured a largely unexpected election victory, dealt a blow to his government from which it never recovered and contributed to the growing eurosceptic divisions within the Conservative Party. Previous economic crises had occurred largely on Labour's watch, while the Conservatives had enjoyed a reputation for economic competence. This was shattered almost overnight. Major's government was also undermined by a series of scandals involving low-level corruption ('cash for questions') and sexual misbehaviour, rendered more serious by Major's call to 'get back to basics', widely interpreted to mean traditional family values. Major delayed the election as long as he could, and the economy did substantially recover, but it was too late.

## New Labour: Blair and Brown (1997–2010)

The 1997 election produced a massive reversal of party fortunes. Labour, whose chances of ever returning to power were once almost written off, swept to victory with the biggest election landslide since 1945. The new government was dominated by Tony Blair, who had led his party since 1994 and successfully rebranded it as 'New Labour' (see Chapters 6 and 7), and the new Chancellor, Gordon Brown who was given wide authority over economic and social policy. A shell-shocked much reduced Conservative parliamentary party went on to elect the then relatively unknown former Welsh Secretary William Hague as their new leader. Meanwhile, the Liberal Democrats doubled their parliamentary representation (on a smaller proportion of the total vote), becoming a credible third parliamentary force.

The dramatic changes in the relative strength of parties made 1997 a landmark election which transformed the political geography of Britain with a massive 10 per cent swing in support from Conservative to Labour, unprecedented in post-war elections. The Conservatives won no seats in Scotland or Wales, while Labour won seats in parts of the south of England which had previously been alien territory for them (see Chapter 5). The Conservatives failed to make any appreciable recovery in the ensuing 2001 election, another landslide victory for Labour. Hague resigned, to be replaced briefly by Iain Duncan Smith, and then, in 2003, by Michael Howard. The Conservatives appeared doomed to ineffective opposition following a third consecutive election defeat in 2005, and Howard resigned, to be succeeded by David Cameron.

The 1997 election had a more marked impact on party fortunes than on policy. To the disappointment of many Labour supporters, the new government did not reverse the Conservatives' trade union reforms and privatization policies but introduced further privatization and extended market reforms of the public services. Some even concluded that Blair was Thatcher's heir. Yet New Labour also introduced other reforms that the Conservatives had opposed, such as a national minimum wage and massive increases in spending on healthcare and education.

Labour's record in social policy is also contentious. Increased spending on health and education produced some improvements, notably reduced waiting times for operations and better exam results in schools. Yet there were some questions over value for money, and rather more over management regimes and the increased role of the private sector (see Chapter 21). Moreover, Labour largely failed to reverse the growth of inequality manifest under the previous Conservative administrations, a damning failure from a socialist perspective (see Chapter 22).

Labour's foreign policy proved much more controversial (see Chapter 24), particularly the close alliance with the United States, involving British forces in several wars, over Kosovo, Afghanistan and Iraq. The last two followed the 9/11 New York attack, and were justified as part of the 'war on terror'. The invasion and subsequent occupation of Iraq from 2003 onwards proved particularly divisive. Although this policy was initially supported by most Conservatives, it split Blair's own party and the country. It also contributed to the alienation of some young British Muslims, who brought terror to Britain with the attacks on London in 2005 and the failed attack on Glasgow airport in 2007.

## Constitutional change and devolution

Labour's most enduring legacy is likely to be the sweeping changes in the system of government. Not all of their ambitious programme of constitutional reform was successfully implemented (see Chapter 10). The failures to reform the House of Lords or change the voting system for the House of Commons particularly disappointed reformers, who have also criticized the lack of overall vision and coherence. Despite these shortcomings the transformation of British government has been substantial and almost certainly irreversible. The Freedom of Information Act and the Human Rights Act have had massive implications, not least for the Labour government. The new Supreme Court is a major reform enhancing the independence of the judiciary and the separation of the powers of the state. The new voting systems involving more proportional

representation introduced for the European Parliament and devolved institutions are important in themselves and increase the pressure for reform of the electoral system for Westminster.

The devolution of powers to Scotland, Wales and Northern Ireland are likely to prove the most important of Labour's constitutional reforms. Plans for devolution in Scotland were substantially agreed between Labour and the Liberal Democrats in the Scottish Constitutional Convention before the 1997 election. The Blair government swiftly introduced referendums in which Scottish voters emphatically, and Welsh voters narrowly, endorsed devolution. This provided popular authority for the substantive legislation that followed, establishing a new Scottish Parliament and Welsh Assembly, both elected by the Additional Member System (see Chapter 5). Devolution now seems irreversible, and has been accepted by the previously opposed Conservatives, although its consequences for Labour have been mixed – the new voting system left them without a majority in either the Scottish Parliament or the Welsh Assembly.

From 1999 to 2007 Labour was the largest party in the Scottish Parliament and took the lead in a coalition government with the Liberal Democrats. The Scottish National Party (SNP) lost votes and seats in the 2003 election, suggesting that devolution had stemmed the nationalist advance, but in 2007 it became the largest party in the Scottish Parliament, forming a minority administration. The SNP did less well than expected in the 2010 UK general election but went on to make sweeping gains in the Scottish Parliament elections of 2011, winning a majority of seats, with the prospect of early referendum on Scottish independence.

Although Labour has been much the largest party in the Welsh Assembly from 1999 it has never commanded a clear majority, forming a minority administration or a coalition, first with the Liberal Democrats then with Plaid Cymu, before winning just half the seats in 2011. In Northern Ireland, Blair was able to build on the initiatives of his predecessor, John Major, whose negotiations with the Irish government and (more covertly) with Sinn Fein had led to an IRA ceasefire in 1995, which broke down the following year. Blair secured a more lasting peace following the Good Friday agreement of 1998. Elections fitfully restored devolved government to Northern Ireland, with power shared between loyalists and nationalists, but with periodic crises over disarmament and policing, that led to a suspension of devolved institutions. In fresh elections in 2007 the more intransigent parties triumphed over the moderates in both communities, yet a previously unthinkable coalition emerged between Ian Paisley's Democratic Unionist Party and Republican Sinn Fein, with initially Paisley as First Minister and Martin McGuinness as his deputy. This remarkable DUP/Sinn Fein coalition survived fresh elections in 2011. Despite continuing occasional atrocities by small dissident republican groups, peace and reconciliation substantially prevail in Northern Ireland. Problems are far from over as a resurgence of violence from small republican groups has demonstrated. Even so, the transformation in Northern Ireland has been remarkable.

With nationalists ruling in Scotland and sharing power in Northern Ireland and Wales from 2007, the end of the Union does begin to appear a real possibility. Whatever the ultimate outcome, British politics and government has already become more multi-layered and complex. (see Chapter 16).

## From Brown's boom to the financial crisis and Labour's defeat

Yet what secured for Labour a second and third election victory was probably none of the above, but its apparently successful management of the economy from 1997 to 2007, with Chancellor Gordon Brown presiding over relatively high employment and economic growth with low inflation. It was this economic success that not only facilitated the substantial growth in public services but also was able to fund Blair's wars. When Blair finally resigned as Labour leader and Prime Minister in 2007, Brown was his obvious successor, and was chosen by the party without a challenge.

Although some hoped, and others feared, that Brown's government would involve a marked change of direction, and perhaps a return to 'old Labour', in practice the differences in government personnel and policy were marginal. Brown promoted some of his own followers and advisers, but many of Blair's closest associates survived the departure of their leader. Brown enjoyed a brief honeymoon period in which he toyed with an early general election in the autumn of 2007 to secure a personal mandate. Yet he hesitated, the opportunity passed, and the 'election that never was' began a slide in his party's support from which it never quite recovered (Kavanagh and Cowley, 2010, pp. 1–17). Moreover, although all parties suffered from the parliamentary expenses scandal of 2009 (see Chapter 13) which further eroded already low public confidence in politicians, it was Labour, as the party in government, that was most adversely affected.

However, far more critical was the banking crisis and ensuing economic recession of 2008–9. Although this was a global crisis, the enduring earlier support for the Labour government substantially reflected the economic prosperity of the Blair and Brown years, (indeed, Brown had incautiously boasted that he had 'ended boom and bust') and the recession inevitably called into question Brown's own record as Chancellor. Critics argued that some of the specific problems in Britain could be attributed to Brown's stewardship: the boom had been fuelled partly by the growth of government and consumer spending, the latter financed by often rash lending by banks only subject to the 'light touch' regulation endorsed by Brown.

Brown earned some credit with other world leaders for his energetic response to the crisis and the massive injection of government, and ultimately taxpayers', money to avoid a complete meltdown in public confidence in the whole financial system. Yet the crisis had happened on his watch and British voters were rather less impressed with the leadership he showed in responding to it. While his own standing in the country plummeted, there were ultimately unsuccessful plots within the Labour party to replace him as leader and Prime Minister. In desperation Brown surprisingly brought back into the Cabinet the key architect of New Labour, Peter Mandelson, following years of bitter enmity between the two men dating back to Blair's election as leader in 1994. The new Business Secretary played an important role in limiting a threatened Cabinet revolt to save Brown's premiership after disastrous European and local elections for Labour in 2009.

Yet, beyond the immediate effect of the crisis on British party politics, the recession has already had much more important consequences for the British economy and society, highlighting once again its over-dependence on financial services and the weakness of manufacturing. It dramatized major weaknesses in the regulation of financial services and publicized the huge rewards Britain's bankers have reaped in salaries, bonuses, share options and pensions, illuminating the massive and increasing inequality in income and wealth within Britain that successive governments had either encouraged or failed to check. One surprising by-product of the crisis was the return of nationalization. The government nationalized Northern Rock in 2007 and has subsequently bailed out and virtually taken into public ownership much larger banks, including RBS, Lloyds and HBOS. It has also renationalized the east coast rail route. All this is supposed to be temporary, yet it involves a significant reversal of the privatization associated with the previous quarter of a century under Thatcher, Major and Blair. Moreover, the need for more government management of the economy was, for a time, widely accepted. To an extent the theories and prescriptions of Keynes enjoyed a temporary renaissance.

There was some shift in the intellectual climate. Greed was no longer good. Wealth did not necessarily 'trickle down' to the poor. The unashamed pursuit of individual self-interest in the free market did not appear to maximize the general welfare. David Cameron, as Conservative party leader in opposition, emphatically declared that there was such a thing as society, contradicting Thatcher's pronouncement to the contrary (although significantly Cameron went on to argue that society was not the same as the state). Cameron's party proclaimed an interest in social justice, and even the promotion of greater social equality, as well as a concern for the environment. Moral philosophers as well as religious leaders enjoined altruistic behaviour in pursuit of the common good. Rational choice theory, long dominant in the study of economics and strongly influential in political science, appeared on the defensive.

## The 2010 election and the Conservative–Liberal Democrat coalition under David Cameron

Opinion polls in 2009 forecast a decisive

Conservative majority at the forthcoming general election, with Brown's personal standing and that of his party hitting new lows. A partial recovery in Labour fortunes early in 2010 proved insufficient for the party to retain power. The result of the 2010 election effectively closed one chapter in British post-war political history, the thirteen years of New Labour, and began another, apparently involving a very different kind of government and politics.

The election produced the first **hung parliament** since February 1974, and prolonged negotiations over a new coalition government between the Conservatives and Liberal Democrats, whose leader Nick Clegg had seen his personal ratings soar after the UK's first televised party leader debates. Other outcomes appeared possible: a minority (Conservative or conceivably Labour) government as in 1974, or a 'traffic-light coalition' of Labour, Liberal Democrats, the solitary Green and others. There was brief discussion of the last option, and some later regretted that the opportunity had been missed (see Comparative Politics 2.2). Yet it was hardly a viable alternative. The Conservatives and the press would have cried 'foul' and perhaps most voters would have agreed. While the Conservatives had failed to win the election, Labour had clearly lost it, even if not as disastrously as some party supporters feared. The sums did not add up sufficiently to create a viable alternative government with more than a vestigial paper majority. Moreover, the continuing financial and economic crisis was widely considered to require tough measures that only a stable government with parliamentary support could deliver.

Thus David Cameron eventually entered 10 Downing Street as the first Conservative Prime Minister for thirteen years, heading the first UK

---

● A **hung parliament** (or a **hung council**) is one where no single political party can command a majority, implying coalition or minority government. Liberal Democrats dislike the term, which they think is pejorative, and prefer 'balanced parliament'. They have a point. A 'hung jury' is one that fails to agree on a verdict. Interestingly, the Northern Ireland Assembly is not described as 'hung' – perhaps because its electoral system and other institutional arrangements were deliberately designed to prevent single party rule and encourage power-sharing. Similarly, the Scottish Parliament and Welsh Assembly are rarely termed 'hung', even though elections for these bodies have yet to produce a clear majority for a single party.

## COMPARATIVE POLITICS 2.2
# The 2010 Australian election

The outcome of the UK general election of May 2010 has been compared with the Australian federal election that took place in August 2010. This also failed to produce a majority for either the defending Labor party, led by Julia Gillard, or the opposition, led by Tony Abbott. However, the Australian result was much closer with both Labor and the main opposition securing 72 seats in the House of Representatives, with the total votes almost equally divided, with a small plurality for Labor. (The Greens will hold the balance of power in the Senate.) After seventeen days of negotiation Labor formed a minority government with the support of the single Green MP and three independents, on the basis of 'confidence and supply' (in other words these MPs would back Labor in a confidence vote and on finance.)

coalition government since 1945, with the Liberal Democrats as junior but significant partners. The perpetual third party outsiders had achieved their first share of power. Nick Clegg became Deputy Prime Minister, with four more of his party gaining Cabinet seats, and others junior government posts.

How far this new political era involves a decisive shift in British politics and a new style of government is not yet clear. Turning points in history are sometimes noticed immediately, more commonly in retrospect. It is possible that Britain will become more accustomed to coalition politics. Before the 2010 general election **hung councils** were already a feature of local government (see Chapter 17). Minority or coalition government has become the norm in Scotland, Wales and Northern Ireland. Yet it is equally possible that coalition at Westminster will prove a short-lived interlude in the general preponderance of single party government since 1945.

While some predicted the new coalition would not last long, the clearly stated intention of both parties was a stable partnership for a whole parliament, with accompanying constitutional changes to facilitate this (see Chapter 10). How far these intentions will be realized remains to be seen, although so far ministers from both parties have worked together amicably. Difficulties are more likely to arise with discontented backbenchers and party members. The new government soon faced a new opposition, as Gordon Brown announced his resignation as party leader as well as Prime Minister, leaving the Labour party to some internal reassess-ment under the surprising winner of the Labour leadership election, Ed Miliband.

The early focus of the coalition government has understandably been on the reduction of the huge public deficit resulting from the banking crisis, economic recession, and (they would argue) Labour's profligacy. All parties were agreed before the election on the need to cut the deficit, although disagreeing over the method and the timetable, and declining to provide detailed proposals. It was soon clear that the coalition was determined to cut the deficit sooner rather than later, and mainly by reductions in public spending rather than increases in taxation (see Chapter 20). This involved potentially massive implications for public services (see Chapter 21) and arguably also for equality and social justice (see Chapter 22). The Labour opposition has argued that the scale and pace of proposed spending cuts put economic recovery at risk and threaten a 'double dip' recession. They also claim that behind the government's plans lies a broader ideological agenda to shrink the state and the public sector, reflecting Thatcherite ideas. This placed increasing strains on the Conservatives' coalition partners. Those Liberal Democrats who have entered government seem broadly sympathetic to the economic liberalism of their Conservative coalition partners. However, many Liberal Democrat MPs and party members still see themselves as on the left, and committed to the social liberalism that has been the dominant political philosophy of the party since the early twentieth century (see Chapter 7).

## British politics today compared with 1945

On the surface much appears unchanged. To judge from the images in the media, power still revolves around Westminster and Whitehall as it did in 1945. The daughter of George VI, Britain's wartime monarch, who became Queen in 1952, remains on the throne, having seen a succession of Prime Ministers come and go, from Winston Churchill onwards. An old Etonian now presides once more in 10 Downing Street, the seventeenth Prime Minister from that school. The same traditional ceremonies are still used for state occasions, such as the opening of Parliament. Yet much has been transformed utterly. The empire has gone, and Britain is now a member of a still expanding European Union that did not exist even in embryo in 1945. Power has been devolved to Scotland, Wales, and Northern Ireland. The British parliament and government contains a significant minority of women, both men and women who are openly gay, and a small but rising number from ethnic minorities and different faiths, partially reflecting more extensive changes in society. Politics reflects new issues and involves new divisions, particularly since the 2010 election. Even so, much of the legacy of the past lives on, not just in the style, but in the substance of modern British politics.

# SUMMARY

- The British political system has been shaped by past history and shows marked stability and continuity, but has been massively transformed by economic, social and political developments.

- British politics in the immediate post-war period were shaped by the development of a welfare state and mixed economy at home, and the Cold War abroad.

- Although people enjoyed rising living standards and low unemployment, Britain continued to suffer relative economic decline, causing political difficulties for successive governments.

- The fast shrinking British empire and the special relationship with the United States were an obstacle to earlier closer engagement with Europe. Britain joined the European Community too late to shape its rules or share early benefits, and the commitment was less than wholehearted.

- From the late 1960s onwards the United Kingdom faced threats to the maintenance of the Union from nationalist movements in Northern Ireland, Scotland and Wales, culminating in the introduction of devolved assemblies and governments in all three countries. It is not clear yet whether devolution will ultimately preserve the Union or lead to separation.

- Changes in population, living standards and lifestyles raised new political issues and involved some rejection of traditional values. It helped spark a politics of protest largely outside the traditional party system.

- The Thatcher government brought a marked shift away from the politics of the post-war decades, involving a rejection of Keynesian economics and a renewed emphasis on market forces.

- Politics under New Labour showed elements of both change and continuity. Labour's constitutional reform programme has transformed the system of government, with unclear implications for the future, particularly in the United Kingdom outside England.

- The credit crunch and recession called into question both Labour's apparent success in managing the economy and the free market ideas associated with Thatcherite Conservatism that had been largely accepted by New Labour. Keynesian ideas enjoyed a modest renaissance.

- The 2010 election ended the New Labour government, but unusually resulted in a hung parliament and coalition government between Cameron's Conservatives and the Liberal Democrats.

## QUESTIONS FOR DISCUSSION

- How far was Britain's great power status an illusion after the Second World War?

- Was there a political consensus in the period after the Second World War, and if so, on what was it based?

- How successful was the application of Keynesian economics by British governments? Why did politicians lose faith in Keynesian remedies from the1970s onwards? Why is Keynes now back in fashion?

- Why were British governments not involved in closer European integration in the 1950s? Why have British governments, and the British people, not engaged more closely with Europe?

- How and why was the unity of the United Kingdom apparently threatened from the 1970s?

- Why do Margaret Thatcher and Thatcherism still inspire so much controversy?

- How far did the election of a Labour government in 1997 involve a turning point in British history, comparable to the election of the Attlee government in 1945 or the Thatcher government in 1979?

- How far did New Labour mark the reversal or continuation of Thatcherism?

- Does a hung parliament and coalition government represent a problem or an opportunity?

## FURTHER READING

There are several useful books on post-war British politics. Sked and Cook (1979) provide a useful survey of the earlier periods and Dutton (1997) a good chronological account up to the dying days of the Major government, with particular emphasis on consensus politics. Morgan and Owen (2001) give an excellent overview of the whole period. Marr (2007) is more populist (it was associated with a television series) but lively, judicious, and relatively up-to-date.

On particular periods, Hennessy (1993) provides a vivid account of politics and life in 1945–51. Pimlott (1992) has written a reliable, sympathetic account of Harold Wilson, while Crossman's diaries provide a fly-on-the-wall insider account of Wilson's 1964–70 government. Campbell (1993) is useful on Heath. The literature on Thatcherism has become voluminous. Kavanagh (1990) provides a very readable introduction, while Hugo Young (1990) gives a lively biography of Mrs Thatcher herself, but see also Thatcher's own account of her premiership (1993). Kavanagh and Seldon (1994) provide a very useful survey of the early part of Major's government, while Major's own autobiography (1999) is frank and readable. The literature on Blair and New Labour is substantial. Rawnsley's (2001) blow-by-blow account of the first term remains useful. Seldon (2001), Ludlam and Smith (2004), Seldon and Kavanagh (2005), and Beech and Lee (2008) are invaluable for analysis of policies and issues. Rentoul (2001) and Seldon (2004) are interesting on Blair, who has now published his own account (2010) of his party leadership and premiership. Bower (2004) is useful on Brown before he became Prime Minister. Useful book sources on Brown's government include Rawnsley (2009, 2010), and Mandelson (2010), and Richards (2010). For Cameron's coalition government, consult newspapers and periodicals as well as appropriate websites until journal articles and books begin to appear.

There is more detailed discussion and fuller references on many of the issues discussed in this chapter in subsequent chapters.

# Economy, Society and Politics

The economic and social circumstances of a country have significant implications for its politics. Marxists have long argued that political power reflects economic power and economic inequality drives political change. British political scientists have acknowledged the importance of economic class divisions especially for party allegiances and voting. Yet it is also clear that other social divisions based on national identity, ethnicity, religion, culture, gender and age also increasingly affect political perceptions and allegiances and the extent of political participation.

Politics is, therefore, substantially shaped by economic and social factors. Yet it is also widely claimed that politics can transform economies and societies. Governments employ a variety of policies to influence the economic and social behaviour of its citizens, for example, to seek employment, avoid anti-social behaviour, increase saving or consumption, avoid discrimination on grounds of gender, ethnicity or religion. State-sponsored services, such as education, health, social and environmental services, aspire to influence the economy and society. Moreover, governments claim, or are given credit for, perceived improvements in the economic and social sphere (for example low inflation or reduced crime figures), while they are widely condemned for perceived failures (rising unemployment or increased drunkenness). When governments are criticized for presiding over increased inequality, it is implied that different policies could promote a more equal society. When David Cameron, in opposition, described Britain as a 'broken society' he was both blaming Labour for the breakdown and claiming that an alternative government could repair it.

In this chapter the main emphasis is on economic and social influences on British politics; the policy chapters in the last part of the book will focus more on the influence of British political activity on economy and society.

## The changing British economy

Britain was the first country to industrialize and once appeared the 'workshop of the world'. Yet even before the end of the nineteenth century, Britain was already being overtaken by the new industrial strength of the United States and Germany, and commentators noted British economic decline (Gamble, 1981, pp. 13–14). The decline was relative. Growth and living standards continued to increase, but at a slower rate than leading competitors (Gamble 1981, pp. 18–23; Gamble in English and Kenny, 2000, pp. 2–10). In the aftermath of the Second World War millions of British workers were still employed in mining, iron and steel, shipbuilding, textiles and clothing, and motor manufacturing.

Since then output and employment in all these industries has declined dramatically, and the British share of world production has shrunk. The United Kingdom still has the sixth largest economy in the world (based on IMF figures for states' gross domestic product, GDP) behind the USA, Japan, China, Germany and France. Yet GDP per head is not only behind all these (except for China) but also behind all the Scandinavian and Benelux countries, some Gulf states, Australia, Canada and even the Irish Republic. Explaining British economic decline has become something of an academic industry (Gamble, 1981; Pollard, 1989; English and Kenny, 2001), as well as a major subject of political debate. Variously attributed to faults in Britain's entrepreneurs and workers, company structure, trade unions, banking system, education system, government intervention and the welfare state, relative economic decline was nevertheless inevitable as multi-national enterprises in an increasingly globalized economy shifted their production where costs were lowest in the industrialized world.

Thus Britain, like other western countries, is adjusting, sometimes painfully, to a post-industrial society, with an economy increasingly centred on services rather than mining and manufacturing. Most British workers are no longer employed in making tangible objects – such as clothes, cars, electrical appliances and 'white goods'. Instead they provide services to each other and the wider world, including education, health and social care, retailing, hotels and catering, maintenance and cleaning, professional and financial services.

As mining, heavy industry and manufacturing have declined, employment has grown in light industry and particularly services. Yet the new jobs were mostly not created in the areas that had suffered the rapid contraction of Britain's staple industries, and for all kinds of reasons people could not easily move to take advantage of economic opportunities elsewhere. The decline of shipbuilding particularly hit Clydeside in Scotland, Belfast in Northern Ireland, and Tyneside in the North-east of England. Pit closures have decimated employment in the coalfields of central Scotland, south Wales and Yorkshire. The rundown of the textile industry has seen the closure of Lancashire cotton mills and Yorkshire woollen mills, and the blighting of once prosperous towns and cities. The contraction of the iron and steel industries has particularly affected the

North-east, Sheffield, the Midlands and south Wales. More recent problems in motor manufacturing have had particularly adverse consequences for the West Midlands. Thus some communities, cities and whole regions suffered disproportionately from economic decline, prompting first UK government and then European Union action to assist the worst affected areas.

Until recently the one apparent success story in the British economy was the continuing strength of its financial services. Successive governments sought to preserve and enhance London as a world financial centre, replacing controls with 'light touch' regulation. Easier credit supplied by banks fuelled much of Britain's economic boom from 1997 to 2007. Although the financial and economic crisis of 2007–9 highlighted the over-dependence of the British economy on its financial sector, politicians hesitated to introduce more controls, fearful of 'killing the goose that lays the golden eggs' and risking the transfer of London's financial services to other countries. The rest of the economy suffered for the mistakes of the bankers, although some parts of the country have suffered more than others.

This crisis, like earlier economic crises, also highlights the extent to which governments and politicians are in the grip of forces they cannot control and to which they can only react. Of course it can be argued that without the prompt action of governments the crisis might have become a catastrophe, that markets cannot ultimately be left to themselves, that political intervention is needed. Governments felt they had little choice but to rescue the banks that had precipitated it. Yet this largely unforeseen global crisis also underlines the limited effectiveness of governments' management of economic forces on their own and the need for international co-operation and concerted action. This is still politics, but at another level, in which governments have to work with each other and with international organizations, both governmental and non-governmental, to tackle the problems they face together.

## The nations and regions of Britain

Britain's economic problems, both older and more recent, have compounded long established differences in Britain's political geography. Although the

**Table 3.1** Population of the United Kingdom of Great Britain and Northern Ireland, 2008

|  | Population in millions | % UK population |
| --- | --- | --- |
| England | 51.5 | 83.8 |
| Wales | 3.0 | 4.9 |
| Scotland | 5.2 | 8.5 |
| Northern Ireland | 1.8 | 2.9 |
| United Kingdom | 61.4 |  |

*Source*: ONS.

United Kingdom is made up of four main component national territories, most of its inhabitants (51.5 million out of 61.4 million) live in England. Thus the Union inevitably appears a rather lopsided affair between the English and the much less numerous peoples inhabiting Scotland, Wales and Northern Ireland (see Table 3.1). The terms 'England', 'Britain' and 'the United Kingdom' are often incorrectly used interchangeably, to the annoyance of the Scots and Welsh.

Differences in culture and institutions arise out of past patterns of settlement and historical influences. Each country has its own religious traditions and divisions. Wales has its own language and an associated distinctive culture. Scotland has its own legal and educational system. Today Scotland, Wales and Northern Ireland not only continue their own political traditions but all enjoy varying degrees of self-government (see Chapter 16). There are also important economic differences. Agriculture is rather more important to Scotland and Wales than England. Heavy industry in central Scotland, South Wales and Belfast was adversely affected by Britain's industrial decline. However, although levels of income per head in Wales and Northern Ireland are substantially below the UK average, they are close to the average in Scotland. Yet while parts of the Scottish economy have flourished, it has recently been rocked by the problems of its hitherto prestigious banking sector.

There are also significant differences in income and other economic indicators (such as unemployment) between English regions, with marked variations in prosperity between a wealthy London and South-east, and the poorest English region, the North-east, which is worse off than Scotland but

similar to Wales and Northern Ireland. Such regional disparities fuel demands for more favourable treatment by government, assistance for inward investment, and improvements to basic infrastructure.

These economic disparities in the performance of Britain's nations and regions have some implications for political allegiances. The North–South divide has become something of a cliché, albeit with some basis in economic and political reality. Not only is the South richer than the North, but Labour's main political support still comes from the industrial North of England, Central Scotland and South Wales, while Conservative strength lies in the South of England and particularly the South-east. The industrial Midlands are politically contested. Although economic inequality and relative deprivation partly explain the distinctive political allegiances of Wales, Northern Ireland and parts of Scotland, cultural factors and the politics of identity, have long been more significant in Northern Ireland, and are increasingly important in Scotland and Wales.

## Town and country, inner cities and outer suburbs

There remain, however, more significant differences in economic activity and thus in income and wealth within than between nations and regions. Yorkshire and the Humber, for example, is among the poorest of Britain's regions, but it contains Leeds which is relatively booming as a major financial, commercial and administrative centre, at least compared with neighbouring Bradford, Sheffield, and Hull. Bradford is now unhappily known for its deprivation, racial tension and riots rather than the woollen industry on which its former wealth was based. Yet within the boundaries of Bradford Metropolitan District is the small commuter town of Ilkley, overwhelmingly white, middle-class and as comfortably prosperous as parts of the Surrey stockbroker belt. Ilkley in turn is part of the parliamentary constituency of Keighley, a formerly prosperous woollen town now inhabited mainly by working-class poor Asian and predominantly white communities which do not inter-relate much. Similar comparisons between neighbouring areas of prosperity and deprivation could be drawn all over Britain.

Thus there are generally marked differences in wealth and living standards between inner urban areas on the one hand and outer suburbs and 'dormitory' towns on the other. Some of the political implications of these economic differences can be charted in the party representation of parliamentary constituencies and local government wards. It is still broadly true that the more deprived urban areas are more likely to be represented by Labour, and the more prosperous outer suburbs and semi-rural areas by Conservatives. However, where economic deprivation is particularly significant there may also be more serious political consequences in terms of alienation, antisocial and criminal behaviour, disturbances to public order, inter-community conflict and the rise of anti-system parties and movements, such as the British National Party and the English Defence League.

## Allegiance and identity

Where people live is less significant for politics than how people think about where they live, and the nations or communities to which they think they belong. The national identity of the substantial majority of people living in England is for the most part unproblematic, but there are divided loyalties among the non-English parts of the United Kingdom (see Curtis, in Hazell, 2000). This is particularly evident in Northern Ireland where the majority of Protestants see themselves as British, and only 2 per cent see themselves as Irish, whereas among Catholics only 9 per cent think of themselves as British while 68 per cent consider themselves Irish. In Scotland opinion is rather less polarized, and many acknowledge a dual identity as Scots and British (see Figure 3.1).

The link between identity and economic experience is contentious. It is certainly plausible that economic problems can fuel dissatisfaction with the United Kingdom, and stimulate distinctive national or regional identities. Yet much of the support for nationalist parties has not come from the most depressed areas of Scotland and Wales, and Scotland is as economically prosperous as England. On the contrary, greater economic

Figure 3.1   National identity in Scotland in 2000

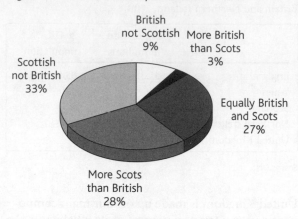

*Source:* Adapted from Curtis in Hazell, 2000, p. 236.

success may boost national pride and confidence in the capacity of an independent Scotland to 'go it alone'.

Perhaps identity is ultimately more to do with culture than economics. Either way, these felt identities may be significant for political behaviour. Thus the percentage who thought of themselves as 'Scottish not British' in 2000 (32 per cent) is not far from the level of support (29 per cent) recorded for the pro-independence Scottish National Party in the first Scottish Parliament elections in 1999 (32 per cent supported the SNP in 2007). Yet only 24 per cent supported an independent Scotland in 2007 (Curtis and Seyd, 2009, p. 122). Rather more of those in Wales acknowledge a dual Welsh and British nationality – there was only a bare majority for a Welsh national assembly in the 1997 referendum (although support for it has increased somewhat since) and only 11 per cent supported Welsh independence in 2000 (Curtis in Hazell, 2000, p. 238). Of course, such felt identities and allegiances can shift further over time, but they have some clear implications for the future of United Kingdom and British politics generally.

To date, there has been little popular demand for elected regional assemblies, partly because regional consciousness remains relatively weak over most of England (apart from the North-east and South-west). In some areas there is more identification with ancient counties going back a thousand years or more, though generally more in connection with sport than politics.

Cities may be more important in this respect, and city identities and loyalties may be stronger today. Rivalries between neighbouring cities are a feature of sub-national politics – between Glasgow and Edinburgh, Cardiff and Swansea, Manchester and Liverpool, Leeds and Sheffield. There are also significant differences in identities and allegiances within urban areas. Some suburban dwellers, who may work in the city and depend on it for shopping and recreation, still strenuously resist the notion that they are part of the city, preferring to identify with the dormitory towns and villages where they live. Yet this may sometimes have more to do with financial self-interest and the fear of higher local government tax bills in city-dominated local authorities than any real sense of community identity. There are also continuing perceived differences between 'town' and 'country', even though only 1 per cent of the UK working population are engaged in agriculture. However, a rather larger number live in and/or identify with the country – hence the apparent political strength and influence of bodies such as the Council for the Protection of Rural England, and more recently, the Countryside Alliance.

Thus, where people live sometimes gives rise to a sense of identity and an allegiance to a particular community. Others, however, may have a greater sense of attachment to other kinds of community, bound together not by physical proximity, but by some other shared membership, for example of a particular ethnic group or faith community.

## Ethnicity

The definition of 'ethnicity' and how it is distinguished from terms such as 'nation' 'culture' 'community' and (most contentious of all) 'race', is problematic (see, for example, Wilson and Wilson in Blakeley and Bryson, 2002). The English or British are sometimes referred to as a 'mongrel' people, the product of waves of invasion and immigration from different ethnic groups over the centuries – Celts, Angles, Saxons, Vikings, Norman French and so on. Though sometimes surviving in place names and surnames, these ethnic origins generally have no lasting political implications.

The tem 'ethnic minorities' today generally refers to non-white ethnic groups (see Figure 3.2).

**Figure 3.2** Non-white ethnic minorities in England and Wales in 2007

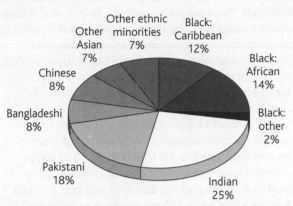

*Note*: Statistics are not collected in similar form in Scotland.

*Source*: ONS Population by Local Authority Statistics 2007.

In England and Wales these total just over five million, with additionally nearly a million of mixed race out of a total) population of just over fifty-four million. Post-Second World War immigration from former British colonies, which produced much of this ethnic minority population, might be described as a legacy of empire. Immigration to the UK, free to Commonwealth citizens until 1962, has been progressively tightened since then.

Yet not all ethnic minorities are 'non-white'. Long resident Jewish or Irish communities and Poles and Ukrainians who settled in Britain after the Second World War are sometimes categorized as ethnic minorities. There are also more recent (mainly white) economic migrants from eastern Europe, resulting from the free movement of labour within the EU. All these may suffer some of the discrimination and prejudice experienced by non-white minorities.

Issues of identity and allegiance can be complicated for ethnic minorities. It is hardly surprising that many relatively recent immigrants and their immediate descendants should have some continuing positive sentiments towards their country of origin, particularly where they retain contacts with relatives there. The United States, which has long had a fairly successful programme of education to integrate immigrants into the American way of life and US citizenship, still has thriving Irish-

American, Spanish-American, Polish-American and Jewish-American communities, among others. Similarly, there are thriving Irish, Polish, and Italian communities in some British cities. These hyphenated identities suggest that allegiances are not mutually exclusive – it is possible to be both Irish and American. It is equally possible to be black or Asian and British, and such a dual allegiance is clearly felt by many.

Yet a more exclusive allegiance may be felt, perhaps as a consequence of disadvantages suffered by ethnic minorities, of which there is, unfortunately, considerable evidence. Thus nearly three-quarters of Bangladeshi children and half of Black African children in Britain grow up in poverty. Black children perform significantly worse in schools and are far more likely to be excluded than white children. (Chinese and Indian pupils, however, outperform whites.) Half of the pensioners living in Bangladeshi or Pakistani-headed households live below the poverty line, compared to around a sixth of the general population (EHRC report, 2010). Following an economic recession, employment levels remain significantly lower for most ethnic minorities, particularly those of Pakistani or Bangladeshi descent (see Table 3.2).

Young Black and Asian school leavers in particular find it much more difficult to secure jobs than their white counterparts. Blacks aged twenty-two to twenty-four are twice as likely to be not in employment, education or training as whites in the same age group. The figure for young Asians is little better (see Table 3.3).

Other economic indicators tell a similar story. Blacks and Asians are less likely to be employed in occupations appropriate to their qualifications, and are more likely to be employed in part-time or casual labour, often involving working unsociable hours. They also encounter discrimination in the housing market. They are more likely to be victims of certain kinds of crime: a quarter of the homicide victims in England and Wales belonged to an ethnic minority. They are far more likely to be stopped by the police and questioned. They also make up a disproportionate part of the prison population (EHRC report, 2010).

While parts of Britain, particularly in London, have become multi-ethnic and genuinely multicultural, more commonly ethnic differences are rein-

**Table 3.2** Percentage of working-age population employed or self-employed, by ethnic group, 2008

| All | 76 |
| White | 78 |
| Black and Black British | 65 |
| Indian | 72 |
| Pakistani/Bangladeshi | 49 |
| Mixed | 66 |
| Other | 83 |

Source: Equality and Human Rights Commission Report, How Fair is Britain? (2010).

forced by residential, social and educational segregation. In some urban areas adversely affected by the decline of a staple industry and rising unemployment, economic deprivation has sharpened mutual suspicions and antagonisms between the white and ethnic minority population. After 11 September 2001, and still more after the London bombings of 7 July 2005, prejudice and discrimination against some ethnic minorities were further complicated by religious differences and Islamophobia.

## Religion

Religious conflict, once a major source of political division, was a running thread in British political history from the sixteenth to the nineteenth centuries. Yet apart from the persecution of the relatively small Jewish minority, religious divisions then were between variants of Christianity. Following the Protestant reformations in both England and Scotland in the sixteenth century,

**Table 3.3** The proportion of young people not in employment, education or training (NEET) by ethnic group, 2009

| | NEET aged 16–18 | NEET aged 19–21 | NEET aged 22–24 |
| --- | --- | --- | --- |
| All | 23 | 23 | 24 |
| White | 23 | 23 | 22 |
| Black | 28 | 31 | 44 |
| Asian | 21 | 25 | 36 |
| Mixed | 29 | 29 | 28 |

Source: Equality and Human Rights Commission Report, How Fair is Britain? (2010).

Roman Catholics became a feared, hated and persecuted minority in Britain, and an oppressed majority in Ireland. The further division between high Anglicanism and Puritanism (or, later, nonconformism) in the seventeenth century was the major cause of Civil War, contributing significantly to subsequent political differences between the rival Tory and Whig parties. While the Church of England was dubbed the 'Tory Party at prayer', it was the 'non-conformist conscience' of Methodists, Baptists and other non-Anglican Protestants that were the bedrock of British nineteenth-century liberalism, and a key strand in the early Labour Party.

Yet if religion was once very important as a source of political inspiration and conflict, its political significance declined rapidly for most of the twentieth century. Today, Anglicans, non-conformists, Catholics and Jews can be found among the supporters of all modern mainstream political parties (in Britain, if not Northern Ireland). Religion has ceased to be an indicator of political allegiance for most of England, apart from areas such as Liverpool, where the Protestant/Catholic divide remains important in sporting loyalties and has a significant if diminishing influence on party support. In Scotland, especially Glasgow, parts of Edinburgh, and the Western Isles, religious differences remained a key factor in explaining political allegiances. In Northern Ireland, however, religious affiliations still correlate closely with political loyalties – particularly for the fundamental unionist/nationalist divide. A problem for unionists is that the number of Catholics is steadily if slowly increasing as a proportion of the total population, so that the Catholic minority could eventually become a majority.

Leaving Northern Ireland aside, there are some signs that religious differences may once more become more politically significant in twenty-first-century Britain, not because of divisions within Christianity, but due to the increasing importance of other religious faiths. The Jewish faith (0.5 per cent of the population) retains a high profile; a strong Jewish identity is still felt by many of Jewish descent, even those with little or no religious belief. Physical evidence of the multi-faith society which Britain has become is provided by the Muslim mosques, Hindu and Sikh temples in British cities.

**Figure 3.3**    Religious affiliation in Great Britain in 2001

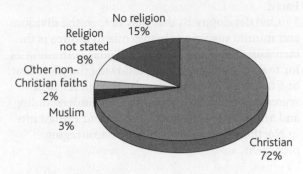

*Source:* Figures derived from 2001 census; for updating see 2011 census, when available.

Of these faiths, Islam is the most visible and important, in terms of numbers of adherents (over one and half million), places of worship and political significance.

Figure 3.3 shows the increased variety of religious faith in Britain, without, however, denting the assumption that Britain has become a predominantly secular society. A quarter of the population either do not state their religion or belong to none; many of those who still routinely claim to be Christian do not attend church services. Religion may be more important in the lives of those belonging to the small but growing non-Christian faith groups; together these only amount to only 6 per cent of the population, though very unevenly geographically distributed within the UK (only 2 per cent of Wales and 1 per cent of Scotland). Many are heavily concentrated in specific localities within London and other large urban areas (Office for National Statistics).

Until recently these religious affiliations had only marginal significance for politics. Yet following 11 September 2001, and more particularly 7 July 2005, Britain's Muslims (just 3 per cent of the population of England) have been subject to scrutiny, much of it hostile and ill-informed, stimulating the growth of what has been termed 'Islamophobia', and reinforcing racist prejudice among some of the white population. Inevitably, prejudice and discrimination has led some among the Muslim community to reconsider their own political allegiance and identity. The Afghanistan and Iraq wars significantly weakened the formerly strong British Muslim support for the Labour Party.

One development that may deepen the divisions and mutual suspicions between faith groups is the increasing demands of some religious communities for their own faith schools, following the precedent of Church of England schools. The influence of segregated education on mutual misunderstanding and antipathies between Catholics and Protestants in Northern Ireland is hardly an encouraging precedent.

## Gender

The division between 'male' and 'female' is in many ways the most obvious and the most persistent of social divisions. Although the position of women in Britain and western society generally has been considerably transformed over the last century or so, and the equality of women is now formally recognized, females continue to suffer discrimination and inequality in many spheres and gender remains an important social division in politics in general.

Women slightly outnumber men in the overall population, by 31.6 million to 30.6 million (ONS estimates, 2010). Girls now regularly outperform boys at every level of education (EHRC report, 2010), yet men continue to outnumber women in the workforce, although the gap is fast closing. The proportion of women of working age in paid employment has grown from 56 per cent in 1971 to 70 per cent in 2008, while over the same period the employment rate for men has fallen from 92 per cent to 78 per cent (ONS, 2010).

Yet these figures are rather misleading as women are much more likely than men to be working part-time (5.2 million compared with 1.2 million). Moreover, women are still expected to undertake a disproportionate share of the burden of domestic work and childcare. They are also far more likely to be involved in the care of elderly relatives (who themselves are more likely to be women, as they outnumber men by three to one among the population aged 85 and over). This dual burden may be one reason (besides discrimination) why relatively few women reach the highest and most well-paid managerial and professional posts. Women's average pay still lags well behind that of

men, despite equal pay and equal opportunities legislation. The gender pay gap is relatively low for the under- thirties, but women aged forty earn on average 27 per cent less than men of the same age. Moreover, differences in income extend into retirement. 60 per cent of women reaching state pension age in 2008 were entitled to less than the full basic state pension, compared to 10 per cent of men (EHRC report, 2010).

As we shall see later, men still substantially outnumber women in formal involvement in politics and government. One consequence of this continued male dominance of the political process, feminists would argue, is that policies are still skewed towards male interests and economic dominance. While gender divisions have not been expressed in terms of separate political parties, they have been politically expressed in a number of other ways. Thus women have worked in pressure groups, through and across existing parties and through the women's movement as a whole, to secure better representation in politics and government and specific reforms to improve the position of women. Yet numerous other divisions, including class, age, ethnicity and religion, cut across the gender divide. Inevitably women find themselves on opposite sides on many political issues (see Chapter 7 on feminism; Chapter 13 on women's representation in Parliament; Chapter 22 for more on gender equality).

## Age

Different age groups are an obvious social division. As members of a particular arbitrarily defined age group we may have some interests and attitudes in common. Yet age groups are an unusual division, as we move between statistical age categories in the course of our lifetime. The old may remember how it feels to be young, while the young may anticipate how their needs, capacities and circumstances will change with age. Even so, the elderly can be the victims of negative stereotypes and they may experience some of the same kind of discrimination and prejudice felt by some other groups; today age discrimination is one of the injustices investigated by the Equality and Human Rights Commission.

There have been significant changes in the age structure of the British population from the nineteenth and even the mid-twentieth century, with considerable implications for politics and economic and social policy. As a result of increasing longevity and decreasing birth rates, in 2008 those of pensionable age (11.8 million) exceeded the numbers of those under sixteen (11.5 milllion). Future projections are complicated by progressive changes in the age of retirement. Thus between 2010 and 2020 it is planned that the age of retirement for women will be brought up to the same age as men (65) and thereafter the state pension age for both sexes will rise in three stages to 68 in 2046. Even so, state pensioners will continue to outnumber the under-sixteens in current projections of population figures up to 2033 and beyond (ONS, 2010).

The elderly have growing political weight. They not only outnumber young voters, but are more likely to use their vote (see Chapter 4). They also have the time and leisure to involve themselves in other political activities, in political parties and a range of pressure groups (see Chapters 6 and 8). The implications of an ageing population are particularly obvious for pensions and health, and it is no accident that these two issues have shot up the political agenda in recent years. Adequate pensions and good healthcare are critical for the quality of life of the elderly, but have massive implications for public expenditure and taxation.

Yet it should not be assumed that the elderly have homogeneous interests. They will differ in family circumstances, mental and physical health, but most of all in income and wealth. Thus the elderly who are largely or wholly reliant on state benefits may experience real poverty while those with good occupational pensions and who own their own home may enjoy a better quality of life than when they were younger. However, both categories of pensioners may, as they age further, suffer physical and mental deterioration to the extent that they become dependent on the care of others, perhaps by relatives, or professional carers in their own home, but more commonly in nursing homes. While such care is increasingly expensive, raising major issues of how the costs should be met, some elderly suffer not only loneliness and boredom but also increasing physical discomfort and pain.

Young adults constitute a smaller proportion of the population than formerly. Their political influ-

ence may be further reduced by their relatively low involvement in conventional politics; although some would argue that this is balanced by their involvement in single-issue pressure groups, the relative political apathy and ignorance of the young has aroused some concern. As with the elderly, generalizations are dangerous, as there are many significant divisions among young adults; between the growing number of university students and graduates and those not involved in higher education, between the full-time employed, casually employed and unemployed, along with differences associated with gender and ethnic divisions. Thus there is some active resentment of students among some poor working-class communities where relatively few have attended university. While some young adults are much more comfortable within a multicultural environment than their elders, others from both the white majority and ethnic minorities are attracted to more extremist or exclusive political involvement, such as racist parties or various forms of religious fundamentalism.

There are clear differences of attitude between age groups on a range of issues, some essentially economic, others based on formative influences when young (e.g. drugs, crime, sexual orientation, race relations). Different generations may have different expectations because of the experiences they have gone through. Prevailing values in society when people were young may condition their own attitudes for a lifetime. There is some evidence to support the assumption that, as they age, people become more set in their ways, less open to change, and conservative (with a small 'c', but perhaps with a large 'C' as well), , although there are some conspicuous exceptions to this generalization.

There is some potential for increased inter-generational conflict, particularly between those in full-time work and pensioners. Fewer of the former can anticipate secure pensions linked with earnings. They have little prospect of early retirement, such as many of their elders have enjoyed. Recent and current students who have piled up debts to finance their higher education are also entitled to regard with some envy an earlier generation who enjoyed not only free tuition bur fairly generous maintenance grants. Yet current and future workers will have to pay increased taxes to support the steadily rising financial costs of maintaining the elderly

(Willetts, 2010). Many will also find there is little prospect of inheriting much from parents and grandparents, as their houses and savings are utilized to help pay for their care. Whether any of this finds significant political expression remains to be seen.

## Families and lifestyles

Families are the smallest social group, but one that to an extent transcends divisions of gender and age, although some feminists see the family as part of the problem for women, while others criticize the growing separation of care of the elderly from the family. As a result of both changes in the law from the 1960s onwards and slower and partial changes in public attitudes more recently, there is now a diversity of lifestyles and families where once the values of traditional marriage and the small nuclear family predominated. What was once called 'living in sin' (couples cohabiting without marrying) has become relatively common. There is no longer a stigma attached to illegitimacy, so that couples who produce children no longer feel obliged to marry. Yet marriage remains popular, with some trying it two or three times or more, as hope triumphs over experience. Moreover, many same-sex couples now seek to regularize their union in civil partnerships, some embracing the same rituals and ceremonies as traditional marriage.

As divorce and remarriage have become common, many families have become more complex, with a web of step-parents, step-grand-parents and step-siblings. Yet while some of these new extended families seem to operate amicably, family breakdown can be a source of enduring trauma for children, and can lead to economic and social problems requiring intervention by social services and other state agencies. Thus issues around the family have become increasingly political. Strengthening 'family values' has become a political mantra.

There is more freedom for individuals to pursue their own lifestyle inside or outside families. Some choose to remain single, perhaps remaining celibate, perhaps pursuing heterosexual or homosexual relationships. The 'gay community' has become politically significant, to the extent that political leaders and parties feel bound to respond to their interests. Yet greater tolerance and understanding among the adult community in the UK does not seem to extend to children. Teachers acknowledge that homophobic bullying is rife in British secondary schools. Two-thirds of lesbian, gay and bisexual students report being bullied.

## Inequalities in income and wealth

Some of the social divisions referred to above – nation, region, ethnicity, gender, age – clearly have an economic dimension. Yet although wealth may be unevenly distributed between these different social categories, they hardly explain poverty. The manifestation of poverty within some of these social divisions reflects a more fundamental division in economic circumstances.

A feature of almost all past and present societies has been gross inequality in income and wealth; the division between the rich and the poor has been seen as the crucial political divide. Commonly, the rich have constituted a tiny minority, and poverty has been the common experience of the majority. Indeed, Plato and Aristotle assumed that democracy, the rule of the many, would be the rule of the poor, while the rule of the few, oligarchy, involved in practice the rule of the rich minority in their own interests.

Once, gross inequality, and poverty for the majority, were widely assumed to be unalterable aspects of human society. The early classical economist, Thomas Malthus (1766–1834), argued that any improvement in the living standards of the poor would lead to an increase in population and a reduction in their circumstances to subsistence levels. While industrialization raised the living standards of whole nations, thus apparently disproving the gloomy assumptions of Malthus, and redistributed income and wealth between groups, it did not reduce inequality within society as a whole, and indeed may have increased it. However, particularly after the Second World War, it was no longer necessarily assumed that governments could or should do nothing about poverty and inequality. Indeed, it was widely believed that progressive taxation on the one hand and state welfare provision on the other were significantly reducing inequality and poverty in countries like Britain (see Chapter 2).

This comfortable assumption of progress towards a more equal society was dented by revela-

**Table 3.4** The distribution of marketable wealth (adults aged 20 or over) in 2002

| Percentage of wealth owned by | (percentage) |
|---|---|
| Most wealthy 1% | 23% |
| Most wealthy 5% | 43% |
| Most wealthy 10% | 56% |
| Most wealthy 25% | 74% |
| Most wealthy 50% | 94% |

*Source*: Adapted from *Social Trends*, 2005.

tions of the failures of the welfare state in certain areas: the rediscovery of child poverty, and the recognition of the economic deprivation suffered by some declining industrial urban areas from the 1960s onwards. It was more severely shaken by the economic problems of the 1970s, which not only involved the return of large-scale unemployment, but led to a more fundamental questioning of the role of the state. Some argued that the growth of government was largely responsible for Britain's economic problems. Governments should not be in the business of redistribution. State welfare and high taxation sapped individual initiative and enterprise and created a dependency culture. Market forces, left alone, would create more wealth and prosperity for the nation as a whole, including the poorest. Attempts to reduce inequality were counter-productive. While this new orthodoxy was never fully acted upon, the growth of public spending was checked and the burden of taxation of the better-off was substantially reduced. There is fairly clear evidence that some apparent progress towards a more equal society in Britain was checked and partially reversed in the last quarter of the twentieth century, for income inequality has grown (Wilkinson and Pickett, 2009).

As Table 3.4 demonstrates, Britain continues to be characterized by wide disparities in the distribution of wealth. The poorest half of the population own only 6 per cent of total marketable wealth. For much of the population the only significant wealth they own is bound up in their houses. If these are excluded from marketable wealth the figures are even more stark. In 2002 the top 1 per cent owned 35 per cent of marketable wealth excluding

dwellings, and the top 50 per cent owned 98 per cent, leaving just 2 per cent of wealth to the other half of the population. These figures have not changed significantly in recent years. It is estimated that the total net household wealth of the top 10 per cent is almost a hundred times higher than the net wealth of the poorest 10 per cent (EHRC report, 2010).

While it is difficult to make accurate comparisons with previous periods, it does appear that inequality in Britain remains more marked than some other advanced industrial nations, and that this has wider adverse implications for the health of Britain's economy and society (see Wilkinson and Pickett, 2009). Democracy, involving the assumption of political equality, has not resulted in much greater economic and social equality. The sources of wealth may have changed considerably over the last two hundred years, and there has been some significant social mobility, but the huge gulf between rich and poor remains.

However, poverty is a relative concept. The poor in Britain today suffer relative deprivation rather than absolute poverty. People feel deprived because they lack commodities or facilities that the bulk of the population take for granted. Where car ownership is almost universal, lack of access to a car appears to have a severely adverse effect on the quality of life. Yet poor Britons clearly do not lack the basic necessities of life. In the mid-nineteenth century it is thought that around a million people in Ireland died as a result of the potato famine, and starvation and emigration reduced the population by some 20 per cent. This level of poverty is unthinkable in modern Britain or Ireland or any developed nation, although unfortunately it remains common enough elsewhere in the world. Nevertheless it is inequality in Britain that is more relevant for British politics and government. Thus it is important to examine in rather more detail the nature and extent of these social divisions by exploring the contentious concept of social class.

## Occupation and social class

It is sometimes suggested that Britain is already, or well on the way to becoming, a classless society. Others not only suggest that class differences are persistent, but that social inequality is increasing.

Some foreign observers are struck by the extent to which Britain remains a class-conscious country. Class remains an important concept in social science in general and political science in particular. It is, for example, still regarded as an important factor in explaining voting behaviour and party allegiance (see Chapters 5 and 6). It is most commonly defined and measured in terms of occupational categories, but different categories are used for different purposes, hinting at problems and ambiguities in fundamental concepts.

Class is a particularly important aspect of the Marxist perspective on power and the state. 'The history of all hitherto existing society is the history of class struggles' (*Communist Manifesto*, Marx and Engels, 1848). Marx, however, used the term 'class' in a distinctive way, linking it with the ownership of productive wealth rather than occupation. He assumed there was a fundamental conflict of interest in a capitalist society between those who owned and controlled the means of production – the capitalists or bourgeoisie, and those who owned only their own labour, the proletariat. These were the two key classes which mattered in a modern capitalist society – others such as the old landed gentry, the *petit bourgeoisie* (shopkeepers etc.) and the peasants were becoming progressively less significant.

Some argue that actual ownership of the means of production may be less important in a modern capitalist society, where ownership can be divorced from effective control, and the key decisions are made by managers. Marx may also have underestimated the power of the professions and the growing state bureaucracy. These developments were more fully appreciated by Max Weber, writing in the early twentieth century. While Weber acknowledged that the ownership of property was a key element in understanding social inequality, he also attached importance to differences in status between, in particular, occupational groups.

Our modern understanding of class owes rather more to Weber than to Marx. A long-established three-class distinction – upper, middle and lower (or 'working') – is long-established, linked in popular usage to hierarchies of social status. The 'upper class' is often relatively ignored, and either linked with the old aristocracy and landed gentry, or used in a quasi-Marxist sense to mean those who are sufficiently wealthy not to have to depend

on their own labour for a more than adequate income.

The terms 'working-class' and 'middle-class', particularly the latter, cover too wide a range to be of much practical value unless broken down into further sub-categories. Thus the middle class is commonly taken to include business owners and directors, both salaried and self-employed professionals, clerical workers, shopkeepers and own-account workers (such as small builders). While some work in the private sector and some own their own businesses, many others work in the public sector. It should be clear that many of this diverse 'middle class' scarcely share the same economic and political interests. Some have a strong interest in low taxation and reduced regulation of business enterprise, others have a vested interest in high public expenditure and thus high taxation. Some are professionally involved in the state intervention and regulation that other members of the middle class complain about. Similarly the manual working class is conventionally subdivided into skilled, semi-skilled and unskilled, and as with the middle class there is a cross-cutting distinction between those employed in the public and private sectors.

The distinction between the middle and working class in the popular understanding is most commonly associated with the division between 'white-collar' (or non-manual) work and 'blue-collar' (or manual) work, and it also underpins some formal classifications for statistical purposes and much academic analysis. However, the division between manual and non-manual work is not always closely aligned with differences in income and wealth. Some 'white-collar' jobs (e.g. junior clerical workers) are relatively poorly-paid, while in parts of Britain some manual workers (plumbers and builders) enjoy comparatively high wages. Moreover, the distinction between a manual working class and a non-manual middle class in no way corresponds to the Marxist distinction between the working class and the 'bourgeoisie' (although this term is often loosely translated as 'middle class'). From a Marxist perspective both blue collar and white collar workers are 'working class'. The (essentially non-Marxist) British Labour Party similarly referred to the familiar distinction between manual and non-manual work, but

## BOX 3.1

# Social or occupational class categories commonly used in Britain

Registrar General's classification formerly used in official surveys

I    Professional
II   Intermediate
III  Skilled (sub-divided into non-manual and manual)
IV   Semi-skilled
V    Unskilled

System of classification used by Institute of Practitioners in Advertising (IPA) and by many political scientists, particularly in the analysis of voting and party allegiance

A    Higher managerial, administrative or professional
B    Intermediate managerial, administrative or professional
C1   Supervisory or clerical, and junior managerial, administrative or professional
C2   Skilled manual workers
D    Semi-skilled and unskilled manual workers

E    State pensioners or widows (no other earnings), casual or lowest grade workers, long term unemployed

Current official classification used for government statistical purposes

1    Higher managerial and professional occupations (e.g. company directors, barristers)
2    Lower managerial and professional occupations (e.g. nurses, police, journalists)
3    Intermediate occupations (e.g. clerks, secretaries)
4    Small employers and own-account workers (e.g. publicans, farmers, decorators)
5    Lower supervisory, craft and related occupations (e.g. printers, plumbers, train drivers)
6    Semi-routine occupations (e.g. shop assistants, bus drivers, hairdressers)
7    Routine occupations (e.g. waiters, building labourers, refuse collectors).
8    Never worked and long-term unemployed.

rejected its significance, in the phrase 'workers by hand or by brain' in the old Clause Four of its constitution.

Academic commentators have often grouped junior white-collar workers with the working class, along with various categories of manual workers, and this makes a great deal of sense in terms of income and economic inequality. Even so, the distinction in assumed social status between white-collar and blue-collar work has proved remarkably persistent, with implications for political behaviour. Thus many poorly-paid white-collar workers have declined to identify themselves with the 'interests of labour' which the Labour Party and its trade union allies claimed to champion.

Yet it is increasingly questionable whether the old and familiar distinction between manual and non-manual work means much any more. Because of the decline of mining and heavy manufacturing industries, and the increased application of technology, most work no longer involves heavy physical labour. At the same time, some white-collar and blue-collar occupations have experienced an element of 'deskilling', while others require more complex skills and training than formerly.

The social classes described in Box 3.1 are for the most part reasonably objective – depending chiefly on occupation. But individuals may think of themselves as working-class or middle-class, and this 'self-assigned' class may not correspond with the categorization of statisticians. Thus a manual worker who earns high wages, owns his own house and car, and adopts a middle-class lifestyle, may think of himself as middle-class. Similarly, some university lecturers (middle-class by classifications based on occupation) may identify with the working class. Self-assigned class may be significant for political behaviour. For example, a manual worker who considers himself middle-class may be more likely to vote Conservative, while it is probably safe to assume that self-proclaimed working-class lecturers will be on the left politically.

## Changing class structure?

There has been much academic debate on how Britain's class structure may be changing. Some argue that the old manual working class is now relatively far smaller and more fragmented (class fragmentation). Others claim that inequalities in income and wealth are as significant as ever and the basic class structure of Britain has not altered (class persistence). Others again believe that old class divisions are being replaced by new (class realignment).

These disagreements relate back to differences in theoretical assumptions and classifications (discussed above). If the working class is identified with manual workers formerly employed in mining and manufacturing, it is clear that numbers have declined in line with these industrial sectors. Moreover, many new jobs in the services sector are commonly counted as middle class, because they appear to be 'white-collar' and 'non-manual'. However, it is at best questionable whether, for example, work in call centres (one major growth area), should be regarded as 'middle class'. It is poorly-paid, relatively unskilled work often undertaken on a short-term or casual basis.

It is certainly true that there is a larger proportion of the population now employed in management and the professions. Moreover it is also true that the working class appears more fragmented –

between employed and unemployed, part-time and full-time, public sector and private sector, as well as along increasingly important gender and ethnic lines. These differences have clearly reduced traditional working-class solidarity, with political repercussions. Moreover, as a consequence partly of the decline of traditional manual occupations, and partly of changes in the law, far fewer workers are now members of trade unions. By 2006 only just over a quarter (25.8 per cent) of all workers were unionised. Today union density is higher among women workers than men, a remarkable turnaround from the days when the British trade union movement was heavily male-dominated (ONS, 2010).

It has been persuasively argued that there are now significant new cleavages in British society, based not on differences within the production process but on differences in the consumption of goods and services. Thus it is claimed that there are significant differences in interest between those who are substantially reliant on public services – particularly transport, education, health and housing services – and those who own their own homes and cars, and use private healthcare and private schools. The former have a vested interest in public services and in higher public spending and taxation, the latter in lower public spending and taxation. Indeed, the poorer public services are, the more their decision to opt out of them seems justified.

**Figure 3.4**   Patterns of housing tenure in Britain, 1971 and 2004

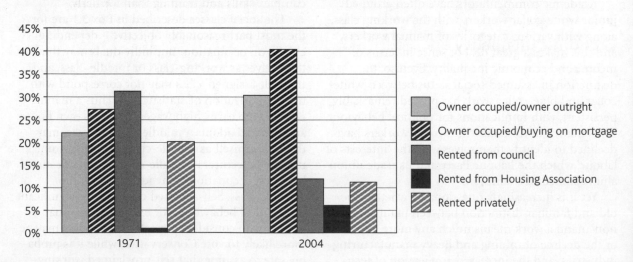

*Source*: Office of the Deputy Prime Minister.

## Housing tenure and the distribution of property

One of the most significant of these 'consumption cleavages' used to be housing tenure. A key distinction was between 'home-owners', who owned their house outright or were buying it on a mortgage, and those who were renting a house from the local authority. While many 'working-class' people lived in council houses, owner-occupation was a badge of middle-class respectability. The council estate was among the most reliable sources of Labour votes, while home-owners were far more likely to vote Conservative. However, the sale of council houses and the transfer of substantial local authority housing to other landlords, both encouraged by Conservative governments after 1979, has substantially altered the pattern of housing tenure (see Figure 3.4).

Thus the number of council houses has been more than halved, a trend which continued under New Labour, when some remaining council estates were transferred to the favoured 'third force' of housing associations. Owner-occupation has become easily the majority form of housing tenure. The substantial rise in house prices was a major factor in the consumption and credit boom that culminated in the financial crisis of 2008. However, since then credit has become tighter, and as a result many young adults are now finding it difficult to obtain the substantial down-payments require for mortgage loans to get a foot on the property ladder.

## Economic inequality and political power

The growth of home ownership is one aspect of what might be seen as a deliberate attempt to give more people a stake in property. A growing proportion of the population has now acquired a large if indirect stake in the stock market through the investment of pension and life insurance funds. Further encouragement was provided by the growth of the unit trust movement and government-sponsored investment schemes. However, the most high-profile stimulus to wider share-holding was provided through the heavily promoted privatizations and flotations of shares in former nationalized industries by the Thatcher and Major governments. The initial flotations were so successful that they were substantially over-subscribed. The cumulative effect was that share-owners outnumbered the (declining) trade union members, which could not have been anticipated in the very different economic and political climate in the years immediately after the Second World War.

This suggests 'popular capitalism' has arrived. Yet the extent of the change can be exaggerated. While many more people seemed to have acquired a stake in property or capitalism, for most of them that stake has remained very small. As Table 3.4 indicates, property ownership has not been significantly spread, but remains heavily concentrated. Income inequality has, if anything, widened. Little significant progress has been made towards either the old Labour ideal of a more equal society or the Conservative 'property-owning democracy'.

The relationship between economic inequality and political power remains contentious. The norms of representative democracy – one person, one vote, one value – suggest political equality and the rule of the majority. To Marxists, the concentration of income and wealth in the hands of the few reflects the effective concentration of political power in the hands of the ruling class. To neoliberals, inequality in income and wealth simply reflects market forces and the effects of the unequal distribution of talents and enterprise in society. Both Marxists and neo-liberals assume the primacy of economics over politics. Social democrats, by contrast, implicitly assume that the political power of the majority can be mobilized to created a more equal society through the ballot box and representative government (Judt, 2010).

## Economic and social divisions – the time dimension

In a book first published in 1941, a leading expert on British politics in the mid-twentieth century, Sir Ivor Jennings, wrote:

Great Britain is a small island with a very homogeneous population. Few think of themselves as primarily English, Scots or Welsh. The sting has long been taken out of religious controversy. The country is so interdependent that there is little economic agitation on a regional basis, as there sometimes is in a large country like the United States. There are class divisions and (what is often the same thing) economic divisions, but they are not wide or deep, and they are tending to disappear through heavy taxation at the one end and high wage rates at the other. We are a closely knit economic unit, with a large measure of common interests and a long political tradition. (From Sir Ivor Jennings, *The British Constitution*, 5th edition, 1966, pp. 8–9)

Anyone acquainted with contemporary British politics (and anyone who has read this chapter) will realize that this description of Britain is hardly valid today. When first written, it reflected reasonably accurately the mood of national unity at the height of the Second World War. Moreover, it preceded many of the substantial changes in society and in political attitudes that have taken place in Britain since the Second World War, often reflecting global change. These have included large scale immigration into Britain and the emergence of a multi-ethnic and multi-faith society, second-wave feminism and the women's movement, the rise of nationalism and devolution, the decline of mining and manufacturing together with manual trade unionism, and massive changes in the management of the economy. The financial crisis and the ensuing economic recession of 2007–9 has inflicted a more recent shock to the system, with major ongoing economic and political implications. Politics is not static but dynamic. British society and British politics have changed dramatically in the years since the Second World War. They are still changing, and will continue to change, perhaps in directions that it is difficult to foresee.

## SUMMARY

- British politics is shaped by ongoing changes in economy and society, although this is a two-way process, as government and politics can in turn influence economic and social change.

- The decline in mining and manufacturing, and the increased importance of (particularly financial) services has major ongoing implications for the distribution of wealth and income and for political attitudes and behaviour. The credit crunch has exacerbated differences between the nations and regions of the UK. While most of the population of the UK live in England, Scotland, Wales and Northern Ireland retain their own distinctive economic interests, cultures and identities.

- Average incomes in Northern Ireland and Wales are lower than the UK average, and there are substantial inequalities between the English regions. The 'north–south divide' has some validity both economically and politically. There is, however, more significant inequality within regions and cities than between them.

- A growing ethnic minority population has resulted from immigration from the 'new Commonwealth' and more recently from eastern Europe. Ethnic differences reinforced by social and educational segregation have fed prejudice and discrimination, and created some political tension between communities.

- Political differences related to variants of Christianity have declined in significance. However, non-Christian faiths are practised by a small but increasing minority. Following 9/11, the Iraq war, and 7/7 Muslims have suffered from Islamophobia and some have felt divided loyalties.

- The role of women continues to change in the workplace, but less in the home. Gender divisions have had only a limited impact on party political allegiances, but women continue to suffer discrimination in many fields, including politics, and there is an ongoing struggle to secure equal rights for women.

- Changes in the age structure of the UK population mean than pensioners now comfortably outnumber children. The 'grey vote' is of increasing political significance.

- Income and particularly wealth remains very unequally distributed in Britain, with some obvious implications for political power, although the relationship remains contentious.

- Changes in occupational class structure overlaid by other social differences have had contentious implications for politics. Differences based on the consumption (public or private) of key goods and services (particularly housing) may be of increased significance.

## QUESTIONS FOR DISCUSSION

- How far and in what respect has Britain declined in relation to other states?

- How politically significant are economic differences between the nations and regions of the UK?

- In what ways have the credit crunch and economic recession increased the differences between the more and less prosperous nations and regions?

- Why are more people in Scotland and Wales identifying themselves as Scots or Welsh rather than British? What might be the political implications?

- How far do ethnic minorities suffer continuing prejudice and discrimination in Britain? Are ethnic tensions rising or declining?

- How significant for politics are differences in religious belief? Should politicians pay more attention to 'faith politics', and if so, why? What are the causes and consequences of Islamophobia?

- How far does the more extensive participation of women in the paid workforce indicate there is no longer significant discrimination against them? Why might gender differences remain important for politics?

- What are the possible political implications of increased 'grey power'? Is there a danger that the political voice of the young may be relatively unheard (and, if so, why)?

- Is social class still important for British politics? How might changes in the class structure have affected political allegiances?

## FURTHER READING

Many of the implications of the social and economic divisions explored here for British politics as whole are addressed in later chapters of this book; see particularly Chapter 5 voting, and Chapters 20–22 on domestic economic and social policy.

The most authoritative and detailed statistics on the UK population are to be found in the full official census,

undertaken every ten years. However, up-to-date statistics will not be obtainable until the results of the 2011 census are available. Even the census is not particularly helpful on some divisions within the UK population (for example on religious allegiances and observance).

The most easily accessible source for up-to-date statistics is from the Office for National Statistics (ONS), which can be viewed online via its website www.statis-tics.gov.uk. A wealth of this official statistical information is regularly published (now annually by Palgrave Macmillan) in the *Annual Abstract of Statistics*, and *Social Trends*. A recent, very full and detailed report by the Equality and Human Rights Commission *How Fair is Britain?* (2010) contains a wealth of detail on

inequality and discrimination by gender, age, ethnicity, religion, sexual orientation and disability, although less on broad inequalities of income and wealth related to occupational category or social class. Wilkinson and Pickett (2009) compare the extent of inequality in the UK with other states, and correlate this with a range of other social characteristics and problems.

# Participating in Politics

If politics is for the many and not just the few, then ordinary people can and should participate in the political process and influence decisions on issues that interest and concern them. This chapter focuses on participation in politics, and serves as an introduction to the succeeding chapters on elections and voting (Chapter 5) political parties (Chapter 6), ideologies, parties and interests (Chapter 7), pressure groups (Chapter 8), and political communication and the mass media (Chapter 9).

The first part of this chapter explores the extent of political participation in Britain today. We then turn to the beliefs and attitudes shaping political attitudes and behaviour, examining political culture and socialization, and the extent to which British political culture may have changed. We go on to explore the meaning of citizenship and community in modern Britain and conclude with a brief discussion of the academic controversy around the term 'social capital'. How far is a perceived decline in political participation linked to a wider decline in social interaction and engagement in modern society?

## Political knowledge and interest

Although political participation is central to democracy, a readiness to participate presupposes some knowledge of, and interest in, politics. In the fifth century BCE Pericles spoke of the extent of participation in Athenian democracy:

Here each individual is interested not only in his own affairs but in the affairs of the state as well: even those who are most occupied in their own business are extremely well-informed on general politics – this is a peculiarity of ours: we do not say that a man who takes no interest in politics is a man who minds his own business; we say that he has no business here at all. (From Pericles' funeral oration, Thucyidides, tr. Warner, 1972, p. 147)

Ancient Athens was of course a direct democracy, arguably requiring a higher level of political involvement among citizens than a modern representative democracy. Even so, if Britain can be regarded as a democracy in a meaningful sense, and if ordinary people do have some real power, then it is still necessary that they should have some knowledge of, interest in, and engagement with, politics. Yet today there is some concern at the extent of political ignorance and apathy in modern Britain.

Most British citizens could hardly be described as 'extremely well-informed' on politics. The Hansard Society (*An audit of political engagement 7*, 2010) found that just over half (51 per cent) of all adults claimed to know 'a fair amount' or 'a great deal' about politics, yet only 44 per cent could name their MP. As might be expected, there was a strong correlation between knowledge of and interest in politics. Thus slightly over half (53 per cent) claimed to be 'very' or 'fairly' interested in politics,

**Figure 4.1**   A hierarchy of political participation

**Activists**
The very small percentage of the electorate who compete to hold office within and between political parties, pressure groups and other political organisations.

**Just voters**
The much greater percentage of the electorate who play a basically passive political role, but who may discuss politics, read political coverage in newspapers and watch political programmes on television. Passive membership of trade unions and pressure groups. Will turn out and vote.

**Almost inactive**
This includes many of the 41 per cent of non-voters in the 2001 general election as well as non-voters in local and European Parliament elections. It contains a disproportionate number of younger people, who may actively avoid talking about politics, reading about it or watching political programmes on television.

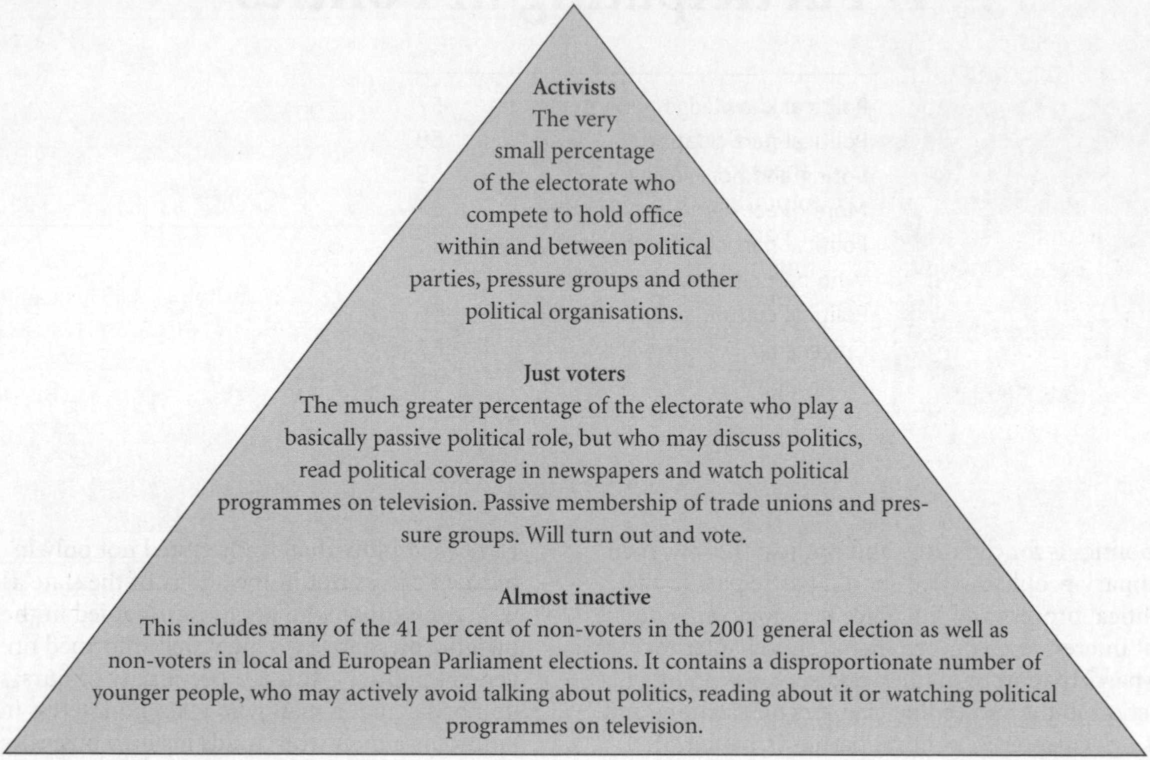

*Source*: Adapted from Milbrath, 1965: 16–22.

a slightly higher level than in previous audits. Women, young voters, manual workers and members of ethnic minorities in particular felt less knowledgeable and less interested in politics. This survey, combined with previous research, indicates that at least a very substantial minority of the population feels alienated and excluded from the political process. These feelings are most evident among the poorest sections of society. Among social classes D and E only 38 per cent claimed an interest in politics compared to 73 per cent of classes A and B.

## Political participation

While other political systems may not necessarily involve extensive participation by ordinary people in politics beyond simply obeying the government, democracy (in theory at least) presupposes active citizen involvement. Yet **political participation** in Britain is limited. Figure 4.1 suggests that the

British people may be divided into three main types of participant: a small number of political *activists;* the majority – *just voters* – whose participation in politics is limited to voting in elections; and a substantial minority who are *almost inactive*, scarcely participating at all. The diagram is derived from distinctions made by Milbrath (1965), but also reflects findings on political participation in Britain (Parry *et al.*, 1992, Bromley *et al.*, 2001, 2002), and recent research by the Hansard Society, who have conducted an annual audit of political engagement from 2004 onwards.

The 2010 Hansard audit identified eight distinct groups, according to the nature and extent of their political engagement. Group 1 were defined as 'politically committed' (10 per cent of the total). Group 2 were 'active campaigners' (14 per cent).

● **Political participation**: Citizen involvement in politics through, for example, voting, or pressure group and party activity aimed at influencing government and public policy.

While the first of these groups was more directly involved, both were regular voters, and keenly followed politics. Together they might roughly correspond to Milbrath's political activists. Group 3 were 'interested bystanders' (14 per cent), group 4 'detached cynics' (17 per cent) and group 5 'politically contented' (6 per cent). All these groups, despite their different attitudes to politics and politicians, were generally regular voters, but not actively engaged in politics and thus similar to those Milbrath described as 'just voters'. Group 6 were 'bored/ apathetic' (6 per cent), group 7, the largest, were 'disengaged/mistrustful' (24 per cent), and group 8 'alienated/hostile' (9 per cent). These last three groups, whatever their different perceptions of politics, might fairly be described as 'almost inactive' politically. They were less knowledgeable about politics, and much less committed to the most basic level of political engagement, voting.

## Voting and non-voting

The most basic form of political participation in a representative democracy is voting. The political system depends on the readiness of people to exercise their right to vote. Substantial non-voting reduces the legitimacy of any elected individual or authority. Low turnout in elections has become a matter of concern in Britain. Turnout in general elections has declined since the 1950s when it averaged over 80 per cent. In 1992, turnout was 77.7 per cent in 1997, 71.5 per cent and in 2001 it was down to 59 per cent, improving only slightly to 61 per cent in 2005 and 65 per cent in 2010. Turnout is lower still in elections for the European Parliament and local elections (see Table 4.1).

Britain is hardly alone in registering low and generally declining levels of electoral participation. Indeed, they appear to be a feature of most western democracies (Hague and Harrop, 2010, p. 194). Some recent US presidential elections (arguably the most important elections in the world today) have only involved around half of American citizens, although the 2008 election that led to Barack Obama's presidency raised turnout to 64 per cent, close to an all-time US record, but still leaving over a third non-voters. Although it is sometimes argued that non-voting reflects contentment, the more

**Table 4.1**   Levels of turnout by British voters

| | |
|---|---|
| London Mayoral election 2008 | 45% |
| European Parliament elections 2009 | 34% |
| UK General Election 2010 | 65% |
| Northern Ireland Assembly elections 2011 | 55% |
| Referendum on Alternative Vote, 2011 | 42% |

general view is that low turnout is a serious cause of concern. Whiteley *et al.* (in Norris, 2001, p. 222), reviewing the 59 per cent turnout in the 2001 general election, observed, 'If this is not a crisis of democratic politics in Britain, then it is hard to know what would be.' For Bill Jones (2003: 24), large-scale abstentions indicate that 'worryingly large numbers of people have little faith in the political system'. Suggested remedies for low and declining electoral turnout depend to a degree on some very different perceptions of the causes of non-voting (see Table 4.2).

All the suggested causes of non-voting have a certain plausibility and most of these suggested remedies have already been tried, many in Britain, and others elsewhere. We have already seen that over half the electorate feel they know little or nothing about politics. Those who are better educated are more interested and more likely to vote. There have been efforts to improve the level of political education in Britain through the national curriculum and through the efforts of campaigning individuals and societies. Political education is intrinsically controversial. Many are worried that it could involve political indoctrination. Yet if it is confined to the safer ground of the political system and process rather than more controversial political issues, it risks being boring. The impact of more political education can only be judged in the longer term, but to date the results are unimpressive. According to the 2010 Hansard survey, the youngest age group in the electorate, those aged between 18 and 24, remain the least knowledgeable (35 per cent), the least interested (38 per cent) and the least likely to vote (27 per cent).

Arguably, low knowledge of, and interest in, politics may be blamed more on the mass media than on any deficiency in political education.

**Table 4.2**  Low electoral turnouts: possible causes and remedies

| The cause? | The cure? |
| --- | --- |
| Voter ignorance of politics and government in general and of local government and the European Union in particular | More political education in schools and colleges |
| | Improved media coverage of government and politics |
| Lack of confidence that voting changes anything, particularly for non-Westminster elections. Lack of a clear impact of voting on government. | More powers for local and devolved government |
| | Increase accountability of European institutions to the elected European Parliament |
| Potential voters put off by 'low-tech' antiquated and inconvenient means of registering choice, by marking a ballot paper in a remote polling station | Penalties (e.g. fines) for non-voting |
| | More convenient polling stations (e.g. in supermarkets) |
| | Reform voting methods by introducing more postal voting, telephone voting and internet voting |
| Potential voters deterred by limited effective choice in British elections and 'unfair' relationship between votes cast and the result in terms of seats won | Reform the electoral system to provide a more proportionate relationship between votes cast and election outcomes, and more effective choice |
| Citizens disillusioned by party politics, elections and the processes of representative democracy | More direct democracy (e.g. through referendums, focus groups, 'citizens' juries'). New forms of politics involving more direct action and involvement. |

Certainly there is evidence of reduced political coverage in the tabloid press and on the main television news programmes. Much of the coverage is also superficial and, in the case of the press, nakedly partisan. Yet those involved in the media might reasonably claim only to be reacting to demand, or in this case the lack of it. The public has shown clear signs of being 'turned off' by the saturation coverage of politics in election campaigns (see Chapter 9 for more on the media and politics).

Some non-voting might reflect not so much political ignorance as a (reasonably accurate?) belief that voting is unlikely to make much difference for anything other than Westminster elections. (Even here the low turnout in 2001 especially could be blamed on the widespread assumption that the result was a foregone conclusion.) Thus low turnout in local elections may be because local councils do not seem to have much power, and perhaps also in many cases because elections are unlikely to lead to a change in party control (see Chapter 17 for more on local elections). Voters may

also perceive that the European Parliament lacks power. Although it has gained increased influence over legislation, the budget and even the composition of the European Commission, it does not effectively control the government of Europe (see Chapter 15). Thus voting in European elections does not appear to make much difference to political decisions in the European Union. Nationalists would argue that one reason for the lower turnout in elections for the Scottish Parliament and, particularly, the Welsh Assembly is that these bodies still do not have enough power (see Chapter 16). Whether turnout would be markedly higher in elections for local councils, devolved assemblies and the European Parliament if these bodies had more power seems debatable, however.

Voting might be encouraged by rewards and/or punishments. Some countries, like Belgium, fine non-voters. Unsurprisingly, this encourages very high turnout (over 90 per cent), yet such a solution has not generally found favour. Compulsion involves some interference with freedom. Moreover, the constrained voter may vote arbitrarily or perversely. Alternatively voters might be rewarded with a modest tax rebate. There may be some merit in allowing positive abstention as an option in elections, for example allowing voters to put a cross next to 'none of the above' under the parties or candidates listed.

In Britain more emphasis has been placed on modernizing and simplifying voting procedures, through the trial use of extended postal voting, and experiments with telephone voting, text messaging, and internet voting. While a generation used to communicating through mobile phones and the internet may find marking a ballot paper with a pencilled cross in a remote schoolroom requisitioned as a polling station both antiquated and inconvenient, there are continuing security concerns over alternatives. Among these, only the relatively 'old-tech' postal voting has led to significantly higher turnout levels, at the cost of increased allegations of electoral fraud, which the Electoral Commission and in some cases the police have investigated. There have also been experiments with rather more user-friendly polling stations, sited in supermarkets. Having elections on a Sunday or public holiday instead of a working day is another option, widely used elsewhere, that might encourage higher turnout in Britain.

Electoral reform might do more to ensure that each vote counts, and thus increase the incentive to vote. At present, turnout is higher in marginal constituencies, and lower in those unlikely to change hands (see Chapter 5). Thus it is at least plausible that a more proportional electoral system would lead to a higher turnout. Yet more proportional electoral systems introduced for elections for the European Parliament, Scottish Parliament and Welsh Assembly have not produced high turnouts. It is even possible that these more complicated electoral systems have confused some electors and put them off.

## More direct democracy?

Finally it is at least possible that the kind of politics that seems inseparable from representative democracy is a 'turn-off' for a section of the electorate. Polls indicate that people distrust politicians and dislike adversarial party politics (particularly

perhaps in the wake of the 2009 parliamentary expenses scandal). More direct democracy might be the solution. One possibility would be increased use of the referendum, enabling all adult citizens to have a direct voice on key issues. The referendum has been occasionally used in Britain for issues of a constitutional nature, and more commonly employed in some other countries like Switzerland. The coalition government that emerged in Britain in 2010 was committed to at least one referendum, on the introduction of the Alternative Vote (see Chapter 5), and this could provide a further precedent for others. A similar device is the initiative used in some American states (e.g. California), where if an issue is raised by a sufficient number of voters it can be placed on the ballot paper. However, not everyone approves of referendums, and many politicians are less than enthusiastic, as they undermine their representative role (see Academic Controversy 4.1).

Most countries use referendums sparingly. However, governments, elected representatives and political parties all make extensive use of opinion polls to guide their own policies and commitments. Local councils and other public bodies frequently engage in public consultation exercises to ascertain people's preferences. Further insights into public thinking may be gained using focus group, in which small, broadly representative samples of people discuss a particular issue or policy in more depth. Local councils sometimes use 'citizens' juries' (or 'citizens' panels') to consult public opinion on key issues in a similar but more thorough and systematic way. Yet although focus groups or citizens' juries may involve a representative cross-section of the population, they have not been chosen by the people and cannot properly represent them. They may enable decision-makers to become better informed on public opinion, but they do not transfer power to the public. They are supplements rather than alternatives to the ballot box.

## Political participation beyond voting

Voting is only the simplest and most basic form of political participation in a modern representative democracy. A rather higher level of political

## Academic controversy 4.1
## The merits and disadvantages of initiatives and referendums

**In favour** of votes on a single issue, it is argued:

- They give people a chance to vote on specific issues that affect their lives, whereas in a general election they can only offer a general verdict on the performance and promises of governing and opposition parties.
- They may help educate citizens on key political issues and stimulate more interest in public policy.
- They may exert pressure on elected representatives to act responsibly, and in the general public interest rather than specific interests with which representatives may be linked.
- Elected representatives may sometimes be out of touch with the views and interests of those they claim to represent.

**Against** such consultation, it may be said that:

- There are commonly problems in framing questions, as it is seldom that an issue can be simplified sufficiently for a yes/no answer. It is not easy to accommodate shades of opinion.

- Frequent referendums arguably require more political knowledge and interest than elections. Although they may help to educate the public, it is equally possible they will produce voter fatigue and apathy.
- Campaigns can be expensive and therefore to the advantage of well-funded groups; business interests have far more scope to influence the outcome than trade unions or consumer groups.
- Initiatives and referendums weaken the role of political parties in the democratic process and undermine the responsibility and accountability of Parliament and other representative bodies.
- They encourage single-issue politics, rather than debate based on a conflict of broad principles.
- Referendums may be used by voters to voice general discontent with the government of the day rather than provide an answer to a specific referendum question.
- Dictators or charismatic leaders have often used referendums not to transfer power to the people but to legitimate their own power and policy.

---

commitment than voting is registered by joining a political party. The modern political parties that developed and flourished in the twentieth century had substantial mass membership, and most voters strongly identified with specific parties. Both active party membership and strong party loyalty have declined markedly over the last half-century over most of the western world and in Britain in particular. Accurate membership figures are difficult to obtain, but it appears the Labour Party has fewer than two hundred thousand individual members, the Conservative Party less than three hundred thousand, and the Liberal Democrats well under a hundred thousand. Altogether only between one and two per cent of voters are party members, and fewer still are actively involved in party meetings, fundraising and canvassing (see Chapter 6). Party

membership thus does not necessarily indicate active participation in politics. Many members do no more than pay subscriptions by banker's order, and some join for the social facilities offered by Conservative or Labour clubs.

It is sometimes argued that the decline in involvement in political parties has been balanced by a rise of participation in single-issue pressure groups. Indeed, the membership of some groups runs into millions, and far exceeds the membership of political parties. However, these figures are hardly reliable indicators of active participation in politics. A more reliable indicator is perhaps provided by membership of campaigning groups such as Greenpeace, Friends of the Earth or Amnesty International (all between a hundred and two hundred thousand). However, even much of

COMPARATIVE POLITICS 4.1

# The French referendum on the European Constitution, 2005

France has long used referendums on constitutional issues, although French voters have sometimes used them to vent their displeasure with the government of the day. In May 2005 they voted to reject the proposed new EU constitution by a margin of 55.6 to 44.4 per cent. According to Timothy Garton Ash, 'the French did not just say no to a particular, cumbersome constitutional treaty...They said no to what the EU has become since the fall of the Berlin wall, no to a much-enlarged

EU where France is no longer in the driving seat. No to the prospect of Turkish membership. No to Anglo-Saxon style economic reform: deregulation, free-market liberalism, Thatcherism imported via Brussels. And, of course, no to lupine Jacques Chirac [then the French President]... This was a no of fear. Fear of losing your job to the now proverbial Polish plumber. Fear of immigration. Fear of change.' (From *The Guardian*, 30 May 2005)

---

this support involves 'cheque book participation' with many members only prepared to make a donation to a cause with which they sympathize, but not to involve themselves further in active campaigning (Maloney, in Dunleavy *et al.*, 2006).

How many people, then, are more actively engaged in politics? Parry and Moyser (1990) found that 23.2 per cent were involved in some other political activity besides voting, but only a very small minority (1.5 per cent) were real political activists, involved in a wide range of political behaviour, including party campaigning, pressure group activity, demonstrating and protesting, and contacting elected representatives. More recently the Hansard Society *Audit of Political Engagement 7* (2010) concluded that 16 per cent of adults are political activists, defined as having done at least three from a list of eight political activities (excluding voting) in the last two or three years (see Table 4.3). Yet even on this relatively loose and generous working definition, it is clear that only a relatively small minority of the population are political activists.

## Who participates, and why?

Political activists are found disproportionately among the higher social classes. Thus over a quarter (28 per cent) of those from social classes A and B are politically active (as defined by the

Table 4.3   Political activism: responses to question 'Which, if any, of the things on this list have you done in the last two or three years?'

| Political activity | Percentage taking part |
|---|---|
| Signed a petition | 40% |
| Boycotted certain products for political, ethical or environmental reasons | 19% |
| Contacted/presented views to a local councillor or MP | 17% |
| Urged someone to get in touch with a local councillor or MP | 15% |
| Been to any political meeting | 8% |
| Donated money or paid membership to a political party | 5% |
| Taken an active part in a political campaign | 5% |
| Taken part in a demonstration, march or picket/strike | 4% |
| None of these | 47% |
| **Three or more activities** | 16% |

*Source*: Poll conducted for Hansard, *Audit of Political Engagement* (2010, p. 81).

## Academic controversy 4.2
# Apathetic young adults?

Research (e.g. Hansard, 2010) indicates that young adults are less interested in politics, less knowledgeable about it and less likely to vote than older generations. This has aroused considerable concern over the alleged political apathy and alienation of young adults, and the prospects for democratic politics in Britain, although some argue that this is simply a life-cycle problem – young people will become more politically engaged as they grow older. Another possible explanation is that the young are 'turned off' conventional party politics but are interested instead in a new politics agenda involving single-issue pressure groups and new social movements.

A survey of young people eligible to vote in elections for the first time found that they had a rather narrow view of politics, involving government, running the country, politicians and political parties. They considered the government unresponsive to the needs and wishes of young people, and had little confidence in their ability to influence parties or the government. Although the research indicated that young people 'had a general attachment to and confidence in the democratic process', they were sceptical about the outcome of elections, and showed 'a deep-seated scepticism towards the political parties and politicians who vie for their votes and political office'. However, the young adults surveyed showed similar levels of interest in political issues to the population as a whole (public services, war, the economy, law and order etc.). The researchers concluded that 'at the heart of young people's declining election turnout and their apparent disenchantment with Westminster politics is a strong sense of political alienation rather than political apathy – the political system in Britain is failing to provide the stimuli necessary for young people to take a greater role in political life' (Henn et al., 2005).

---

Hansard Society – see above) compared with 8 per cent of C2s and just 5 per cent of Ds and Es. Political participation increases with levels of education. Education builds self-confidence, increases political knowledge and provides communication skills, all useful for significant political participation. Whites are more politically active (17 per cent) than those from non-white ethnic minorities (4 per cent). Gender differences in political participation, once significant, have largely disappeared. Women (16 per cent) are as well represented as men (15 per cent) among the politically active. Young adults are less likely to be active (only 9 per cent) than older generations, although for perhaps obvious reasons political activism beyond voting falls away among the over 65s (Hansard report, 2010, p. 82).

Why do some people participate more in politics than others? Political activists may be more confident that their efforts may make a difference. The Hansard survey (2010) found that just 37 per cent of the public agreed that 'when people like me get involved in politics they really can make a difference'. Those believing political participation is futile and ineffective may not even try to influence decisions that affect them. They are thus unlikely to have their interests taken into account, confirming the view that 'no one takes any notice of people like us'. Yet they may be right, at least in part. Governments may be more responsive to some interests than others, while some sections of the population have fewer resources and skills for effective participation (see Chapter 8). There seems to be a fairly widespread dissatisfaction with popular influence on government and policy, and considerable mistrust of Parliament and politicians. However, the Hansard survey surprisingly found that there had been no significant collapse of trust in the wake of the 2009 parliamentary expenses scandal (see Chapter 13) 'in large part because levels of confidence or trust were already low'. Thus the scandal 'has merely confirmed and hardened

## BOX 4.1

# The new politics of participation

**The Anti-Poll Tax Movement** employed a wide range of methods of protest, including lobbying of MPs and councillors, petitions and demonstrations; on occasion, it was involved in violent disturbances such as the March 1990 Trafalgar Square riot which ended with over 140 being injured. More significantly, its massive campaign of non-payment tapped into a long tradition of civil disobedience in Britain. In the first six months of 1992 alone, nearly 4 million people were summonsed for failing to pay the tax. This popular non-cooperation, driven by a combination of moral outrage and self-interest, forced the government to back down and withdraw the tax.

**Anti-roads protests** were coordinated from 1991 by Alarm UK, an umbrella organization for 250 groups, involving direct action against a large number of road schemes, including extensions to the M3, M11 and A30. 'Eco-warriors' engaged in a large variety of obstructive activities on new road sites, including occupation of houses and tree-houses, barricading themselves in tunnels, chaining themselves to concrete lock-ins and occupying offices of construction companies.

**Protests against the export of live animals** in 1995, involving demonstrations and obstruction, succeeded in reducing the number of ferry companies and ports handling the trade, but protesters were far from satisfied with the new EU rules on the live transport of animals agreed in July 1995.

**Protests against GM (genetically modified) crops** (1999 onwards). Greenpeace and other environmental groups opposed trials of GM crops by the company Monsanto, fearing cross-pollination with native plants and other damaging environmental effects. Protests included the trashing of GM crops. Hostile public opinion led to a moratorium on the commercial growing of GM crops.

**The fuel protests.** In September 2000, militant French road hauliers blocked fuel supplies in a protest against the rising cost of diesel. This encouraged British farmers, lorry drivers, taxi drivers and in some places fishermen to take similar action with blockades at oil refineries and fuel distribution depots. The opposition leader William Hague described the blockade as a 'taxpayers' rebellion' which appeared to be supported by 95 per cent of public opinion. The fuel protesters showed that, using the new technologies of communication, relatively few activists could create disproportionate national disruption. It was estimated that only two thousand individuals were involved directly in the fuel blockade, yet within days the country was plunged into crisis. Panic buying by the public left garages without fuel and created food shortages in supermarkets.

the public's widely held scepticism about politicians rather than changed their views' (Hansard Society, 2010, p.3).

Higher than average political participation may also be related to political values. Those holding strong or extreme political views tend to participate well above average, with overall participation in all fields of political activity highest on the extreme left. By contrast, the moderate centre tends to under-participate. This may be because they are more satisfied with the way the country is run, and so less inclined to indulge in political activities to secure change. (The 2010 Hansard survey found that just 28 per cent felt that the present system of governing the country worked well while 69 per cent felt it could be improved either 'a great deal' or 'quite a lot'.)

Political values associated with the 'new' or 'post-materialist' politics of environmentalism, peace and feminism are linked to higher than average participation, although this may be expressed through collective and direct action far more than through more conventional forms of participation (see Box 4.1 and Chapter 8). Civil disobedience strategies have been most evident in anti-poll tax demonstrations in the 1980s and early 1990s, and more recently in animal rights protests and campaigns against new roads, airport runways, nuclear and coal-fired power stations and similar environmental protests. While a majority only support orderly, peaceful methods of political protest, willingness to engage in more threatening forms of direct action such as site occupations, destruction of crops, refusals to pay taxes, and blocking roads appears to have increased. The London bombings of July 2005 and the attack on Glasgow airport in 2007 show that a small minority are even prepared to countenance indiscriminate violence against ordinary members of the public in pursuit of political objectives.

## Political culture and socialization

Some would link the changes in political participation described in the first part of this chapter with a broader change in political attitudes and behaviour, or what is sometimes described as **political culture**. It used to be argued that Britain had a political culture characterized by moderation, mutual toleration and respect for the law. Almond and Verba (1965), in a comparative study of five cultures, suggested that Britain enjoyed substantial political participation, social trust and civic organization. More recent analysis suggests this culture has changed. Social trust and more specifically trust in government and politicians has declined markedly. There is now less readiness to defer to authority. There has been a corresponding reduction in traditional forms of political participation (voting, party membership and identification), perhaps offset by a rise of participation in direct action (see Box 4.1), and an increasing resort to illegal and even violent behaviour.

What can explain this apparent change in political culture? The process by which people come to understand and mentally absorb the culture of their society is referred to as socialization, and the process by which they acquire knowledge of their political culture is known as **political socialization**. Political knowledge, values, attitudes and beliefs are informally learned in a process that begins in childhood and continues throughout adult life. Although political socialization is continuous, certain phases seem to be particularly important. Because of the malleability of the young and

their greater exposure and susceptibility to influences, it is generally held that the pre-adult years are of critical significance to political socialization, even though political attitudes learned when young may be modified or changed as a result of later experiences and pressures.

Key agencies influencing political socialization include the family, local community, peer groups, education, workplace experience and the media. The manner in which these agencies combine varies for each individual. Often, because of the depth and intensity of the emotional relationships it involves, the family is the predominant influence. It passes on an ethnic, religious and class identity, which normally is associated with a particular set of political orientations, and it powerfully shapes a child's attitude to authority, to gender roles, and to values which have clear implications for political behaviour. But family influences, however powerful, may not determine political outlooks permanently. Some may rebel against their parents as teenagers or grow away from their family values as adults.

The main agencies of political socialization are themselves continually evolving. The considerable increase in recent decades of divorce and birth outside marriage may be weakening the family, thereby undermining its effectiveness as a mechanism for transmitting political culture. The proportion of the population with qualifications at all levels has risen steadily and in the longer term an educated population may be expected to participate more. Changes in the media may also have an impact on the political socialization process, with the growing predominance since the 1970s of television as the major source of public information about politics, although the political agenda remains strongly influenced by the (still predominantly right-wing) tabloid press. The significance of 'new media' is also increasing (see Chapter 9).

Finally, an important theory of social change is the generation theory: the idea that the political outlook of each generation is powerfully shaped by the dominant ideas and institutions of the age into which they are born and brought up. In seeking to understand political attitudes and behaviour, it makes sense to consider the often sharply contrasting experiences of 'political generations'. Thus successive generations may have been moulded by

---

● A **political culture** is the pattern of understandings, feelings and attitudes that dispose people towards behaving in a particular way politically. It is the collective expression of the political outlooks and values of the individuals who make up society.

---

● **Political socialization** is the process by which political beliefs and attitudes are learned or acquired particularly in childhood, but throughout life.

*Academic controversy 4.3*
# Participation and democracy

The nineteenth-century thinker John Stuart Mill assumed that representative democracy required both the political education and full participation of its citizens (Mill, 1861). Like the French writer Alexis de Tocqueville he hoped that local government would provide an education in democracy. (However, today there is less public knowledge of and participation in local government and politics than central government and parliamentary elections).

In contrast the American political thinker Joseph Schumpeter (1943), chose to redefine democracy and limit the extent of citizen participation to an occasional choice between rival teams of political leaders and programmes, demanding less political knowledge and engagement.

Albert Hirschman's book *Exit, Voice and Loyalty* (1970) listed in its title the three main mechanisms available to individuals to influence issues and decisions affecting them. As Stoker (2006) points out, 'exit' is the classic economic mechanism. In a free market, if consumers are dissatisfied they can go elsewhere. In politics 'exit' clearly has a place; thus party members and voters can switch their allegiance, and ultimately a dissatisfied citizen may be able to seek refuge in another state

(although as David Hume long ago pointed out, this is often not a realistic option). More commonly, faced with a monopoly state provider of public services, the consumer has no effective exit option (as neo-liberal economists emphasize). Thus 'voice' is the characteristic political mechanism, but as Stoker (2006, p. 75) acknowledges, 'voice ... carries more costs for the individual than exit'. Campaigning and protesting is harder work, and particularly frustrating if no-one appears to be listening. Thus the political process is intrinsically more difficult than the simple market mechanism, which is why it is a 'turn-off' for many. There is also 'designed-in disappointment' as 'the outcomes of the political process are seldom clear cut and are often messy compromises' (Stoker, 2006, p. 82). Yet he is sceptical over some proposed remedies involving increased public participation, arguing that most people do not want to devote much more of their time to politics. 'Overloading citizens with information or access to decision-making processes ignores the attraction of the division of labour in representative politics. From the citizen's viewpoint, somebody else – their elected representative – is taking the time and trouble to investigate the issues' (Stoker, 2006, p.166). He concludes (p. 205): 'we need a politics designed for amateurs so that citizens can engage in politics and retain a life'.

---

the carnage of the First World War, the 1930s Depression, the post-1945 welfare state, the 'permissive society' of the 1960s, the Thatcherite era of free markets and 'enterprise', and most recently, the New Labour economic boom, abruptly ended by the credit crunch.

## Citizenship

A key term in the debate on political participation is citizenship. Citizenship implies full membership of a particular nation or state. To be a subject implies passive obedience to government and the state, to be a citizen implies willing, active involve-

ment in a political community. Citizenship is widely taken to involve a common identity with fellow-citizens, a core of shared values, generally agreed rights and responsibilities, including an entitlement to participate in the nation's affairs.

In some countries, such as the USA, citizenship is only granted after formal tests in which applicants demonstrate their knowledge of a country's history, culture and political institutions, and an oath of allegiance. In Britain there are no such formal requirements, although more recently courses and ceremonies have been introduced for new British citizens, reflecting a growing concern that citizenship in Britain does not necessarily involve a common identity and shared values. Some British citizens may identify with only part of the territory of the United Kingdom, and a minority may reject any allegiance to the British state. Yet quite apart from these ambiguities over the very nature of the British state, many British citizens (as we have seen) may fall short of the ideal of active citizenship and full membership of the political community.

Citizenship is generally considered to involve both rights and obligations. Marshall (1950) categorized citizen rights under three headings – civil rights, political rights and social rights. Civil rights are rights necessary for individual freedom – freedom of speech and conscience, property rights, equality before the law. Political rights involve the right to participate in political life, through the right to vote and stand for election. Social rights include the right to education, health treatment, housing etc. These rights were progressively recognized over different periods in Europe – civil rights in the eighteenth century, political rights in the course of the nineteenth, and social rights with the growth of the welfare state in the twentieth century. Yet rights carry with them obligations, not simply to obey orders, but to participate willingly and conscientiously in the political community. High levels of citizen participation have often been considered a necessary condition for democracy (see Academic Controversy 4.3).

Although many British politicians and thinkers and all mainstream British political parties have favourably invoked the term 'citizen', it remains a hotly contested concept, used in different ways. Thus socialists have stressed the social rights of citizens to adequate levels of education, health and housing, effectively requiring extensive state intervention. Neo-liberals, however, have tended to deny or minimize social rights, and downplay rights to political participation, emphasizing instead the civil rights of the citizen against the state, the rights of individuals to live their own life free from state interference, and their right to choose as consumers of public services.

Blair's Labour government gave citizens statutory powers to enforce their rights through the Human Rights Act (see Chapter 14). Otherwise, New Labour emphasized that citizenship involved obligations as well as rights, and sought to engage

those who suffered from 'social exclusion' by promoting citizenship education as part of the national curriculum, providing services (e.g. parenting classes, homework clubs and childcare facilities) to help local communities, combined with new controls (e.g. anti social behaviour orders, increased electronic surveillance). Yet some individuals and whole communities remained alienated, apparently 'socially excluded' by choice. Thus David Cameron spoke of a 'broken society' and a 'broken Britain' which needed to re-engage its citizens. Whether his coalition government will be more successful than New Labour in combating political alienation and apathy and engaging citizens in Cameron's 'big society' remains to be seen.

## Community

While citizenship relates to the rights and duties of individual men and women, community is about groups of people and wider social interaction. Although it commonly conjures up images of small face-to-face local communities, such as a village or neighbourhood, it is also applied to much larger collective bodies – the national community, the European Community, the international community. Moreover, community is not invariably linked with territory. Thus in other contexts we have professional communities, the academic community, ethnic minority communities or the Catholic community. There may be distinctive communities living alongside each other within a specific area, as Catholics and Protestants do in Northern Ireland, but scarcely interacting socially.

Community, like citizen, has positive connotations, so much so that it is sometimes employed as an all-purpose sanitizing term to promote particular initiatives (community care, community policing), institutions (such as the now defunct Community Health Councils) or even taxes (the Community Charge, the official description of the notorious poll tax, abolished in 1993). More positively, it is a term linked with certain values and ideas, such as co-operation, fellowship and solidarity. It implies that people do have interests in common, that they are not just a mere aggregate of individuals motivated exclusively by their own self-interest, but capable of fellow-feeling, group loyalty, and a sense of social obligation.

## Academic controversy 4.4
# Social capital and a decline in social and political engagement?

Robert Putnam (1995, 2000) has developed a complex theory linking a decline in political participation with a general reduction of what he calls *social capital*. Basically, social capital reflects how much individuals interact with each other face-to-face as neighbours, members of clubs and other forms of association. High levels of such interaction encourage the development of civic attitudes (including voting in elections). The more individuals play passive, isolated roles in society, such as staying at home, watching television and videos, and surfing the internet, the more likely they are to withdraw from public activities such as voting, and from active involvement in political parties and pressure groups. Putnam supports his theory with a wealth of research in the United States, indicating a strong correlation between a decline in social capital and decline in active citizenship and political engagement.

Theda Skocpol (1996, pp. 20–5) objected that Putnam's approach assumes that 'spontaneous social association is primary and government and politics are derivative'. Others suggest that Putnam has been too pessimistic and one-sided over the social changes he has described. Social capital theorists have tended to see television and the internet as a threat to participatory democracy, through the reduction in face-to-face communication and social interaction. Yet it can be argued that they offer new forms of communication and opportunities for increased participation, through for example internet chat rooms and interactive television (Margetts in Dunleavy *et al.*, 2002).

Some critics suggest that Putnam's American findings do not necessarily apply to Britain. Thus Maloney (in Dunleavy *et al.*, 2006, pp. 114–15) cites evidence of increased political engagement and involvement in the voluntary sector in Britain and relatively high levels of social and political trust.

Indeed, a whole communitarian school of political thought has grown up to counter the narrow individualism associated with classical liberalism and, more recently, the neo-liberal New Right (Mulhall and Swift, 1996). These ideas have been popularized by, among others, Amitae Etzioni (1995) and briefly taken up by politicians like Tony Blair and, more recently, David Cameron. Community in this sense is highly compatible with the notion of active citizenship, involving wider social engagement and mutual rights and obligations. Both citizenship and community are terms which have acquired a strong normative flavour, recommending how people should behave.

Some, however, would suggest that a sense of community, and obligations to the community, have declined markedly in the modern world. Thus we no longer live, work and interact within small face-to-face communities, but live fragmented, isolated lives, loosely linked to a range of barely related 'communities' with little feeling of identity or loyalty. We do not necessarily know or care for our neighbours, having nothing in common beyond physical proximity. Robert Putnam (2000) in particular has linked the decline of political participation with a reduction in 'social capital', a more general decline in social interaction and engagement in the modern western world.

# SUMMARY

- Democracy appears to require higher levels of political interest, knowledge and involvement than other political systems.

- Nevertheless up to half of British adults have little knowledge of and interest in politics. A substantial and growing minority do not even vote, and the majority of the population do not participate in politics beyond voting.

- Various practical remedies have been tried or proposed to counter this apparently widespread political ignorance and apathy, including more political education, making it easier to vote, electoral reform and the encouragement of other forms of political involvement.

- Some argue that a decline in traditional political engagement through voting, parties and representative institutions has been offset by a rise in new forms of political activity involving social movements, campaigning groups and more direct action.

- Democracy may be felt to require active citizenship. In practice the term 'citizen' has been extensively used in political debate in Britain but with a wide variety of meanings.

- Community is another key term in the debate over political participation; it is imprecise, but carries strong normative overtones and is freely applied to different levels and types of social organization.

- Social capital theorists have linked declining political participation with reduced levels of social interaction and community engagement more generally in modern society. The analysis is suggestive but contentious.

# QUESTIONS FOR DISCUSSION

- How far do low and declining turnout figures in elections suggest a crisis for democracy?

- Should voting be compulsory? How else might people be encouraged to vote? Does voting change anything?

- How else can individuals participate in politics beyond voting? How many do in fact participate significantly beyond voting?

- How far are there significant differences in the political outlook and behaviour of different generations? Are younger people less interested in politics, and if so, why, and how might this be remedied?

- Does the apparent increase in the politics of direct action involve a threat to rational democratic debate, or a healthy alternative to outdated and limited traditional means of political involvement?

- Should there be more education in citizenship? Should language or other tests be a requirement for British citizenship? What does, or should, citizenship involve?

- Has there been a general decline in social interaction and engagement in modern Britain, and what are the implications for politics?

# FURTHER READING

On political participation, a key source is still Parry, Moyser and Day (1992), *Political Participation and Democracy in Britain*. This should be supplemented by the British Social Attitudes surveys, (www.natcen.ac.uk) produced annually, and the annual reports on political engagement produced by the Hansard Society from 2004 onward (e.g. Hansard Society, 2010) which can be consulted on their website. For a valuable survey of participation, citizenship and associated academic debates see the chapters by Margett and Frazer in Dunleavy *et al.* (2002). For more specific analysis of political culture and voting participation see Evans in Dunleavy *et al.* (2003). A useful recent short article is Bill Jones, 'Apathy: Why don't people want to vote?'

(*Politics Review*, April 2003). Lynch discusses new voting methods in 'Goodbye Ballot Box, Hello Post Box' (*Talking Politics*, September 2002). For a discussion of non-participation by the young see O'Toole *et al.* (2003), *Political Quarterly*, vol.74, no. 3, and Henn *et al.* (2005), *Political Studies,* vol. 53, no. 3. For 'Political Participation beyond the Electoral Arena' see Maloney in Dunleavy *et al.* (2006).

On political culture, the classic work is Almond and Verba (1965), *The Civic Culture*. See also the same authors' *The Civic Culture Revisited* (1980). On social capital see Putnam (2000), *Bowling Alone: The Collapse and Revival of the American Community*.

**Elections and Voting**

Elections are central to modern representative democracy. They reflect the principles of popular sovereignty, that ultimate power rests with the people, and governments derive their authority from the people's support. Yet the composition of the UK parliament and government may only imperfectly reflect the preferences of voters, due in part to a disproportionate electoral system. Defenders of this system have long argued that it delivers strong stable government, although parties (such as the Liberal Democrats and Greens) who are under-represented have demanded electoral reform. A variety of more proportional systems have already been introduced for devolved government in Scotland, Wales and Northern Ireland (see Chapter 16), for London government (see Chapter 17) and for British elections to the European Parliament (see Chapter 15). These systems (new in the UK but long familiar in other countries) have produced markedly different results in terms of voters' behaviour, the choice of representatives, relative party strengths and the nature and style of government. Largely as a result of proportional representation, coalition or minority government has become familiar in Scotland, Wales and Northern Ireland, as it has long been on most of the European continent.

This chapter begins with an analysis of the general election of May 2010, which was distinctly unusual in, even without electoral reform, failing to deliver a majority of seats for any party for the first time since February 1974. In other respects, it reflected recent trends in voting behaviour. Generally, the electorate has become more volatile and party allegiances appear weaker. The formerly marked correlation in Britain between voting and occupational class has declined, although it remains more significant than most other objective social divisions. Identity politics – who people think they are – may have increased significance for voting behaviour.

## The 2010 general election

On 6 May 2010 voters in the United Kingdom went to the polls to elect 650 Members of Parliament. The three previous general elections, in 1997, 2001 and 2005, had resulted in victories for the Labour party, albeit with a declining proportion of the popular vote. The 2010 election (see Table 5.1) involved a marked reversal of fortunes for the two main parties at Westminster, and in this respect was a watershed election (like those of 1979 or 1997). The main losers were clearly Labour, whose share of the vote dropped to 29 per cent (their poorest showing since 1983) and who lost 98 seats. The Conservatives comfortably overtook Labour as the largest party, gaining 109 seats, a very substantial advance, although not enough for an outright majority. This was a significant disappointment for a party that had earlier enjoyed a huge lead in the opinion polls, and led to some recriminations over the Conservative electoral strategy. It was perhaps a greater disappointment for the Liberal Democrats, in view of the strong surge in their poll ratings after Nick Clegg performed well in the televised leader debates, but who only secured a modest increase in their share of the vote and lost five seats. Their substantial consolation was that they held the balance of power, a position they have exploited vigorously to end up as coalition partners with the Conservatives (see Chapter 11), obtaining their first cabinet seats since Churchill's wartime coalition government.

Thus the 2010 election was unusual in producing a 'hung parliament', in which no party secured an overall majority. The only other post-war election which similarly failed to produce a clear winner was February 1974,when Labour emerged as the largest party, and went on to form a minority administration under Harold Wilson that secured a small overall majority in a second election six months later. In the fevered speculation that followed declaration of the results in 2010 many predicted that a second election would follow similarly within a few months. Instead the deal struck between the Conservatives and the Liberal Democrats appears to promise a lasting stable government.

Yet in other respects the 2010 election exhibited similar features to previous UK elections. Indeed it hardly fulfilled some of the more lurid predictions and expectations that preceded it. Thus there were few indications of the widespread political apathy and disgust with the old parties that many detected in the wake of the parliamentary expenses scandal and the credit crunch. Turnout rose to 65 per cent (compared with 61 per cent in 2005 and 59 per

**Table 5.1** The result of the 2010 general election (2005 in brackets)

| Party | % votes | Number of seats | % seats |
| --- | --- | --- | --- |
| Conservative | 36 (32) | 307* (197) | 47 (30) |
| Labour | 29 (35) | 258 (356) | 40 (55) |
| Liberal Democrats | 23 (22) | 57 (62) | 9 (10) |
| Others** | 12 (11) | 28 (30) | 4 (5) |

\* The results in 649 seats were declared in May 2010. The poll in Thirsk and Malton was postponed following the death of one of the candidates during the campaign. It was later retained by the Conservatives, increasing their number of seats to 307.

\*\* Other parties that won seats were Northern Ireland parties (18), SNP (6), Plaid Cymru (3), Green Party (1).

cent in 2001). In England especially the election involved a battle between the candidates of the established three main parties. The anti-EU United Kingdom Independence Party (UKIP) and the far-right British National Party (BNP), which had both performed strongly in the 2009 European Parliament elections, came nowhere near winning a single Westminster seat. The anti-war party Respect lost its only MP. An assortment of independents (including some celebrities) hoping to capitalize on the disgust with mainstream party politicians also performed poorly. Even the lone Independent Richard Taylor lost the Wyre Forest seat he had held through two parliaments to the Conservatives. The only MP elected from outside the three main parties in England was Caroline Lucas, the Green Party leader. The other 27 MPs who were elected for different parties all came from the other nations that make up the United Kingdom. They included 18 from Northern Ireland, six Scottish nationalists (SNP) and three Welsh nationalists (Plaid Cymru). Yet the nationalists in Scotland and Wales made no significant progress. The SNP in particular failed to fulfil their leader Alex Salmond's ambitious hopes of twenty seats.

Table 5.1 shows that there was no close relationship between the percentage of votes secured by a party and the percentage of seats won in the House of Commons. Both the two major parties won a much larger share of seats than their share of the votes. The Conservatives ended with 47 per cent of the seats on 36 per cent of the vote. Labour held 40 per cent of the seats on just 29 per cent of the vote. By contrast the Liberal Democrats secured only 9 per cent of the seats at Westminster on 23 per cent of the vote. A glance at the figures in brackets for the 2005 election indicates that this disproportionate relationship between seats and votes was not a freak feature of 2010. Indeed, in 2005 Labour won a comfortable overall majority of seats (55 per cent) on a marginally smaller proportion of the vote that the Conservatives obtained in 2010 – 35 per cent.

There has been a long-running debate over the electoral system, the **single member plurality system** (or 'first past the post') used for choosing members of the House of Commons, a system which is now relatively uncommon in the western world. The debate has intensified as the UK party system evolved from the substantially two-party contest in the immediate post-war years to a three- or multi-party system in recent decades. This has led to an increasingly erratic relationship between the proportion of votes cast and seats won by particular parties.

Those who defend the single member plurality system include most Conservatives and many in the Labour party. They make the following points:

- It is a simple and readily understood system, unlike most other electoral systems involving more proportional representation.
- It normally produces a clear result quickly (although not in 2010!).
- It preserves a strong link between the electors in each constituency and their Member of Parliament, who has a powerful incentive to listen to constituents and represent their inter-

ests and that of the area in Parliament in order to secure re-election.
- Because it normally exaggerates the winning margin of the leading party and delivers a clear majority of seats in the House of Commons, it provides stable government.

Critics of the Single Member Plurality System argue that it is unfair because:

- It produces often grossly disproportionate results in terms of seats won compared with votes cast, commonly over-representing the leading party.
- However the party that wins the most votes does not necessarily win the most seats. In 1951 the Conservatives had 200,000 fewer votes than Labour but won a majority of the seats and formed the government. In February 1974 Labour won fewer votes but more seats than the Conservatives and formed the government.
- It particularly penalizes third and minor parties whose support is widely dispersed over the country as a whole (e.g. the Liberal Democrats, Greens, UKIP). Thus in 1983 the Labour Party received 27.6 per cent of the popular vote and won 209 seats. The recently formed Liberal-SDP Alliance, close behind with 25.4 per cent of the popular vote, won only 23 seats (3.5 per cent of the total).
- It can also penalize major parties in parts of the UK. Thus the Conservatives won no seats at all in Scotland and Wales in 1997, and have not improved their representation much since. Labour wins few seats outside London in the south of England.
- Under the system, most votes are effectively wasted. All votes for losing candidates and all surplus votes for winning candidates may be considered wasted as they do not contribute to the election of representatives. (To win, a candidate only needs one vote more than the number received by any other candidate. A constituency majority of 20,000 or more may be impressive, but does not make any difference to a party's representation.)
- Because most parliamentary seats are considered 'safe' as there was a substantial majority for the party that won last time, there is little incen-

---

- The **single member plurality system** (SMPS), often called 'first past the post',* used for the House of Commons, involves the election of a single Member of Parliament for each electoral area (or constituency) into which the country is divided. The candidate for election who wins a plurality of votes (that is, more votes than any rival candidate) wins, regardless of whether he or she has a majority of the total votes cast. This system is disproportional because there is no necessary relationship of the overall proportion of seats gained to votes won by a party over the whole country.

* Most political scientists prefer 'single member plurality system' as a more accurate description of the electoral system for Westminster than the more familiar term 'first past the post' used by the media.

## COMPARATIVE POLITICS 5.1

# Parliamentary representation of German Free Democrats and the UK Liberal Democrats

The German Free Democrats (FDP) have generally secured between 5 and 10 per cent of the vote in elections in the German Federal Republic since 1949, but under the German electoral system they always received a broadly comparable proportion of seats in the *Bundestag* or federal parliament. Because it has been rare for a single party to secure an overall majority of seats the FDP have held Cabinet seats in a coalition government for most of the period since 1949. In 1949–1957 and 1961–5 they were in coalition with the Christian Democrats and from 1969 to 1983 they partnered the Social Democrats, returning to share government posts with the Christian Democrats from 1983 to 1998. Since 2009 they have been back in government as junior partners with the Christian Democrats under Angela Merkel. The British Liberal Party and its successors has consistently won a larger share of the national vote than the FDP since 1974, sometimes achieving twice or three times the FDP's share of the vote. Yet the Liberal and their successors have been substantially under-represented at Westminster, and never shared in government nor held a single Cabinet post from 1945 until 2010, when they entered coalition with the Conservatives.

tive to vote in such seats. Only more marginal seats are likely to change hands. This is one explanation for low turnout. Turnout can be much lower in safe seats than marginals, for example (in 2010), 44.3 per cent in Manchester Central, a safe Labour seat, compared with 75.8 per cent in Winchester, a marginal that changed hands from Liberal Democrat to Conservative.

- The system can distort voters' preferences. Voters may fear to vote for their main preferred candidate or party for fear of letting in the party they most dislike. Thus voters may vote 'tactically' for their second or third choice. Such tactical voting has increased markedly since 1997.

The main losers from the current system, the Liberal Democrats, have long advocated electoral reform involving more proportional representation. They have a reasonable grievance, as can be seen by comparing their electoral support and role in government with that of their German sister party, the Free Democrats (FDP) (see Comparative Politics 5.1).

Although the Liberal Democrats have long championed a change in the electoral system, there seemed little prospect of achieving this for UK general elections as the two major parties benefited from the existing system. While the 1997 Labour government introduced a variety of new electoral systems for UK elections to the European Parliament and for devolved parliaments and assemblies in Scotland, Wales, Northern Ireland and London, they did not hold a promised referendum on electoral reform for the House of Commons. It was only in the lead-up to the 2010 election that Labour indicated support for further electoral reform. Only after a hung parliament materialized did the Conservatives reluctantly agree to a referendum on a limited reform, the Alternative Vote (held 5 May 2011; see below).

## Electoral reform

The case for electoral reform depends not only on the perceived defects of the single member plurality system, but on the alternatives available. Ideally an electoral system should deliver the following:

- Real choice for voters – involving a range of candidates and parties.
- Simplicity – a system that is readily comprehensible to voters.

- Fair treatment of parties and candidates – each vote as far as possible should count equally.
- Effective representation of local communities or constituencies.
- Effective representation of the gender, age, ethnic, religious and occupational class divisions in the population at large.
- Parliaments or assemblies that can sustain stable government.
- Accountable government, with a clear link between elections and the making and breaking of governments.

Yet in practice there is no ideal system that can meet all these objectives, but a range of options, each of which offers advantages and disadvantages. There is long experience of a range of different electoral systems operating in other countries, some of which have been introduced in the UK for elections for the European Parliament, devolved parliaments and assemblies in Scotland, Wales, and Northern Ireland, the Greater London Assembly, and mayoral elections. As Curtice (in Dunleavy *et al.*, 2003, p. 100) has observed, 'Britain has become a laboratory of electoral experimentation and change'.

## The Alternative Vote (AV)

One simple, widely advocated reform of the current single member plurality system used for Westminster elections is the Alternative Vote (AV). This would keep single member constituencies but allow voters to express their preferences in order, with the bottom candidates being progressively eliminated and their votes transferred to second or subsequent preferences until one candidate emerged with an overall majority of the votes cast. A simple plurality of votes (more than any other candidate) would not be enough. AV is used in Australia. In Britain a more limited form of preferential voting involving just second preferences (called the supplementary vote) is now used for mayoral elections (for example, in London).

The Alternative Vote was belatedly proposed by Gordon Brown before the 2010 election. David Cameron has since promised a referendum on AV to secure Liberal Democrat partnership in coalition, but indicated that his party would campaign against change. AV would prevent MPs being elected on a share of the vote sometimes well below 50 per cent. Thus in 2010 Caroline Lucas won the Brighton Pavilion constituency for the Greens with 31 per cent of the votes cast, while Simon Wright gained Norwich South for the Liberal Democrats with just 29 per cent. It would also remove the need for tactical voting for a second or third choice candidate to prevent the election of a feared alternative. However the Alternative Vote would not produce **proportional representation**. A party obtaining 20 per cent of first preference votes over the country as a whole might still end up with no seats. Moreover, many seats would remain 'safe', reducing the incentive to vote, and for parties to campaign, in those constituencies. Many votes would still be 'wasted' as surplus votes for winning candidate and all votes for losing candidates would not contribute to the election of any MPs.

Proportional representation can only be achieved by other electoral systems. One option is a regional party list systems, already now used for British elections to the European Parliament. Another is the Single Transferable Vote (STV) used for elections for the Northern Ireland Assembly (and incidentally the Dail, the parliament of the Irish Republic). A third option is the Additional Member System (AMS) already used for elections to devolved government in Scotland and Wales, and for the London Assembly.

## Regional party list systems

A party list system can deliver a closely proportional relationship between seats and votes. Each party draws up a list of its candidates in order. Thus in a national list system involving a 100-member legislature a party securing 40 per cent of the vote would see its first forty candidates elected. However larger countries that use the list system divide the country into regions, where

---

● **Proportional representation**: An electoral system that delivers for each political party a share of elected representatives proportionate to its share of the total national vote. Thus a 20 per cent share of the vote for a party should produce close to a 20 per cent share of the seats in the elected parliament, assembly or council.

each party has its own regional lists of candidates. Voters may be given the option of expressing their own order of preferences for candidates within parties (open list systems) rather than simply having to accept the official party list order (closed list systems). Party list systems are widely used in continental Europe and Latin America. A closed regional party list system was introduced in Britain for the election of Members of the European Parliament from 1999 onwards (see Chapter 15), similar to that used by most other EU member states.

The system is fairly simple and delivers proportional representation. It does not provide effective constituency representation, and critics suggest it gives too much power to the party nationally (or regionally) responsible for drawing up lists of candidates, marginalizing local party members. It may also lead to the representation of a number of small and possibly extremist parties (the BNP won two seats in UK elections for the European Parliament in 2009). It can render stable government more difficult.

## The Single Transferable Vote (STV)

This is the most complex system that can produce results close to proportional representation. Under the system the country is divided into a number of electoral areas that each elect a number of representatives (multi-member constituencies), but where each voter only has a single vote that is transferable between candidates. To secure election, a candidate has to win a proportion of the total vote in the electoral area or constituency, according to the following formula:

$$\frac{\text{Total number of votes cast}}{\text{Number of seats} + 1} + 1$$

Initially, only first preferences are counted. Any candidate who achieves the quota is deemed elected, and any surplus votes above the quota are redistributed according to second (and later subsequent) preferences. If no candidate achieves the quota on the first or subsequent count, the bottom candidates are progressively eliminated and their second (and subsequent) preferences are distributed until all the seats are filled.

It sounds complicated, but can be best illustrated with reference to Northern Ireland Assembly elections, where the system has been used since 1998. Each constituency elects six members of the Northern Ireland Assembly. To be elected a candidate needs (according to the formula above) one vote more than a seventh of the total number of votes. In practice the leading parties put up not one but several candidates, hoping to get as many as possible elected in each constituency. Thus in Belfast North in 2007 one Ulster Unionist (UUP), two Democratic Unionists (DUP), two Sinn Fein and one member for the Social Democratic and Labour Party (SDLP) were elected. Belfast West elected five Sinn Fein members and one SDLP. In Fermanagh and South Tyrone two Sinn Fein candidates were elected, two UUP and one each for the DUP and SDLP.

The system combines constituency representation with overall results close to proportional representation. Broadly speaking, the more members elected for each constituency, the more proportional the whole system will be. The Irish Republic has used STV for many years, but most constituencies only elect three members, leading to a rather less proportionate relationship between a party's seats and votes than in Northern Ireland, where the system was adopted to ensure that all communities and shades of opinion were represented, as part of the ongoing peace process. There was also hope that moderate parties might profit, and indeed the small non-sectarian Alliance Party managed to retain seven seats in 2007, while it would not have come close to winning any under the single member plurality system (for more on elections in Northern Ireland, see Chapter 16).

## The Additional Member System (AMS)

Under the Additional Member System (sometimes called the German system) voters have two votes, one for their local constituency, and a second vote, designed to compensate parties that are under-represented in the constituencies, by electing additional members through national or regional party lists. It is often referred to as a hybrid system, combining a clear link between directly elected representatives and constituencies with overall results close to proportional representation. It has long been used in Germany, where, however, parties can only gain additional members if they secure more than 5 per cent of the national vote, a threshold designed to exclude very small parties and prevent the fragmentation of representation in the German parliament.

AMS has already been used in the UK for elections to the Scottish Parliament, Welsh Assembly and Greater London Assembly. In Scotland the results provide a clear contrast with the general election, where Scottish MPs are still elected under 'first past the post'. In general elections from 1997 onwards Labour has won a comfortable overall majority of seats in Scotland (41 out of 58 in 2010). Yet in elections for the Scottish Parliament under AMS, Labour fell well short of a majority in both 1999 and 2003, and formed a coalition with the Liberal Democrats. In 2007 the SNP won 47 seats to Labour's 46 and went on to form a minority government. They secured a remarkable overall majority, never achieved by Labour, after making sweeping gains in 2011, and incidentally demonstrating that proportional representation does not necessarily lead to minority governments or coalition (see Chapter 16).

It is worth adding that the Conservative party has also benefited from AMS in Scotland. Although Conservative representation of Scotland at Westminster has been almost wiped out (no seats in 1997, only one in 2001, 2005 and 2010), they have secured representation in the Scottish Parliament more proportionate to their share of the vote. By contrast they won 17 MSPs (Members of the Scottish Parliament) in 2007 and 15 in 2011. The Additional Member System may also make it easier to secure a more equal share of seats by gender. Thus half the members of the Welsh Assembly are women.

## Single party and coalition government

Arguments over proportional representation are bound up with the debate over the relative advantages and disadvantages of single party and coalition government. Some argue that coalition government involves too many compromises, and often too much influence for small (sometimes extremist) parties on whose support the coalition depends for survival. Thus coalition government may appear weak and unstable, unable to take tough decisions. Alternatively, there may be a virtually permanent governing coalition with opposition parties effectively locked out of power, with no real viable alternative for voters. Others argue that concession and compromise are vital parts of the democratic process. Single party governments with large majorities can behave in high-handed ways, ignoring popular opposition to policies, and riding roughshod over minorities. Critics point out that contentious British policies such as the poll tax would probably not have been implemented by a coalition government. However, the 2010 coalition government controversially trebled university tuition fees and raised VAT despite previous Liberal Democrat opposition.

## Further electoral reform in Britain?

Electoral reform only seems to excite political 'anoraks', and has never been much of an issue with most voters. Yet electoral systems can make a crucial difference to the fortunes of parties and the form and nature of government, as some of the examples above indicate. Were proportional representation ever to be introduced for Westminster elections, it would lead regularly to minority or coalition government, if current voting patterns were maintained. In practice it might also change voting behaviour, perhaps encouraging more support for minor parties, as in Scotland. What then are the prospects for further electoral reform in Britain, particularly for UK general elections and local elections in England and Wales now still conducted under the single member plurality system?

In 1997 Labour promised a commission on electoral reform with a subsequent referendum. The commission, chaired by Lord Jenkins, a former deputy leader of the Labour Party, and former leader of the Social Democratic Party (SDP), reported in 1998. It recommended the introduction of the Alternative Vote (AV) to elect 80 to 85 per cent of the House of Commons, with

## COMPARATIVE POLITICS 5.2

# Coalition government in Britain and elsewhere in Europe

From 1945 until 2010 Britain has had nothing but single party government, and most of those governments have enjoyed a fairly comfortable majority in the House of Commons. Had British elections been conducted under a system of strict proportional representation, no party would have won a majority of seats because no party secured a majority of votes over the whole period. The consequence would have been minority or coalition government, which have been rather rare in Britain outside wartime. (The Lloyd-George wartime coalition continued into peacetime, until it broke up in 1922, and there was a Conservative-dominated National Government from 1931 that became more Conservative with time.) Recently there has been more experience of coalition government in parts of Britain, for example in Scotland, Wales and Northern Ireland (under a more

proportional electoral system) and on many local councils (still elected under the single member plurality system).

Coalition government is the norm rather than the exception elsewhere in Europe (Bale, 2008, pp. 105–11; Hague and Harrop, 2010, pp. 327–31). Germany and the Netherlands have long provided examples of stable and generally successful coalition government. By contrast, France under the Fourth French Republic and Italy until recently experienced weak, unstable coalition government, sometimes only lasting for weeks before collapse. Coalitions have also proved less durable in post-communist Eastern Europe. Further afield, proportional representation in Israel has left coalition governments sometimes dependent for their survival on the votes of small extremist parties.

---

the rest elected by a list system. This system (sometimes described as 'AV plus') would have led to increased representation for other parties had it been in place in 1997, although Labour would have had a smaller, but still comfortable, overall majority on 44 per cent of the vote. Thus it fell well short of proportional representation. In practice the report was ignored and there was no referendum.

There was some renewed debate over electoral reform leading up to the 2010 election, with Labour promising a referendum, probably just on the Alternative Vote but conceivably AV plus. In the inter-party negotiation that followed the election the Conservatives under Cameron pledged a referendum on the AV, which became part of the programme of the coalition government. Possible further reforms may include some form of primary elections (as in some US states), widening the selection of parliamentary candidates to include voters and not just party members, and the right of

voters to recall MPs for misconduct (following the 2009 expenses scandal).

## Persistence and change in voting behaviour

We move now from considering the mechanics of electoral systems to examine why people vote as they do. It has long been argued that most people are habitual voters who support the same party from one election to the next, and relatively few are floating voters, prepared to change their vote. Indeed, many people seem to determine their party allegiance young, perhaps at their first election, or maybe even earlier, and stick with that party through its fluctuating fortunes subsequently, in much the same way as many continue to support the same football team, regardless of success or failure. Indeed, most elections in Britain since the war have involved a relatively small shift in votes from the previous election, with the '**swing**' between the parties commonly less than 3 per cent, although some recent elections (such as 1997 and 2010) have involved much larger swings.

There is some evidence that the electorate may be becoming more volatile. The 1997 general election was a political earthquake with an almost unprecedented swing of over 10 per cent from Conservative to Labour, although subsequent elections in 2001 and 2005 involved more modest shifts in party support. 2010 involved an average swing of around 5 per cent from Labour to Conservative, considerable, but substantially less than the pro-Labour swing in 1997, and less than was required for a Conservative majority.

The average swing conceals considerable variations. Back in the 1960s and 1970s a leading political scientist, Robert McKenzie, used a 'swingometer' to predict the results of general elections on television after the first handful of seats had been declared. The predictions were generally very accurate, because then the whole country appeared to swing together, and there were only minor variations between particular constituencies.

More recently there have been more marked differences in the size of the swing. Thus the average swing in 2010 from Labour to Conservative

of around 5 per cent masked huge variations. These range from a Labour to Conservative swing of 14.4 per cent in Hemel Hempstead to a 4.3 per cent swing the other way in Cumbernauld. Local issues can still make a difference. A vigorous and effective constituency party campaign may buck the trend, as can the record and personality of individual candidates. Votes for 39 Labour MPs implicated in the expenses scandal dropped by an average of 6.5 per cent, one and a half percentage points above the figure for other incumbent Labour MPs. Similarly, Conservative MPs who were implicated fared less well than other sitting Conservatives, and by a similar margin (see Curtis *et al.* in Kavanagh and Cowley, 2010, pp. 393 and 398). Yet overall the scandal seems to have had less impact on the election than anticipated, perhaps because some of the more notorious offenders had been persuaded or compelled to stand down.

## The shaping of party allegiances

Why do people support a particular party? In many cases childhood socialization (see Chapter 4) will play an important part. Political attitudes and behaviour may be learned from the family, peer group, schooling and local community. Yet some young adults may have received mixed messages if there are divided allegiances in the immediate family, school or neighbourhood. In other instances experiences at university or in work may expose people to different interests and ideas and change attitudes. Some may rebel against their background and adopt diametrically opposed political views. Even so, it still appears that most people determine their political allegiance relatively early, perhaps by the time they cast their first vote, and many stick with it. However, there is also some evidence for the widespread assumption that some people become more conservative, with a small 'c' and perhaps with a large 'C' also, as they grow older.

Much of this is common sense, once some of the jargon is decoded. However, voting is also a topic that can be subjected to sophisticated statistical analysis. Voting has been correlated with a wide range of social characteristics and divisions – housing tenure, car ownership, newspaper readership, age, gender, religion, ethnicity, region and,

---

● **Swing** measures the shift in support between parties between elections. The two-party swing between elections can often be simply measured by adding the increase in votes for one party to the decrease in votes for the other and dividing by two. It becomes slightly more complicated if the votes for both parties increase or decrease (because of changes in votes for other parties). Here swing is measured by the formula

$$\frac{(C2 - C1) + (L1 - L2)}{2}$$

where C1 is the percentage of Conservative votes obtained in the first election and C2 the percentage at the second, while L1 and L2 are Labour's share of the vote in the two election.

The swing needed for a party coming second in one election to win the next is more easily measured: simply halve the difference in the percentage of votes of the leading two parties. Thus if Labour had 40 per cent and the Conservatives had 34 per cent at the previous election, the Conservatives would need a 3 per cent swing to win next time. In other words three voters in a hundred would have to switch support between the two parties.

Note, however, that in elections where several parties are competing, the two-party swing can be misleading. In 2005 there was a 4 per cent swing from Labour to Conservative, but most of this was the result of defections from Labour to other parties rather than a positive swing to the Conservatives, whose proportion of the vote scarcely increased.

above all, social class. Some of the analysis should be interpreted with care. A **correlation** does not prove a cause. Thus there may be a significant correlation between owning two cars and voting Conservative, but this does not necessarily mean that owning two cars makes someone a Conservative. It is perhaps more likely that the occupation and income that enables someone to own two cars may increase the likelihood of voting Conservative. The direction of causation may also be problematic. Thus there is a significant positive correlation between reading the *Daily Mirror* and voting Labour. Does this mean the *Daily Mirror*, a paper long committed to the Labour cause, influences its readers to vote for that party? It is certainly quite plausible. Yet it is also possible that those whose background and interests incline them to Labour choose to buy a Labour paper. Perhaps a little of both goes on, and reading the *Daily Mirror* and voting Labour are mutually reinforcing. (There are also of course many exceptions to even fairly strong positive correlations. Thus some two car owners vote Labour, and some *Daily Mirror* readers vote Conservative.)

## Social class and voting behaviour

Social class has long appeared a key factor explaining voting in Britain, although there is evidence that it is less important than previously. Labour, as the name implies, was the party established to represent the interests of the working class, particularly the manual working class who were members of trade unions affiliated to the Labour Party. The Conservative Party was associated with the interests of the property-owning middle class. Indeed, back in 1967 British political scientist Peter Pulzer (1967) claimed 'class is the basis of British politics; all else is embellishment and detail'. Analysis of voting by class then provided substantial justifica-

**Table 5.2**   Voting by social class, 1945–58

|  | AB | C1 | C2 | DE |
|---|---|---|---|---|
| Conservative | 85 | 70 | 35 | 30 |
| Labour | 10 | 25 | 60 | 65 |

*Source*: Tapper and Bowles (1982, p. 175).

tion for Pulzer's bold assertion (see Table 5.2). The further down the social scale (classes C2, D and E on this common classification – see Chapter 3) the greater the support for Labour, while the professional and managerial classes (A and B) were then overwhelmingly supporters of the Conservatives. Routine white-collar workers (C1s), often described as 'lower middle-class' were twice as likely to vote Conservative as Labour.

Even then, however, it will be noted that significant minorities did not support the party associated with their class. Thus around a fifth of the middle class (ABs + C1s) in post-war elections voted Labour, while around a third of the manual working class voted Conservative. Political scientists sought to explain this 'deviant voting', particularly the working-class Conservatives. Some saw the explanation in terms of the deference of some workers to their social superiors. Others considered that affluent workers (such as Midland car workers) were increasingly acquiring middle-class characteristics and attitudes (including voting Conservative). Indeed, left-wing analysts feared that growing affluence was, over time, eroding Labour's working-class vote.

Subsequently, class allegiances have become more blurred. Mrs Thatcher made a particular pitch for the skilled working-class vote (the C2s), with some success, although a substantial minority of skilled workers had supported the Conservatives throughout the twentieth century. From a Labour perspective these were worrying trends (see Chapter 3). The manual working class was not only declining as a proportion of the population, but also appeared increasingly fragmented on lines of ethnicity and gender, and between public and private sector employment. Labour could no longer hope to win elections by securing most of the vote of the manual working class, but had to appeal to a wider cross-class constituency if it was ever to

● A **correlation** measures the strength of the association between two variables. **Correlation coefficients** can be calculated between −1 and +1. A negative score indicates a negative or inverse correlation between two variables (e.g. those in higher income groups may be less likely to support Labour). A positive score indicates a positive correlation (e.g. Muslims predominantly support Labour). A score close to zero (e.g. between − 0.2 and +0.2) suggests a weak association that may not be statistically significant.

**Table 5.3**   Voting by social class, 2005

|                   | AB | C1 | C2 | DE |
|-------------------|----|----|----|----|
| Labour            | 28 | 32 | 40 | 48 |
| Conservative      | 37 | 36 | 33 | 25 |
| Liberal Democrat  | 29 | 23 | 19 | 18 |
| Other             | 6  | 9  | 8  | 9  |

*Source:* MORI poll, reported in *The Observer*, 8 May 2005.

return to power. This they seemed to achieve spectacularly in 1997, making dramatic gains across all social classes, but particularly among the C1s and C2s. Middle-class support for Labour was further consolidated in 2001 with small swings to Labour among the ABs and C1s, while the Conservatives made gains among the C2s and DEs. In 2005 there was a swing to the Conservatives in all social classes, but this was more marked among the working than the middle class, further reducing the association between support for parties and social class (see Table 5.3).

Nevertheless there was still a correlation between social class and voting in 2005. The proportion of votes for Labour increased, while the Conservative vote decreased, the further down the social scale. However, in 2010 the picture was far more confused (see Table 5.4). At the top and bottom ends of the social spectrum there was no substantial change. The party allegiances of the higher social classes (ABs) remained broadly similar to 2005, and Labour still did much better than other parties among the lower classes (DEs). However, the intermediate C1s (lower middle-class) and C2s (skilled working-class) showed marked increases in support for the Conservatives and a pronounced fall in Labour voting. Thus, remarkably, a smaller proportion of C2s and C1s

**Table 5.4**   Voting by social class, 2010

|                   | AB | C1 | C2 | DE |
|-------------------|----|----|----|----|
| Labour            | 29 | 26 | 22 | 44 |
| Conservative      | 36 | 42 | 39 | 28 |
| Liberal Democrat  | 28 | 26 | 24 | 15 |
| Other             | 7  | 6  | 15 | 13 |

*Source:* IPSOS MORI poll, reported in *The Observer*, 9 May 2010.

supported Labour than ABs. Curtis *et al.* (in Kavanagh and Cowley, 2010) argue that Labour did particularly badly in seats with high unemployment and a high proportion of manual workers. However, the Labour vote held up better in seats with an above average proportion of workers in the public sector. The Liberal Democrats did best among the higher social classes, and had significantly less support among the lowest classes, DE.

## Age and voting

Conservative support increases and Labour's decreases with age. The only age group in which the Conservatives led Labour in 1997 and 2001 was the over-65s. By 2010 the Conservatives led Labour comfortably among the over-55s, by 39 per cent against 27 per cent for men and by 44 to 30 per cent for women. The Conservatives also led Labour more narrowly among the 35 to 54 age group (by 34 to 28 per cent for men and 35 to 32 per cent for women). Owing to increased longevity and a declining birth rate, older people are an increasing proportion of the population and they are also more likely to vote. Thus 'grey power' is becoming increasingly significant.

Two explanations are advanced for this apparent link between age and Conservative voting. One is the familiar notion that people become more conservative (with a small and large 'C') as they grow older. They may be increasingly disturbed by change. They may become better off, with more to lose. Another explanation is linked to the notion of political generations. If most people forge their political allegiance as they reach adulthood and tend to stick with the same party, they may be particularly influenced by the prevailing political climate when they first have the right to vote. Those who first voted in the 1950s during a period of Conservative dominance might be more inclined to remain with that party subsequently. Those who came of age in the mid-1960s when Labour under Harold Wilson came to power might maintain a Labour allegiance. Others, who reached maturity in the late 1970s and 1980s, are more likely to be 'Thatcher's children', their political attitudes shaped by free market ideas hostile to state intervention. Finally, of course, others will have been influenced by the political climate surrounding the Labour landslides of 1997 and 2001. There is something in this argument, first advanced by Butler and Stokes in 1969. However, more recent research suggests increased electoral volatility, with more voters prepared to switch their votes between elections, and party identification correspondingly weaker. Thus the notion of political generations with enduring preferences seems rather less persuasive (Denver, 2003, pp.182–3).

## Gender and voting

A higher proportion of women than men used to support the Conservatives. This gender effect almost disappeared when Britain acquired its first woman Prime Minister in Mrs Thatcher, briefly reappeared when Major succeeded Thatcher, and then disappeared again in 1997 and 2001. More recent polls suggest that while older women remain more likely to support the Conservatives, younger women favour Labour (perhaps as a consequence of increases in family benefits and nursery provision under Labour governments). In 2005, polls suggested that among men both major parties were neck and neck on 34 per cent while women backed Labour with 38 per cent to the Conservatives' 32 per cent. This suggests it was women who helped to keep Labour in power with a comfortable overall majority (see Table 5.5).

**Table 5.5**    Gender and voting, 1987–2005

|      |       | Conservative | Labour | Liberal Democrat |
|------|-------|--------------|--------|------------------|
| 1987 | Men   | 44           | 33     | 25               |
|      | Women | 44           | 31     | 25               |
| 1992 | Men   | 38           | 36     | 19               |
|      | Women | 44           | 34     | 16               |
| 1997 | Men   | 31           | 44     | 17               |
|      | Women | 32           | 44     | 17               |
| 2001 | Men   | 33           | 42     | 18               |
|      | Women | 33           | 42     | 20               |
| 2005 | Men   | 34           | 34     | 22               |
|      | Women | 32           | 38     | 23               |

*Sources*: *The Guardian*, 15 June 1987; *The Daily Telegraph*, 14 April 1992; *The Sunday Times*, 4 May 1997; *The Observer*, 10 June 2001; *The Observer*, 8 May 2005.

## Religion and voting

In the nineteenth century there were close links between religious and party political affiliations. The Church of England, it was humorously suggested, was 'the Tory party at prayer', while protestant non-conformists (e.g. Baptists, Methodists) provided the Liberal Party's core support. In the twentieth century the Labour Party inherited much of the non-conformist vote – it was sometimes said that Labour owed more to Methodism than Marxism. However, with the growth of a more secular society, religion became of decreasing political importance, outside Northern Ireland of course, and with some significant exceptions elsewhere – especially Liverpool and parts of Scotland. Catholics are more likely to support Labour in Liverpool, Glasgow and Edinburgh, although it does not necessarily follow that those with other faiths will favour Labour's opponents in these areas. Outside these areas, the religious convictions of election candidates were regarded as almost totally irrelevant. Anglicans, Roman Catholics, nonconformists, Jews and atheists can be found across all parties.

Today religion is becoming of more political importance in some parts of Britain as a result of the increased allegiance to non-Christian faiths associated with some ethnic minorities, for whom ethnicity and religion are inseparably bound together as part of their identity. Following the 'war on terror' and more especially the war in Iraq, some Muslims deserted Labour for the Liberal Democrats or other anti-war parties such as Respect in 2005. In 2010 it seems that the Muslim vote was again predominantly Labour (see Curtis *et al.*, in Kavanagh and Cowley, 2010, pp. 391–2).

## Ethnicity and voting

Ethnicity hardly figured in earlier analyses of voting, as ethnic minorities were then insufficiently numerous to make much difference. Today non-white ethnic minorities amount to over five million in a total population of 60 million. While this is still a relatively small minority in the country as whole, the proportion in some cities is much higher and in a few parliamentary constituencies the 'ethnic minority' population constitutes the

**Table 5.6**   Black and Asian voting in the 2001 general election

|  | Black | Asian |
|---|---|---|
| Conservative | 9 | 11 |
| Labour | 76 | 69 |
| Liberal Democrat | 4 | 4 |
| Other | 1 | 2 |
| Refused an answer | 10 | 14 |

*Source*: Courtesy of Operation Black Vote.

majority. Until very recently this ethnic vote was overwhelmingly Labour (see Table 5.6. on Black and Asian voting in 2001).

What has happened since 2001? Perhaps not much for Afro-Caribbeans and non-Muslim Asians, although as we have seen, there was a significant drop in the Muslim Labour vote in 2005. However, despite the efforts of Cameron to secure more ethnic minority candidates in winnable seats in 2010, the ethnic minority vote (and, it seems, the Muslim vote) remained predominantly Labour (Curtis *et al.* in Kavanagh and Cowley, 2010, pp. 391–5).

## A north–south divide? Regions and neighbourhoods

The notion of a political north–south divide has some basis in reality. Even a casual perusal of the political map of Britain reveals substantial Conservative strength south of a line from the Bristol Channel to the Wash. Back in the 1980s Labour only held a handful of seats outside London below this line. In 1997 they made significant gains in the south, but lost a few of these in 2001 and rather more in 2005. By 2010 Labour representation in the south was reduced once more to odd specks of red in a sea of blue and the occasional yellow of the Liberal Democrats. Thus they won just four out of 78 seats in the South-east, three seats out of 58 in the South-west (where the Liberal Democrats had 15), and just two out of 58 in eastern England (both in Luton). By contrast, the Conservatives only managed to hold one seat out of 59 in Scotland, although they gained five seats in Wales to hold eight out of 40. Yet despite

making significant gains they still won relatively few seats in the North-east of England (nineteen out of 83) and the North-west (23 out of 75). London, the East and West Midlands were more closely contested between the major parties. The main Liberal Democrat territory used to be the 'Celtic fringe' – the South-west of England, rural Wales, and northern Scotland. Yet more recently they have made gains in middle-class suburban areas and some inner city areas. Their leader (and now Deputy Prime Minister) Nick Clegg represents Sheffield Hallam.

Generalizations about regional party strengths conceal substantial intra-regional differences. There is also something of an urban–rural divide. Even though only one per cent of the British workforce derive their living from the land, there are many more rural dwellers, some commuting into the cities, others retired or working from home. Many identify with the countryside even if they work, shop and seek entertainment in the towns. Such semi-rural areas are predominantly Conservative with a Liberal Democrat challenge in some constituencies. Thus there are strong Conservative areas in parts of a predominantly Labour North.

Some of these regional differences reflect class differences. Thus there is a rather higher proportion of manual workers in the North of England and Scotland, rather more professional and managerial workers in the South. Yet there may also be a neighbourhood effect. Those living in strongly Labour or Conservative neighbourhoods may be influenced by the locally prevailing political attitudes. Thus manual workers in Bournemouth may be more likely to vote Conservative than manual workers in Barnsley. Similarly, doctors or solicitors in Barnsley may be more inclined to support Labour than their fellow professionals on the south coast. Yet it is impossible to be sure about the causal connection. It may simply be the case that doctors and solicitors with Labour sympathies are more likely to live and practise in poorer areas where they do more good.

## Issues, values and preferences

Studies of voting behaviour suggest this rarely involves a dispassionate analysis of party programmes by rational voters. Indeed earlier research indicated that most voters were not even aware of some of the issues that politicians debated, and if they were, this did not seem to affect their choice of party. Thus in the 1950s and 1960s, according to opinion polls a majority of those who supported Labour opposed its 'central policy of nationalisation' (Denver, 2003, p. 98). Yet more recently, some political scientists have argued that issues, values or preferences are increasingly affecting voting.

Thus issues such as health, education, crime and immigration not only loom large in election campaigns but may have a significant impact on the choice of parties. Even so, not all elections have confirmed the importance of issues. Thus in 1992 polls showed that Labour was ahead on what were then perceived as the key issues of health, education and unemployment, but still lost the election. However, in 1997 Labour had a substantial lead on five key issues, and won by a landslide. Yet sceptics suggest that this does not mean that voters necessarily have much grasp of party policy on key issues. They may simply make up their mind which party they are supporting, and then declare that they have the best policies on particular issues (Denver, 2003 pp. 99–104). Others argue that it is broader principles, values or ideologies that lie behind party choice. Issues are transitory; values, principles or ideological outlook are more enduring and can be related to more or less accurate perceptions of where the parties stand on, for example, the promotion of greater equality or the defence of individual freedom.

Some argue that there is one issue that tends to dominate all others – the government's handling of the economy, or people's perception of general economic prospects and their own sense of well-being – the so-called 'feel-good factor'. People may tell pollsters that the most important issue is health, or education, or unemployment and may claim that they would be prepared to pay more in taxes for better services or more effective policies. However, in the privacy of the polling booth they may vote according to what they perceive is in their economic self-interest. Thus David Sanders (1995) found a close correlation between economic expectations (strongly influenced by changes in interest rates) and the popularity of the government in the period 1979 to 1994. Yet in 1997 the Conservative government plunged to its worse defeat for over a century, despite a fast-improving economy. Even so, as Denver (2003, p. 117) points out, economic considerations remained important in that election: 'Following the ERM disaster the Conservatives simply lost their longstanding reputation for being competent managers of the economy and they never recovered it.' Reputation and perception may be more important than reality. The economy remained Labour's trump card in 2005. Brown's established reputation as a prudent and successful manager of the economy drowned out warnings of underlying economic problems and troubles on the horizon. When these became acutely obvious from 2008 onwards with the banking crisis and recession, Brown and Labour received much of the blame, and this was a key factor in their defeat in 2010. Curtis *et al.* (in Kavanagh and Cowley, 2010, p. 389) conclude that 'those parts of the country that had suffered most from the recession were indeed the most likely to have lost faith in Labour's ability to govern'.

It is worth noting that most analysis of voting focuses on the electorate as a whole, understandably, because it is how the mass of voters behave that determines the outcome of elections. Yet particular sections of the electorate may be strongly influenced in their choice of parties by issues that matter to them, and this can make a critical difference in individual constituencies. Thus polls indicated that Iraq was well down the list of most voters' concerns in 2005 (14th on one assessment), yet it clearly was the decisive influence in some constituencies with a substantial Muslim population. Immigration seems to have preoccupied voters more in 2010 than 2005, even though the Conservatives under Cameron emphasized the issue less than Michael Howard had in the previous election. Some predicted the BNP could win their first Westminster seat on the issue, perhaps at Barking where the BNP leader was standing against Labour's Margaret Hodge. Yet she held the seat with a comfortable majority of over 16,000 , with the BNP coming a poor third. Even so, it appears that Labour lost some working-class voters to the BNP in 2010. Curtis *et al.* (in Kavanagh and Cowley, 2010, pp. 405–6) conclude that the 'BNP was most successful in relatively deprived urban constituencies' where a large rise in unemployment added to concerns over immigration.

## Party leaders

The media have long tended to treat elections as gladiatorial contests between rival leaders and prospective Prime Ministers. In recent elections both television and the press have focused on party leaders, to the exclusion of even their closest colleagues. In 2010 this occurred more than ever with the introduction of the first televised leaders' debates. These gave the Liberal Democrat leader Nick Clegg equal time, and a huge boost to his media profile. After the first debate, which he was widely reckoned to have won, his party's poll ratings soared to the extent that some polls put them in first place briefly, while many showed them ahead or level with Labour. The barrage of hostile publicity from the other parties and from the Conservative-supporting tabloids, coupled with improved performances by Cameron and Brown in the subsequent debates, seem to have partially reversed the Clegg bandwagon, so that the eventual result was a considerable disappointment for his party. Even so, the Liberal Democrats slightly improved their share of the vote. Had it not been for the televised debates they might have been effectively squeezed out by the big parties. Thus elections are becoming more presidential with voters choosing between individual leaders rather than parties. Some lament this Americanization of British politics, but it is perhaps inevitable. In any case, televised leaders' debates are almost certainly here to stay, and may contribute to raising interest and turnout.

The debates, inevitably perhaps, elevated issues of appearance, personality, body language and communication skills over policy substance. They also further marginalized other important politicians who were not party leaders. This did Labour, whose leader appeared least telegenic, no favours. Indeed much has been made, both before and after the election, of Brown's personality defects (Rawnsley, 2009; Mandelson, 2010; Blair, 2010).

## Party images

Whatever people think of leaders, parties conjure up associations and images that influence people's attitudes towards them. Internal post mortems into Conservative defeats in three successive elections in 1997, 2001 and 2005 concluded that the party suffered from an unflattering image. It was seen as nasty, racist, narrow, intolerant, anti-women and homophobic. Although xenophobia and intolerance may be attitudes found in the ageing party membership in the country, they were not the attitudes on which election victories

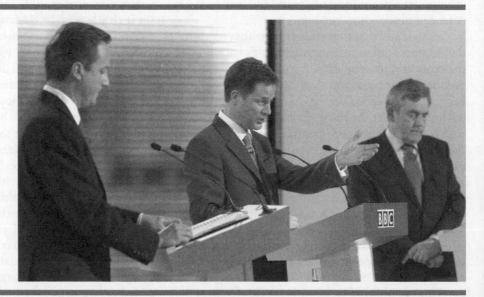

**Image 5.1  Televised leaders' debate during the 2010 general election campaign**

(*Left to right*) David Cameron, Nick Clegg and Gordon Brown.

These were the first televised party leader's debates in a UK General Election, and transformed the campaign. It seems certain they are here to stay and will be a feature of future elections.

could be won in a broadly progressive society. Some political commentators drew unflattering contrasts between the middle-class, mostly male and almost entirely white body of Conservative MPs and the composition of wider society. Successive Conservative party leaders, aware of the problem, have tried to address it, Cameron most determinedly, securing the acceptance of more women, gays and ethnic minority candidates. Indeed, the 2010 election saw the return of eleven non-white ethnic minority MPs compared with just two in 2005. Although this rise in ethnic minority candidates did not appear to significantly increase ethnic minority vote for the Conservatives, it has helped to 'detoxify' the image of the party. Even so, the leading Conservative members of the new Cabinet (apart from the party chair, Lady Warsi), were white, predominantly male, and privately and Oxbridge educated, like Cameron himself.

## Party campaigns

The conventional wisdom is that party election campaigns generally make little difference to the outcome. Most voters, it is argued, have made up their minds before the start of the campaign (less true perhaps in 2010) and recent elections indicate only minor fluctuations in party support leading up to polling day. Even so, the campaign may make a crucial difference where the parties are seen to be neck and neck, as in 1964, 1974 or 1992. Thus particular incidents or perceived mistakes made in the course of these campaigns figure prominently in accounts of these elections. In 2010 Gordon Brown was responsible for the worst gaffe of the campaign, when he forgot his radio microphone was still on following an encounter with a life-long Labour supporter who tackled him on immigration. He referred to her as a 'bigoted woman' in what he imagined was the privacy of his car. Clips of his comments and his subsequent live appearance on BBC radio were endlessly replayed on world as well as UK media. Perhaps 'bigotgate' (as it was called) only confirmed opinions of Brown, rather than lost him the election, but it was one of the defining moments of the campaign.

Yet in one respect at least, the conduct of election campaigns does clearly affect voters' behav-

iour. It has long been recognized that the outcome of elections is determined by the outcome in key marginals. Most parliamentary constituencies are 'safe seats' where it would take a political earthquake for them to change hands. Both nationally and locally party resources are directed towards marginal seats that they must hold or win, away from other seats where the outcome is virtually certain. Party leaders and other prominent figures tour the marginals, zigzagging round the country by helicopter, train or coach. Within marginal seats parties seek to ensure that their own core supporters vote, ignore their opponents' core support, and concentrate their main efforts on possible swing voters, with the help of sophisticated computer analysis and market research indicating where these potential swing voters live and what they care about. The consequence is that the mass of voters, particularly those in safe seats, are relatively neglected, to the extent that there are few signs that an election is in progress, while targeted voters in marginal constituencies are deluged with visits, phone calls and mail.

This focus on marginal constituencies and relative neglect of safer constituencies seems to have an appreciable impact on turnout. The average turnout in 2010, 65 per cent, conceals huge variations, with some more marginal constituencies securing turnout levels nearly twice as high as in safer seats. This may partly reflect the lack of effort by party workers to persuade voters to go to the polls in safer seats. It is, however, the electoral system rather than the conduct of electoral campaigns that is ultimately responsible for low turnout in safe seats. Indeed it may be argued that what is surprising is not how few people turn out to vote in safe seats, but how many do, in spite of the clear evidence that their cross on the ballot paper will almost certainly not affect the result.

## Media influence

Before the 2010 election there was much discussion of the growing influence of the new media, particularly the internet, in the wake of Obama's successful 2008 presidential election campaign in the United States. Some argued that the traditional mass media, television and press, would be much less influential than in previous elections. Certainly there was less emphasis on poster campaigns and party election broadcasts, prominent features of earlier elections. Indeed some posters proved counter-productive, as countless imaginative spoof alternative versions appeared online, sometimes generating more publicity than the originals.

All the major parties certainly sought to make far more use of the new media. Election manifestos were available online and far more were down-loaded than printed copies sold. Party election broadcasts were released online. Candidates, partic-ularly in marginal constituencies, used their own websites as part of their campaigning. Yet Kavanagh and Cowley (2010, p. 185) observe that 'those who were seeking evidence to prove that 2010 was Britain's first internet election – a claim that has now rather tediously been made for every contest since 1997 – tended to be frustrated'. However, they conclude that 'the internet is now a mainstream tool of political campaigning in the UK where the new media has meshed with the old'.

Thus the new media supplemented rather than supplanted the more traditional media. Television coverage proved more crucial than ever and domi-nated the campaign, with the leaders' debates in particular attracting a huge audience and extensive subsequent analysis by the press. The national press (particularly the tabloids, apart from the *Mirror*) returned to the vigorously pro-Conservative, anti-Labour style and content that characterized elec-tions before 1997. Indeed, after the first leaders' television debate that boosted Clegg and the Liberal Democrats, the pro-Conservative papers vehe-mently turned their fire also on them. In an envi-ronment where the major television channels are legally obliged to provide balanced coverage (which is not the case in all western democracies), the unbridled bias of the popular press may still influ-ence perceptions of parties and leaders, even in the new internet age (see Chapter 9).

## Electoral trends: weakening support for the two major parties and increased electoral volatility

Fewer people today identify strongly with political parties. As party loyalties have weakened so electoral *volatility* has increased. More voters are prepared to switch to another party or decide not to vote at all. There has been a more or less steady decline in the percentage of the total vote won in general elections by the Conservative and Labour parties. For example, in 1951 nearly 97 per cent of voters supported either Labour or Conservative. After touching a low point of 72 per cent in 1983, the percentage rose to 78 in 1992, but fell back to 74 in 1997, and reached its lowest level in 2010 – 65 per cent.

The corollary of the decline in support for the two major parties has been growth in support for the Liberal Democrats, and for other parties, most notably the nationalists. Even with an electoral system which penalizes third and smaller parties, particularly those whose support is relatively dispersed, three-party politics has clearly arrived in Britain (and four-party politics in Scotland and Wales). The Liberal Democrats had already become a significant third force at Westminster in succes-sive elections, even before entering a full coalition with the Conservatives in 2010. Their future party fortunes will depend heavily on how that coalition survives and performs.

## Tactical voting

One explanation for the growth of three- or multi-party politics despite the 'first past the post' elec-toral system is the emergence of tactical voting. This can involve supporting a second or third choice party rather than one's first preference in order to prevent the election of a feared alternative. As a rational response to the current electoral system, tactical voting will continue to thrive as long as the single member plurality system is retained for Westminster elections. Election analysts used to be sceptical about the real extent of tactical voting, not least because it seemed to require rather more political sophistication than they assumed most voters had. Yet tactical voting had long been evident in parliamentary by-elec-tions, enabling disgruntled voters to use opinion polls to discern which opposition candidates were best placed to beat the governing party's candidate and 'send a message to Number Ten'.

However, tactical voting was used on a larger scale in the 1997 general election. Both the size of Labour's majority and the increase in Liberal

Democrat seats (on a smaller national vote) can be attributed to tactical voting against the Conservatives, encouraged by pressure groups and some media publicity. In the campaign leading up to the 2010 election, even some Labour ministers advised tactical voting (Kavanagh and Cowley, 2010, p. 186), and this may have contributed to the Conservative failure to obtain an overall majority.

## Coalition politics: the 2011 referendum and elections

The Conservative–Liberal Democrat coalition government that eventually emerged from the 2010 election takes British politics into unfamiliar territory. Yet coalition government is the norm over most of the European continent, and much of Britain already has had experience of coalition before 2010, in local and devolved government.

Initially relations between the Conservative and Liberal Democrat coalition partners appeared remarkably harmonious. Potential conflicts on issues such as nuclear power and Europe failed to materialize. Pre-election differences over the pace of deficit reduction, spending cuts and taxation were resolved, as the Liberal Democrat ministers backed Osborne's judgement. They also contradicted firm election pledges by supporting controversial proposals to treble university tuition fees (see Box 21.2, p. 381), to the dismay of many of their backbench MPs, party members and voters. Thus it was the Liberal Democrats, and particularly Deputy Prime Minister Nick Clegg, who suffered most from public criticism of unpopular government decisions. To reassert their own influence and party identity within the coalition they sought to slow and modify Andrew Lansley's contentious NHS reforms. Yet it was over the referendum on the Alternative Vote (AV) that a far more bitter rift opened up between the coalition partners.

AV involves only a very limited reform of the voting system, yet precipitated the first full UK wide referendum since 1975. Much more extensive and far-reaching changes have been introduced to the system of voting for the European Parliament and devolved assemblies, without any apparent need for popular endorsement. The AV referendum pledge was the minimum Liberal Democrats would accept, and the maximum the Conservatives were prepared to concede in their coalition negotiations. The interests of the two parties were diametrically opposed. According to one estimate (Curtice *et al* in Kavanagh and Cowley, 2010, p. 417) had the 2010 election been held under AV the Liberal Democrats would have won 79 instead of 57 seats, while the Conservatives would have been reduced to 281 rather than 307. (However, a post-coalition election held under AV could substantially alter the distribution of second preferences, and the result).

The referendum campaign generated more heat than light. Some used it to vent their rage at Nick Clegg and his party for entering coalition. The 'NO campaign' (funded almost entirely by the Conservative party) freely exploited Clegg's unpopularity in their material, reminding voters of his broken promises and arguing 'The only vote that would count under AV would be Nick Clegg's' (NO campaign leaflet). While supporters of AV exaggerated its advantages, its opponents employed misleading analogies, dubious evidence and highly specious cost figures. Liberal Democrat ministers expressed their outrage at some of these tactics in Cabinet. Chris Huhne claimed Clegg had been smeared and demanded Cameron sack any Conservative official linked to the offending campaign literature.

The referendum involved a massive defeat for AV and an endorsement of 'first past the post' by 68% of voters on a 42% turnout. The margin of defeat would appear to rule out AV and any other electoral reform for the foreseeable future, a huge blow for Clegg and his party. The scale of the defeat had not been anticipated. Early polls had suggested a vote for AV. Yet electoral reform was not high on the list of voter's concerns. Party allegiance seems to have largely determined the outcome, with Conservative supporters overwhelmingly voting against change, particularly after the decisive intervention of David Cameron, against the (much diminished) ranks of the Liberal Democrats, with Labour voters as evenly divided as their MPs, despite Miliband's support for AV. Thus the next General Election will be fought under the old rules. Moreover, a reduction in the size of the Commons, and an increase in the average size of constituencies (not subject to a referendum) is expected to favour the Conservatives over Labour.

The AV referendum was only one of many ballots held on 5 May 2011, which involved massive losses for the Liberal Democrats in elections for the Scottish Parliament and Welsh Assembly (see Chapter 16) and English local elections (see Chapter 17). Labour made substantial gains in town halls in the north of England, but made little progressive in the south, while gaining seats in Wales, and losing badly in Scotland to the SNP. The two big winners were David Cameron, whose party's support held up well and even made some gains in Wales and English local elections, and Alex Salmond, whose SNP swept to a remarkable overall majority at Edinburgh, making Scottish independence and the end of the Union a real prospect. British politics has been transformed, and the future is uncertain.

## SUMMARY

- Single party majority UK government was the norm from 1945 until 2010 but this reflected an electoral system (single member plurality) involving a markedly disproportionate relationship between the votes and the seats won by political parties.

- Since 1997 a variety of new electoral systems have been introduced for elections for the European Parliament and the Scottish Parliament, other devolved assemblies and mayoral elections. These have further stimulated a trend towards multi-party politics in Britain.

- The 2010 election, still fought under the single member plurality system, produced a hung parliament and eventually a coalition between the Conservatives and Liberal Democrats. There is a commitment to a referendum on the introduction of the Alternative Vote, but not proportional representation, long demanded by Liberal Democrats.

- There has long been a close link between social class and support for the two main parties. This has declined markedly, but there was still a clear if diminishing correlation between party support and class in recent elections.

- Some other social divisions are also significant for party support. Older people are more likely to support the Conservatives. Women, once slightly more likely to vote Conservative, are now slightly more supportive of Labour. The ethnic minority vote has been predominantly Labour, although the Iraq war alienated some Muslims, who switched to the Liberal Democrats or other candidates in 2005.

- There is still a pronounced North–South divide in British politics, with the Conservatives stronger in the South of England, and Labour in Scotland, Wales and the North of England, with the Midlands more closely contested. Urban Britain is more Labour, suburban and rural Britain more Conservative.

- Issue voting appears to be on the increase, although it is difficult to measure with any precision.

- Party leadership and party image can exert a significant influence on party support. The televised leader debates in 2010 had an immediate dramatic impact and dominated the campaign, but were a more mixed influence on the eventual result.

- In recent general elections tactical voting has helped increase the parliamentary strength of the Liberal Democrats and the development of three-party politics. Further electoral reform might accelerate the trend towards multi-party politics in Britain.

# QUESTIONS FOR DISCUSSION

- How far does the result of the 2010 election advance the case for electoral reform?

- Why have so many different kinds of electoral system been introduced for various levels of government in the United Kingdom?

- What have been the effects of different electoral systems on party politics?

- How far and why does the association between voting and social class appear to be declining?

- What other social divisions seem to have important implications for voting?

- How far do issues and ideas influence voters?

- How much difference do leaders make to party support? What other factors may make a difference to the fortunes of political parties?

- How significant is tactical voting? In what circumstances can it be effective?

- Is coalition politics here to stay? What are the prospects for the next general election?

# FURTHER READING

Denver (2006), *Elections and Voters in Britain* is the best short guide to this subject. It is fuller on voting behaviour than electoral systems, although it does give a brief account of the different electoral systems now operating in the UK, with a succinct criticism and defence of first past the post. Hague and Harrop (2010), Chapter 10, gives a broad comparative perspective on elections and voting, while Chapter 6 of Bale (2008) is good on European comparisons. Curtice (in Dunleavy *et al.*,2003) and Leach (2004) provide a critical appraisal of the effects of different electoral systems in the UK; see also Game (2001). Past election statistics are available from a range of sources, including Butler and

Butler (2000), *Twentieth Century Political Facts* and (2006), *British Political Facts Since 1979*.

Full accounts of particular UK elections are provided in the Nuffield series, with which David Butler has been associated since 1951. Recent books in the series include Butler and Kavanagh (1997, 2001, 2005) and, most recently Kavanagh and Cowley (2010), with a forward by David Butler. There are many other accounts of specific elections that can be consulted for comparison. Also very useful are the increasing number of publications of the Electoral Commission, some of which can be consulted on its website www.electoral-commission.org.uk.

Politics is commonly associated almost exclusively with 'party politics', a specialist and rather unpopular activity undertaken by party politicians. This very narrow interpretation of politics is misguided, yet it does underline how important parties have become in modern political systems. As we saw in the last chapter, elections are fought substantially between parties. That chapter reviewed the shifting support for political parties in the post-war era and some of the reasons for increased volatility in the choice of parties. This chapter concentrates on the functions, types, organization and finance of political parties. It explores briefly the need for parties, reviews the rather unusual party system in Britain, and goes on to explain how and why it is changing. It explores some conventional distinctions between different types of parties, as a prelude to an analysis of the organization and distribution of power and influence within major British parties, and particularly the relationship between the party leadership, parliamentary parties, party members and voters. The controversial issue of party finance is considered in a separate section. The chapter concludes with an examination of the future of political parties, and more specifically of the British party system, in the light of declining party membership and activism, on the one hand, and coalition government and politics on the other.

## Why parties?

It is not immediately obvious why political parties are necessary in a modern representative democracy. Why could not voters simply choose the best men and women for the job, regardless of party labels? Parties may seem to bring more division than necessary to politics. Often it is suggested that a certain issue should be 'taken out' of party politics, or that party politics should play no part in, for example, local government. Could we not dispense with parties altogether? The answer to that question is, almost certainly, no. Parties have developed in just about every political system involving representative democracy, which suggests that they are necessary for the operation of the system (see Box 6.1).

## Party systems

Competition for power between political parties has become almost a defining condition of modern western democracy. In most modern democracies this involves a contest between several parties for control of government by either a single party or, more commonly, a coalition of parties (see Comparative Politics 6.1 for the range of party systems in other countries).

Until recently the United Kingdom could be fairly described as a two-party system.

**BOX 6.1**

# The functions of political parties

- **Political choice** – parties are the principal means by which voters are given an effective choice between different teams of leaders, ideas and policies. Without parties it would be very difficult for voters as a whole to have much influence on the shape of the government to emerge or the policies to be pursued.
- **Political recruitment** – parties recruit and train people for political office and government. Virtually all MPs and most councillors are first nominated as candidates by political parties. In Britain parties also recommend individuals for appointment to other posts such as school governors or Justices of the Peace.
- **Political participation** – belonging to and taking an active role in political parties is one way in which ordinary citizens can participate in the political process besides voting. As party members they can help to choose candidates for Parliament and local councils, join in the election of party leaders and other party positions, and influence party policy, both directly through party conferences and policy forums and indirectly through other channels of communication with the party leadership.
- **Reconciling and aggregating interests** – parties involve coalitions of interests. They bring together various sectional interests in society and assist in transforming a mass of demands into a coherent programme that can be placed before voters at election times. They help to balance conflicting interests on the many issues confronting governments.
- **Communication** – parties provide a two-way channel of communication between political leaders and their supporters. The party leadership uses various channels of communication including speeches, websites and party publications to persuade their members and voters they are doing their best to meet their needs and aspirations. Members and supporters can express their concerns through, for example, representations to MPs and councillors, resolutions to party conferences, and views voiced in party meetings, surveys, focus groups and the media.
- **Accountability and control** – parties effectively take control of the government of the United Kingdom and other levels of government. Thus it is through parties that the government, at various levels, is held accountable for its performance, particularly at elections. Through parties, voters can clearly identify who is in charge, and either reward them by giving them another term in office or reject them and elect a government of another party or parties.

---

- Only two parties have formed governments since 1945. Labour has governed from 1945–51, 1964–70, 1974–9 and 1997–2010; the Conservatives have governed from 1951–64, 1970–4, 1979–97, alone until the formation of the coalition in 2010.
- Through most of British history over the last 200 years there has appeared to be two-party duopoly: Whigs and Tories, then Liberals and Conservatives, more recently Labour and Conservatives.
- Most of the seats in the House of Commons (and sometimes nearly all of them) have belonged to the two major parties since 1945.
- The whole British system of government assumes a confrontation between two parties. There is a Government and Opposition, a Cabinet and a Shadow Cabinet, a House of Commons with two sets of benches facing each other (compared with semi-circular assemblies, common elsewhere).

It could be argued, however, that Britain's two-party system was in large part a product of an electoral system which severely penalizes other parties, particularly those (like the Liberal Democrats or Greens) whose support is widely dispersed and not concentrated in particular areas (see Chapter 5). The introduction of more proportional representation in elections for the House of Commons and local councils would almost certainly establish a multi-party system and coalition government, as in most of continental Europe. However, even without further electoral reform there has already been a marked trend away from two-party politics.

- An increasing number of voters are no longer opting for the two major parties, Labour and

## COMPARATIVE POLITICS 6.1
# Party systems in other countries

- **No party systems.** These are now relatively rare and confined largely to traditional autocracies dominated by a ruling family (e.g. Saudi Arabia).
- **One-party systems.** In most former communist states only one party was permitted. In some former colonial states a nationalist party which led the struggle for independence achieved a virtual monopoly of political life. In both cases there is no competition between parties, although there may be competition between candidates and factions within the party.
- **Dominant party systems.** In some states more than one party may contest elections, but one party dominates membership of the legislature and government, and there seems little real prospect of a change in power (in the short term at least). This was the position for many years in post-independence India, where the Congress Party dominated, and in Japan, where government was monopolized by the Liberal Democratic Party until recently.
- **Two-party systems.** Two parties win most of the seats in the legislature and alternate in government, e.g. competition between Democrats and Republicans in the USA. (Note that third party groups or candidates have sometimes challenged in US elections, but have not succeeded in changing the two-party duopoly.)

- **Systems involving two major parties and smaller parties.** Two major parties compete to lead government, but may not be able to form a majority government alone without the support of a smaller third party. This has been the position in Germany for several decades. Christian Democrats (CDU/CSU) and Social Democrats (SPD) are the two major parties who rely on the smaller Free Democrats (FDP) or Greens for support in coalition governments.
- **Stable multi-party systems.** Although many parties are represented and normally none can command a majority in the legislature, it is relatively easy to form stable coalition governments between parties, perhaps because ideological differences are not too deep. The Netherlands, France and Denmark might be included in this category.
- **Unstable multi-party systems.** It is difficult to form coalition governments, and once formed such governments often prove short-lived. (Examples include France under the former Fourth Republic, Italy until more recently, and Israel.) One problem may be the existence of substantial anti-system parties that are excluded from coalition-building.

*Note:* An important question is how far party systems reflect particular electoral systems or significant divisions in society.

---

Conservative. The combined two-party share of the vote has declined markedly from a high point (97 per cent) in 1951 to around 75 per cent in more recent general elections, 68 per cent in 2005, and 65 per cent in 2010. Liberals and Liberal Democrats have averaged around a fifth of the vote in elections since 1974.

- The number of MPs not formally attached to the two major parties at Westminster has increased from 9 in 1951 to 85 (including 57 Liberal Democrats) in 2010 (slightly down on the 92 MPs elected for other parties in 2005).

- Multi-party politics is already well established in Scotland, Wales and Northern Ireland, particularly in elections for new devolved assemblies.
- In parts of England the main conflict today is not between Labour and Conservative, but between Conservative and Liberal Democrat, or between Labour and Liberal Democrat
- Some relatively new parties (such as the UK Independence Party (UKIP) and Respect) and some older fringe parties (like the Greens or the British National Party) have also secured some support and occasional electoral success.

- In local government there are virtual one-party systems (e.g. Barnsley or Rotherham in South Yorkshire, and parts of the south coast), dominant party systems (e.g. Labour in Manchester), multi-party systems (e.g. Calderdale) and even no party systems (e.g. rural Wales, parts of Lincolnshire and North Yorkshire).

Party politics in Britain today seem more fluid and unpredictable. Trends may not be sustained; new parties may prove ephemeral. Even the substantial Liberal Democrat advance may not last, particularly if coalition with the Conservatives strains party loyalty and causes division. A two-party system of some sort may be re-established at Westminster if there is no change in the electoral system. However, multi-party Britain is already the reality even under the current system (Childs in Dunleavy *et al.*, 2006, p. 58) and would almost certainly become the norm with a more proportional voting system.

## Mass parties?

British political parties developed in the eighteenth and early nineteenth centuries as **cadre parties** based on Parliament, with only rudimentary organization in the country. The growth of a mass electorate in the nineteenth century made it far more important for the Liberal and Conservative parties to recruit and identify supporters in the constituencies, and ensure those eligible were registered to vote. Both the existing major parties went on to establish national organizations to look after their new mass membership. By contrast, the Labour Party was actually founded outside Parliament (as the Labour Representation Committee in 1900).

---

- In the analysis of political parties a distinction has been made between **cadre parties**, based around loose groups of MPs and local notables, and **mass parties**, with an extensive active party membership in the country (Duverger, 1964). In many western countries early parties were of the cadre type, while subsequently socialist and social democratic parties were organized as mass parties. Many (but not all) older parties then acquired their own mass organization.

Both Conservative and Labour could at one time fairly claim to be **mass parties**. Party membership figures rose to a peak in the early 1950s, but have declined significantly since. Conservative party membership has plummeted from nearly three million then to below three hundred thousand in the early twenty-first century. The decline is particularly marked at the younger end. Once there was a thriving Young Conservative membership. Now half the party's members are retired. Comparisons with Labour are complicated by the question of affiliated organizations (largely trade unions). However, Labour's affiliated membership has declined, together with trade union membership from the 1980s onwards. Individual membership has fallen more sharply, from a peak of over a million in the early 1950s, to less than 200,000 in 2010. The long decline was briefly halted and partially reversed in the run-up to the 1997 election, but many of the new members then recruited later failed to renew their subscriptions. The Liberal Democrats have fewer than 100,000 members.

The problem is perhaps worse than the membership figures suggest. Only a relatively small proportion of the members are active, while many do nothing beyond paying their annual subscription. Local political meetings are commonly too poorly attended to be worth the time and expense of organizing, and social events are not well supported. Some constituency parties are effectively run by a handful of members. Indeed, it may be questioned whether parties are in any sense still 'mass parties'.

Does this matter? It has some serious consequences for the parties themselves. Members bring in money through subscriptions and other fund-raising; they provide invaluable voluntary labour, particularly at election times, and an important sounding board for both MPs and the leadership. Yet there are more fundamental concerns. Some of the key functions of parties within a healthy system of representative democracy, notably recruitment, participation, reconciling and aggregating interests, and two-way communication can only be effectively performed by parties with a substantial membership.

## British parties: ideological or pragmatic?

Another distinction is sometimes drawn between **ideological** (or 'programmatic') parties and **pragmatic parties**. In the past, Labour was seen as an ideological party, with its socialist objectives defined in the old Clause 4 of its constitution. The Conservative Party, by contrast, was perceived as essentially pragmatic, mainly interested in the pursuit of power, and thus avoiding ideology and theory. More recently, it is commonly argued, the distinction has been reversed. While Mrs Thatcher introduced ideology and 'conviction politics' into the Conservative Party, Blair subsequently transformed Labour into a pragmatic **'catch-all party'**, prepared to steal the opposition's clothes. In practice both parties have always involved a blend of ideology and pragmatism, particularly when in office.

Indeed, the distinction between ideological and pragmatic parties is, at most, relative. Parties can hardly avoid ideological assumptions. More positively, they need ideals and a message to enthuse their supporters. They also need to show some consistency if they are to be taken seriously. Their ideas may have to evolve and change with the times, but too many sharp reversals of position in pursuit of votes cause confusion and mistrust. But while parties are inevitably ideological, if they are to succeed they have to interpret their ideology flexibly, and adapt to changed circumstances or face permanent exclusion from power and thus lose the opportunity to implement any of their ideas and policies. There are numerous instances of British parties behaving pragmatically – Labour abandoning previous commitments to leave the European Community and to renationalize privatized industries, the Conservatives abandoning their previous opposition to devolution and the minimum wage after 1997, the Liberal Democrats reversal of firm pledges on university tuition fees in 2010. Similar instances of policy reversals can be found throughout the history of British parties.

Other terms are sometimes used to describe modern parties. It is also argued that, with a declining active membership, parties (Panebianco, 1988) are increasingly dominated by careerist professionals. Some critics use the term cartel party (Katz and Mair, 1995) to suggest that established parties collude to cut out competition from new parties, drawing up rules for elections, the state funding of parties, or party election broadcasts that effectively exclude competitors.

Some of these terms could be used to describe major parties in Britain. Thus Labour, Conservative, and perhaps the Liberal Democrats might be considered 'catch-all' parties, and increasingly also 'electoral-professional' parties, dominated by professional politicians who have never had a significant career outside politics. (Four of the five candidates for the Labour Party leadership in 2010 were political advisers before entering Parliament, as were both David Cameron and Nick Clegg.) Could they also be described as cartel parties? The two big parties benefit from an electoral system and rules on political broadcasting. However, they do not substantially benefit from state funding of parties, as do parties in some other political systems. Moreover, if Labour and the Conservatives are operating a cartel, designed to limit competition, they have not been conspicuously successful in the light of increased support and representation for the Liberal Democrats, nationalists, UKIP, Greens and others (Childs in Dunleavy *et al.*, 2006, p. 68). Indeed both major parties have shown a willingness to seek coalitions with the Liberal Democrats and sometimes other parties in local, devolved and, in 2010, national government.

---

● An **ideological party** is explicitly committed to a specific ideology and political programme. This might be stated in the party's name, formal objectives, and constitution. Such a party will not be prepared to compromise its ideals and principles in pursuit of popularity or power, but rather will seek to convert voters to its own ideology and programme.

● A **pragmatic party** is more concerned with the pursuit of power than the implementation of programmes, and is prepared to adjust policies to the perceived preferences of voters, relying on common sense or 'what works' rather than theoretical assumptions.

● A **'catch-all' party** (Kirchheimer, 1966) attempts to maximize electoral support by appealing to as many classes and interests as possible. One influential older interpretation of party competition is that in order to maximize votes, parties need to seek the middle ground, and must carry any ideological baggage lightly (Downs, 1957).

## Parties and pressure groups

Distinctions are commonly drawn between political parties and pressure groups. Parties pursue *power* by fighting elections and forming governments. Groups seek *influence* over government and public policy. Moreover, while groups commonly represent a single interest, parties, if they are to be successful, must involve coalitions of interests. Thus, to use the jargon, groups *articulate* interests while parties *aggregate* them. Once more the distinction is hardly watertight. Some parties seem more concerned with protest than power, and some are linked closely with a particular interest (e.g. UKIP or Respect). By contrast, some interest groups may put up candidates at elections, but often more to win publicity than with the expectation of victory (although some single-issue groups have occasionally been successful in winning seats at Westminster and for the Scottish Parliament).

The British Labour Party from its origins has had a close relationship with a particular interest – trade unions. As they used to provide nearly all the party's membership and money, the relationship was a source of considerable strength to Labour, although it also provided ammunition for Labour's opponents, who have often argued that the unions controlled the party and its policies. The unpopularity of unions, particularly in the 1970s, the reduction in size and the fragmentation of the old manual working class, and the decline in union membership rendered the trade union connection a depreciating asset. Moreover, unions now only provide some 30 per cent of Labour's income. In seeking to reassure business and appeal to 'middle England', Labour leaders from Wilson to Miliband have sought to distance the party from the unions, to the extent that some unions have increasingly questioned the value of the Labour Party link. Yet the 'contentious alliance' (Minkin, 1992) between Labour and the unions survives because, on balance, both sides have more to lose than to gain from divorce.

The Conservative Party has been (less formally) linked with landed interests and subsequently business interests, and more broadly with the middle classes. Such interests provided the party with much of its finance and active membership. Yet if Labour needed to reach out beyond its class base to win and retain power, this was even more true for

the Conservatives, as the interests with which they were linked involved a far smaller proportion of the electorate. To win power the Conservatives needed to appeal to at least a sizeable minority of the working class, including trade union members. For much of the twentieth century it was the breadth of the party's appeal that brought it considerable success.

## Party cohesion – factions and tendencies

Any successful party arguably needs to involve a broad coalition of ideas and interests. Too narrow a focus will restrict its appeal and limit its chances of winning support. This is particularly the case in Britain where the electoral system heavily penalizes smaller parties. However, the range of interests and ideological perspectives within a single party can be a constant source of tension, with the periodic threat of open dissent, rebellion and even a fundamental party split. The appearance of party unity is important, as openly divided parties do not often win elections.

There are significant divisions, or **factions** and **tendencies** within all major British parties. These sometimes arise over particular issues (e.g. the European Union for Conservatives). Sometimes they have more to do with immediate tactics or medium-term strategies (e.g. Liberal Democrat attitudes to coalition with other parties). Sometimes they reflect deeper ideological differences (e.g. between free market and One Nation Conservatives, between socialists and social democrats in the Labour Party, between economic and social liberals among Liberal Democrats). Not infrequently, personal differences and rivalries complicate other divisions (as with Blair and Brown in the Labour Party).

If the internal tensions and divisions within a party develop, a split may result. Splits can be very damaging, perhaps even leading to the demise of the

---

● A **party tendency** is sometimes defined as a loose and informal group within a party sharing a particular ideological perspective or policy stance.

● A **party faction** is a more stable, enduring group, sometimes with a constitution and formal organization and membership.

**Table 6.1**    Crossing the Floor: recent changes of party by sitting MPs

| Date | Name | From (party) | To (party) |
|------|------|--------------|------------|
| 1995 | Alan Howarth | Conservative | Labour |
| 1996 | Emma Nicholson | Conservative | Liberal Democrat |
|      | Peter Thurnham | Conservative | Liberal Democrat |
| 1997 | Sir George Gardiner | Conservative | Referendum Party |
| 1998 | Peter Temple-Morris | Conservative | Labour |
| 1999 | Shaun Woodward | Conservative | Labour |
| 2001 | Paul Marsden | Labour | Liberal Democrat |
| 2003 | George Galloway | Labour | Respect |
| 2004 | Andrew Hunter | Conservative | Democratic Unionist Party (DUP) |
| 2005 | Robert Jackson | Conservative | Labour |
| 2007 | Quentin Davies | Conservative | Labour |

*Note:* In 2008 Conservative MP Bob Spink resigned the party whip and said he would join UKIP, but it seems unclear whether he ever did so (Kavanagh and Cowley, 2010, p. 117).

party as a serious political force. One cause of the rapid decline of the old Liberal Party was a series of damaging divisions, in 1886, 1916–8 and 1931–2. Labour's internal divisions, long a source of electoral weakness, led to a major split in 1981 when some leading Labour 'moderates' left the party to form the Social Democratic Party (Crewe and King, 1995). Some commentators concluded that Labour was effectively finished as a credible party of government. More recently, divisions within the Conservative Party severely weakened John Major's government and contributed to the party's defeat in 1997; some Conservative MPs 'crossed the floor' to Labour or the Liberal Democrats (see Table 6.1), while a few former Conservatives switched to the Referendum Party or UKIP. Although a diminishing number of pro-Europe Conservatives have remained within the party, they have increasingly appeared an embattled minority.

The Labour Party in particular has been periodically concerned about the dangers of infiltration or 'entryism' by groups or tendencies which do not share the party's commitment to parliamentary methods and its own moderate interpretation of socialism. Apart from the internal divisions and conflict caused by such groups, the perception that a party has been infiltrated by 'extremists' can be electorally damaging. Although the Labour Party has suffered most from association with extremists ('reds under the beds'), instances of former BNP

and National Front activists working within the Conservative Party have sometimes undermined its recent attempts to appear more inclusive and welcoming towards ethnic minorities.

## The organization of parties: power and decision-making

The above analysis suggests it is very important for a party to manage internal divisions and maintain an appearance of unity and cohesion. One of the problems here is that modern political parties are extremely complex organizations that operate at a number of levels. Key elements of their organization normally include:

- A clearly identified party **leadership,** including a single acknowledged leader who has considerable prestige and authority, and commonly a deputy leader, surrounded by a team which together constitute the collective party leadership.
- A **parliamentary party** (assuming it has parliamentary representation) including party committees and a whip system to maintain party unity and discipline.
- A **mass membership** in the country (which for the major parties is organized at regional, constituency and ward levels).

- **Party conferences** to represent the party as a whole (supplemented increasingly by postal and online communications with party members).
- A **national organization** and **party bureaucracy** involving both full- and part-time officials who serve the party and provide it with administrative, promotional and often research support.

Key questions arise over the inter-relationship between these various parts of a modern political party.

## The party leadership – choosing leaders

A credible and popular leader can make a substantial difference to the fortunes of a political party. The leader of a majority party who is also Prime Minister wields considerable power and responsibility, and may change the course of history. It follows that the method of choosing leaders is extremely important both for parties and for the country as a whole. The selection or election of leaders has often been controversial and the major parties have all changed their rules, in some cases several times.

For most of the twentieth century the Parliamentary Labour Party (PLP) elected its own leader and (subsequently) deputy leader. Where there were more than two candidates a series of ballots was held, with the bottom candidate dropping out, until one candidate emerged with an overall majority. Some of these elections were very closely contested. Thus when Harold Wilson resigned as Prime Minister in 1976 there were six candidates to succeed him, and James Callaghan eventually emerged as party leader and Prime Minister in the third ballot.

The Conservative Party did not have a formal system for electing their leader until 1965. When a Conservative Prime Minister resigned other than because of an election defeat, the monarch invited another leading Conservative to head a new government, normally after consultation with senior figures in the party. This informal system operated without significant difficulties until Harold Macmillan suddenly announced his resignation as Prime Minister on the eve of the 1963 Conservative Party conference. The resulting frantic competition for support by candidates for

the succession and a somewhat flawed process of consultation led eventually to the emergence of Sir Alec Douglas-Home as Prime Minister and leader – and the refusal of two Cabinet ministers to serve in his government in protest against his appointment. This shambles reflected badly on the party, which in opposition moved to a system of formal election by MPs, as in the Labour Party, although with rather different rules.

This system produced several close and bruising leadership contests. It was first used in 1965 to elect Edward Heath, who went on to become Prime Minister in 1970 and then to lose two close general elections in 1974, after which his leadership was successfully challenged by Margaret Thatcher in 1975. She, in turn, after three election victories, faced challenges to her leadership, first in 1989, and then more seriously in 1990 from Michael Heseltine, who had dramatically resigned from her Cabinet over the Westland affair in 1986. Although Thatcher won more votes than Heseltine in the first ballot, she narrowly failed to secure the simple majority plus 15 per cent of the votes required in the party rules. She was persuaded to stand down for the second ballot, when John Major and Douglas Hurd entered the contest, leading to a decisive victory for Major. In 1995 Major himself, frustrated by attacks on his leadership, challenged his critics to 'put up or shut up', and defeated his former Cabinet colleague, John Redwood, who however secured enough votes (89) and abstentions (20) to further damage Major's weakening position. The last time this system was used was in 1997, after John Major resigned as leader following the Conservative defeat at the general election, when William Hague defeated Kenneth Clarke on the third ballot.

By this time the other parties, beginning with the Liberals, had moved to a system of election involving their wider party membership. In 1975 David Steel was elected in a postal vote of Liberal Party members voting in constituency associations. When the Liberals and the short-lived Social Democratic Party (SDP) merged to form the Liberal Democrats, Paddy Ashdown was elected as leader in a postal ballot of members in 1988. After Ashdown's resignation as leader in 1999, Charles Kennedy defeated Simon Hughes in a similar election. When Kennedy was effectively forced out

**Table 6.2**    Labour Party leadership election, September 2010

|                | First ballot | Second ballot | Third ballot | Fourth ballot |
|----------------|--------------|---------------|--------------|---------------|
| Ed Miliband    | 34.33%       | 37.47%        | 41.26%       | 50.65%        |
| David Miliband | 37.78%       | 38.89%        | 42.72%       | 49.35%        |
| Ed Balls       | 11.79%       | 13.30%        | 16.02%       | Eliminated    |
| Andy Burnham   | 8.68%        | 10.41%        | Eliminated   |               |
| Diane Abbott   | 7.42%        | Eliminated    |              |               |

after his parliamentary colleagues lost confidence in him, Menzies Campbell was elected leader by party members in 2006, and following his resignation in 2007, Nick Clegg narrowly defeated Chris Huhne.

After considerable pressure for more internal party democracy within the Labour Party, a new leadership election process was adopted after a special conference held at Wembley in 1981. One problem for Labour was that the party had both individual members, attached to parliamentary constituencies, and affiliated members (mainly from trade unions affiliated to the Labour Party). The rather clumsy solution was an electoral college in which originally trade unions had 40 per cent of the votes, constituency parties 30 per cent and the Parliamentary Labour Party 30 per cent. The system was first used in a contest for the deputy leadership in September 1981 when Dennis Healey very narrowly defeated Tony Benn. It was subsequently used when Neil Kinnock and Roy Hattersley were elected leader and deputy leader in 1983, and again in 1988, when they were unsuccessfully challenged. Using the same system, John Smith and Margaret Beckett were elected leader and deputy leader in 1992.

After the 1993 Labour party conference the system of election was slightly modified, adjusting the proportions in the electoral college to give one-third of the votes to each of the constituent elements. More significantly, unions and constituency parties were obliged to ballot members individually and divide their votes accordingly, thus meeting the demand for 'one member, one vote' (OMOV). Using this modified system Tony Blair and John Prescott achieved a clear majority in the 1994 elections for leader and deputy leader in each category as well as overall.

When Blair resigned in 2007, Gordon Brown was elected without opposition, although Harriet Harman eventually defeated five other candidates for the post of deputy leader.

Following Brown's resignation as Prime Minister and party leader following the 2010 election, five candidates stood for the leadership. However, it was soon clear that it was essentially a two-horse race between the Miliband brothers. Following a four-month interregnum in which Harman was acting leader, Ed Miliband defeated his older brother David by the narrowest of margins, once the second preferences of those who voted for eliminated candidates were taken into account (see Table 6.2).

There was some criticism from both inside and outside the party on the rules under which the contest was fought, particularly as it was clear that Ed Miliband owed his victory to trade union votes. Ed Miliband was supported by a minority of MPs and MEPs (46.57 per cent) and party members (45.59 per cent) but overtook David by securing 59.80 per cent of the votes of members of affiliated organizations (largely trade unions). However, since the reforms of the 1990s, individual trade unionists who have not opted out of the political levy paid to the Labour Party vote individually in a secret ballot, just like other party members. Nevertheless, there is some legitimate criticism of the way in which some individuals can acquire multiple votes by qualifications in different categories. Thus a Labour MP is also a party member, and may have additional votes in other categories by being a member of one or more affiliated organizations.

The Conservative Party, which had been slow to introduce a formal system of electing its leader by MPs in 1965, became the only major party restrict-

**Image 6.1 Candidates in the 2010 Labour leadership contest**

(*From left*) Andy Burnham, David Miliband, Diane Abbott, Ed Balls, Ed Miliband.

The long campaign for the Labour leadership, the complex voting system and close result in which Ed Miliband narrowly defeated his brother, the early front runner, David Miliband, perhaps did the party few favours.

ing the election of leader to MPs alone after 1981. In a reform aimed at giving more power and influence to ordinary members after the general election defeat in 1997, William Hague introduced a new method of election that gave them the final decision on the leadership. MPs would nominate candidates for the leadership, followed by ballots within the parliamentary party to narrow the choice down to two, with the final decision involving a ballot of ordinary party members. This system was used for the first time in 2001 when Hague resigned after the 2001 general election defeat. Five initial candidates were reduced to three, and in the final MPs' ballot Kenneth Clarke won 59 votes, Iain Duncan Smith 54 votes and Michael Portillo 53 votes. Portillo was thus eliminated, and Duncan Smith went on to win the members' ballot by 61 to 39 per cent.

Party members had chosen a leader who was the first choice neither of Conservative MPs nor ordinary voters (according to opinion polls). Opposition to Duncan Smith's leadership grew when he failed to make an impact in Parliament or the country. In October 2003 he faced a vote of no confidence within the parliamentary party, and went on lose by 90 votes to 75. This seemed to pave the way for another bruising leadership contest, yet after some discussions within the parliamentary party only one candidate, Michael Howard, was

nominated, and party members were effectively denied a choice. There were, however, few howls of outrage. The party rallied behind their new leader (who had come a poor fifth in the 1997 contest and had not even stood in 2001).

It seemed Duncan Smith might prove to be the last and only leader to be elected by Conservative members. By late 2004 there were moves to change the method of election once again to give the final say to MPs. Following the 2005 general election Howard announced that he would resign once a new system for electing a leader was in place. However, a ballot in September 2005 produced insufficient support for a rule change, and the Conservative leadership election proceeded under the system introduced by William Hague. Conservative MPs eliminated Kenneth Clarke and Liam Fox, leaving party members a choice between the early front runner, David Davis, and the relatively unknown David Cameron, who, after a strong performance at the Conservative party conference, eventually triumphed by a margin of two to one.

Thus all major parties now involve their ordinary party members in the election of the party leader. However, it should be noted that this move towards more internal party democracy has developed over a period when the numbers of individual party members has steeply declined, and are only a

**BOX 6.2**

## The authority of Labour and Conservative leaders compared

Labour leaders have appeared weaker in theory than their Conservative counterparts because:

- they are bound by Conference decisions according to the Labour Party constitution;
- they are constrained by the National Executive Committee (NEC) between conferences, and have not always enjoyed a majority on the NEC;
- they do not control the appointment of their own deputy who is separately elected;
- they can not even choose their own Shadow Cabinet in opposition, which is formed from a parliamentary committee elected by a vote of the Parliamentary Labour Party;
- they do not fully control the party bureaucracy.

However, in practice Labour leaders have generally enjoyed considerable power over their parties – at times ignoring Conference decisions. When Labour leaders have also been Prime Minister they have enjoyed all the considerable constitutional powers associated with that office and have had as much authority as their Conservative counterparts.

perhaps voters). So there is plenty of continuing potential for tensions between MPs, party members and voters. Yet open leadership elections help to secure legitimacy for leaders, and can help build support for them among voters. The Labour Party did itself and its new leader no favours when Gordon Brown was elected without a contest in 2007.

### The power of party leaders

While the Conservative Party has traditionally emphasized the importance of leadership, Labour historically was suspicious of the leader's power and has sought to restrain it. Yet in practice Labour leaders from Wilson onwards have been less vulnerable to formal challenges within the party. The only sitting Labour leader who has faced a leadership contest over the last forty years was Kinnock, who easily saw off a challenge from Tony Benn. Over the same period Heath, Thatcher, Major and Duncan Smith have all faced challenges, which only Major survived. Perhaps one reason for the greater vulnerability of Conservative leaders is that their party has grown accustomed to success, and is unforgiving of failure, or the prospect of failure.

It should not be forgotten that while most of the media attention is focused on the individual who is party leader, he or she is normally surrounded by other politicians with their own positions, power bases and popularity within the party. The leader has to try to satisfy the political ambitions of those who may be real or potential rivals, but also needs to draw on their talents so as to present a credible collective leadership of actual or potential ministers, and convince the voters of their collective competence. Within the leadership group, some politicians may come to seem indispensable, as Whitelaw was to Thatcher and Heseltine became to John Major. Both these were disappointed candidates for the leadership who gave full loyalty to the victors. By contrast, Gordon Brown, who was reluctantly persuaded to forego his own leadership hopes in 1994, evidently retained ambitions to lead the Labour Party in which he remained a hugely important figure, with real power in his own right.

small proportion of party voters. There is clearly a risk that parties may end up with leaders who enjoy neither the confidence of parliamentary colleagues nor the support of the wider electorate which has the critical voice in the making of a Prime Minister at a general election. Thus Conservative MPs and members repeatedly rejected the leadership candidate who had most support in the country, Kenneth Clarke. Ironically, Charles Kennedy was forced out of the leadership of the Liberal Democrats in 2006 by his parliamentary colleagues when he still enjoyed support among party members and voters. Ed Miliband became Labour's leader in 2010, despite being the second choice of the party's MPs and individual members (and

## Parliamentary parties

Parties in Britain began in Parliament, flourishing long before any formal party leadership roles were acknowledged. Although it is sometimes suggested that modern parliamentary parties are mere 'lobby fodder', coerced to troop through the division lobbies at the behest of their powerful leaders, they still retain a crucial role at the very centre of the modern party system. The most gifted politicians are powerless without a significant parliamentary party behind them. Lloyd George, perhaps the ablest orator and administrator in twentieth-century British politics, was effectively forced out of office in 1922, at the height of his powers, never to return, because he did not have a united parliamentary party with a majority behind him. His position depended on the support of the Conservatives, a party not his own, and this was withdrawn once Conservative backbenchers voted to fight the election as a separate party, against the advice of most of their leaders, who wanted to maintain the Lloyd George coalition.

The power of ordinary Conservative backbenchers, revealed then, was subsequently formally recognized with the establishment of the 1922 Committee, which consisted of backbenchers when the party was in government up until 2010, and whose elected officers remain figures of real status and influence within the party. It is the 1922 Committee that acts as the sounding board for ordinary Conservative MPs, alerts the leadership to the concerns of the backbenchers, and organizes leadership elections. David Cameron upset his backbenchers when he became Prime Minister in May 2010 by pushing through a change in the rules to allow ministers to attend the 1922, although he agreed, in a compromise, that they should not vote.

The Parliamentary Labour Party (PLP) continues to form a similar function within the Labour Party. When the party is in opposition the PLP elects a Parliamentary Committee, which becomes in effect the Shadow Cabinet. The leader is obliged to offer shadow posts to all those elected, although others who are not elected may be given a front bench role as well. When the Labour Party is in government, the leader chooses his own Cabinet, (although normally constrained initially to offer Cabinet posts to former elected Shadow Cabinet members), and the PLP chooses a small Parliamentary Liaison Committee to provide a link between the parliamentary party and the government.

Both the Labour and Conservative parties have their own system of specialist party committees covering a range of government functions, which allow MPs to use and develop specialist interests and expertise. These committees provide an additional channel of influence as well as a pool of more experienced MPs who may become members of key all-party Parliamentary Select Committees, or gain reputations which may earn them a government post when the party is in office. In the 2010 coalition government the Liberal Democrats established committees to shadow departments in which there were no Liberal Democrat ministers.

Party cohesion and discipline is promoted by the party whips, who play a key role in the modern parliamentary party (although the name and post date back to the eighteenth century). Today both major parties have a whip's office, led by a chief whip assisted by junior whips. The whips may use a combination of threats, bribes and cajolery to keep members of their party in line. A disaffected MP may risk losing some valued perks of the job – for example trips abroad on parliamentary delegations, membership of prestigious parliamentary committees, an honour, or the prospect of promotion. In more extreme circumstances, the whips may threaten to communicate their displeasure to an MP's constituency association (which could lead to their deselection as party candidate at the next election), or to withdraw the party whip, so that the MP is no longer considered a member of the parliamentary party. For offences which are regarded as particularly heinous they may be expelled from the party, although the party cannot expel an MP from Parliament. Only the House of Commons, or ultimately the voters, can do that.

However, such weapons are not always effective, particularly against MPs who have no further political ambitions or realistic expectations of promotion. Even the withdrawal of the whip may not prove too damaging to an MP who retains the support of his or her constituency party. In 1994 the whip was withdrawn from eight Euro-sceptic Conservative MPs who had consistently refrained from voting with the party on European issues and one sympathiser voluntarily resigned the whip. These 'whipless nine' continued to constitute a separate parliamentary grouping until the whip was restored without promises of future good behaviour a year later. Rebellion has not always proved a bar to promotion, and in retrospect has sometimes appeared a good career move. Former rebels who have gone on to become party leaders include Winston Churchill, Harold Macmillan and Iain Duncan Smith among Conservatives, and Harold Wilson and Michael Foot on the Labour side.

Party splits are perceived as damaging to a party's electoral prospects and hence to the prospects for re-election of individual MPs, who normally owe their position almost completely to party endorsement. Although much party discipline is self-discipline, it has weakened of late, with more backbench rebellions. One possible explanation is that large government majorities (enjoyed by both Thatcher and Blair) allow the luxury of rebellion without any risk to the survival of the government, and also make it more difficult to satisfy the political ambitions of increased numbers of MPs, who may consequently become restive. Blair's government faced huge backbench revolts on some of its policies, notably on the Iraq war and student top-up fees (Cowley, 2005). Coalition government complicates the position further. Many backbench Liberal Democrats rebelled against their ministerial colleagues over university tuition fees in 2010.

Yet the power of ordinary backbench MPs is not to be measured by the size and frequency of rebellions. Much of their influence springs from the leaders and whips anticipating what the backbenchers will not stand for, and altering course accordingly. While most MPs want their party to succeed and want to remain loyal, they all have a 'bottom line', issues of principle on which they are not prepared to budge, as the party whips realize. Indeed the whips' job is not just to persuade or coerce recalcitrant backbenchers, but often, more importantly, to convey backbench feeling to the party leaders, and warn them against proceeding

with policies or decisions in the teeth of substantial opposition from their own MPs. A celebrated example was when Wilson's Labour government backed down from its proposed trade union reforms after the Chief Whip informed the Cabinet that he could not get the reforms through the parliamentary party. More recently, Brown was persuaded to reverse several decisions following backbench pressure on, for example, some of the tax changes he had proposed in his last budget in 2007, such as the abolition of the proposed 10p starting rate for income tax. The Brown government also quietly dropped proposals to extend the 28 days of detention without charge for terrorist suspects to 42 days after a near-defeat in the Commons was followed by rejection in the Lords.

## Party conferences

Each party holds an annual conference for a week in the autumn, together with other occasional or more specialized conferences. In theory there is a massive difference between the role of the Labour Party Conference as the party's own 'parliament', supreme over party policy, compared with that of the conference in the Conservative Party with no constitutional power. Indeed, one past Conservative Prime Minister, Balfour, said he would rather take advice from his valet than the party conference. Yet in practice the Labour conference was never as powerful as the party constitution suggested, while Conservative conferences were often influential despite their lack of formal power (McKenzie, 1955). Labour leaders could, and effectively did, disregard conference decisions that they opposed, while the Conservative leadership was sometimes influenced by strong expressions of conference opinion, not always in the party's longer-term interest. One example is Thatcher's ill-fated poll tax that helped to remove her from Downing Street. A more recent illustration was the popular pledge to reduce inheritance tax at the 2007 Conservative conference, a commitment that proved embarrassing in the altered economic climate from 2008 onwards.

Even so, until recently there were still considerable differences between the parties in the way in which the conferences were conducted. Labour party conferences often involved furious rows and party splits. The party leadership lacked effective control of the agenda, or who could speak (even leading Cabinet Ministers had no right to speak). One celebrated example was in 1960, when the leader Hugh Gaitskell defiantly declared, to the jeers of his audience, that he would 'fight and fight and fight again' to reverse a Labour conference decision in favour of unilateral nuclear disarmament. Another came in 1985 when Neil Kinnock denounced Labour's (Militant-dominated) Liverpool Council to a mixture of cheers and boos. All this made for dramatic television, but also reflected badly on a divided party. By contrast, Conservative annual conferences were generally carefully stage-managed and relatively docile. Contentious motions and issues were kept off the conference agenda. Essentially they were viewed as rallies of the party faithful, rewarding loyal members with an opportunity to meet their leaders in a friendly social setting, and more importantly, allowing leading politicians to display some effective platform oratory and secure abundant valuable free publicity for the party.

This contrast is much less obvious today. Labour conferences under Blair and Brown were more carefully managed. For all parties, conferences now seem to be more about public relations than policy. A successful conference for any party can result in a significant (if often only temporary) boost in its poll ratings. The Liberal Democrats, who have particular problems in securing publicity for their politicians and policies, have learned the value of the conference shop window, and significantly have also sought to impose more discipline and control over delegates, so as to appear more moderate and responsible. Yet ironically party conferences now attract less media coverage and have less impact on the public, partly because they no longer seem to decide important political issues. A carefully organized Conservative conference demonstration of loyalty to Iain Duncan Smith in October 2003 did not prevent Conservative MPs passing a vote of no confidence in his leadership later in the same month.

## Party bureaucracy

Parties with a substantial mass membership require complex organizational structures to manage the relationship between the parliamentary leadership and the extra-parliamentary party, operating at various levels in the country. Major parties now require extensive permanent bureaucracies to meet their needs. This has meant employing increasing numbers of paid staff – particularly at the centre, but also in the regions and in constituencies, as well as using large numbers of unpaid party activists. Professional expertise is required for a range of purposes – raising money and controlling spending, marketing and advertising, policy-oriented research, legal advice, party management and administration. All major parties retain paid permanent agents in marginal constituencies, who play a crucial role in maintaining the party organization at constituency level, and maximizing the party's vote at election times.

At national level the Conservative Party is organized from Conservative Central Office, founded in 1870. The party's Chair is directly appointed by the leader, and Central Office has been described as 'the personal machine of the leader'. Its main tasks are fund-raising, the organization of election campaigns, assistance with the selection of candidates, research and political education. While Central Office has enjoyed substantial power and prestige in the past, it has become increasingly subject to criticism following poor election results and other evidence of the party's decline. Some party activists (e.g. in the Charter Movement) would like to see Central Office become more accountable and subject to democratic control. Pressure for reform and more internal democracy in the party following the landslide defeat of 1997 led William Hague to introduce a range of changes (published as *The Fresh Future*), although the increased influence given to a diminishing and elderly membership has sometimes proved problematic.

The organization of the Labour Party nationally has been subject to extensive change in recent years. Labour headquarters were long located at Transport House, in the offices of the Transport and General Workers Union, symbolizing the close links of Labour with the trade unions. The party's organization was not always efficient. In 1955, Harold Wilson famously described Labour's party machine as a rusty penny-farthing bicycle in the era of the jet plane (Pimlott, 1992, p. 194). In 1980

**Table 6.3**   The new National Executive Committee of the Labour Party

| Number | Who? | How selected? |
|--------|------|---------------|
| 2 | Leader, Deputy Leader | Ex officio (previously elected through an electoral college) |
| 1 | Treasurer | Elected by all members |
| 10 | Members of affiliated trade unions | Elected at annual conference |
| 2 | Representatives of socialist societies | Elected at annual conference |
| 6 | Constituency party members | Elected by all members Cannot be MPs |
| 3 | Parliamentary Committee | Elected by Parliamentary Committee (Shadow Cabinet) |
| 3 | MPs/MEPs | Elected at annual conference |
| 2 | Labour Councillors | Elected from Association of Labour Councillors |
| 1 | Young Labour representative | Elected at youth conference |
| 1 | Leader of the European Parliamentary Labour Party | Elected by Labour MEPs |

*Source*: Adapted from official Labour Party material.

the party moved to its own modest headquarters in Walworth Road, but it was still criticized as ineffective, until a substantial reorganization started under Kinnock's leadership (Minkin, 1992, Chapter 19). From 1995 key staff moved to the new campaign and media centre at Millbank Tower, which came to symbolize New Labour's slick public relations and 'spin doctoring'. Both the expense and the (increasingly unfavourable) image of Millbank led in 2002 to another move, to more modest but central premises in the heart of Westminster at Old Queen Street.

In the past Labour leaders lacked the control over party organization enjoyed by Conservative leaders, partly because the party's official governing body (between conferences) is not the Cabinet or Shadow Cabinet or even the PLP, but the National Executive Committee (NEC). This was once dominated by the trade unions, and, to a lesser degree, members chosen by constituency associations (largely left-wingers). In the 1970s and early 1980s

the majority of the NEC was hostile to the party leadership. As the NEC had to approve the party manifesto and controlled key appointments in the Labour Party, including the post of General Secretary, there was often division at the top.

In 1997 there was a significant reorganization of the party's central machinery. The affiliated organizations (mainly unions) retained 12 seats on an NEC increased from 29 to 31 members (see Table 6.3). Party members could vote for six constituency party members, who could no longer be MPs (MPs and government ministers are represented separately). Separate women's representatives were abolished and replaced by new rules requiring a minimum number of women in different categories of NEC members. The new NEC has caused fewer problems to the leadership (particularly since the introduction of postal ballots for party members), and the party has appeared less divided.

Whereas the Labour Party national organization in the past often appeared divided and shambolic while the Conservative organization seemed ruthlessly united and efficient, the image of the two parties was almost reversed from 1995 to 2005. Thus the Conservatives sought to imitate aspects of Labour's successful electoral machine. Yet Labour paid a price for its greater discipline and professionalism. The Labour leadership was accused of acting like 'control freaks', seeking to manipulate all key roles in the party, while the party's slick public relations have become increasingly identified with manipulation and 'spin' (see Chapter 9). Alastair Campbell, Labour's most formidable 'spin doctor', resigned as the Prime Minister's Director of Communications in 2003. Following the Phillis Report (2004) the party became less reliant on 'spin' by anonymous spokespersons, with more direct communication by ministers in televised press briefings.

## The party membership and constituency parties

All major parties have recently sought (ostensibly at least) to give more power and influence to ordinary members. Party members have always had one very significant power: choosing party candidates for local and general elections. Although in certain circumstances the national party may seek to influence the choice of parliamentary candidate, and exceptionally may block the selection of a particular candidate, in general it is the members voting at constituency level who choose. Moreover, particularly in the Labour Party, members have sometimes exercised powers to deselect sitting MPs with whom they have become dissatisfied. Beyond that, as we have seen, all major parties over the last 30 years or so sought to involve party members in the choice of the party leader, and made some show of involving them more in the policy-making process.

Internal party democracy may not necessarily help a party to win elections, however, and can be positively detrimental, particularly as active members become fewer and less representative of potential party voters. Most people who vote for a party are not party members. Active party members almost by definition are unusual creatures with views and preferences that may be similarly untypical. Thus the problem for parties is that they serve two very different political 'markets'. Policies that please active members may not appeal to ordinary voters. Labour Party members in the 1980s wanted left-wing policies (including more nationalization and unilateral nuclear disarmament) which the electorate rejected. Today, Labour's constituency activists and candidates are increasingly middle-class professionals, often out of touch with the party's core manual working-class voters in northern urban housing estates.

The problem for the Conservatives may be worse. William Hague, Iain Duncan Smith, Michael Howard and, most of all, David Cameron, have all sought a broader, more inclusive, party. However, its existing dwindling membership is elderly, overwhelmingly white and middle-class. Although women are well represented among party activists, many hold very traditional views on gender relations and the role of women in society and the workplace. No Conservative leader has dared to introduce all-women shortlists, although Cameron's preferred 'A-list' candidates contained many career women and representatives of ethnic minorities whom he sought to advance. Yet central influence on candidate selection is still much resented and has led to rows and splits within constituency parties. The internal Conservative differences over policy have more generally been muffled in the interests of election victory. Yet the policies which appeal to members (such as tax and public spending cuts, a hard line on crime and immigration, and support for 'family values') alienate some of the new target voters the party is trying to attract, including ethnic minorities, unconventional families, gays, and young people generally.

Similarly, Liberal Democrat activists often seem to have different ideas and priorities from those of Liberal Democrat voters, and more recently their leaders. Surveys and polls suggest that many of those who vote Liberal Democrat are hazy over Liberal Democrat policies. Most Liberal Democrat seats were originally taken from Conservatives, and the views of some of their voters in these seats appear well to the right of activist Liberal Democrat members. Many of the latter see themselves as on the left, indeed to the left of New

Labour. These radical party members had already clashed with the new party leadership under Clegg, well before the formation of the coalition with the Conservatives. The party leadership began a switch away from the higher taxation proposed by Kennedy to fund increased spending on education, and sought to modify the party's opposition to university tuition fees. This was strongly resisted by party members (Kavanagh and Cowley, 2010, pp. 108–10) and has become a major source of internal party conflict as the coalition government proceeded to treble tuition fees.

All main parties seem to have a problem recruiting and keeping younger members. Recent research suggests that Liberal Democrat activists are predominantly male and middle-class with an average age in the late 50s. Perhaps the real problem is that older forms of political activity, such as attending ward and constituency meetings, no longer appeal. Increasingly, the parties are pursuing other methods of communicating with their members through postal ballots and surveys and interactive websites. Yet it seems most unlikely that the long-term decline in active party membership will be reversed.

One pessimistic answer is that people are not interested in more participation in politics. There are more diverting ways for people to spend their leisure time in a modern consumer society. Another possible answer is that in so far as people have the energy and inclination to participate in politics, it is increasingly in single-issue pressure groups rather than political parties (see Chapters 4 and 8). Parties, involving coalitions of interests, inevitably require compromise. Those whose ideals motivate them to become involved in politics may be turned off by the messy and sometimes grubby processes of accommodation and compromise within mainstream parties. For them, political parties are part of the problem rather than the solution, (all the more so after the 2009 parliamentary expenses scandal), contributing to the alienation of ordinary people from the political process rather than offering an opportunity for involvement. Whatever the explanation, the UK political system depends to a degree on competition between mass political parties which hardly exist any longer. It is not a problem confined to the UK, as a decline in party membership seems to be an almost universal problem in modern western democracies, affecting parties across the political spectrum, from communist and socialist parties on the left to Christian democrat parties on the right.

## The finance of political parties

The financing of political parties has become such an important and controversial issue that it requires a separate section. Parties need money for many purposes, for example, servicing their permanent organization, paying administrators and agents, commissioning policy research, financing elections, political advertising and market research. There are three main possible sources of finance: subscriptions from ordinary members, donations from organizations and individuals, or state funding (Outhwaite, 2004).

Ideally, perhaps, money should come from party members, through ordinary party subscriptions, but it is virtually impossible for a dwindling membership to provide the funds required. Much higher membership fees would deter potential recruits at a time when all parties are desperately seeking to encourage a larger and wider membership. Many 'unwaged' members (e.g. the large number who are retired) do not pay the full membership rates.

Thus additional sources of finance are solicited, from individual donors, from business organizations, trade unions, and other friendly bodies. Yet this can cause problems for parties, as has been only too evident in recent years. How far are contributors to party finances effectively buying influence or status? There is a long history of allegations of the award of honours in return for donations to political parties. Lloyd George, the Liberal leader and coalition Prime Minister (1916–22), sold honours almost openly. More recently there have been charges that knighthoods and peerages have been given by Conservative governments to individual donors and directors of companies that have made donations to the Conservative Party.

More damaging are allegations of influence on policy. The Conservative Party for many years routinely received contributions from particular sectors of business, such as brewers, tobacco companies, and construction companies, and there

# Academic controversy 6.1
## Internal party democracy

From the late nineteenth century onwards, mass political parties appeared increasingly important as a means of participation by ordinary citizens in the political process, and potentially as a bridge between the political mass and the political elite, particularly as they became more open and inclusive. Internal party democracy would ensure that leaders served the mass membership rather than the other way around. However, in 1911 Robert Michels [1968] argued that power in political parties (including even those which strongly proclaim their attachment to democracy) naturally gravitates to the parliamentary leadership and permanent bureaucracy. This may be because large organizations are inevitably oligarchies (the argument of Michels) or because parties, particularly in Britain, operate within a centralized political system, or because of media focus on leading personalities, or perhaps because leaders betray (or more subtly manipulate) their followers.

The last argument has been most commonly heard within the Labour Party. 'Betrayal' has been a familiar theme since Ramsay MacDonald ignored his own party and formed a National Government with the Conservatives in 1931. Much of the argument over organizational reforms in the 1980s barely concealed a battle for power between the moderate parliamentary leadership and a left-wing active membership. Giving power to the members was interpreted to mean giving power to activists who turned up to meetings, rather than those whose involvement was largely confined to paying their subscription.

However, subsequent reforms since 1987 and more particularly under Blair have been interpreted (Webb in Dunleavy et al., 2002 p. 158) as 'motivated by the desire to enhance the autonomy of the leadership (at the expense of backbenchers and grassroots activists)'. In particular, critics point to the development of 'plebiscitary democracy' within the party. This effectively bypasses party activists and 'empowers' (through postal ballots) the 'ordinary members' who are perceived as 'more docile and more likely to endorse the policies (and candidates) proposed by the party leadership' (Mair, in Katz and Mair, 1994). Those voting on candidates or issues by post are also more likely to be influenced by the (business-dominated) mass media rather than the debate within the party. While this may be true it is hard to argue against reforms that appear to involve more members in decisions. If members are increasingly unwilling to give up their time to attend meetings, other ways of consulting them have to be found.

A bigger problem is that party members constitute only a tiny and unrepresentative minority of party voters. Because many constituency parties are now effectively run by a few activists there is even the danger (illustrated by the success of the Trotskyist Militant Tendency in the Labour Party in the early 1980s) that a small unrepresentative group opposed to some of the party's core principles could take them over. While internal democracy within competing parties with an active mass membership may complement representative institutions and enhance democracy, grass roots power in parties which no longer involve the masses could deny them effective choice and subvert rather than assist the wider democratic process.

---

were suggestions they were particularly open to influence in these areas as a result. Particularly controversial were contributions from wealthy foreign businessmen. Until Hague's leadership most large donations to the Conservatives were secret – so there were allegations of hidden influence.

Labour had long openly depended financially on contributions from trade unions, provoking accusations that the party was effectively run by the unions. More recently, Labour has courted business, and Blair's Labour government was embarrassed by a large donation from Bernie Ecclestone, the Formula One boss, in 1997. The subsequent

BOX 6.3

## Recommendations of the Neill Committee on party funding, 1998

- Public disclosure of donations to parties of more than £5,000 (or more than £1,000 to parties locally)
- A £20 million cap on any party's general election campaign spending
- An end to 'blind trusts'
- A ban on foreign donations by non-citizens
- A ban on anonymous donations to political parties of more than £50
- Scrutiny of nominations for honours where nominees have donated more than £5,000 to a political party within the last five years
- An independent and impartial Electoral Commission to monitor the new regulations
- More public money to finance political parties in Parliament

exemption of F1 events from bans on tobacco companies sponsoring sporting events was thought to reflect his influence. The problems surrounding party donations led to the Labour government establishing the Neill Committee on party funding, which reported in 1998.

Most of the Neill report recommendations were implemented, including the establishment of the impartial Electoral Commission. Labour hoped that more transparency would end allegations of sleaze. Instead, the publication of donations has made it easier for journalists to allege some connection between gifts and a possible impact on policy. Publicity given to some donors has also sometimes upset party members. Thus in 2002 the revelation that the new owner of the *Express* group of newspapers had given the Labour Party £120,000 aroused anger from party members (including some ministers) that the party had accepted money from an individual who also owned a number of pornographic publications.

Such scandals have led to renewed interest in another possible source of party finance – state funding, ultimately out of taxation. Some countries

already use such state funding. In the UK there is already some limited state financial help for opposition parties to fund their administration and policy research. This problem was addressed in 1975 by the then Labour government which introduced payments to opposition parties to enable them to carry out their parliamentary role more effectively.

More controversial is the notion of state funding for party election expenditure and party propaganda generally. Particularly with the current emphasis on image and marketing it may be argued that the best-financed parties have a distinct advantage. In the past the Conservative Party regularly outspent the Labour Party, but these two far exceeded the financial resources of other parties. In 1997 Labour almost matched Conservative spending (£25.7 million to £28.3 million), while the Liberal Democrats spent just £2.3 million.

In the 2001 general election, under the new rules administered by the Electoral Commission set up following legislation in 2000, the Conservatives spent £12,751,813, Labour £10,945,119, and the Liberal Democrats only £1,361,377, which was less than double the £693,274 of the tiny UK Independence Party. In the 2005 election, according to the Electoral Commission's Report, both the two main parties spent nearly £18million, with Labour slightly outspending the Conservatives and the Liberal Democrats spending £4.3million. By 2010 it appears that the Conservatives comfortably outspent Labour, both in the period leading up to the election, and in the campaign itself. Particularly controversial were the large sums donated by the non-domiciled Conservative peer, Lord Ashcroft, directed at the crucial marginal constituencies.

## The future of the British party system

Will the 2010 election prove a decisive turning point in the fortunes of British political parties and, perhaps, the party system as a whole? 1997 was a landmark election that redrew the British political map, in ways which were seemingly confirmed in 2001 and, with some significant exceptions, 2005. Eighteen years of Conservative Party dominance had given place to 13 years of Labour dominance, although in both cases this was exaggerated by the vagaries of the electoral system (see Chapter 5), and the divisions and sometimes poor leadership of the main opposition party. Thus the Conservative Party appeared in total disarray, seemingly unable to present a credible challenge from 1997 to 2005. Yet the 2005 election did involve some significant shifts in party allegiances. Labour won a substantial working majority on just 35 per cent of the vote, less than any party gaining a majority of seats had ever secured. It no longer held most seats in England, being dependent on the votes of Labour MPs from Scotland and Wales, a significant development in view of the devolution of power that had transferred some services and issues to Edinburgh and Cardiff. Moreover, while some Labour supporters were still prepared to vote tactically for Liberal Democrats to keep out the Conservatives in relevant seats, Labour was no longer benefiting much from similar tactical voting by Liberal Democrats after the Iraq war. Yet although those two parties were now further apart than they had been, there were few signs then of a potential coalition between the Liberal Democrats and the Conservatives. Even if the 2005 election had produced a hung parliament (a possible outcome that would have better reflected the distribution of the popular vote), it is difficult to imagine a Conservative-Liberal Democrat coalition headed by their then party leaders, Michael Howard and Charles Kennedy.

Developments in the 2005–10 parliament involved significant changes in all three parties and the relations between them. Changes in the leadership of all of them made a difference. Brown lacked the breadth of appeal and communication skills of Blair. Clegg initially made less of an impact than his predecessors, Ashdown and Kennedy, although he moved the Liberal Democrats to a more equidistant relationship with the other two parties before improving his own and his party's fortunes in the election campaign. Cameron substantially transformed his party's image and prospects, and made an early pitch for liberal support by emphasizing his own progressive credentials. Thus even before the election a Conservative–Liberal Democrat coalition was no longer unthinkable, and indeed was already foreshadowed by local government coalitions in cities such as Birmingham and Leeds.

The 2010 General Election (see Chapter 5) showed few signs of rejection of the old parties and the old politics that some had predicted. In terms of seats, fringe parties failed to make a breakthrough, apart from the solitary Green victory in Brighton. Independents did badly. Representation in England especially is still through long-established political parties. There seems little imminent prospect of the party-less democracy some commentators have talked about. Even so, outside the diminishing ranks of the party faithful, there is little enthusiasm for the old parties.

Can the Conservative–Liberal Democrat coalition that emerged from the 2010 election last, and what impact will it have on the future of British parties and the party system generally? The coalition may survive a full Parliament. Liberal Democrats, in government for the first time since the war, can hardly dare precipitate another early election for which they are financially ill-prepared, unless severely provoked. Cameron and the Conservatives have more incentive to try to secure an overall majority, but would find it difficult to engineer a dissolution without accusations of bad faith after the compact agreed between the two parties. In any case the Liberal Democrats remain useful to Cameron in keeping his own party under control and providing a convenient scapegoat for popular resentment against coalition policies. While Conservative support has substantially held up it is the Liberal Democrats who have aroused more opprobrium for spending cuts and broken promises.

Yet a lasting coalition would frustrate Conservatives keen to advance their own party agenda, and also the ambitions of many Conservative MPs, effectively deprived of government office by the need to accommodate the Liberal Democrats. They, in turn, would be threatened with the loss of their separate party identity if they became perpetual junior partners in a Conservative-dominated coalition. To maintain their independence it is essential for the Liberal Democrats to keep their options open, including the possibility of a future alliance with Labour (which many of their activists and some of their MPs would still prefer). That this could be possible is shown by the example of the German Free Democrats, who have formed coalitions with both the major parties in Germany over decades. Yet while this has given the Free Democrats a fairly regular share in government it has scarcely advanced their electoral fortunes overall.

Thus the role of junior coalition partner may not advance Liberal Democrat dreams of an electoral breakthrough eventually perhaps allowing them to form a government of their own. Indeed, after the first full year in government, it was the Liberal Democrats who bore the brunt of unpopular coalition decisions and spending cuts, with substantial losses in local council elections in England and elections for the Scottish Parliament and Welsh Assembly in May 2011. Overall they experienced their worst results for decades, threatening a return to fringe party status. Whether this slump in their support can be checked may depend on the speed and extent of economic recovery (see Chapter 20).

As for Labour, much will depend on how far the party is able to renew itself in opposition under the leadership of Ed Miliband. It is unlikely to repeat the divisions that plagued Labour in the 1950s and 1980s. There is no longer a substantial Labour left with a credible alternative leader. The Blairite–Brownite divisions, never primarily about policy, have largely evaporated with the departure of the personalities involved. Labour, however, may have problems in rebranding itself, now that New Labour, as both Milibands recognized, is over.

Labour will not be helped by the planned reduction in the size of the House of Commons and new constituency boundaries, which are expected to help the Conservatives. A bigger problem for Labour may be retaining or regaining its old power bases in Scotland and Wales. Scots and Welsh have been prominent in the Labour Party from its foundation until the demise of the Brown government, in which the Prime Minister and his Chancellor were both Scots who sat for Scottish constituencies. Until 2009 the Speaker of

the House of Commons was also a Scot (and a Glaswegian Labour MP). Although Labour did relatively well in Scotland, and not badly in Wales in the 2010 election, it is perhaps significant that the subsequent 2010 Labour leadership election was contested by English and largely London-based politicians. There is a chance that both the Westminster parliament, and perhaps the Labour Party itself, will be increasingly viewed by Scots and Welsh as essentially English and alien. To regain power Labour has to renew itself in Scotland and Wales as well as England.

While Labour did well in the elections for the Welsh Assembly in 2011, the elections for the Scottish Parliament were a disaster, with substantial losses to the SNP, whose 2007 narrow minority administration under Alex Salmond was triumphantly returned with a remarkable overall majority (see Chapter 16). This paves the way for an independence referendum. Needless to say, if Scotland became independent, and no longer sent MPs to Westminster, Labour's hopes of ever forming a government again would be much weaker. Polls still suggest there is still insufficient support in Scotland to end the Union, but it does now seem a distinct possibility.

Further electoral reform for UK general elections might have changed calculations, but this is now off the agenda for the foreseeable future following the 'no' vote in the 2011 referendum on the Alternative Vote, to the great satisfaction of Cameron and his party. A more proportional electoral system would make multi-party politics and coalition government the norm in the United Kingdom, as it in many other countries. As it is, without electoral reform and on recent voting trends (see Chapter 5) a return to two party dominance and single party government seems rather more likely, at least for the UK government and parliament.

# SUMMARY

- Political parties fulfil important functions in modern representative democracies.

- Although the Conservative and Labour parties still largely dominate politics at Westminster and have monopolized UK government since the Second World War, multi-party systems and coalition government are now a feature of devolved parliaments and assemblies and many local councils.

- Party leaders have considerable influence over policy and strategy. An effective and credible leader seems to be crucial for a party's electoral prospects. Methods of choosing new leaders and challenging existing leaders are therefore important and often controversial. All major parties have moved towards involving ordinary members in leadership elections, although the Conservatives are having second thoughts.

- Parliamentary parties are often accused of being too subservient to the party leadership. There are strong inducements to loyalty, not least because divided parties do not prosper. Even so, MPs are becoming more rebellious.

- Party conferences are not generally occasions for important political decisions, and now only rarely involve major controversy. All parties now seem to use their party conferences as, primarily, opportunities for promoting the party, its policies and leading personalities.

- Parties in Britain, as elsewhere, have experienced a significant decline in their active membership. Fewer than one in 40 voters are now party members. It is questionable how far British parties can still be described as mass parties. Party members are predominantly elderly and in other respects unrepresentative of the wider population.

- Local constituency members normally choose candidates for parliamentary and other elections, and have more recently been given a role in leadership elections. Their influence on policy is less easy to assess. In so far as members are influential they may damage a party's electoral prospects, as the views of party activists are generally untypical of those of voters.

- Parties need money to compete effectively, but their finances are very unequal. Subscriptions from a diminishing membership are inadequate, and parties rely on donations from corporate bodies (particularly business firms and trade unions) and from rich individuals, leading to concerns over the purchase of influence. Reforms have made party funding more transparent, but this has raised further questions about the sources of party finance. One possible solution is state funding of political parties.

- The 2010 election, leading to the first coalition in Britain since the war, has potentially massive significance for the future of British parties and the party system.

# QUESTIONS FOR DISCUSSION

- Could modern representative democracy operate successfully without political parties?

- Is Britain's former two-party system now defunct?

- Why might more internal party democracy possibly risk adverse electoral consequences?

- In what sense, if any, are British political parties still mass parties?

- What are the arguments for and against the state funding of political parties?

- To what extent is Britain experiencing a significant party realignment? What implications does the Conservative–Liberal Democrat coalition have for the future of the British party system?

- Is party-less democracy a realistic prospect?

# FURTHER READING

Useful but now inevitably rather dated books on British political parties include Garner and Kelly (1998), *British Political Parties Today*; Ingle (2000), *The British Party System*; Webb (2000), *The Modern British Party System*. The chapter by Sarah Childs in Dunleavy *et al.* (2006) is excellent, but like other source requires updating.

More specialist books include a, now dated, dissection of Conservative party members, *True Blues* (1994) by Whiteley, Seyd, and Richardson, and a rather more recent broader dissection of party activism in Britain by Seyd and Whiteley (2002). Bale (2010) is the most useful source on Cameron's Conservative party. Still worth consulting on the Labour party is Lewis Minkin's (1992) monumental study of the *Contentious Alliance* between the unions and Labour, and Eric Shaw's analy-

sis of *The Labour Party since 1945* (1996). New Labour can be explored through Fielding (2003), Ludlam and Smith (2001, 2004), Coates (2005), and Beech and Simon (2008). See also Rawnsley (2001, 2010). Useful sources for updating include journals such as *The Political Quarterly, British Politics, Politics Review* and most recently *Political Insight.* Party websites can also be consulted, including www.conservative-party.org.uk, www.labour.org.uk and www.libdems.org.uk. The Electoral Commission is a key source on party funding and electoral competition.

A useful introduction to the comparative study of parties is Chapter 10 in Hague and Harrop (2010). Chapter 5 in Bale (2008) is good on European political parties and party systems.

CHAPTER **7** # Ideologies, Parties and Interests

The importance of political ideas and rival political ideologies has been briefly explored in Chapter 1. Here we consider the relationship between ideologies, political parties and material interests. Ideologies are commonly linked to political parties (see Chapter 6) and this chapter seeks to explore in more depth the competing mainstream ideologies of liberalism, conservatism and socialism in British politics and the changing interests they represent. While these ideologies transcend national boundaries, their British interpretations are distinctive and have evolved over time, along with their internal tensions and differences. We review how far they have converged or remain distinctive. The formation of a Conservative–Liberal Democrat coalition has ideological implications (potentially lasting) for both parties and for the Labour opposition.

We conclude with a discussion of other ideological perspectives that are outside the traditional mainstream, including feminism, nationalism, racism and green thinking, some of which cut across or transcend the traditional 'left–right' ideological spectrum and have increasing implications for British government and politics. While some of these other ideologies also find expression in political parties, others are more clearly linked with pressure groups and less formally constituted broad political movements (see Chapter 8).

## Ideology and pragmatism

Some argue that ideas are not so important in British politics, which is often associated with pragmatism and common sense. Thus many Conservatives distrust abstract theory, and have a positive aversion to ideology, while Labour, never a Marxist party, has largely avoided the doctrinal debates of socialists and social democrats elsewhere. New Labour emphasized its pragmatism in the slogan 'What matters is what works'.

Yet politics requires both ideology and pragmatism. Politics can hardly be conducted without reference to values and principles (or ideology), but it also requires flexibility and compromise (or pragmatism) in pursuit of ideological goals. Indeed, a dogmatic insistence on pragmatism, and a denial of the possibility of radical change based on clear principles, reflects distinctive ideological assumptions over human nature, behaviour and motivation, and the scope and limitations of government.

## Mainstream ideologies and political parties in Britain

Accounts of political ideologies may include creeds such as nationalism, fascism, feminism, anarchism

## BOX 7.1

# Core liberal values

- **Individualism.** Liberal analysis starts with individual men and women, rather than nations, races or classes. Individuals, it is assumed, pursue their own self-interest. The interests or rights of individuals take priority over society or the state, which is only the sum of individuals composing it. Social behaviour is explained in terms of some fairly basic assumptions about individual human psychology.
- **Liberty (or freedom).** Individuals must be free to pursue their own self-interest. Liberals demand full freedom of thought and expression, and particularly religious toleration. Yet liberals have often differed over the interpretation of freedom. Early liberals emphasized freedom *from* tyranny and oppressive government (negative liberty) and championed the free market. In the early twentieth century New Liberals

sought freedom *to* fulfil individual potential (positive liberty), which might require state welfare services and state intervention to secure full employment.
- **Rationalism.** Liberals assume humans are rational creatures who are the best judge of their own self-interest. Many liberals followed Bentham in assuming that the universal pursuit of rational self-interest would promote the greatest happiness of the greatest number.
- **Political and legal equality.** Liberals generally emphasized an equality of worth, advocating equality before the law and political equality. In the economic sphere liberals have advocated equality of opportunity, but not equality of outcome. Indeed freedom in the economic sphere has commonly resulted in marked inequality.

and environmentalism (or green thinking), but they commonly focus chiefly on three 'mainstream' ideologies: liberalism, conservatism and socialism. In Britain these ideologies can be linked with three significant political parties: the Liberals (and today's Liberal Democrats), the Conservatives and Labour. Yet it is a mistake to identify ideologies wholly with the parties with which they are linked. Those who call themselves socialists, both within and outside the British Labour Party, often disagree passionately over the nature and definition of socialism. Some would deny that Labour is, or ever has been, a socialist party. Similarly, both Conservatives and Liberals agonize over the true meaning of conservatism and liberalism. Such debates suggest some ideal conception of conservatism, liberalism and socialism against which the programmes, policies and performance of parties can be measured.

This implies it might be better to examine political ideologies without linking them to parties. Yet this would not do either. The key point about political ideologies, as opposed to traditional political theory, is that they are 'action-oriented'; they have implications for political behaviour. Political parties are key vehicles for translating ideas into practice. Thus parties which call themselves 'liberal'

seek to bring about, over time, their own version of a liberal society.

Moreover, political ideologies are expressed at a number of levels – by leading thinkers, by practising politicians who adapt the ideas of more original minds in speeches and slogans, by parties in election manifestos and programmes, and by the masses, if often in simplified and perhaps vulgarized form. Indeed, some ideologies, such as nationalism, or fascism, are fairly thin in theoretical terms. While there are some important theoretical sources for British conservatism, much of it has to be inferred from the policy and practice of the British Conservative Party. So it is neither possible nor desirable to separate the study of mainstream political ideologies from their distinctive and sometimes highly contested expression by political parties.

## Liberalism

### Core interests and values of liberalism

It is particularly important not to identify liberalism entirely with the British Liberal party and modern Liberal Democrats, as liberal ideas have been so influential that they have permeated all

# Key thinker: John Stuart Mill

John Stuart Mill (1806–73) survived an intensive education supervised by his father, James Mill, that turned him into an infant prodigy and provoked an early mental breakdown, to become the leading nineteenth-century liberal thinker, and a continuing source of inspiration to modern liberals. His essay *On Liberty* (1859) was a passionate plea for full freedom of expression and toleration of difference. His *Considerations on Representative Government* (1861) advocated the principle and practice of representative democracy, which Mill thought required extensive citizen participation beyond simply voting. Unlike his father, Mill argued that the vote should not be confined to males. As an MP he introduced a bill to give votes to women. His feminism was influenced by his intellectual partnership with Harriet Taylor, whom he subsequently married. In *The Subjection of Women* (1869) he compared the condition of Victorian wives to that of black slaves, denounced the violence and abuse suffered by many women, and advocated full and equal partnership between the sexes. His writings on political economy show a gradual shift from orthodox free market economics towards some sympathy with trade unionism and even socialism.

mainstream British political parties. The term liberalism was not commonly used until the nineteenth century. However, the foundations of European liberal thought are much older, springing from the religious reformations of the sixteenth and seventeenth centuries, the eighteenth-century enlightenment, the French revolution, but most of all from the economic, social and political transformation brought about over time by industrialization. Indeed the growth of liberalism is closely linked with the growth of capitalism, representative democracy, and the modern world. In that sense it is the hegemonic ideology of the modern age.

Liberalism has been closely linked with the class interests of the industrial bourgeoisie (capitalists, or more loosely, the middle class). In early nineteenth-century Britain, following the arguments of classical economists such as Smith and Ricardo, liberals championed the free market and free trade, and opposed government intervention in the economy. Thus they saw a very limited role for the state, summed up in the French expression *laissez-faire* – suggesting government should refrain from interfering with individual freedom and the beneficial operation of free market forces. Their political programme involved an extension of the vote and parliamentary representation to the new industrial centres, leading to a gradual transfer of power and influence from the old landowning aristocracy to the manufacturing classes.

Yet to achieve power Liberals increasingly had to appeal to a wider constituency, including the growing ranks of the professions and the skilled working class. The Liberal Party that Gladstone led, four times as Prime Minister, contained an awkward coalition of old Whig landowners and successful businessmen, supported by middle- and working-class religious nonconformists who favoured radical reform. This helps to explain some of the tensions within British liberalism as it evolved in the course of the nineteenth century. While early, or classical, liberalism advocated limited constitutional government and free markets, subsequently British liberalism became identified with full representative democracy, as advocated by John Stuart Mill. However, the extension of the vote to the working classes increased pressures for more state intervention, for example, to provide free education for all children. Some liberals, such as Herbert Spencer (1820–1903) still vehemently opposed such state intervention.

## The New Liberalism

Mill was a transitional figure between the classical free market liberalism and the interventionist New Liberalism of the late nineteenth and early twentieth centuries. New Liberals such as T. H. Green, Leonard Hobhouse and John Hobson argued that state intervention was not a restriction on liberty,

BOX 7.2

## Maurice Duverger on the problems faced by centre parties

The French political scientist Maurice Duverger (1964, p. 215) has trenchantly observed 'The fate of the Centre is to be torn asunder, buffeted and annihilated: torn asunder when one of its halves votes Right and the other Left, buffeted when it votes as a Group first Right then Left, annihilated when it abstains from voting.' Duverger's point applied to centre parties in general. It is certainly a fair description of the unhappy predicament of the British Liberal party from the 1920s through to the 1960s. It is still a problem for today's Liberal Democrats holding the balance in a hung parliament.

but would enlarge the freedom of each individual to make the most of their own potential. The Liberal government of 1906–14 introduced old age pensions, labour exchanges and health and unemployment insurance, and laid some of the foundations for the welfare state.

The First World War split the Liberal party, which declined rapidly. Many former Liberals moved to the Conservatives or Labour, and by the 1950s the party was reduced to just six MPs in the House of Commons. Yet New Liberal ideas permeated the other parties. Keynes and Beveridge, whose work and thought underpinned the post-Second World War political consensus, were both small and large 'l' liberals (see Chapter 2). The inspiration of the policies pursued by post-war Labour and Conservative governments arguably owed more to New Liberalism than to traditional conservative or socialist thinking.

### Neo-liberalism

Ironically, when this ideological consensus was challenged in the 1970s, the challenge came from a revival of an older version of liberalism, the free market liberalism derived from Adam Smith and the classical economists. This 'neo-liberalism' (not to be confused with New Liberalism) was energetically promoted by key thinkers such as Hayek and Friedman and taken up by Conservative politicians such as Keith Joseph and Margaret Thatcher. Thus the second half of the twentieth century in Britain can be interpreted as much as a conflict between different versions of liberalism as a battle between conservatism and socialism.

### Liberalism and the Liberal Democrats

Meanwhile the Liberal party achieved a modest revival of fortunes, initially on its own and then, from 1981, in alliance with a breakaway party from Labour, the Social Democratic Party (SDP). This culminated in a merger to form the current Liberal Democrats, which after an uncertain start has become an established third force in British politics. The Liberal Democrats retain a characteristic liberal interest in individual rights and civil liberties, support for New Liberal type welfare policies, a strong commitment to constitutional reform (particularly devolution and electoral reform) and an internationalist, humanitarian approach in foreign affairs. They preserve links with other liberal parties around the world and form part of the Alliance of Liberals and Democrats for Europe in the European Parliament.

The Liberals and their Liberal Democrat successors have long been associated with the centre ground of British politics, occupying a middle position on the ideological spectrum between the Labour left and Conservative right. A centre party can sometimes appear to occupy a rather difficult and uncomfortable position in politics (see Box 7.2).

Yet some leading Liberal and Liberal Democrat politicians, and many party activists, saw themselves on the left rather than the centre. Indeed, the progressive New Liberal tradition of the British party has long appeared to place them well to the left of some of their continental cousins. This perception has been somewhat strengthened by the Liberal alliance and subsequent merger with the

Social Democratic Party (SDP), and by the Liberal Democrats' co-operation with Labour on devolution and other issues before and after the 1997 election (see Chapter 10). It was the party's united opposition to the 2003 Iraq war that sharply divided Liberal Democrats from both major parties and this radical stance helped the Liberal Democrats win some seats from Labour in 2005.

Yet changes in the party's leadership led to some shift in emphasis. After the departure in rapid succession of Charles Kennedy in 2006 and Menzies Campbell in 2007, the party narrowly elected a former Liberal Democrat MEP, Nick Clegg, who was not well-known by the wider public and only elected to Westminster in 2005. Clegg followed a series of Liberal and Liberal Democrat leaders (Steel, Ashdown, Kennedy and Campbell) who were clearly ideologically closer to Labour than the Conservatives but he favoured a more equidistant relationship with the other two parties.

There was already a growing ideological debate within the party, which had echoes of the argument between free market Liberals and New Liberals a century or more ago. Thus a party pressure group Liberal Future challenged the commitment to tax and spend policies. David Laws called for a return to economic liberalism, and co-edited an influential book of essays *The Orange Book: Reclaiming Liberalism* (Marshall and Laws, 2004) to which Clegg, Chris Huhne and Vince Cable contributed. According to Gray (2010b, p.3) the aim was 'to reaffirm a version of liberalism they believed had been lost: one in which support for small government and the free market goes with a strong commitment to civil liberties and freedom of lifestyle'. Gray goes on to cite a speech made by Clegg at the London School of Economics in January 2008 where he rejected the social democratic strand in liberalism. While 'the state was necessary to secure a proper funding of public services ... once it had done that, government should "back off" and allow services to be provided privately'. Gray observes that 'Clegg and his fellow market liberals were engineering a fundamental reorientation in the party's values'.

In the lead-up to the 2010 election the party apparently reaffirmed its commitment to social justice and progressive taxation. Thus it remained solidly opposed to raising university tuition fees, and committed to their ultimate abolition, a pledge signed by its candidates that won support for the party from many students. However, following their entry into Cameron's coalition government, Clegg and his fellow Liberal Democrat ministers have moved away from the centre-left project of Blair and Ashdown. They accepted the case for faster and deeper public spending cuts to reduce the budget deficit, departing from an economic policy that seemed closer to Labour before the election. They now appear to endorse the Conservatives' smaller state agenda, accepting the end of universal Child Benefit, and the sharp rise in university tuition fees that they were pledged to abolish. Unsurprisingly, many backbench Liberal Democrat MPs as well as party members and supporters in the country are increasingly unhappy about the direction of their party.

While both coalition partners have made concessions, it is the Liberal Democrats who face the bigger risk of losing their separate party identity. Indeed, past coalitions between Liberal Unionists and Conservative before the First World War and between national Liberals and Conservatives in the 1930s led to their absorption by the Conservatives. It will take determination for the party to maintain its independence and its readiness to seek other coalition partners in different circumstances. Yet the Liberal Democrats in government seem increasingly locked into the ideological agenda of the Conservative leadership, and it could take a major new upheaval within the party to recreate any prospects for a Lib-Lab combination.

# Conservatism

## Traditional conservatism

There are significant internal tensions and contending schools of thought within all major ideologies, which may evolve and change considerably over time. This should be borne in mind in relation to modern **conservatism**. Those more

---

● **Conservatism** suggests 'conserving', keeping things as they are, resisting radical change. It implies a defence of the existing social and political order and of traditional institutions. However, British conservatives are prepared to accept limited reform that grows out of the past.

## Key thinker: Edmund Burke and the conservative tradition

Edmund Burke (1729–97), a lifelong Whig politician, is now regarded as a key source of inspiration for conservatives. Like all Whigs he celebrated the Glorious Revolution of 1688 that had expelled James II and established limited constitutional monarchy. Like most Whigs he also supported the American revolution. However, he broke with the leaders of his own party over the French revolution, which he condemned in his critical essay *Reflections on the Revolution in France* (1790). Here he argued for gradual reform that would grow out of tradition, rather than radical revolution inspired by 'naked reason'. His hostility to radical change, his reverence for tradition and his suspicion of rationalism became key elements of conservative ideas (as, for example, outlined by the twentieth-century conservative thinker, Michael Oakeshott (1901–90).

familiar with the free market ideas embraced by leading modern British Conservatives may be surprised to learn that in the 1950s and 1960s Conservative governments accepted the principles of Keynesian demand management, the welfare state, the mixed economy and even a form of economic planning (including incomes policy). Mrs Thatcher and her successors rejected much of this One Nation conservatism in pursuing neo-liberal or New Right free market ideas. While there were important elements of continuity between Thatcherism and older conservative thinking, Mrs Thatcher's leadership marked a watershed in the development of British conservatism. However, older interpretations of conservatism are not just of historical interest, but reflect continuing strands of thought within the party, some of which are evident in Cameron's party.

Whereas early liberalism favoured change and reform, nineteenth-century conservatism was generally suspicious of, and resistant to, change. The Conservative party in Britain emerged from the old Tory party that originated in the seventeenth century. Tories supported the monarchy and the Church of England, and defended the rights and interests of landowners. While liberalism was a product of the eighteenth-century enlightenment, the American and French revolutions, and, most of all, industrial capitalism, Toryism and subsequently conservatism involved a reaction against all these. It was suspicious of the 'age of reason' and the threat

this seemed to present to traditional religious and secular authority. It was hostile to the language of freedom, equality and fraternity. It was fearful of many of the changes resulting from industrialization and the ideas associated with it. The eighteenth-century politician and writer Edmund Burke expressed many of these ideas.

If liberalism was (initially at least) the ideology of the rising capitalist class, Toryism and conservatism at first reflected the interests of the declining but still powerful landed interest. Conservatives sought to maintain the current economic, social and political order against the pressures for change that could only result in a decline in their influence and power. Yet, had conservatism remained wedded to a declining landed interest, it would have fast faded as a political creed. Instead, it held its own in conflict with liberalism in the nineteenth century and proceeded to dominate twentieth-century politics in Britain. It achieved this remarkable success by flexible adaptation to new circumstances, although it can also be argued that some of its core principles have been fairly consistently maintained.

Thus, although British Conservatives have opposed radical change, they have not generally been reactionary. They have often subsequently accepted changes introduced by their political opponents rather than seeking to put the clock back, and indeed have sometimes initiated gradual reforms themselves. Flexibility, gradualism (a preference for gradual rather than radical reform) and pragmatism have been key aspects of British conservatism in action for most of the last two centuries.

To survive, Conservatives had to seek a wider base of support as the franchise was progressively extended to the middle classes, skilled workers and then the entire adult population. Increasingly, the Conservative party came to be identified with the interests of property in general, rather than landed property, winning the support of many business-men who once supported the Liberals. Moreover, from the late nineteenth century the Conservatives under Benjamin Disraeli and subsequent leaders made a determined attempt to woo the working classes, particularly skilled workers, through social reform at home, combined with the pursuit of British national and imperial interests abroad (Beer, 1982a). In the course of the twentieth century they also sought to give the workers an increased stake in property through encouraging home ownership and wider share ownership.

Their political opponents saw this as a patent 'con trick', to persuade those with little or no prop-erty to support the Conservative cause and reject policies of social reform and redistribution advo-cated by socialists. Conservatives themselves have generally argued that the various classes are bound together by ties of mutual dependence in an organic society, which is more than the sum of its individual parts. This organic theory of society and the state (derived from Burke) has often been contrasted with the individualism of liberalism. Disraeli had sought to transcend class differences and create 'one nation'. He argued that wealth carries with it obligations, including an obligation to assist those less fortunate. This 'paternalism' might entail a duty of voluntary charity, or an acceptance of state-sponsored social reform.

Such an approach marks off traditional conser-vatism from older forms of liberalism. While early liberals thought individual human beings could achieve social progress by pursuing their own rational self-interest in a free market, traditional conservatives did not generally share this optimistic faith in human reason, goodness and progress. Conservatism has been described as a 'philosophy of imperfection' (Quinton, 1978). Most conserva-tives do not believe in the perfectability of humankind, but rather assume that there is an 'evil

streak' (which Christians might describe as 'original sin') in human nature. This implies a need for authority – a strong state and strong government to maintain law and order and restrain violent and anti-social behaviour (Leach, 2009, pp. 54–67).

Thus conservatives were once far from being enthusiastic supporters of the free market and free trade. They supported the protection of British agriculture and 'fair trade' as opposed to 'free trade' in the nineteenth century. In the early twentieth century the party was converted by Joseph Chamberlain to tariff reform and 'imperial prefer-ence', a policy which his son Neville Chamberlain sought to put into practice as Chancellor and later Prime Minister in the Conservative-dominated National Government of the 1930s (Beer, 1982a, chapter 10).

In the post-Second World War era modernizers in the Conservative party adopted Disraeli's 'one nation' slogan to embrace social reform and state intervention. This One Nation conservatism became the new party orthodoxy. Thus Conservative governments between 1951 and 1964, particularly that of Harold Macmillan (1957–63), supported Keynesian demand management, state welfare provision, the mixed economy, and consen-sus and compromise in industrial relations. These policies did not seem far removed from those of the Labour Party. Indeed, Macmillan had written a book entitled *The Middle Way* in the thirties and had once provocatively declared that conservatism was a kind of paternal socialism. For some modern Conservatives this whole period is an aberration in the long history of the party, although for others it remains the very essence of the authentic Tory and Conservative tradition (Gilmour, 1992, 1997). Yet according to one influential interpretation, British conservatism involves an ongoing tension between two rival libertarian and collectivist strands of thought, with each appearing to be dominant at different periods (Greenleaf, 1973, 1983).

## Thatcherism and the New Right

The controversy over the nature of conservatism is at the heart of the continuing debate over the modern Conservative party. It is difficult to discuss conservatism after 1975 without extensive reference to the lady who gave her name to a political

## Key thinker: Hayek, neo-liberalism and the New Right

Friedrich von Hayek (1899–1992), born in Austria, spent much of his working life teaching in Britain at the London School of Economics. He was a fervent opponent of economic planning, not only Soviet communist planning but also the moderate state intervention favoured by social democrats, New Liberals and One Nation Conservatives. State interference with the free market informed *The Road to Serfdom* (1944). Hayek's ideas were later taken up with enthusiasm by Margaret Thatcher, Keith Joseph and the New Right in both Britain and America. Significantly, Hayek described himself as a liberal rather than a conservative, but his liberalism was the older free market *laissez-faire* liberalism of the nineteenth century, rather than the social liberalism advocated by many twentieth-century liberals.

doctrine, Thatcherism. For some, Margaret Thatcher and her allies hijacked the Conservative Party, and introduced alien individualist free market ideas at odds with the One Nation tradition of social reform (Gilmour, 1978, 1992, 1997). For others, Thatcherism involved the rediscovery of true conservatism. Yet both critics and true believers perhaps exaggerated the break with the immediate past.

Margaret Thatcher is widely regarded as a conviction politician, who broke with the consensus politics of the post-war era, and rejected traditional conservative pragmatism for the ideology of the free market and competition. There is clearly some truth in this picture. Under Margaret Thatcher's leadership the neo-liberal ideas of Hayek and Friedman became the new orthodoxy. Keynesian demand management was rejected and Adam Smith's 'invisible hand' of the free market restored to favour. Many of the policies pursued by her governments, such as the sale of council houses, the privatization of the nationalized industries, the injection of competition into the public sector, and the attempts to 'rein back' the state and cut public spending and taxation, reflected free market ideas (Kavanagh, 1990).

Yet Thatcherism can be seen as the consequence rather than the cause of the breakdown of Keynesianism and the post-war consensus. Keynesian policies had been applied with some apparent success in the post-war decades, but by the late 1970s they no longer seemed to work, and

had been effectively abandoned by Callaghan's Labour government. Similarly, concerns over the growth of government, the cost of the welfare state, trade union power and poor industrial relations were already widespread before Mrs Thatcher became leader of the Conservative party in 1975. The party and its new leader adapted to altered circumstances as British Conservatives had managed so successfully in the past.

Moreover, while in office (1979–90) Thatcher was generally more pragmatic and cautious than is sometimes imagined. Thus, although she embraced the rhetoric of the free market with some fervour, she declared that the National Health Service is 'safe in our hands', rejected the privatization of British Rail and the Post Office, and continued policies of state-financed urban regeneration (while slashing regional aid). Despite some real cuts in spending programmes and significant changes in the distribution of taxation, Conservative governments after 1979 were not particularly successful in reducing public spending and the overall burden of taxation. The state was restructured rather than 'reined back'. It was only more towards the end of her premiership that she dogmatically and disastrously pursued policies such as the poll tax (incautiously described as 'the flagship of Thatcherism') which ultimately helped to bring her down (see Chapter 17).

Indeed, the ideology of Thatcherism or the New Right is best seen not as a pure free market

**Image 7.1  Margaret Thatcher, Prime Minister 1979–90**

The inspiration for 'Thatcherism'. Although not a particularly original thinker herself, she enthusiastically embraced the free market ideas of others and sought to apply them in government, and dominated the British political scene in the last quarter of the twentieth century.

doctrine but as a blend of these ideas with some traditional conservative elements, a mix of neo-liberalism and neo-conservatism, 'the free economy and the strong state' (Gamble, 1988). Thus 'reining back the state' in the economic sphere did not entail weakening government. On the contrary, Thatcherism involved a reaffirmation of the traditional Tory commitment to strong government, leadership, defence, law and order and the authority of the state. Mrs Thatcher and her successors continued to exploit the sentiments of nationalism and patriotism which had appealed so well in the past to the British electorate, most obviously in relation to the Falklands, the Gulf War and Europe. Both Mrs Thatcher and her successor John Major strongly opposed devolution and continued to champion the Union of the United Kingdom. Both also employed the rhetoric of traditional family values that always played well with their party.

For a period Thatcherism played well with the electorate also. Ideologies are held at various levels. While the sophisticated version of Thatcherism reflected the economic theories of Smith, Hayek and Friedman, the popular version was more about vivid imagery and slogans: 'The Iron Lady', 'Stand on your own two feet', 'The Nanny State', 'Get on your bike' (to look for work). Some of this rhetoric appealed to sections of the working class as well as the Conservative Party rank and file, although the popularity of Thatcherism can be exaggerated. Indeed, parliamentary landslides depended more on the electoral system and weaknesses and divisions in the opposition rather than positive support for Mrs Thatcher's brand of conservatism.

Moreover, this blend of neo-conservative and neo-liberal ideas inevitably involved some tensions and contradictions. One important illustration of the problems of reconciling free market and traditional conservative ideas was over Britain's relations with Europe. Thatcher had supported joining the European Community and was an enthusiastic advocate of the single market, which seemed to fulfil her own free market values. Indeed, membership of the EC had been sold to the Conservative Party and the British people as a 'Common Market' entailing economic benefits for Britain. However, closer European integration threatened another core Conservative value, national and parliamentary sovereignty. Conservative schizophrenia over Europe was intensified by the Maastricht Treaty, signed by John Major, and subsequently the issues of monetary union and the European constitution.

Altogether, Thatcherism and Margaret Thatcher herself were rather more compatible with the mainstream Tory and Conservative tradition than is sometimes imagined. Even so, in one respect at least Mrs Thatcher was untypical. Her instincts were radical rather than gradualist. She was a warrior rather than a healer. She was impatient with dissent to the extent of quarrelling not only with ideological opponents within her party but with many of her earlier allies, including Nigel Lawson and Geoffrey Howe. Ultimately she was brought down by a coalition of the enemies she had made in the Cabinet and on the back benches, yet the bitterness caused by the circumstances of her departure has left a legacy of internal division in a party whose loyalty was once declared its secret weapon.

The strength of conservatism in the past has been its flexible pragmatism, its ability to adapt to new circumstances. While it might be fairly claimed that Mrs Thatcher successfully reinter-preted conservatism for a new age, she made it more difficult for her successors to perform a similar feat. Her own influence helped tip the scales against candidates for the leadership who might have changed direction – Heseltine, Clarke and Portillo – in favour of those more likely to protect her legacy – Major, Hague, Duncan Smith and Howard.

## Conservatism from Major to Howard

John Major's political style was more consensual, but otherwise his premiership did not mark a significant break from Thatcherism, although Mrs Thatcher herself became sufficiently disappointed with her chosen successor to effectively disown him. Yet apart from scrapping the poll tax, Major continued and extended his predecessor's policies, privatizing the railways, developing the internal market in the health service and competition in schools, pursuing managerial centralization through executive agencies in the civil service, and resisting devolution. Of his own initiatives. the Citizen's Charter was widely if not entirely fairly dismissed as an essentially cosmetic exercise, 'back to basics' was misinterpreted, and local government reorganization disastrously backfired, but none of these could be interpreted as a departure from the Thatcher legacy. He received most criticism from Thatcherite loyalists over Europe who conveniently

forgot that it was Mrs Thatcher who had signed the Single European Act and accepted UK entry into the Exchange Rate Mechanism (Kavanagh and Seldon, 1994).

The next three Conservative leaders neither wished nor dared to challenge the Thatcher legacy. Hague (party leader 1997 to 2001) sought to make the party more internally democratic, while attempting also to promote a more caring, inclusive conservatism. The two aims proved mutually incompatible, aimed at two very different audi-ences, a socially diverse electorate and a dwindling, ageing and unrepresentative party membership whose views on most issues were diametrically opposed to those of the disillusioned ex-voters and new voters the party had to woo. Subsequently neither Duncan Smith (leader 2001–3) nor Howard (leader 2003–5) managed to revive significantly their party's fortunes. Obliged to disown any apparent retreat from Thatcherism, they failed to reinvent conservatism and present a credible alter-native message.

Thus while Mrs Thatcher successfully changed the terms of political debate to the extent that Labour was eventually obliged to accept much of her free market ideology, from 1997 Labour domi-nated the political agenda. Conservatives in turn felt constrained to accept much of Labour's programme from 1997, including Bank of England independence, the minimum wage, devolution and increased spending on public services. On other issues they criticized without conviction, or presenting credible alternatives. After a third successive election defeat in 2005 and the resigna-tion of a third opposition leader who had failed to restore Conservative fortunes there was a growing acceptance within the party that it needed to change to win back support.

## Cameron's Conservatism

Accordingly, Howard's successor David Cameron enjoyed more freedom than his predecessors to reposition and modernize the party, or as commen-tators put it, 'detoxify' the Conservative brand. Thus he promised to maintain Labour's spending on health and education, and particularly empha-sized his full support for the National Health Service. He also distanced himself from

Thatcherism, declaring 'there is such a thing as society' but adding that it was not the same as the state. Thus he could both reaffirm the social concerns of One Nation conservatism, while still maintaining the Thatcherite criticism of 'big government'. Perhaps the initiative that resonated most with the wider public was his enthusiastic embrace of the environmental cause.

Cameron also sought to transform the composition of the Conservative parliamentary party, effectively through more central influence over the selection of parliamentary candidates. Ironically this meant selecting fewer candidates with the upper-class, Eton and Oxbridge background that Cameron himself shared with some of his leading colleagues, and increasing the number of women candidates and those from ethnic minorities. Here the parliamentary expenses scandal (see Chapter 13) contributed to the early retirement of some of the old 'knights of the shire' and aided the recruitment of candidates from a more diverse background, although Cameron encountered some resistance from local Conservative Associations.

Thus Cameron could not altogether avoid the dilemma of his predecessors: how to extend the appeal of the party to the wider public without alienating core supporters. However, Conservative activists were prepared to swallow some unpalatable changes in pursuit of victory. Yet he also had to enthuse his own party, by telling them what they wanted to hear. This he did initially on Europe, giving a 'cast-iron pledge' of a referendum on the Lisbon Treaty, and promising in his leadership election to take Conservative MEPs out of the centre-right European Peoples' Party to join with other more Euro-sceptic MEPs. Both pledges perhaps reflected his own preferences, but could reduce the appeal of UKIP as well as please his own increasingly Euro-sceptic party, yet both later came back to haunt him. He abandoned his pledge of a referendum after the Lisbon Treaty was ratified, handing further ammunition to UKIP. The association of Conservative MEPs with a ragbag of right-wing MEPs from eastern Europe both threatened loss of influence within the European Union, and also invited criticism that some of their new associates were reportedly anti-semitic and/or homophobic.

He also pleased party loyalists and perhaps the wider public on tax. Thus the pledge to slash inheritance tax made by Shadow Chancellor George Osborne was enthusiastically received by the 2007 Conservative Party conference and also seems to have contributed to a surge in public support. Yet this pledge proved a hostage to fortune as the recession took hold, allowing Brown to pillory Cameron and Osborne for promising tax relief to the relatively wealthy at a time when many of those on middle and lower incomes were suffering.

Aware of the changing public mood, Cameron later refrained from giving priority to reversing Labour's increases on income tax for higher earners. At the 2009 party conference both Cameron and Osborne criticized Labour's record on helping the poor and reiterated their own commitment to social justice.

Cameron's slogan in the period leading up to the 2010 election was 'big society, not big government', once more distancing himself from Thatcher as well as Labour. Here he drew on so-called progressive 'red Tory' ideas (Blond, 2010), which in turn seemed heavily dependent on the early twentieth-century Catholic thinkers Hilaire Belloc and G.K. Chesterton, and notions of community, voluntary endeavour and mutual aid rather than state intervention (Raban, 2010). Whether 'empowering people' could effectively replace state action and funding seemed questionable to critics who objected that 'people power will provide cover for the break-up of the welfare state' (Seamus Milne, *The Guardian*, 15 April 2010).

There was still some perceived mismatch between the Conservative promises on taxation and their new progressive social agenda. The response of Cameron and Osborne to the credit crunch and recession was to demand urgent action to cut the mounting government deficit. It was clear that they proposed to do this primarily through cuts in government spending rather than increased taxation. Thus they promised to reverse Labour's planned increase in National Insurance contributions, denouncing it as a 'tax on jobs', proposing instead more 'efficiency savings'.

The conduct of the 2010 election campaign and its failure to secure an overall majority for the Conservatives led to renewed criticism of the Conservative leadership. Many MPs and party

# Mainstream ideologies and industrialization

**Toryism and traditional conservatism** harked back to a pre-industrial, ordered society. Tories sought to protect traditional landed interests and agriculture, were wary of the upheavals involved in industrialization and urbanization, and suspicious of the rising manufacturing and mercantile interests.

**Liberalism** was essentially the ideology of industrial capitalism, and reflected the interests of manufacturing and commerce. Liberals were critical of traditional institutions and values and favoured reforms that would increase the political influence of growing towns and cities, and remove restrictions on trade and enterprise.

**Socialism,** like liberalism, was essentially a product of modern industrial capitalism, but socialism reflected the interests of the growing industrial workforce and sought to overthrow or transform capitalism. Socialists sought a radical redistribution of income and wealth, and favoured a planned rather than a free market economy.

members remained unhappy with the new image and policies of the party and Cameron's close control over it. This criticism was muted once Cameron moved into Downing Street as the Prime Minister of a Conservative-dominated coalition. However, this may have far-reaching implications for the future direction of the party. Concessions to Cameron's junior coalition partners involve a softening of the party's recent marked Euro-scepticism, and some shift in priorities over taxation. Thus there are no early plans to reduce inheritance tax or reverse Labour's tax increases for high earners, while paying for the Liberal Democrat commitment to remove many more pensioners and low earners from income tax involves increases in other taxes (e.g. capital gains tax) that some Conservatives may find painful. The abolition of Child Benefit for higher-rate tax payers and the steep rises in university tuition fees will hurt the middle classes on whose support the Conservatives depend. Yet there are also suggestions that Cameron is not unhappy with the compromises following from coalition politics, and the dropping or postponement of some manifesto pledges. The alliance with the Liberal Democrats helps him reposition his own party, and marginalize the right. Yet only time will tell what Cameron's 'big society' really means and how far his 'progressive Conservatism' differs from that of his predecessors.

## British socialism

### Early socialism

While conservatism involved a defence of traditional social arrangements, and liberalism a justification for moderate constitutional and social reform, European socialism developed as a radical or revolutionary ideology involving a fundamental challenge to both traditional interests and industrial capitalism. As Britain was the first country to industrialize, at some initial cost to the living conditions of the labouring poor, it might appear a fertile environment for revolutionary ideas. Yet the British working class largely rejected the revolutionary movements which swept through much of the European continent.

Robert Owen (1771–1858) secured some popular support for his interpretation of socialism, derived initially from his own experiences of running a model factory, but subsequently from his involvement in early British trade unionism in the 1830s and the co-operative movement from the 1840s. His socialism depended on grass roots working-class self-help rather than the total overthrow of the existing economic and political system demanded by revolutionary socialists. Thus he was criticized by Marx as a 'utopian socialist' with no realistic strategy for achieving socialism. Yet Marx's own socialism found less support in Britain (the country where he spent the bulk of his working life) than in Germany, France, Italy or even (but ultimately especially) Russia.

## Socialism and the Labour Party

The mainstream British version of socialism, the socialism of the Labour party, developed relatively late and was distinctly unusual. Indeed, some question whether it should be called socialism at all. The Labour party was effectively formed in 1900 from an alliance between some trade unions seeking parliamentary representation to protect union rights, and three small socialist societies, of which one, the Marxist-inspired Social Democratic Federation, left within a year. The other two were the tiny but influential Fabian Society, committed to gradual, parliamentary state-sponsored socialism, and the Independent Labour Party, which preached a quasi-religious ethical socialism based on the universal brotherhood of man rather than the revolution arising from inevitable class conflict taught by Marxists. In practice, Labour's reformist ideas were not so dissimilar from those of radical Liberals, some of whom were to switch subsequently to the new party.

Trade union ideas and interests dominated the early history of the Parliamentary Labour Party that had been established to serve the wider interests of the labour movement. Trade unions were more concerned with improvements in wages and conditions through 'free collective bargaining' rather than the overthrow of capitalism. Beyond that, the largely moderate trade union leadership was content to leave parliamentary tactics and policy to the Parliamentary Labour Party and its leaders.

While socialists of sorts were part of the broad labour coalition from the start, the Labour party only became formally committed to a socialist programme in 1918 with the adoption of **Clause Four**, and the celebrated commitment to the 'common ownership of means of production' (see Box 7.4). However, the detailed plans for imple-

> ### BOX 7.4
>
> ## Clause Four of the Labour Party Constitution (1918–95)
>
> To secure for the workers by hand or by brain the full fruits of their industry and the most equitable distribution thereof that may be possible, upon the basis of the common ownership of the means of production, distribution, and exchange, and the best obtainable system of popular administration and control of each industry and service.

---

## Key thinker: Ralph Miliband

Ralph Miliband (1924–94) was a leading British Marxist historian and political thinker who discussed the problematic relationship between the British Labour party and socialism. His book *Parliamentary Socialism* (1963) argued that Labour was always more committed to parliamentary institutions and values ('parliamentarism') than socialism, and, by implication, that the parliamentary route to socialism was inherently flawed. He and his friend the historian John Saville (1988) employed the term 'labourism' rather than socialism to describe the ideas of the Labour party. In *The State and Capitalist Society* (1969) he argued power was effectively concentrated in the hands of inter-connected elites, which provoked a celebrated debate with Poulantzas, a leading structural Marxist, in the *New Left Review* (1969, 1970). At the end of his life and after the collapse of the Soviet Union, Miliband reaffirmed his own socialist convictions in *Socialism for a Sceptical Age* (1994). Ironically, its publication was overseen by his sons David and Ed, already influential in New Labour, and later to become Cabinet ministers, and then close contenders for leadership of the party whose commitment to socialism their father had doubted.

**Figure 7.1**    Influences on the ideology of the Labour Party

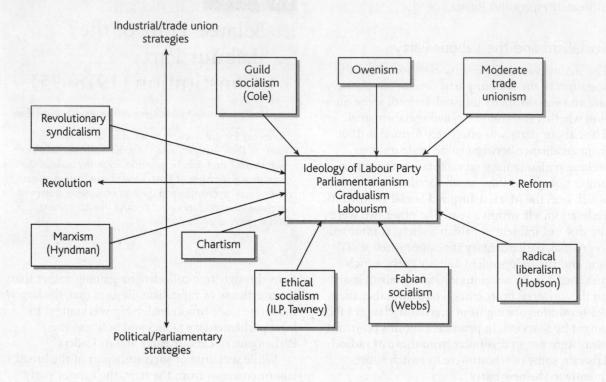

menting this ambitious goal were never formulated. Instead the Labour Party in practice
remained committed to gradual parliamentary
reform rather than a fundamental transformation
of the economic, social and political order. This
was demonstrated by the cautious record of the
two minority Labour governments of 1924 and
1929–31, as well as the whole labour movement's
peaceful and constitutional record in the General
Strike of 1926. Socialism for the Labour party was a
distant aspiration, dependent on the achievement
of a parliamentary majority, and step-by-step
gradual reform. Other variants of socialism, including Marxism, syndicalism, guild socialism, co-operation, and local socialism, were rejected or
marginalized. Critics suggested the Labour Party
was always more committed to parliamentarism
than to socialism.

Labour achieved its first parliamentary majority
in 1945. The record of the Attlee government
(1945–51) has come to define the Labour interpretation of socialism, both what it was, and what it

was not. Nationalization of the 'commanding
heights of the economy' (largely energy and transport) involved an extensive and controversial
extension of the role of the state, although not the
wholesale common ownership envisaged by some
socialists. The industries taken into state ownership
were already largely municipalized (electricity, gas)
and/or perceived to be declining (gas, rail, iron and
steel). Left-wing critics complained that the
method of nationalization (through Public
Corporations) involved 'state capitalism' rather
than workers' control. Labour's economic policy
followed the principles of Keynesian demand
management rather than the detailed socialist planning of a command economy. Labour operated a
mixed but essentially still capitalist economy, albeit
with more government regulation. The government's most important achievement was the establishment of the welfare state. It not only largely
implemented the welfare proposals of the 1942
Beveridge Report, but also established the National
Health Service, and expanded municipal housing.

## Key thinker: Anthony Crosland and revisionism in the Labour Party

Anthony Crosland (1918–77) was the most influential thinker on the social democratic right of the Labour Party. In his key book *The Future of Socialism* (1956) he argued that Marx 'has little to offer the contemporary socialist either in respect of practical policy, or of the correct analysis of our society, or even of the right conceptual tools or framework'. Pure capitalism had been replaced by a mixed economy. Socialism thus needed revising and updating. Ownership of industry was irrelevant. Instead, socialists should pursue greater equality through progressive taxation and improved welfare provision. Crosland served in Wilson's government, promoting comprehensive schools and the expansion of higher education. He opposed cuts in public spending at the time of the 1976 IMF loan crisis. He died in office as Foreign Secretary under Callaghan.

## Socialism and social democracy

The second half of the twentieth century saw a long battle between the Labour left and right which began with the resignation of Bevan, Wilson and Freeman from the Attlee government, in protest against the Labour Chancellor Gaitskell's imposition of charges for teeth and spectacles in 1951. Bevan became the unofficial leader of the left, which championed more nationalization and opposed German rearmament and Britain's independent nuclear deterrent. Revisionists or social democrats on the right were convinced that the party had to modernize, and abandon further nationalization, which was electorally unpopular. Gaitskell, who defeated Bevan for the leadership of the party in 1955, sought to scrap Clause Four, and even considered changing the party's name. He fought to reverse a 1960 party conference decision in favour of unilateral nuclear disarmament.

The conflict if anything became more bitter following the deaths of Bevan in 1960 and Gaitskell in 1963, after which Harold Wilson, the candidate of the left, became leader, while Roy Jenkins eventually emerged as the standard bearer of the Gaitskellites. The problems faced by the Wilson and Callaghan governments further polarized opinion within the party. Left-wing socialists favoured more nationalization, unilateral nuclear

disarmament and internal party democracy, and mostly opposed membership of the European Community. The right supported NATO, nuclear weapons and Europe while opposing further nationalization. After the election of the old Bevanite, Michael Foot, as leader in 1980, some 'moderates' left Labour to form the Social Democratic Party (Crewe and King, 1995), while others such as Healey and Hattersley stayed to fight from within. Healey narrowly defeated Tony Benn (by now the standard bearer of the left) for the deputy leadership in 1981, but the party went on to its most disastrous defeat in 1983 on a left-wing manifesto which included commitments to further nationalization, nuclear disarmament and leaving Europe.

## From old to New Labour

Under the leadership of Neil Kinnock (1983–92), John Smith (1992–94) and finally Tony Blair, the Labour Party gradually restored its electoral fortunes. Kinnock faced down the hard-left Militant Tendency which had infiltrated the party, instituted a policy review which led to the abandonment of the pledges which some considered had lost the party support, and modernized the image and presentation of the party (including the introduction of the red rose logo). Smith introduced 'One person, one vote' (OMOV) for the trade union membership rather than the old system of block votes. Blair boldly persuaded the party to change Clause Four (see Box 7.5), which Gaitskell had earlier sought and failed to scrap. Blair's modernization programme also involved an (unofficial) rebranding of the party as New Labour.

Much has been written on the transition from old to New Labour. The party's programme clearly changed considerably from the election defeat in 1983. Some would see the change in terms of a shift from socialism to social democracy. Indeed, New Labour embraced many policies of the old SDP. Others argue that Blair not only abandoned socialism but social democracy as well, and was effectively Thatcher's heir. Certainly Blair accepted the free market. His government from 1997 onwards did not reverse the Conservative privatizations, and made controversial use of public–private partnerships and the Private Finance Initiative to fund public sector investment. Yet at the same time the Blair government pursued many policies that the Conservatives previously opposed, including devolution as part of a radical programme of constitutional reform. Labour also introduced a national minimum wage, ratified the Social Chapter of the Maastricht treaty, instituted the new deal of 'welfare into work', and incorporated the European Convention of Human Rights into UK law.

The rejection of 'old Labour' did not involve just the rejection of left-wing socialism but 'labourism', the moderate trade unionist and working-class values and interests which permeated the Labour Party. In this sense, the most symbolic change was not the redrafting of Clause Four which had never really reflected the aims of Labour in practice, but the dropping of the old Labour Party logo with its manual workers' tools for the red rose. While the party had never preached class conflict, it had been mainly identified with the interests of (largely male-dominated and white) manual workers and trade unionists, although increasingly led by middle-class graduates and professionals. The problem for Labour was that the working class was both a smaller proportion of the population and more frag-

mented on gender and ethnic lines as well as between skilled and unskilled, public and private sector workers (see Chapter 3). It was no longer possible for Labour to win elections just through the support of the old manual working class of Britain's industrial heartlands. Appealing to 'middle England' and consumer as well as producer interests was an electoral necessity.

It is less easy to explain New Labour ideas and values. Blair himself used 'buzz words' which had been part of Labour's vocabulary since its beginnings: 'society', 'community' 'solidarity', 'co-operation', 'partnership', 'fairness'. He argued that Labour's values were unchanged, but needed re-interpretation in the modern world. A number of fashionable concepts and strands of thought were initially linked to the New Labour project, such as stakeholding (Hutton, 1995), Christian (or ethical) socialism, and the Third Way (Giddens, 1998). Yet, to some critics, New Labour involved a retreat from ideology, and a search for the political middle ground, embracing the pragmatism which was once a hallmark of conservatives: 'what matters is what works'.

New Labour certainly achieved electoral success, securing an unprecedented three terms of government. These owed much to the apparently successful management of the economy by Chancellor Gordon Brown, which not only erased memories of the economic problems experienced by previous Labour governments but also helped finance a massive increase in public spending on health and education. However, Labour's foreign policy divided both party and country (Kampfner, 2004), while the 'war on terror' at home led to increased state surveillance and restrictions on civil liberties. Some erstwhile Labour supporters switched to the Liberal Democrats, others to a variety of left-wing groups. Thus Labour won the 2005 election on a much reduced share of the vote.

## From Blair to Brown

By then Gordon Brown was established as Blair's heir presumptive, although he was not to succeed until 2007. Some hoped that Brown's leadership would involve a return to old Labour or a reinvigorated social democracy. It was soon clear that while Brown's style was different (and less effective), the policy substance was very similar. Indeed, the man who had presided over the British economy as Chancellor for ten years could hardly present his government and party as new. It took a global banking crisis to force a change in direction. Brown's government effectively took a large slice of the British banking industry into temporary public ownership, imposed some more controls over financial services, and raised income tax for higher earners, not to demonstrate his socialist convictions but in response to the worst economic crisis the world had faced since 1929. If any ideas were resurrected, it was not Labour's old Clause Four, and still less Marxism, but the economic analysis and prescriptions of Keynes. Thus Brown borrowed heavily to inject more demand into the economy, by cutting taxes and maintaining public spending.

Economic shocks inevitably damaged Labour's recently acquired reputation for successful economic management, and Labour, as the party in power, was also badly damaged by the 2009 parliamentary expenses scandal. At the ensuing 2010 election it was difficult for a party that had been in government for 13 years to present itself as the party of change. In the event Labour did better than some predicted, well enough to prevent an outright Conservative majority, but not for a credible centre-left coalition of the kind that Blair and Ashdown once sought.

Brown's resignation as Prime Minister and party leader paved the way for the party's renewal under new leadership in opposition. The leadership election resulted in the close and contentious victory of Ed Miliband over his older and more experienced brother David, who was perhaps damaged by his record as a Blair insider, while Ed asserted his own opposition to the Iraq war. Yet in other respects there appear to be negligible ideological differences between them. Ed's victory was greeted rather more enthusiastically in the Conservative party than his own. Only time will tell whether he will make an effective opposition leader and potential Prime Minister, and how the image and substance of his party may change.

## Ideological divergence or convergence?

Although the main British political parties draw inspiration from what were originally very different ideologies serving different interests, their ideas have appeared to converge at various times, particularly the post-war Keynes-Beveridge consensus (see Chapter 2). This appeared to break down completely in the late 1970s and early 1980s, as the Conservatives under Mrs Thatcher moved to the right, and the Labour Party appeared dominated by the left. By the 1983 election the two major parties once more appeared to stand for strongly contrasting principles and programmes, allowing a third grouping (the SDP-Liberal Alliance) considerable ideological space in the centre ground.

Subsequently successive Labour leaders abandoned much of its left-wing programme and edged back to the centre. Indeed some suggested that after 1997 there was a new Blairite consensus around acceptance of the free market coupled with increased spending on public services (Gray, 2010a). Moreover, there was general acceptance of Labour's constitutional changes, some of which had been earlier resisted by the Conservatives (particularly devolution). All the major parties professed a strong commitment to protecting the environment and tackling climate change. There was also cross-party backing for much of Labour's foreign policy up to 2003, and even the Iraq war had Conservative (but not Liberal Democrat) support. The only issue that really divided the major parties was hunting, which provoked some of the biggest protest demonstrations against the government until Iraq. All parties employed a similar rhetoric, using the same 'buzz words': 'community', 'society', 'fairness' (or 'social justice'), 'choice', 'competition', 'hard-working families'.

The economic recession threw up new challenges and some confused responses. Some of the disagreement was over the cause of the crisis. Thus the former opposition parties, understandably, sought to pin blame on Labour's (and particularly Brown's) management of the economy, while Brown insisted that it was a global crisis which had adversely affected all countries, some more than Britain. However, very few politicians saw the crisis coming. Both Labour and the Conservatives favoured the 'light touch regulation' of financial services that some have since blamed for the near collapse of major banks.

Yet significant ideological divergence between the parties soon developed over future economic strategy. Thus at the 2009 party conferences Cameron and his Shadow Chancellor Osborne attacked 'big government' in speeches reminiscent of Thatcher. Cameron claimed 'It is more government that has got us into this mess', while Brown attacked the Conservatives as a do-nothing party, and proposed more state action to rescue Britain from recession. This seemed to suggest a return to 'politics in primary colours' as one commentator, Andrew Rawnsley, described it (*The Observer*, 11 October 2009, p. 29), based on a fundamental ideological divide over the respective roles of the state and the free market.

This became clearer after the election, when the coalition of Conservatives and (predominantly) *Orange Book* Liberal Democrats proposed a substantial reduction in the state and the public sector as the main means to reduce the massive deficit (Gray, 2010b), while Labour opposed both the size and pace of the cuts. How far the new government will succeed in cutting state spending and services, and how far cuts will affect the wider economy and public opinion remains to be seen. The future shape of British conservatism and more especially liberalism may be strongly influenced by the outcome of the coalition's strategy. For the present, economic liberalism has recovered ascendancy over the social liberalism that dominated the Liberal party and Liberal Democrats for much of the last century. To those who will suffer from the Cameron government's massive cuts, it may appear that 'compassionate conservatism' is a thin cover for the return of a more extreme version of Thatcherism. It is also unclear whether Labour, under the new leadership of Ed Miliband, will be able to articulate a coherent and credible alternative programme that resonates with the public. New Labour may be over but the ideological flavour of the post-Blair and Brown party has yet to emerge.

## Other ideologies: beyond left and right?

Whatever is thought of the notion of consensus politics, mainstream British parties often seem to offer only a restricted choice. A marked feature of British politics over the last 40 years or so has been the development of political ideas that cut across the traditional left–right ideological spectrum. Most of these new ideological currents have little in common, except that they are not primarily concerned with the interests and values of traditional ideologies centred on attitudes to state intervention, but reflect other issues and priorities. While some of these non-mainstream ideologies are represented by political parties, others are largely articulated by pressure groups or social movements.

## Feminism

Feminism is one example. Although some leading figures are associated with the left, feminists can also be found on the right and centre, bound together by the common aim of securing justice for women and combating **sexism**.

Feminism in some shape or form has been around for a long time, fuelling ultimately successful demands for property rights, education and opportunities at work, as well as votes for women. However, in Britain as in most of the western world a 'second wave' of feminism from the late 1960s

---

● **Sexism** involves attitudes and behaviour that discriminate against women or demean them. Unequal pay and prospects for women, demeaning images of women in the media or pornography, and the use of language that neglects or diminishes women are all examples of sexism.

**Table 7.1**  Varieties of feminism

|  | Liberal feminism | Socialist or Marxist feminism | Radical feminism |
|---|---|---|---|
| *Who?* | (first wave) | (first wave) | Germaine Greer |
|  | Mary Wollstonecraft | William Thompson | Kate Millett |
|  | John Stuart Mill | Friedrich Engels | Shulamith Firestone |
|  | Harriet Taylor | (second wave) | Eva Figes |
|  | The suffragettes | Juliet Mitchell | Susan Brownmiller |
|  | (second wave) | Michelle Barrett | Angela Dworkin |
|  | Betty Friedan |  | 'Ecofeminists' |
| *Key ideas and terms* | Application of liberal principles to women; gender equality; freedom of opportunity. | Economic exploitation of women as 'industrial reserve army'; women's role in reproduction of labour. | Patriarchy and male dominance; 'The personal is political'; sexual politics; celebration of women's difference. |
| *Aims* | Extension of rights of man to women; legal and political rights; women's education; equal opportunities; equal pay. | Politicization and unionization of women; nurseries and workplace crèches; wages for housework? | Alternatives to nuclear family; a woman's right to choose (on abortion); end of violence against women; end of pornography; lesbian rights; green issues; peace. |

onwards drew attention to the continuing severe disadvantages suffered by women despite their formal political and legal equality. Thus few women reached the top in business, government or the professions, while average women's pay lagged well behind that of men. Moreover, women continued to bear the major responsibility for child-rearing, housework and care for elderly relatives.

Conventionally, three principal strands of modern feminism are distinguished – liberal feminism, socialist or Marxist feminism and radical feminism (see Table 7.1), although there is in practice considerable overlap between these categories, while some feminists are difficult to categorize and resist labeling.

Liberal feminism goes back a long way. Early feminists like Mary Wollstonecraft (1759–97) sought to extend the rights liberals demanded for men to women. They built on liberal assumptions and values but sought to apply them to both sexes. They sought equal rights for women, on the assumption that (apart from some obvious physical differences) women were much the same as men in terms of their nature and capacities. Liberals also assumed that they could persuade both men and

women of the justice of the demand for equal rights by rational argument. Liberal feminism was largely responsible for the formal establishment of women's legal and political equality, and other advances such as the expansion of education opportunities for females. Modern liberal feminists have continued to press for further changes in the law and increased political representation for women. Yet they have had some difficulty in explaining why formal legal and political equality has fallen well short of achieving actual equality for women.

Socialist or Marxist feminists explain women's inequality in terms of social pressures and in the context of wider inequality in a capitalist society. Low wages in what was once still a predominantly male full-time paid workforce could only be sustained through the unpaid domestic and child-care labour provided by women. Women in the workforce, many part-time and not members of trade unions, also constituted an 'industrial reserve army', particularly important when there were labour shortages, but always useful to employers in keeping wages down. Working-class women were doubly exploited, both as members of a subordi-

## Key thinker: Simone de Beauvoir

Simone de Beauvoir (1908–86) was an influential French feminist whose key work *The Second Sex* (1949) anticipated much of the analysis of 'second-wave' American, Australian and British feminists some 20 years later. She sought to explain why women constituted a 'second' or inferior sex in society with less freedom to shape their own destiny. She attacked contemporary images of passive femininity, and advocated full equality for women in a balanced relationship between the sexes, in which both men and women enjoyed freedom. She sought to exemplify this in her own life-time partnership with the existential philosopher, novelist and playwright Jean-Paul Sartre.

nate class, and because of their gender. Socialist feminists sought to raise the political consciousness of women, persuade them to join trade unions and secure more effective protection for part-time and casual work. One contentious proposal, wages for housework, was opposed by some feminists because it appeared to legitimize the unfair domestic burden placed on women. Thus many socialist feminists saw the solution in terms of a dramatic extension of paid maternity leave and nursery provision. While Marxism provided a body of theory that could explain some of women's subordinate role in modern western society, it could not explain all of it, nor inequality in other non-capitalist socieites.

Radical feminists concluded that the real problem was not the lack of formal political and legal rights for women, nor inequality in society generally, but simply men and men's power over women, **patriarchy**, in the family and society more generally. Male power was exercised sometimes through crude physical force and violence against women (including rape), often through more subtle social and educational conditioning. One radical feminist target was the images of women in the media and pornography, another the subliminal messages conveyed by everyday language (chair*man*, business*man*, *his*tory), and by literature from Jane

Austen onwards, suggesting that women's ultimate fulfillment lay in love and marriage to a man.

Liberal feminists (and subsequently most socialist feminists) had sought equality and partnership with men and were only too happy to campaign alongside sympathetic men, such as John Stuart Mill. Radical feminists argued that women had to achieve their own liberation. While liberal and socialist feminists assumed there were no fundamental differences between the minds and mental capacities of men and women, some radical feminists celebrated the differences between the sexes. Women thought and behaved differently. While men were inherently competitive and prone to violence, women were more co-operative and pacific. Thus men were largely excluded from the women's movement and from some women's political initiatives (such as the Greenham Common women's peace camp).

Radical feminism has helped transform the way people think about politics. No longer is politics confined to the public sphere. Radical feminists argued that much of women's oppression takes place in the private sphere – in the family and in personal and sexual relationships. A particular concern remains continuing violence against women, especially rape (including rape within marriage). Thus for radical feminists, 'the personal is political'.

Radical feminism has perhaps contributed most to changing attitudes towards women, yet it has provoked some divisions within the women's movement and a broader backlash against what were

● **Patriarchy** means literally rule of the father. The term is used by feminists to mean the habitual domination of men over women in the family and wider society, even in states where equal rights are enshrined in law.

perceived as the excesses of 'women's lib', not least among some women. The hostility of some radicals to men, to heterosexual relations, to marriage, motherhood and family, and to any manifestation of femininity upset many women who otherwise supported the broad aims of the women's movement. Thus some feminists have reasserted the value of motherhood (Freely, 1995). Eco-feminists, who combine feminism with environmental concerns and emphasize the nurturing role of women, often reject abortion, in marked contrast to earlier feminists who strongly proclaimed women's right to control their own bodies. Other 'new feminists', dismissed by Germaine Greer as 'lipstick feminists', have defended feminine clothes and makeup as empowering women, enabling them to feel good, while asserting the continued importance of the women's movement in the struggle for equality (Walter, 1999).

Some critics have suggested most modern feminists belong to the white middle class, and their concerns are not necessarily those of working-class women, black or Asian women. Today the voice of black feminism is being heard rather more, however. In some respects these differences and even conflicts within the women's movement testify to its richness and diversity, although they also raise a question mark over the direction of feminism.

## Nationalism

**Nationalism** has been defined as 'a political principle which holds that the political and the national unit should be congruent' (Gellner, 1983). In other words **nations** should form independent sovereign states, and states should consist of nations (**nation states**). The simple principle of **national self-determination** had dangerous implications for old

---

● **Nationalism** is a political doctrine that holds that nations should form independent sovereign states.

---

● A **nation** is a community of people bound together by some common characteristics (real or imagined).

---

● A **nation state** is an independent sovereign state whose inhabitants belong to a single national community.

---

● **National self-determination** requires that a nation should be able to pursue its own future, normally involving a free and independent sovereign state.

dynastic states that included various national or ethnic groups, such as nineteenth-century Austria or Russia. Nationalists demanded political unification for Germany and Italy, and independence for nations then subject to foreign rule, such as Greece, Poland, Hungary or Norway. In the twentieth century nationalist movements demanded and secured independence for the colonies of imperial powers, including Britain.

Many nationalists were less concerned with nationalism as a universal principle than the advance of their own specific **nation**, which might involve the rejection of other nationalist claims. Indeed, for Breuilly (1993, p. 2) a basic assertion of nationalism is that the interests and values of the nation take priority over all other interests and loyalties, (although some forms of nationalism seem more prepared to accommodate multiple identities and allegiances).

Yet what precisely is a nation? There are no easy definitions or clear criteria. Language, ethnicity, religion, culture and history may all contribute to a sense of nationhood, but ultimately a nation exists in the minds of its members; it is an 'imagined community' (Anderson, 1991), although it is also clear that a sense of national identity can evolve and change over time.

Nationalism was associated with liberalism in the early nineteenth century, and more closely linked with conservatism and the right subsequently. Over the last century it has sometimes been associated with racism and fascism, although anti-colonial nationalism was often socialist and sometimes explicitly Marxist. Thus nationalism is something of a chameleon ideology, taking colour from the political context in which it develops. In Britain nationalist ideas were absorbed into the mainstream parties, particularly the Conservatives, and at one time seemed to reinforce the British political system and culture.

Yet the impact of nationalism on British politics has changed significantly over the last forty years or so. From the late 1960s support for separatist nationalism in Northern Ireland, Scotland and Wales posed an increasing threat to the survival of the British state. How far this threat has been reduced or increased by the peace process in Northern Ireland and by devolution of powers in Scotland and Wales remains to be seen. However,

## BOX 7.6

# Fascism and racism in British politics

Before the Second World War Oswald Mosley's British Union of Fascists was subsidized by Mussolini and Hitler and attracted some initial media support (notably from the *Daily Mail*). Fascism, it was claimed, offered a middle way between capitalism and communism, but its main appeal was to xenophobia and anti-semitism. After the war Mosley attempted a political comeback, exploiting concerns over 'coloured' immigration rather than anti-semitism. However, it was new quasi-fascist and racist parties like the National Front or more recently the British National Party that attracted more publicity and support. Yet although advances in by-elections, local elections, and European Parliament elections have sometimes raised

alarm, neither has come remotely closely to winning a seat at Westminster. The electoral failure of racist parties may not reflect a determined rejection of racism by British voters, but rather of politicians and parties linked with Britain's wartime enemies. In that respect the Anti-Nazi League slogan 'The National Front is a Nazi front' was highly effective. Nick Griffin, the leader of the British National Party, has given his party a more outwardly respectable image. Nazi-type uniforms have been replaced by smart suits, and the tone of public pronouncements has been moderated, leaving racist language for more private meetings.

---

from 2007 nationalist parties shared power in Northern Ireland, Scottish nationalists ran the government in Edinburgh, and Welsh nationalists briefly joined a coalition with Labour in the Welsh Assembly. Thus separatist nationalism has appeared stronger than ever in the non-English territories of the United Kingdom (see Chapter 16).

## Populist radical right ideologies: racism and populism

Separatist nationalism within Britain coupled with anti-European and anti-globalization sentiments have fuelled an English backlash, manifested in support for the UK Independence Party and the British National Party (BNP). Despite their names, these have secured the bulk of their support in England. Significantly, the cross of St George has increasingly displaced the Union Jack as a right-wing nationalist symbol in England.

Some of this English nationalism (particularly that associated with the BNP and the English Defence League) is explicitly racist, feeding on hostility to ethnic and religious minorities perceived as a threat to the values and culture of the native British or English. This racism is commonly linked with fascism, and indeed some far-right racists have embraced the full fascist

ideology. However fascism has never had much appeal for most British voters, partly because it is associated with Britain's wartime enemies. In so far as extreme right-wing parties have achieved significant support in parts of Britain from time to time, this has been because of their racism rather than other elements of fascism.

While racism is officially repudiated by mainstream parties and politicians, there is abundant evidence that racism is widespread in British politics and not just confined to the political fringe. 32 per cent of Britons surveyed have described themselves as 'very or quite racist' (Parekh, 2000b, p. 119). More recently, particularly since the attack on the Twin Towers on 11 September 2001, and the bomb attacks in London in July 2005, religious differences have exacerbated racist suspicions and fears. The term 'Islamophobia' has been employed to describe hostility to Muslims. The English Defence League has organised provocative demonstrations to exploit both concerns over immigration and rising Islamophobia. Thus for many members of minority ethnic and religious communities racism remains part of their everyday lives, as they continue to suffer substantial discrimination and prejudice.

Some of BNP's support in Britain has come from former Labour voters among deprived sections of the white working class, hostile to a

## COMPARATIVE POLITICS 7.1
# The rise of right-wing populism in Europe

Much of the rhetoric of extreme right parties in Britain is populist and anti-establishment. This is in line with the rise of similar right-wing populism (sometimes verging on neo-fascism) elsewhere in Europe. Such parties include the Front National in France, the Alleanza Nazionale in Italy, the Flemish party Vlaams Belang in Belgium, the Jobbik party in Hungary and, many commentators would add, the Austrian Freedom Party, the Swiss People's Party and the National Democratic Party in Germany. These parties raise diffi-cult questions of definition and classification. While some might be fairly described as neo-fascist or racist, others are just xenophobic and nationalist, and reject European integration. Some are anti-tax parties. Commonly they have charismatic leaders, and are populist and anti-establishment in their appeal. (See Mudde, 2007, and the Review Symposium on his work in *Political Studies Review*, volume 7, number 3, September 2009.)

---

multicultural society and multicultural values (Ford and Goodwin, 2010). Once the orthodox official answer to ethnic tension was to stress the importance of integration and assimilation, yet the more recent response has been to celebrate difference within a multicultural society, and the benefits to be derived from diversity. Multiculturalism has been advanced as a counter-ideology to racism, although it has also been criticized by some Conservatives for eroding a sense of British identity. Yet others argue there is no contradiction between British and other identities as 'Multiple identities are a natural feature of the human condition' (Davies, 2000, p.874). Thus people can be both 'Black' and 'British', or 'Muslim' and 'British' unless discrimination and prejudice over time renders these identities less compatible (see Chapter 22 for further discussion of racism and multiculturalism).

## Green thinking

Green thinking is often referred to as 'environmentalism' or 'ecologism'. Yet as the name and colour 'green' has become almost universally identified with concern for the environment, there seems little point in using less familiar terms for what has become an important and distinctive political ideology. Other ideologies focus on the interests and needs of humankind in general or a particular section of humanity – a class, a nation, a race or gender. The green slogan 'Earth First!' subordinates the future of humankind to the future of the planet, although of course Greens would argue that the futures of both planet and people are bound up together.

Although many green activists are associated more with the left, they draw support across the political spectrum. Indeed, the green slogan 'not left, not right but forward' transcends conventional political divisions. While mainstream ideologies and parties from left to right welcome economic growth as a means of satisfying conflicting human interests and demands without necessarily making anyone worse off, Greens insist there are limits to growth. Many of the resources on which our current standard of living depends are non-renewable and thus finite. Unless renewable energy resources are utilized to replace the dwindling stocks of fossil fuels, humans will ultimately exhaust those supplies. Pollution is also causing irreversible damage to the environment, and climate change that could prove catastrophic. The relentless pursuit of growth to satisfy the needs of a still fast-expanding human population threatens not only other species but future generations (see Box 7.7).

While some green thinking has permeated all major parties and sections of big business, radical

BOX 7.7

# Green ideas: key points

- **'Earth first!'** The needs of the planet should have priority over the needs and wishes of humankind. This is sometimes called an **eco-centric** approach rather than an **anthropocentric** approach, putting ecology ahead of humanity.
- **Limits to growth.** There are limits to the increases in productivity that can be derived from the exploitation of finite natural resources (an argument distantly derived from the economist Thomas Malthus). Greens have also identified significant costs to the pursuit of growth in terms of potentially irreversible damage to the environment.
- **Sustainability.** Thus humans should only pursue policies that can in the long run be sustained without irreversible damage to the resources on which the human species and other species depend. Any growth has to be sustainable
- **Protect future generations.** Those alive today may not pay the price for unsustainable policies, but our descendants will. We need to consider the interests of future generations, and should leave the earth in no worse shape than we found it. Climate change from human activity could ultimately make the earth uninhabitable.
- **Animal rights.** Many (but not all) Greens are strong supporters of animal rights, and refuse to eat or wear dead animals. (Greens also argue that the production of meat consumes too many resources compared with the production of cereals and vegetables.)
- **'Think global, act local'.** While Greens believe environmental issues and problems are global, they stress the need for action at the local level. Many Greens are suspicious of central government and the state and believe (with the economist Schumacher, 1973) that 'small is beautiful'.

Greens suggest much of this is relatively superficial 'greenspeak'. It falls well short of the massive changes in policy and lifestyles they feel are necessary to avoid further irreversible damage to 'planet earth' through pollution and climate change. The Green Party has contested elections for many years in Britain, and has had some success particularly in elections involving proportional representation (e.g. Scotland, London, European Parliament). In 2010 their leader Caroline Lucas won her party's first Westminster seat. Yet green pressure groups (e.g. Friends of the Earth, Greenpeace) have been rather more influential than the Green Party (for more on the environment see Chapter 23).

## Mainstream and other ideologies

None of the ideologies discussed in this section are concerned primarily with the relationship of the individual to the state, or the argument over how far the state can and should interfere with free market forces, which are major concerns of the traditional mainstream ideologies. In so far as these ideologies are concerned with equality and social justice, it is with other divisions of the human race than social class, or in the case of Greens, future generations, other species and the planet. Together they have enlarged political discourse, extending ideological debate well beyond the confines of the established two- or three-party debate, reflecting a wider range of political interests and conflicts.

# SUMMARY

- In Britain the mainstream ideologies of liberalism, conservatism and socialism (or labourism) have developed within a British context, and show distinctive features.

- British liberalism is a broad ideology which has evolved over time, with some tension between older free market liberalism and the more interventionist New Liberalism of the late nineteenth and twentieth centuries. These ideas are still important for the Liberal Party and the modern Liberal Democrats, but have also influenced both Conservatives and Labour.

- British conservatism has generally sought to preserve the existing social and political order and resist radical change, emphasizing tradition, authority and the interdependence of classes against the individual freedom and rational self-interest of liberalism. Yet from Disraeli onwards Conservatives have favoured limited social reform to benefit the less fortunate.

- The New Right (or Thatcherism) combined some traditional conservative themes (patriotism, leadership, law and order) with free market liberalism (competition and privatization). Thatcher's successors were unable to escape from her shadow.

- David Cameron, however, has shifted the public perception of his party through his new emphasis on the environment, his efforts to make Conservative candidates more representative and his ostensibly progressive social agenda. However, in government he and Osborne have sought to cut the state and public spending more than Thatcher.

- British socialism (or 'labourism') has been gradualist rather than revolutionary, influenced by progressive liberalism and moderate trade unionism, but with a tension between its more socialist and reformist (or social democratic) wings. From 1945 onwards Labour was associated with the welfare state and mixed economy.

- New Labour under Blair and Brown formally abandoned its commitment to nationalization, and embraced market competition, but also increased spending on public services and pursued constitutional reform.

- The banking crisis and recession has forced all parties to re-examine their positions on state intervention and regulation, particularly with respect to management of the economy. There was a brief revival of Keynesian ideas. Yet the nationalization of banks was seen as a temporary expedient.

- While there been some apparent ideological convergence in terms of rhetoric, with all three parties stressing fairness, there remain substantial differences between the major parties particularly on attitudes to the state and public spending.

- Outside the traditional mainstream, other political perspectives that prioritize different concerns beyond the role of the state and the market are attracting increasing interest and support, with continuing implications for British politics, government and policy.

- Feminism has prioritized gender issues, while radical feminism in particular has extended the sphere of politics to encompass personal and family relations.

- Nationalists have re-opened debates over the borders and nature of the state.

- Greens raise issues over the relationship between humankind and the environment that transcend old issues and conflicts within current human society, concerning generations yet unborn, other species and the very survival of the planet.

# QUESTIONS FOR DISCUSSION

- How did the New Liberalism differ from older liberalism?

- What exactly do Liberal Democrats stand for today?

- What are the core values of traditional conservatism?

- How far was Mrs Thatcher more a nineteenth-century liberal than a traditional conservative?

- Does Cameron's progressive conservatism involve anything really new?

- What is socialism? Has the British Labour Party ever been a socialist party?

- How might New Labour be distinguished from old Labour?

- When, and in what respects, has there appeared to be a political consensus in Britain since 1945?

- Where do other ideologies, such as nationalism, feminism and green thinking, fit on the left–right ideological spectrum? Are the terms 'left' and 'right' still meaningful?

- How far has feminism or green thinking redefined what politics is about?

# FURTHER READING

McLellan (1995) has written a good brief introduction to the contentious concept of ideology. For a fuller analysis see Seliger (1976) and Freeden (1996). Definitions of key terms and brief accounts of important thinkers can be found in specialist dictionaries of politics and political thought (e.g. Williams, 1976, , Miller, 1991, Scruton, 2007, Bottomore, 1991). There are now many useful introductions to political ideologies in general, e.g. Heywood (2007). Leach (2009) relates ideologies specifically to British politics, as does Adams (1998). More extensive interpretations of British political thinking can be found in Beer (1982a), Greenleaf (1983) and Freeden (1996).

The literature on specific ideologies is massive. Among useful readers are Eccleshall (1986) on liberalism, Eccleshall (1990) on conservatism and Wright (1983) on British socialism. Readable general accounts of specific ideologies include Gray (1986) on liberalism, Davies on the ideas of the Labour and Conservative Parties (1996a and 1996b). On more recent developments in mainstream ideologies, it is difficult to select one or two titles from the daunting literature on Thatcherism and the New Right – Gamble (1988) and Kavanagh (1990) are among the more accessible. See also Ludlam and Smith (1996), and Gilmour and Garnett (1997). On Cameron's Conservatism see Bale (2010), Snowdon (2010) and Blond (2010). The literature on New Labour already almost rivals that on Thatcherism: see Driver and Martell (1998, 2002), Ludlam and Smith (2001, 2004), Fielding (2003), Coates (2005), and Beech and Lee (2008). On the Third Way see Giddens (1998, 2000). On the ideological divisions within the Liberal Democrats a short article by Mark Rathbone (2005b) is helpful. Gray (2010a) is provocative on mainstream party thinking immediately before the election, and (2010b) after the establishment of the coalition and its cuts programme.

On feminism see Bryson, *Feminist Political Theory* (2003). Celebrated classical feminist texts include Wollstonecraft (1792, ed. Tauchert, 1995) and Mill (1869, ed. Okin 1988). Modern classics include Greer (1970), Millet (1977) and Figes (1978). More recent contributions to debates within feminism are Freely (1995) and Walter (1999). On nationalism see Gellner (1983) and Breuilly (1993). On racism see Miles (1989, 1993) Solomos and Back (1996) and Solomos (2003). On the BNP see Ford and Goodwin (2010) On green thinking see Dobson (2007). Lovelock (2007) is an important British green thinker with maverick tendencies.

# CHAPTER **8** Pressure Groups and Social Movements

Pressure groups perform a vital role in modern democracies. While elections and parties are crucial to the theory and practice of representative democracy they do not necessarily involve much popular participation in day-to-day government and decision-making. Elections are infrequent and blunt instruments offering only a restricted choice between rival teams and programmes. Political parties are no longer mass parties and provide limited opportunities for participation. By contrast, pressure groups offer opportunities for ordinary people to participate in the political process on a continuous basis over specific issues that concern them. Pressure groups normally seek influence over, rather than direct control of, government. However, pluralists argue that power in society is effectively dispersed through the widespread influence of countless groups on government and policy making. Others suggest that some groups are vastly more influential than others, both in Britain and in modern capitalist society generally, and that power remains effectively concentrated in the hands of the few. Thus analysis of pressure group behaviour is closely tied up with theories about the distribution of power. There are also concerns over some forms of pressure group activity, which may either be almost invisible or only too visible. While some criticize the sinister influence of powerful 'hidden persuaders' behind the scenes, others point to the potential of small special interests that are strategically placed to 'hold the country to ransom'. One important question is how far protestors are justified in pursuing forms of direct action, sometimes involving breaking the law, in pursuit of a cause in which they passionately believe.

Starting with the definition and classification of pressure groups, this chapter analyzes their role in the political system and considers recent trends in their activities as well as the emergence of new social movements. We consider the various targets for pressure group influence and the factors affecting their success. We conclude with an analysis of the contribution of pressure group activity to the theory and practice of democracy.

## What are pressure groups?

This simple definition will serve as an introduction, but some aspects are not unproblematic. Many pressure groups are highly organized, with formal constitutions, containing clearly stated aims and objectives, rules and procedures, including the election of officers and the management of resources. Yet some groups may begin with a much looser informal structure, while others may prefer to retain non-hierarchical organizations from ideological preference or practical considerations. Thus radical green or feminist groups may consciously reject formal structures with leadership roles for a

---

● A **pressure group** is any organized group that seeks to seeks to influence government and public policy at any level. Pressure groups thus

- are *organized* – they are not just a section of the public with an interest in common;
- seek *influence* rather than formal positions of political power (unlike political parties);
- are *outside* rather than inside government.

more loose and democratic means of operating, while groups on the fringe of the law (such as some animal rights groups) prefer informal and clandestine procedures.

While pressure groups (unlike parties) do not normally contest elections, they may seek to influence elections (for example, advising voting against particular candidates) and occasionally may fight (and even win) elections in pursuit of a particular interest or cause. Thus the Campaign for Nuclear Disarmament (CND) did sporadically put up candidates for elections, while more recently members have been elected to the Westminster parliament and the Scottish Parliament on pressure group platforms. Moreover, some formally constituted political parties are essentially single-issue pressure groups (e.g. the Referendum Party which contested 547 seats in the 1997 election, and UKIP which contested a record 558 seats in 2010).

Although pressure groups are formally outside government, some groups work so closely with government that they are part of the process of governance. Government, both at national and local level, may seek the active co-operation and partnership of business groups and voluntary organizations, and may even delegate important tasks to them. Such groups may continue to put pressure on government, but as recipients of government contracts, grants and other benefits they are also clients of government. Decisions may emerge as a result of an ongoing debate within a network of public, private and voluntary organizations, all with an interest in a particular area of policy (see discussion of policy networks in Chapters 17 and 18). It may even be possible on occasion for a government department or agency to be effectively captured by the interests they are responsible for regulating (such 'agency capture' has sometimes occurred in the United States). It is also worth noting that some parts of government seek to influence other parts of government, often using familiar pressure group tactics. Thus local councils and local government in general (through the Local Government Association and appropriate professional bodies) often seek to influence the decisions of central government and the European Union.

Ultimately, the distinction between influence and power is at best relative. Large banks, major manufacturers and media organizations may all seek to exert influence on government, but they also, through their own operations, directly affect and even perhaps determine political outcomes. As we have seen, some ideological perspectives assume that real power is not exercised by politicians and governments but by big business or the 'military-industrial complex'.

## Types of pressure group

Pressure groups are so numerous and varied that many attempts have been made to distinguish between types of group, to bring some order into the analysis of a very crowded field. One fundamental distinction for political scientists is that between groups with a clear political purpose (e.g. Plane Stupid or the Taxpayers Alliance) and groups which exist primarily for social purposes, and may engage in politics rarely, if at all. Yet even an allotment association or sports club, ostensibly non-political, may from time to time seek political influence, over ground rents or council grants for example, or more seriously over plans for roads or buildings which might threaten their survival. Charitable organizations, such as Oxfam or the RSPCA, may frequently engage in political lobbying as part of their primary purpose (although they have to be careful not to endanger their charitable status).

Another simple distinction might be made about the level at which groups operate. Some are purely local, seeking to influence decisions and services in the immediate community. Others are national, although they might have local or regional branches (e.g. the NFU, the NUS, the NUT). An increasing number of groups operate at the European level (e.g. Association of European Automobile Constructors). Some of these European groups act as **peak** or **umbrella groups** for long-established national groups in EU member states. Finally, some groups are genuinely international in their membership and concerns (e.g.

---

● **Peak** or **umbrella groups** involve formal associations of a large number of similar groups. The most well-known of these in the UK are the Trades Union Congress (TUC), to which nearly all British trade unions are affiliated, and the Confederation of British Industry (CBI) of which most (but not all) large and medium-sized firms are members.

Amnesty International, Greenpeace) although such groups commonly have links with national organizations or national branch structures.

Two systems of classifying groups have been widely used by political scientists: the first describes groups in terms of *what or who they represent*, the second in terms of *their strategies and relations with government*.

## Interest and cause groups

The first approach distinguishes two main types of pressure group: (1) interest groups, seeking to defend the interests of a particular section of the population (alternatively, these may be described as 'sectional' or 'defensive' groups); and (2) cause (or promotional) groups.

**Interest groups** include business firms, trade associations, professional bodies and trade unions and other groups involved with industry and employment. Examples include the Confederation of British Industry, the Trades Union Congress, the British Medical Association (BMA), the Law Society and the National Union of Teachers. Members of churches, sports bodies, residents' associations and groups representing particular minority communities may also be described as groups concerned primarily, although not exclusively, with defending their own interests.

**Cause groups** by contrast come into existence to promote some belief, attitude or principle. They are also referred to as promotional, attitude, ideological or preference groups. Examples are Greenpeace, the Child Poverty Action Group, the League Against Cruel Sports, Amnesty International, Liberty and Plane Stupid.

There are two main differences between the two types of group. First, whereas membership of a sectional group is limited to those with a shared background, membership of a cause group is open to all those sharing the same values. Second, whereas the purpose of the sectional group is to protect the interests of its own members, the aim of the cause group is generally to advance other interests (the environment, children, animals, prisoners of conscience) or the public welfare as perceived by its members.

Yet the distinction between interest and cause groups is not always clear-cut. First, interest groups may pursue causes. The BMA, for example, not only looks after the professional interests of doctors but also campaigns on more general health issues such as drinking and smoking. Second, whilst in terms of their overall goals and motives many groups are clearly cause groups, such groups also often have material interests to defend. A charity such as Oxfam owns property and employs professional staff with careers to advance.

Many groups may combine a mixture of self-interest and more altruistic concerns. Thus groups opposed to specific developments (e.g. a new airport runway or a bypass) can involve both those promoting the broad cause of environmental conservation and others with a more self-interested objection to the proposed development's impact on their personal well-being and their property values. While some opponents reject almost all new roads or airports as part of a radical alternative transport strategy, others simply want the proposed development somewhere else – 'not in my back yard' (NIMBY). Moreover, as a matter of tactics, to win wider public support, particular sectional interests often claim they are acting in the wider public interest. University lecturers seeking salary increases stress the benefits to higher education and the country. Foxhunters opposing a ban on their leisure pursuits broadened the debate to encompass the cause of rural protection (the Countryside Alliance).

Despite these complications, the straightforward classification of groups into sectional and cause remains useful. However, an additional typology, based on the distinction between **insider** and **outsider groups** (Grant, 2000, p. 19) is also widely employed.

## Insider and outsider groups

One important virtue of this typology is that it sets groups firmly within *a relationship with*

---

● **Interest groups** are concerned to defend or advance the interests of their members, whereas **cause groups** are based on a shared attitude or values.

---

● **Insider groups** are consulted on a regular basis by government whilst **outsider groups** either do not want to become closely involved with government or are unable to gain government recognition.

*government*. It refers both to the *strategy* pursued by a group – whether or not it seeks acceptance by government – and to the *status* achieved or not achieved as a result of its efforts. Yet this distinction is also not clear-cut. While insider groups operate mainly behind the scenes, rather than indulging in the politics of protest, in part because they do not want to put at risk their good relations with government and their influence in the 'corridors of power', they may on occasion campaign publicly. Indeed, some groups that are too powerful or important to ignore, such as the BMA and NFU (National Farmers Union) regularly use both behind the scenes influence and public campaigns.

However, other groups dependent on government funding or official recognition may become client or prisoner groups. Some outsider groups may lack the contacts and skills to become insiders, while others may be potential insiders, who seek to be consulted and may achieve this over time. Others may fear that a close relationship with government could jeopardize their independence and blunt their capacity for radical criticism and action. Radical groups committed to direct action (for example, the Animal Liberation Front or Plane Stupid) may reasonably suspect their aims and methods will make them unacceptable to government in any case.

This classification cuts across the interest/cause distinction. Interest groups are perhaps rather more likely to be insiders than cause groups. However, some cause groups have managed to achieve insider status, (e.g. MENCAP and the Howard League for Penal Reform), while some interest groups (e.g Fathers 4 Justice) have been conspicuously excluded from government consultation. Status can also change over time. Thus trade unions were regularly consulted on employment issues, incomes policies and economic and social policy generally by both Labour and Conservative governments up until 1979 when they lost insider status. They only recovered some (but by no means all) of their extensive former influence under New Labour. By contrast, all radical environmental groups began as outsiders, but while Greenpeace remains an outsider group, Friends of the Earth has acquired a degree of insider status. Questions of definition and perception as well as apparent changes over time illustrate some problems with the insider/outsider distinction as a basis for classifying groups.

## Pressure group targets and methods

Whom do pressure groups seek to influence and what methods do they use? It is reasonable to consider these together as the methods adopted may clearly depend on potential targets. Moreover, in choosing their strategy much depends on the aims and resources of particular groups and the level at which they are operating.

Potential targets include:

- the 'core executive' – government ministers (including the Prime Minister) and civil servants (Whitehall);
- Parliament (both Houses);
- political parties;
- informed opinion (more disrespectfully described as 'the chattering classes');
- wider public opinion (mainly through the mass media);
- local institutions, including local government;
- the European Union.

### Influencing the government

Why do groups seek to influence the government and why is the government ready to listen? The answer to the first question is perhaps fairly obvious. Groups seek to defend and advance their own interest or cause, and government policy or specific government decisions may affect them, adversely or beneficially. Therefore they have a strong motive to seek to influence government, especially as power in the British political system is heavily concentrated with the core executive. Thus a change in taxation may significantly affect business profitability or the living standards of particular sections of the population. A change in the law may similarly affect business costs, employment opportunities or individual freedom. As law-making is largely an executive function in Britain, the natural target for influence is again the government.

# The National Farmers' Union and foot and mouth disease

The foot and mouth disease crisis which struck British agriculture in 2001 led to divisions among farmers and within their union, the NFU. Many farmers were distressed by the government's policy of slaughtering animals to stop the spread of the disease. Often this meant killing healthy animals that were not infected, as a precaution. Some farmers wanted to have these healthy animals vaccinated against foot and mouth disease rather than slaughtered. The NFU leadership argued that there was no satisfactory alternative to the slaughter policy. The leadership was accused of representing the interests of big farmers and agri-businesses, and not the interests of small stock farmers. It was argued that 60,000 farmers were members of the NFU, most of them small farmers, yet it was the minority of big farmers that most influenced NFU official policy.

Small farmers complained that the NFU had never consulted them to find out their views and consequently the union was not representing them in a democratic manner. As a result, a number of small farmers left the NFU because other rival agricultural organizations represented their interests more accurately. A dilemma for large interest groups such as the NFU is that its membership is diverse. In the case of the NFU it speaks for big and small farmers, arable and livestock farmers, and they each have different interests and priorities, and favour different policies.

Government decisions on benefits, grants and subsidies and on specific projects such as hospitals, schools, roads and airports may profoundly affect particular sections of society and specific communities. Those groups affected want information on the government's early thinking and draft proposals, because it is often easier to influence the government before it has gone public and committed itself. They want the chance to influence both the substance and detail of government policy, for if they cannot change the government's mind on the principle, they will want to ensure that the detailed implementation damages their interests as little as possible. Once a law is passed, a tax introduced or a planning decision announced, affected interests may continue to seek its amendment or repeal. Influence on the core executive is commonly the most direct and effective way to look after those interests, and groups may only seek to influence Parliament, political parties or public opinion when this direct route fails.

There can be risks involved in becoming too close to government, however. Groups may fear to criticize government for fear of losing their valued insider status. In so doing they may risk upsetting some of their own members, who may feel their interests and views are being ignored or unrepresented. Something of this sort happened to the NFU in the 2001 foot and mouth disease outbreak, although their difficulties were increased by differences of interest within the farming community (see Box 8.1).

It is perhaps less easy at first sight to see what the government gains from contacts with pressure groups, although this is at least as important. Government needs, first, information and specialist knowledge and advice, which is not generally available in Whitehall. Second, government will want some idea of the likely reaction to specific initiatives from those likely to be affected. Prior consultation may avoid potential trouble later. Third, if possible, government wants support from relevant interests. If a minister can claim that those with an interest in a particular policy or initiative have been fully consulted and support the proposals, this will help win the argument in Parliament, the media and the country. Finally, on many issues the government needs the active co-operation of outside bodies, if it is to be successful. Thus a reform of the NHS should preferably have the support of health service professionals.

Much effective influence may not involve high-profile meetings with ministers, but routine behind the scenes discussions with officials. Many group representatives sit with civil servants on the large number of committees advising government. Many group spokespersons will have frequent formal and informal contacts with their 'opposite numbers' in Whitehall.

## Influencing Parliament

Attempts by pressure groups to influence Parliament often secure more media publicity than attempts to influence the executive (because much of this is behind the scenes). Thus television news frequently broadcasts pictures of particular groups lobbying Parliament, and occasionally more dramatic interventions, such as the purple dye 'bombing' by Fathers 4 Justice of the Commons chamber, or its invasion by protestors against the ban on hunting. Although Parliament has long been seen by most established groups as a less effective target for influence than the executive, survey evidence suggests a growing use of parliamentary channels. Reasons for this include the increase in backbench independence and the growth in size and number of backbench revolts, the increasing importance of departmental select committees that provide another channel for influence, and the growth of Westminster-based professional consultancies, often employing MPs or their researchers. The semi-reformed House of Lords has also become an increased target of pressure group influence, particularly as it has demonstrated more readiness to amend and delay government legislation (see Chapter 13).

Groups may seek to influence Parliament by submitting petitions, lobbying Parliament and individual MPs, circulating all MPs and peers with letters and information packs, and using friendly MPs to ask questions, raise issues, and introduce amendments to legislation, or sometimes even a bill (through private members' legislation). Much of this activity is open and legitimate, although sometimes it has involved more questionable inducements, which have led to scandals and increased scrutiny, particularly from the Committee on Standards and Privileges.

Groups may seek to influence the legislative process at every stage. As nearly all the legislation passed by Parliament are government bills, much of this influence is targeted at the executive, particularly in the formative pre-parliamentary stages when the need for new legislation is discussed and the government is consulting outside interests.

However, while a bill is going through Parliament, groups will seek to target both government and Parliament, particularly with regard to the details of legislation, often at the committee stage using sympathetic MPs or peers to introduce amendments drafted for them. On controversial bills groups will hope to influence the votes of MPs, particularly backbench MPs on the government side, who may be persuaded to defy the government whips. Even after a bill is passed and becomes an Act of Parliament, groups may often be involved in the crucial implementation of the Act, and in influencing delegated legislation (although much of this influence will be directed at the executive rather than Parliament). If a group remains dissatisfied with the law as it stands, it will campaign for new legislation, using the channels of influence, and the whole process may start again.

Groups may particularly target Parliament and individual MPs and peers on private members' legislation (bills introduced by Members of Parliament who are not members of the government). Although very few of these succeed, certain controversial political questions, particularly those involving moral issues, have often been left to private members' legislation (e.g. changes in the law on homosexuality, divorce, abortion) partly because these cut across party lines. As such issues are normally left to a free vote of MPs, there is more scope for pressure group influence. Sometimes outside groups draft whole bills and seek to persuade MPs who have won a place in the annual ballot for a chance to present private members' bills to introduce their measure (see Figure 8.1). (For more on pressure groups and Parliament see relevant sections of Chapter 13.)

## Influencing political parties

Influencing Parliament and individual MPs inevitably involves influencing parties, as almost all MPs and most peers belong to parliamentary parties. Yet groups may seek to influence parties more directly. They may do this in a number of ways. The most obvious way is to make donations to political parties, as do both the trade unions (to Labour) and business (now again mainly to the Conservatives). Between 1986 and 2005, trade union contributions to the Labour Party declined from three-quarters to

**Figure 8.1**   Pressure group influence on Whitehall and Westminster: the main stages

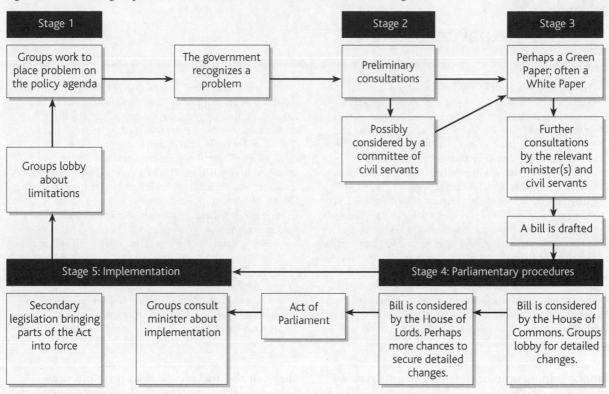

*Source*: Grant (1995, p. 48).

under a third of its total funds. whilst business contributions have grown, at least until recently.

Some cause groups, such as the anti-hunting and anti-abortion lobbies, try to influence parties' choice of parliamentary candidates. Others again attempt to persuade parties to include detailed commitments in their manifestos. In return for influence, such groups campaign for the party supporting their cause. Sometimes group and party membership overlaps, and this may help the groups achieve a favourable reception from parties.

Targeting a particular party may have draw-backs for a group, however. It may alienate opinion in other parties and thus is only likely to be successful if the targeted party is in power or has reasonable prospects of reaching power, and even then past commitments may not be honoured. However, Labour was more receptive to some inter-ests (e.g. trade unions, ramblers, groups opposed to blood sports) and it made sense for relevant groups to target the party to fulfil prior commitments on the minimum wage, access to the countryside, and

hunting legislation after 1997. Other organizations such as the Countryside Alliance and the Taxpayers' Alliance have found a more sympathetic audience from Conservatives.

## Influencing informed opinion

Because many public policy issues are relatively specialist and do not attract much interest from the mass media or the wider public, it may often be more important to target what might be called 'informed opinion' or what are sometimes more disrespectfully called 'the chattering classes'. This may be achieved, for example, through influencing important professional bodies, and through more specialist media, including minority television channels and programmes, the 'quality' daily press, and weeklies (such as *The Economist*, *Spectator* or *New Statesman*). Such bodies and media outlets may be far more influential than their membership or audience figures may suggest, as they are noticed by those who matter. Winning the argument

## BOX 8.2

# The Taxpayers' Alliance

The Taxpayers' Alliance (TPA) was founded in 2004. According to the TPA's own website (www.taxpayersalliance.com) its mission is 'to reverse the perception that big government is necessary and irreversible, to explain the benefits of a low tax economy and to give taxpayers a voice in the corridors of power'. To this end it 'opposes all tax rises' and seeks 'the abolition of inheritance taxes'. Thus although it claims to stand for taxpayers in general, it particularly champions the interests of those whose levels of income and wealth render them liable to high taxes rather than those who pay relatively low taxes, but are heavily dependent on public services and welfare benefits. The corollary of its support for low taxes is its opposition to big government and high public spending. Thus it regularly publicizes allegations of 'wasteful and unnecessary' government spending. The TPA itself is well-staffed and well-funded and claims 18,000 registered members. As a limited company it is less restricted in its political campaigning than other groups fearful of losing their charitable status. Its work is regularly cited in the media, but although it claims to be independent of parties, there is a considerable overlap between its leading members and donors and membership of and support for the Conservative Party. It was influential while the party remained in opposition. The TPA campaign to scrap inheritance tax was surprisingly endorsed by Shadow Chancellor George Osborne at the 2007 Conservative Party Conference. It maintained a high profile at the 2009 conference, supplying delegates with bags and balloons proclaiming their love for low taxes. Whether it will remain so influential with the 2010 coalition government remains to be seen. While the Cameron government is committed to huge cuts in public spending, the size of the deficit precludes significant tax cuts, while Conservative pledges on reducing inheritance tax and scrapping Labour's 50p tax on high-income earners have so far been shelved.

among leading opinion-formers may often prove decisive in the long run in swaying the decisions of ministers, civil servants and MPs, even sometimes where the mass media and wider public opinion is pushing in another direction. For example, while the mass media dramatized a possible link between the triple MMR (measles, mumps and rubella) innoculation programme and autism, health professionals and informed opinion reached a clear consensus that there was no such link and the government held firm, despite an initial panic.

## Influencing wider public opinion

Much of the most visible pressure group activity involves influencing public opinion, although this can be time-consuming and expensive in resources, and may be less effective than other channels. Thus groups can seek to raise public awareness of an issue by various forms of protest and direct action (Jordan and Mahoney, 1997). These include legal and non-violent methods including public petitions, marches and demonstrations (such as those by the Countryside Alliance or the Stop the War Coalition), or consumer boycotts of goods. But they can also include the disruptive but non-violent tactics used by radical campaigning groups such as Greenpeace or Plane Stupid (see Box 8.3). More rarely the use of violence and intimidation is employed; for example, supporters of the Animal Liberation Front have broken into laboratories, released animals, and targeted the persons and property of any individual remotely connected with experiments on animals.

Some experienced pressure group campaigners make only very sparing use of public demonstrations, because they can be not only ineffective but even counter-productive, particularly if they get out of hand and alienate public opinion and decision-makers. Thus the mobs which went on the rampage attacking suspected paedophiles (often wholly innocent victims of mistaken identity) harmed the cause they were seeking to advance. Yet more disciplined peaceful mass demonstrations can have relatively little effect. Thus the Campaign for Nuclear Disarmament (CND) annually organized massive four-day marches between the nuclear research establishment at Aldermaston and London from the late 1950s onwards without having any appreciable impact on government defence policy.

### BOX 8.3

# Plane Stupid

Plane Stupid was set up in 2005 to oppose airport expansion and the aviation industry generally. The group argues that the projected expansion of aviation contributes substantially to carbon emissions and climate change, and must be stopped. Like several other radical groups within the environmental movement it lacks a formal organizational structure or clear leadership, and campaigns through direct action rather than the more conventional methods of petitions, lobbying Parliament and legal challenges. They have organized demonstrations and occupations of buildings and facilities at several UK airports including East Midlands (2006), Manchester (2007), Heathrow and Stanstead (2008), Southampton, Aberdeen and London City (2009). Other protests that have attracted publicity included rooftop demonstrations at the Houses of Parliament and Scottish Parliament (2008), and throwing green custard over Labour's Business Secretary, Peter Mandelson (2009) (see photo). Such tactics have secured publicity, although not always public sympathy. In their opposition to expansion at specific airports they have shrewdly aligned themselves with local residents'

groups adversely affected by proposed developments. They have a harder task in halting the growth of air travel generally, particularly through cheap flights offered by budget airlines that remain popular with the wider public, despite their environmental impact.

More recently, what was estimated to be the largest public demonstration ever, that against the Iraq war in March 2003, did not succeed in its objective of stopping the war.

Rather more successful in influencing public opinion have been much smaller more targeted demonstrations, such as those employed by Greenpeace. One of the most successful of these was the brief occupation by protestors of the Brent Spar oil rig in 1995, in protest against proposed plans to dump it at sea. The episode was filmed and shown on the main television news. The publicity embarrassed the Shell oil company and the government to such an extent that the plans to dispose of the rig at sea were abandoned. Whether this was the right decision is still subject to debate. However, there can be little doubt that the demonstration was successful in changing policy (Jordan, 2001).

This example illustrates the importance of the mass media if a pressure group demonstration is to be effective in influencing public opinion. Without the free publicity given by the media, only those few people directly involved would have known

about the occupation of the Brent Spar oil rig. Other protests have been taken up and extensively amplified by the tabloid press, particularly those by the Countryside Alliance from 1997 onwards, the fuel protests of September 2000, the anti-council tax protests of 2003–4, and Joanna Lumley's successful campaign to secure rights to British citizenship for the Ghurkhas (see photo overleaf), which illustrates the value of a prominent public celebrity to a cause in securing news coverage and the attention of politicians.

## Influencing local government and other local institutions

Many important decisions that affect people's lives are still made locally (see Chapter 17). Small local community groups with relatively few resources can sometimes be very effective in influencing these local decisions, such as the proposed closure of a school or hospital, or decisions on planning applications, or policy on roads and traffic regulation.

**Image 8.1  Joanna Lumley, David Cameron and Nick Clegg celebrate with Gurkhas gathered outside the Houses of Parliament**

Lumley celebrates with (then) opposition politicians Cameron, Huhne and Clegg, and Ghurkhas, after her successful campaign to secure British residence and citizenship for former Ghurkha soldiers and their dependants who served in the British army.

An organization can spring up very quickly, and can often tap local expertise to mount a professional campaign. There are some clear targets for influence. The local MP may be a potentially useful and influential ally, even if the issue involves local institutions rather than central government. Individual councillors, local government officers and the council as a whole are an obvious target for issues that are a local authority responsibility, although sometimes a government department may also be contacted if a minister has the final say. Doctors, nurses and other health service professionals, together with affected patients, readily attract sympathetic coverage on any health service issue. Meetings and demonstrations can invariably get free publicity from the local press and radio, and sometimes also regional television if there is a story that is newsworthy.

## Influencing the European Union

At the other extreme, many decisions that affect people in Britain are made by the European Union (see Chapter 15). Although this seems to many Britons a remote body, it is still highly susceptible to influence from organized groups. Business and farming interests, trade unions, professional associations such as the BMA and the Law Society, and environmental groups all lobby at European Union level. Some British groups have offices in Brussels and lobby directly. Many others employ consultancy firms to lobby on their behalf. Commonly, British groups seek allies in other EU member states and work through Europe-wide umbrella groups such as UNICE (Union of Industrial and Employers' Confederations of Europe), ETUC (European Trade Union Confederation), COPA (Committee of Professional Agricultural Organizations), BEUC (European Bureau of Consumers' Associations) and EEB (European Environmental Bureau). A potential disadvantage of such Eurogroups, however, is that they sometimes find it hard to agree on policy because of national differences.

Pressure groups have long sought primarily to influence the European Commission, but as the powers of the European Parliament have increased, that too has become an important target. It is rarely possible for groups to have any direct influence on the Council of Ministers, so here they have to rely on their national government to protect their interests. However, they may be able to influence the

Committee of Permanent Representatives (COREPER), which serves the Council of Ministers and prepares papers on which Council decisions are made. Relatively few groups seem to make much use of the Economic and Social Committee in Brussels, which was an institution designed to reflect the interests of employers, employees and consumers.

Some British groups (such as trawlermen) undoubtedly feel they have little or no influence over decisions made in Brussels that affect their livelihoods. Other groups, however, make use of EU directives and regulations to put pressure on their own government, and cite examples of practices in other EU member states to demand improved services and higher standards in Britain (see Chapter 15 for more on pressure groups and the European Union).

## New social movements

The term 'social movement' has been employed to describe a much looser informal and less organized coalition of individuals or groups supporting a broad interest or cause. It is customary to define a pressure group as an *organization* which aims to influence policy by seeking to persuade decision-makers by lobbying rather than by standing for election and holding office. Paul Byrne described a social movement as something which is relatively *disorganized* (Byrne, 1997). While a pressure group is a formal organization that has *members*, a social movement is an informal and loosely organized network, with *supporters* rather than members. Examples of what are termed 'new social movements' are the women's movement, the peace movement, the green movement, or the anti-capitalist movement (to be contrasted with older social movements such as the labour movement). All these include some specific organized groups, and many individuals who may be members of one or more such groups, but also others who may not belong to any organized group but still identify strongly with the interest or cause. Thus the women's movement is much more than a coalition of interest groups, but represents a broad swathe of interests and opinion in society that has already promoted significant social change.

A loose informal movement may be preferred to a formal organization for ideological reasons. Some

feminists associate formal organizations, with their rules and hierarchies, with a male preference for order, authority and status, and seek more spontaneous and co-operative methods of working. Similarly, some peace campaigners or green activists positively reject leadership roles as part of a wider rejection of the existing social and political order based on traditional values.

Radical social movements favour alternative ways of organizing politics and society and thus want changes that will fundamentally change the existing order. While pressure group members may work through parliamentary parties, social movement supporters are more likely to reject such traditional institutions and lead their own private lives in ways shaped by their alternative values and ideologies. Whereas many pressure groups broadly accept the current political and governmental system, and are content with traditional channels of influence, supporters of a social movement may challenge the values of the governing elite, question its authority and replace conventional politics with the 'new' politics of direct action (see Box 8.4).

Many protest movements challenging the legitimacy of government and Parliament, and prepared to use direct action, sometimes involving deliberate breaches of the law, have been associated with the radical left. However, Labour's dominance from 1997 to 2010 saw the emergence of a number of right-wing protest movements. These include the Countryside Alliance, the fuel protests of September 2000, and the anti-council tax protests, which unlike the campaign against the poll tax originated among those with relatively high-value properties in middle-class rural and suburban areas. One obvious explanation is that until 1997 the rural gentry, the road transport lobby and middle-class homeowners felt reasonably well-served by a Conservative government. Under a Labour government some of these interests felt outside the political mainstream and resorted to the methods of mass demonstrations and sometimes direct action traditionally used by those who feel excluded from power and influence. They turned back towards more conventional methods of political influence as the electoral prospects of the Conservatives improved.

## BOX 8.4

# The anti-capitalist movement

Anti-capitalist protests and direct action against multi-national companies have grown. This new social movement has no established leaders, and no organization in the sense of having a headquarters staffed by office workers, but involves a loose international network linked by the internet. It has been described as a 'global, anarchic and chaotic' body, but nevertheless has become a significant political force. Much campaigning takes place against the 'iron triangle' of global capitalism: the World Trade Organization, the International Monetary Fund and the World Bank. Much additional grassroots campaigning takes place against multi-national companies such as McDonald's, Coca-Cola, Nike, Texaco, Shell, Microsoft, Disney and Gap. The protesters' causes range from anti-consumerism and environmentalism to anti-slavery and the promotion of human rights. Some oppose successfully advertised junk food replacing locally produced real food. Some oppose the use of 'sweatshop labour' by women and children in the third world to produce expensive designer-label products in the West.

More recently there has been a resurgence of populist far-right political movements, such as the English Defence League, ostensibly formed in 2009 to counter militant Islam, but whose provocative demonstrations have appeared indiscriminately Islamophobic and racist, and have commonly led to violent confrontations with anti-fascist groups. It draws support particularly from among white football supporters. It has developed links with the US Tea Party movement.

## Pressure groups, power and democracy

The debate over the role of pressure groups in the political process is closely bound up with arguments over the distribution of power and the extent of democracy, both in Britain and in other modern western political systems.

Pluralists argue that power is effectively dispersed in modern western democracies in large part through the activities of countless freely competing groups. They point to the apparent influence of pressure groups in numerous case studies of decision-making. They claim that pressure groups promoting one interest or cause (such as legalized abortion, a ban on blood sports or low taxes) stimulate the growth of rival groups to counter their arguments, as has happened in Britain. These rival groups, through their activities, promote democratic debate, help educate the public on the issues and lead to better-informed decisions which reflect the net sum of influence

# Key thinker: Robert Dahl

Robert Dahl (born 1915) was a leading US political scientist, particularly associated with the study of power. He was a key figure in the community power debate between pluralists, who argued power was widely dispersed, and elitists, who claimed it was concentrated in the hands of the few. His book *Who Governs?* (a study of decision-making in New Haven, Connecticut) concluded that there was no single elite guiding decisions, but that power was dispersed through the influence of numerous groups on specific policy areas. His theory of democracy (he preferred the term 'polyarchy') rested heavily on the ability of ordinary people to influence government decisions through their participation in pressure group activity.

## BOX 8.5

# Who really represents the disabled?

In lobbying government, disabled people are represented by numerous voluntary sector charities and agencies. These are very fragmented, and there is no single influential voice but rather many competing forces. Even so, these groups have greater resources and access to government than 'newer groups led by disabled people themselves' (Drake, 2002, p. 373). A crucial issue for disabled people is how far a voluntary body staffed by people who are not disabled can really represent the disabled themselves. Some charities are almost as concerned with helping the families and relatives of disabled people as with helping disabled people themselves. In other words, the interests of the carers and the disabled become combined, yet what serves the best interests of relatives might not be in the best interests of the disabled. Furthermore, some charities provide services based on their professional judgements rather than on the needs expressed by disabled people.

The problem might be resolved if disabled people held positions in charities for the disabled, but in reality disabled people have found it very difficult to get established and hold positions in the most powerful charities.

Governments 'hear only what they want to hear', and may exclude certain strands of opinion, effectively controlling the type of advice it is likely to receive (Drake, 2002). Large traditional charities are always likely to be included but smaller groups, especially if they are radical and out of line with government thinking, are more likely to be excluded. However, since disabled people are more likely to be involved in the latter type of group they tend to be excluded from the political process. This results in the political agenda concerning disability being controlled more by professionals such as social workers and therapists than the disabled.

and the balance of public opinion. Thus pressure group activity is the very essence of a free democratic society. Indeed, some modern theories of democracy (notably those of Robert Dahl) depend heavily on the role of pressure groups.

Elitists, by contrast, argue that power remains concentrated in the hands of the few. The contest between groups, they claim, remains profoundly unequal, in part because of massive differences in resources. Some have abundant finance, effective leadership and communication skills, but above all access to decision-makers, while others do not. Much of the most effective influence takes place behind the scenes rather than in the open. Government listens to some interests and ignores or rejects others. Within a capitalist system business groups have much more influence than groups representing labour or consumers not only because of their greater resources and access to government, but because their role is crucial if the economy is to be managed successfully. Some interests (the poor, the sick, the elderly) are more difficult to organize than others.

Although the numbers involved in some pressure groups are impressive, and far larger than

those involved in parties, group policy is commonly determined by leaders and spokespersons. Some group leaders are elected by members, but most are not, and can be virtually self-appointed. Although some, like the once influential Mary Whitehouse and her National Viewers' and Listeners' Association, claimed to speak for the 'silent majority', while the majority remains silent there is no way of testing such claims. It is also sometimes questionable how far some groups really represent those whose interests they are ostensibly serving (see Box 8.5). Moreover, much of the most effective influence is behind the scenes in the 'corridors of power' rather than in the open. Thus some of the most effective pressure groups are 'hidden persuaders' rather than contributors to a democratic public debate.

While some of the criticism of the role of pressure groups in modern politics has come from the left, because of marked inequalities in group resources and influence, some has come from the right, particularly the New Right. New Right thinkers and politicians have argued that increases in public spending and taxation have been pushed by an alliance of unions of public sector workers

# Pressure groups in the USA and France

The academic study of pressure groups goes back a long way in the United States, at least as far back as the work of Bentley (1908). They have been viewed as not only a necessary but as a highly beneficial part of the political process, increasing competition and spreading influence. Under Robert Dahl they have become the vital ingredient of a modern theory of democracy or 'polyarchy'. Among the national pressure groups considered particularly well-supported and influential in the American political system are the National Rifle Association (NRA), the National Organization of Women (NOW), and the American Association for Retired Persons (AARP).

In France the political culture seems less compatible with pressure group politics, perhaps reflecting a tradition of thought going back to Rousseau, who saw special interests as articulating a 'partial will' opposed to the 'general will' of the French people. Thus the Fifth French Republic 'one and indivisible' is less responsive to special interests than the American political system with its elaborate checks and balances. Groups representing labour and business are smaller and weaker than elsewhere in northern Europe. Although some French workers are often involved in disruptive action, such as strikes, obstruction and boycotts, this may reflect their relative lack of influence in government circles. However, farmers remain an important exception to the relative lack of influence of special interests in French politics.

and dependent client groups with a vested interest in higher spending, against the interests of the broad mass of voters and taxpayers. The excessive influence of these groups, it was argued, interfered with the operation of free market forces, to the detriment of economic efficiency and prosperity. The Thatcher government in particular reacted against a particular form of economic decision-making involving peak organizations representing employers and workers, known as tripartism or corporatism. The election of the Thatcher government virtually ended corporatism. Lord Young, a leading member of her Cabinet, claimed 'We have rejected the TUC; we have rejected the CBI. We do not see them coming back again. We gave up the Corporate State' (*Financial Times*, 9 November 1988).

Finally, it may be noted that pressure groups are viewed variously in other political cultures, influenced by their own traditions of thought and practice. Thus, while pressure groups are widely seen as integral to the process of democracy in the United States, they tend to be viewed rather differently in a country like France (see Comparative Politics 8.1).

# SUMMARY

- Pressure groups offer more scope for direct involvement in the political process than political parties.

- Pressure groups may operate at various levels. Distinctions are commonly made between interest (or sectional or defensive) groups and cause (or promotional) groups, and between insider and outsider groups.

- Insider groups may enjoy a mutually beneficial relationship with government, although there may be a risk that groups get too close to government and become effectively emasculated. Government departments or agencies may sometimes be effectively captured by their client groups.

- Groups may have a variety of targets, including ministers, civil servants, Parliament or the wider public. In the British political system influence on the executive is generally seen as more effective than influence on the legislature, although some policy areas can be exceptions.

- A recent phenomenon has been the growth of broad, loosely organized 'new social movements' often involving the politics of direct action. Although these have generally been associated with the left, under the Labour government there was some increased use of direct action by groups and movements on the right.

- While some claim that competition between countless pressure groups helps to disperse power (pluralism) and enhance democracy, others claim that group resources and influence are grossly unequal, and the system favours established interests. The New Right by contrast has argued that vested interests can interfere with free market forces, and encourage high government spending and taxation.

# QUESTIONS FOR DISCUSSION

- How far is the distinction between interest groups and cause groups valid and useful?

- How far do most pressure groups have a choice in becoming an insider or outsider group? Are there any disadvantages to insider status?

- Why do most pressure groups prefer to target the executive rather than the legislature in the British political system? What exceptions are there to this general rule?

- Why do governments bother with consulting pressure groups? How far is government an impartial arbiter of group pressures?

- What purposes might a public demonstration or protest seek to serve? Why might they sometimes be ineffective or even counter-productive?

- What is a 'new social movement' and how might such a movement be distinguished from a pressure group?

- Are there more right-wing protests and demonstrations, and if so, why?

- How far is power effectively dispersed and democracy assisted through the activities of pressure groups?

# FURTHER READING

Good recent texts on pressure groups in Britain are those by Grant (2000), *Pressure Groups and British Politics*, Byrne (1997), *Social Movements in Britain* and Coxall (2001), *Pressure Groups in British Politics*. Baggott (1995) remains useful. Jackson (2004) provides a useful brief overview in *Politics Review* 13.4. Jordan and Richardson (1987), Marsh and Rhodes (1992), and Smith (1995) all illustrate the policy networks approach. See also Maloney in Dunleavy *et al.* (2006). Greenwood (2007), provides valuable insights and examples of pressure group influence on the European Community. Richardson (1993), *Pressure Groups* affords a useful comparative perspective as does Chapter 12 of Hague and Harrop (2010). Some further examples of pressure group activity are provided in later chapters of this book: see especially Chapter 19 and the succeeding issues and policies chapters .

More information on specific groups can be found from their websites, e.g the British Medical Association www.bma.org.uk; the Campaign for Nuclear Disarmament www.cnduk.org.uk; the Confederation of British Industry www.cbi.org.uk; Countryside Alliance www.countryside-alliance.org, Friends of the Earth www.foe.co.uk; Greenpeace www.greenpeace.org.uk; the Howard League for Penal Reform www.howardleague.org.uk; the Law Society www.lawsociety.org.uk; the League Against Cruel Sports www.league.uk.com; The National Farmers Union www.nfu.org.uk; Stop the War Coalition www.stopwar.org.uk; the Trades Union Congress www.tuc.org.uk.

# Political Communication and the Mass Media

Communication is inseparable from politics, and a vital part of any political system in any age. However, the development of the mass media in the course of the twentieth century hugely enlarged the scope of political communication. Dictators like Hitler, Mussolini or Stalin, with almost exclusive control of the press, film and radio, as well as the education system, could shape how people thought about politics. Yet the same mass media were equally important for the functioning of a democratic system that assumed effective two-way communication between political leaders and people. The new media (including cable, satellite and digital television, and particularly the internet) have dramatically expanded further the potential for interactive public debate, enabling all kinds of special interest groups to communicate with each other and with the wider public in a globalized communication system.

While a free and diverse media enabling a wide expression of views is a necessary condition for democracy (see Chapter 1), it is debatable how effectively the media in Britain meet that condition. They may be substantially free from direct government censorship, and they may offer a range of views, yet they are inevitably subject to other forms of bias, arising from their relatively restricted ownership and control. Moreover the nature of

each medium of communication substantially influences the message that is transmitted, while content is ultimately determined by market considerations in a capitalist economy where profit, circulation and market share are more important considerations than the wider public interest. This chapter examines the role of the mass media (including the new media) in modern political communication in Britain. It also explores the role of government and political elites in shaping the nature and extent of political debate, and influencing opinion.

## The mass media and society

Most of what people think they know about government and politics comes through the **mass media**. Relatively few people participate much in politics (see Chapter 4). Government and politicians do not, most of the time, communicate directly with voters, but through the prism of the mass media. The mass media enable government

---

● The **mass media** refers to all those forms of communication where large numbers of people are exposed to an identical message. The mass media include the press, film, radio and television and the internet. The mass media provide the ideas and images which help most people to understand the world they live in and their place in that world.

and politicians to reach far more people, but their message is shaped and sometimes transformed in the process. Moreover, those who own and control the media may have their own political agenda.

## Traditional and new media

The mass media include not only newspapers, magazines, cinema, video, radio and terrestrial television, but also, more recently, multi-channel satellite, cable and digital television, the internet and mass text messaging. This growth implies greater choice for the individual as well as easier access to global mass communication. New media channels allow individual access to a far wider range of information, including political information, but also provide scope for new ways of political involvement. Recent advances in media technology have increased opportunities for more specialist communication to niche audiences. Thus the move from analogue to digital has reshaped television, with many more channels made available. An expansion of sub-genre themed interactive channels has replaced what was once a choice from only a few national or regional channels. In other words, 'narrowcasting' allows transmission of political and other content to 'niche or even individualised consumer segments' of the public audience (Cornford and Robins in Stokes and Reading, 1999, p. 109).

Even more important has been the massive expansion of access to the internet. This has already had important consequences for traditional media. Television faces a formidable rival in the production of up-to-date news and comment, and a rival not subject to the same controls. Thus the BBC has developed its own extensive website, BBC Online. The internet has further accelerated the decline in newspaper circulation. Although traditional newspapers are still printed, circulated, purchased and read, younger readers in particular have become used to getting most of their news online, and many may never acquire the habit of buying newspapers. (Indeed, there are available freely circulated freesheets.) The major national papers now also publish extensively online, and their websites are a major source of news, opinion and information. Some fear the end of the press, rendered obsolete by the new media. Rupert Murdoch and his News Corporation now charge for content on the inter-

net. However, many who obtain their news and comment free are averse to paying for it.

Some political scientists have speculated that, driven by this technological change, the world of media conglomerates will be replaced by 'a perfect marketplace of ideas' leading to a massive growth in decentralized, grassroots politics. In this new media world, some have argued, any individual with access to the web has the same potential political power as *The Sun*. Add to this the mobilizing impact of the internet for bringing together individuals who share political values, then it is possible to argue that technological change in the media will result in a new, more democratic, political order.

However, while the new media have the capacity to transform political communication and encourage different forms of political behaviour, it is only a minority who use the new media for political purposes. Most of the population still receive their political messages from more traditional media, including particularly terrestrial television and the national press. The new media have also, more disturbingly, provided a platform for cranks, extremists and terrorists to disseminate propaganda and a message of hate and violence. Garbage can be accessed as readily as wisdom. Altogether, the capacity of the internet to revitalize democracy has been exaggerated (Morozov, 2011).

## The medium is the message?

A celebrated media guru from the 1960s, Marshall McLuhan, coined the snappy formula 'the medium is the message'. What he meant by this is that each medium of communication has its own distinctive characteristics that shape the message that is put across. There are some obvious differences between the media. Some are wholly or largely visual, for example posters or silent films, while radio is wholly aural – your mind has to supply the pictures. Some, like film and television, are both visual and aural, although arguably the main message comes through the visual images rather than the soundtrack, and pictures have more impact than the spoken word.

Thus it has been argued that radio manages serious political debate better than television. Yet radio abhors silence, even for a few seconds. Questions have to be answered instantly – there is no time for reflection or rephrasing. Ideas and complex arguments may be better expressed in print, where the writer has time to develop and refine his ideas, perhaps through a succession of drafts, and readers can digest matter at their own speed, rereading what they may not have grasped initially.

There are also major differences in the circumstances in which the audience receives communications. Although the term 'mass media' implies a mass audience, that mass is generally made up of countless individuals and small groups. A national newspaper may have a huge circulation but each copy is usually read by just one person at a time. Radio and television may have an audience of millions, but normally this is made up of individuals and families who receive the same message in separate households. Prime Minister Harold Macmillan observed of his own television broadcasts, 'Someone once said to me "there will be twelve million people watching tonight". I just had the sense to say to myself, no, no, two people, at the most three. It is a conversation, not a speech.' He grasped that television was essentially an intimate domestic medium. It was necessary to talk to people in a quiet relaxed fashion, as if he was a guest in the room, rather than speak at them as if he was addressing a mass meeting.

Television may be contrasted with films, viewed by large audiences in cinemas, at least before the video age. Hundreds and sometimes thousands in cinemas all over Germany would have viewed together Leni Riefenstahl's film of the Nazi party rally at Nuremberg, *Triumph of the Will*, and been moved by collective emotion, as if they had been part of the crowds at the rally themselves, carried away by the experience. Yet it has been observed 'Hitler's demonic manipulation of the masses would not have been possible today because his performance would have looked ridiculous on television' (Henry Porter, *The Guardian*, 12 October 1995).

Each medium works differently. Politicians adept at one form of communication may never master another that requires a different approach. Looking and sounding good on television has become a crucial skill that ambitious politicians have to learn. The former Labour leader Michael Foot was a powerful platform and parliamentary

orator, and an engaging writer, but he never mastered television. By contrast, the more relaxed conversational style of James Callaghan or John Major was well suited to 'the box'. Harold Wilson became a good television performer after his advisers persuaded him to replace his emphatic hand gestures with a calming pipe that became his trademark. Margaret Thatcher's appearance, clothes and strident voice were initially off-putting, until she sought advice, learned to soften her image and became an effective television performer. Blair was a more natural communicator, particularly for the television cameras, but his successor, Gordon Brown, never quite mastered the medium.

## The British press

Despite the rise of radio and television, and more recently the new media, most adults in Britain still read newspapers (although circulation is now generally declining). While over a thousand newspaper titles are published in Britain, more than half being 'free papers' wholly dependent on advertising for revenue, the press remains dominated by ten national daily papers (plus linked Sunday papers). Scotland has its own dailies alongside the London press, but the few regional morning dailies elsewhere in Britain have a relatively small circulation. This is in marked contrast to some other countries, where the regional press is stronger than the national press.

The rack of papers seen outside any newsagents symbolizes the British class system. *The Times, The Daily Telegraph, The Guardian, The Independent* and the *Financial Times* are read overwhelmingly by the higher socio-economic groups. These papers used to be known as the 'broadsheets' from the size of paper used, although this term is no longer applicable, as *The Times* is now available in tabloid size, while *The Guardian* has adopted the mid-size *Berliner* format. There are two papers (the *Daily Mail* and the *Daily Express*) competing in the mid-market area for middle-class readers, whilst the mass circulation *The Sun, Daily Mirror* and *Daily Star* have predominantly working-class readers. There is relatively little crossover in readership between these different titles (Sparks, in Stokes and Reading, 1999, pp. 47–50), and thus little effective competition.

**Table 9.1**    National daily newspaper circulation and ownership, 2010

| Title | Circulation | Group | Proprietor |
|---|---|---|---|
| *The Sun* | 2,956,000 | News Corporation | Rupert Murdoch |
| *The Times* | 507,000 | News Corporation | Rupert Murdoch |
| *Daily Mirror* | 1,240,000 | Trinity Mirror | Sir Ian Gibson |
| *Daily Express* | 666,000 | Northern and Shell | Richard Desmond |
| *Daily Star* | 823,000 | Northern and Shell | Richard Desmond |
| *Daily Mail* | 2,096,000 | Daily Mail & General Trust | Lord Rothermere |
| *The Daily Telegraph* | 683,000 | Press Holdings International | Barclay brothers |
| *Guardian* | 289,000 | The Scott Trust | |
| *The Independent* | 188,000 | Independent Print Limited | Alexander Lebedev |
| *Financial Times* | 387,000 | Pearson plc | |

Treatment of the news varies enormously between papers. The quality papers contain much more of what might be described as 'hard news' in addition to comment and editorial. The mass circulation papers more closely resemble adult comics and are designed for looking at rather than reading, containing 'soft news' and features that have interest but not immediate newsworthiness. Much space is taken up with photographs and large-print headlines. Where the quality press covers international events and city news, the mass circulation papers rarely fail to devote considerable space to 'scandal' of one sort or another, often involving celebrities.

The number of national dailies declined steadily until the 1980s when the introduction of new technology destroyed the power of the old print unions, and seemed for a time to enable new papers to start and thrive. However, only one of the new titles launched then, *The Independent*, still survives, rather precariously. Most papers have suffered a decline in circulation in recent years (see Table 9.1). *The Sun* remains the market leader, followed by the long-established *Daily Mail*, whose circulation has held up better than its main rivals in an era of overall decline. The so-called 'quality press' (the *Times, Daily Telegraph, Financial Times, Guardian* and *Independent*) survive on a much smaller circulation than the 'tabloids' because their readers come predominantly from the higher social classes and enjoy more income and spending power, which is significant for advertising revenue.

Ownership of the press is concentrated in the hands of a few major groups, often with an influential controlling proprietor, such as Rupert Murdoch, Lord Rothermere, and Richard Desmond. Some of these have other extensive media interests. Thus Rupert Murdoch's News Corporation owns papers in many other western countries, and also has major interests in satellite and digital television, radio, cinema and books. The Mirror Group has extensive magazine interests, and controls many regional and local papers. Richard Desmond also has a major stake in magazines (including a number of 'soft porn' titles).

Does the concentration of media ownership matter? Editors have responsibility for the overall style and content of papers, but owners appoint (and can sack) editors, and this alone gives them substantial influence. Some owners, like Rupert Murdoch, have a more hands-on approach, and enjoy the power they wield that extends to the party political allegiance of their papers.

## British radio and television

Radio and television began in Britain as state-sponsored services financed by a licence fee paid by listeners and viewers, controlled by an arms-length public corporation, the British Broadcasting Corporation (BBC) with a charter and statutory obligation to show balance in its political reporting. The BBC monopoly was broken in the 1950s with the inauguration of commercial television and radio, with programmes financed by advertising

## COMPARATIVE POLITICS 9.1
# Political advertising in Britain and the United States

A marked feature of American election campaigns is the volume of political advertising on American television. Candidates, parties and special interests can buy television time to promote themselves, just like the advertising of commercial goods and services. Thirty-second or one-minute political commercials are a familiar feature of the American political scene. Candidates who run out of cash to finance advertising campaigns lose visibility. Well-funded groups like the National Rifle Association, or those with a vested interest in private medicine, are able to purchase substantial airtime to communicate their message in debates over gun control or healthcare. However, not all groups have the financial resources to enable them to put across their case.

In Britain, parties, candidates for elections and political groups are not allowed to buy advertising time on radio and television. British political parties are, however, allotted a number of party political broadcasts (and, during an election campaign, party election broadcasts), on a formula that takes into account the seats they contest and the votes they secure at elections. (Thus the British National Party first qualified for a party election broadcast during the 2005 election campaign.) The broadcasting time and basic studio facilities are free, although parties may purchase the services of film-makers, advertising agencies or public relations consultants to secure more professional promotion of their cause. A few party election broadcasts have made sufficient impact to become important news stories, with a measurable immediate effect on party support. Normally they have little impact, and are generally treated by viewers as a 'kettle opportunity' – to take a break from viewing to make coffee or tea. Some question their continuing value. They do, however, continue to provide an opportunity for relatively poorly financed parties (like the Liberal Democrats) to put their case to the public, helping to provide a more level playing field between competing parties. However, it is now widely reckoned that the televised leader debates, introduced into British politics for the first time in 2010, have further marginalized party election broadcasts.

---

revenue, although the statutory obligation on the Independent Broadcasting Authority (from 1990 replaced by the Independent Television Commisson, and later by Ofcom) of balanced political coverage remained. Thus the BBC monopoly was replaced by a BBC/ITV duopoly. This was only marginally affected by the slow emergence of new television channels, BBC2, Channel 4 and finally Channel 5, before the arrival of satellite, cable and digital television considerably expanded the range of choice open to viewers. In the context of this explosion of options, the continued survival of the BBC as a public service broadcaster with a global reputation is remarkable. In most other countries public service broadcasting has shrivelled in the face of competition (Curran and Seaton, 2003, p. 231).

The television audience is now far more segmented than it was. At one time, a large part of the population viewed the same national events and news at the same time, often as a family, in front of the single set in the house. This helped to create what was substantially a shared national political culture. Today many households have several television sets, with individual household members viewing programmes geared to their tastes in separate rooms, with playback facilities enabling them to watch programmes at different times. Thus television no longer brings the nation together, as it once did. It is now also easier to avoid material that individuals may prefer not to see. Thus the mute button on the remote control or the fast speed on the video can silence or eliminate commercials or party political broadcasts, or news programmes. Alternatively, they can be avoided by simply switching channels. Thus it is possible for those who are apathetic or antagonistic towards politics to avoid overt political communication

## Alastair Campbell, the BBC and the Hutton Report

In the events leading up to the invasion of Iraq, Alastair Campbell, then the government's Director of Communication and Strategy, had a key role in the presentation of the government's case for war. A political storm broke after a BBC journalist, Andrew Gilligan, alleged on the *Today* programme on 29 May 2003 that the government had embellished or 'sexed up' the case for war based on intelligence reports. Gilligan alleged specifically that the claim that Saddam Hussein could launch chemical and biological weapons within 45 minutes was included although the government 'probably knew' it was wrong. Campbell demanded that the BBC 'should accept for once that they got it wrong'. The BBC Chairman, Gavyn Davies, and Director General, Greg Dyke, stood by their reporter. The row became a major crisis after the source of Gilligan's allegation, David Kelly, a scientific adviser to the Ministry of Defence and a former weapons inspector, committed suicide shortly after giving evidence to the Commons Foreign Affairs Committee. An official inquiry set up under Lord Hutton to investigate the circumstances surrounding Kelly's death exonerated the government, and criticized the BBC. Campbell declared, 'What the report shows very clearly is this: the Prime Minister told the truth, the government told the truth, I

told the truth. The BBC, from the Chairman and Director General down, did not.' Both Davies and Dyke resigned, a consequence that the government had not initially expected or desired. Ironically, the earlier appointment of both men had been criticized by the Conservative Party because of their known Labour connections. Events proved the 45-minute claim was wrong, although the government continued to argue it was based on available intelligence. Some feared that the outcome would inhibit BBC political reporting.

almost entirely, because there is always something else to watch, even for those who rarely consider the drastic alternative of switching the set off.

## The British media, political bias and democracy

A free and diverse media expressing a range of political views is widely seen as a necessary condition for democracy. The media assist the working of a democratic system through facilitating free speech and unrestricted public debate. In Britain a variety of political opinions are aired in the media, and many of them are hostile to the government of the day. However, it is often argued that there is a political bias in the media that inevitably influences public opinion.

Much of the debate over media bias is around the issue of overt or covert party political bias.

Here there is a clear difference between the electronic media and the press. Both commercial radio and television as well as the BBC are bound by charter and by law to show balance between parties and impartiality in reporting and treating the news. This is interpreted to mean balance between the major parties and opinions within the political mainstream. The only programmes exempted from this requirement to political impartiality are party political broadcasts and party election broadcasts (see Comparative Politics 9.1).

Despite the obligation to maintain political balance, smaller parties and minority interests often feel broadcasters disregard their views. Moreover the major parties may allege party bias in individual broadcasters or programmes. The left has long been critical of television's coverage of political news, particularly industrial disputes, where they detect an anti-union bias. By contrast, some in the Conservative party have portrayed the

**Table 9.2**   Changing party support of national daily newspapers

| Newspaper | 1992 | 1997 | 2001 | 2005 | 2010 |
|---|---|---|---|---|---|
| *Daily Mirror* | Labour | Labour | Labour | Labour | Labour |
| *Daily Express* | Conservative | Conservative | Labour | Conservative | Conservative |
| *The Sun* | Conservative | Labour | Labour | Labour | Conservative |
| *Daily Mail* | Conservative | Conservative | Conservative | Not Labour | Conservative |
| *Daily Star* | Pro-Conservative | Labour | Labour | No endorsement | No endorsement |
| *Daily Telegraph* | Conservative | Conservative | Conservative | Conservative | Conservative |
| *Guardian* | Labour/Lib Dem | Labour | Labour | Labour | Lib Dem |
| *The Times* | Conservative | Euro-sceptics | Labour | Labour | Conservative |
| *The Independent* | None | Labour | Not Cons. | More Lib Dems | Lib Dem |
| *Financial Times* | No endorsement | Labour | Labour | Labour | Conservative |

*Sources*: Butler and Kavanagh (1992, 1997, 2001, 2005); Kavanagh and Cowley, 2010.

BBC as the 'Bolshevik Broadcasting Corporation', a hotbed of radicalism, hostile to mainstream conservative values. Yet in 2003 a major and bitter conflict between the Labour government's former Director of Communications, Alastair Campbell, and the BBC arose over its coverage of the government's case for war with Iraq. This conflict resulted in the resignations of the BBC's Chairman and Director General after the publication of the Hutton report (see box 9.1).

The press has no obligation to maintain impartiality, and indeed most British national newspapers make no secret of their own political sympathies and party preferences, freely selecting and interpreting the news in accordance with these. The political bias of newspapers often reflects the established preferences of its readers. Most *Daily Telegraph* readers are Conservative, while *Mirror* readers are predominantly Labour. Thus editorial policy arguably reflects market considerations. Any attempt to turn *The Daily Telegraph* into a staunch Labour paper would spell disaster for its circulation.

Yet most people do not buy papers for their politics, and may notice only subliminally, if at all, shifts in their political stance. Thus although *The Sun* arose from the ashes of the old *Daily Herald*, which was a Labour paper when Rupert Murdoch acquired it in 1974, he turned it into a highly partisan supporter of Margaret Thatcher's Conservatives, an allegiance initially maintained when Major succeeded Thatcher. By 1997 Murdoch, however, had switched to support Blair

and New Labour, and *The Sun* endorsed Labour again in 2001, and once more in 2005. Yet *The Sun* became increasingly critical of the Labour government after Brown succeeded Blair, and it was no surprise when it dramatically announced it was abandoning its support for the party in the midst of the Labour conference in 2009. In the 2010 election campaign its coverage was markedly pro-Conservative and critical of both Labour and the Liberal Democrats. *The Times* also switched to the Conservatives, as did the *Financial Times,* while the left-leaning *Guardian* endorsed the Liberal Democrats. By 2010, only the *Mirror* still backed Labour, representing a massive swing in the political coverage of the press, back to the anti-Labour bias of the pre-1997 period (see Table 9.2).

So far, bias has been explored almost exclusively in terms of *party* bias. Yet it has often been alleged that the British media display other forms of political bias. Feminists have long complained that the media portray women in a demeaning or degrading way, reinforcing and perpetuating their inferior status in society, sometimes even stimulating, through pornography, the degrading or violent treatment of women. Ethnic minority groups used to complain that they were invisible in the media, or shown in subordinate, stereotypical roles, although this is now less evident than before. Gays were shown, if at all, as comic figures. 'BBC English' once reflected southern middle-class accents, in a way that appeared to marginalize other parts of Britain and other social backgrounds.

More generally, the media, it has been argued, inevitably reflect dominant interests in society, the views of the establishment, of business rather than the workers, of 'the haves' rather than 'the have nots' and of private enterprise and free market capitalism. This is perhaps more particularly the case for newspapers and commercial television, substantially dependent on advertising revenue, and both directly and indirectly celebrating commercial values. Some have claimed that a globalized media reflects the interests of global capitalism.

The British media are thus far from neutral. News does not just happen, rather it is made. News items are selected and placed in order, in an implicit hierarchy of importance. Selection and ordering inevitably reflects bias of some kind. This may be a bias in favour of home rather than foreign news, of stories with 'human interest', and, for television, a bias in favour of visually interesting material. Some of this bias may substantially reflect what it is assumed readers, listeners and viewers want. Thus the sex life of a minor British celebrity, particularly if accompanied by revealing pictures, may command more media space and time than a humanitarian disaster in a remote continent, and this both reflects and in turn influences people's values.

## The power and influence of the media

The Conservative leader Stanley Baldwin once famously observed that newspaper proprietors exercised 'power without responsibility, the prerogative of the harlot throughout the ages' (a phrase apparently suggested by his cousin, the writer Rudyard Kipling). Few would deny that the press and the media generally do have political power and influence, although there is considerable debate about its nature and extent (see Academic Controversy 9.1).

How far does media bias translate into real media power and influence? In one interpretation, perhaps not as much as might be imagined. It has been persuasively argued that people do not just passively accept the political communication imparted by the media, but 'filter out' messages that do not match their own preconceived ideas, and only accept communications that reinforce those ideas. They do this through a process of selective exposure, selective perception and selective retention. Thus people tend to read newspapers or watch programmes that support their own political viewpoints. They re-interpret the hostile material they do encounter to fit in with their own preconceptions. Moreover, they remember selectively, only recalling evidence and arguments that fit in with their own ideas and forgetting those that do not (Trenamen and McQuail, 1961; Blumler and McQuail, 1967; Denver, 2003, pp. 132–4).

Yet as Denver (2003) points out, the key research supporting the filter model was carried out a long time ago, and largely focused on television, and more specifically on party election broadcasts, and their influence on voting. The bias in party election broadcasts is both transparent and generally unsubtle, and perhaps consequently less influential. Outside the special case of party broadcasts, television coverage is constrained by obligations to balance, particularly in election campaigns, and thus largely follows the parties' own agendas, rather than the independent judgement of television programme producers and reporters. However, television may still influence political choice in some respects. Television is primarily a visual medium, so the physical appearance, clothes and body language of candidates and leaders may influence voters, consciously or unconsciously. In a television era politicians need to 'look good on the box'. This was particularly apparent in the party leaders' debates in 2010.

Although most people trust television more than newspapers as a reliable source of news, the press may still be more politically influential, in part because it is uninhibited by any obligation towards balance. Moreover, it is not just editorials and comment columns that show bias, but the way in which news is selected and interpreted. Even those who turn straight to the sport or 'page 3' can hardly help registering, if only subconsciously, headlines that carry a strong political message. While people may believe they are uninfluenced by papers showing a manifest bias, they also think they are not influenced by commercial advertisements. If this were the case, companies could save money by scrapping their extensive advertising

## Academic controversy 9.1
# The role and power of the media

Three main models of the role and power of the media have been advanced.

The **pluralist model** suggests that Britain has a free press, with other media not controlled by the government. The media present a wide diversity of views, aiding public debate and the democratic process, enabling people to make up their own minds on important political issues. The media also have an important 'watchdog' role on behalf of the people, over government and powerful interests in society, and promote more effective public accountability.

The **dominant values model** suggests that the media portray news and events in such a way as to support the dominant values of political elites. As Marx claimed, 'The ruling ideas in every age are the ideas of the ruling class.' Ownership and control of the media is heavily concentrated, reflecting the concentration of wealth, income and power in society. The media reflect only a relatively narrow range of views, and minority perspectives are given little space or airtime. The media also 'scapegoats' minority social groups perceived as 'deviant' from prevailing norms – single mothers, social security scroungers, striking workers, asylum seekers.

The **market model** suggests that the media are driven largely by market or commercial considerations. Owners, editors, and producers seek to maximize profits by increasing circulation or audience share. Thus the media deliver what the public wants. The reduction of serious political content and overseas news in the press and mainstream news programmes reflects public taste and preference.

---

budgets. They advertise because their market research indicates it is effective, if sometimes subliminally. It is also difficult to believe that the 'drip, drip, drip' of political propaganda has no effect on readers over a period of years, rather than the three or four weeks of an official election campaign. As Denver (2003, p. 143) points out, this influence is likely to be stronger still now that fewer people identify strongly with particular parties. He concludes that 'the conditions are ripe' for increased media influence on voters' opinions 'with the development of a more free-floating and easily mobilized electorate'.

It is also plausible that the press helps to determine the political agenda, and influences public opinion on specific issues, such as the European Union, crime, or asylum seekers. The capacity of television to shape the political agenda is limited by the obligation to maintain balance, particularly during election campaigns. Thus television news coverage and most current affairs programmes tend to follow the parties' own agenda or the press agenda. If the press has managed to raise an issue that the parties have ignored, then it becomes 'news' and television can report it. Otherwise, if television producers choose to raise issues that parties have deliberately avoided, they risk accusations of bias. On particular issues the press can distort, and publish scare stories, and even plain untruths. Past examples include allegations that 'loony left' councils had banned black binliners as racist, or that the European Union was going to ban curved bananas. Some such stories are harmless nonsense, although the relentless hostility of most of the press towards the European Union goes some way towards explaining the prevailing Euro-scepticism in Britain.

## The 'dumbing down' of politics?

Some suggest that the media, and particularly the press, influence more general attitudes towards politics and government in Britain. Thus the media have been blamed both for 'dumbing down' political coverage, and encouraging a cynical negative attitude to parties, politicians and politics generally,

BOX 9.2

## Press influence on voting: the 1992 and 2010 general elections

In 1992 opinion polls predicted victory for Labour and its leader, Neil Kinnock. *The Sun* campaigned ruthlessly against both Labour and particularly Kinnock himself. On the eve of the election *The Sun* published a nine-page special fronted with the banner headline 'Nightmare on Kinnock Street' graphically predicting the horrors to come if Labour won. On polling day itself *The Sun* announced to its readers that if Kinnock won, 'We'll meet you at the airport.' After Major won, and Kinnock resigned the Labour leadership, some analysts found evidence that the Tory tabloids, and particularly *The Sun*, influenced a late and decisive swing to the Conservatives, prompting Murdoch's paper to boast 'It was *The Sun* wot won it.'

*The Sun* backed Labour in elections from 1997 to 2005, but in 2009 it transferred its support back to the

Conservatives and campaigned vigorously against Labour. It also turned its fire on the Liberal Democrats and Clegg after the first televised leaders' debate. Among readers of *The Sun* that had supported Labour in the three previous elections, there was a massive swing of 17.5 per cent to the Conservatives in 2010 (IPSOS MORI, reported in *The Observer*, 9 May 2010). Thus perhaps 'it was *The Sun* wot won it' or 'hung it' in 2010. The shifts in allegiance of *The Sun*, still the market leader, exemplify the power of a single newspaper proprietor, Rupert Murdoch. However, it can also be argued that the shifts in *The Sun*'s party allegiances reflected changes in wider public opinion and thus market considerations. Plausibly also, Murdoch wanted to retain influence with the party appearing most likely to form the next government.

with damaging consequences for political participation and the democratic process (Lloyd, 2004).

There is today more political information in the public domain than ever before, as a consequence both of the proliferation of new media channels, and the continuing pressures for more open government. Yet while there is far more information out there for those who want to access it, paradoxically the majority of the public are less exposed to politics than they were, and unsurprisingly feel less well-informed (see Chapter 4). For all the growth of new media channels, and new sources of information, most people still learn about politics from newspapers and mainstream television. However, serious political coverage by the popular press has declined markedly in recent decades, to be replaced by gossip, scandal and features. The private lives of politicians can attract a vicious media feeding frenzy, while their ideas and policies are relatively neglected, unless they upset the prejudices of journalists or readers. Even the so-called quality press devotes far less space to some aspects of politics than previously, most notably parliamentary business. Full coverage of parliamentary proceedings, including summaries of speeches, has

been replaced by short humorous reviews of (most commonly) Prime Minister's Questions. The main television news programmes have also moved down market, devoting more time to celebrities, sport and idiosyncratic items. Most members of the public have scarcely ever heard a full-length political speech involving a developed argument, only very short 'soundbites' – memorable sentences or phrases plucked out of context (Franklin, 2004).

Some consider the mass media have steadily reduced the intellectual demands made on readers, listeners and viewers. Americans call this process 'dumbing down'. Serious political coverage is reduced to increase market share. Within ITV, for example, 'there are undoubtedly pressures to reduce and popularize news output' (Crisell, in Stokes and Reading, 1999, p. 69). The BBC is affected by similar pressures, despite its role as a non-commercial public service broadcaster, partly because if its market share declines significantly it becomes politically more difficult to justify finance through the licence fee. Of course, it can be argued that far more news is now available on a 24- hour basis on minority channels for those who want it. Yet the channels that most people watch have cut their serious news content, and it is much easier for the politically apathetic to avoid informing themselves about politics.

Others argue that the growth of cynical hostile interrogation of politicians and negative reporting has encouraged a general distrust of the political process and democracy (Lilleker *et al.*, 2003; Lloyd, 2004). If interviewers assume that all politicians are crooks or liars, it is hardly surprising that viewers and listeners come to share the assumption. Politicians have hardly helped to improve their own image by the strategy they commonly adopt when confronted by sneering cross-examinations by 'rottweiler' interviewers, simply repeating their own prepared '**soundbites**', almost regardless of the questions posed. Such confrontations may sometimes make good television but rarely contribute much to the sum total of public political knowledge.

## Politicians and the media – the uses and abuses of image and spin

So far the emphasis in this chapter has been on the power and influence of the media on government and the political process. Yet government and political leaders generally are far from being helpless victims of the mass media. As they inevitably make news by their pronouncements and decisions, they can seek to control the news, by the timing and manner of the release of information. They can seek to manage the media, to use whatever channels of communication are available to put their message across.

They and their advisers can also manage the presentation of their own image. Graham Wallas (1920, p. 31) a pioneer British social scientist, grasped the value of photographs in projecting a favourable image of candidates for political office. 'Best of all is a photograph which brings his ordinary existence sharply forward by representing him in his garden smoking a pipe or reading a newspaper.' The casual, seemingly spontaneous appearance would in reality be carefully posed, the back-

ground, clothes, and props deliberately chosen, the body language conveyed by expression and posture considered. Later, the posed photograph was replaced by the televised 'photo-opportunity', the context providing an appropriate political message – Mrs Thatcher cuddling a day-old calf, John Major visiting a DIY store, Tony Blair beginning an election campaign at a school, David Cameron riding his bike to work. All these photo-opportunities were professionally stage-managed to create an impression of informal spontaneity. More recently, politicians and their advisers have learned how to project their own image more effectively through websites. The technology may change, and some of the skills, but the essential art of image projection is as old as politics.

Similarly, skilful leaders and politicians have always grasped the importance of putting a favourable gloss on events, of getting their version of the story accepted. This is essentially what 'spin' is about. 'Spin doctors' are those skilled in presentation and interpretation. The use of the term in British politics is relatively new, but the activity is very old. Thus although 'spin' has become particularly associated with New Labour, it was effectively practised in British politics long before. Indeed, one of the old Labour party's problems was that they were not as good at political communication as their opponents. While the Conservatives hired the best advertising agencies available to put their message across, Labour was distrustful of advertisers and 'selling politics like cornflakes'. Moreover, Labour had to contend with a generally hostile press, particularly in the 1980s and early 1990s. Labour's 'spin machine' grew from the bitter experiences of opposition. They learned the importance of good political communication, of party unity and 'staying on message' – agreeing the story and sticking to it. They also appreciated the need for better relations with the media, particularly the press. While many in the party loathed Rupert Murdoch and *The Sun* newspaper, Blair and his advisers actively sought to win and retain Murdoch's support, in the process converting a substantially anti-Labour press into a generally supportive press.

'Spin', moreover, is not confined to politicians, parties and their advisers. Radio, television and newspaper journalists are constantly putting their

---

● '**Soundbites**' are short snappy memorable phrases, frequently extracted from the broader context of a speech or document. Thus mainstream television rarely broadcasts whole speeches or even substantial extracts from speeches but brief 'soundbites'. Research suggests that soundbites are becoming shorter.

## BOX 9.3

# 'Becoming the story': some prominent spin doctors

**Peter Mandelson** has been credited with successfully rebranding the Labour Party as New Labour, and making it electable. A very successful backroom operator, he had political ambitions of his own, becoming Labour candidate for Hartlepool, which he won in 1992. He played a key role in the emergence of Blair as leader in 1994, and in the revision of Clause Four of Labour's constitution. Curiously, he was much less effective in spinning himself than his party, and was twice obliged to resign Cabinet posts in controversial circumstances in 1998 and 2001. His return to the Cabinet as Business Secretary under Gordon Brown in 2008, after a period as a European Commissioner, was a real surprise. However, selling Brown proved beyond him.

**Alastair Campbell** became a key adviser to Blair in opposition, later the Prime Minister's press secretary and after 2001 his Director of Communications and Strategy, before resigning in 2003 shortly after the David Kelly affair and the Hutton Report (see also Box 9.1). An outspoken, belligerent, but generally effective champion of Labour and its Prime Minister, he antagonized many journalists by his bullying, threatening manner. He continued to advise Blair more informally, and later helped Brown.

**Jo Moore** served as Labour minister Stephen Byers' spin doctor, and was responsible for an infamous email sent on the occasion of the 9/11 attack on the Twin Towers. This, she suggested, was a good day to publish and 'bury' departmental bad news. Releasing bad news under cover of some bigger story is a familiar technique, but this was an appallingly insensitive example. Byers unwisely stood by his adviser, (although eventually she had to go), and this contributed to events leading to his own resignation in 2002.

**Andy Coulson** became the Director of Communications and Planning for the Conservative party in 2007 soon after he resigned from his post as editor of the *News of the World* after journalists at the paper were involved in phone hacking the royal family, politicians and celebrities. Coulson denied any personal knowledge of phone hacking when he appeared before a Commons Select Committee. When *The Guardian* made fresh allegations about the extent of phone hacking by *News of the World* journalists, Cameron was urged to sack Coulson. He refused, saying he believed in giving people a second chance. Yet ultimately Coulson felt obliged to resign in January 2011. The spinner had become the story.

own interpretation, or 'spin', on news stories. Confronted with a complex mosaic of facts and unsubstantiated rumour, journalists try to reveal the 'real story'. Often the first in the field determines what the story is, unless a rival can provide a convincing new interpretation. Far from being some kind of New Labour invention, 'spin' may be seen as a universal activity.

Ultimately, New Labour 'spin' became counterproductive. The most successful and effective 'spinning' is that which is so unobtrusive as not to be noticed; people are led to believe that they are given the plain unvarnished and incontrovertible truth, rather than a selective and partisan interpretation of events. The problem with Labour's spin doctors was that they became too high-profile. Rather than anonymously and successfully purveying good stories, they themselves became the story and in the process damaged the product they were hired to

promote (see Box 9.3), as Campbell for one seemed to appreciate.

Political communication is important in any political system, but particularly crucial in those states claiming to be democratic. Democracy requires more than effective government communication, for it implies a two-way interactive communication between government and people. A government that does not listen is unlikely to remain long in power. However, western democracy also assumes a continuous competitive struggle for power and influence by individuals, interests and parties in which those who manage to put across the most persuasive stories are more likely to prevail. The stakes can be high, helping to determine 'who gets what, when, how' in Lasswell's terse definition of politics (see Chapter 1). Effective communication of the message of a politician, party or group may make the difference between winning and losing. In a complex world there are inevitably many sides to difficult questions, not a single version of the truth. Effective communication generally requires selection, simplification and graphic illustration, which can easily lead to accusations of manipulation and 'spin'. While the media can perform a watchdog role, they are also participants, with their own interests to defend and their own conflicting but strongly held interpretations of the pubic interest to advance. In such circumstances it is difficult for the public to know whom to believe. Routine accusations of deliberate deception on the part of government or the media undermine public trust, are corrosive of democracy, and increase alienation from the whole political process (Lloyd, 2004).

## The internet and traditional media: the 2010 election

The internet has become increasingly important in British politics, particularly perhaps the growth of political blogs, providing a much more extensive range of easily available instant reactions to political developments. Much more political information has become accessible including some (such as the revelations of Wikileaks) that governments would much rather keep secret. It has been argued that the internet enables a much wider and more democratic market of ideas.

It was widely predicted (again!) that the UK 2010 election would be the first in which the web displaced more traditional channels of political communication, particularly following the 2008 US presidential election in which the internet was extensively and successfully used by the Obama campaign. The prediction proved accurate only up to a point, and most obviously in a negative sense. Thus some claimed that the imaginative range of spoof alternative election posters instantly created on the web has killed off the traditional billboard poster campaign, a prominent feature of recent elections, dating back to the celebrated Saatchi and Saatchi 1979 'Labour isn't working' poster featuring

a dole queue. The ritual unveiling of new posters had, until recently, even featured prominently on television election coverage. In 2010 it proved only too easy to generate mocking variations of the main parties' expensively created posters. Thus Cameron's allegedly airbrushed image next to the words 'We can't go on like this. I'll cut the deficit, not the NHS' spawned an avalanche of creative alternatives. The series 'I've never voted Tory before but …' led to an imaginative range of mocking imitations. Similarly, Labour's slogan 'A future fair for all' was endlessly reinterpreted. Other bloggers generated their own spoof election slogans and pictures. Much of this, originally viewed by many thousands online, was picked up by newspapers and reproduced for the edification of millions of readers. Thus the traditional media were largely responsible for circulating much of the information, comment, analysis and satire on the web to a wider audience. As a result some party advertising proved counter-productive. More people may have laughed over the spoofs than saw the originals. Elsewhere there was much instant comment and feedback on the web on the daily conduct of the election campaign, and this considerably amplified the range and depth of political coverage. Both major parties made increased use of the internet to put their message across and reach niche audiences (although here the Liberal Democrats seem to have been less effective).

Yet the traditional mainstream media still dominated the election. The central talking point of the campaign that stirred new interest and perhaps raised turnout was the televised leaders' debates and their endless analysis and re-interpretation in the press. One by-product of the focus on these unscripted events was the eclipse of the carefully constructed party political broadcasts that have often featured prominently in past elections. The gaffe of the campaign, Gordon Brown's encounter with 'that bigoted woman' and subsequent comments caught on a live microphone, were also endlessly replayed on mainstream television, and seized on by the press.

# SUMMARY

- Most of what people think they know about politics and government does not come from direct personal experience. Political communication between government and people is largely through the mass media.

- Each media channel has its own particular characteristics (and limitations) strongly influencing the messages they transmit. Thus television is primarily a visual medium; the pictures rather than sound commentary convey the main message.

- The British press is dominated by ten national dailies (and associated Sunday papers) competing in segmented markets. Ownership of the press is substantially concentrated, and some proprietors have other extensive media interests.

- British radio and television have charter and statutory obligations to maintain political balance, unlike the highly partisan national press.

- The extent of media power and influence is contentious. Thus it has been argued that media influence on voting is very limited, although not everyone agrees. Others suggest that there is a pervasive media bias in favour of the establishment or free market capitalism.

- The media have been accused of reducing and 'dumbing down' political coverage, and more recently of encouraging alienation and apathy.

- The handling of party and government communication and management of the media has also come under increasing criticism. Blair's Labour government has become associated with 'spin', putting a favourable interpretation on events and developments.

- The 2010 election confirms the rising significance of the new media, especially the web. Yet the traditional mainstream media still had more impact on the campaign, and perhaps its outcome.

# QUESTIONS FOR DISCUSSION

- How far do different media require different political communication skills? In what ways might television trivialize political debate?

- How far does the concentration of ownership of the press and media generally pose problems for democracy?

- How far and in what ways is the British press and British television biased?

- In what ways has the internet transformed political communication in Britain? How far does it facilitate genuine two-way communication between citizens and government? How might it transform democracy?

- How much real political power and influence do the media have?

- What evidence is there that the British press, or the media generally, have significantly influenced political views and party choice?

- To what extent has media coverage of British politics been 'dumbed down'?

- What is spin and how new is it? How far was New Labour spin effective?

- How far and in what ways might the new media encourage more political participation and interactive public debate? Do the new media pose any problems for politics?

## FURTHER READING

Raymond Kuhn (2007) provides an excellent overview of *Politics and the Media in Britain* that contains extremely useful summaries of most of the relevant research and controversies around political communication over the last forty years. John Street (2001) is broader in scope, though less up to date, but contains a particularly useful analysis of media bias. The sixth edition of Curran and Seaton (2003), *Power Without Responsibility: The Press and Broadcasting in Britain* remains one of the best guides to the traditional British media. This can be supplemented by Stokes and Reading (1999), *The Media in Britain: Current Debates and Developments*. On media influence on British politics, and specifically voting, see the discussion in

Chapter 6 of Denver (2003). The influence of the media on recent general elections is discussed extensively in chapters in the Nuffield election studies. See especially relevant material in Kavanagh and Cowley (2010) on the 2010 election. On the growing literature on government communication and news management see Franklin (1994, 2004), Jones (1996, 1999) and the extracts from Gaber, Franklin and Jones in *The New Labour Reader*, edited by Chadwick and Heffernan (2003). Wring, in Dunleavy *et al.* (2006) covers New Labour's political communication. Lloyd (2004) is critical of the influence of media political reporting on the style and content of British politics. Evgeny Morozov (2011) is provocative on the internet and democracy.

# The Changing British System of Government

In this and subsequent chapters the emphasis shifts from the wider political processes involving (to a greater or lesser degree) the whole people to the relative few directly involved in the institutions and workings of government. British government long appeared a model of stability in a changing world. Since the upheavals of the seventeenth century, culminating in the Glorious Revolution of 1688, and the 1707 Act of Union, Britain has not experienced the revolutions and regime changes that have characterized, for example, French government and politics for over 200 years. Instead the British system of government has evolved gradually towards a constitutional monarchy and later a parliamentary democracy, a process substantially completed at the end of the First World War. Reforms were grafted onto traditional institutions. The new was painlessly absorbed into the old and familiar. There appeared no need to spell out the functions of different parts of government, nor the rights of citizens in any authoritative written constitution, such as other states possessed. Indeed, what was sometimes described as 'the Westminster model' was widely admired at home and abroad.

More recently the British system of government has appeared, to many, rather less admirable. Criticisms of core institutions and even of fundamental constitutional principles fuelled a strong movement for constitutional reform from the late twentieth century onwards. Thus both the Labour government that took office in 1997 and the coalition government formed in 2010 were pledged to radical constitutional change. The cumulative impact of recent and proposed constitutional change involves a massive change to Britain's traditional system of government. Yet it is by no means clear how far the Westminster model has been superseded, as reforms, past and ongoing, have proceeded piecemeal and grafted on to traditional institutions and principles without much apparent thought being given to the implications for the system as a whole. Some critics feel that the tensions and ambiguities inherent in the still evolving new system of government can only be resolved by a written constitution.

This chapter examines Britain's still unwritten constitution, its sources, and the core principles that have been attributed to it. It explores the attitudes of political parties to the constitution, and the criticisms that have fuelled demands for further constitutional reform. It proceeds to examine recent and proposed reforms, and explores the implications for traditional British constitutional principles. Finally, the case for further reform and a written constitution is considered. More detailed aspects of British government are, however, treated in later chapters.

## BOX 10.1

# The major sources of the British constitution

- **Statute law** - law passed by Parliament, some of which is of a constitutional nature, e.g. Acts determining the composition of the electorate and the conduct of elections, and Acts laying down the powers and composition of the House of Lords.
- **Common law** - theoretically the immemorial law of the people, in practice the law as determined by decisions of courts. The remaining 'prerogative powers' of the crown (now exercised by the government of the day) derive from common law.
- **Conventions** - unwritten rules of constitutional behaviour which are widely accepted and observed (largely because of the political difficulties which would follow if they were not). Most of the powers relating to the Prime Minister depend on convention. Conventions may evolve over time, and may be difficult to date precisely (e.g. the convention that a Prime Minister must sit in the House of Commons).
- **The law and custom of Parliament.** Many of the rules relating to the functions, procedures, privileges and immunities of each house are contained in resolutions of both houses, conventions and informal understandings. These are listed and described in Erskine May's *Treatise on the Law, Privileges, Proceedings and Usages of Parliament.*
- **Works of authority.** In the absence of other authoritative written sources, works by eminent experts on the British constitutions are consulted, e.g. Walter Bagehot, *The English Constitution* (1867); A. V. Dicey, *The Law of the Constitution* (1885); and Sir Ivor Jennings, *The Law and the Constitution* (1933).
- **European Union law.** Since the UK joined what was then the European Community in 1973, EC/EU law has been binding on the UK and applied by British courts. This has implications for the constitutional principle of parliamentary sovereignty. Additionally, some specific EU rules are of a constitutional nature.
- **The European Convention on Human Rights.** This was (in effect) incorporated into UK law by the 1998 Human Rights Act, which came into force in 2000. This Act appears to have a higher status than ordinary parliamentary law, which may be declared incompatible with the ECHR (thus limiting parliamentary sovereignty). Conservatives have proposed replacing the European Convention on Human Rights with a British Bill of Rights.

## The constitution

A **constitution** provides a framework of rules and principles for the conduct of government and politics in a particular state. For almost all states today these are contained in a single written document, which commonly proclaims key political values, details the functions and powers of state institutions, and the rights and responsibilities of state citizens. Britain unusually lacks such a single authoritative written document on its system of government.

However, this does not mean that Britain lacks a constitution, in the sense of well-established rules for the conduct of government, and widely accepted constitutional principles. Some of these rules *are* written down, as part of the law of the land, contained in Acts of Parliament, or decisions on cases decided in the courts. Thus, strictly speaking, the British constitution is uncodified (in the sense that it has not been collected into a single document), rather than unwritten. Some key aspects of the British system of government, however, *are* unwritten, as they are not contained within any formal written document, but rest on conventions, agreed usages which are so widely accepted they have long been undisputed. However, these conventions, 'unwritten' in the sense that they have not been authoritatively recorded in some law or charter, have been extensively analyzed and dissected by constitutional lawyers and political scientists.

Many argue, on the principle 'If it ain't broke, don't fix it', that Britain does not need a written constitution as its system of government works well enough without one. Indeed, written constitutions are generally imperfect guides to political reality –

---

- A state **constitution** is simply a set of rules and conventions that lays down the powers and functions of state institutions and their relationship with each other.

to the actual as compared with the supposed distribution of power within a state. For example, many constitutions either omit or scarcely mention the roles in the political process of such institutions as political parties, pressure groups and public bureaucracies. Much important political behaviour occurs outside the formal legal framework. Many bald statements in constitutional documents require supplementing by a body of custom and practice. Some provisions may be positively misleading or rendered ineffective (such as the electoral college that supposedly chooses the US President). Moreover, some constitutions have proved hardly worth the paper they were written on, torn up or simply ignored by usurpers and dictators.

Yet, while written constitutions are incomplete guides to political practice, they do matter for a number of reasons. They commonly include the most important procedural rules of a political system. They frequently also contain statements of key political principles and commitments to basic rights and freedoms. They give legitimacy to a particular system of government, and to the distribution of power within a state. They can be widely revered by both governors and governed. They may be used and interpreted by courts of law. Alongside moral codes and cultural norms, they provide a means of restraint on politicians and state officials.

## The powers of the state

In the analysis of any system of government the powers of the state are widely grouped under three headings: **legislative**, **executive** and **judicial**.

In many other countries the separation of legislative, executive and judicial powers has long been established as an important constitutional principle. Thus it is a key feature of the American constitution, and of many other constitutions that have been established since. In the United States the executive is the Presidency, the legislature, Congress, while the Supreme Court heads an inde-

- The **legislature** is responsible for *making law*.

- The **executive** is charged with the day-to-day government of the country, responsible for making policy and *administering law*.

- The **judiciary** is responsible for *adjudicating on the law* and legal disputes.

pendent judiciary. There are checks and balances in the American Constitution that are designed to prevent any part of government from becoming too powerful.

Back in the eighteenth century, British government appeared to involve a separation of powers between King, Parliament and an independent judiciary. Yet in practice the executive was increasingly not so much the king but a Cabinet of leading ministers dependent on a parliamentary majority. This effectively involved a fusion of executive and legislative powers. Today, the British executive remains a parliamentary executive, dependent on a continuing Commons majority, but dominating the work of Parliament. Moreover, until very recently (2009) the upper house of the legislature, the House of Lords, was also Britain's highest court, involving a mixture of the legislative and judicial roles. While recent reforms appear to have strengthened the independence of the judiciary, Britain's new Supreme Court lacks the prestige and power of the American Supreme Court.

## Changing the constitution

Although constitutions (written or unwritten) may be treated with great reverence, they are not 'above politics' but remain part of politics. Constitutions embody the current rules of the political game. These advantage some interests and disadvantage others, so they can become acutely controversial. Thus some politicians and political activists may seek to modify, radically reform or, if they are revolutionaries, overthrow the existing constitution. Yet even if there is a broad consensus supporting key elements of the existing constitution, inevitably ongoing technological and social change may require amendments to institutions, procedures and, sometimes, constitutional principles.

So constitutions are not immutable, although it is widely agreed that they should not be lightly altered. Thus constitutional law often has the status of a higher form of law, only alterable by special procedures. In many countries more than a simple parliamentary majority is required for a constitutional amendment – such as a two-thirds majority in each house of parliament. Some constitutions additionally stipulate the support of the people in a

## COMPARATIVE POLITICS 10.1
# The American constitution

The American constitution was originally drawn up in 1787. Much of the text still accurately describes features of the US system of government, including the separation of legislative, executive and judicial powers.

- 'All legislative Powers herein granted shall be vested in a Congress of the United States, which shall consist of a Senate and a House of Representatives' (Article 1, Section 1).
- 'The Executive Power shall be vested in a President of the United States . . .' (Article 2, Section 1).
- 'The Judicial Power of the United States shall be vested in one Supreme Court . . .' (Article 3, Section 1).

However, although the constitution was proclaimed in the name of 'We the people of the United States', it was not a document originally designed to give much real power to the people. Yet over time the United States became more democratic, in part because some features of the system, such as the Electoral College for choosing the President, never operated as the Founding Fathers intended. A conspicuous flaw in American democracy was the survival of slavery until the American civil war, and the treatment of blacks as second class citizens for more than a century afterwards.

The constitution continues to be treated with reverence by American politicians and citizens. It is a constant reference point when major disputes over government arise. Even so, it is not always an accurate guide to American government and politics. On other important issues such as the rights of the states, city and local government, political parties and organized groups, the constitution is vague or silent.

*Note*: The text of the US constitution and amendments is available online and reproduced in many books on American politics.

---

referendum. Federal systems of government additionally will normally require the support of all or most of the member states for a constitutional amendment.

Britain's unwritten (or uncodified) constitution remains highly flexible. Indeed, interpretation of the constitution has altered almost imperceptibly over time. Thus at one time a Prime Minister could come from either house of parliament, and in the nineteenth century most came from the House of Lords. In the twentieth century this seemed incompatible with democratic assumptions, and over a period it has become a convention that the Prime Minister must sit in the House of Commons, although this has not been officially laid down in any law. Some parts of the British constitution can be found in Acts of Parliament (e.g. those relating to the powers of the House of Lords). However, such laws with constitutional implications can be changed, effectively by a simple majority in the House of Commons. While a number of issues with constitutional implications have been submitted for a popular vote in a referendum from 1975 onwards, there is no obligation on government to hold such referendums, nor is Parliament bound by the results (see below).

A flexible constitution may enable a system of government to evolve with the times, but may appear vulnerable to ill-considered change, or subversion. By contrast, a constitution that can only be changed with great difficulty may lack the capacity to adapt to new pressures and altered circumstances, perhaps of a kind that its original designers could hardly anticipate. Yet judicial interpretation can lead to significant change even in countries with an apparently 'rigid' constitution. Thus the American Supreme Court's interpretation of the constitution has evolved with the times, with, for example, considerable implications for racial segregation and civil rights.

## COMPARATIVE POLITICS 10.2
# Amending constitutions

Procedures for amending the **US constitution** are described in Article 6 of the constitution. Congress can propose amendments that have been approved by a two-thirds majority in each House. Any such amendment must also be approved by three-quarters of the state legislatures before it takes effect. Thus amending the US constitution is very difficult. Even so, a number of important amendments have been passed. These include:

- The Bill of Rights, the name given to the first ten amendments, ratified in 1791, which includes a number of basic citizen rights including free speech and religious toleration, the right to a fair trial and the notorious second amendment, the right to bear arms.
- The abolition of slavery (13th amendment, 1865).
- Prohibition of the manufacture, sale, or transportation of intoxicating liquors (18th amendment, 1920, subsequently repealed in the 21st amendment, 1933).
- The enfranchisement of women (19th amendment, 1920).
- The limitation of the Presidential period of office to two terms (22nd amendment, 1951).

In **Australia** constitutional amendments require the support of both houses of parliament, then a referendum which must receive majority support overall and in a majority of states.

In **Germany** constitutional amendments need a two-thirds majority in both houses of parliament, but the federal system and the rights of German citizens cannot be amended.

**France** has two methods for making constitutional amendments:

- Amendments can be made by a majority in both houses of the French parliament voting on an identical motion, followed by ratification of three-fifths of Congress (the two houses combined). The Fifth Republic has been amended seven times using this method.
- Amendments can also be made by a constitutional referendum, after an identical motion passed in both houses of parliament.

(See Hague and Harrop, 2010, ch. 13.)

## Key features or principles of the British constitution

Written constitutions commonly contain some statements of principle, for example a commitment to democracy, or a republic or an established religion. In Britain there is no authoritative statement of the principles on which the (unwritten) constitution rests, and these in practice have been inferred by constitutional lawyers and other experts. The British constitution has long been described in terms of the following key features or principles:

- A unitary state (rather than a federal state)

- A constitutional monarchy (rather than a republic)
- Parliamentary sovereignty (rather than a separation of powers)
- Representative democracy (rather than direct democracy)
- The rule of law

All of these principles require some further explanation and discussion. Some are contentious, particularly in the light of relatively recent and proposed changes in UK government (discussed later in the chapter). This section outlines how the principles have been traditionally explained and interpreted, and goes on to explore some of the questions and ambiguities now surrounding them.

## A unitary rather than a federal state?

The United Kingdom is, as its name suggests, a unitary rather than a federal state. Besides the separation of executive, legislative and judicial powers, some constitutions divide the functions of the state between different levels. Under a federal system sovereignty is deliberately divided between two or more levels of government. Each level of government is, in theory, sovereign (or supreme) in its own sphere.

**Federalism** was virtually invented by the founding fathers of the American constitution. Some earlier political thinkers like Thomas Hobbes (1588–1679) had declared that **sovereignty** (or supreme power) could not be divided. Yet those who devised the American constitution had to reconcile the rights of the original thirteen American states with the need for some overall co-ordination of (especially) defence, foreign policy and inter-state trade. Thus powers were effectively divided between the federal government and state governments. This solution was attractive to other countries where there was a similar need to accommodate both unity and diversity, particularly where different ethnic, cultural and national groups were located within the same territories. Thus today there are many federal states, including the USA, Canada, Switzerland, Australia, Germany, India and Belgium (Hague and Harrop, 2010, pp. 273–80).

A federal state virtually requires a written constitution. If each level of government is supreme in its own sphere, there has to be some authoritative document determining those spheres, laying out the functions of the federal and state governments. This could involve listing the functions of each (perhaps with some powers exercised 'concurrently'), or merely listing the functions of one level, and ascribing all remaining powers to the other level. Thus the American constitution details the powers of the federal government, reserving all other powers to the states. Inevitably, this does not preclude tensions between the levels of government. A major theme of the history of American government has been the alleged encroachment of the federal power on states' rights.

Most states are not federal states. Some particularly emphasize their unity. Thus the French Fifth Republic is 'one and indivisible'. This does not preclude other levels of government (regional and local), but these are legally subordinate to the sovereign state. The United Kingdom (like France) is still a unitary state, at least in legal form. Legally and constitutionally the recent **devolution** of power to Scotland, Wales and Northern Ireland affects neither the unity of the United Kingdom nor the sovereignty of the Westminster parliament. (However, some argue that devolution in practice involves a quasi-federal system of government.)

## A constitutional monarchy

The United Kingdom, again as its name implies, remains a monarchy, but a limited or constitutional monarchy. Thus it is generally reckoned that the Queen 'reigns but does not rule' and has little or no political power. The personal political power of the monarch has been eroded gradually over the centuries and is now vestigial. Constitutional experts used to debate the monarch's discretion over the choice of a Prime Minister, or a requested dissolution of Parliament, but the circumstances in which there might be scope for discretion now seem remote. After the inconclusive result of the 2010 election, for example, advisers and experts agreed that the Queen must in no way be personally involved in the making of a new government. She had to wait for the main parties to resolve the deadlock, and for Brown to resign, before she could ask Cameron to form a government whose shape had already been determined. The Queen, in the

---

● **Federalism** involves the division of sovereignty between two or more levels of government. In a federal system each level of government is sovereign (or supreme) in its own sphere.

● **Sovereignty** means supreme power. Within a state it refers to the ultimate source of legal authority. When used of states in their external relations, sovereignty means a state's ability to function as an independent entity – as a sovereign state.

---

● **Devolution** is a term coined to describe the delegation of powers in the United Kingdom downwards to institutions in Scotland, Wales and Northern Ireland. Devolution is distinguished from federalism because it does not, in theory, involve any transfer of sovereignty, nor any breach of the constitutional principle of the unity of the United Kingdom.

words of Walter Bagehot, the nineteenth-century authority on the constitution, retains the right to be consulted, the right to encourage and the right to warn. The Prime Minister still has regular meetings with the sovereign, and the present Queen's experience of successive governments and Prime Ministers from Churchill onwards may well sometimes make her advice worth listening to.

However, if the personal power of the monarch is too negligible to be a live political issue, the institution of the crown and the royal prerogative are more contentious. Ministers, members of the armed forces and civil servants are officially servants of the crown rather than the public or 'the state'. There is no positive injunction to serve the people or the public interest. Until recently it was not even possible to sue the crown or servants of the crown. Moreover, some of the former powers of the sovereign which are no longer exercised by the Queen have not been abolished but transferred, mainly to the Prime Minister. Thus it was the Prime Minister who effectively inherited the former 'royal prerogative' powers to declare wars, make treaties and dissolve Parliament. A Prime Minister, until very recently, could involve Britain in war without seeking ratification from Parliament. While some of these prerogative powers are now being restricted or abolished, others remain. .

The monarchy has rarely been a political issue since the later nineteenth century, even if the removal of the principle of heredity from the second chamber may be thought to have implications for a hereditary head of state. No major political party has dared propose the abolition of the monarchy (although some maverick MPs have done so). If Britain were to become a republic, a President or formal head of state would probably be necessary, in addition to the Prime Minister as head of government, as in most other modern democratic republics (see Comparative Politics 10.3).

## Parliamentary sovereignty

Parliamentary sovereignty has long been considered a key British constitutional principle. Parliamentary sovereignty effectively denies the principle of the separation of powers. The executive in Britain is a parliamentary executive, whose existence depends on the continuing confidence of Parliament. The judiciary is bound to accept law passed by Parliament.

What parliamentary sovereignty means in practice is that, in formal terms, parliamentary authority in the United Kingdom is unlimited. William Blackstone, the eighteenth-century jurist, declared that Parliament 'can do everything that is not naturally impossible'. According to the principle of parliamentary sovereignty, statute law, law passed by Parliament, is supreme over other kinds of law. No person may question its legislative competence and the courts must give effect to its legislation. Part of the principle is that no parliament can bind its successors. This looks like a limitation on the power of Parliament, but clearly if an Act of Parliament contained a clause that it could not be repealed, this would effectively end parliamentary sovereignty.

However, the long maintained principle of parliamentary sovereignty does not mean that Parliament is particularly powerful in practice. Indeed, the decline in the power and effective influence of Parliament is often lamented (see Chapter 13). As Andrew Marr (1996, p. 160) has observed 'Here is the crucial conundrum for the British Parliament, which it alone can answer: if it is sovereign, indeed absolute, then why is it so weak?'

## Representative democracy

Representative democracy may be considered a more fundamental principle of the British system of government than parliamentary sovereignty, even if it is a principle less discussed by constitutional lawyers. It is a mark of the evolutionary nature of the British system of government that it is difficult to pin down precisely when Britain became a democracy (and some critics would deny that it is, in some important respects, even now). Yet the extension of the vote was accompanied by a gradual acceptance of democratic principles over time, and this in turn prompted the emergence of new conventions embodying the spirit of democracy. Thus it came to be established that the peers should not frustrate the will of the democratically elected House of Commons, particularly on issues which had been submitted to the people in a manifesto by the governing party. Similarly, it became an unwritten rule that the Prime Minister and head of government should be a member of the House of

## COMPARATIVE POLITICS  10.3
# Constitutional monarchies and republics

In France, the United States, and in most other countries regarded as democratic, republicanism is regarded as the natural corollary of democracy. The retention of the principle of heredity for filling the post of head of state appears incompatible with democratic values. Thus many democracies have a non-hereditary head of state. Sometimes the head of state is also head of the government, as in the United States. More commonly, there is a separate formal head of state with little effective power, either directly elected by the people, or indirectly elected by parliament.

However, while the retention of the institution of monarchy is rare it is not unique among countries with a reasonable claim to democracy. Belgium, the Netherlands, Sweden, Denmark and Spain are among examples in Europe of democratic states that retain hereditary monarchs, who in all cases have negligible personal political power. In addition, several Commonwealth countries still acknowledge the Queen as their head of state, (although the issue has become politically contentious in Australia).

Commons, and, normally, the elected leader of the majority party.

Of course, British democracy involves representative (or parliamentary) democracy rather than direct democracy (see Chapter 1). There is an implied contradiction here between the principles of **parliamentary sovereignty** and **popular sovereignty**. It is elected representatives of the people rather than the people themselves who decide. How far these representatives are truly representative of the people is itself a contentious issue (see Chapter 5 on voting, and Chapter 13 on Parliament). Yet is clear that parliamentary decisions do not always coincide with public opinion. Thus Parliament legislated to abolish capital punishment even when opinion polls suggested continuing public support for it.

## The rule of law

The leading jurist A. V. Dicey (1835–1922) saw the rule of law as a fundamental characteristic of the

British constitution, viewing it as of equal importance to the doctrine of parliamentary sovereignty. Although in strict constitutional terms, the rule of law is subordinate to parliamentary sovereignty, the rule of law remains of key significance. It affirms that, while the executive and legislative branches of state are 'fused', the judicial branch is largely independent and separate and can check the executive. Second, the rule of law enshrines principles such as natural justice, fairness and reasonableness that can be applied by the courts through the process of judicial review.

The fundamental principle is that people are subject to the rule of law, not to the arbitrary will of their governors. No-one is above the law. Ministers and public authorities are bound by the law. Actions without the authority of law can be challenged in the courts. Citizens should have redress for illegal or arbitrary acts by public authorities, through the ordinary courts, administrative tribunals or other special machinery, such as complaints to the various 'ombudsmen' over what is termed 'maladministration'. (For more on the rule of law, and its application, see Chapter 14. For further analysis of the principle see Bingham, 2010.)

The constitutional principles described above, particularly the unitary state, and parliamentary sovereignty rather than a separation of powers, also

---

● **Parliamentary sovereignty** means that Parliament has supreme power. **Popular sovereignty** means that supreme power rests with the people. There is clearly potential for tension or open conflict between these two doctrines. The views of the elected representatives of the people clearly may not always coincide with the views of the people themselves.

## BOX 10.2

# The Westminster model

The traditional British system of government is often described in shorthand as the 'Westminster model', involving a fusion and centralization of executive and legislative power at Westminster. Indeed, most mature representative democracies (the USA is a prominent exception) have such a parliamentary executive, with the government emerging from, and dependent on, a parliamentary majority. However, the British Prime Minister and Cabinet appear to control Parliament to a far greater extent than parliamentary executives in many other countries. This is partly because of the (substantially) two-party system and single party majority government that the British government at Westminster has involved for almost the entire period from 1945–2010, mainly as the consequence of its markedly disproportionate electoral system.

emphasize the centralization of political power on Westminster and Whitehall. The Westminster model, to its admirers, delivers strong, responsible and responsive government, and promotes national unity and homogeneity. Indeed, features of the system of government have been admired and sometimes imitated in other countries, particularly former British colonies. Yet more recently, as we shall see, the Westminster model has been much criticized.

## British parties and the constitution: from consensus to conflict

While constitutions can be acutely contentious, consensus in British politics has often extended to constitutional issues. Thus after a period of intense constitutional controversy in the years leading up to the First World War, there appeared to be a substantial consensus between the two major parties in support of the system of government lasting up until the 1970s. However, this apparent agreement conceals some very different assumptions on the constitution that help to explain the marked differences in attitude to constitutional

reform that subsequently emerged between the parties in the late twentieth and early twenty-first centuries.

Both major parties that have dominated British government and politics since the war showed relatively little interest in constitutional reform until relatively recently. Throughout their history Conservatives have generally defended the existing constitution and its traditional institutions, including the monarchy, the House of Lords and the established church. However, they rarely sought to reverse any constitutional reforms introduced by their opponents. Thus they came to accept the principle of representative democracy by the end of the nineteenth century, although 'Tory democracy' continued to emphasize the need for firm government and strong leadership. They have sometimes initiated changes of their own (e.g. the introduction of life peers, 1958). It was also a Conservative government (Heath's) that finally negotiated UK entry into the European Community (later Union). However, Conservatives in government and opposition resisted other changes to Britain's system of government. From the nineteenth century, when they strongly opposed home rule for Ireland, Conservatives were strongly committed to the preservation of the Union; they opposed Labour's devolution proposals from 1974–9 and in 1997 elections (although devolution, once implemented, was subsequently accepted). The party has also generally resisted electoral reform.

For much of its history the Labour party was surprisingly uninterested in radical constitutional reform, although it intermittently pursued House of Lords reform, and occasionally toyed with other constitutional changes. Labour wished to capture and control the state rather than reform it. Their priorities were social and economic reform, and it was assumed that this could be achieved through the existing state apparatus (Bogdanor, in Seldon, 2001, pp. 139–42). Labour, like the Conservatives, endorsed strong government, but for different reasons. Once they had achieved a parliamentary majority and a mandate from the people, Labour wanted to be able to enact their social and economic programme unchecked (Dunleavy, 1997, p. 130). Labour, like the Conservatives, also benefited from an electoral system that protected the two major parties from third-party competition.

While Conservatives have strongly defended the existing constitution, and Labour was generally content to work within it, Whigs, Liberals and more recently Liberal Democrats have placed more emphasis on constitutional reform. Thus in the nineteenth century, Liberals championed parliamentary reform and, from 1886 onwards, Irish home rule (and subsequently 'home rule all round'). In the early twentieth century the Liberal government took on and defeated opposition from the House of Lords, and reduced its powers. After the Second World War the Liberal Party was the first to support entry into the European Economic Community, and they continued to support devolution to Scotland and Wales as well as English regional government. They have sought to defend civil liberties and individual rights, and to strengthen the role of Parliament. Unsurprisingly, they have consistently campaigned for electoral reform, as the simple plurality single member system has particularly penalized them. The Liberal Democrats, under Ashdown, Kennedy and most recently Clegg, have maintained this commitment to constitutional reform.

On the fringes of British politics there were always those who sought to overthrow rather than reform the state. These have included small groups on the far right or the far left of the political spectrum who rejected most of the key institutions of the British state, but also, and increasingly significantly, varieties of nationalists. It was the growing support for separatist nationalism in Ireland which led to the establishment of the Irish Free State (and later Republic). Nationalism in Scotland and Wales took longer to make an impact, and was generally committed to peaceful change, although they also sought the break-up of the British state. They only began to make an impact after nationalist pressures re-ignited in Northern Ireland in the late 1960s and early 1970s, at around the same time as the debate over British membership of the European Community was raising concerns over British national sovereignty.

These pressures had a particular impact on the Labour Party. The rise of nationalism threatened its own heartlands in Scotland and Wales, and converted Labour to devolution. At the same time Labour was split from top to bottom by the issue of Europe, and opted for a referendum on EC membership as a way out of its own divisions, before referendums were also held (and lost, in 1979) on Labour's devolution plans for Scotland and Wales. The introduction of referendums was a potentially significant development for parliamentary sovereignty and representative democracy. In opposition after 1979, Labour became increasingly committed to constitutional reform, with important implications when they finally exchanged opposition for power in 1997.

## Incremental constitutional reforms in the UK 1945–97

Although neither of the major parties that dominated British politics in the post-war years put forward radical programmes for constitutional reform, there were important incremental changes in the system of government. Thus Attlee's Labour government further reduced the delaying power of the Lords in the Parliament Act of 1949. Of rather more significance was the introduction of life peers in 1958 by Macmillan's Conservative government. This, over time, was to transfer the Upper House from an almost entirely hereditary chamber to a largely appointed one. Wilson's 1964–70 Labour government (rather unsuccessfully) sought further parliamentary reform, including the introduction of more specialist Commons committees to scrutinize the government. (It was under the Thatcher government that committee scrutiny became both more permanent and comprehensive.)

Of more importance than any of this was probably UK entry to the European Community (later Union), although its constitutional significance was played down at the time. The European Communities Act (1972) gave the force of law in the United Kingdom to obligations arising under the EC/EU treaties and it made EU law general and binding authority within the United Kingdom. It provided that Community law should take precedence over all inconsistent UK law; and it precluded the UK parliament from legislating on matters within EC competence where the Community had formulated rules. Some argued that parliamentary sovereignty was not impaired, because membership of the EC/EU had not broken the principle that Parliament cannot bind its future

**Image 10.1  The former prime minister, Edward Heath, signs the UK treaty of accession on 22 January 1972**

Prime Minister Edward Heath signs the treaty of accession of the UK into the European Community in January 1972, with membership becoming efective from the beginning of 1973. UK membership of the EC had considerable implications for the British constitution, particularly for national and parliamentary sovereignty, and significantly affected the practice of British government and politics.

action. Thus, the European Communities Act could be repealed, and indeed had the subsequent 1975 referendum on Britain's membership of the EC gone the other way, the United Kingdom would almost certainly have withdrawn from the Community. Yet while the UK remained a member of the Community, it soon became apparent that parliamentary sovereignty was affected. Moreover, the introduction of a popular referendum to resolve the issue of UK membership (and divisions within the Labour party) also created a precedent with potentially significant constitutional implications.

## Radical constitutional reform: Charter 88 and New Labour

Constitutional reform was a cause that became increasingly fashionable from the late 1980s onwards. Compared with earlier proposals in the 1960s and 1970s, which had been limited to specific issues, this new phase was about fundamentals and produced radical proposals for reform. An important step was the formation of the influential pressure group, Charter 88, symbolically three hundred years on from the Revolution of 1688 (see Box 10.3).

There was some support for constitutional reform on the right of the political spectrum, notably from the neo-liberal think tank, the Institute of Economic Affairs, and individuals such as a former head of Margaret Thatcher's Political Unit, Ferdinand Mount (1992). However, most of the interest in constitutional change then came from the centre and left of the political spectrum (Hutton, 1995, Chapter 11; Barnett, 1997). In March 1997, the two centre-left parties, Labour and the Liberal Democrats, which had already been co-operating closely in the Scottish Constitutional Convention (on devolved Scottish government), produced an agreed raft of proposals for constitutional reform, including:

- Select committee on modernization of House of Commons
- Abolition of hereditary peers
- A Scottish Parliament and Welsh Assembly elected by proportional representation
- Referendums on an elected London authority and elected English regional assemblies
- Incorporation of European Convention of Human Rights into UK law
- An electoral commission to recommend alternative to present voting system
- Freedom of Information Act

Labour enacted a substantial part of this reform programme in government after 1997. There were referendums on devolution in Scotland and Wales (1997), and Northern Ireland (1998), and on a new system of government for London. Support for change was soon followed by legislation for a new Scottish Parliament, a Welsh Assembly, a Northern Ireland executive and assembly, and a directly elected mayor and authority to govern London. Thus Labour fulfilled its commitment to devolution, but only partially met pledges on electoral reform. While the additional member system was introduced for the new assemblies in Scotland, Wales and London, the Single Transferable Vote system for Northern Ireland and regional party lists for elections to the European Parliament, Labour did not introduce its promised referendum on a new system of voting for Westminster. However, other pledges were met. The Labour government legislated to incorporate the European Convention on Human Rights into British law and eventually passed a Freedom of Information Act. All this amounted to a major transformation of the British system of government, with far-reaching constitutional consequences.

Yet other proposed constitutional reforms ran into trouble. Labour had originally intended to complement Scottish and Welsh devolution with some devolution to the English regions, but although new Regional Development Agencies were introduced, plans for elected regional assemblies were abandoned after they were rejected in the single region (the North-East) where a referendum was held in 2004. More seriously, the government's plans for Lords reform (after they had removed most hereditary peers) were rejected but no new alternative proposals for the composition of the second chamber could be agreed upon. Blair's government did however eventually proceed with plans in its second term to replace the judicial functions of the Lords with a new Supreme Court, finally established in 2009. While some changes were introduced to the timetables and procedures of the House of Commons, these had rather less impact, and did nothing to reduce executive dominance of the legislature.

A number of criticisms have been levelled at Labour's constitutional reforms. An early criticism was they were insufficiently 'joined-up' and not

---

**BOX 10.3**

## Constitutional reform: the main demands of Charter 88

- A Bill of Rights to ensure key civil rights
- Freedom of information and open government
- A fair electoral system based on proportional representation
- A reformed democratic, non-hereditary second chamber
- The subordination of the executive to a 'democratically renewed parliament'
- An independent, reformed judiciary
- 'An equitable distribution of power between local, regional and national government'
- A written constitution

---

informed by any coherent vision (Bogdanor, in Seldon, 2001, pp. 149–50). Thus Labour did not seek to introduce a written constitution, which would have required resolving fundamental issues that the government preferred to avoid, over parliamentary sovereignty and the unitary state. Flinders (in Dunleavy *et al.*, 2006, pp. 117–37) described it as a 'half-hearted revolution' which failed to transform the old Whitehall and Westminster model of the constitution into 'a new multi-level polity'. Evans (in Beech and Lee, 2008, p. 87) compared Blair to the 'Sorcerer's apprentice in Walt Disney's *Fantasia*, desperately trying to stem the flood of unintended consequences that flow from constitutional reform'.

## The Conservative and Liberal Democrat coalition and constitutional reform

The parliamentary expenses scandal of 2009 gave renewed impetus to constitutional change. Although all the major parties were affected by the scandal, it was Labour as the party in power who were most tarnished by it, and the opposition parties who were better placed to profit from the new impetus for reform. Thus both the Conservatives and Liberal Democrats before the 2010 election advocated widening the selection of candidates, giving voters the right to recall erring MPs, and reducing the number of MPs. Both also promised Lords reform. Even before the 2010 election their programmes involved some significant common elements.

However, the Liberal Democrats also demanded a fairer voting system, involving proportional representation, which the Conservatives firmly rejected. Moreover, the parties differed sharply over future UK relations with the European Union, with the Conservatives proposing the repatriation of some powers to Westminster, while the Liberal Democrats remained fully committed to the EU, and sympathetic in principle to the single currency, the euro.

When the election produced a hung parliament both parties soon agreed a constitutional reform programme. This included changes to the Commons that they both favoured (fewer MPs and more equal constituencies), and a largely elected House of Lords. The pledge of a referendum on the introduction of the Alternative Vote was regarded by Liberal Democrats as an inadequate but modest step towards fairer voting. Significantly, the new Deputy Prime Minister Nick Clegg was given responsibility for this programme of constitutional reform, which he claimed involved the most sweeping changes to Britain's system of government since the 1832 Reform Act. The claim was exaggerated, but certainly promised significant further constitutional upheavals, with potential far-reaching consequences for the British system of government.

## Where is the British constitution today?

The changes to the British system of government introduced over the last few years, coupled with other reforms still in progress, already amount to a constitutional revolution that calls in question some of the key features or principles of the British constitution described earlier in the chapter. Britain's constitutional monarchy remains largely unquestioned, and the rule of law has, if anything, been strengthened by the growth of judicial review,

the incorporation of the European Convention on Human Rights into British law and the clearer separation of the legislative and judicial functions of the state. However, the unitary state and parliamentary sovereignty are now more questionable.

## The end of the unitary state?

The official orthodoxy is that the United Kingdom remains a unitary state, despite devolution. Yet one obvious consequence of devolution is increasing diversity within the UK as devolved executives increasingly exercise their powers in different ways. This diversity was less evident from 1999 to 2007, when Labour both ruled at Westminster and dominated the devolved governments of Scotland and Wales. Yet an SNP government in Scotland from 2007 and a Conservative mayor of London from 2008 have led to increased disagreements and some demarcation disputes between different levels of government. Britain is already arguably a 'quasi-federal state', and, as pressures for more devolution of powers increase, could be en route to a fully federal state.

A fully federal Britain is, however, only one possible longer-term outcome of the constitutional reform process. For Irish, Scottish and Welsh nationalists devolution and federalism are only stages on the road to separation and the break-up of Britain. Some who have opposed devolution all along (including many Conservatives and some Labour critics, like Tam Dalyell) have feared that it is a 'slippery slope' on the road to independence, as indeed nationalists wish. By contrast, Labour and the Liberal Democrats hope that devolution will satisfy the legitimate demands of many in Scotland and Wales to have a greater say in decisions which affect them, and that devolution will ultimately strengthen rather than weaken the British state. It is impossible to know the eventual outcome. The various peoples of the United Kingdom have embarked on a journey where the final destination is unknown.

## The end of parliamentary sovereignty?

The principle of parliamentary sovereignty has been eroded by UK membership of the European Union. The 1972 European Communities Act

BOX 10.4

## UK parliamentary sovereignty and the European Union: the Factortame case

Britain's legal subordination to Brussels was underlined by an important legal case in 1991, *R.* v. *Secretary of State for Transport ex p. Factortame Ltd no. 2* (the Factortame case). The European Court of Justice in effect quashed sections of a British Act of Parliament (the Merchant Shipping Act 1988) which provided that UK-registered boats must be 75 per cent British-owned and have 75 per cent of crew resident in the UK. The Act had been designed to prevent boats from Spain and other EC countries 'quota-hopping' by registering under the British flag and using the UK's EC fishing quotas. The European Court of Justice had overturned British legislation before, but no earlier case had provoked such an outcry.

recognized that in areas of EU legislative competence, EU law is supreme and is given precedence over national UK law where the two conflict. The implications were not perhaps fully appreciated at the time, but became clearer when UK and EU law clashed (see 10.4).

Vernon Bogdanor (in Seldon, 2001, pp. 145–6) claims that parliamentary sovereignty has been further reduced by at least three other developments: the employment of referendums, the Human Rights Act, and devolution.

Following the precedent of the 1975 referendum on EC membership, subsequent British governments have occasionally had recourse to popular referendums on essentially constitutional issues. Thus referendums were held on devolution to Scotland and Wales (1979, and again in 1997), London government (1998), the Northern Ireland agreement (1998), and on a projected elected assembly for the North-east (2004). All these were conducted while Labour was in office. However, the Conservatives in opposition were committed to a referendum on the EU Lisbon treaty (before it was ratified by all member states), and the coalition government pledged a referendum on the introduction of the Alternative Vote for 2011. Thus the referendum has become (an occasional but significant) part of the UK constitution.

Referendums require the passing of a specific Act of Parliament, and the result of a referendum remains theoretically advisory, so the principle of parliamentary sovereignty is officially maintained. Yet it would be politically suicidal to hold a referen-

dum and ignore the result. Thus Bogdanor argues that in practice 'a referendum which yields a clear outcome on a reasonable turnout binds Parliament'. The sovereignty of the people is substituted for the sovereignty of Parliament. The more referendums become a regular part of the British system of government, the further the principle of parliamentary sovereignty is eroded.

The Human Rights Act does not give judges power to reject Westminster legislation, but 'nevertheless alters very considerably the balance between Parliament and the judiciary' (Bogdanor in Seldon, 2001, p.146) so that Parliament will feel obliged to respond to judicial decisions that a statute is incompatible with the European Convention of Human Rights. While the sovereignty of the Westminster parliament is theoretically unaffected by devolution, in practice English MPs have lost responsibility for legislation on devolved functions, particularly in Scotland. Bogdanor (Seldon, 2001, p. 151) argues that the Human Rights Act and the Scotland Act 'have the characteristic of fundamental laws. They, in practice, limit the rights of Westminster as a sovereign parliament, and provide for a constitution which is quasi-federal in nature.'

The official answer here is clear. Devolution is not the same as federalism. Power devolved is power retained, because sovereignty or supreme power is unaffected, and thus any functions which are devolved can be called back. Devolution itself may be reversed, as the suspension of the Stormont parliament in 1972 and the resumption of direct rule of Northern Ireland after 50 years of devolved government demonstrates. Indeed, following the Good Friday Agreement (1998), the Northern Ireland Assembly and Executive were suspended four times, reinforcing the point.

Yet Northern Ireland is a special case. Any reversal of devolution to Scotland and Wales now seems inconceivable, unless wanted by a clear majority of Scots and Welsh. However, all the pressures are now the other way – for more devolution to the Scottish Parliament and Welsh Assembly. Thus it is arguable that Britain is evolving towards a quasi-federal system of government which entails the end of UK parliamentary sovereignty (these points are discussed further in chapter 16).

The political impossibility of reversing devolution illustrates the practical limitations on the power of the Westminster parliament. Yet it is not just devolution that illustrate the limitations of the legislative authority of Westminster. Sometimes Acts of Parliament apparently embodying the full force of law can become virtually unenforceable. Trade union resistance wrecked the 1971 Trade Union Act and widespread popular revolt helped destroy the poll tax (introduced by the Thatcher government, and abolished by Thatcher's Conservative successor, Major). This suggests that parliamentary sovereignty can in practice be limited by what the people will stand (or, effectively, by democracy).

## Direct democracy rather than representative democracy?

Parliamentary sovereignty implicitly places limits on the sovereignty of the people. It is the representatives of the people who ultimately decide, not the people themselves, whose role was traditionally confined to choosing the representatives who would control the government. While the occasional use of referendums has given individual voters a say on a very few specific (essentially constitutional) issues, it has hardly undermined the general principle of representative democracy, as practised in Britain by political parties in Parliament.

Yet the 2009 parliamentary expenses scandal has been the catalyst not only for a loss of public trust in elected representatives, but also for a range of new reform proposals. One proposed reform (based on US practice) would enable voters to recall MPs with whom they had become dissatisfied (e.g. in relation to their expenses claims). This would, it is argued, make MPs more responsive to those they represent. Another proposal is to open out the selection of MPs, for example through the introduction of primary elections (as in the USA) rather than selection by relatively few local party members. This would, it is argued, help to bring into Parliament MPs from different, less conventional backgrounds, less constrained by party machines. The Conservative party under Cameron has already experimented with widening candidate selection beyond party members.

Others, pointing to the decline in support for the major parties in terms of voting and particularly active membership, advocate a democracy less dependent on political parties. This might involve increased use of referendums (which could be demanded by the initiative of voters, another US practice). It might involve more direct popular participation in decision-making through citizens' juries, perhaps selected by lot, an ancient Athenian practice. All these projected reforms reflect a widespread public distrust of Parliament, parties, MPs and the whole traditional system of representative democracy as it has operated in Britain.

## A written constitution?

Demarcation disputes arising from devolution and the eroded sovereignty of the Westminster parliament may ultimately necessitate some kind of written constitution, with provision perhaps for judicial arbitration over disputes. A written constitution is one part of the Charter 88 package of proposals that Labour ignored or rejected, but it may prove the logical culmination of reforms already implemented. A written constitution, particularly if it contained safeguards against hasty amendment by a bare Commons majority, would effectively mean the end of parliamentary sovereignty, and in so far as it spelt out the respective functions of different levels of government, would also involve the end of the unitary state.

## The end of the 'Westminster model'?

The Westminster model described earlier in this chapter has long provoked criticism, both as a descriptive and prescriptive model. Some dissenters have argued that this portrayal of a strongly centralized British state is exaggerated, and that government was always more diverse, and power in practice more decentralized, than the Westminster model implied (Bulpitt, 1983; Rhodes, 1988, 1997). Indeed, although British government was clearly more centralized than in federal systems such as the United States, Canada, Germany or Switzerland, it long appeared much less centralized than the 'one and indivisible' French Republic.

However, rather more critics from across the political spectrum agreed that political power in Britain was indeed substantially centralized, but deplored the fact. Thus a former Conservative Lord Chancellor, Lord Hailsham, criticized what he described as Britain's elective dictatorship. Similar criticism helped inspire an influential constitutional reform movement demanding more decentralization and diversity in the last years of the twentieth century (Holme and Elliot, 1988; Mount, 1992; Hutton, 1996; Marr, 1996; Barnett, 1997). Substantive constitutional changes from 1997 onwards have had significant but contentious implications, not least for the survival of the Westminster model (see also chapter 18 and chapters by Flinders and Dunleavy in Dunleavy *et al.*, 2006).

## The coalition and the constitution

The 2010 election, like other elections from at least 1983 onwards, confirmed that Britain is no longer a two-party system, but also, more crucially, failed to produce a parliamentary majority for a single party for the first time since February 1974. Whereas the consequence in 1974 was a short-lived minority government, the 2010 election has resulted in the first coalition government since the Second World War. Coalition government may prove a brief aberration from the normal pattern of single party majority government. Alternatively it could become the norm in Britain, as it has long been in most other countries on the European continent.

How far the coalition's rhetoric on 'returning power to the people' is implemented remains to be seen. Referendums, widening candidate selection and proposals for recalling MPs all emphasize popular rather than parliamentary sovereignty. Fixed-term parliaments may remove an important power of Prime Ministers, but hardly strengthens the power of Parliament to control the executive. Indeed a smaller parliament with fewer MPs could lead to increased executive dominance, unless there is a parallel reduction in the total number of ministers who constitute a substantial 'payroll vote' in any parliament.

Yet, even without this latest package of constitutional reforms, the British system of government already appears much altered. Key constitutional principles such as parliamentary sovereignty and the unitary state have been criticized on normative grounds, and progressively eroded by a series of constitutional reforms, particularly UK membership of the European Union, devolution and the Human Rights Act. A unitary state centred on Westminster and Whitehall has been transformed, some would argue, into a new system of multi-level governance (see Chapter 18), with some powers transferred upwards, some downwards.

Both the 2010 election and the coalition government that emerged from it may increase the tensions between the UK government and devolved governments in Scotland, Wales and Northern Ireland. Scotland returned only one Conservative MP to Westminster, while the old Ulster Unionists in Northern Ireland, now realigned with the Conservatives, failed to win a single seat, although the Welsh Conservatives made gains. Cameron's coalition partners at Westminster were recently coalition partners of Labour in Scotland, and, more briefly, in Wales, and many Scottish and Welsh Liberal Democrats are uncomfortable with their new allies. This could boost support for the nationalists in both countries, and increase prospects for independence in Scotland especially, particularly if cuts in public spending are particularly noticeable north of the border. Thus the United Kingdom could break up.

Whatever view is taken of recent and proposed constitutional reforms, and their possible implications, it would be widely conceded that there are continuing tensions and ambiguities in the emerging new British system of government. Perhaps these tensions and ambiguities may remain unresolved as they reflect the inconsistent convictions and preferences of the British political elite, and perhaps the British people also. Devolution in particular is a classic fudge, which seeks to satisfy both those who want more self-government for the nations that make up the United Kingdom and those who maintain the unity of the state. Tensions between these two substantially irreconcilable positions may ultimately led to the break-up of Britain, but it is also quite possible that the awkward status quo will be maintained, because this is what most people want, however unsatisfactory or contradictory it may appear to some on both sides. Similarly, many people may want both popular sovereignty and parliamentary sovereignty, even though these two principles are ultimately inconsistent. Of course, a written constitution might oblige both the British government and people to confront and resolve these contradictions, and decide their ultimate values. Perhaps this is one reason why such a written constitution, long advocated by reformers, may take a long time to materialize.

# SUMMARY

- Britain does not have a written constitution. There is no authoritative description of the British system of government contained in a single document.

- In the absence of a written constitution, major sources of the British constitution include relevant statute law, case law, conventions and the law of the European Union.

- Key constitutional principles include constitutional monarchy, parliamentary sovereignty, representative democracy and the rule of law. In contrast to the United States and many other countries, there has been no clear separation of executive, legislative and judicial powers in the United Kingdom.

- There was a two-party consensus on most aspects of the constitution until relatively recently. This consensus was broken when Labour became committed to specific constitutional changes amid a growing movement for extensive constitutional reform.

- The New Labour government initiated major constitutional reform, although the pace slowed subsequently, as some initiatives failed or ran into substantial difficulties.

- An extensive new programme of constitutional reform is promised by the Conservative and Liberal Democrat coalition that took office in 2010. These have further profound implications for the British system of government.

- The final outcome of recent and ongoing changes to the UK system of government remains unclear, but the future of the 'Westminster model' is questionable. Britain could be moving towards a quasi-federal system of government. Another possibility is the break-up of Britain.

## QUESTIONS FOR DISCUSSION

- Is a hereditary monarchy compatible with the principle of democracy? Should Britain get rid of the monarchy and establish a republic?

- What is parliamentary sovereignty? Why is there a potential conflict between parliamentary sovereignty and popular sovereignty?

- How far have changes in Britain's system of government since 1973 eroded the principle of parliamentary sovereignty?

- How far were Labour's constitutional reforms part of a coherent vision for the future government of Britain? Why did the reforms appear 'insufficiently joined-up?'

- Is the United Kingdom still a unitary state? Should it be?

- How far do the Cameron and Clegg reform proposals amount to significant decentralization and a return of power to the people?

- Does Britain need a written constitution, and if so, what should be included in it?

## FURTHER READING

Britain's constitution and constitutional reform has become a difficult and fast-changing topic. An account from a lawyer's perspective is provided by Jowell and Oliver, *The Changing Constitution* (2007). Vernon Bogdanor (2009), *The New British Constitution* is now a key source. For earlier commentary on Labour's reforms see works by Robert Hazel and the Constitution Unit, such as *Constitutional Futures* (1999), *The State and the Nations* (2000) and *The State of the Nations* (2001, 2003), Bogdanor in Seldon (2001), and chapters by Flinders and Dunleavy in Dunleavy *et al.*, (2006). The chapter by Evans in Beech and Lee (2008) is also worth consulting. Newspapers, periodicals and the internet provide early material on the coalition government reforms, pending the appearance of journal articles and books.

On arguments for constitutional reform see the publications of the pressure group Charter 88 and its website www.charter88.org.uk. Holme and Eliot (1988) provides the background to its formation and programme. Thoughtful although now dated reflections on the principles and practice of the traditional British constitution include Ferdinand Mount (1992), *The British Constitution Now*, Andrew Marr (1996), *Ruling Britannia*, Will Hutton (1996), *The State We're In* (Chapter 11) and Anthony Barnett, *This Time* (1997). Chapter 13 in Hague and Harrop (2010), *Comparative Government and Politics* provides some useful comparative background against which the very unusual British constitution can be assessed.

# Prime Minister and Cabinet

In this chapter we consider the institutions which make up the core executive in British government, the Prime Minister and Cabinet, and their supporting staff. We saw in Chapter 10 that the executive in Britain is not separate from the legislature, as it is in many other countries. The British executive is a parliamentary executive. It is not directly elected (as for example is the US President). The key politicians who are members of the executive, the Prime Minister, Cabinet and junior ministers outside the Cabinet, are all members of the House of Commons or the Lords. Moreover, the government, or executive, normally has a working majority in the Commons and dominates its work.

At the centre of the executive is the Prime Minister. We examine the various roles of the Prime Minister, the sources of his or her power and the limitations on that power. We look at the growth in size and importance of the Prime Minister's Office, and discuss the case for a Prime Minister's Department. We then consider the role of the Cabinet, Cabinet committees and the Cabinet Office in the British system of government, and explore the implications of the principle of collective Cabinet responsibility.

Britain has become accustomed to single party government. The Cabinet from 1945 until 2010 consisted entirely of ministers from either the Conservative party or the Labour party. The formation of a coalition government of Conservatives and Liberal Democrats in 2010 breaks new ground in British post-war politics, although it is common in other parliamentary democracies. We review how far running a coalition government involves new problems, or perhaps new opportunities.

It is periodically alleged that prime ministerial government has effectively replaced Cabinet government in the British system. Although we review the arguments fully, we suggest that the traditional debate over prime ministerial power involves a misleading oversimplification of relations at the heart of government. The influence of individuals and institutions not only fluctuates markedly with political circumstances but is heavily constrained by all kinds of external forces. The levers of power do not always secure the effective delivery of policy. Moreover, the government of Whitehall and Westminster is now only part (although still the most important part) of a complex system of multi-level governance which affects the lives of British people.

## The executive in the United Kingdom

It is not easy to define the executive in the United Kingdom. It is generally accepted that the UK is a plural executive rather than a single person executive (such as the US Presidency) yet the extent of the executive and the distribution of power and influence within it has long been contentious. A description now 50 years old still seems broadly accurate.

> The country is governed by the Prime Minister who leads, co-ordinates and maintains a series of ministers, all of whom are advised and backed by the civil service. Some decisions are taken by the Premier alone, some in consultation between him and the senior ministers, while others are left to heads of departments, the Cabinet, Cabinet committees or the permanent officials. Of these bodies the Cabinet holds the central position because, although it does not often initiate policy or govern in that sense, most decisions pass through it, and Cabinet ministers can complain that they have not been informed or consulted. (Mackintosh, 1962)

Today one might additionally mention the Cabinet Office (which did exist then) and the Prime Minister's Office (which did not), and the increasing number of special advisers independent of the permanent civil service brought in by successive governments. But otherwise John Mackintosh captures well the complexity and ambiguity surrounding British government at its centre. Some more recent writers prefer to use neutral terms such as 'the central executive territory' (Madgwick, 1991) or 'the **core executive**' (Heffernan in Dunleavy *et al.*, 2006) for British central government, avoiding more familiar but loaded definitions such as 'Cabinet government' or 'prime ministerial government'.

● **Core executive**: The term 'core executive' refers to the key institutions at the centre of government. It covers the Prime Minister, Cabinet and its committees, the Prime Minister's Office and the Cabinet Office, co-ordinating departments such as the Treasury, the government's law officers and the security and intelligence services.

Even so, whatever language is used to describe British central government, it remains the case that in popular perception this involves especially the Prime Minister and Cabinet and these will be the focus of much of the rest of this chapter.

## The Prime Minister

The **Prime Minister** is the effective head of British government. The post of Prime Minister emerged in the course of the eighteenth century, although it long remained an unofficial position, and the title only found its way into official documents in the latter twentieth century. Sir Robert Walpole, the leading minister from 1721 until 1742, is generally regarded as the first Prime Minister. The government then was still the king's government in more than name, but the Cabinet, consisting of senior ministers, had become the effective executive. As the king no longer chaired Cabinet meetings this crucial role fell to the leading minister. Walpole's official post was First Lord of the Treasury (a title retained by modern Prime Ministers). This crucially put him in charge of patronage – the distribution of jobs in government – and gave him pre-eminence in the Cabinet. In the course of the eighteenth century, Cabinets became increasingly dependent on parliamentary support rather than royal favour, and the Prime Minister became the real head of government. In the process, the Prime Minister effectively acquired the right to exercise most of the old prerogative (or personal) powers of the Crown.

Prime Ministers in the eighteenth and nineteenth centuries could come from either house of parliament, and many sat in the Lords (Lord Salisbury, who resigned in 1902, was the last peer to serve as Prime Minister). However, the post had long required the support of a majority in the House of Commons, and increasingly democratic assumptions required a head of government who had been elected as an MP. Even so, the convention that a Prime Minister must sit in the House of

● **The Prime Minister**: A head of government whose power normally derives in Britain from leadership of the largest party in the legislature, more exceptionally from enjoyment of the confidence of a cross-party parliamentary majority. The Prime Minister is not the head of the state.

## COMPARATIVE POLITICS  11.1
# Prime Ministers and Presidents

The position of a UK Prime Minister is often compared with heads of government in other western democratic countries, such as the USA, Germany or France.

- The US President is (effectively) directly elected by the American people and combines the role of head of government with head of state. He is the acknowledged head of the armed forces, and the focus of national loyalty. Yet as head of government the US President may often have less control of policy than a British Prime Minister, particularly if he does not have a majority in Congress, which is not uncommon. The main reason that a UK Prime Minister can seem more powerful is because of the fusion of the executive and legislature in Britain compared with the constitutionally separate executive and legislature in the USA.

- However, the US President is a rather unusual type of President. Many other Presidents around the world are formal heads of state, not heads of government, with little political power (for example the Presidents of Germany, Italy and Ireland). Most are not subject to direct popular election.
- The French Fifth Republic comes somewhere between the US and German models. It is sometimes characterized as a 'dual executive' because it has both a directly elected President with significant powers, particularly in foreign affairs, and a Prime Minister (who has to command a majority in the French Assembly) largely responsible for domestic policy.

(See Hague and Harrop, 2010, ch. 16; Helms, 2005; Cole et al., 2008.)

---

Commons only gradually emerged in the twentieth century.

Modern Prime Ministers derive much of their authority and democratic legitimacy from their position as elected leader of the majority party in the House of Commons, although the formal election of party leaders only developed in the course of the twentieth century. Gordon Brown (Prime Minister 2007–10) won neither a general election, nor a contested Labour leadership election (although he was formally elected by his party). Some argued his position was weaker as he lacked a personal mandate. However the British executive is a parliamentary executive, and the head of government has never been directly elected by the people. Many Prime Ministers, like Brown, have succeeded to the position in mid-parliament, without a general election (e.g. since 1945, Eden, Macmillan, Home, Callaghan, Major).

The modern office of Prime Minister involves a formidable concentration of power, although much of this depends on convention rather than law. In summary, the Prime Minister is responsible for forming a government; for directing and coordinating its work; and for general supervision of the civil service. The Prime Minister also has special responsibilities in the sphere of national security. Alongside these formal responsibilities the Prime Minister in practice can exercise a strong influence over any specific policy or service, and many recent holders of the position have taken a particular interest in defence, foreign affairs and the management of the economy. Finally, the Prime Minister is the national leader, as evidenced by his or her role in representing the country at international conferences and meetings, signing treaties and playing host to leaders of other states (see Comparative Politics 11.1 and Box 11.1).

## Patronage ('hiring and firing')

The most important element of prime ministerial patronage is the power to select the one hundred or so politicians – drawn mainly from the majority party in Commons but including some from the Lords – who at any given moment form the government. The Prime Minister appoints not just the Cabinet of normally between 20 and 23 members but also ministers of state, under-secretaries of state, whips and law officers such as the Attorney General. Occasionally a Prime Minister may wish to appoint a minister who is not already a Member of Parliament, but convention dictates that such individuals have to become MPs or peers.

A coalition government imposes some further restraints on a Prime Minister's freeedom of action – in that the distribution of posts will involve negotiation with coalition partners, as it clearly did in 2010, and had done previously in 1915, 1931 and 1940, when new coalition governments were formed. Clearly also the Prime Minister of a coalition government faces some constraints in dismissing and replacing ministerial colleagues who do not belong to his or her party. However, even with single party government there are significant practical political constraints on appointments and dismissals, as all parties involve coalitions of views and interests and a Prime Minister must be wary of upsetting influential factions and tendencies within the party.

Whether the government is drawn from a single party or a coalition of parties, a substantial proportion of MPs (normally from a quarter to a third) of the governing party or parties can expect to be in office. By no means all politicians seek ministerial office but most probably do. The continuing power to 'hire and fire' is a formidable source of control for the Prime Minister.

The Prime Minister also plays a key role in the selection of individuals to fill a wide variety of other leading posts in national life. This influence extends over the creation of peers as well as over the appointment of top civil servants at the permanent secretary and deputy secretary levels, the heads of the security services and the chairmen of royal commissions. In addition, the Prime Minister has ultimate responsibility for recommendations of honours.

## Direction and organization of the government

The Prime Minister is responsible for directing and organizing the work of the government at the highest level. This involves setting broad policy

| BOX 11.1 |
| --- |

## The role of the Prime Minister: key aspects

- **Appoints ministers** (and others to leading roles). The Prime Minister 'hires and fires'.
- **Organizes government**, including setting up, reorganizing and abolishing departments of state, and overseeing organization of the civil service and other parts of government.
- **Steers government.** PM directs and co-ordinates government policy and strategy, chairs Cabinet, and has special interest in key policy areas.
- **Controls House of Commons** through leadership of a disciplined majority party (normally).
- **Gives leadership to nation**, particularly in time of national crisis (e.g. war), but has high political profile always, and represents country at home and abroad.

objectives (within the framework of party ideologies and party manifestos) and devising short-term and long-term strategies for attaining these goals. The leadership, of course, is always in the collective context of the Cabinet system: the Prime Minister is not a single person executive like the US President. Within that framework, there are clearly differences in style. Margaret Thatcher is well known for having led from the front, and the same might be said of Tony Blair. Harold Wilson and John Major both had a more consensual style. However, the Prime Minister expects all ministerial colleagues to support government policy according to the convention of collective responsibility .

The Prime Minister not only has overall responsibility for government, but can take a particular interest in key policy areas. Thus many Prime Ministers (particularly Brown, but not Blair) have taken a decisive role in the determination of economic policy in consultation with the Chancellor of the Exchequer and the Treasury. Others, notably Churchill, Thatcher and Blair, have played a leading part in foreign and defence policy, sometimes overshadowing their foreign and defence secretaries. However, issues may arise over the whole field of government in which the Prime

Minister either has to get involved or chooses to take a particular interest. Thus Prime Ministers in the 1960s and 1970s were unavoidably involved in industrial, trade union and pay policies. Margaret Thatcher took a direct personal interest in the management of the economy, in Europe and foreign policy generally, in trade unions and industrial relations, in changes to the civil services and NHS, and in the introduction of the poll tax in local government. Major and Blair were both centrally involved in the development of the peace process in Northern Ireland. Brown, because of his long experience of economic policy, continued to play a leading role nationally and internationally in coping with the credit crunch and recession after he became Prime Minister.

The Prime Minister draws up the Cabinet agenda and decides the composition, terms of reference and chairs of Cabinet committees. (In the case of Cameron's coalition government this involved consultation with the minority coalition party.) As well as playing a key part in deciding the nature, timing and ordering of issues reaching the Cabinet, the Prime Minister chairs Cabinet meetings. This can give the Prime Minister considerable influence over the direction and outcome of Cabinet discussions, by making his or her views known before and during the meeting, by determining who is called to speak and in what order, and by summing up 'the sense of the meeting'. In the process, they may deploy various 'manipulative arts' of chairmanship including delay, verbosity, deliberate ambiguity, sheer persistence and authority. Votes are rarely taken in Cabinet: they encourage division, dilute collective responsibility and are vulnerable to 'leaks' and misleading reports in the media. But it is the task of the Prime Minister to summarize the decisions reached, taking into account the weight of opinion for or against a course of action.

Finally, the Prime Minister has overall responsibility for the work of the civil service (the Cabinet Secretary is head of the civil service).

Developments since 1979 have seen a significant strengthening of the Prime Minister's position in relation to Whitehall. The Thatcher–Major era saw large-scale changes in the organization and management of the civil service (see Chapter 12). Blair continued and expanded the practice of his predecessors in bringing in external special advisers on short term contracts and establishing special cross-departmental units which upset some senior permanent civil servants, some of whom felt marginalized (Norton in Beech and Lee, 2008, p. 95).

## Managing Parliament

As the Prime Minister heads a parliamentary executive, he must be an elected Member of Parliament and depends for survival on maintaining a majority in the House of Commons, the management of Parliament is clearly an important concern. The Prime Minister's performance in Parliament is always the subject of close scrutiny. Every Wednesday for half an hour the premier appears in the House of Commons to answer Prime Minister's Questions. (This was the result of a change introduced by Blair; formerly it was two fifteen-minute sessions a week.) This is by far the most common prime ministerial activity in Parliament. Prime Ministers can expect to answer about 1,000 questions per session, a large proportion of them on economic and foreign affairs. Many of the questions appear as 'supplementaries' that are more difficult to prepare for. Question Time is a testing ordeal, at which much is at stake, including personal reputation, control of party and the authority of the government. In particular the verbal duels between the Prime Minister and the leader of the opposition can attract considerable media publicity, and may affect the morale of their respective parties. While Blair excelled in verbal sparring with his opposite number, Brown was frequently worsted in his weekly duels with David Cameron. Since exchanging opposition for office Cameron has only occasionally been embarrassed at question time.

When Parliament is sitting, premiers may expect to be constantly preoccupied with it in other ways, too. Their concerns include the progress of government legislation, set-piece speeches in full-dress parliamentary debates and, more generally, the state of party morale. 'Parliamentary business' is always an item on Cabinet agenda. However, modern Prime Ministers only attend the Commons for a specific purpose, and normally only for brief periods. Indeed Blair was criticized for devoting

BOX 11.2

# The Prime Minister's Office

Although the Prime Minister wields extensive powers and normally dominates the entire governmental system, he or she does not head a large department but is directly served by a Prime Minister's Office of around a hundred people, of whom around one-third are senior officials and advisers. It was only in 1974 that a policy unit was established within the Prime Minister's Office at 10 Downing Street to give the Prime Minister an independent source of policy advice. John Major's policy unit had just eight special advisers, while Tony Blair initially had twelve (Hennessy, 2000, p. 487). The Blair government also introduced a new Strategic Communications Unit in November 1997 to co-ordinate press relations of the various departments and ministers (which led to some tension between the Labour Party's 'spin doctors' and the permanent civil servants responsible for government information). Further changes were introduced in subsequent years.

The expansion and increased status of what has become the Prime Minister's Office has increased the Prime Minister's capacity 'to oversee government strategy, to monitor departmental work and to initiate policy from the centre'. Contemporary Prime Ministers are better informed about what is happening across the whole range of government and there is an increased tendency for business to flow to the Prime Minister's Office and for ministers to consult Number Ten before launching policy initiatives.

Some argue that the Prime Minister's Office has effectively become a Prime Minister's Department of the kind that some centralizing reformers have advocated (Hennessy, 2000, pp. 485–6). Holliday (in Dunleavy et al., 2002, pp. 94–6) claims the increased integration and coordination of the Prime Minister's Office and the Cabinet Office 'makes them, in effect, a single executive office'. Yet Riddell (in Seldon, 2001, pp. 31–2) points out that 'the Number 10 operation is still small by comparison with the executive offices in presidential systems, such as the United States and Germany, and even in prime ministerial systems such as Australia and Canada'.

little time and attention to Parliament (Norton, 2005, p. 243) and having 'the worst voting record of any modern Prime Minister' (Norton in Beech and Lee, 2008, p. 97).

Yet it was Blair who introduced twice-yearly meetings of two and a half hours with the Liaison Committee consisting of the chairs of the parliamentary Select Committees, who were able to question him in depth over a wide range of topics (Cowley in Dunleavy et al., 2006, p. 47).

## The end of the Prime Minister's power to recommend a dissolution of Parliament

The power to dissolve Parliament was one of the former prerogative powers of the Crown inherited by the Prime Minister. Until 2010 Prime Ministers have had the exclusive right to recommend to the monarch the timing of the dissolution of Parliament at any time within a five-year period. This meant that they effectively controlled the date of the general election, as the monarch could not refuse such a request without appearing to take sides in party politics. The 2010 coalition government is committed to legislation for fixed-term parliaments of five years, removing the power of Prime Ministers to call an election at the time of their choosing. This is a significant surrender of power, as Prime Ministers were formerly able to choose an election date most favourable for their party's prospects (e.g. soon after a generous budget or a diplomatic triumph). Critics argued that this was not only unfair, but damaging to the country, because of the resulting uncertainty over the election date and prospects for a new parliament and government (financial markets in particular can be affected by such uncertainty).

However, although the power to dissolve Parliament was potentially useful, past Prime Ministers did not always use it effectively. Brown's indecision over a snap election in the autumn of 2007, soon after he had succeeded Blair as Prime Minister, not only seriously damaged his reputation in the short term (Rawnsley, 2010), but was almost certainly a miscalculation in the long run. Labour might have won a majority in 2007, and could scarcely have done worse than in 2010. Similarly, Heath and Callaghan both arguably failed to choose the most opportune election date for their parties. Wilson, however, successfully called early elections in March 1966 and October 1974 to improve his parliamentary support.

It was also once argued that this power to dissolve Parliament could be used to discipline a Prime Minister's ministerial colleagues and back-benchers when faced with internal party dissent. However, a Prime Minister who called an election with a divided government and party would almost certainly face defeat, while rebel MPs in safe seats would survive. Yet this might have been a useful weapon for the Prime Minister of a coalition government, particularly in circumstances where other parties, including junior coalition partners, might be disadvantaged by an early election. Thus without the commitment to fixed-term parliaments David Cameron would have been free to recom-mend a further dissolution of Parliament after a few months in the hope of securing an overall Conservative majority, when other parties, includ-ing the Liberal Democrats, would be financially ill-equipped to fight another election. The commitment to fixed-term parliaments was arguably necessary to remove Liberal Democrat fears of an early snap election and provide stability for the coalition government.

There is now something approaching an all-party consensus in favour of fixed-term parlia-ments, and many constitutional reformers agree, because it removes the potential advantage to the incumbent of being able to select the election date. Yet the UK was by no means the only country accustomed to variable-term parliaments. One possible advantage is that they keep the parliamen-tary opposition in a constant state of readiness to challenge the government, and this is good for them and the country, rather than allowing them to keep a low profile until the fixed date of election arises (Hamlin, 2010).

## National leadership

The Prime Minister occupies a special role in the life of the country that distinguishes the occupant of the office from other Cabinet members – as national leader. This is always the case but becomes especially apparent at times of national crisis such as war, natural or man-made disasters or serious economic problems, such as the world banking crisis and economic recession of 2008–9 , and the subsequent budget deficit from 2010 onwards. Prime Ministers are expected to provide leadership in such circumstances and may be criticized if they fail to do so.

## The Prime Minister, communication and the media

Effective national leadership requires effective communication. Contemporary Prime Ministers need to pay particular attention to the way they and their governments are presented in the media. They inevitably spend much of their lives in public – being interviewed on television, briefing lobby correspondents, making speeches at public func-tions, responding impromptu to queries about the latest crisis, scandal or leak. If they succeed in presenting a decisive image, they will be given credit for their handling – or, more pejoratively, for their 'manipulation' – of the media. If they are tripped up, fluff their lines or give a less than posi-tive impression, their own reputation and that of the government will suffer. In other words, self-presentation through the media has become another vital prime ministerial concern. While Blair excelled as a communicator, Brown appeared wooden and sometimes indecisive. Brown's personal poll ratings plummeted from the autumn of 2007, and remained sufficiently low to fuel peri-odic speculation over a challenge to his leadership.

The Prime Minister's relations with party, Parliament and the media are often closely linked to the authority with which Prime Ministers are able to carry out their executive and national lead-ership roles. It is as the leader of the majority party that a Prime Minister gains office in the first place; it is the continuing regular support of that party in Parliament that maintains the Prime Minister's authority to govern. Relationships with the party, therefore, are of the greatest significance and these are two-way. The Prime Minister seeks to maximize control of the party while the party strives for influence over the Prime Minister.

## BOX 11.3

# Removing Prime Ministers

- **Election defeat.** Most commonly Prime Ministers are brought down by a defeat in a general election. Since the Second World War Prime Ministers Churchill (1945) Attlee (1951) Home (1964) Wilson (1970) Heath (1974) Callaghan (1979) Major (1997) and Brown (2010) were effectively removed by the electorate. It was once fairly common for defeated Prime Ministers to return for a second or subsequent period in charge, but since 1945 only Churchill and Wilson have returned for second premierships. Some defeated Prime Ministers have resigned their party leadership immediately (Major, Brown) or soon afterwards (Home, Callaghan).

- **Death or serious illness.** No post-war Prime Minister has died in office. Illness was the ostensible reason for the resignations of Churchill (1955) Eden (1957) and Macmillan (1963), although political difficulties played a part in the departures of the last two in particular, and all three lived for many years after resigning.

- **Resignation after a serious challenge from Cabinet colleagues and/or the parliamentary party).** Thatcher was the only Prime Minister to resign after a formal challenge to her position as party leader in 1990. Major provoked and defeated a similar challenge in 1995. Neither Blair nor Brown ever faced a formal challenge to their leadership.

Faced with recalcitrant backbenchers, the Prime Minister can appeal to personal ambition (the power of patronage is a potent weapon) and party loyalty (a general desire to do nothing to assist the opposition). In general, Prime Ministers are strongest in their relations with their parties in the months following victory in a general election or leadership election. Such 'honeymoon' periods may be very brief indeed, as John Major's experience in 1992 showed. His unexpected election victory in April was a personal triumph, but by early November he had become the most unpopular Prime Minister since records began. Blair, by contrast, remained well ahead in the opinion polls from his election victory in 1997 until the unexpected fuel protests of September 2000, by which time the Prime Minister had enjoyed a 'honeymoon' of over three years. Brown's brief honeymoon period was abruptly terminated by 'the election that never was' in September 2007 (see Chapter 1).

Prime Ministers are at their weakest when government policies seem not to be working and provoke popular hostility and opposition. It was Thatcher's mounting unpopularity as a result of high interest rates, a stagnant economy and the poll tax that led the party to revolt against her in November 1990. Economic problems and increasing divisions over Europe provoked a formal challenge to Major in 1995. The Iraq war, foundation hospitals and student tuition fees caused increasing problems for Blair from the Parliamentary Labour Party from 2003 onwards (leading him to contemplate stepping down in the early summer of 2004). Falling poll ratings for Brown during the financial crisis and economic recession led to unsuccessful plots against his leadership in 2008 and 2009 (Rawnsley, 2010). However, the failure of plots against Brown, and of many similar challenges to former Prime Ministers, indicates the difficulty in unseating an incumbent premier (see Box 11.3).

## The Cabinet

The Cabinet is the country's top executive committee. However, status within the Cabinet is not equal and most Cabinets divide into a small circle of ministers who may expect to be frequently consulted by the Prime Minister and an outer circle who count for less. The 'plum' jobs are the posts of Chancellor of the Exchequer, Foreign Secretary and Home Secretary, which a victorious party's leading few politicians may expect to occupy. Also key posts today are Justice Secretary (combined with the traditional post of Lord Chancellor) and Business Secretary. Other posts may become particularly important because of external circumstances or special government priorities.

On occasion, and notably in times of war, a small inner Cabinet has been formed, as during the Falklands War for example. Thus, although the decision to commit the Task Force in 1981 was taken by full Cabinet, Margaret Thatcher formed a small War Cabinet of five to run the war on a day-to-day basis. Blair similarly formed what was effectively a smaller War Cabinet over Kosovo in 1999, although there were regular reports to the full Cabinet (Hennessy, 2000, p. 504–5). Some have called for a smaller Cabinet in peace-time, arguing that a Cabinet of over twenty is too large for the efficient conduct of business. However, political difficulties would arise if a major department and its associated outside interests were not seen to be represented at the 'top table', or if particular areas of the country or sections of the population, or important strands within the party were excluded.

## Cabinet business

Cabinet meetings became more numerous throughout the twentieth century down to the 1960s but declined thereafter, slowly at first but then dramatically under Thatcher to a much lower level, which was continued under her successors. The full Cabinet normally now meets once a week when Parliament is sitting, although in times of crisis it may meet more frequently. Under Blair the length of Cabinet meetings noticeably shortened, commonly to an hour or less (Hennessy, 2000, p. 481).

Very few decisions in the modern Cabinet system are actually *made* by full Cabinet although virtually all the major policy issues come before it in some form. Its agenda over a period of time consists predominantly of three kinds of matter:

- *Routine items* such as forthcoming parliamentary business, reports on foreign affairs and major economic decisions.
- *Disagreements referred upwards for Cabinet arbitration,* e.g. from Cabinet committees or from departmental ministers in dispute.
- *Important contemporary concerns* – a broad range, including national crises such as a war, issues of major controversy such as a large-scale strike and other matters of political sensitivity.

---

**BOX 11.4**

# The role of the Cabinet

- **Formal approval** of decisions taken elsewhere
- **Final court of appeal** for disagreements referred from below
- **Crisis management** of emergencies and issues of major political controversy
- **Debating forum** and sounding board for leading ministers
- **Legitimizer** conferring full legitimate authority upon government decisions
- **Symbol of collective executive** rather than single person executive in Britain

## Cabinet committees

Because of the sheer volume and complexity of modern governmental business, the bulk of decisions within the Cabinet system are taken by Cabinet committees. Cabinet committees either take decisions themselves or prepare matters for higher-level decision, possibly at Cabinet. Official committees (of civil servants) underpin ministerial committees and prepare papers for their consideration (Burch and Holliday, 1996, p. 44). Cabinet committee decisions have the status of Cabinet decisions and normally a matter is referred to full Cabinet only when a Cabinet committee cannot reach agreement. The Prime Minister or senior Cabinet ministers chair the most important committees. The committee chairman must agree any request to take a dispute to full Cabinet, but such appeals are discouraged. Treasury ministers, however, in 1975 gained the right of automatic appeal to Cabinet if defeated on public spending in committee (James, 1992, p. 69).

The establishment, composition, terms of reference and chairmanship of Cabinet committees are the responsibility of the Prime Minister. Before 1992 their structure was supposedly a secret, although details did gradually come to light from the 1970s on as a result of ministerial memoirs and partial statements by the Prime Minister. After the 1992 general election John Major decided to make public the entire system of Cabinet standing committees and the subjects they deal with. This information has been routinely available since.

Cabinet committees have become central to decision-making in the post-war period. Thatcher and Major reduced the number of committees and the frequency of meetings. Blair and Brown maintained the system of Cabinet committees but also set up a number of ad hoc working groups, while Blair in particular often relied on bilateral discussions with relevant departmental ministers. The relative informality of this decision-making (dubbed 'sofa government') aroused some criticism (e.g. in the Butler Report, 2004, and Chilcot Inquiry, 2009–11).

## The Cabinet Office

The Cabinet Office is another institution at the heart of the core executive that has developed in response to the large growth in the volume of government business. Dating from 1916, its most important component is the Cabinet Secretariat, a group of some 30 senior civil servants on secondment from other departments working under the direction of the Cabinet Secretary. Over the years a number of new special offices and units have been brought within it, often covering policy issues which cut across departmental boundaries. The Cabinet Office now works closely with the Prime Minister's Office.

## Cabinet minutes

Cabinet minutes are the responsibility of the Cabinet Secretariat. Like the minutes of most meetings, they involve a brief record of decisions and conclusions rather than a full account of any preceding discussion. As such they are very important as they are binding on the whole government machine. Controversy has occurred over the extent of prime ministerial involvement in the process, with certain members of past Labour Cabinets suggesting that this could be considerable (Castle, 1980, p. 252). But the then Prime Minister, Harold Wilson, denied it, and later provided what is now widely accepted as the correct account of routine procedure: 'The writing of the conclusions is the unique responsibility of the Secretary of the Cabinet . . . The conclusions are circulated very

promptly after Cabinet, and up to that time no minister, certainly not the Prime Minister, sees them, asks to see them or conditions them in any way' (Wilson, 1976, cited in King, 1985, p. 40).

## Collective responsibility

The doctrine of **collective responsibility**, which holds that all ministers accept responsibility collectively for decisions made in Cabinet and its committees, is the main convention influencing the operation of the Cabinet. The document *A Code of Conduct and Guidance on Procedure for Ministers* (1997, previously *Questions of Procedure for Ministers*) is the first Cabinet paper a new minister is handed. This document declares: 'Decisions reached by the cabinet or ministerial committees are binding on all members of the government' (not just the Cabinet). The argument behind the doctrine is that an openly divided government could not work together and could not command the confidence of Parliament or the wider public.

The doctrine of collective responsibility is clearly of value to the Prime Minister in the control of Cabinet colleagues. On the other hand, it does lay reciprocal obligations on the Prime Minister, first, not to leak decisions and, second, to run the government in a collegiate way, making sure that ministers have reasonable opportunities to discuss issues. One problem for ministers is that they often play a limited part in making the decisions to which they are required to assent. This latter point has implications not only for the conduct of Cabinet itself but also for the composition of Cabinet committees which – if they are to take authoritative decisions in the name of the Cabinet – must be representative of the Cabinet as a whole.

Collective Cabinet responsibility obliges all ministers to support government policy or resign. Although such resignations are relatively uncommon, when they occur they can have serious and sometimes devastating implications for the future of the government and the Prime Minister in particular, especially if senior figures with a following in the party and Parliament are involved. Thus

---

● **Collective responsibility**: The convention of Cabinet government requires all ministers to support publicly decisions of Cabinet and its committees, or resign from the government.

## BOX 11.5

## The practical implications of collective Cabinet responsibility

- **Cabinet solidarity**. Ministers may disagree until a decision is made, but are expected then to support it publicly or, at least, not express their lack of support for it. If they feel they must dissent publicly, they are expected to resign. If they fail to resign, it falls to the Prime Minister to require them to do so. The underlying purpose of this is to create and maintain the authority of the government which public squabbling between ministers could be expected to damage.
- **Cabinet secrecy**. A precondition of Cabinet solidarity is that Cabinet discussion is secret. Ministers need to feel free to speak their minds secure in the knowledge that their views will not be divulged to the media. Ministers who are known to disagree with a policy

may be expected to have little commitment to it; well-publicized disagreements, therefore, have potentially damaging consequences for public confidence in government.
- **Cabinet resignation** if defeated on a Commons vote of confidence. The convention requires that the Cabinet – and therefore the entire government – should resign if defeated on a Commons vote of confidence. Thus when the Labour government elected in October 1974 was defeated on a vote of confidence on 28 March 1979, the Prime Minister James Callaghan immediately requested a dissolution. However, such defeats are very rare because governments usually enjoy a comfortable overall Commons majority.

the resignations of Defence Secretary Michael Heseltine (1986), Chancellor of the Exchequer Nigel Lawson (1989) and finally Deputy Prime Minister Geoffrey Howe (1990) progressively damaged the Conservative government of Margaret Thatcher and substantially contributed to her fall. The resignation of Leader of the House, Robin Cook, in 2003 over the decision to invade Iraq was a serious blow to Blair's government, particularly as Cook had been Foreign Secretary from 1997 to 2001 and could speak with some authority on the subject. The resignation of more Cabinet ministers would have indicated a significant Cabinet split. However, Clare Short, the International Development Secretary, who had openly expressed disquiet over Blair's 'recklessness' was persuaded to stay on to assist in the rebuilding of post-war Iraq. She eventually resigned but the delay reduced the impact and limited the damage to the government.

There were two earlier occasions when the principle of collective responsibility was formally suspended. In 1932 there was an 'agreement to differ' over tariffs among members of the National Government. In 1975 members of Wilson's Labour government were allowed to campaign on both sides of the referendum on whether the United

Kingdom should remain in the European Community.

## Managing a coalition government

These precedents are significant for the Conservative–Liberal Democrat government that took office in 2010 after protracted negotiations between the Conservative and Liberal Democrat parties, following the inconclusive general election on 6 May. The Liberal Democrats obtained their first ministerial posts since 1945. Although negotiating teams from the two parties were able to agree a substantially common programme for government, involving concessions and compromises on both sides, there were some issues on which the coalition partners appeared divided, particularly electoral reform, nuclear power, university tuition fees and relations with Europe. Thus while there was a commitment to a referendum on the introduction of the Alternative Vote, the coalition parties remained free to campaign on opposite sides. A similar 'licence to differ' on other 'red line issues' may prove necessary in due course to prevent the break-up of the coalition. Liberal Democrat ministers face difficulties if they support policies that they have previously strongly opposed, if the party wishes to maintain its separate identity and maintain credibility with party members and voters.

However the problems of managing a coalition government are not so wildly different from managing a single party government. All major parties involve coalitions of values and interests, and Prime Ministers and Cabinets have always had to consider the impact of policies and decisions on factions and tendencies within the governing party. Indeed both former Conservative and Labour governments faced considerable internal dissension and often significant rebellions among ministerial colleagues, parliamentary parties and wider party members.

## The Coalition Cabinet

The Coalition Cabinet contained 23 members (Table 11.1), 21 from the House of Commons and two from the House of Lords (Lord Strathclyde and Lady Warsi). Four Cabinet Ministers were women (all Conservative), fewer than the seven that had once featured in Blair's Cabinet. However, this marks an advance on previous Conservative Cabinets, which between 1979 and 1990 generally contained just one woman, the Prime Minister, Margaret Thatcher, while John Major's first Cabinet was all-male.

For a party with just 57 MPs, or 9 per cent of the seats in the Commons, a total of five Cabinet posts for the Liberal Democrats looks generous, although rather less generous if their 23 per cent share of the total vote is compared with the Conservatives' 36 per cent. While their leader Nick Clegg became Deputy Prime Minister with special responsibility for political and constitutional reform, the party obtained none of the traditional great offices of state, the Exchequer, Foreign Office and Home Office. Vince Cable secured the post of Business Secretary (previously occupied by Labour's Lord Mandelson), taking charge of a department whose abolition he had previously advocated. Chris Huhne became responsible for Energy and Climate Change, David Laws, Chief Secretary to the Treasury, while Danny Alexander became Scottish Secretary (a less important responsibility in post-devolution Scotland).

Following the resignation of David Laws later in May after revelations over his parliamentary expenses, Danny Alexander replaced him at the Treasury and another Liberal Democrat, Michael Moore, became Scottish Secretary. The Liberal Democrats also picked up a number of ministerial posts outside the Cabinet, involving them in most government departments.

Otherwise, at 23 the Cabinet is on the large side, made larger still by the number (5) of non-Cabinet ministers (all Conservative) routinely attending Cabinet, with others attending as required. Some of these non-Cabinet ministers include prominent members of the former Conservative Shadow Cabinet, who might reasonably have expected to be full Cabinet ministers, had the Conservatives secured an overall majority.

The Conservative–Liberal Democrat coalition reduced the number of full Cabinet committees, but introduced some new ones, notably the Coalition Committee, of which the party leaders are co-chairs. Otherwise most committees are chaired by Conservatives with Liberal Democrat deputies. This ensures the two parties are involved in debates and decisions on virtually all aspects of coalition government policy (see box below).

---

**Coalition Committee**
  (Co-Chairs: David Cameron and Nick Clegg)
**National Security Council**
  Chair: David Cameron; Deputy Chair: Nick Clegg)
**NSC (Threats, Hazards, Resilience and Contingency**
  (Chair: Cameron;;Deputy: Clegg)
**NSC (Nuclear Deterrence and Security**
  (Chair: Cameron; Deputy: Clegg)
**European Affairs Committee**
  (Chair: William Hague; Deputy: Chris Huhne)
**Social Justice Committee**
  (Chair: Iain Duncan Smith)
**Home Affairs Committee**
  (Chair: Nick Clegg; Deputy: Kenneth Clarke)
**Economic Affairs Committee**
  (Chair: George Osborne; Deputy: Vincent Cable)
**Banking Reform Committee**
  (Chair: George Osborne; Deputy: Vincent Cable)
**Parliamentary Business and Legislation Committee**
  (Chair: Sir George Young; Deputy: David Heath).

**Table 11.1**  The Conservative and Liberal Democrat Coalition Cabinet, May 2010

| | | |
|---|---|---|
| Prime Minister, First Lord of the Treasury, Minister for the Civil Service | David Cameron | Conservative |
| Deputy Prime Minister, Lord President of the Council | Nick Clegg | Lib Dem |
| Secretary of State for Foreign and Commonwealth Affairs | William Hague | Conservative |
| Chancellor of the Exchequer | George Osborne | Conservative |
| Lord Chancellor, Secretary of State for Justice | Kenneth Clarke | Conservative |
| Secretary of State for the Home Department and Minister for Women and Inequalities | Theresa May | Conservative |
| Secretary of State for Defence | Liam Fox | Conservative |
| Secretary of State for Business, Innovation and Skills, President of the Board of Trade | Vincent Cable | Lib Dem |
| Secretary of State for Work and Pensions | Iain Duncan Smith | Conservative |
| Secretary of State for Energy and Climate Change | Chris Huhne | Lib Dem |
| Secretary of State for Health | Andrew Lansley | Conservative |
| Secretary of State for Education | Michael Gove | Conservative |
| Secretary of State for Communities and Local Government | Eric Pickles | Conservative |
| Secretary of State for Transport | Philip Hammond | Conservative |
| Secretary of State for Environment, Food and Rural Affairs | Caroline Spelman | Conservative |
| Secretary of State for International Development | Andrew Mitchell | Conservative |
| Secretary of State for Culture, Olympics. Media and Sport | Jeremy Hunt | Conservative |
| Chief Secretary to the Treasury | Danny Alexander* | Lib Dem |
| Leader of the Lords, Chancellor of the Duchy of Lancaster | Lord Strathclyde | Conservative |
| Secretary of State for Northern Ireland | Owen Paterson | Conservative |
| Secretary of State for Scotland | Michael Moore* | Lib Dem |
| Secretary of State for Wales | Cheryl Gillan | Conservative |
| Minister without Portfolio (and Conservative Party Chair) | Lady Warsi | Conservative |
| **Also attending Cabinet** | | |
| Leader of the Commons, Lord Privy Seal | Sir George Young | (Conservative) |
| Minister for the Cabinet Office, Paymaster General | Francis Maude | (Conservative) |
| Minister of State (policy advice to Prime Minister) | Oliver Letwin | (Conservative) |
| Minister of State, Universities and Science | David Willetts | (Conservative) |
| Parliamentary Secretary to the Treasury and Chief Whip | Patrick McLoughlin | (Conservative) |
| **Attending when required** | | |
| Attorney General | Dominic Grieve | (Conservative) |

\* Changes following the early resignation of David Laws as Chief Secretary to the Treasury after revelations over his parliamentary expenses (see below and Chapter 12).

## Constraints on prime ministerial government

In practice, prime ministerial power can vary considerably according to the disposition of the individual Prime Minister to exploit the capacities of the office and political circumstances such as size of parliamentary majority and simply how 'events' fall out. Constitutional, political, administrative and personal constraints prevent the Prime Minister from achieving the degree of predominance suggested by the prime ministerial government thesis.

Britain's top decision-making body remains a collective executive and the Prime Minister's role therefore is to provide leadership within a Cabinet system in which collective responsibility remains the rule. Constitutionally, the Prime Minister has a free hand in the making of government appointments, but politically selection is constrained by the pool of talent within a particular party, by party standing

**BOX 11.6**

# The first coalition Cabinet meeting, May 2010

This historic photograph shows the first meeting of the Cameron Conservative-Liberal Democrat coalition government, which was also the first of any UK coalition government since 1945. It was, however, soon out of date, as it shows the Cabinet before the early reshuffle caused by the resignation of the Liberal Democrat Chief Secretary to the Treasury, David Laws (see Box 12.9, page 221). (Laws is prominent on the left of the picture.) Opposite him sits the Minister without Portfolio and Conservative party chair, Lady Warsi, herself symbolizing a significant transformation in the presentation of Cameron's party. Relatively few women, and none from an Asian background, had sat in any previous Conservative Cabinet. The full list of the post reshuffle Cabinet and other ministers regularly attending Cabinet is provided in Table 11.1, page 202.

and by the need to please sections of the party (and in Cameron's case another party also). This means in practice that Cabinets often include individuals whom the Prime Minister would rather be without. Cabinets also generally contain one or two politicians of the highest calibre who are actual or potential rivals for the party leadership. Political considerations also constrain the Prime Minister's power of dismissal and demotion. Brutal sackings can backfire, as did Macmillan's removal of a third of his Cabinet in 1962 (the so-called 'Night of the Long Knives'), or Thatcher's big Cabinet reshuffle of July 1989, which included the demotion of the reluctant Sir Geoffrey Howe from the post of Foreign Secretary. Later Prime Ministers were more cautious. Major, in a celebrated aside, revealed he would not sack hostile colleagues because he did not want 'three more of the bastards' on the backbenches (Major, 1999, p. 343). Blair rejected advice from Mo Mowlam to sack his powerful Chancellor, Gordon Brown. Brown himself reportedly drew back from replacing Alistair Darling as Chancellor with his long-term ally Ed Balls in 2009, when it was clear that Darling would not accept another post.

While party is a source of support for a Prime Minister it is often a constraint on freedom of action. Thus Europe has caused serious problems of party management for Prime Ministers from Macmillan onwards. Wilson suspended collective responsibility and held a referendum to avoid splitting Labour, and Major resigned the party leadership in 1995 in an attempt to end incessant Cabinet and party dissension over Europe. Ultimately, the party may even remove a sitting Prime Minister, but this has happened to only four Prime Ministers in the last 100 years and only one since the war, Thatcher (see Box 11.3).

Finally, there are personal limits to the power of the Prime Minister – the limits of any single individual's ability, energy, resources and time, together with the (very considerable) extent to which decisions are shaped by circumstances beyond any individual's capacity to control. Moreover, the Prime Minister's special concerns (foreign affairs, the economy and security) are particularly vulnerable to setbacks that rebound swiftly on the popularity and even credibility of the premier (as Blair found over the Iraq war and Brown discovered on economic management).

Coalition government does not fundamentally alter the relations between Prime Minister and Cabinet. David Cameron has to keep another party

## *Academic controversy 11.1*
# Prime ministerial government?

It was Bagehot ([1867] 1963), writing in the mid-Victorian period, who identified the Cabinet as the key link between the executive and the legislature and the 'efficient secret' of the constitution. In a new introduction to Bagehot's classic text almost a century later, Richard Crossman (1963) declared that prime ministerial government had replaced Cabinet government. Crossman drew heavily on (and somewhat exaggerated) the analysis of John Mackintosh (1962). However the prime ministerial government thesis was vigorously criticized, notably by G. W. Jones (1965). Anthony King (1969) edited a book, *The British Prime Minister,* that included extracts on both sides of the argument. Much of the debate at the time focused on Wilson's 1964–70 government of which Crossman himself was a leading member. His diaries (Crossman, 1975, 1976, 1977), the writings of other Cabinet ministers and Wilson himself (1976) contributed further to the controversy.

Subsequently, the contentious government of Margaret Thatcher revived the debate. King (1985) produced a second edition of *The British Prime Minister* in which he contributed a substantial analysis of Thatcher's premiership. King (1985, p. 137) claimed she had 'been pushing out the frontiers of her authority ever since she took office in 1979' but he was suitably cautious as to whether she had 'fundamentally changed the office of prime minister' (King, 1985, p. 136). In 1990 Thatcher was brought down by a parliamentary party and Cabinet revolt, precipitated by former ministers with

whom she had acrimoniously parted. This suggests significant constraints on prime ministerial power.

The debate was taken to another level when Foley (1993, 2000) claimed that modern UK Prime Ministers wielded presidential authority. Early commentators on the post-1997 Labour government freely used the term 'President Blair'. Rawnsley (2001, p. 50) claimed that from the beginning Blair's premiership 'was designed to be a presidential premiership' (see also Hennessy, 2000). Norton (in Beech and Lee, 2008, p. 99) suggested that Blair 'exhibited the characteristics of presidentialism ... on an unprecedented scale'. Yet after the Iraq war Blair's dominance was reduced to the extent that he contemplated resignation in 2004 and was talked of as a 'lame duck premier' when he confirmed he would not fight another election after 2005. Subsequently Gordon Brown faced several plots against his own leadership, and never acquired the ascendancy of his predecessor (Rawnsley, 2010).

In retrospect, much of the debate over prime ministerial or presidential power drew on the earlier years of the Wilson, Thatcher and Blair premierships. The Wilson government of 1974–6 and the later years of both Thatcher and Blair suggest more limitations to prime ministerial power, as did the governments led by Callaghan, Major and Brown. Thus the power of the prime minister inevitably fluctuates with the personality of the holder of the post and the political circumstances of the time. As the first coalition Prime Minister since the war, David Cameron faces new constraints and new opportunities.

---

reasonably happy, besides his own Conservatives, and that is an additional complication. Yet in some respects the coalition with the Liberal Democrats provides him with a handy excuse for not satisfying his own MPs and party members. He can argue, correctly, that he lacks a majority to fulfil all past party manifesto pledges, without bringing down the government and risking the return of Labour to power. Potential rebels may be deterred from

pursuing causes that may precipitate such an outcome. Thus it may be easier for Cameron to manage his own party, despite some backbench dissatisfaction with his leadership, while it seems he has little to fear from his coalition partners, keen to avoid an early election.

In some respects David Cameron is more fortunate than some previous Prime Ministers, in that he has no obvious rivals for his job, even though

**Table 11.2**  Prime ministerial power and constraints on prime ministerial power: a summary

| Prime ministerial power | Constraints on prime ministerial power |
| --- | --- |
| PM's power of patronage – to 'hire and fire' – appointment of Cabinet, junior ministers, other posts, recommendation of honours, etc. | Political constraints on exercise of patronage – need to satisfy powerful rivals, sections of party, interests in the country, etc. |
| PM's position as majority party leader (normally following a party election) | Party a constraint on power as well as source of power – potential party revolts and challenge from party rivals |
| PM's parliamentary majority and dominance of parliamentary business | Problems in managing parliament – increasing backbench rebellions (PMs devote little time to parliament beyond PM's Questions) |
| PM's position as Chair of Cabinet – heading whole machinery of government | PM can be outvoted in Cabinet, and can face Cabinet revolts and threats of resignation |
| PM's control over civil service (as Minister for Civil Service) | PM's limited authority over civil service, which has tradition of political neutrality |
| PM's power to intervene personally in any area of government | Opportunity costs to PM's intervention in any policy area – cannot intervene everywhere |
| PM's standing in country enhanced by modern communication through mass media | PM can be undermined by failures in communication |
| PM represents the country at home and abroad | PM is not a head of state (cf. US President) |

his Cabinet includes two former Conservative party leaders (William Hague and Iain Duncan Smith) and other past leadership candidates (Liam Fox and Kenneth Clarke). Clarke remains a formidable politician, but his age and declining support within the party means he is hardly an alternative Prime Minister.

To summarize, the British Prime Minister has very considerable powers – and these were stretched to the limit by a dynamic Prime Minister such as Thatcher and more recently by Blair also. But the constraints upon the premier make 'prime ministerial government' an inappropriate description. Is 'Cabinet government' a more apt one? Our earlier discussion suggested that the Cabinet itself neither originates policy nor takes more than a small proportion of major decisions. Most policy decisions in British government are taken in departments. However, the Cabinet retains what may be described as 'a residual and irreducible' authority; it has not sunk into merely 'dignified' status (Madgwick, 1991, p. 259). It remains strong

enough to help depose a dominant Prime Minister and also to provide a collective shield to protect both a Prime Minister and his or her leading ministers when they get into political difficulties. The British system of decision-making at the top has grown more complex, diffuse, and extensive but, arguably, it is still a collective executive in which the Prime Minister provides leadership within a Cabinet system.

## Prime ministerial power: an irrelevant debate?

Although the argument over whether Britain has Cabinet or prime ministerial or perhaps even presidential government has rumbled on for 50 years, some modern academics consider that it is largely irrelevant to the understanding of political and governmental power in modern Britain (see e.g. Smith, 1999, chapter 4; and Smith in Dunleavy *et al.*, 2003, pp. 62–5).

- In assuming a bipolar struggle between Prime Minister and Cabinet, the traditional debate oversimplifies the complexity of Britain's core executive and the role of other players within that core executive, including the Treasury, departmental ministers, senior permanent civil servants, special advisers, and Cabinet committees.
- It fails to distinguish sufficiently between the power of Cabinet ministers as heads of departments with real resources at their disposal and interests behind them, and the power of the Cabinet as a collective body.
- In focusing on the power of institutions it underestimates the importance of relationships between key players and the resources they can deploy in bargaining – resources which may shift significantly over time.
- It underestimates the importance of the context in which conflicts within government are fought out. Factors such as the size of a government's majority (or lack of one), the governing party's discipline and cohesion, and the opinion poll standing of the Prime Minister and leading rivals are not minor incidental features, but crucial to power relationships.
- It focuses too much on the traditional centre of British government in Whitehall and Westminster, ignoring the shift towards multi-level governance, in which the Prime Minister and Cabinet are only operating at one level (Rhodes, 1997). Thus it is suggested that the Prime Minister now has 'more control over less' (Rose, 2001). 'While a Prime Minister may be increasingly powerful in the Whitehall world, policy making in the real world has increasingly shifted from that arena . . . power has shifted upwards to the international arena, outwards to the private and voluntary sector, and downwards to agencies, quangos and devolved institutions' (Smith in Dunleavy *et al.*, 2003, p. 79).

# SUMMARY

- The executive in Britain is a parliamentary executive. The Prime Minister, the head of government, is not directly elected by the people. His or her authority derives normally from being leader of a party which gains a parliamentary majority in a general election.

- The key powers of the Prime Minister include appointments to government and public office, steering and organizing government, and giving leadership to the nation.

- The Prime Minister is served directly by the Prime Minister's Office, which has grown in size and importance but is relatively small compared with the staff of many other heads of government.

- The Cabinet is chaired by the Prime Minister and consists of some 20 to 23 ministers. Most head major government departments. Most are members of the House of Commons, although a few (normally only one or two) may come from the Lords.

- Outside the Cabinet are junior ministers, who mostly sit in the Commons, although a few may sit in the Lords. The whole government, including Cabinet and junior ministers, numbers around a hundred.

- Alongside the Cabinet a complex system of Cabinet committees has grown up. Some of these are chaired by the Prime Minister, others by senior ministers. Junior ministers as well as Cabinet ministers may be members of Cabinet committees. Many decisions are taken in committees and not referred to Cabinet.

- All members of the government are bound by the principle of collective responsibility. They are expected to support all government policy in public (or at least refrain from public dissent). Any member of the government who wishes to make public their disagreement with any item of government policy is required to resign their ministerial post.

- The formation of a coalition Cabinet involves some new issues for the management of government but has not fundamentally altered Britain's core executive system.

- Although it is widely alleged that the power of the Prime Minister has grown at the expense of the Cabinet there remain important constraints on the exercise of prime ministerial power, which in any case has fluctuated markedly between and also within premierships, according to personalities and circumstances.

- The reduction of Britain's power in the world, globalization and the growth of multi-level governance have in any case markedly reduced the capacity of the British central executive to control events and deliver policy.

## QUESTIONS FOR DISCUSSION

- What are the sources of the power of the British Prime Minister? In what respects might a British Prime Minister sometimes seem to have more power within his or her country's governmental system than an American President?

- Should the Prime Minister still be able to determine the date of the general election, or should there be fixed-term parliaments?

- Is the British Cabinet too large? Why is it difficult to reduce its size?

- Has the growth of Cabinet committees involved the bypassing of Cabinet?

- Why is there an apparent need for collective Cabinet responsibility, and what are the implications in practice?

- Has Cabinet government been effectively replaced by prime ministerial (or presidential) government?

- Why might the debate over prime ministerial power be regarded as only marginally relevant to the real issue of power in British government?

- What special problems (or advantages) might there be in managing a coalition government?

## FURTHER READING

On the Prime Minister, a key source is Peter Hennessy (2000), *The British Prime Minister: the Office and its Holders since 1945*. Older useful sources include King (1985) and Foley (1993, 2000). Brief summaries of the continuing debate on prime ministerial government are provided by Mark Garnett (2005) in *Politics Review*. Dennis Kavanagh and Peter Riddell provide thoughtful complementary analyses of Blair as Prime Minister during his first term in Seldon (2001), while Kavanagh extends his analysis to cover the second term in Seldon and Kavanagh (2005). See also Heffernan in Dunleavy *et al.* (2006). Philip Norton provides a critical overall review of Blair's premiership in Beech and Lee (2008). Rawnsley (2010) is revealing on the Brown premiership. On the Cabinet and the central executive generally see Rhodes and Dunleavy (1995), Burch and Holliday (1996) and Smith (1999). Useful brief discussions of developments since the 2001 election can be found in Holliday (in Dunleavy *et al.*, 2002) and Smith (in Dunleavy *et al.*, 2003).

Useful websites include 10 Downing Street: www.number-10.gov.uk; Cabinet Office: www.cabinet-office.gov.uk

# CHAPTER 12

# Ministers, Departments and the Civil Service

The last chapter focused on the central direction and co-ordination of policy in Britain by the Prime Minister and Cabinet. However, relatively few government decisions are sufficiently important or controversial to be taken to Cabinet. Most are made in departments. Whenever new government responsibilities are created by legislation, Parliament confers them squarely upon ministers and departments, not on the Cabinet or the Prime Minister. How decisions are taken within departments is consequently of vital significance in British government. Are ministers the real decision-makers? How far does the real power lie with civil servants or, perhaps now, special advisers? This chapter considers the major departments of state, and the respective roles of the ministers who head them and the permanent civil servants and more temporary advisers who staff them. We explore the radical changes in the civil service introduced by the Conservatives after 1979 and substantially maintained, but with some shifts in emphasis, by Labour. We consider the rise in numbers and importance of special advisers brought by ministers into the heart of government. We look at the impli-

cations of these and other developments on the traditional civil service principles of permanence, neutrality and anonymity. We examine issues of accountability and responsibility that have arisen in the relationship between elected politicians, civil servants and special advisers. We conclude with a discussion of the distribution of power and influence within government.

## The organization of British central government

The central government of the United Kingdom is organized into a number of departments of varying size and importance. Ministries or departments have emerged rather haphazardly over the centuries, and particularly over the last century, as the responsibilities of government have expanded. Moreover, ministries or departments have frequently been merged or sub-divided in periodic reorganizations, and often renamed in the process.

Is there any coherent rationale behind these departmental reorganizations? Back in 1918 the

Haldane Report into the machinery of government reckoned that there were two main principles under which the tasks of government might be grouped: by function (e.g. education, health, transport) or by client group (children, pensioners, disabled, unemployed). Haldane came down in favour of the functional principle. There are two other ways in which tasks might be allocated: by area or by work process (e.g. departments of architecture or accounting).

It should be clear that the actual organization of British central government does not completely follow any one of these principles. While most departments follow Haldane's functional (or service) model, there are also others that deal with particular areas of the United Kingdom – Scotland, Wales and Northern Ireland (but see below for the impact of devolution). In addition, ministers (if not departments) have sometimes been appointed for particular client groups. Thus we have had ministers for the disabled, and a minister for women and recently in Brown's government a Department of Children, Schools and Families. Organization by work process has rarely been explicitly used in central government (although it was once common in local government, e.g. departments of engineering, surveying, architecture).

Administrative fashion has sometimes influenced organizational change. In the 1960s and 1970s there was a general presumption in favour of large-scale organization in both the private and public sectors. 'Big was beautiful', because, it was argued, it could yield economies of scale, and lead to better co-ordination of policy. Thus a number of 'giant departments' were created which merged previously separate ministries, for example the Department of Trade and Industry (DTI), the Department of Health and Social Security (DHSS), the Department of the Environment (DoE). Subsequently there was a reaction against 'big government', and also against large departments, which were held to produce problems for effective management, and thus diseconomies rather than economies of scale. Thus the DHSS, and for a time the DTI were re-divided, while a separate Transport Department was hived off from the DoE. After 1988, disaggregation went further with the introduction of Executive Agencies (see below).

More often, organizational change seems to have reflected political factors rather than administrative theory. Thus the creation of a new department may be intended to signal the importance the government attaches to a particular responsibility. Thus Harold Wilson formed a new Ministry of Technology in 1964, Tony Blair established a separate Department of International Development in 1997. Occasionally a new Department has been created to provided a senior post for a particular politician, such as the deputy leader of the Labour party, John Prescott, for whom a new special Department of the Environment, Transport and the Regions (DETR) was created in 1997. (It was subsequently broken up from 2001 onwards.)

## The impact of constitutional reform on the organization of central government

Labour's constitutional reform programme had a more fundamental impact on the organization of UK central government. Devolution to Scotland and Wales inevitably reduced the role and importance of the Secretaries of State for Scotland and Wales, and the Scottish and Welsh Office. Most of the staff were transferred to the new Scottish and Welsh executives, while the ministerial posts were effectively downgraded, becoming second jobs for Cabinet ministers whose main responsibilities lay elsewhere. However, interestingly, David Cameron has given full Cabinet posts without additional responsibilities to the Secretaries of State for Scotland, Wales and Northern Ireland, despite the ongoing transference of additional powers to their devolved governments. Yet the Secretary of State for Northern Ireland has retained extensive administrative responsibilities, (particularly as the Northern Ireland assembly and executive were suspended four times up to 2007), as well as a delicate political role in maintaining the impetus of the peace process. (Responsibility for policing was finally transferred in 2010.)

Far more controversial was the Blair government's reorganization of the Lord Chancellor's Department, which raised a political storm. The original intention was simply to abolish the post, as part of a package of reforms, which included the introduction of a new Supreme Court, and a clearer separation of executive, legislative and judicial powers. A new Department for Constitutional Affairs was established, which in turn was swallowed up, along with some former Home Office responsibilities, in the new Ministry of Justice in 2007 (see Chapter 10 and particularly Chapter 14). The title of Lord Chancellor is now combined with that of Secretary of State for Justice.

Cameron's coalition government has signalled its own commitment to constitutional change by giving special responsibility for constitutional reform to Deputy Prime Minister Nick Clegg, the leader of the Liberal Democrats. Otherwise he has largely continued the departmental responsibilities of his Labour predecessors, although he has reverted sometimes to simpler titles (such as the Department for Education).

## The internal organization of government departments: politicians and civil servants

Departments are officially directed and run by politicians drawn mainly from the House of Commons, although a few come from the Lords. Today virtually all the ministers who head departments are of Cabinet rank, and most of these now hold the title of Secretary of State. Below the Secretary of State each department frequently contains at least one minister of state and two or more parliamentary under-secretaries of state. These junior ministerial appointments are the route by which aspiring politicians gain experience of government and often but not invariably lead in time to promotion to full ministerial rank. Yet memoirs of junior ministers suggest that they do not feel they have much power or influence (see Mullin, 2009).

Ministers are the political and constitutional heads of departments. Departments, however, are largely composed of permanent officials. Below the ministerial 'team' there is a body of civil servants headed by the permanent secretary, the most senior official in the departmental hierarchy. In addition to acting as the minister's top policy adviser, the permanent secretary is in charge of the daily work of the department, is responsible for its staffing and organization, and is also its accounting officer.

Below the permanent secretary, in order of rank, are the deputy secretaries, under-secretaries and three other grades down to principal. Broadly speaking, each department is normally divided up, first into several areas of policy, each the responsibility of a deputy secretary, and then into a number of functional units (or branches), each with an under-secretary in charge. Figure 12.1 brings together the points made so far about departmental structure in diagrammatic form.

## The civil service: size and distribution

In 2009 total **civil service** staff (full-time equivalent) numbered just under 490,000 (Office for National Statistics). Their numbers had declined from 735,000 in 1979 as a result of a deliberate policy carried out by successive governments designed to prune the bureaucracy. However, these figures somewhat exaggerate the reduction in bureaucracy as many of these workers continued to be employed elsewhere in the public sector. The civil service only constitutes about 10 per cent of all public sector employees (others are employed in local government, the health service, the armed forces, and a variety of appointed agencies, often called 'quangos').

Although the civil service is still widely associated with London, and more specifically Whitehall, it is increasingly geographically dispersed. Just 16 per cent of UK-based civil servants work in London and a further 10 per cent work in the rest of the South-east whilst almost three quarters work in other English regions, Scotland, Wales and Northern Ireland, or overseas. However, it remains true that the majority of the most senior civil servants remain London-based.

Perhaps more significant than geographical decentralization is the increasing managerial decentralization of the modern civil service. Most management (as opposed to policy advice) func-

---

● **The civil service**: Civil servants are 'Servants of the Crown, other than holders of political or judicial offices, who are employed in a civil capacity and whose remuneration is paid wholly and directly out of moneys voted by Parliament' (The Tomlin Commission, 1931). It includes all those directly employed by government departments and executive agencies.

**Figure 12.1**   Structure of a typical department of state

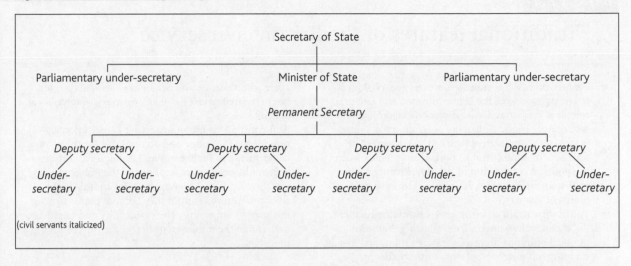

(civil servants italicized)

tions of the civil service are now carried out by **executive agencies** which have been established under the Next Steps programme (1988) to improve management in government and the delivery of services (see below). Today 78 per cent of the civil service work in over a hundred Next Steps agencies or on Next Steps lines. Each agency is headed by a Chief Executive, who generally reports to a minister. The minister sets the Chief Executive output, financial and quality of service targets for each year.

However, this chapter is primarily concerned with the 4,700 members of the Senior Civil Service (SCS). These constitute only one per cent of the entire civil service, but they advise ministers (now along with short-term special advisers) and help 'run the country'. There are in addition 31,900 in grades 6 and 7 (the next highest grades below the SCS), 217,500 in executive grades and 225,400 in administrative grades.

## Traditional features of the British civil service

British constitutional theory has always made a clear distinction between the *political* role of minis-

ters and the *administrative* role of civil servants. Ministers are in charge of departments and responsible to Parliament for running them, whilst civil servants advise ministers on policy and implement government decisions. Three features of the civil service have been traditionally linked to this distinction: permanence, political neutrality and anonymity (see Box 12.1).

Although senior civil servants are not allowed to play a formal (party) political role, as key ministerial advisers they have always been heavily involved in the politics of bargaining for influence *within* departments, *between* departments, *with* outside interests and *in their relations with* ministers. Moreover, in recent decades the traditional neutrality and anonymity of the civil service has been significantly eroded (see below and especially Box 12.8).

## Recruitment of the higher civil service: issues of expertise and bias

For much of the nineteenth century civil servants were recruited by a system of patronage, by *who* they knew rather than *what* they knew, which was hardly likely to promote efficient government. Following the 1854 Northcote-Trevelyan report, competitive examinations were introduced, with the aim of recruiting the best and brightest gradu-

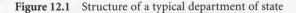

● **Executive agencies** (often referred to as Next Steps agencies) are organizations with some managerial autonomy within the civil service that are responsible for the management of a specific function or service.

## BOX 12.1

# Traditional features of the British civil service

- **Permanence.** While ministers are temporary, subject to the patronage of the Prime Minister, and electoral fortunes, civil servants are career officials enjoying security of tenure. Unlike the position in the United States (see Comparative Politics 12.1), where large numbers of administrative posts change hands when the political complexion of the government changes, in Britain civil servants are expected to serve governments of any party.
- **Political neutrality.** British civil servants are required to be politically impartial, not allowing their own political opinions to influence their actions and loyally carrying out government decisions, whether they

agree with them or not. Senior civil servants are still not permitted to engage in any open partisan political activity.

- **Anonymity.** Because ministers are constitutionally responsible for policy, and accountable for their departments to Parliament and public, civil servants have traditionally been kept out of the public eye. It was the role of civil servants to offer confidential advice to ministers and if they became public figures, this might compromise their neutrality and might also undermine the frankness of the advice offered to ministers.

ates into the higher civil service. This aim was substantially achieved. In the twentieth century the British higher civil servants generally had outstanding academic records with first-class degrees from the older and more prestigious universities. However, in the latter part of the twentieth century there were increasing criticisms of top British civil servants on two main grounds: their lack of relevant skills and expertise, and their narrow and unrepresentative social and educational background.

While there was little doubt that the senior civil servants recruited by the rigorous selection process were, in general, exceedingly able, critics argued that they usually lacked relevant knowledge of the services they were called on to administer, and appropriate managerial skills. Nor were these deficiencies systematically addressed through in-service training. Moreover, as most were recruited straight from university, they had little direct experience of the outside world, particularly commerce and industry. The professional and technical expertise of British senior civil servants was compared unfavourably with their French equivalents (see Comparative Politics 12.1).

The Fulton Report (1968) called for changes in civil service recruitment, promotion and training. Fulton recommended the recruitment of graduates with more relevant degrees, a considerable expan-

sion of late entry in order to enable people from many walks of life to bring in their experience, and the widening of the social and educational base from which top civil servants were recruited. The idea of demanding 'relevance' was rejected but, although expansion of late entry had disappointing results, from the mid-1980s there was a significant programme of two-way temporary secondments between Whitehall and industry, commerce and other institutions (Hennessy, 1990, pp. 523–4). By 1996, there had been a dramatic increase in recruitment from the private sector, with a quarter of the 63 posts advertised in the senior civil service going to private sector applicants. Secondments outside Whitehall had also increased, with 1,500 civil servants on medium- to long-term attachments in 1996. The Blair government established a new group headed by the Cabinet Secretary and the President of the Confederation of British Industry to oversee the development of shorter, more flexible secondments from the civil service into industry, especially of junior level civil servants from outside London.

A rather different criticism was that the senior civil service was socially and educationally unrepresentative of the public they served. It was perhaps inevitable that the aim to recruit the best brains would result in an unrepresentative civil service, but a persistent bias in favour of the recruitment of

## COMPARATIVE POLITICS 12.1
# Public bureaucracies in the USA, France and Britain

**USA**. The American public bureaucracy is highly complex, fragmented and at higher levels more politicized than the British. The complexity partly reflects the US federal system and division of powers. Thus bureaucracies exist at federal, state and local levels, but there is also a bewildering proliferation of departments, bureaus and agencies, often with overlapping responsibilities. Whereas British higher civil servants are expected to be politically neutral, many senior posts in the USA change hands when control of government changes (the 'spoils system'). American public officials do not generally enjoy the same prestigious status as their British or French equivalents

**France**. A strong, technocratic and highly prestigious bureaucracy serves the French 'one and indivisible' Republic. While senior British civil servants had the reputation of being able generalists without much specialist background or training, senior French public officials tend to be specialists with technical or profes-sional expertise. However, the French public service is not necessarily a career service on the lines of the British civil service. Although leading bureaucrats are recruited from the elite *Ecole Nationale d'Administration* (whose graduates are referred to as *Enarques*), some subsequently move into politics, and others transfer into the private sector, and sometimes back into the state service. This more specialist education combined with a greater breadth of experience may help to account for the prominent role of French officials in modernizing the economy and implementing prestigious projects.

*However*, changes in the British system of government (e.g. devolution, executive agencies, special units) have increased the complexity of the British bureaucracy. Moreover, changes in recruitment (more special advisers, short-term appointments, secondments to and from industry, etc.) have reduced the permanence and uniformity of the old higher British civil service.

Oxbridge graduates did tend to reinforce the rather exclusive and distinctly untypical social and educational background of senior servants. Broadening the base of recruitment away from Oxbridge-educated arts graduates has occurred very gradually, although canvassing for recruits at 'red brick' and 'new' universities intensified from 1991.

Another concern has been the gender and ethnic bias. Women make up just over half (53 per cent) of the total number of civil servants, but they are still disproportionately employed at lower levels, although the gender balance is fast changing. In 2009 women comprised 33 per cent of the senior civil service, and 39 per cent of grades 6 and 7 (see Figure 12.2). 9 per cent of civil servants come from ethnic minorities (rather more than their proportion in the economically active population), although only just over 4 per cent are in the Senior Civil Service. Just over 7 per cent of all civil servants and 4.3 per cent of the Senior Civil Service are disabled. In 2009 median earnings for all civil service employees were £22,100. The gender pay gap was 13 per cent. While these figures could be still further improved they compare favourably with national employment and pay figures (figures from Office for National Statistics).

Overall, the civil service is becoming more representative of the public it serves. Yet the composition of the highest ranks in a career service almost inevitably reflects patterns of recruitment twenty or 30 years ago from a society which was different in important respects. It will take time before change is perceptible among the permanent secretaries, deputy secretaries and under-secretaries who constitute the highest levels within the service. As senior civil servants advise ministers and influence policymaking, it is a matter of some continuing concern that important sectors of the community are under-represented in their ranks. If relatively few top civil servants have had direct experience of

**Figure 12.2**    Women employed in the civil service by grade, 2009

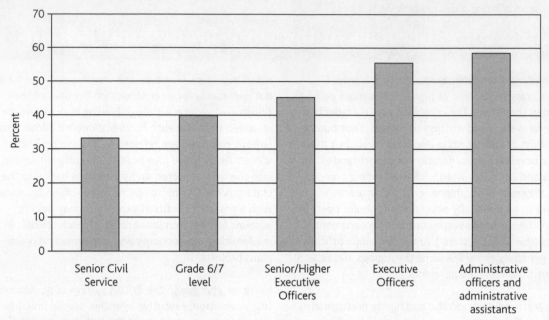

*Source*: Office for National Statistics.

state schools or ordinary universities they may be less competent to advise on education. If relatively few have had to juggle the demands of their professional work with the domestic work, childcare or care of the elderly and infirm which remains disproportionately a female responsibility in British society, they will have little direct insight into the problems of working women. If they have never felt at first hand the prejudice and discrimination which is the routine experience of most blacks and Asians, they can scarcely appreciate the attitudes and behaviour of ethnic minority communities and the problems of living in modern multi-cultural Britain. While senior civil servants may strive to give disinterested and impartial advice, their attitudes will inevitably reflect their own educational and social background, and their ignorance of very different environments. They have also sometimes been accused of other forms of bias (see Box 12.2).

## Reforming the civil service: the Thatcher and Major governments

The civil service has long been regarded as the core of what was described as public administration in

Britain, with a distinctive public sector ethos quite different from the practice and principles of the private sector. More recently there have been persistent attempts to introduce some of the characteristics of the private sector into the management of the public sector. The term 'New Public Management' (NPM) is often applied to the extensive changes inspired by the private sector introduced into managing public services, not only in Britain, but in many other countries in the western world. Indeed, many of the theoretical assumptions behind New Public Management, and many key initiatives, originated elsewhere, particularly in the United States. In Britain it is argued that New Public Management has increasingly displaced the values and processes associated with traditional public administration, not just in the civil service but in other parts of the public sector such as local government and the National Health Service. Although there were differences in interpretation and emphasis across varieties of organizations and services, New Public Management involved a number of generally recognizable features (see Box 12.3).

The new approach to managing the public sector in Britain was particularly associated with the Thatcher and Major governments, although it

## BOX 12.2

# Possible forms of bias in the civil service

**Party bias?** Although some Labour sources have accused senior civil servants of a Conservative bias, past Labour Prime Ministers and Cabinet ministers have generally testified to the loyal support they have received from the civil service.

**Establishment bias?** Radical critics have argued that the untypical social and educational background of senior civil servants gives them a bias in favour of establishment (or elite) values and interests. There are some continuing concerns that the higher civil service is socially unrepresentative.

**Liberal arts and social science bias?** Other critics suggest that the restricted academic background from which most top civil servants are drawn means few have knowledge or understanding of business or science and technology (see

also comparison with the French civil service in Comparative Politics 12.1).

**Consensus bias?** Both left-wing socialists and right-wing Conservatives have sometimes accused civil servants of a bias in favour of moderate consensus politics and hostility towards radical change. Civil servants, obliged to serve governments of different parties, may prefer continuity to change, and may react negatively to radical proposals from the left or the right.

**Bias towards their own interests?** New Right thinkers use the assumptions of classical economics to argue that civil servants pursue primarily their own self-interest and favour policies most likely to preserve and enhance their own pay, conditions and prospects (see also Academic Controversy 12.1, p. 223).

was largely maintained by Labour from 1997 to 2010. Conservative reforms were inspired by free market assumptions, involving distrust of big government and the public sector. They assumed that public sector organizations not subject to market competition were inherently wasteful and inefficient. Following free market economists such as Buchanan, Tullock and Niskanen, they considered that senior civil servants essentially pursued and protected their own interests rather than the wider public interest. The remedy was to cut the public sector down to size, and expose it to competition, introducing private sector norms and practices.

Conservative reforms between 1979 and 1997 constitute the most radical change in the civil service since the Northcote-Trevelyan reforms of 1854. They substantially reduced the numbers of civil servants from 735,000 to 494,300 between 1979 and 1996, a drop of over 32 per cent (although much of this involved the reclassification of jobs rather than their disappearance). From 1979, an Efficiency Unit headed by Sir Derek (later Lord) Rayner initiated a series of scrutinies of departments with the aim of reducing costs and streamlining procedure. From 1982, a variety of

## BOX 12.3

# Features of New Public Management

- A managerial culture that reflects private sector norms and practices rather than those of traditional public administration
- The promotion of competition, markets and quasi-markets within the public sector
- More managerial delegation, decentralization and organizational disaggregation
- An emphasis on economy, efficiency and effectiveness ('the three Es')
- Performance measurement, standards and targets
- Flexibility of pay and conditions (sometimes including performance-related pay)
- A greater emphasis on customer choice and service quality
- The contracting out of some service provision to the private sector, with the separation of purchaser and provider (or client and contractor) roles
- Privatization of some former public services – with state regulation rather than state control

## BOX 12.4

## Example of an executive agency: the Driver and Vehicle Licensing Agency

The Driver and Vehicle Licensing Agency:

- Sets itself clear targets (e.g. to reduce average waiting time for driving tests, and to reduce delays in issuing driving licences);
- Has shown considerable enthusiasm for marketing, e.g. customized number-plates;
- Has cut costs by putting provision of security and cleaning services out to private tender.

management information systems (such as the Financial Management Initiative – FMI) were designed to enable ministers to discover 'who does what, why and at what cost?'

The overall aim was to transform the civil service culture along business lines, to enhance the role of civil servants as managers of people and resources and to downgrade their role as policy advisers. In 1988 Sir Robin Ibbs produced a report entitled *Improving Management in Government: The Next Steps*. This argued that there had been insufficient focus on the delivery of services, even though the vast majority of civil servants (95 per cent) were in service delivery rather than policy advice roles. The report advocated the division of the civil service into a small 'core' engaged in supporting ministers with policy advice within traditional departments, and a wide range of executive agencies responsible for the delivery of services. Departments would set the policy and budgetary objectives and monitor the work of the agencies, but within that framework, each agency, headed by a chief executive, would have considerable managerial independence, with control over the recruitment, grading, organization and pay of their staffs. By the end of the twentieth century three-quarters of civil servants were working in Next Steps Agencies or along Next Steps lines. One such agency, Job Centre Plus, now employs 100,000 staff, and its annual budget is £4 billion. Many

other executive agencies are relatively small, with fewer than a thousand staff and annual budgets of a few million pounds.

It was argued that the new agencies improved service delivery, increased cost-effectiveness and produced significant savings. Another advantage claimed for the transfer of activities to executive agencies was a reduction in ministerial overload, although critics argued it also weakened ministerial accountability and effective political control, particularly in politically controversial area such as the Prison Service or the Child Support Agency.

The Conservatives increasingly involved the private sector in the delivery of public services. During the 1980s, compulsory competitive tendering (CCT) was introduced in local government and the NHS, allowing the private sector to bid for contracts to provide certain public services (see Chapter 17). Following a White Paper *Competing for Quality* (1991), market testing was extended to the civil service. By January 1995, over £1 billion of work had been transferred to the private sector. Privatization of some agencies had been envisaged by the Ibbs Report from the outset, although only eight small central government organizations were transferred to the private sector between 1992 and 1995.

The implicit and often explicit criticism of public service in these reforms was demoralizing for public sector workers. John Major's Citizen's Charter involved a rather more positive campaign to raise standards in the public services, although critics suggested it was more cosmetic than substantial. Each service was required to publish performance targets and results against set targets and establish well-publicized and readily available complaints and redress procedures. By 1995, nine agencies had published individual charters specifying standards that customers and clients were entitled to expect (e.g. the Jobseekers' Charter).

## Standards in public life

The reform programme from the 1980s onwards was primarily about improving the efficiency of government. The probity of government was more often taken for granted. However, a series of scandals in the 1990s reawakened concerns over ethical standards among politicians and office holders. Some of the concerns were over the conduct of

## BOX 12.5

# The Nolan Report, 1995: the seven principles of public life

- **Selflessness.** Holders of public office should take decisions solely in the public interest. They should not do so in order to gain financial or other material benefits for their family or their friends.
- **Integrity.** Holders of public office should not place themselves under any financial or other obligation to outside individuals or organizations that might influence them in the performance of their official duties.
- **Objectivity.** In carrying out public business, including making public appointments, awarding contracts, or recommending individuals for rewards and benefits, holders of public office should make their choices on merit.
- **Accountability.** Holders of public office are accountable for their decisions and actions to the public and

must submit themselves to whatever scrutiny is appropriate to their office.
- **Openness.** Holders of public office should be as open as possible about all the decisions and actions that they take. They should give reasons for their decisions and restrict information only when the wider public interest clearly demands.
- **Honesty.** Holders of public office have a duty to declare any private interests relating to their public duties, and to take steps to resolve any conflicts arising in a way that protects the public interest.
- **Leadership.** Holders of public office should promote and support these principles by leadership and example.

MPs (see Chapter 13). Several ministers were forced to resign, some for personal or sexual misconduct which had little to do with their government duties, but others in circumstances with wider implications. Beyond these scandals there were also concerns over the rules and principles covering those who held public office, whether as ministers or civil servants, and the relations between them. Thus Prime Minister John Major set up the Nolan Committee on Standards in Public Life in October 1994. Nolan's terms of reference were to examine current concerns about standards of conduct in public office-holders and to make recommendations as to any changes required to ensure the highest standards of propriety in public life. His brief covered Parliament (see Chapter 13); ministerial appointments to quangos (see Chapter 18); and central government. Nolan responded (Report, 1995) by laying down the 'seven principles of public life' (see Box 12.5).

The Nolan Report made a number of more specific recommendations regarding the conduct of ministers and civil servants which were largely accepted and incorporated into a non-statutory Civil Service Code (1996) and a revised Code of Conduct for Ministers (1997).

## Labour and the civil service: competition and co-ordination

Labour policy towards the civil service largely involved the consolidation and extension of Conservative initiatives, rather than their reversal. Thus the Blair government accepted most of the Conservative reform programme, including the introduction of competition and market values into the management of the public sector, and administrative decentralization through executive agencies. Yet there was also an important shift in emphasis towards more co-ordination between departments and agencies, and towards a wider co-operation between the public, private and voluntary sectors in the interests of 'joined-up government'. 'Departmentalism' is a familiar difficulty of government. Problems and policies are viewed through the often narrow perspectives of individual departments. Yet specific issues (e.g. drugs, child poverty, care of the elderly) frequently transcend departmental and agency boundaries, and require people from different organizations to work together.

Co-ordination may sometimes be improved by the reorganization of government departments, such as the replacement of the former Ministry of

## BOX 12.6

## Cabinet practice: a Code of Conduct and Guidance on Procedure for Ministers

This paper (Cabinet Office, July 1997) lays down guidelines to ministers and civil servants in the operation of Cabinet government. It requires ministers:

- To uphold the practice of collective responsibility;
- To account to and be held to account by Parliament for the policies, decisions and actions of their Departments and Next Steps Agencies;
- To give accurate and truthful information to Parliament, correcting any inadvertant error at the earliest possible opportunity; ministers who knowingly mislead Parliament are expected to offer their resignations to the Prime Minister;

- To be as open as possible with Parliament and the public, refusing to provide information only when disclosure would not be in the public interest;
- To require civil servants who give evidence before Parliamentary Committees on their behalf or under their direction to provide accurate, truthful and full information in accordance with the duties set out in the Civil Service Code;
- Not to use resources for party political purposes; to uphold the political impartiality of the Civil Service and not to ask civil servants to act in any way which would conflict with the Civil Service Code.

Agriculture, Fisheries and Food with the new Department of the Environment, Food and Rural Affairs. Yet no matter how far functions are reshuffled between different departments, there will always remain a need for co-operation across departments on specific issues (see Box 12.7). Labour attempted to ease the problem by creating a number of special cross-departmental units (e.g. the Social Exclusion Unit, the Women's Unit, the UK Anti-Drugs Co-ordination Unit). However, to an extent the new co-ordinating machinery has increased the sheer complexity and, ironically, even the fragmentation of government. Responsibility and accountability are blurred.

Moreover, there was a continuing tension between the New Labour 'third way' approach to management, emphasizing networks, mutual trust and co-operation and the earlier New Right-inspired emphasis on markets, competition and consumer choice, which Labour substantially endorsed. Thus schools and hospitals were still encouraged to *compete* for pupils and patients to promote more efficiency and value for money in the delivery of public service, but urged also to *co-operate* with their main rivals by sharing information and methods, which might reduce their own competitive advantage.

## The rise of special advisers

The Labour government, like its Conservative predecessors, was no longer content to rely on the permanent civil service for most of its policy advice. What New Labour required of the civil service was similar to what the Thatcher government wanted – loyal and effective implementation of government policy. All the emphasis was on policy delivery. The Labour government preferred to draw its policy advice from a range of sources including party research, independent think tanks, and most important of all, its own special advisers (or 'SpAds' for short), appointed on short-term contracts and brought into the centre of the government machine.

Special advisers were not new. They were employed alongside the permanent civil service by successive governments. However their number and more particularly their influence has steadily grown. Although still heavily outnumbered by senior civil servants, special advisers were by repute hugely influential on key areas of Labour government policy. Indeed, some special advisers, such as Ed Balls, a key economic adviser to Gordon Brown, and Andrew Adonis, initially an education adviser, were later to become ministers and influential

## BOX 12.7

## The need for departmental and agency co-ordination: the case of food

Food production was long seen as the almost exclusive responsibility of the old Ministry of Agriculture, Fisheries and Food, with its understandable concern for British farming. The new Department of the Environment, Food and Rural Affairs (DEFRA), established by the Blair government, involved a more explicit focus on food production and its relationship with broader environmental concerns. Yet other departments retained a strong interest in aspects of food. Thus the Department of Health clearly had an interest in the safety and quality of food. Other aspects of food production and marketing raised issues for the Department of Business (e.g. the dominance of major supermarkets over food retailing), Transport (e.g. the long distance carriage of live animals) and International Development (e.g. fair trade in agricultural produce). Each of these departments has its own associated agencies and outside interests to consider. Thus food policy in the fullest sense requires co-operation between a number of government departments and agencies and extensive consultation with all kinds of groups and interests outside government.

figures in Brown's Cabinet. Particularly controversial were a number of Labour advisers with responsibility for government communication, who acquired a high media and public profile as New Labour's spin doctors.

Some of the special advisers who served earlier governments (such as Wilson's) found themselves isolated and effectively neutralized by the permanent civil service. More recently special advisers have become some of the most influential figures at the heart of government, while top civil servants have found their traditional pre-eminence in policy advice considerably eroded. Smith (in Dunleavy, 2003) observes 'To some extent, top officials have been excluded almost completely from policy making.' Even with the qualifications this is an exaggeration. A permanent secretary's length of experience and first-hand knowledge of past policy failures and difficulties remains enormously valuable to ministers. Yet the permanent secretary is no longer substantially the voice of the department, and some have felt their role has been significantly diminished.

Some see the growing influence of special advisers as contributing to a decline in the traditional neutrality of a permanent career civil service (see Boxes 12.2 and 12.9). Yet special advisers are here to stay. Indeed, it is not unreasonable for a government to bring in some experts who share their general political philosophy to give advice on policy. In many other countries there is a far larger turnover in officials when the government changes hands. However, the rise to prominence of special advisers has caused tension with permanent civil servants in some departments, most spectacularly in the Department of Transport, culminating in the pressures which led to the resignation of two special advisers and then the minister, Stephen Byers, in 2002. Special advisers have the ear of ministers but are outside the hierarchy of permanent staff, leading to demands for more clarification of their role, particularly over how far they can issue instructions to civil servants. Their status remains unclear.

## Ministerial responsibility revisited

The convention of **individual ministerial responsibility** governs relations between ministers, civil servants and Parliament. Ministerial responsibility means that ministers are required to inform Parliament about their work and explain their own and their departments' actions. Individual minis-

---

● **Individual ministerial responsibility**: The constitutional convention by which each minister is responsible to Parliament for the activities of his or her department and 'carries the can' for failure.

**BOX 12.8**

## The impact of reform on key attributes of the civil service (cf. Box 12.1)

- **Permanence.** Traditionally, the Civil Service was a career service, characterized by security of tenure. The permanence of the civil service underpinned its public service ethos and commitment to impartial service of the government of the day. Market testing and some privatization have eroded the traditional job security of the civil service. The majority of civil servants now work for executive agencies, which have substantial responsibility for recruitment, pay (sometimes involving an element of payment by results) and conditions. Approximately one-quarter of agency Chief Executives and some top civil service posts were appointed from outside the service, while ministers have appointed more special advisers to provide the policy advice formerly given by senior civil servants. Today, a unified, career civil service with a single hierarchical organization, and common pay and conditions, no longer exists.

- **Neutrality.** In traditional theory, top civil servants are politically neutral, obliged to give ministers honest and impartial advice. Yet the 1983 Armstrong Memorandum asserted that the civil service has 'no constitutional personality or responsibility separate from the duly elected government of the day' and stressed that the duty of the civil servant was first and foremost to the ministerial Head of Department

(rather than Parliament or the public). This overriding duty of responsibility to a (party) government can inevitably create some problems for their political neutrality. Critics suggest that the civil service has become progressively more politicized under recent governments, Conservative and Labour. The Major, Blair and Brown governments have been accused of involving permanent civil servants in the promotion of policies for partisan objectives.

- **Anonymity.** The anonymity of civil servants – an important corollary of ministerial responsibility – has been considerably eroded. As ministerial willingness to assume responsibility for the mistakes of officials has declined, so the practice has grown of naming and blaming individual bureaucrats. Some of the chief executives who head the more controversial Next Steps Agencies have attracted considerable media attention and, sometimes, personal criticism. They are also more directly accountable to Parliament. Civil servants are increasingly summoned for interrogation by Departmental Select Committees. It was following his appearance before the Foreign Affairs Committee, which was investigating the government's use of intelligence in the lead-up to the Iraq war, that Dr David Kelly, the weapons expert, committed suicide in July 2003.

ters constantly explain and defend departmental policy before Parliament – at Question Time, during the committee stage of legislation, before Select Committees and privately to MPs. Ministerial answers to political questions are not always entirely full or satisfactory and sometimes they are downright evasive. None the less, individual ministerial responsibility in its first meaning of 'answerability' or 'explanatory accountability' still applies.

Ministerial responsibility used to mean that ministers – and ministers alone – are responsible to Parliament for the actions of their departments. However, the delegation of managerial responsibility, a key aspect of executive agencies, clearly implies some reduction of direct ministerial

responsibility. Chief executives of agencies have been summoned to appear before parliamentary committees, and their replies to parliamentary questions are published in *Hansard*. Of course, ministers remain in charge of policy, but there is a difficulty in dividing responsibility neatly between 'policy' and 'operations' (for which chief executives are responsible).

In the last resort, ministerial responsibility may entail resignation, yet relatively few ministers have felt obliged to 'carry the can' for policy failure. The most celebrated example of such resignations was that of the Foreign Secretary Lord Carrington and the whole Foreign Office team of ministers who resigned in 1982 for failure to foresee and prevent the Argentinian invasion of the Falklands, although

## BOX 12.9

# Examples of ministerial resignations for personal failings and political misjudgements

**Jonathan Aitken,** Chief Secretary to the Treasury, resigned in 1995 to fight a libel action against *The Guardian* newspaper that had alleged financial misconduct. The paper was later able to prove its allegations and Aitken was convicted for perjury and sent to prison.

**Peter Mandelson** resigned twice, firstly as Trade and Industry Secretary in December 1998 after his secret £373,000 home loan from fellow minister Geoffrey Robinson was made public. Then after he was brought back into government he resigned as Northern Ireland Secretary in 2001, following his failure to give a coherent account of his earlier involvement in the fast-track passport application by the Indian businessman, S. P. Hinduja.

**David Blunkett,** like Mandelson, resigned twice. In 2004 he resigned as Home Secretary following lurid publicity over his affair with *Spectator* publisher, Kimberly Quinn, culminating in acrimonious paternity disputes, and damning allegations that Blunkett had fast-tracked a visa application for his former partner's nanny. Brought back into government after the 2005 election as Secretary for Work and Pensions, he resigned again in November after revelations that he had failed to consult the independent committee that advises outgoing ministers on business posts he had taken up before the election. Thus he had

failed to observe all the principles of public life declared by Lord Nolan in 1995 and he had failed to follow specific recommendations in the revised Code of Conduct and Guidance for Ministers.

**David Laws** was an early Liberal Democrat resignation from the coalition Cabinet in May 2010, following revelations in *The Daily Telegraph* that he had incorrectly claimed parliamentary expenses for accommodation in his partner's flat. Laws maintained that he had sought to keep his gay relationship secret for family reasons. His situation aroused some sympathy among colleagues, but it was also accepted that he appeared to have broken the rules, and could not remain in office as the minister substantially responsible for cutting public spending.

---

the Defence Secretary, John Nott, survived. A more recent case involved the resignation of Estelle Morris as Education Secretary in October 2002, following a series of embarrassing failures in the service and department over which she presided, culminating in the A-level marking scandal, in which thousands of students were given the wrong grade. It is not entirely clear how far the failings here were the fault of the minister or officials, but the minister accepted responsibility. With this doubtful exception, there is no clear recent case of a minister resigning for mistakes made by officials.

While there has indeed been a stream of forced ministerial resignations in recent decades, most of these have been due to personal rather than policy failings, commonly sexual misconduct or financial

impropriety, while some others might be ascribed to political misjudgements and mistakes (see Box 12.9). In a few instances there was a fairly clear breach of the ethical principles governing the holding of public office (and formalized by Lord Nolan in 1995; see Box 12.5). In other cases, resignation followed lurid publicity of a minister's private life and a prolonged media 'feeding frenzy' which made the minister's position untenable.

The principle of individual ministerial responsibility should be distinguished from the convention of collective Cabinet responsibility requiring all ministers to support government policy in public (discussed in Chapter 11). Yet the distinction is by no means always clear-cut in practice. Thus a policy which was the collective responsibility of the

## BOX 12.10

# Constraints on the effective power of ministers

- *Numbers*: Ministers are substantially outnumbered by leading civil servants.
- *Permanence*: Civil servants are permanent while ministers are 'birds of passage' who change jobs frequently. The average tenure of a specific ministerial office since 1945 is just over two years. It takes ministers a lengthy period to master the business of their department, and during this time they are largely dependent on official briefing.
- *Weak preparation for office*: Few ministers, on taking office, have specialist knowledge of their department, and frequent moves to do not help them acquire expertise. Ministers rarely come to office with clearly defined policies, priorities or objectives. Unexpected situations which arise during their terms of office further increase their dependence upon officials.
- *Ministerial workload*: Ministers face multiple demands upon their time – from Cabinet, Parliament, party, constituency, media and increasingly from the EU in addition to their department; on average, they spend about two-thirds of their working week on other than departmental matters.
- *Control of information*: Top civil servants retain substantial influence over information going before ministers, the way in which it is presented and its timing, all of which gives them a formidable capacity to shape decisions.
- *Coordinating role*: Both formally through official committees and through informal contacts with their opposite numbers in other departments, top civil servants prepare and to a varying extent predetermine the work of ministers.
- *Implementation*: Civil servants can employ a variety of tactics to thwart implementation of policy, including delay and finding practical difficulties.

*However*, ministers, both individually and collectively, appear to have increased capacity in recent governments to control policy making, partly as result of the increased numbers of special advisers and partly because of institutional changes.

government as a whole may be treated as a matter of individual responsibility to minimize loss of public confidence in the government. Accordingly, an individual minister may feel obliged to accept responsibility for a policy that was really a collective decision. However, a matter of individual responsibility is sometimes transformed into a case of collective responsibility in order to shield a particular minister, whom a Prime Minister is anxious to retain.

## Where does power lie? Decision-making within departments

The constitutional position is that ministers make policy and civil servants implement policy. Yet it was commonly argued that senior civil servants in practice had a much larger role in the making of British public policy, and indeed were the real decision-makers. Ministers and civil servants, it was argued, had an adversarial relationship in which

the latter had distinct advantages in terms of numbers, permanence, information, expertise and time. Ministers were not well prepared for office, lacked time to learn on the job because of frequent Cabinet reshuffles, and had too many other parliamentary, party and constituency duties to concentrate fully on running their departments (see Box 12.10).

The notion that top civil servants were the real rulers of Britain was popularized by a comedy television series of the 1980s, *Yes, Minister* (and subsequently *Yes, Prime Minister*) which portrayed ministers as innocent dupes of their sophisticated and manipulative permanent secretaries. Judging from the surprising success of sales of the series abroad, the theme evidently struck a receptive chord in many other countries also. Yet, ironically, the *Yes, Minister* view of the relationship between ministers and civil servants acquired widespread acceptance in Britain at a time when the power and influence of civil servants was already under sustained attack from the Thatcher government.

## Academic controversy 12.1
# The bureaucratic over-supply model

The *bureaucratic over-supply model* came to the fore in the 1970s and is mainly but not exclusively linked with the New Right critique of government and civil service growth in previous decades. It drew on the analysis of public or rational choice theory advanced by William Niskanen and others. Niskanen (1971, 1973) applied classical liberal economic assumptions of the pursuit of individual self-interest to the public sector. In the absence of market constraints and the profit motive, public sector bureaucrats would seek to maximize the size of their own 'bureau' or department and its spending, because this would favour their own pay, promotion prospects, conditions of service and status. Such growth would involve the supply of more public services and more public spending and a bloated, inefficient and wasteful bureaucracy (bureaucratic over-supply). New Right analysis was not just descriptive but prescriptive, and pointed to its own solutions: both the bureaucracy and 'big government' needed 'cutting down to size', through transferring some activities to the private sector and subjecting others to competition. Thus the bureaucratic over-supply model provided much of the theoretical under-pinning for the Thatcher government's programme of civil service reform.

One influential study (Dunleavy, 1991) has applied public choice assumptions to argue that bureaucrats will engage in bureau *shaping* rather than bureau *maximizing*. Size (of budgets or staff) does not necessarily matter to senior bureaucrats, who do not always like managing large numbers of (sometimes difficult) junior staff. Indeed, the most prestigious departments are often among the smallest (e.g. the Treasury). Cuts in public spending and institutional change have rarely affected senior bureaucrats. While competition and market testing has often adversely affected the pay and conditions of routine manual and clerical workers, it has generally involved increased opportunities and more managerial autonomy for senior officials. In pursuit of their own self-interest, they do not necessarily want or need 'big government'.

---

Indeed, reality was always more complicated than the simple adversarial view of the relationship between ministers and civil servants portrayed in *Yes, Minister*. Civil servants, it has been argued, prefer strong ministers who know their own mind rather than weak ministers who can be manipulated. Strong ministers are not only more interesting to work for; they are more likely to be successful in fighting the department's battles in Cabinet and Cabinet committees. Indeed, relationships between ministers and top civil servants are commonly more collaborative than competitive. They are often on the same side, battling together against ministers and civil servants from other departments over administrative territory, public spending, policy priorities and legislative time. Moreover, many senior politicians and top civil servants come from a similar social and educational background, share many values, interests and aspirations, and belong to the same relatively small, enclosed Whitehall world (Heclo and Wildavsky, 1974). Many of the special advisers brought into government work closely and harmoniously with permanent civil servants to the extent that it can be difficult for casual observers to distinguish between the two.

There is no simple answer to the question: who rules, ministers or top officials? One answer could be both, another might be neither, bearing in mind the constraints of powerful outside interests, and the often intractable problems with which government has to wrestle. Moreover, government today is far more complex. It no longer consists substantially of a number of great Whitehall departments, each headed by a minister and a permanent secretary, but now involves a mosaic of departments, executive agencies, quangos, cross-cutting units and task forces, sometimes operating at different levels

(Rhodes 1997, Bevir and Rhodes 2003). The key personnel may include not only elected politicians and career civil servants, but also many other appointed public officials, special advisers, as well as representatives of powerful outside interests who have the ear of ministers. Government is in a constant state of flux, so that the real movers and shakers at any one point in time may no longer be influential soon afterwards.

## Managing coalition government

Some of the points above are all the more relevant following the emergence of a coalition government. Although this involves a complete change of ministerial personnel and special advisers, the new government will continue to work with most of the top civil servants who served the Brown government. Some of the latter may prove more influential and others less so with the new administration, depending on their own areas of expertise and their developing personal relations with new ministers. An additional problem, or perhaps opportunity, for top civil servants is having to work with ministers drawn from two parties. Although initially the combined team of ministers has appeared particularly harmonious, there are bound to be some differences of emphasis arising from their respective party backgrounds.

Certainly the preparations for a new government that the civil service made prior to the 2010 election were somewhat upset by the subsequent emergence of a coalition. There is an established tradition of top civil servants talking to the opposition before an election, as well as studying their manifesto and other party policy documents available, so as to enable the smooth transition, if the former opposition take office. Yet the hung parliament and complex prolonged negotiations between the two opposition parties involved the ditching or delay of some Conservative commitments, the acceptance of some Liberal Democrat policies, and some compro-

mises. Thus the new government's programme is not the same as that foreshadowed in the Conservative manifesto. Nor does the Liberal Democrat manifesto, to which civil servants paid little close attention until the party's surge in the election campaign, provide a reliable guide either. Thus civil servants were required to help implement a programme that was only cobbled together in the feverish days after the election. Yet the machinery of government managed the transition to a novel coalition calmly and without manifest difficulty.

Whether more problems emerge in the future remain to be seen. Yet although coalition is unfamiliar at Westminster and in Whitehall, it is the norm in most other western democracies, and there is ample experience of it elsewhere in the United Kingdom, in the devolved administrations in Scotland, Wales and Northern Ireland and in local government. Whitehall civil servants will have to grow used to coalition, as public bureaucrats elsewhere have long been used to it. Cynics might suggest that it may provide civil servants with ample opportunity to play off one coalition party against another, and have their own way. Certainly there are now representatives of both parties in most of the leading departments, so there may be scope for such tactics. Yet there were few early signs of inter-party friction in the new government, as the new ministers initially showed a closely united public front. Moreover, many civil servants will enjoy confronting new ideas and new challenges. Indeed, some top civil servants who felt marginalized under the previous government welcomed their new masters. However, deep cuts in the public sector may increasingly sharpen divisions between the coalition parties, and perhaps sour relations between ministers and civil servants. Top civil servants were soon adversely affected by freezes on pay and cuts in bonuses and fringe benefits, even if they did not face the threat of redundancy or geographical relocation like many more humble public sector employees.

# SUMMARY

- The bulk of decisions made by central government are made in departments by ministers and civil servants rather than by the Cabinet.

- Most departments are based on the function or service principle, although there is no single coherent rational principle behind the structure of central government. Departments have been frequently reorganized for a mixture of administrative, political and personal reasons.

- Departments are headed by politicians, usually a Secretary of State and several junior ministers. They are staffed by civil servants. The most senior civil servants who advise ministers are permanent secretaries and, beneath them deputy secretaries and under-secretaries.

- The traditional characteristics of the British civil service include permanence, neutrality and anonymity, although changes over the last 30 years call much of this into question.

- There are around half a million civil servants, geographically dispersed around the United Kingdom, although the majority of senior civil servants continue to work in London.

- Although women and ethnic minorities are well represented among the civil service as a whole, they are under-represented among the senior civil service, whose social and educational background remains restricted in other ways.

- The unrepresentative character of the civil service may influence their outlook. Although it is generally conceded that senior civil servants do not show a party bias, it is sometimes argued they show other forms of bias.

- The civil service has been extensively reformed over the last 30 years, along the lines of the New Public Management (NPM). This has involved a reduction in size, administrative decentralization, and increased competition. Most civil servants are expected to concentrate more on the management of departments and agencies and the delivery of services rather than advice to ministers.

- Renewed concern over ethical standards, prompted by scandals in the 1990s, led to the formalization of principles and codes of practice for both ministers and civil servants.

- The Blair and Brown governments largely maintained previous Conservative reforms but emphasized the need for increased co-ordination and co-operation ('joined-up government') alongside competition.

- The rise in numbers and importance of special advisers to ministers, and the implications for the responsibilities of career civil servants, has raised some concerns.

- There is no easy answer to the question, where does power lie, with ministers or civil servants? The relationship is often more collaborative than competitive. Permanent civil servants may have ceded some influence to ministers and special advisers, but government has become more complex, shifting and multi-layered, so generalizations are difficult.

- Civil servants now have to serve two masters in a coalition administration, but there are abundant precedents elsewhere and few indications that this will raise any serious problems.

# QUESTIONS FOR DISCUSSION

- Why are government departments so frequently reorganized in Britain?

- How far is the higher civil service unrepresentative? Does it matter? How might the service be made more representative?

- In what ways, if at all, might senior civil servants show bias?

- How far are senior civil servants in Britain suitably qualified for the work they are required to do?

- In what ways have changes introduced into central government and the civil service over the last 30 years affected the traditional permanence, neutrality and anonymity of senior civil servants?

- How is the principle of individual ministerial responsibility upheld in practice? Who carries the can for policy failure? For what reasons are ministers obliged to resign?

- How far are senior civil servants the real rulers of Britain?

- Will a coalition government increase the problems or opportunities for senior civil servants?

# FURTHER READING

For extracts from a wide range of sources, including some key public documents, see Barberis (1996), *The Whitehall Reader*. Among broad surveys see Pyper(1995), *The British Civil Service*. On the post-war history, Hennessy (1990), *Whitehall*, and Theakston (1995b), *The Civil Service since 1945* should be consulted. On relations between minister and civil servants, see Theakston (1995a) in Pyper and Robins (1995) and Smith *et al.* in Rhodes and Dunleavy (1995). For analysis of the role and power of senior civil servants see Theakston (1999) .

On civil service reform since 1997 see the White Paper *Modernising Government* (1999) and subsequent Cabinet Office papers. Gavin Drewry in Blackburn and Plant (1999) and in Jowell and Oliver (2007), Andrew Massey in Savage and Atkinson (2001) and Rod Rhodes in Seldon (2001) devote rather more space to

discussing New Labour's 'administrative inheritance' and speculating about the future than analyzing substantive reforms. There is a very useful brief discussion of the changing relations between ministers and civil servants in Martin Smith's chapter on *The Core Executive* in Dunleavy *et al.* (2003, pp. 69–81). Tony Butcher (2004) provides a helpful review of 'The Civil Service under the Blair Government' in *Developments in Politics,* volume 15.

### Websites

Home Office: www.homeoffice.gov.uk

Foreign Office: www.fco.gov.uk

Department of Health: www.doh.gov.uk

Civil service: www.civil-service.gov.uk

# Parliament and the Legislative Process

We now turn from government to parliament and from the executive to the legislative process in the British political system. Britain's parliament at Westminster is very old, dating back to 1265. It began as an English parliament, adding Welsh, Scottish and Irish representatives with successive Acts of Union, and losing most of its Irish representatives with the establishment of a separate Irish state in 1922. The Houses of Parliament provide a visual symbol of the heart of British government, the very centre of political power. Indeed, the sovereignty of Parliament has long been regarded as the key principle of the British constitution. Yet it is often argued that despite its age and prestige, Britain's parliament is no longer very powerful. The government dominates the House of Commons, while the indefensible composition of the House of Lords has long rendered it incapable of exercising real power. It is also questioned how far Parliament really represents the people. Moreover, the Westminster parliament is now not the only representative assembly elected by British citizens, but is just one among a number of levels of representative bodies. The prestige of both Houses has been further gravely damaged by the 2009 parliamentary expenses scandal, leading to demands for further radical reform.

In this chapter we explore the composition and functions of both chambers of the Westminster parliament. We begin with the House of Commons, by far the more important. We examine how far and in what sense it represents the British people, and how effectively it fulfils its main functions, particularly its role in law making and its scrutiny of the executive. We then turn to the linked issues of the composition and powers of the upper chamber within the context of the ongoing reform process. We conclude with a discussion of the future of the Westminster parliament in a multi-level system of representative bodies.

## The functions of the House of Commons

The House of Commons has five main functions:

- Representation
- Recruitment and maintenance of a government
- Scrutiny of the executive
- Legislation
- Forum for national debate

### Representation

The representative character of the House of Commons underpins its other roles. The House of Commons has long been held to represent the common people of Britain, and this claim was strengthened by the extension of the vote to the

## BOX 13.1

# Unrepresentative MPs

- Women remain considerably under-represented, despite a significant advance in 1997 when 120 women were elected (compared with 60 in 1992). In 2010 the number of women MPs rose to 143, or 22 per cent of all MPs. Most of these (81) are Labour, a result of the party's efforts to secure more female candidates through, for example, all-women shortlists for some seats, but David Cameron encouraged the selection of more women candidates for the Conservatives, which has helped boost the total of Conservative women to 49 (still only a fifth of the parliamentary party).
- Ethnic minorities have long been under-represented at Westminster, although in 2010 the number of ethnic minority MPs almost doubled from 15 to 27, including 11 Conservatives, compared with just 2 in 2005. The other 16 are Labour. There are still no successful Liberal Democrat MPs from non-white ethnic minorities.

- 35 per cent of all MP were educated at fee-paying schools (54 per cent of Conservative MPs, 40 per cent of Liberal Democrat MPs and 15 per cent of Labour MPs) compared to 6 per cent of the UK population. 20 MPs (19 Conservatives, including the new Prime Minister, and one Liberal Democrat) came from a single fee-paying school (Eton). 9 out of 10 MPs attended university (30 per cent Oxbridge).
- The 2010 intake of MPs brought in many more with experience of management consultancy and banking and fewer teachers and doctors. Only a very small and declining number of Labour MPs were previously manual workers, and almost none from other parties.
- A large intake of new MPs has slightly reduced their median age from 48 in 2005 to 47. 15 MPs from the 3 main parties are aged 29 or under, 15 are over 70.

whole adult population in the nineteenth and early twentieth centuries. Thus it represents the people of Britain because they have chosen it.

Yet while the House of Commons represents the people it is not typical of the wider population and does not represent them in the sense of being a *social* microcosm of the nation, MPs still being predominantly white, male, middle-aged and middle-class (see Box 13.1). Does this matter? It can be argued that electors want representatives with the skills to perform their roles effectively, and these skills are unequally distributed through the nation. It is thus perhaps no accident that occupations with an emphasis on communication skills (law, education, journalism) are well represented in the House of Commons.

On the other hand, a significantly unrepresentative parliament may lack the range of experience necessary for informed deliberation and legislation. If women are under-represented there is a risk that a woman's perspective will be insufficiently taken into account, not only on what may be traditionally thought of as 'women's issues' (such as equal rights, childcare, abortion and

violence against women) but on the whole range of economic and social policy. If ethnic minorities and non-Christian faiths are under-represented, the reality of racial and religious discrimination routinely experienced by minorities will not inform debate on these issues. If relatively few MPs have shared the kind of education, housing and employment of most of their constituents, there is almost bound to be some lack of understanding of their problems. Beyond that, some voters seem increasingly disenchanted with, and alienated from, the politicians who supposedly represent them.

While the House of Commons collectively represents the whole people, each individual MP represents a particular geographical area or parliamentary constituency. Groups of MPs also represent sections of the national community, most obviously political parties, but also various other organized interests, some of which raised concerns (see below). However, following the parliamentary expenses crisis of 2009, some voters concluded that MPs were more concerned with furthering their own interests.

## The representation of constituencies

The House of Commons consists of 650 MPs, elected by single-member parliamentary constituencies. Candidates for Parliament may stand as representatives of a party but, once elected, each MP is expected to represent the interests of the constituency as a whole and to be at the service of all constituents. Through this constituency role MPs collectively may be said to represent the entire country, which would not be true of their roles as party and group representatives.

Yet if each MP represents a particular constituency, that does not necessarily mean that he or she has to represent the views of their electorate, at least according to an influential theory of representation derived from the eighteenth-century Whig politician and thinker Edmund Burke: 'Your representative owes you, not his industry only, but his judgement; and he betrays, instead of serving you, if he sacrifices it to your opinion.' Parliament, in Burke's view is 'a deliberative assembly of one nation' rather than 'a congress of ambassadors from different and hostile interests'. (Burke, speech to his electors at Bristol, 1774, quoted in Hill, 1975, p. 158). Thus Parliament should lead public opinion rather than simply reflect it

This contrasts with the delegate theory of representation – part of the ideology of radical democracy – in which the elected representatives are considered to be the agents of, and directly accountable to, their constituents.

Most MPs take their constituency responsibilities seriously and the burden of work can be considerable. MPs' constituency work falls into two main categories. First, there is the local welfare officer/social worker role, dealing with a wide variety of problems (e.g. housing, education, health and social security) on behalf of individual constituents. MPs tackle the problems at the appropriate level, conducting a voluminous correspondence with ministers, government departments, local authorities and other local offices, and so on. Also MPs can raise constituents' grievances through parliamentary questions and debate and, if all these means fail, they can refer cases of alleged public maladministration to the Ombudsman (see Chapter 14). Second, MPs seek to look after the interests of the constituency as a whole. Thus they may try to attract new commercial and industrial investment, to get roads built, to find solutions for local industrial disputes, and to prevent local factories, schools and hospitals from closing. Cowley (in Dunleavy et al., 2006, pp. 38–41) argues that the constituency role of MPs has grown substantially in recent years, sometimes leaving little time for them to fulfil properly other important responsibilities.

## The representation of parties in the House of Commons

MPs are elected (almost always) as representatives of a party, and party underpins their activities once in the House. Table 13.1 shows how party determines the composition of the House of Commons, involving two parties that make up the coalition government, Conservatives and Liberal Democrats, the main opposition party, Labour and several smaller parties (including varieties of nationalists, the Democratic Unionist Party of Northern Ireland and a single Green. However, although MPs clearly represent parties, the distribution of seats does not

**Table 13.1** Number of party seats in the House of Commons after elections, 1997–2010

| Party | 1997 | 2001 | 2005 | 2010 |
|---|---|---|---|---|
| Labour | 418 | 412 | 355 | 258 |
| Conservative | 165 | 166 | 198 | 307* |
| Liberal Democrat | 46 | 52 | 62 | 57 |
| Scottish National Party | 6 | 5 | 6 | 6 |
| Plaid Cymru (Welsh Nationalist) | 4 | 4 | 3 | 3 |
| Ulster Unionist | 10 | 6 | 1 | 0 |
| Democratic Unionist Party | 2 | 5 | 9 | 8 |
| Sinn Fein** | 2 | 4 | 5 | 5 |
| Social Democratic and Labour Party | 3 | 3 | 3 | 3 |
| Independent*** | 1 | 1 | 2 | 1 |
| Respect | – | – | 1 | 0 |
| Green Party | 0 | 0 | 0 | 1 |
| Speaker | 1 | 1 | 1 | 1 |
| Total seats | 659 | 659 | 646 | 650 |

\* Including the Conservative MP elected at Thirsk and Malton, after the general election poll was postponed following the death of a candidate.
\*\* Sinn Fein MPs do not take their seats.
\*\*\* Sylvia Hermon, for North Down.

## BOX 13.2

# The organization of parties in the House of Commons

- **Cabinets and Shadow Cabinets.** The Cabinet is normally drawn from the party (or, from 2010, parties) with a majority in the Commons, and thus provides a collective leadership for the governing party or parties. The inclusion of ambitious potential rival leaders in the Cabinet renders a dangerous back-bench revolt less likely and reinforces party unity. Shadow Cabinets provide collective leadership for the official opposition party. When the Conservatives are in opposition the leader chooses their Shadow Cabinet. When Labour is in opposition its Shadow Cabinet is elected by the Parliamentary Labour Party, although the leader allocates Shadow Cabinet portfolios and appoints additional shadow ministers.

- **The Whip system.** Whips play a central role in linking the party leaderships with the backbenchers. The whips try to ensure that backbenchers support party policy in divisions (or votes) of the House of Commons. Party MPs are sent a weekly outline of parliamentary business with items underlined once, twice or three times, depending on whether an MP's attendance is merely requested (a one-line whip), expected (a two-line whip) or regarded as essential (a three-line whip). Defiance of a three-line whip constitutes a serious breach of party rules. Yet whips are personnel managers rather than disciplinarians. They rely mainly on persuasion (which may sometimes include veiled inducements and hints of honours or promotion). The ultimate sanction against a party rebel – withdrawal of the party whip (i.e. expulsion from the parliamentary party) – is rarely used, and can prove counter-productive, as the Major government discovered when the whip was withdrawn from

eight Conservatives in 1994, only to be restored in 1995.

- **Party meetings.** Meetings of the parliamentary party provide an important channel of communication between party leaders and backbenchers, allowing the airing of grievances and concerns. The Conservative Party meets weekly in the 1922 Committee when Parliament is sitting, and includes all MPs except the leader when the party is in opposition. Historically, when the party was in government, only backbenchers attended, but Prime Minister David Cameron attempted to involve all Conservative MPs including ministers, a move that upset backbenchers. Under a compromise, ministers can now attend but not vote. The chairman of 'the 1922' plays a key role in the party especially in times of controversy and crisis. When in opposition, the Parliamentary Labour Party (PLP) is attended by all Labour MPs including members of the Shadow Cabinet. When the party is in government, Labour ministers attend meetings of the PLP when the work of their Departments is under discussion, with liaison between the government and its backbenchers maintained by the Parliamentary Committee whose members include ministers and backbenchers.

- **Specialist party committees.** Each major party also forms a large number of specialist committees, which may enable backbenchers to influence party policy on specific subjects. (These purely party committees should not be confused with all-party committees, such as the increasingly important Departmental Select Committees, which may lead to a cross-party consensus which could erode discipline and cohesion within parties.)

---

reflect the distribution of support for parties in general elections. Nor do parliamentary parties necessarily closely mirror the opinions of the party members who selected them as candidates, or the voters who elected them, although MPs with markedly different views may face criticism and ultimately perhaps deselection. Alternatively, MPs who become unhappy with their party may leave it and seek to join another party

Government is party government; consequently it is crucial for governments to retain their parliamentary majority by maintaining the support of

their parliamentary party, or parties (and preferably the party in the country). Discipline and cohesion, especially in formal activities such as voting in Parliament, are almost as important for opposition parties as for the government if they are to have parliamentary and electoral credibility. Open divisions are damaging to a party and encouraging to its rivals. For a government, they may jeopardize the passing of legislation and, for an opposition, destroy any chance to embarrass or defeat the government. The worst eventuality is that a party will split and, as may happen as a result, suffer electoral defeat – as

## BOX 13.3

## MPs and the representation of interests: some areas of concern

- *Payment of fees to MPs to serve as advisers, consultants or directors*: the Nolan Committee (1995) found that 168 MPs (including 145 Conservatives, 15 Labour and 6 Liberal Democrats) shared 356 consultancies. (Publicity has led to a marked reduction in the number of such consultancies.)
- *Access to the Commons as MPs' research assistants and aides*: the use of House of Commons photo-identity passes by organizations as a cover for commercial lobbying activities, in return for services to the MP concerned, first became evident in the late 1980s.
- *Lobbying of MPs by professional consultancy firms*: this kind of lobbying developed into a multi-million pound industry during the 1980s.
- *Financing of all-party parliamentary groups by outside interests* (e.g. individual businesses, groups of companies, trade associations, lobbying firms and charities).
- *Specialist assistance on an ad hoc unpaid basis*: a wide range of groups provide information and support for MPs' parliamentary activities, such as Select Committees and Private Members' bills.
- *MPs' pursuit of outside occupations*: outside interests are represented in the House of Commons through MPs' part-time occupations as, for example, journalists, lawyers and company directors.
- *Sponsorship of election candidates through a particular party*, such as Labour Party candidates by trade unions. This practice ended in 1995. Formerly, unions could not instruct MPs how to speak or vote (as that would be a breach of parliamentary privilege) but they did expect MPs to watch over their interests.

Labour did from 1983 to 1992 after splitting in 1981. Thus each parliamentary party appoints whips to maintain party discipline. However, although there are strong inducements for MPs to maintain party loyalty (see Box 13.2), the number and size of rebellions has increased (Cowley and Stuart in Beech and Lee, 2008, pp. 103–19).

Party, then, dominates Parliament, but the reverse is also true. Parliament equally clearly dominates party. Thus virtually all UK parties accept the legitimacy of Parliament, and have as their major aim the winning of seats in the House of Commons. Almost inevitably, the parliamentary party assumes far greater importance than the party in the country. Parliament provides the main arena for the party battle between elections, and this parliamentary conflict, through the media, influences the shifting public support for rival parties.

### The representation of interests

MPs not only represent parties, they also, less formally (and sometimes less openly) represent a range of interests. Some of this arises naturally from their past (and sometimes continuing) occupations, their membership of a range of organizations, their personal and family connections and leisure pursuits. It is only to be expected that a former teacher or miner will retain not just an interest in their old occupation but also useful experience and expertise to contribute to debates on the subject. Similarly, MPs who are keen church-goers, fox hunters or ramblers have an interest which they will naturally seek to defend and promote where relevant. They may hold a position (honorary or otherwise) in an organization which gives them an additional obligation to look after its interests. Much of this is relatively uncontroversial, and indeed may enrich the deliberations of Parliament. However, some representations of interests by MPs have raised rather more concern (see Box 13.3).

### Representing themselves? Sleaze and the parliamentary expenses scandal

A more cynical view is that some MPs are more concerned with pursuing their own interests than those of others. In the 1990s newspaper allegations that some MPs were receiving 'cash for questions'

**Image 13.1 'Duck Island' protest against the parliamentary expenses scandal of 2009**

An expenses claim for a duck island came to symbolize the parliamentary expenses crisis of 2009, which brought parliament and MPs into disrepute.

were upheld and two Conservative backbenchers were reprimanded by the Commons and suspended without pay for 20 and 10 days respectively. Soon afterwards, the Committee on Standards in Public Life, initially under the chairmanship of Lord Nolan, was appointed (see Chapter 12). The recommendations of the Nolan Committee (May 1995) were substantially implemented. The key moves were the banning of paid advocacy, the adoption of a new Code of Conduct and the appointment of a Parliamentary Commissioner for Standards. The Nolan restrictions on paid advocacy contributed to a 66 per cent drop in the number of consultancies declared by MPs in the 1997 Register of Members' Interests (from 240 to 80). However, more recent registers show that some MPs continue to make substantial sums from lucrative second jobs, particularly directorships and consultancies, public speaking and journalism, with incomes that sometimes exceed their parliamentary salaries. As these interests are transparent they raise fewer ethical issues, although extensive outside occupations inevitably reduce the time and energy devoted to the MP's role, which critics argue should be full-time.

The 2009 parliamentary expenses crisis dwarfed earlier concerns over political sleaze. MPs' expenses claims were leaked to *The Daily Telegraph*, which published a steady drip of damaging details in May and June 2009. It was not just the size of the claims (some substantial) that made headlines but sometimes their frivolity. Thus claims for duck islands and moat cleaning illustrated the gulf between the lifestyles of some MPs and their constituents, while others for dog food and toilet seats appeared petty. A more serious criticism was of the apparently widespread practice of MPs 'flipping' their main residence and second home to maximize their expenses and minimize their tax bills. Speaker Michael Martin was effectively forced out after his perceived mishandling of the crisis.

Revelations led to numerous humiliating public apologies and repayments of wrongly claimed expenses by MPs. Many parliamentary careers were effectively ended as some members voluntarily or under pressure declined to stand for re-election. The most serious cases of false claims led to criminal prosecutions. David Chaytor, the former Labour MP for Bury North, was the first to be convicted, receiving a prison sentence (for eighteen months) in January 2011.

All parties suffered from the allegations, and party leaders were not exempt from criticism. Gordon Brown had some difficulty explaining his complicated cleaning expenses, while David Cameron agreed to repay a claim for removing wisteria from his cottage chimney. Yet Cameron won some credit by appearing to deal quickly and toughly with erring MPs in his own party, while

## BOX 13.4

# Reasons for government control of the House of Commons

Government control of the House of Commons rests on four main factors:

- *Possession in normal circumstances of a majority, allied with the habit of loyal voting by its own supporters.* Out of 18 general elections between 1945 and 2010, in only February 1974 and 2010 did one party fail to win an overall majority of seats, although in four others (1950, 1964, October 1974, 1992) the governing party only enjoyed small majorities. Far more commonly, governments have enjoyed comfortable majorities, coupled with generally strong party discipline.
- *Power to determine the parliamentary timetable.* Although some Commons business is initiated by opposition parties and backbenchers, three-quarters of Commons time is devoted to the consideration of government business (but see Wright Committee reforms, below).

- *Ability to curtail debate.* The government can restrict debate by employing the closure and the guillotine. The closure – the request 'that the question be now put', stopping debate if successful – is rarely used now to restrict debate on government business. The guillotine – an 'allocation of time' motion regulating the amount of time to be spent on a bill – is normally used when the government considers that progress on a major piece of legislation is unsatisfactory at committee stage. In recent years, guillotine motions have been used more frequently.
- *Control over legislation.* The legislative process, from initiation to completion, is dominated by the Cabinet, Cabinet committees and the Departments, and is essentially now a function of the executive (see section on legislation, below).

---

Labour perhaps suffered most from the crisis as the party in government. Controversial Labour claimants included Alistair Darling and Hazel Blears (accused of being serial 'flippers'). One late victim of the newspaper's allegations was Liberal Democrat David Laws (see Chapter 12). Few MPs came out well, although *The Daily Telegraph* listed some fifty 'saints' whose claims were modest and reasonable.

In mitigation it can be argued that MPs were virtually encouraged to claim additional expenses to compensate for salaries deemed inadequate by many (but not by low-paid and unemployed voters). Moreover, the rules were complex, designed to meet some of the extra costs incurred by MPs, particularly those with constituencies well outside London, requiring the maintenance of two homes. There was also an element of hypocrisy among some of the critics. Tax avoidance and over-claiming expenses are rife among the self-employed and some professions, including journalists who castigated MPs. Yet the scandal undermined trust in politicians that may take years to restore, and led to pressure for reforming not just the system of parliamentary expenses, but the House of Commons more generally (see below). However,

expectations that the scandal would lead to lower turnouts, a backlash against the established three parties and the election of more independents were not substantially realized in the 2010 election.

## Recruitment and maintenance of a government

A key (but often insufficiently emphasized) function of the House of Commons is the recruitment and maintenance of a government. The executive in Britain is a parliamentary executive. Members of the government are drawn from Parliament and must retain the confidence and support of a majority in the House of Commons. It might be assumed that this would render governments weak, dependent on parliamentary support that might be withdrawn at any time. Yet in practice governments normally dominate Parliament and control its business. It is virtually impossible in normal circumstances (i.e. government possession of a working majority) to bring a government down and, in practice, very difficult to engineer a significant government defeat in the House of Commons. Thus executive dominance of Parliament is the general rule (see Box 13.4).

Although an opposition can make life awkward for a government in a number of ways, they normally lack the numbers to defeat the government on their own. The only time that a government has suffered defeat on a motion of confidence since the Second World War was in March 1979, when Callaghan's government, which had already lost its overall Commons majority, was defeated by one vote on a censure motion. In more normal circumstances when a government enjoys a comfortable majority it can only be defeated if some of its own backbenchers combine with the opposition. Backbench rebellions have increased in size and frequency in recent decades. Conservative rebellions seriously embarrassed John Major's 1992–97 government, whose small initial majority of 21 declined steadily as a result of by-election defeats and removal of the party whip from rebel Conservatives. Blair's government, cushioned by substantial majorities, was able to survive sizeable Labour rebellions, most notably on Iraq, when the main opposition party supported its policy. His government came closer to defeat over university tuition fees, when Labour rebels combined with Conservatives and Liberal Democrats (Cowley and Stuart in Beech and Lee, 2008).

Although in Britain it is taken for granted that ministers are drawn from Parliament, and predominantly from the House of Commons, it is not necessarily the case in other democratic states. Indeed, in some countries where there is a stricter separation of executive and legislative powers, government ministers are not even allowed to serve as members of the legislative assembly. Elsewhere it is more common than in Britain for some ministers to be drawn from the worlds of business, finance or academia, without serving as elected representatives. One consequence is that the Prime Minister is effectively limited in choosing ministerial colleagues by the pool of party talent available in Parliament and particularly the House of Commons. Prime Ministers have sometimes sought to recruit ministers from outside Parliament, but such ministers have been obliged by convention to obtain a seat in the Commons (through a parliamentary by-election) or in the House of Lords. However, such appointments have been few, and not always successful. Businessmen and trade unionists without prior experience of Parliament have often found it difficult or frustrating to cope with parliamentary conventions and procedures.

Thus anyone seeking high office in government must normally first seek election to the House of Commons, and gain recognition there. Election to, and successful performance in, the House of Commons are the main criteria for political advancement and promotion into government in the British political system. It is in the Commons that ambitious politicians first attempt to make, and then as ministers sustain, their reputations. Yet the skills of parliamentary debate are widely acknowledged to be no real preparation for running a Department, nor are the two kinds of ability invariably present in the same person. Outstanding parliamentary orators do not necessarily make good ministers. Some potentially outstanding ministers may not be discovered through the British system of recruiting and training for government office.

## Scrutiny of the executive

Governments are accountable to Parliament, and through Parliament to the voters. Thus it is in Parliament that the government must explain and defend its actions. Major opportunities for scrutinizing and influencing the government through the procedures of the House of Commons are Parliamentary Questions; general, adjournment and emergency debates, Early Day Motions, Select Committees and correspondence with ministers (Table 13.2).

Parliamentary questions remain the most celebrated means of calling the Prime Minister and ministers to account for their conduct of government. Questions for written answers enjoy less publicity, but can be a useful means of extracting information from government. Not all questions for oral answer can be dealt with in the time allotted, and ministers together with their civil servants have plenty of time to prepare answers to the pre-submitted questions, although ministers can sometimes be embarrassed by unexpected supplementary questions. Overall, the effectiveness of Question Time as a means of providing effective scrutiny of the executive is rather diminished by party point-scoring – particularly in Prime Minister's Question Time.

**Table 13.2**    Main methods of Commons scrutiny of the executive

| | |
|---|---|
| Questions | • Backbenchers may submit oral and written questions to ministers<br>• Written questions and replies are recorded in *Hansard*<br>• Ministers reply to oral questions daily, Monday to Thursday<br>• Prime Minister's Question Time 1–1.30 pm Wednesday<br>  (NB MPs may ask one (unscripted) supplementary question) |
| Debates | • General – on Queen's Speech, no-confidence motions (rare) and motions tabled by government and opposition<br>• Adjournment debates – opportunity to raise general or constituency issues<br>• Private Members' motions – 11 days per session allocated to these<br>• Emergency debates – can be demanded but rarely conceded by Speaker |
| Early Day Motions | • Proposing and signing early day motions enables MPs to express their views – gains publicity, but no debate follows |
| Select Committees | • Able to scrutinize executive away from the floor of the Commons<br>• Powers to send for 'persons, papers and records'. Can interrogate ministers<br>• Includes 16 Departmental Select Committees and others (e.g. Public Accounts, Public Administration, European Legislation, Statutory Instruments, Standards and Privileges)<br>• Party balance on Select Committees reflects that of the House as a whole. (Unanimity difficult – may divide on party lines) |
| Letters to ministers | • Main way in which MPs pursue cases and issues raised by constituents |

Further opportunities for backbenchers to raise issues are provided through general debates initiated by government and opposition, Private Members' motions and adjournment debates, and through the largely symbolic device of signing Early Day Motions. However, more effective scrutiny is provided not so much by the Commons as a whole but by Select Committees.

An old and important Select Committee is the Public Accounts Committee (PAC), which has a central role in the Commons' scrutiny of government expenditure. Control of finance was once considered a crucial function of the Commons, but today, in as far as the Commons has any effective influence over government finance, it is largely through the PAC. It is composed of 15 members and chaired by a senior member of the opposition. It is particularly concerned to ensure the taxpayer gets value for money from public spending. Since 1983 it has been powerfully assisted by the National Audit Office, an independent body directed by the Comptroller and Auditor-General (CAG) with a staff of 900 which produces around 50 Value for Money reports every year. Reports of both the PAC and the

National Audit Office are often extremely critical of government departments. However, PAC reports are rarely debated by the House and, when they are, are poorly attended and receive little public attention.

Parliamentary reformers from the 1960s advocated the greater use of Departmental Select Committees (DSCs) to improve scrutiny of the executive. A new system of Select Committees to provide regular scrutiny of the work of every government department was implemented in 1979. The task of these new DSCs was 'to examine the expenditure, administration and policy in the principal government departments . . . and associated bodies' and to make reports with recommendations. In conducting their investigations, they can send for 'persons, papers and records'.

Departmental Select Committees undoubtedly constitute a marked improvement on the Commons machinery for scrutinizing the executive available before 1979. However, critics point out that, despite the frequent excellence of their reports and the occasional publicity achieved by their investigative sessions, they lack real clout. Thus their occasional effectiveness is offset by their more

**Table 13.3**    Advantages and limitations of Departmental Select Committees (DSCs)

| Advantages | Limitations |
|---|---|
| ● Powers to send for 'persons, papers and records' improve scrutiny and accountability of executive<br>● Coverage of proceedings aids open government<br>● DSCs may have pre-emptive or deterrent effect – deterring Ministers and civil servants from behaviour which they might be unable to justify before Committee<br>● Committee investigation and reports may ultimately persuade government to change course<br>● Committee membership helps develop specialization and expertise – and Committees can seek outside advice and assistance | ● Party whips' influence on membership of DSCs has compromised their independence (but see Box 13.5).<br>● Many members of DSCs lack necessary motivation, knowledge and skills.<br>● Most DSCs lack the staff and budgets for substantial independent research.<br>● Limited powers: ministers normally attend when requested, but are not obliged to answer questions. Civil servants may withhold information in the interests of 'good government' or national security.<br>● Lack of influence: few DSC reports are debated on the floor of the House of Commons, and ministers can (and generally do) ignore them. |

frequent lack of impact. They are still part of an executive-dominated parliamentary system and lack the resources or prestige to sustain the powerful inquisitorial role that US congressional committees have long enjoyed.

## Law making

Law making is ostensibly the most important function of Parliament, which is after all a legislature. Law passed by Parliament remains supreme over other forms of British law, such as common law, even if it has to accept European Union law. Yet although Parliament devotes much of its time to considering legislation, it may be questioned whether Parliament effectively makes the law. Westminster legislation today is substantially an executive function. Government dominates the legislative process from start to finish. Although ordinary backbench MPs retain some limited opportunities to initiate legislation, they normally have little chance of converting their draft **bills** into law. Most of the time devoted by Parliament to the scrutiny of legislation is spent on government bills, and it is almost entirely government bills which ultimately successful in passing through all their stages to become **Acts**. Parliament's effective influence on the principles and even the details of government legislation is usually limited. Although significant amendment and, very occasionally, even

defeat of a government bill remains a possibility, the government's majority normally ensures that its legislation emerges from its passage through Parliament more or less in the form intended.

Parliament, it may be said, *legitimates* rather than *legislates*. Although it is government rather than Parliament that substantially makes law, Parliament's assent remains vital to the establishment of the *legitimacy* of that legislation. Thus the formal parliamentary stages of legislation (outlined in Table 13.4) remain important. Yet they do not tell us very much about how law is really made in Britain. Where do the ideas for new laws come from? Who decides that legislation is necessary?

---

● *Definitions of parliamentary legislation (pp. 236–40)*

**Bill**: A bill is a draft Act of Parliament. It remains a bill until it has passed all its stages.

**Act**: An Act of Parliament (also known as a **Statute**) is a bill which has passed though all its stages and received the royal assent.

**Public Bill/Act**: A Public Bill or Act is one that affects the whole country. It may be introduced by the government (**Government Bill**) or an ordinary backbencher (**Private Member's Bill**).

**Private Bill/Act**: A bill or Act which affects only part of the country or community. (A local authority, for example, may seek to acquire special powers in its area through a Private Act).

**Delegated legislation** (sometimes referred to as secondary or subordinate legislation – the technical name is **Statutory Instruments**). Many Acts are outline in form, giving authority to ministers or to other public bodies to make necessary orders or regulations under the authority of the parent Act. Thousands of Statutory Instruments are published every year.

**Table 13.4**   The formal parliamentary stages of legislation

| Stage | Where taken | Comments |
|---|---|---|
| First Reading | Floor of House of Commons (unless introduced in Lords) | Purely formal – no debate |
| Second Reading | Floor of House of Commons | Debate on principles – very unusual for a government bill to be defeated at this stage |
| Committee stage | Normally in Standing Committee on which government has a majority. Some bills taken in Committee of the Whole House. | Considered in detail, clause by clause – amendments can be made but only those introduced by ministers have much chance of success. Can take weeks. |
| Report stage | Floor of House of Commons | Report on amended bill; further amendments can be made |
| Third reading | Floor of House of Commons | Debate (often short) on final text, and approval of bill – generally a formality |
| Lords stages (or Commons stages if bill introduced in Lords | Bill passes through similar stages in other chamber. Committee stage normally taken on floor of Lords. | Lords may amend bill (some further amendment may be introduced by government). If bill is amended it returns to the Commons for consideration. |
| Consideration of Lords (or Commons) amendments | Floor of House of Commons | Lords' amendments may be accepted, if not the Lords usually give way. Otherwise bill can be re-introduced and passed without Lords' consent under the Parliament Act. |
| Royal assent | Monarchy | Last refused in reign of Queen Anne |

Which interests influence the shape and content of legislation, and how? Is the formal completion of the parliamentary stages with the royal assent really the end of the process? How are Acts implemented and adjudicated upon? How far are they successful in fulfilling the intentions of the legislators? To answer such questions it is important to go beyond the formal parliamentary stages of legislation, to consider the crucial formative pre-parliamentary stages of the legislative process, the extra-parliamentary influences on the formal parliamentary stages, and the all important process of implementation, adjudication and review.

## Introducing new laws

Where does the legislative process really start? Normally, not in Parliament. The initial idea may come from a variety of sources, perhaps from a government department or an official report such as a Royal Commission, or possibly from a party manifesto or a pressure group or media campaign. Whatever the initial inspiration, the idea for legislation will not normally get far unless it wins government favour and eventually receives the backing of the Cabinet, and finds a place in the government's legislative programme.

Before a government decides to legislate it will consult widely across departments and other relevant public bodies, and often extensively with outside interests (see Chapter 8). This process of consultation not only provides the government with more information and expert opinion, but also may be crucial in winning the argument in Parliament and the country. If the government is able to claim that they have consulted widely with affected interests and secured their support this reduces the scope for effective opposition. In some cases the government seeks not just the acquiescence of key interests but their active co-operation (e.g. any reform of the National Health Service is likely to depend on the willing support of the medical profession for successful implementation).

Thus only after much initial consultation will the department principally concerned begin the process of drafting a bill using the services of expert parliamentary law drafters, Parliamentary Counsel. Drafts are circulated to other interested departments and consultation with outside interests will continue. It may take a year or two before the government feels ready to introduce a bill in Parliament. Thus often much activity will have taken place before Parliament gets the opportunity to consider a government bill. Debates on the Queen's Speech may provide some opportunity o comment on proposals to legislate, and sometimes the government will announce its intentions through a **Green** or **White Paper**. Normally, however, Parliament's first opportunity to debate a bill is at the Second Reading, as the First Reading is purely formal.

## Parliamentary scrutiny of government legislation

Bills can be first introduced into either the Commons or the Lords, although more controversial measures are normally introduced in the Commons. The First Reading of a bill is purely formal, with no debate. A dummy copy of the bill is placed on the Speaker's table, and a date announced for the Second Reading. Only after the First Reading is the bill printed and circulated. (Note, however, that draft bills are now sometimes published for Parliament's consideration.) The Second Reading normally involves a full debate on the principle of the bill, which can be defeated then, but this would be a most unusual fate for a government bill. If it passes its Second Reading the bill proceeds to the committee stage, normally

---

- A **Green Paper** is a consultative document, implying the government has not finally made up its mind.

- A **White Paper** normally involves a firmer statement of government intention.

(However, sometimes ministers may observe that a particular White Paper 'has green edges', indicating a readiness to listen to arguments and make changes.)

---

taken by a standing committee, although a Committee of the Whole House may consider very important bills with constitutional implications, or at the other extreme, relatively simple and non-controversial bills. It is also now possible for bills to be referred to a Select Committee, or a special standing committee, enabling a more rigorous examination of the evidence and contributions from outside witnesses, although these procedures remain uncommon (Norton, 2005, pp. 86–7, 255).

During the committee stage the bill is considered in detail, line by line and clause by clause, and amendments may be proposed, either by the government, seeking to tidy up and improve the bill, or by government or opposition party MPs. The process of consultation with outside interests will continue throughout the committee stage. Friendly committee members may sometimes be prepared to introduce amendments drafted by such outside groups. If the governing party has a substantial majority in the Commons as a whole, it will have a commensurate majority on all committees. Thus most of the amendments passed by the committee will be the government's own amendments, although it may accept amendments proposed by its own backbenchers, and occasionally even an opposition amendment. This process may help improve the legislation, closing loopholes, removing obstacles to successful implementation, and perhaps securing the goodwill of important interests whose full co-operation may be crucial to ensure that the Act achieves its intentions.

After the committee stage comes the report stage when the amended bill is reported back to the House of Commons as a whole. Further amendments may be considered here, before the House proceeds immediately to a debate on the Third Reading. If the bill passes its Third Reading, it proceeds to the House of Lords (assuming the bill was initiated in the Commons) and follows similar stages there, with further opportunities for consultation and amendment. After a bill has passed all its stages in both Houses it goes to the monarch for the royal assent (last refused in the reign of Queen Anne, three centuries ago). It then becomes an Act, and the law of the land.

It looks like a very thorough scrutiny, yet it is not always as effective as it appears. Governments normally seek to push through a large and complex

## COMPARATIVE POLITICS  13.1
# The legislative roles of the UK Parliament and the US Congress

The United States Congress is a legislature in the full meaning of the term. It makes laws. 'All legislative powers herein granted shall be vested in a Congress of the United States' (American Constitution). Both houses of Congress, the House of Representatives and the Senate, play an important role in the legislative process and both have to agree before legislation can go forward for presidential approval. If the President declines to approve laws passed by Congress, this veto can be overridden by a two-thirds majority of both houses of Congress. Although the President can propose laws, these may be substantially modified or rejected by Congress, which is quite often controlled by a different party to that of the President, as they are elected separately and for different terms. The system is one of 'checks and balances', deriving from the separation of powers in the US constitution.

By contrast, the executive dominates the legislative process in the UK Parliament. Virtually all government bills are passed, while most bills introduced by ordinary MPs fail, and can normally only succeed if the government does not oppose them. The subordinate role of the British parliament stems from the fusion of executive and legislative powers in the Westminster system, compared with the separation of powers in the US constitution. Thus, the British parliament is controlled by the government by means of its (usually) disciplined majority in the House of Commons. The British parliament, like most in western Europe, is essentially a reactive, policy-influencing assembly that may modify or even (very exceptionally) reject government legislative proposals, but has negligible opportunities to initiate legislation. Unlike the US Congress, it is not a legislature in the full meaning of the term.

---

legislative programme as quickly as possible without significant concessions. Thus MPs on the government side in standing committee often appear to have taken a vow of silence. By contrast, opposition MPs are only too voluble, speaking at length to numerous amendments – some essentially 'wrecking amendments' undermining the whole principle of the bill, to delay proceedings as long as possible. This may go on until the government loses patience and 'guillotines' debate through a timetabling measure. Often this can mean that important parts of a bill are never scrutinized in committee, although sometimes the omission is remedied in the Lords. Yet governments normally get their way.

## Implementation of legislation

While the royal assent may seem to mark the end of the legislative process, a new Act often requires extensive subsequent **delegated legislation** if it is to be successfully implemented. Thus the Act may confer on ministers or other public bodies the authority to lay detailed regulations and orders having the force of law. Thousands of such **Statutory Instruments** are published annually. They are no longer regarded as a sinister threat to the power and sovereignty of Parliament, but as an essential adjunct to modern governance, allowing regulations to be amended with changing circumstances, and permitting useful experiments. Often they will involve further consultation with affected interests. For example, a change in the list of dangerous substances that cannot be sold over the counter might involve discussions with chemists, doctors and the police.

With or without the addition of delegated legislation, Acts still have to be implemented. Often implementation is not the responsibility of the central government but of other agencies, such as local authorities, which may proceed slowly and reluctantly, arising from their own opposition to a particular measure. Alternatively, they may complain they have been given statutory

## BOX 13.5

# Limitations on Private Members' bills

- They are not supposed to entail the expenditure of public money (which requires a money resolution).
- Lack of time is a crucial constraint. Ordinary backbenchers lack the procedural devices used by the government to curtail debate, and thus most bills run out of time. Normally, only the first half-dozen or so of the 20 bills introduced have a chance of passing all their stages and becoming law.
- Bills are unlikely to make progress if the government is opposed, because the government with its majority can use the whip system to destroy a bill. (In practice, some Private Members' bills may be government

measures in disguise, with the government offering its own facilities and benevolent support for a backbencher sponsoring a bill which the government favours but has no time for in its own legislative programme).

- Even if the government is not opposed, a bill which arouses strong animosities among a minority of MPs may often be blocked. It may be 'talked out' by opponents 'filibustering', and thus run out of time, or 'counted out' because too few MPs can be persuaded to attend on Fridays (in the absence of pressure from party whips).

responsibilities without adequate resources. Or there may be political problems in the way of implementation. Thus some Acts are not fully implemented, and a few have never been implemented at all. On other Acts there may be considerable discretion given over methods of implementation. Problems with implementing law may be reported to Parliament but Parliament has no formal responsibility for overseeing implementation. Finally, Acts are open to interpretation and adjudication in courts of law. Although judges must accept an Act of Parliament, they may sometimes interpret it very narrowly. In such judicial interpretation only the wording of the Act will be taken into account, not the pronouncements of governments or speeches in Parliament. Moreover a judge may now declare that an Act 'appears inconsistent' with the European Convention of Human Rights, effectively requiring its amendment (see Chapter 14).

Thus the legislative process in Britain is largely executive-dominated from start to finish. Parliament has a negligible role in the origination and formulation of legislation (with the exception of **Private Members' Bills** – see below), and no role in implementation beyond its generally inadequate scrutiny of delegated legislation. On the parliamentary stages of legislation, government backbenchers generally have more influence than the opposition, for the simple reason that the

opposition cannot normally threaten the government's majority, while dissent in its own ranks can. Thus governments may be prepared to make some concessions to critics on their own side. Beyond that, governments can expect to carry most of their legislative proposals substantially unchanged. 'Once bills have been introduced by government, they are almost certain to be passed' (Norton, 2005, p. 102).

## Private Members' legislation

The only partial exceptions to executive control of the legislative process are **Private Members' bills**. These are bills introduced by MPs who are not members of the government, including backbench members of the governing party or parties and members of the opposition. They can be introduced under various procedures, but the only method which normally stands any chance of success is through the annual ballot under which up to 20 backbenchers secure the right to introduce bills on a number of Friday sittings set aside for Private Members' measures. They then go through the same stages as government bills. Yet there are a number of practical limitations on Private Members' bills (see Box 13.5).

Thus only a very small proportion of Private Members' legislation reach the statute book. Even so, some Acts introduced by Private Members have been important, transformed lives, and changed attitudes. Thus Private Members' legislation changed the law on capital punishment, homosexuality, divorce and abortion in the 1960s, outlawed video 'nasties', compelled front-seat passengers to wear seat belts, restricted advertising on cigarettes in the 1980s and banned cruelty to wild animals in the mid-1990s. Such controversial social issues with a strong moral dimension often cut across normal party lines: thus both government and opposition parties find it more convenient to leave them to a free vote.

## Forum for national debate

In addition to the functions outlined above, the Commons is also reckoned to provide a forum for national debate. On occasions the Commons has appeared to rise above party conflict to change the course of history. A celebrated instance was when the Conservative Leo Amery famously called out to Labour's Arthur Greenwood 'Speak for England, Arthur' in the 1940 Norway debate which was to bring down Neville Chamberlain and make Churchill head of a coalition government. On this occasion a debate in Parliament had momentous consequences, which decisively transformed the conduct of the Second World War and perhaps changed the course of history. Yet critics suggest that such occasions are very much the exception. More commonly, debates take the form of relatively narrow, almost ritualistic combat between rival teams of party gladiators urged on by compact stage armies of supporters. Thus the proceedings in Parliament often seem to amount to little more than episodes in a continual election campaign, rather than offering a more open and wide-ranging forum of national debate.

Indeed, Parliament is not always even given the opportunity to debate issues of national importance. Parliament is not in session for substantial periods of the year, including some three months in the summer. While events may lead to demands for a recall of Parliament, this is rarely conceded. Even when Parliament is in session it is not easy to organize an extensive debate on some unanticipated development. Much of the parliamentary timetable is determined well in advance. While emergency debates may be demanded, they are rarely conceded by the Speaker. Explicit parliamentary approval is not required for some of the most momentous decisions that a government can take. The British Prime Minister has inherited most of the old prerogative powers of the crown and does not need express parliamentary sanction for such crucial and potentially far-reaching acts as signing treaties and even declaring war. As Hennessy (2000, p. 89) has observed, 'here, the royal prerogative is all. Unless primary legislation is required, Parliament does not have to be routinely involved at all.'

In practice, a wise Prime Minister will normally try to involve Parliament as much as possible over national crises and war. Churchill during his wartime premiership treated the Commons with 'high respect', addressing numerous 'secret sessions' which gave MPs 'a sense of being privy to special knowledge' (Jenkins, 2001, p. 622). Eden, by contrast, failed to carry Parliament with him over Suez in 1956, refused a request for the recall of Parliament from the Leader of the Opposition (Hennessy, 2000, p. 245), and (it is now clear) lied to the House of Commons on the crucial issue of foreknowledge of Israeli plans. Mrs Thatcher wisely agreed to an exceptional Commons debate on a Saturday over the Falklands crisis, and this perhaps helped her to maintain a level of bipartisan support for the subsequent task force. There were major Commons debates on the eve of the Iraq war on 26 February and 18 March 2003, when Blair secured a parliamentary majority despite the opposition of 139 Labour rebels. It is now accepted that Parliament must debate and vote before British forces are sent into action.

However, Parliament does not always provide an effective forum for national debate. Even if Parliament is generally given the opportunity to debate issues of national importance it no longer appears to be at the centre of national debate. The proceedings of Parliament are now much less reported even in the quality press. Although the Commons reluctantly let in the television cameras after a long delay, and it is now possible for members of the public to follow parliamentary proceedings on minority channels, the main BBC and commercial news and current affairs programmes devote only cursory treatment to Parliament. Indeed, much of the real national debate now seems to take place through the media.

## Reform of the House of Commons

While the House of Commons in theory is the centre of democracy in Britain, it has often seemed to operate more as a private club determined to keep the public at arms' length. When the television cameras were finally allowed in and the public could hear and see their representatives, they were unimpressed by MPs' behaviour and the quality of debate in an often near-empty chamber. The House remains cramped and ill-equipped, and its procedures antiquated. Thus while town halls have long used push-button voting, votes in the Commons are decided first by acclamation (shouting) and then by queuing in the division lobbies to be counted manually by tellers, a process which can take twenty minutes or more. For long periods, particularly over the summer, the House does not meet, and until 2003 its daily timetable began at 2.30 and continued without an official break until 10.30, and sometimes on into all-night sittings. Although some of its more meaningless mumbo-jumbo has been simplified, quaint language and rituals continue to bewilder outsiders.

Reform of the Commons has been long debated, and indeed some important reforms have been carried through in recent decades. Thus Departmental Select Committees were introduced in the 1980s, with a Standards Committee to provide more effective safeguards against corruption and 'sleaze'. Improved office and secretarial facilities have been provided to help MPs to work more effectively. Recent reforms have focused on the Commons timetable and methods of working. The Blair government reduced the frequency of Prime Minister's Questions from twice to once a week, which some critics thought weakened the Prime Minister's accountability to Parliament (even though the total time given to them remained the same). Norton (in Seldon, 2001, p. 54) maintained Blair spent 'less time to parliamentary activity than his predecessors'. Partly in answer to such criticisms Blair inaugurated in 2002 twice-yearly Prime Ministerial appearances before the Liaison Committee of the House of Commons, composed of chairs of Select Committees. This has proved a more successful innovation.

The Select Committee on the Modernisation of the House of Commons, appointed in 1997, recommended a number of reforms, mostly to be tried initially on an experimental basis. Some of these have been implemented. Thus Westminster Hall has been utilized as a 'parallel chamber' for debates not involving votes, increasing speaking opportunities for MPs. Some changes in the scrutiny of legislation were also introduced. When the reform-minded Robin Cook became Leader of the House after the 2001 election, there was some further impetus for change. In October 2002 the Commons finally voted for a revised parliamentary day, starting in the morning and finishing in the early evening, and for a shorter summer recess. This made the House more amenable to the increased number of women MPs as well as some of their more family-minded male colleagues. However, many on both sides of the House opposed the new timetable, and in 2005 a fresh vote led to a compromise which seems unlikely to satisfy either side. Philip Norton (in Seldon, 2001, p. 48) observed that the Blair reforms 'appeared limited and failed to change significantly the relationship between the legislature and the executive'. Thus the government rejected 'modest' proposals for the reform of the appointment and scrutiny of Select Committees. However, the issue was revived in 2009 and a new Select Committee on reform of the House of Commons chaired by MP Tony Wright appointed (see Box 13.6).

The Wright Committee proposals were generally approved by the House, and the new coalition government agreed that they should be fully implemented in May 2010. The reforms should improve the independence and effectiveness of Departmental Select Committees, and enhance the control of the Commons as a whole, and backbenchers in particular, over its own business.

However the Hansard Society, while welcoming reforms to strengthen the influence of backbench MPs, considered other proposals for involving the public in the parliamentary process were disappointing.

In the wake of the 2009 parliamentary expenses crisis the 2010 coalition government is committed to other reforms of the Commons, including a reduction in its size, and the introduction of a voters' right of recalling erring MPs. However the reform that could do most to reduce executive

BOX 13.6

# The Wright Committee reforms

The Wright Committee's report, 'Rebuilding the House', was published in November 2009. Its proposals included:

- A reduction in the number and size of Departmental Select Committees
- Chairs and member of departmental and similar Select Committees to be elected by secret ballot of MPs
- Backbench business to be determined by the Commons rather than the government
- One backbench motion to be debated each month

dominance of Parliament is a reform of the voting system, particularly if this were to involve proportional representation. This would almost certainly make hung parliaments the norm rather than an exception and end single-party majority government. However, following the decisive rejection of AV in the 2011 referendum, both AV and any further electoral reform seem off the agenda for the foreseeable future.

## The House of Lords

The British Parliament, like many, but by no means all, legislatures around the world (Hague and Harrop, 2010 pp. 296–8), is bicameral; in other words it has two chambers or houses. In many other countries the second chamber has a significant role. Thus the US Senate is actually rather more powerful and prestigious than the US lower house, the House of Representatives. However, the British upper house, the House of Lords, because of its bizarre composition (until recently composed largely of hereditary peers), has long been of marginal significance to British government and politics. One indication of its declining role is that while in the nineteenth century many Prime Ministers and other leading ministers came from the House of Lords, since

1902 there have been no Prime Ministers who have sat in the Lords, and very few senior ministers. The powers of the Lords are limited. Although it can delay legislation for up to a year, its undemocratic composition has generally inhibited their lordships from exercising even this limited power too often.

## Powers and functions of the Lords

The main functions of the House of Lords are as follows:

- *Legislation*: revision of House of Commons bills, giving ministers the opportunity for second thoughts; initiation of non-controversial legislation, including government bills, bills by individual peers, private bills (promoted by bodies outside Parliament, e.g. local authorities), and consideration of delegated legislation.
- *Deliberation*: the provision of a forum for debates on matters of current interest.
- *Scrutiny*: the Lords subjects government policy and administration to scrutiny through questions and through the work of its Select Committees (e.g. European Communities, Science and Technology).

## Legislation

Constitutionally, despite its reduced powers, the upper house remains an essential part of the legislative process, and spends over half its time on legislation. By the Parliament Act of 1911, the Lords completely lost their power to delay or amend money bills, which receive the royal assent one month after leaving the House of Commons, whether approved by the Lords or not. It retained the power to delay non-money bills for up to two years (reduced to one by the Parliament Act of 1949).

In practice the Lords has accepted further limitations on its own power of delay. The main guiding rule – firmly established by Conservative opposition peers in the immediate post-war period – is that the upper house does not oppose measures included in the governing party's manifesto at the previous election (the Salisbury/Addison doctrine). In addition, the Lords rarely press an amendment or delay a measure to the point where the

## The end of the Lords' function as the supreme court of appeal

One important historic function of the Lords has recently been abolished. Until 2009 the Lords not only contributed to making the law, but also adjudicated on the law in its role as the supreme court of appeal. In 2005 the Constitutional Reform Act transferred the Lords' judicial powers to a new UK Supreme Court, which became effective in 2009. This has contributed to a clearer separation of the legislative and judicial powers of the state (see Chapters 10 and 14).

Parliament Acts have to be invoked (although the partially reformed House has recently proved more difficult – see below).

The House of Lords can cause political embarrassment to the government of the day, but no more. The upper house has on numerous occasions impeded government legislation and forced concessions, although generally on minor issues. Although it is far from being a major constitutional obstacle to the party in power, during periods of substantial government majorities and weak opposition in the House of Commons, the Lords have sometimes offered more substantial if ultimately ineffective resistance to government.

A significant trend in recent decades has been the greater use made of the Lords by governments to revise and generally tidy up their legislation. Because much of this tidying-up process has to be done hurriedly at the end of sessions, one peer has described the upper chamber as 'a gilded dustpan and brush'. Suggested causes for this development include inadequate consultation, government indecisiveness and poor drafting in the early stages of legislation, but whatever the reasons, it has made the House of Lords an increasingly attractive target for pressure groups seeking to influence the detailed amendment of bills.

## Deliberation and scrutiny

The House of Lords – which devotes approximately one day a week to general debate – is often praised for the quality of its debates but their overall impact is questionable. Its exercise of its scrutiny functions (through Questions and Select Committees) is of greater consequence. The House of Lords Select Committee on the European Communities, which considers initiatives proposed by the EU Commission, is well-staffed, able to consider EU proposals on their merits, and expert. It produces over 20 reports a year which, like other Lords Select Committee reports but unlike their equivalents in the Commons, are all debated. Overall, however, the House of Lords has made no attempt to establish through its Select Committees a mechanism for consistent, comprehensive scrutiny of government but has rather used them to fill gaps left by the Commons Select Committee system.

## The composition of the House of Lords

If the powers of the Lords have been controversial, the traditional composition of the upper chamber has come to be regarded as unsustainable in a modern democratic era. The House of Lords long consisted of lords temporal (holders of hereditary titles) and lords spiritual (the archbishops and senior bishops of the Church of England). In the nineteenth century specialist law lords, appointed for life, were added to assist the upper chamber in its (then) judicial capacity as the highest court in the land. The composition of the House of Lords was more significantly affected by the Life Peerages Act 1958, which empowered the Crown (effectively the Prime Minister) to create life peers and peeresses. The Peerages Act 1963 allowed hereditary peers to disclaim their titles, and admitted hereditary peeresses into the House of Lords in their own right. These two Acts had the incidental effect of introducing a small proportion of women (now 7 per cent) to what had been an all-male chamber. Rather more significantly, the upper chamber was transformed over a period from an almost entirely hereditary chamber to a chamber in which appointed life peers outnumber hereditary peers in the work of the Lords. This occurred because, whereas most of the hereditary peers did not attend regularly, many of the life peers were 'working peers' and these constituted the bulk of the active membership. However, the hereditary peers retained a nominal majority, which could become effective when a subject dear to their hearts was debated.

However, the composition remained bizarre, and not only because the majority of members still claimed their seats from an accident of birth. The only religion represented as of right is the established Church of England, which hardly seems appropriate in what has become a multi-faith Britain. Moreover, while appointment may constitute an advance on heredity as a qualification for membership, the life peers owe their appointments to prime ministerial patronage (although the Prime Minister normally accepts recommendations from the leaders of opposition parties), which hardly seems much more democratic. In practice, retired ministers and long-serving MPs are among those who are commonly offered peerages. Thus debates in the Lords often feature elderly politicians, who were once household names but are now largely forgotten, giving substance to a quip of the former Liberal leader, Jo Grimond, that the House of Lords proves there is life after death.

A final objection to the composition of the unreformed upper chamber was its unbalanced representation of political parties. Although a substantial minority of peers are crossbenchers who are independent of party allegiance, among those who took a party whip Conservative peers outnumbered Labour peers by 300 up to 1997. This built-in Conservative advantage had a marked effect on the Lords' function as a revising chamber. On average, whereas the Lords inflicted 70 defeats a year on Labour governments between 1974 and 1979, it defeated Conservative administrations only 13 times a year between 1979 and 1997. Unsurprisingly, the Labour government that took office with a huge Commons majority in 1997 sought to correct this party imbalance, as part of an intended comprehensive reform of the second chamber.

## Reform of the House of Lords

While it has long been recognized that the hereditary second chamber is indefensible in a democratic era, reform of the Lords has proved difficult.

As Robert Hazell (1999, p. 114) has observed, 'it is impossible to decide a satisfactory system for Lords' membership without first deciding what interests peers are there to represent'. This is not easy in Britain. The key function a second chamber performs in a federal state is to represent the interests of the states, as the Senate does in the USA or the Bundesrat in Germany. It is more difficult to establish such a clear function in a unitary state, as the UK remains, at least in theory. It would be easier to devise a logical role for a second chamber if British government evolves towards a quasi-federal or ultimately perhaps a fully federal system. Although Lords reform is long overdue, and some would argue that it has come a century late, it is perhaps premature while the final outcome of the devolution process remains unclear.

Another solution to the Lords reform dilemma is simply abolition. Unicameral legislatures have become more common. In 2009, 114 of the world's 191 national parliaments had only one chamber, after some mature democracies abolished their second chamber and many new and post-communist states opted for a single chamber (Hague and Harrop, 2010, pp. 296–7). Yet this solution has never found much favour in Britain, although Labour proposed it for a time. It is commonly argued that a second chamber provides an opportunity for second thoughts on over-hasty legislation from the lower house. If it is accepted that some kind of revising chamber is necessary or desirable, it is then a question of deciding how that chamber should be composed. While many favour a wholly or largely elected second chamber, a problem here is that this could challenge the legitimacy and primacy of the House of Commons.

Because previous reform proposals had foundered on the failure to agree on the composition and powers of the second chamber, Blair's Labour government opted for a two-stage model of reform. Stage one was to involve simply removing the hereditary peers, stage two a more long-term and comprehensive reform. The government moved quickly towards the abolition of the right of hereditary peers to sit in the Lords, but faced with the prospects of a prolonged battle with the upper house, instead reached a compromise. This allowed the hereditary peers to elect 92 of their number to remain as members of the transitional House

**Table 13.5** Old and interim composition of the Lords, after House of Lords Act 1999

|  | Old com-position | Interim new House |
|---|---|---|
| Spiritual peers (archbishops and senior bishops of Church of England) | 26 | 26 |
| Hereditary peers | 777 | 92 |
| Law Lords | 27 | 27 |
| Life peers | 525 | 525 |
| Total | 1355 | 670 |

pending a more fundamental final reform. After the 92 peers were chosen, the rest of the hereditary peers lost their powers to speak and vote in the Lords. (The interim composition of the half-reformed House of Lords, compared with its former composition is shown in Table 13.5 and Figures 13.1 and 13.2.)

The projected second stage of Lords Reform has proved far more difficult. The government adopted a time-honoured device for dealing with politically awkward questions, appointing an independent Royal Commission chaired by Lord Wakeham, a former Conservative minister. Its report favoured a largely appointed house with only a minority of elected peers, but a government White Paper in 2001 that largely endorsed Wakeham's proposals met wide-ranging opposition. The government then set up an independent joint committee of both houses to undertake widespread consultation and propose options for reform. Yet when both houses in 2003 were given the chance to vote on seven options ranging from a wholly appointed to a wholly elected upper chamber, none commanded a clear majority. The government then proposed simply removing the remaining hereditary peers, but following opposition in the Lords this was abandoned and the reform of the composition of the Lords has remained in limbo since. Labour is far better represented (and now over-represented) in the Lords than previously (see Figure 13.3). However, ironically this partially reformed upper chamber caused rather more problems for the Labour government.

**Figure 13.1** Composition of unreformed House of Lords, pre-1999

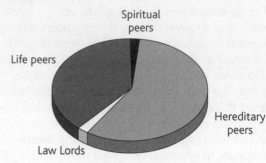

**Figure 13.2** Composition of interim House of Lords, 1999

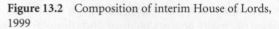
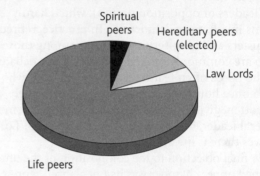

**Figure 13.3** Party affiliations of members of the House of Lords, 2010

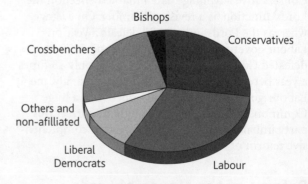

*Sources for all*: Parliament website.

## The 2010 coalition government and the Lords

The coalition government is committed to a mainly elected upper chamber. There are also suggestions that they wish to change the balance in the Lords, reducing the proportion of Labour peers. Detailed proposals have yet to emerge. However the experience of the Labour government and indeed of previous governments over the last century, suggest that it will not be easy to achieve a reformation of the composition of the Lords that will command the support of both houses.

## The Westminster parliament and other parliaments

Although the Westminster parliament remains at the centre of British politics, formally at least, in the sense that its sovereignty remains a key principle of the unwritten (or uncodified) British constitution, it is no longer the only parliament with which British politics is concerned. UK membership of the European Union has meant that representatives are also elected to the European Parliament. While this used to be dismissed as a mere talking shop, its influence on European Union decision-making, and hence on decisions that affect Britain, has grown steadily in recent years (see Chapter 15). Indeed, some would argue that it has become a more effective policy-influencing body than the Westminster parliament. Additionally, since 1999 the Westminster parliament now co-exists with a Scottish Parliament with legislative powers, and assemblies for Wales and Northern Ireland (see Chapter 16). There is also a new Greater London Assembly although the additional prospect of elected English regional assemblies has receded. Thus the Westminster parliament may increasingly appear as one of many representative assemblies in the evolving British system of governance. The existence of these other parliaments and assemblies have considerable and potentially increasing implications for the role and functions of the Westminster parliament, and require considerable liaison and coordination.

UK membership of the European Union already has considerable if contentious implications for the sovereignty of the Westminster parliament. Under the Treaty of Rome and subsequent treaties, European Union law is binding on member states. Parliamentary sovereignty seems increasingly circumscribed, despite attempts to improve the legislative accountability of European Union to national parliaments. With an increasing proportion of legislation emanating from the European Union, Westminster surveillance of European directives and regulations is a matter of some importance. The task involves both Houses of Parliament. In the Commons the Select Committee on European Legislation (the 'Scrutiny Committee') refers EU legislation that it sees as requiring further scrutiny and debate to one of the two Standing Committees. The House of Lords also has a scrutiny committee, the Select Committee on the European Communities (1974), whose task is to decide which of the hundreds of EU documents deposited with it each month require scrutiny because they raise important questions of policy or principle or for other reasons. Six sub-committees, whose reports are normally debated by the House, undertake this scrutiny. The scrutiny of European legislation seems likely to remain a dual function of the European Parliament and the parliaments of member states. That being so, there is clearly a need for improved co-operation between national parliaments and the European Parliament. From a party perspective there may be some divergence of interests between a party's national and European representatives, especially as the latter are part of wider European parties (see Chapter 15).

The longer-term implications of the devolution of power to the Scottish Parliament and Welsh and Northern Ireland assemblies also have profound implications for the role and perhaps ultimately composition of the Westminster parliament. Much of the law passed at Westminster will now be English (or English and Welsh) law rather than UK law, while law passed in the devolved assemblies may have knock-on implications for Westminster. At the very least there is a need for considerable liaison between the various parliaments and assemblies. Initially the potential for serious conflict between parliaments was somewhat lessened by Labour or Labour-dominated governments at Westminster, Edinburgh and Cardiff. More problems were predicted when a Conservative–Liberal

Democrat majority at Westminster in 2010 faced a minority SNP government in Edinburgh and a Labour–Plaid Cymru coalition in Cardiff. Some of the implications of these developments for long-established British constitutional principles, particularly the sovereignty of the Westminster parliament and the unity of the United Kingdom, are discussed in Chapters 14 and 16.

## SUMMARY

- Although the Westminster parliament is very old, prestigious, and constitutionally sovereign, critics allege it is not in practice very powerful, nor particularly effective.

- MPs represent electoral areas called constituencies. They are not socially representative of those who elect them, nor are they expected to reflect their views. Almost all represent parties, and all of them also reflect a range of outside interests. While this can be very useful, some outside interests raise ethical questions.

- The 2009 parliamentary expenses scandal raised more concerns over the conduct and financial interests of MPs, with serious implications for public trust in Parliament, politicians and parties, and demands for further reform.

- Government is recruited from and maintained by Parliament (essentially the House of Commons). There has long been a close interdependence between the executive and legislature in British politics. In practice the government dominates the Commons.

- Traditional means of parliamentary scrutiny of the executive have been supplemented by the development of Departmental Select Committees that oversee all ministerial departments.

- Most of the legislation examined in the Commons and almost all the laws that are passed are government measures. Legislation is in practice substantially an executive function.

- The 2010 coalition government is proposing further reforms of the Commons in the wake of the parliamentary expenses scandal and the 2010 election resulting in a hung parliament.

- The upper house has only powers of delay over legislation. Its undemocratic composition restricts its legitimacy and authority.

- Although most hereditary peers have been removed, detailed proposals for further reform of the upper house have failed to secure broad support, and it remains a mainly appointed chamber. The 2010 coalition government is proposing new reforms.

- The former judicial functions of the House of Lords have been transferred to a new Supreme Court.

- The Westminster parliament is no longer the only representative assembly elected by UK voters. There is a need for more liaison with the European Parliament and with the new devolved Scottish Parliaments and Welsh and Northern Irish assemblies. The results of recent elections may potentially lead to increased tensions between devolved institutions and Westminster.

# QUESTIONS FOR DISCUSSION

- Should MPs vote according to their constituents' wishes?

- Should MPs be full-time? What restrictions (if any) should be placed on MPs' pursuit of outside interests?

- How representative are MPs of those they are elected to serve? How does this compare with other parliaments and assemblies around the world? How might the Commons become more socially representative? Does it matter?

- How might MPs be given a more effective role in the legislative process?

- How might the House of Commons be given more effective influence over the executive?

- How can trust in Parliament be restored, following the parliamentary expenses scandal?

- Should the number of MPs be reduced? What might be the effect of this on relations between the executive and legislature?

- Why does Britain need an upper house? Should the House of Lords simply be abolished?

- If members of the second chamber should be wholly or mainly elected, how should they be elected, and whom should they represent?

# FURTHER READING

Philip Norton's (2005) *Parliament in British Politics* can be recommended as a reasonably up-to-date introduction to the subject by a leading academic who is also a Conservative peer. Older, but still useful is Griffith Ryle (1989), *Parliament*. Ridley and Rush (1995), *British Government and Politics since 1945* contains valuable essays on aspects of Parliament, whilst Rush (1990), *Parliament and Pressure Politics* considers the relationship between Parliament and pressure groups. For developments under the Labour government see the chapters by Norton (in Seldon, 2001) Cowley and Stuart (in Seldon and Kavanagh, 2005) Cowley (in Dunleavy *et al.*, 2006) and Cowley and Stuart (in Beech and Lee, 2008). There was much analysis of the compo-

sition of the 2010 post-election House of Commons in the press. Criddle (in Kavanagh and Cowley, 2010) has since provided a more authoritative analysis of party election candidates and elected MPs. Chapter 15 of Hague and Harrop (2010) is invaluable for a comparative perspective on legislatures. On the 2009 parliamentary expenses crisis *The Daily Telegraph* published 'The Complete Expenses file' in June 2009 and all documentary evidence was made available on the paper's website, www.telegraph.co.uk.

Website

Parliament (links to House of Commons and House of Lords): www.parliament.uk.

# The Law, Politics and the Judicial Process

The state is involved in law making (Chapter 13), executing the law through its ministers and public officials (Chapters 11 and 12), and adjudicating on the law, which is the subject of this chapter. Some political theorists have long argued that these functions should be kept strictly separate. While this separation of powers has been enforced as far as practicable in some constitutions (notably the US constitution), this has not previously been the case in Britain. Yet constitutional reforms first announced in 2003, involving the establishment of a separate Supreme Court (finally established in 2009), changes in the system for appointing judges and the reform of the office of Lord Chancellor were intended to emphasize the independence of the judiciary from both the executive and legislature.

These reforms involve a significant shift in constitutional theory and practice. They may appear to separate the administration of the law further from government and politics. However, in this chapter we argue that inevitably (and particularly in Britain) the law and politics are closely intertwined. The language of the law and legal concepts permeate the theory and practice of politics. Lawyers still play a leading role in government and Parliament, and figure prominently in public bureaucracies and business. Court judgements can have significant political consequences, affecting both governments and the lives of ordinary people, particularly following the substantial growth in the practice of judicial review of executive decisions. Judges themselves continue to wield massive power and influence, not just through the courts but in politics and government generally, and questions can and should be asked about their social and educational background, and their personal and political views. These are among the issues that we seek to address in this chapter.

Questions can also be asked about the efficiency and effectiveness of the judicial system in Britain. Does it deliver justice, fairly, quickly and reasonably economically? How might it be improved? There are also important issues surrounding the enforcement of law and the pursuit of prosecutions by the police. Finally, there are other vital questions about the protection of human rights and civil liberties in Britain, and the effectiveness of the various channels for securing redress of grievances against the state and public authorities.

## The rule of law

The rule of law has long been considered one of the fundamental principles of the unwritten (or uncodified) British constitution. It has, however, been variously interpreted over time. Today, the rule of law involves a number of assumptions, which in turn each involve some qualification or raise some questions.

- **Everyone is bound by the law.** No-one is above the law. Ministers and public officials are subject to the law and have no authority to act beyond the powers conferred on them by law (the *ultra vires* principle). *However*, British ministers are usually in a strong position to change the law because of executive dominance of the parliamentary legislative process, coupled with the traditional principles of parliamentary sovereignty and the supremacy of statute law.
- **All persons are equal before the law.** All citizens have legal rights and can have recourse to the law, and the law is supposed to treat all citizens on an equal basis. *However*, there are some doubts over equality before the law in practice. The law, like the Ritz Hotel, is open to all. Legal proceedings can be expensive, and although there is legal aid for those with limited means, it is restricted (for example, it is not available for libel cases). Some would argue that the law in practice has systematically favoured property owners and established interests.
- **Law and order must be maintained** through the officials and institutional machinery of the state, which has a monopoly of the legitimate use of force within the state's borders. Citizens should be protected from violence and disorder, but should be forcibly restrained from taking the law into their own hands. *However*, the maintenance of law and order may lead to restrictions on individual liberty, such as restrictions on freedom of movement and detention of suspects without trial. The 'war against terror' has been used to justify restrictions on civil liberties, particularly after the London bombings of July 2005.
- **Legal redress is provided for those with complaints** against other individuals, organizations or the state. *However*, doubts are still expressed over the effectiveness of some of these remedies.
- **The law and legal processes and personnel should be independent and free from political interference.** The courts are generally reckoned to be free from political pressures in practice. Labour's Constitutional Reform Act (2005) was supposed to establish more formally the separation of powers and the independence of the judiciary. *However*, judges still complain about the interference of politicians, particularly over judicial sentencing.

## English, Scottish, European and international law

It is difficult to summarize briefly the legal and judicial system in the United Kingdom, because there are marked differences within the state, particularly between English and Scottish law and their respective judicial systems. Scottish law, by contrast with that of England, is, like continental European law, influenced by Roman law and involves distinctive principles and practice and a separate system of administration. Although Scottish law, like English law, remains bound by the theoretical sovereignty of the Westminster parliament, the devolution of legislative powers to the new Scottish Parliament has already led to some

---

● Law is conventionally subdivided into a number of categories, such as **criminal**, **civil** and **administrative**.

---

● **Criminal law** provides standards of conduct as well as machinery (police, courts system) for dealing with those who commit crimes. Crimes are normally classified as (1) against the state (treason, public order); (2) against the person (murder, assault, rape); and (3) against property (robbery, malicious damage). A successful *prosecution* in a criminal case leads to a *sentence* (e.g. fine, imprisonment, community service, probation).

---

● **Civil law** is concerned with the legal relations between persons. Normally, proceedings in a civil court depend upon a *plaintiff* pursuing an *action* against a *defendant* and they generally result in some *remedy*, such as damages, specific performance (where the defendant has to keep his side of the bargain), or a 'declaration' of the plaintiff's legal rights. While cases in criminal law have to be proved 'beyond reasonable doubt', actions in civil law are decided on the 'balance of probabilities'.

---

● **Administrative law** is 'the body of general principles which govern the exercise of powers and duties by public authorities' (Wade, 1988). Administrative law is more systematically developed on the European continent than in Britain. However, this sphere of law has grown considerably in Britain over the last century with the growth of the welfare state and public services. A variety of judicial and quasi-judicial institutions (the ordinary courts, tribunals, the Ombudsman) apply a framework of rules within which public authorities act. Administrative law is particularly involved in citizen rights and redress of grievances.

## COMPARATIVE POLITICS  14.1
# English common law and law in other European countries

The English law and judicial system differs markedly from that prevailing over most of the European continent. While continental law is generally based on written codes deriving ultimately from Roman law, English law is based on common law, assumed to be the immemorial but uncodified law of the English people, and declared by judges in court cases. Thus the law is essentially contained in decisions on past cases which are binding on subsequent cases of a similar nature. Although judges are theoretically only declaring the law, they can in effect make new law, particularly when new circumstances arise. However, statute law is supreme over common law, so the law made by Parliament (and effectively by the government) overrides judge-made case law.

---

further significant divergences between English and Scottish law, and these differences seem likely to become more marked over time.

Besides these differences between legal principles and practice within Britain, law in Britain is subject to growing supranational influence and control. Thus the British government ratified the European Convention on Human Rights in 1951, and allowed individual petitions from 1966, permitting British citizens to take their case to the court at Strasbourg. The Human Rights Act (1998) enabled judges to declare that legislation appeared incompatible with the European Convention on Human Rights.

From 1973 the United Kingdom has also been a member of the European Community (now Union). Thus the UK is subject to EU law and to the decisions of the European Court of Justice at Luxembourg (not to be confused with the European Court of Human Rights at Strasbourg, which formally is nothing to do with the European Union). Naturally EU law is strongly influenced by the mainstream European continental legal tradition, and this in turn has had some impact on English law, particularly perhaps, the growth of judicial review. It seems likely that over a period of time there will be more convergence between legal principles and systems within Europe.

On top of this, the United Kingdom is increasingly influenced by international law and conventions. Thus critics of the Iraq war argued that it was illegal under international law without clear United Nations authorization. The Attorney General, a member of the government and its official legal adviser, eventually declared that the war was legal, although it was alleged that the short published version of his advice omitted qualifications and reservations indicated in an earlier longer judgment. It remains a contentious issue.

## The courts

The UK system of courts is complicated. Scotland and Northern Ireland have their own rather different court systems. Most of what follows applies particularly to England and Wales (see Figure 14.1). Minor criminal cases are tried without a jury in magistrates' courts, by legally qualified, full-time stipendiary (paid) magistrates in the cities and by part-time lay magistrates advised by legally qualified clerks elsewhere. More serious criminal cases for 'indictable' offences and appeals from the magistrates' court are heard in the Crown Court before a judge and jury (unless the defendant pleads guilty, which is commonly the case, when a jury is not required). Appeals from conviction in the Crown Court are usually to the Criminal Division of the Court of Appeal. The Court of Appeal consists of Lords Justices of Appeal and other judges who are members *ex officio*. A further

**Figure 14.1**    The system of courts in England and Wales

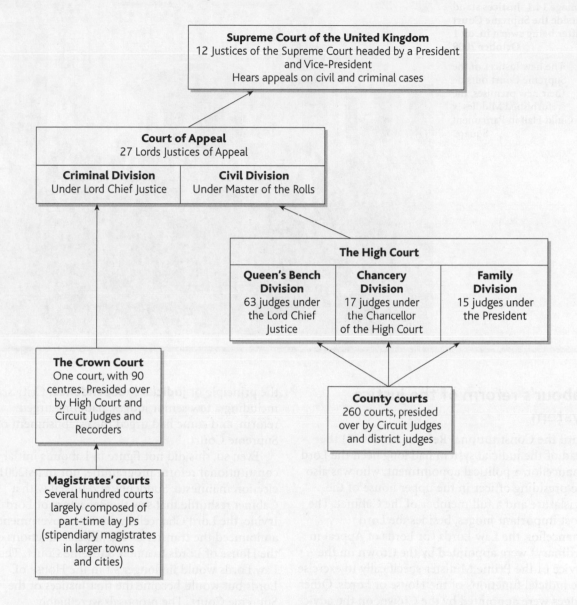

appeal on a point of law may be allowed to the Supreme Court which became operative in 2009 (formerly appeals were made to the House of Lords, sitting as a court).

A few minor civil cases are heard in magistrates' courts but most minor cases are heard by county courts, presided over by circuit judges. More important cases are heard in the High Court, which is split into three divisions: Queen's

Bench Division, dealing with common law, Chancery Division, dealing with equity, and the Family Division, dealing with domestic cases. Appeals from lower courts are heard in the appropriate Division of the High Court. Appeals from the High Court can be made to the Civil Division of the Court of Appeal, and from there to the new Supreme Court.

**Image 14.1  Justices stand outside the Supreme Court after being sworn in, on 1 October 2009**

The new Justices of the Supreme Court outside their new premises, the refurbished Middlesex Guild Hall in Parliament Square.

## Labour's reform of the justice system

Until the Constitutional Reform Act (2005) the head of the judicial system had long been the Lord Chancellor, a political appointment, who was also the presiding officer in the upper house of the legislature and a full member of the Cabinet. The most important judges, besides the Lord Chancellor, the Law Lords (or Lords of Appeal in Ordinary) were appointed by the Crown on the advice of the Prime Minister specifically to exercise the judicial functions of the House of Lords. Other judges were appointed by the Crown, on the advice of the Lord Chancellor. This entanglement of the judicial functions of the state with its executive and legislative functions appeared thoroughly confusing and even downright dangerous to critics familiar with the stricter separation of powers in the constitutions of other states such as the USA and France. Although many commentators in the UK conceded that in practice the judiciary was independent and largely free from political interference, the unreformed system did not guarantee the principle of **judicial independence**. Critics, including a few senior judges, had long urged reform, and some had urged the establishment of a Supreme Court.

Even so, this did not figure in Labour's initial constitutional reform programme, nor in its 2001 election manifesto. Suddenly, and linked with a Cabinet reshuffle that saw the departure of Lord Irvine, the Lord Chancellor, the Blair government announced the transfer of the judicial functions of the House of Lords to a new Supreme Court. The Law Lords would no longer sit in the House of Lords but would become the first Justices of the Supreme Court. The proposals were highly contentious. Traditionalists lamented the projected abolition of the Lord Chancellor (subsequently the title was maintained but the role transformed and reduced), while critics suggested the Labour government's proposals did not go far enough.

● **Judicial independence:** The constitutional principle that in order to protect individual freedom the judiciary should be independent from the other branches of government, the executive and the legislature.

The new Supreme Court began operating in October 2009. It is housed in the refurbished Middlesex Guild Hall in Parliament Square, close to the Houses of Parliament and some of the great departments of state. It is composed of twelve Justices of the Supreme Court. Most of these were formerly Law Lords (or Lords of Appeal in Ordinary) in the House of Lords. The senior Law Lord, Lord Phillips of Worth Matravers became the first President, and Lord Hope of Craighead became Deputy President. Five of the justices were over seventy when appointed, and the rest in their sixties. Only one was a woman (Baroness Hale). All but one were Oxbridge graduates, six from Cambridge and five from Oxford. (Lord Kerr of Tonaghmore is a graduate of Queen's University, Belfast.)

The new Supreme Court 'of the United Kingdom' does not receive appeals on criminal cases from Scotland, as the Law Lords did not hear such cases in the past. The only new powers transferred to the Supreme Court not previously exercised by the Law Lords were over appeals on jurisdiction under the Devolution Acts, previously the responsibility of the Judicial Committee of the Privy Council. It is only on such devolution issues that decisions of the Supreme Court are binding throughout the United Kingdom. Moreover, the UK Supreme Court does not closely resemble some other supreme courts. Unlike the US Supreme Court it is not able to invalidate legislation contravening the constitution, as this would undermine the principle of parliamentary sovereignty. Thus the Supreme Court is not the guardian of the constitution.

## Lawyers, judges, and politics

The new Supreme Court for all its important constitutional implications will probably not have much impact on the nature and character of the British legal profession. This is divided between some 4,000 or so barristers, who alone can plead cases in the higher courts, and around 50,000 solicitors who deal directly with the public, and among their other duties prepare the cases for barristers to plead. This division of labour is relatively unusual in other countries, and some critics suggest that it is, in effect, a restrictive practice that benefits lawyers rather than their clients. The cost and length

of training for barristers in particular, and the uncertain rewards in the early years in the profession have tended to restrict entry into the legal profession predominantly to those from well-to-do family backgrounds. Yet if they do become successful, the rewards for a sought-after barrister can be huge. Thus while lawyers may frequently have to defend the interests of the poor and marginalized in British society, very few successful barristers share the social background of their clients.

It is from the ranks of senior barristers that judges are mainly drawn. Once appointed, they are virtually irremovable before the obligatory retirement age, which was reduced from 75 to 70 in 1993. Unsurprisingly, senior judges are drawn almost exclusively from the ranks of the white, male, upper middle class. There were no Justices of the Supreme Court, nor Heads of Division nor Lords Justices of Appeal and only three per cent of High Court and Circuit Judges from ethnic minorities in 2009. Rather more women are now being appointed as judges, but few to the higher ranks of the judiciary (see Table 14.1). As judges are normally only recruited after a long career at the Bar, and are not obliged to retire at the same age as most of the working population, they are also predominantly elderly.

Judges are powerful and often controversial figures. They may become celebrated or notorious public figures because of their sentencing in criminal cases, their comments during the course of a trial and their observations in summing up (for which they cannot be sued). Politicians and the media have sometimes criticized judges for passing sentences that are considered too light. Judges in their turn have deplored mandatory sentences for certain categories of crime, which reduce judicial

**Table 14.1**  Senior judges by gender, 2009

| Level of judiciary | Men | Women | % Women |
| --- | --- | --- | --- |
| Supreme Court | 10 | 1 | 9 |
| Heads of Division | 5 | 0 | 0 |
| Lords Justices of Appeal | 34 | 3 | 8 |
| High Court Judges | 92 | 16 | 15 |
| Circuit Judges | 579 | 101 | 15 |
| Recorders | 1032 | 201 | 16 |

*Source*: www.judiciary.gov.uk.

discretion, and have roundly criticized interference by politicians. As law and order is an emotive political issue, it is perhaps unsurprising that politicians and judges are drawn into conflict. Because of their role in declaring (and sometimes effectively making) the law, they are inevitably helping to shape public policy and influence public attitudes. In addition to their judicial activities, judges because of their public standing and legal expertise are often invited to conduct or chair major enquiries into controversial political areas. Examples include the Scott Inquiry on the arms to Iraq scandal in 1996 or the 2003 Hutton Inquiry into the circumstances surrounding the death of the weapons inspector David Kelly and government and media handling of communications leading up to the Iraq war.

The orthodox view is that the judicial system is impartial, symbolized by the blindfold figure of Justice above the Central Criminal Court. Judges balance the scales of justice fairly, without fear or favour. The acknowledged impartiality of the judiciary legitimizes the whole administration of justice in the United Kingdom. Judges are moreover sometimes seen also as stout defenders of the rights and freedoms of citizens against arbitrary and unjustified acts by governments and public authorities. The growth of judicial review over the last thirty or forty years (see below) provides some support for this perspective. The 1998 Human Rights Act has provided further opportunities for judicial intervention against government.

Yet critics argue that judges are almost inevitably biased in their attitudes and decisions because of the kind of people they are. While they may strive earnestly to appear impartial, their own highly restricted and exclusive social background is almost bound to affect their assumptions and outlook, which is inevitably conservative with a small 'c' and, critics allege, generally with a large 'C' also (Griffith, 1997). Indeed, some judges almost seem to pride themselves on their ignorance of popular culture and common language. More disquietingly, critics argue they sometimes appear more sympathetic to 'white-collar' criminals than their working-class counterparts, have on occasion shown marked leniency to men in rape cases, and send more blacks than whites to prison for longer periods for equivalent offences.

The Labour government was committed to more diversity within the judiciary, although this was not made explicit in the 2005 Constitutional Reform Act. By contrast, the Scottish and Northern Ireland commissions for appointing judges were required to bring about a judiciary more reflective and representative of the community, and less overwhelmingly male and white. Yet, given the type and length of legal experience required of a judge, and the relatively restricted social background of senior barristers, it will be difficult to achieve significant changes in the short to medium term. Although it could be argued that juries composed of ordinary citizens provide protection against the (perhaps largely unconscious) bias of an unrepresentative judiciary, jury trials are only used in a minority of cases, and there are proposals to restrict their use still further, for example in fraud cases (see Box 14.1).

## The police and policing

All states require police to enforce the criminal law and prevent disorder. It is the most vulnerable members of society, such as the old, the young, women and minorities facing discrimination and prejudice who most need the protection of an efficient and impartial police force. Yet, even more than judges, police appear to represent the coercive role of the state. Although a good police force is a requirement for any civilized nation, the police in many countries are feared and hated, while the chief of police has become a familiar figure of demonology. It says something for the British police that they long avoided this unenviable reputation. While fictional portrayals in novels, music hall, and early films and television occasionally showed police officers as bumbling, they were rarely portrayed as harsh or corrupt. If this image of the friendly 'British bobby' was always somewhat idealized, it was not altogether a myth. Unusually, the ordinary police did not (and still do not) carry guns, indicating an uncommon degree of mutual trust between the police and public. This trust still survives in many parts of the country. However, confidence in the impartiality and efficiency of the police in Britain was never universal and now appears lower than it used to be.

Just as there are issues over the possible bias of the judiciary, there are similar concerns over the

## BOX 14.1

# Trial by jury under threat?

Trial by jury was enshrined as a principle in Magna Carta (1215) and is still widely regarded as an important right and the essence of a 'fair trial'. Yet most trials no longer involve a jury. Jury trials are expensive and time-consuming, not least for those summoned for jury service. Indeed, it is sometimes alleged that juries no longer represent a fair cross-section of the community because some sections of the population successfully plead to be excused. In criminal cases many police believe jury trials lead to more acquittals of defendants they 'know' are guilty. There are also cases where jurors have been threatened or intimidated. It is also suggested that juries are not competent to decide on complex legal issues, such as fraud cases. Anecdotal evidence suggests that the deliberations of some juries may involve a muddled compromise between diametrically opposed gut reactions of individual jurors, even if most of the time they seem to follow the guidance of the judge. Yet juries can sometimes show an obstinate independence and perhaps more common sense than legal experts.

police. This is not because the police are recruited from a very restricted social and educational elite (as could be said of judges). On the contrary, most police have been recruited from lower white-collar and working-class family backgrounds. In spite or perhaps even because of this, it is widely alleged that the police behave in a more deferential manner towards 'respectable' people. Moreover, it is suggested that they are less concerned, or less well equipped, to pursue 'white-collar' crime.

However, possible class bias has received rather less scrutiny of late than the alleged sexist, homophobic and racist attitudes of sections of the police. It is sometimes alleged that women police officers (roughly one in six of the total force) do not fit easily into the rather 'macho' police culture, and have found it difficult to secure promotion to the highest levels. This culture sometimes led in the past to the unsympathetic treatment of female victims of rape and male violence, with the police particularly reticent over intervention in 'domestic' issues. This was one factor in the reluctance of women to report rape and other crimes of violence, although more recently many police forces have made more strenuous efforts to treat such crimes sympathetically and pursue them seriously. The same macho culture has sometimes contributed to a marked lack of sympathy and sometimes hostility towards homosexuals. Again, attitudes are changing, perhaps more slowly, but sufficiently to allow a

few police themselves to 'come out' and even join in 'gay pride' marches.

Allegations of police racism have received considerable publicity in recent years. It has to be said that racism in the police largely reflects racism in wider society, although the problems have perhaps been more pronounced in some forces. Relatively few blacks and Asians have been recruited into the police (less than 2 per cent), and they have often found it difficult to obtain acceptance from their white colleagues and secure promotion. This has tended to reinforce mutual suspicion amounting sometimes to marked antipathy between the police and minority communities. Members of ethnic minorities are far more likely to be stopped and searched than members of the majority white community. There is also evidence of routine racist abuse of blacks and Asians, and some cases of violent maltreatment of black suspects. Tragically there have also been high-profile police failures to secure convictions of those responsible for crimes of violence against black victims, most notably Stephen Lawrence and Damilola Taylor. It was the Macpherson Inquiry into the handling of the murder of Stephen Lawrence that led to acknowledgement that there was institutional racism in the Metropolitan Police and other police forces (see Chapter 22).

The efficiency and effectiveness of the police has also been called into question by some high-profile miscarriages of justice and failures to solve crimes.

Some miscarriages of justice were perhaps the consequence of intense media and public pressure on the police to secure convictions, leading to hasty and ill-prepared prosecutions, but in a few cases involved the extraction of dubious confessions from suspects and even the fabrication of evidence. Some former police officers have been jailed for corruption, undermining faith in the integrity of the police.

There has also been criticism of police handling of protests and demonstrations. Thus police efforts to contain demonstrators and prevent damage to property have sometimes caused distress and injury to peaceful protesters and even innocent bystanders, as in the 2010 student protests over increased university tuition fees. Rather more sinister have been the revelations over police covert operations involving long-term infiltration of radical environmental groups, which surfaced in January 2011. While such undercover operations may be legitimate where national security is at risk, it is difficult to justify similar activities against lawful protesters.

All this raises important concerns over the accountability and control of the police, an issue in many countries. It is considered important on the one hand that the police should be independent from direct control by party politicians, but on the other that they should be fully accountable to the public or their representatives. Squaring that circle is difficult and in Britain, police accountability and responsibility is somewhat blurred. The police used to be a local authority responsibility, but control by elected councillors, never very effective, particularly on operational issues, has been progressively weakened as a consequence of police force amalgamations and reduced councillor representation on Police Authorities. Today these are virtually quasi-autonomous local public bodies, often covering several local authorities. Chief Constables retain substantial operational control. The coalition government is pressing ahead with proposals for elected police commissioners, with the aim of improving the public accountability of the police force, but these proposals have been heavily criticized by the police, Police Authorities and others.

If local accountability is not particularly effective, what of accountability at the centre? Nationally, the minister in charge of crime and the police is the Home Secretary, who only ever had direct responsibility for London's Metropolitan Police, and even this was, in 2000, transferred to the Metropolitan Police Authority. Thus the Home Secretary is not answerable in the Commons for the conduct of Police Authorities and local police forces. Despite having overall responsibility for the police, successive Home Secretaries have found it difficult to pursue reorganization and modernization of the police.

Machinery for handling complaints against the police has improved but remains controversial. Formerly, the investigation of complaints was wholly in the hands of the police themselves (although officers from another force might be brought in for serious cases). A Police Complaints Board was introduced to supervise the process in 1976. Following the 1984 Police and Criminal Evidence Act this was replaced by a beefed-up Police Complaints Authority, which supervises the investigation of serious complaints, although the actual investigation is still carried out by police officers, so it is still questioned whether this amounts to a genuinely independent enquiry.

Policing, together with law and order generally, can hardly be taken out of politics. Indeed it remains a hotly contested political issue. Thus the last Labour government tried to counter the accusation that the party was 'soft on crime'. Blair first came to national prominence as Shadow Home Secretary, with his soundbite that Labour would be 'tough on crime and tough on the causes of crime'. New Labour's first two Home Secretaries – Jack Straw from 1997 and David Blunkett from 2001 – were notably 'tough', and both Blair and Brown made periodic interventions on law and order issues. The coalition government has sent out more mixed messages. On the one hand, Justice Secretary Kenneth Clarke is seeking to reduce the prison population (one of the highest in the western world), while other Conservatives are keen to reassert their party's traditional toughness on crime, and the message that 'prison works'. However, the drive to cut public spending may help Clarke win this argument within the party.

## Human rights and civil liberties

The hallmark of a liberal democratic state, it is often said, is the effectiveness with which a range of basic citizen rights or civil liberties is guaranteed.

These rights or liberties have long been enthusiastically extolled by British people, and it is vital, therefore, to examine to what extent this confidence in the security of such rights is justified. Three points provide a context for this discussion:

- Virtually all British civil liberties stem from a fundamental principle: that people may do what they like so long as no law prevents them.
- Legal protections against infringements of this fundamental freedom in specific instances (e.g. freedom of expression, meeting, association and so on) have been established gradually throughout British history. They were not codified or enshrined in any particular statute until the Human Rights Act, which came into force in 2000.
- The question of citizen rights or liberties has both a positive and negative aspect: the right to do certain things *and* the right *not* to have certain things done to you.

## Administrative law: protecting civil liberties and redressing grievances

How are the rights and freedoms set out in Box 14.2 in practice protected? What channels of **redress** do citizens, groups and organizations have if they feel they have been illegally, unfairly, unreasonably or arbitrarily treated by a public official or public authority? Of course, aggrieved citizens will commonly first pursue a complaint with the organization directly concerned. They may ask to see the manager, or follow a publicized complaints procedure within the organization. However there are a number of other recognized channels which may be taken to achieve a remedy. While the first of these is a political channel, the others are judicial or quasi-judicial:

- Contact an elected representative – a Member of Parliament or local councillor

- Appeal to the ordinary courts for judicial review and remedy
- Appeal to an administrative tribunal
- Provide evidence to a public inquiry
- Complain to an Ombudsman
- Invoke the European Convention on Human Rights

## Judicial review

Recourse to the courts for **judicial review** can often be expensive and time-consuming, and is normally only effective where a clear breach of the law is involved. Often citizens are complaining about the merits of a particular decision rather than a breach of the law. However, the ordinary courts have been interpreting more administrative behaviour as involving a breach of the law, and providing more effective remedies. While critics have often accused the judiciary of having a pro-establishment or pro-government bias, over the last thirty or forty years the political role of the courts in scrutinizing the actions of government and public officials has become steadily more important.

The grounds on which an application for review can be made were summarized by Lord Diplock in the GCHQ case (1985) as illegality, procedural impropriety and irrationality, to which proportionality can now be added (Box 14.3).

There are however some significant limitations to judicial review in Britain:

1 Judges work within the framework of parliamentary sovereignty. Because Parliament is sovereign, judges cannot strike down legislation as unconstitutional. Thus, in the UK judicial review means preventing public authorities from doing anything which the ordinary law forbids or for which they have no statutory authority. By contrast, in codified constitutions such as the United States, the Supreme Court from the early days of the Republic assumed the role of striking down legislation deemed unconstitutional.

---

● **Redress of grievances**: The legitimate expectation by a citizen in a democratic society that complaints against public officials will be considered fairly and impartially and that legal remedies for wrongs will be available should malpractice be found.

● **Judicial review**: The constitutional function exercised by the courts to review the legislation, regulations and acts of the legislative and executive branches of government.

---

**BOX 14.2**

# Civil rights established over centuries in the UK (and some limitations)

---

- **Political rights,** including the right to vote, guaranteed by Representation of the People Acts (1918, 1928, 1948, 1969).
- **Freedom of movement,** includes right to move freely within, and the right to leave, Britain (but note powers to detain suspected terrorists, and police powers to stop and search on suspicion).
- **Personal freedom,** including freedom from detention without charge (Magna Carta 1215, *habeas corpus* legislation in eighteenth century (but note exceptions, especially detention without charge in Northern Ireland, and more recently for suspected terrorists in Britain).
- **Freedom of conscience,** includes right to practise any religion, right of parents to withdraw children from religious instruction in state schools, right of conscientious objection to conscription into the armed forces.
- **Freedom of expression,** includes right of individuals and the media to communicate information and express opinions (but note freedom of expression is limited by laws on treason, sedition, blasphemy, obscenity, libel, incitement to racial hatred, defamation, contempt of court and the Official Secrets Act).

- **Freedom of association and meeting,** includes right to meet, march and protest freely (but note some restrictions on public order grounds, and restrictions on 'secondary picketing' in industrial disputes).
- **Right to property,** includes right to property and to use it, and not be deprived of it without due process (but note compulsory purchase orders, planning restrictions etc.).
- **Right to privacy:** a general right to privacy is contained in article 8 of the European Convention of Human Rights, now incorporated into UK Law through the 1998 Human Rights Act (but note exceptions in interests of state security, which is used to justify political surveillance, phone tapping etc.).
- **Rights at work,** including protection against unfair dismissal, the right to a satisfactory working environment, and freedom from racial and sexual discrimination (all embodied in a series of Acts of Parliament).
- **Social freedoms,** including freedom to marry and divorce, to practise contraception and seek abortions, to practise homosexuality between consenting adults (contained in several post-war Acts of Parliament).

---

2 Judges in Britain cannot pronounce on the merits of legislation – that is, they are not justified in substituting what they would have done for what Parliament enacted on a given occasion. Judges distinguish clearly between matters of policy on which Parliament is the only authority and matters concerning lawfulness on which the courts may legitimately intervene. (However, judges can now declare that legislation appears incompatible with the European Convention on Human Rights – see below.)

3 Judicial review can be subject to statutory exclusion (specific Acts of Parliament may rule it out).

4 The courts themselves have imposed strict limitations on their own power to scrutinize executive decisions made under the royal prerogative. They were defined by Lord Roskill in the

GCHQ case to include the making of treaties, the defence of the realm, the prerogative of mercy, the grant of honours, the dissolution of Parliament and the appointment of ministers (Madgwick and Woodhouse, 1995, p.88).

## Administrative tribunals

Appeal by an aggrieved citizen to an administrative tribunal may be more appropriate where a particular decision which does not involve a clear breach of the law is involved – for example the refusal of a grant, or a pension or a licence. Tribunals are a very important part of the British system of administrative justice. They are normally established by legislation and cover a wide range of functions, many of them in the field of welfare. Thus, there are tribunals for national insurance, pensions, housing,

## BOX 14.3

# Grounds for judicial review

*Illegality.* The principle here is that exercises of power by public authorities must have specific legal authority. The fundamental doctrine invoked by the courts is *ultra vires* (beyond their powers), which prevents public servants taking actions for which they have no statutory authority, i.e. acting illegally. When courts investigate an administrative action under an enabling statute, they consider whether the power in question was directly authorized by the statute or whether it may be construed as reasonably incidental to it. They can also consider whether a minister or other public authority abused their powers by using them for a purpose not intended by statute or whether, in exercising power, a decision-maker took irrelevant factors into account or ignored relevant factors.

*Procedural impropriety.* The courts also allow executive decisions to be challenged on the grounds that the procedures laid down by statute have not been followed. In reviewing administrative actions, the courts may also invoke the common law principles of natural justice. These are twofold: first, the rule against bias (no one to be a judge in his own cause); and second, the right to a fair hearing (hear the other side). Under the first rule, administrators must not have any direct (including financial) interest in the outcome of proceedings; nor must they be reasonably suspected of being biased or of being likely to be biased. Justice must not only be done but should be seen to be done. The right to a fair hearing requires that no one should be penalized in any way without receiving notice of the case to be met and being given a fair chance to answer that case and put one's own case.

*Irrationality.* This ground for review dates back to a case in 1948 when the judge held that a decision made by an authority would be unreasonable if 'it were so unreasonable that no reasonable authority could have come to it'. Although the test of unreasonableness has been used since then to strike down local authority actions, its use is rare.

*Proportionality.* The use of proportionality as a ground for judicial review in the 1990s reflects the increasing influence of European Union law on British judges, especially the European Court of Justice. Thus the Treaty of Maastricht declares, 'Any action by the Community shall not go beyond what is necessary to achieve the objectives of the Treaty.'

---

education, the National Health Service (NHS) and immigration. Claims arising out of injuries at work, industrial disputes, unfair dismissal and redundancy are dealt with by industrial tribunals.

Tribunals are usually composed of a chairman with legal qualifications (often a solicitor) and two lay members representing interests related to the concerns of the particular tribunal. They are independent and not subject to political or administrative interference from the Departments under whose aegis they usually work. Their functions may be described as quasi-judicial: to hear appeals against initial decisions of government agencies or, sometimes, disputes between individuals and organizations. Their role is to establish the facts of each case and then apply the relevant legal rules to it, thus in the majority of instances to decide what the statutory rights and entitlements of the aggrieved actually are. Except where the parties request privacy, tribunals hear cases in public. They provide simpler, cheaper, speedier, more expert and more accessible justice than the ordinary courts in their specific sphere of responsibility. It is possible to appeal against their decisions – normally to a superior court, tribunal or a minister. For a small number of tribunals, however, including the National Health Service Tribunal, the Social Security Commissioners and the Immigration Appeal Tribunal, no appeal is available.

Back in 1957 the Franks Committee on Administrative Tribunals and Inquiries recommended that tribunals move towards 'greater openness, fairness and impartiality'. Proceedings should be held in public and reasons for decisions should be given. The parties before tribunals should know in advance the case they had to meet, should have the chance to put their own case either personally or through representatives, and should be able to appeal against decisions. Finally, proceedings should not only be impartial, through stronger safeguards regulating their composition, but also be seen to be impartial by no longer being held on the premises of government departments. The general trend of the last half-century has been towards making the procedure of tribunals more judicial, but without forfeiting the advantages of tribunals over ordinary courts. These are greater informality, specialization, capacity to conduct their own investigations and flexibility in terms of the formulation of reasonable standards in their own spheres.

## Public inquiries

Often aggrieved citizens are concerned about some proposed, rather than past, action of a public authority – such as a planned new road, housing development or airport runway. The standard method for giving a hearing to objectors to a government proposal is the public inquiry. Proposals have to be adequately publicized, and third parties have to be afforded the opportunity to state their cases before decisions are taken. Decisions of inquiries may be challenged in the High Court within six weeks of the decision either on the grounds of procedure or the substance of the decision.

Courts hearing appeals from inquiry decisions have sought to safeguard the rights of the public. For example, they have ruled that objectors at an inquiry should be able to take 'an active, intelligent and informed part in the decision-making process' (1977) and that they must be given 'a fair crack of the whip' (1976) in putting their case. From the point of view of public authorities, major inquiries have often been unduly expensive and time-consuming. From the perspective of objectors to planning proposals, the dice are heavily weighted against them. They lack the expertise, time and resources available to government and developers. Often objectors claim the terms of reference are too narrow. Thus they may be permitted to raise objections to a particular route for a road, but normally not to the need for a road. Yet they do provide a forum where objectors can make their case, and oblige planners to defend their proposals with evidence.

## The ombudsman system

As well as legal rights, citizens have a more general right to a good standard of administration. In 1967 the Parliamentary Commissioner for Administration (PCA) was established (commonly referred to as 'the Ombudsman', the term long used in Sweden from where the idea came). The Ombudsman's brief is to investigate and, if possible, remedy complaints by individuals and corporate bodies who feel that they have experienced 'injustice in consequence of maladministration' at the hands of central government. Maladministration relates to the way in which decisions are made, and can include:

> corruption, bias, unfair discrimination, harshness, misleading a member of the public as to his rights, failing to notify him properly of his rights or to explain the reasons for a decision, general high-handedness, using powers for a wrong purpose, failing to consider relevant materials, taking irrelevant material into account, losing or failing to reply to correspondence, delaying unreasonably before making a tax refund or presenting a tax demand or dealing with an application for a grant or license, and so on. (De Smith and Brazier, 1990, p. 649)

Appointed by the Crown on the advice of the Lord Chancellor, the Parliamentary Commissioner for Administration enjoys an independent status similar to that of a High Court judge, and a staff of about 55, largely drawn from the civil service. During investigations, which are conducted in private, the Ombudsman can call for the relevant files of the Department concerned, and can compel the attendance of witnesses and the production of documents.

Complaints must be referred to the Ombudsman through MPs. This was because MPs were concerned that the Ombudsman should supplement rather than supplant their own historic role in securing redress of constituents' grievances. Normally only a small proportion of complaints are accepted for investigation – complaints are rejected if they do not involve maladministration, or if there is a right of appeal to a tribunal. The Ombudsman issues a report on each investigation to the referring

MP, with a copy to the Department involved. Where maladministration is found, a Department is expected to correct it – for example. by issuing an apology or financial recompense to the aggrieved person – but the Ombudsman has no power to compel it to do so. If the Department refuses to act, the Ombudsman may first bring pressure to bear on it by means of the Commons Select Committee on the PCA, and if this fails, can lay a Special Report before both houses of Parliament.

Initially limited to the investigation of maladministration in central government, the ombudsman system was later enlarged by the addition of ombudsmen for Northern Ireland (1969), the National Health Service (1973), and local government in England and Wales (1974) and Scotland (1976). Unlike the position with regard to the PCA, direct access to these ombudsmen is allowed (in the case of local government, only since 1988), and both the health and the local government commissioners receive a much larger volume of complaints than the PCA. As with the PCA, however, neither local nor health commissioners have any enforcement powers. If a local authority in mainland Britain chooses not to comply with an adverse report by a local ombudsman after various efforts have been made to persuade it, the ombudsman can require it to publicize the reasons for non-compliance.

Ombudsmen have made a less dramatic impact on British public administration than their early advocates hoped, partly because of lack of public awareness of the system, and inadequate powers of enforcement. The only powers of the ombudsmen against a recalcitrant public authority are those of publicity. However, most of their recommendations are accepted and implemented by the Departments and authorities concerned, and they have secured on occasion substantial compensation for victims of maladministration. More usually, small-scale payments in compensation follow a report, and sometimes just an apology.

## The European Convention on Human Rights and the Human Rights Act

The European Court of Human Rights has long played a part in upholding and enlarging civil liberties in Britain although between 1966 and 1997 it did so in a somewhat roundabout way. The United Kingdom ratified the European Convention on Human Rights in 1951 and allowed individuals to petition it from 1966. Although these were not legal rights in Britain and therefore not enforceable in British law, they turned out to be an important influence on civil rights. British courts could take note of the Convention and presume Parliament did not intend to legislate inconsistently with it. Moreover, the UK government normally complied with judgements of the European Court. However, these rights were not enforceable in British law because, although Britain renewed its ratification of the Convention every year, unlike the other countries who have signed the document, it did not, until 1998, incorporate the Convention into British law. Hence, British citizens were not able to use the Convention to appeal to British courts when their rights were infringed. They were able to appeal to the European Court at Strasbourg, but only after they had tried and failed to find remedies in the British courts. No legal aid was available, and the Court took a long time to reach its judgements – an average of five years for a case to move through the entire process. In all, up to 1997, the Court pronounced on 98 British cases and found violations of human rights in 50 of them. (The United Kingdom lost more cases before the European Court than any other signatory state.) The decisions of the European Court were not, strictly speaking, enforceable in the United Kingdom. But the UK government agreed to respect the decisions made by the Court and, in practice, its verdicts were observed, normally by changing British law accordingly. (Box 14.4 lists the rights available under the European Convention on Human Rights and its Protocols.)

Following its 1997 manifesto promise to incorporate the European Convention on Human Rights into British law, the Labour government passed a Human Rights Act in 1998, which came into force in 2000 (Wadham in Blackburn and Plant, 1999; Wadham and Mountfield 2000; Lester and Clapinska in Jowell and Oliver, 2007). This means that British citizens who consider that their rights have been infringed are now able to take their cases to British courts rather than to the European Court of Human Rights in Strasbourg. The Act makes it

## BOX 14.4

# Rights under the European Convention on Human Rights and its Protocols (summarized)

### Articles of the Convention

2. Right to life
5. Freedom from torture or inhuman or degrading treatment or punishment.
6. Freedom from slavery or forced labour
7. Right to liberty and security of person
8. Right to a fair trial by an impartial tribunal
9. Freedom from punishment for an act which did not constitute a criminal offence under law when it was committed.
10. Right to respect for family and private life, home and correspondence
11. Freedom of thought, conscience and religion
12. Freedom of expression
13. Freedom of peaceful assembly and association, including the right to join a trade union
14. Right to marry and found a family
15. Right to an effective remedy before a national authority *(not included in Human Rights Act 1998)*
16. Freedom from discrimination on grounds of sex, race, colour, language, religion, etc.

### Protocol No. 1

1. Right to peaceful enjoyment of possessions
3. Right to education. Parental right to the education of their children in conformity with their own religious and philosophical convictions
4. Right to free elections with a secret ballot

### Protocol No. 4
*(not ratified by UK, nor in Human Rights Act 1998)*

1. Freedom from imprisonment for debt
3. Freedom of movement for persons
4. Right to enter and remain in one's own country
5. Freedom from collective expulsion

There are other Protocols which are yet to be ratified by the UK and not included in the Human Rights Act (Wadham and Mountfield, 2000, pp. 142–8). However, Protocol No. 6 (abolition of death penalty except in time of war) is included in the Human Rights Act 1998.

---

illegal for public authorities, including the government, the courts and public bodies discharging public functions to act in a way incompatible with the European Convention on Human Rights.

In theory, the Human Rights Act preserves parliamentary sovereignty. Judges do not have the power to strike down Acts of Parliament (as they do in Canada, for example). Instead, they are able to declare a law 'incompatible with the Convention', which should prompt the government and Parliament to change the law through new fast-track procedures. However, Bogdanor (in Seldon, 2001, pp. 146–8) argues that the Act 'alters considerably the balance between Parliament and the judiciary' and enables judges 'to interpret parliamentary legislation in terms of a higher law, the European Convention'. Thus 'the Human Rights Act in effect makes the European Convention the fundamental law of the land.' The argument is contentious. Morris (also in Seldon, 2001, p. 378) seems sceptical

of the argument that 'major social and political change will be driven by judges rather than legislators', pointing out that 'there is little evidence of this in those countries in which the Convention has long been domestically incorporated'.

While it is perhaps too early to assess the longer-term impact of the Human Rights Act on the British constitution and the relations between the judiciary and the legislature, it has certainly had some significant immediate implications for British politics and law. Thus the European Court of Human Rights declared in 1998 that some provisions in the Representation of the People Act limiting election expenditure violated the Convention, requiring the rewriting of UK legislation on political funding. In 2001 the Court upheld an action by residents in the Heathrow area which claimed that night flights involved an infringement of a basic human right (to sleep), a judgment that was later overturned. Yet, ironically, the Human Rights Act has not prevented some British citizens from being deprived of what is generally regarded as a far more basic and important right. Following the attack on the Twin Towers on 11 September 2001, the British government introduced emergency legislation to deal with terrorism, including powers to hold terrorist suspects without trial, which would normally infringe Article 5 of the Convention – the right to liberty. However, Article 15 allows the suspension of rights in an emergency. Further measures to counter terrorism followed after the bomb attacks on London in July 2005, and the failed attack on Glasgow airport in 2007. The courts have a delicate balance to strike over increased government restrictions on civil liberties in response to the very real threat of terrorism.

## SUMMARY

- Britain has not in the past accepted the need for a strict separation of powers between legislature, executive and judiciary. Reforms initiated in 2003 and completed in 2009 involved the transfer of the House of Lords' judicial functions to a new Supreme Court.

- Judges remain unrepresentative of the communities they serve. They are predominantly elderly, white, male and come from an upper middle-class background.

- While the image of the police in Britain has generally been positive, parts of the police force have been accused of racist, sexist and homophobic attitudes and behaviour, although efforts have been made to remedy this.

- There is no clear coherent system of administrative law in Britain, although there are a number of channels for citizens wishing to make a complaint against government and public authorities, including the ordinary courts, tribunals, public inquiries and the ombudsman system.

- Although Britain was an early signatory to the European Convention on Human Rights, this was only incorporated into British law in 1998. This has implications for the constitutional principle of parliamentary sovereignty, even though this is formally maintained, as judges have not been given the power to strike out laws incompatible with ECHR.

## QUESTIONS FOR DISCUSSION

- Why was the new UK Supreme Court introduced? How far is it comparable with other supreme courts, such as the US Supreme Court?

- How far and in what respects might some judges be considered to be biased?

- How far can the police be trusted to act impartially towards all sections of the community? Are procedures for complaints against the police adequate?

- Should trial by jury be retained?

- Are human rights adequately protected in Britain?

- Has the Human Rights Act effectively destroyed the sovereignty of Parliament?

- How far is it possible to reconcile requirements to protect the community from terrorism with full respect for individual human rights and freedoms?

# FURTHER READING

On key themes covered by this chapter, including the rule of law, the executive and the courts and redress of grievances, see Madgwick and Woodhouse (1995), *The Law and Politics of the Constitution*, and for New Labour's constitutional reforms see Jowell and Oliver (2007) and Bogdanor (2009). Books on constitutional and administrative law include Alder (2009), Carroll (2009) and Barnett (2009).

On the judiciary, Griffith (1997), *The Politics of the Judiciary* is still worth reading, although it needs updating.

On rights, and the debate leading up to the Human Rights Act, 1998, see Klug *et al.* (1996), the special issue of *Political Quarterly* (1997), 68:2, April–June, and Freeman (1997). Contrasting views of the Human Rights Act can be found in the comments of Bogdanor and Morris in Seldon (2001), *The Blair Effect*. Further background and critical analysis is provided by the director of Liberty, John Wadham, in Blackburn and Plant(1999), *Constitutional Reform* and by Lester and Clapinska in Jowell and Oliver (2004), *The Changing Constitution*. A more detailed account, including key texts, is provided in Wadham and Mountfield (2000), *Human Rights Act 1998*.

For the UK Supreme Court and associated constitutional reforms, see Ryan (2004). For more depth refer to Le Sueur in Jowell and Oliver (2004). See the Ministry of Justice, www.justice.gov.uk and also www.judiciary.gov.uk for key documents and latest developments.

# Britain and Europe

The UK's membership of the European Community (later Union) from 1973 has had massive implications not only for Britain's politics and public policy, but also for its whole system of government and fundamental constitutional principles. Yet Britain's long involvement with the European Union has become increasingly contentious, dividing existing parties, and assisting the emergence of new ones hostile to the whole European project. The European Union itself now faces many difficult challenges, soon after arguably its greatest triumphs: the establishment of a single European currency in 2002, and the political unification of a continent once divided by the Iron Curtain, following the enlargements of 2004 and 2007. These challenges now include a massive ongoing financial and economic crisis, on top of new divisions within a larger, more diverse European Union, and difficult relations with the USA, Russia, China and the developing world over trade, the environment and security issues. This chapter analyzes in more depth the development, institutions and processes of the European Union, and the often problematic relationship between Britain and Europe. We conclude with a brief examination of the future of the EU, and UK's role within it, or conceivably outside it.

## Britain and Europe 1945–97

The overriding objective of Robert Schuman and Jean Monnet, the founding fathers of the new Europe, following centuries of conflict, was the prevention of future war, although it was certainly hoped that closer European integration would also help rebuild European agricultural and industrial production. The Schuman Plan (1950) sought to lock the economies of France and Germany so closely together as to render another war between them impossible. It envisaged an ongoing process of integration of key policy areas that would lead over time to closer union, as states and peoples experienced the practical benefits of co-operation. Thus in 1952 France, Germany, Italy and the Benelux states (Belgium, the Netherlands, and Luxembourg) formed the **European Coal and Steel Community** (ECSC) with extensive powers to regulate the coal and steel industries in the

● **The European Coal and Steel Community** (ECSC) Precursor of EC/EU established in 1952 following Treaty of Paris

member states. The same countries went on to sign the Treaty of Rome in 1957. This inaugurated the **European Economic Community** (EEC), which established a customs union with internal free trade and a common external tariff, and the European Atomic Energy Authority (Euratom). The Common Agricultural Policy (CAP) initially absorbed three-quarters of the EEC budget, although subsequently increasing funds were devoted to social and regional policies.

British governments initially took no part in these developments. At the end of the Second World War British concerns and interests appeared different from the countries that formed the EEC. Britain retained the illusion of great power status, one of the 'big three' which had defeated Nazi Germany, with a still extensive overseas empire. Its political system was stable, its economic and financial interests remained world-wide. Not having experienced the miseries of defeat and occupation, British politicians and the British public generally saw no imperative need for closer economic and political integration with other European states. Britain's empire and Commonwealth, coupled with the 'special relationship' with the United States of America, provided strong alternative influences on Britain in the period immediately after the war. Although Winston Churchill called for 'a kind of United States of Europe' in a speech at Zurich in 1946, he made it plain that Britain would be among the 'friends and sponsors of the new Europe' rather than an integral part of it. Thus Britain did not join the European Coal and Steel Community in 1952, nor the European Economic Community (EEC) in 1958. Indeed, the UK government took the lead in establishing a rival trading block, the European Free Trade Association (EFTA).

Political and economic developments combined to provoke a rapid reassessment of Britain's relations with the EEC from the late 1950s onwards. The rapid liquidation of the British Empire was one factor. The opposition of the USA and even some Commonwealth countries to the disastrous 1956 Anglo-French Suez expedition was a defining moment, which destroyed lingering illusions of Britain's world power status. Continuing economic problems evidenced by low growth, adverse trade balances and recurring sterling crises contrasted with the strong economic performance of the six EEC countries after 1958. Thus Harold Macmillan's Conservative government sought entry in 1961. Diplomatic negotiations were abruptly terminated in 1963 with the veto of the French President, General de Gaulle. Wilson's Labour government met a similar rebuff when it tried to enter the EEC in 1967. It was only the removal of de Gaulle from power which finally enabled Heath's Conservative government to join the **European Community**, along with Ireland and Denmark, in 1973.

Yet the British commitment to Europe was never wholehearted, either at elite or mass level. EC membership was sold to the British public on the basis of presumed economic benefits – higher growth and living standards. The European Community's political implications, evident from its founding fathers and from the Treaty of Rome, were largely ignored. This was not (as has sometimes been suggested) a deliberate conspiracy by British governments to keep people in the dark. It simply reflected a widespread British view that joining the **Common Market** (as it was then widely called in Britain) was essentially an economic or 'bread and butter' issue. (Indeed, opponents made much of the projected effect of entry on the price of a standard loaf and a pound of butter.).

While the costs of membership in terms of increased food prices were soon evident, the economic benefits were not immediately obvious. This was partly because the UK joined too late to influence the shape and early development of the EC. Thus the UK had to sign up to rules designed by others to meet the economic needs of the original six member states. The British economy with its relatively small agricultural sector was unlikely to benefit significantly from the Common Agricultural Policy. Moreover, 1973, the year of UK entry, was

---

● **The European Economic Community** (EEC) Established 1958, along with Euratom (European Atomic Energy Community) after the 1957 Treaty of Rome

---

● **The European Community** (EC) – or **The European Communities** Technically resulted from merger of ECSC, EEC and Euratom in 1965

---

● **The Common Market** Term used in Britain to describe the EEC in its early years. The Rome Treaty did involve a Common Market, but promised more.

also the year of the energy crisis which signalled the end of the post-war economic boom. While the original members of the Community had enjoyed substantial growth rates and sharply rising living standards which ensured the continuing popularity of European integration, the early years of UK membership were accompanied by 'stagflation' rather than the promised sustained higher rates of growth. Britain had joined the party too late.

Thus Community membership remained politically controversial in Britain. The only mainstream political party consistently in favour were the Liberals, and subsequently Liberal Democrats (and even they contained a few dissidents). The majority of Conservatives supported, with varying degrees of enthusiasm, membership of the European Community sought by the party leadership, although an (initially small) minority remained strongly opposed. The controversial former Cabinet Minister Enoch Powell argued that entry into the European Community involved the destruction of national and parliamentary sovereignty. In the 1974 election he advised a vote for Labour, who had promised a referendum on EC membership, and he himself left the Conservatives for the Ulster Unionists.

Labour was split over Europe. Although Prime Minister Wilson had sought entry to Europe in 1967, after the election defeat in 1970 most of the party switched to oppose entry. Much of the left saw the European Community as a rich man's capitalist club, providing the economic underpinning for NATO, although Labour's social democrats, led by deputy leader Roy Jenkins, remained enthusiastically pro-Europe. The return of a Labour government under Wilson in 1974 entailed a (largely cosmetic) renegotiation of the terms of entry and a referendum in 1975, resulting in a two-thirds majority for staying in. Yet although the Labour government officially recommended a Yes vote, a third of the Cabinet campaigned on the opposite side, and Labour remained deeply divided on the issue. In 1981 some pro-European social democrats left the party for the new SDP. By 1983 Labour, now led by the veteran left-winger Michael Foot, was pledged to withdrawal from the European Community without a referendum.

Most Conservatives were then far more enthusiastic about Europe. After all, Britain's membership of the EC was a Conservative achievement, strongly supported by Mrs Thatcher in her early years as leader. Although she had belligerently demanded and obtained a rebate from the EC budget, she went on to sign and endorse the 1986 Single European Act, regarded as the embodiment of free market principles. It was only towards the end of her premiership that Thatcher's own reservations on European integration and the threat it presented to Britain's national sovereignty became clearer:

> We have not successfully rolled back the frontiers of the state in Britain only to see them re-imposed at a European level with a European superstate exercising a new dominance from Brussels. (Margaret Thatcher, speech at Bruges, 1988)

Even so, Thatcher (rather reluctantly) agreed to UK entry to the Exchange Rate Mechanism in October 1990, and it was only after her fall from power soon afterwards that her opposition to the whole European project intensified. John Major, her successor, seemed more enthusiastic about Europe:

> My aim for Britain in the Community can be simply stated. I want us to be where we belong. At the very heart of Europe. Working with our partners in building the future. (John Major, speech, 1991)

However, the Maastricht Treaty was to mark further divisions with Britain's European partners, as John Major's government negotiated an opt-out from the Social Chapter and monetary union. Indeed, the problems that Major's government encountered over Britain's brief membership of the Exchange Rate Mechanism and the ensuing catastrophe of 'Black Wednesday' in 1992 (see Chapter 2) fuelled increasing euroscepticism on the Conservative benches. At the same time the Labour Party leadership of Kinnock, Smith and Blair reversed its earlier hostility and became steadily more favourable to what was now called the **European Union**. Labour liked the Social Chapter (which afforded some protection to workers) and

---

● **The European Union** (EU) Term adopted after the Treaty of the European Union (TEU or Maastricht Treaty) 1992

approved the expansion of EU regional policy that benefited some of the more deprived areas of the United Kingdom where Labour was traditionally strong. They were not opposed in principle to European monetary integration. Thus the two major parties had almost reversed their positions compared with 20 years previously.

## The development of the European ideal: integration and enlargement

The history of the European Union can be presented as a triumphal process towards ever deeper European integration and a steady expansion in membership, population and boundaries. Yet the progress has often been slow and uneven, while there been some increasing tension between enlargement and integration, between widening and deepening the European Community/Union. Needless to say, both enlargement and integration had considerable implications for the government and politics of the United Kingdom

One indication of the success of any club is the enthusiasm of new members to join it. By that token the European Union has been very successful. The original six members of what began as the European Economic Community in 1958 were joined in 1973 by three more, the United Kingdom, Ireland and Denmark. Greece joined in 1981 and Spain and Portugal in 1986. German reunification following the fall of the Berlin Wall in 1989 led to a significant increase in the size of both the German state and the population of the EU. In 1995 Austria, Finland and Sweden joined, bringing the number of member states to 15. In 2004 a further ten states, mainly from former communist eastern Europe, became part of the EU, following the enthusiastic endorsement of membership by their citizens in referendums. Bulgaria and Romania brought the number of member states to 27 in 2007. Meanwhile a start date of 3 October 2005 was agreed for the beginning of accession talks with Turkey (*The Guardian,* 17 December 2004), although the proposal remains contentious. Other states, such as Croatia and Serbia, remain eager to join the club.

Thus the EU remains fairly popular not only with the original six founding states, but among a substantial majority of the peoples of states which joined from 1973 onwards. Ireland appeared to prosper economically from EU membership, at least until the 2008 recession. For Greece, Spain and Portugal, which had only recently escaped from dictatorships, joining the European club brought both political and economic benefits. Many of the former eastern European states, and new states established following the collapse of the USSR, similarly hoped for increased political stability and economic growth from being locked into the western European political and economic system.

Progress towards closer economic and political integration was initially rendered more difficult by the unanimity rule, as common policies required the full consent of all member states and could be prevented by the veto of any member. Thus after the early progress of the European Communities, the pace of European integration slowed in the 1970s and early 1980s. Crucially, non-tariff barriers to trade still impeded the development of a full European internal market. It was only in 1986 that the Single European Act established a timetable for the elimination of non-tariff barriers to trade and competition by 1992.

The 1992 Maastricht Treaty or Treaty of the European Union (TEU) marked further progress towards closer integration, particularly towards monetary union and the adoption of a Social Chapter by 11 of the 12 member states (with Britain initially opting out). It also involved agreement on a common foreign and security policy, and co-operation on justice and home affairs. The new momentum towards closer integration was maintained with the Treaties of Amsterdam (1997) and Nice (2000) and particularly with the formal inauguration of the common currency, the Euro, in 1999 and the introduction of notes and coins to replace national currencies in 12 member states in 2002. However, the Euro did not become the single European currency for the whole of the European Union, as some older member states (UK, Denmark, Sweden) declined to participate, and new member states who joined in 2004 and 2007 were not ready.

Indeed, enlargement of the European Union raised some doubts on the capacity of the EU to absorb so many new states without impeding

**Map 15.1**    Europe and EU Membership

Founding members (1952 ECSC; 1958 EEC and Euratom): Belgium, France, (West) Germany, Italy, Luxembourg, Netherlands. The territory of the German Democratic Republic (East Germany) was incorporated into a united Germany in 1990.

First enlargement (1973): Denmark, Ireland, United Kingdom.

Mediterranean enlargement: Greece (1981); Portugal, Spain (1986).

EFTA enlargement (1995): Austria, Finland, Sweden.

2004 enlargement: Cyprus, Czech Republic, Estonia, Hungary, Latvia, Lithuania, Malta, Poland, Slovakia, Slovenia.

2007: Bulgaria, Romania.

Key
1 Croatia
2 Bosnia and Herzegovina
3 Serbia
4 Montenegro
5 Former Yugoslav Republic of Macedonia
6 Albania
7 Switzerland
8 Moldova
9 Slovenia

*Source*: Originally used in Andrew Heywood, *Global Politics*, Palgrave Macmillan, 2011, p. 497.

further progress towards closer integration. Each of the previous enlargements from 1973 to 1995 had shifted the balance of power and interests within the EC/EU, and each put some strain on existing institutions and policies. The 2004 and 2007 enlargements, involving 12 new member states, required an extensive modification of institutions and procedures. There was also a need for some adjustments to existing EU policies, particularly the Common Agricultural Policy. The increased disparities between regions following enlargement required a significant redirection of social and regional funds, which inevitably involved some reductions in regional aid directed to poorer regions of older member states, including Britain.

## Britain and Europe 1997–2010

Blair came to power in 1997 with an apparently much more positive attitude to the European Union, and his government quickly signed up to the Social Chapter (from which John Major had secured an opt-out). Yet after three full terms of Labour in power, the divisions between Britain and much of continental Europe remain, particularly on the key issues of monetary union, economic policy and foreign policy.

Monetary union is perhaps the most significant step towards European integration that has been taken since the establishment of the European Community, yet Britain remains outside. While Blair insisted that the government was committed to joining the Euro in principle, his Chancellor, Gordon Brown, sounded a more cautious note, laying down five stringent economic conditions. Following Labour's second landslide election victory in 2001 over a Conservative party fighting to 'Save the pound', there were predictions that Labour would seek entry early in the new Parliament. Yet this did not happen. The real obstacle was less perhaps Brown's economic conditions than Labour's commitment, made in opposition, to hold a referendum should the government seek to join the Euro. Opinion polls continued to suggest that the government would have great difficulty in winning such a referendum. The prospect of Britain joining the Euro has since receded (although some economists have argued that, following the credit crunch and recession of

2008–9 and the depreciation of the pound against the Euro, it might now be in Britain's interests). Others have maintained that the problems of the Eurozone from 2009 amply justify Brown's caution.

In 2004 Blair did commit his government to a referendum, planned for 2006, but on the issue of the proposed new European constitution rather than the single currency. The rejection of that constitution by French and Dutch voters appeared to the Labour government to render a British referendum unnecessary, although the new Conservative leader David Cameron disagreed (see Box 15.1). However, Prime Minister Brown alongside other European leaders signed the replacement Lisbon Treaty in 2007. This was finally ratified by all member states after a second Irish referendum and reluctant agreement by the Czech President in 2009.

Other issues have continued to divide the UK from Europe. Despite acceptance of the Social Chapter, the Labour government continued to champion flexible labour markets in the face of the more corporatist approach of the European Union and most other member states. New Labour appeared to prefer the American free market model of capitalism rather than the more interventionist 'Rhineland' or European alternative. More significant perhaps were differences over foreign policy, with the Labour government and the then Conservative opposition providing consistent support for the USA, in marked contrast to increasing French and German reservations over American policy in general and on Iraq and Israel in particular. The old tensions between Britain's relationship with Europe and its 'special relationship' with the USA that had plagued previous governments re-emerged.

Thus the UK is still widely perceived as an 'awkward partner' (George, 1998) in Europe. Yet other European countries have sometimes shared British reservations over the pace and extent of European integration. France has at times also appeared an 'awkward partner' particularly under President de Gaulle, who feared that French national sovereignty and interests might be subordinated in a federal Europe. Since then France has often been slow to implement EU regulations. Voters in Denmark initially rejected the Maastricht Treaty. Both Denmark and Sweden, along with the

# The row over the European Constitution and the Lisbon Treaty

Enlargement of the EU clearly required some revision of institutions and procedures. A new European Constitution was drafted to replace existing EU treaties (from Rome to Nice). Heads of government approved the text in 2004, but it required ratification by all member states. Most proceeded to ratify the constitution through parliamentary procedures, but several governments, including Britain, promised referendums. In the Netherlands and France referendums in 2005 resulted in the rejection of the constitution, which was now effectively dead. Following a 'period of reflection' member states agreed a new treaty signed in Lisbon in 2007, and finally ratified by all states in 2009.

This provoked a major row in Britain. All three major parties had promised a referendum on the European constitution. The Labour government argued Lisbon differed from the draft constitution and that a referendum was not required for an amending treaty. (A referendum had not been conceded by previous British governments on former treaties such as Maastricht, nor by most other EU member states.) The Conservatives, under new leader David Cameron, and worried by increasing support for the eurosceptic United Kingdom Independence Party (UKIP) on its right flank, gave a 'cast iron guarantee' of a referendum on the replacement Lisbon Treaty. They claimed this embodied key elements of the defunct constitution, including a new President and Foreign Minister. However, following the ratification of the Lisbon Treaty by all member states in 2009 ahead of the UK general election, Cameron dropped his proposed referendum, insisting instead that he would negotiate on the return of some EU powers to Britain. UKIP denounced this apparent U-turn.

UK, initially declined to join the Euro. Germany and France long resisted overdue reforms of the Common Agricultural Policy. The Irish threatened to derail the Nice Treaty (together with EU enlargement) by voting to reject it, a decision reversed by a second referendum in 2002. The rejection of the EU constitution in 2005 by voters in two of the original six member states, France and the Netherlands, was an even bigger shock. This was followed by the Irish voters' initial rejection of the replacement Lisbon Treaty (to be followed by acceptance in a second referendum, after reassurances). However, it is the British who are still widely perceived as the most reluctant Europeans.

## The European Union: superstate or inter-governmental organization?

From its beginning there has been controversy over the nature of the European Community/Union and the direction in which it is going. Some talked from the start of a United States of Europe, whose political and economic clout would match that of the USA. They had no reservations in proposing a federal system on US lines, in which supreme power or sovereignty would be effectively divided between two or more levels of government. Others envisaged a weaker form of association, sometimes termed a confederation rather than a federation. General de Gaulle, the former French President, talked of a *Europe des Patries*, essentially an inter-governmental association of sovereign nation states. Fifty years after its original establishment the nature and scope of Europe's political union remains both unclear and contentious.

Much of continental Europe is untroubled by talk of federalism. Countries such as Germany, Belgium or Spain, already federal or quasi-federal countries, see the European Union as just another tier in a system of multi-level governance. Sovereignty is not lost, but pooled. For a substantial body of opinion in Britain, however, federalism is the dreaded 'f-word.' Euroscepticism and europhobia have been fed by fears of the EU's political agenda and the threat to British national identity and the sovereignty of the Westminster parliament represented in particular by European monetary

## TIMELINE 15.1

# *Europe and the United Kingdom*

| | |
|---|---|
| **1950** | The Schuman Declaration (or Schuman Plan) |
| **1951** | Treaty of Paris to establish the European Coal and Steel Community (instituted in 1952) involving France, Germany, Italy, Benelux countries |
| **1957** | Treaty of Rome to establish European Economic Community (EEC) and Euratom (established in 1958) |
| **1960** | UK with six other states forms the rival European Free Trade Association (EFTA) |
| **1961** | UK (Macmillan Conservative government) applies to join EEC (French veto by President de Gaulle terminated negotiations in 1963) |
| **1967** | Second UK attempt to join EEC by Labour (ended by fresh French veto) |
| **1973** | UK (Heath Conservative government), Ireland and Denmark join the EC |
| **1975** | Labour government recommends 'Yes' vote in referendum on whether UK should stay in EC after renegotiation of terms. Two-thirds vote 'Yes'. |
| **1979** | First direct elections for European Parliament |
| **1981** | Greece joins the European Community |
| **1983** | Labour Party pledged to UK withdrawal from EC without a referendum |
| **1986** | Spain and Portugal join the EC |
| **1986** | Single European Act signed |
| **1990** | UK (Thatcher government) joins Exchange Rate Mechanism (ERM) |
| **1990** | After reunification of Germany, former East Germany becomes part of EC |

| | |
|---|---|
| **1992** | Maastricht Treaty (TEU). John Major secures opt-out from Social Chapter and monetary integration. 'Black Wednesday' – UK forced out of ERM. |
| **1995** | Austria, Finland and Sweden join European Union |
| **1999** | The Euro becomes the official currency for 11 EU member states |
| **1999** | European Commission resigns following fraud and corruption allegations |
| **2000** | Nice Treaty |
| **2002** | Euro notes and coins replace national currencies in 12 EU member states |
| **2004** | Ten more countries join European Union |
| **2004** | Blair promises a referendum on the new constitution for the EU |
| **2004** | EU leaders agree start date (October 2005) for accession talks for Turkey |
| **2005** | Voters in France and the Netherlands reject the proposed new European constitution. Blair scraps plans for a referendum in Britain. |
| **2007** | Heads of government sign up to replacement Lisbon Treaty |
| **2007** | Romania and Bulgaria join EU |
| **2008** | Irish voters reject Lisbon Treaty in referendum |
| **2009** | Lisbon Treaty is finally ratified after a second Irish referendum |
| **2009** | Crisis in Eurozone following economic recession, e.g. Greek and Irish bailouts |

union and the supremacy of European Union law over the law of member states.

It was fears of the growing power of EU institutions which led to the formal declaration at the Maastricht Treaty of the clumsily-named **principle of subsidiarity**. The Treaty requires the Community 'to take action . . . only if and in as far as the objective of the proposed action cannot be sufficiently achieved by the Member States' and can 'by reason of its scale and effects be better achieved by the Community'. This may be seen as an application of a wider principle that decisions ought to be taken at the lowest level consistent with efficiency. One implication is that decisions might be devolved below the nation-state level to regional government or local government. Indeed, the Maastricht Treaty gave some encouragement to such devolution of power, establishing a new Committee of the Regions to represent such sub-national interests. The devolution of power to national executives and assemblies in the UK, and some former pressure for English regional government fitted into this agenda.

## The institutions and processes of the European Union

The controversy over the very nature of the European Union discussed in the last section is an essential preliminary to any appreciation of the issues surrounding its very complex institutions and processes. From the start there was a tension between the interests of the EC/EU as a whole and the interests of the separate member states and this tension is fully reflected in EC/EU institutions. Those who wish to see and those who fear the development of a European 'superstate' or a federal United States of Europe can find in the suprana-

tional institutions all the elements of a sovereign state. There is a kind of executive in the form of the European Commission, a legislature (at least potentially) in the shape of the European Parliament, and a judiciary in the European Court of Justice (see Table 15.1). Other supranational bodies include the Economic and Social Committee, the Court of Auditors, the European Central Bank and the European Investment Bank. Yet alongside these institutions which are all supposed to serve the interests of the EC/EU as a whole there are others which look after the interests of member states. These include the Council of Ministers, consisting of national politicians served by their own national civil servants in the Committee of Permanent Representatives (COREPER), but increasingly more important than either, the European Council, involving regular meetings of the heads of government of member states. Moreover, the Treaty of Lisbon provides for a larger role for national parliaments, along with increased power for the European Parliament.

Even in the early days when there were only six member states, decision-making was not made easy in the Council of Ministers by the unanimity rule, which meant that the government of any single member state could prevent action by using their veto. In 1965 French ministers refused to attend the Council of Ministers, effectively preventing any decisions. The 'empty chair crisis' was eventually resolved by the 'Luxembourg compromise' under which the veto was retained for issues of great importance to member states. However a system of qualified majority voting (QMV) is used for other issues. Progressive enlargement of the EC/EU has made it more necessary to streamline decision-making, and this was extended in the Lisbon Treaty. Today some matters are decided by simple majority, many others by qualified majority, but the right of veto is still jealously guarded by member states, particularly the UK, for some key policy areas.

While some of these procedural issues are of mind-boggling complexity, the crucial point is not too difficult to grasp. The European Union involves a curious constitutional hybrid, part embryo state, part intergovernmental organization. Throughout its history there has been a built-in tension between its quasi-federal and inter-governmental institu-

---

● **Principle of subsidiarity** 'The Community shall act within the limits of the powers conferred on it by this Treaty and of the objectives assigned to it therein. In areas which do not fall within its exclusive competence, the Community shall take action, in accordance with the **principle of subsidiarity**, only if and in as far as the objectives of the proposed action cannot be sufficiently achieved by the Member States and can therefore, by reason of the scale or effects of the proposed action, be better achieved by the Community. Any action by the Community shall not go beyond what is necessary to achieve the objectives of this Treaty.' (*Article 3b of the Treaty Establishing the European Union*).

**Table 15.1**    The location, composition and functions of key European Union institutions

| Institution | Location | Composition | Functions | Comments |
|---|---|---|---|---|
| European Commission | Brussels | 1 Commissioner for each member state – serves for 5 years President and Commission approved by the European Parliament | Proposes laws Drafts budget Administers laws and policies | Commissioners swear allegiance to EU, head Directorates |
| European Court of Justice | Luxembourg | 27 judges, 1 from each member state | Rules on EU law Adjudicates in disputes | EU law supreme over state law |
| European Parliament | Strasbourg and Brussels | MEPs directly elected by voters in member states (by regional list system) | Largely consultative, but increasing role in legislation and budget | MEPs sit in European parties, not in national blocks |
| Economic and Social Committee | Brussels | Representatives of interests | Purely consultative | Marginalized in modern EU |
| Committee of the Regions | Brussels | Representatives of regions of EU | Consultative role, particularly on regional policy | Established after Maastricht Treaty |
| Council of Ministers | Largely in Brussels | Relevant ministers of member states | Defends member state interests | Unanimity still needed on major issues |
| COREPER (Committee of Permanent Representatives) | Brussels | Civil servants on secondment from member states | Bureaucracy serving Council of Ministers | Does initial work for Council of Ministers |
| European Council | Peripatetic | Heads of government | Forum for resolving key issues | From 1974, now crucial |

tions and interests. Where the balance of power really lies is partly a matter of perception, but partly also may vary over time and particularly over policy areas.

The introduction under the Lisbon Treaty of two new posts, a European Council President and a High Representative of the Union for Foreign Affairs and Security Policy, aroused further concerns among Eurosceptics. The former UK Prime Minister Tony Blair was mentioned as a potential EU President, although his name was never formally put forward. Once the Treaty was

ratified, complex negotiations within EU institutions and member states resulted in the appointment of the former Belgian Prime Minister Herman van Rompuy as the new President, and the relatively little-known Labour peeress, Lady Ashton, as the High Representative. This outcome was widely interpreted to mean that real power would be retained by leaders of the major member states, and so far this seems to be true. Confusingly, there is still a President of the European Commission (José Manuel Barroso), as well as the President of the Council.

## The European Commission

The European Commission is commonly perceived as the centre of the EU's supranational authority. Although it has not become the effective executive for a federal Europe envisaged by Jean Monnet, it retains a key role in the initiation of legislation and new regulations, and has detailed responsibility for the administration of the European Union. While Commissioners are nominated by member states, they are not supposed to look after the interests of their own country but have to swear an undertaking to serve the Union as a whole. They each take charge of at least one of the Commission's Directorates responsible for a particular policy area or service. Until the 2004 enlargement the larger member states nominated two Commissioners each, while the smaller countries nominated one. Now each country regardless of size nominates one. The President of the Commission is a key political figure. Past Presidents include Britain's Roy Jenkins and the controversial French politician, Jacques Delors.

While Eurosceptics lament the power of the European Commission it is often suggested that this supranational body has progressively lost its leadership role (Nugent, 2010, pp. 135–7). From the start the Commission was relatively less dominant than the equivalent High Authority in the European Coal and Steel Community, and the Commission by itself proved unable to lead and develop further European integration in the face of French opposition under de Gaulle. It was only intergovernmental conferences that finally succeeded in breaking the deadlock and restoring some forward momentum to the European project. This reflected the reality of the power of the member states. Since then the Council of Ministers and the European Council (effectively a new supreme intergovernmental institution not envisaged by the founding fathers) have gained at the expense of the Commission. In 1984 the Secretary General of the European Commission complained of the 'institutional drift away from the spirit, and indeed the letter, of the Treaties of Rome'. He argued that 'the Community system is gradually degenerating into intergovernmental negotiation', which he blamed on the unanimity rule and 'the constant intervention of the European Council'. The prestige of the Commission was further damaged by revelations of fraud and corruption. These led to the resignation of the entire Commission in 1999 and the initiation of a reform programme. These developments obliged the Commission to take more notice of the European Parliament, which in 2004 declined to accept the proposed new Commission until changes were made in key posts.

## The European Court of Justice

The Court of Justice is the supreme judicial body in the European Union. One judge is nominated by each member state for a six-year period (renewable). The Court interprets and rules on European Union law and adjudicates in disputes between EU institutions and member states. European law overrides the national law of member states and has to be implemented, although implementation has sometimes been delayed. The increasing workload of the ECJ led to delays in obtaining judgements, so that a subsidiary General Court (formerly the Court of First Instance) was introduced to speed up the judicial process. However, national courts are also required to apply European law and existing case law of the European Court of Justice. This principle has already been accepted by the House of Lords (Craig in Jowell and Oliver, 2004).

## The European Parliament

The European Parliament gained some additional authority and legitimacy following the introduction of direct elections in 1979, although consistently low turnouts by voters in Britain and increasingly in other countries suggest some lack of interest in democracy at the European level. Part of the problem is that these elections do not appear to decide very much. National elections in Britain, France, Germany and other countries may lead to the fall of governments and, sometimes, significant changes in policy. However, elections for the European Parliament have little if any immediate impact on the government and decision-making of the European Union, even though it has gained additional powers from the Single European Act and Maastricht Treaty.

Each member state elects a number of MEPs (Members of the European Parliament) roughly in

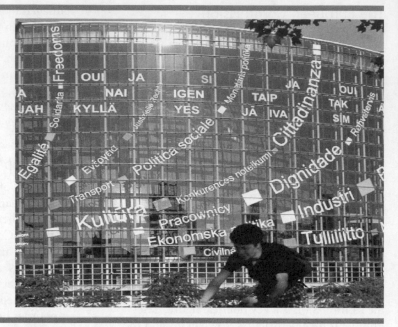

**Image 15.1  The European Parliament building, Strasbourg**

Often dismissed as a talking shop, the European Parliament has acquired more powers in recent years. The multi-lingual slogans on the parliament building in Strasbourg underline the practical problems involved in the large and growing number of official languages in which EU institutions have to conduct their business. MEPs can address the parliament in their own language. An army of translators almost instantaneously converts the speech into all the official EU languages, so that MEPs, officials and visitors can listen to it in their own language through headphones. Another problem is multi-site working. While most mains sessions are held in  Strasbourg, much committee work is undertaken at Brussels, and administrative support is provided from Luxembourg.

proportion to the size of population, but allowing some over-representation of the smaller states. Germany has 99 MEPs, France, the UK and Italy 78 each, other countries fewer, down to Malta with just five. There are currently 732 MEPs in all. Until 1999 elections for the European Parliament in Britain were conducted under the 'first past the post' system, leading to wildly fluctuating party representation at Strasbourg. Other member states used some version of proportional representation, mostly a regional party list system, which Britain adopted in 1999.

In practice, elections for the European Parliament involve large remote electoral areas, generally little-known candidates, and predominantly national rather than European issues, which may help to explain the low and declining turnout figures. Until 2004 the turnout in Britain was invariably the lowest by far in the European Union – only one in four bothered to vote in 1999. In 2004 UK elections for the European Parliament were held on the same day as local elections, while trials of postal ballots also raised turnout levels to 38 per cent, but in 2009 it fell back to 34.3 per cent. Meanwhile turnout levels fell markedly in some older member states. Surprisingly, some of the new member states recorded even lower voting figures in both 2004 and 2009 (see Comparative Politics

15.1) despite the enthusiasm their citizens had earlier shown for joining the EU. Only those countries where voting is compulsory (e.g. Belgium) have high turnouts. The average EU-wide turnout figure is 43.2 per cent.

Once elected, MEPs do not sit in national blocks but in European party groups. Thus British Labour MEPs form part of the Alliance of Socialists and Democrats (S&D), while the Liberal Democrats belong to the Alliance of Liberals and Democrats for Europe (ALDE). Conservative MEPs used to belong to the European People's Party (EPP), but after the 2009 elections they are now part of a much smaller new party, the European Conservatives and Reformists (ECR) group, some of whose members are perceived as further to the right. The 13 UKIP MEPs belong to the Europe of Freedom and Democracy group (EFD), critical of the EU. Two British Green Party MEPs, two SNP and one PC belong to the Greens/European Free Alliance (Greens/EFA). Four other British MEPs (including 2 BNP) are not attached to any official group. No party has an overall majority. The European People's Party (EPP), with 265 MEPs after the 2009 election, but with no UK members, is the largest party.

Although European Parliament elections should be about EU institutions and policies, in practice

## COMPARATIVE POLITICS 15.1
# Turnout for the 2009 European Parliament election

| Over 60% | 50–60% | 40–50% | 30–40% | Under 30% |
|---|---|---|---|---|
| Belgium 90.3 | Cyprus 59.4 | Austria 45.3 | Bulgaria 38.9 | Czech Republic 28.2 |
| Italy 66.5 | Denmark 59.5 | Estonia 43.2 | Hungary 36.2 | Lithuania 20.9 |
| Luxembourg 91 | Greece 52.6 | Finland 40.3 | Netherlands 36.9 | Poland 24.5 |
| Malta 78.8 | Ireland 57.6 | France 40.1 | Portugal 37.0 | Romania 27.4 |
|  | Latvia 53.1 | Germany 43.3 | UK 34.3 | Slovakia 19.6 |
|  |  | Spain 46.0 |  | Slovenia 28.3 |
|  |  | Sweden 45.5 |  |  |

*Sources:* Nugent (2010, p. 191) and European Parliament website.

voters tend to be influenced rather more by the record of parties nationally, sometimes punishing parties in government. The 2009 elections, conducted in the wake of the credit crunch and recession, involved a swing to the right in many member states. Christian Democrats gained, partly at the expense of socialists and social democrats. One trend is some increase in support for eurosceptic or anti-European parties. Thus in Britain UKIP outpolled Labour and won 13 seats, compared with 12 in 2004 and just three in 1999.

Much criticism has been directed at an alleged 'democratic deficit' – the apparent weakness of democratic control and accountability within Europe. Yet while the European Parliament is often denounced as a mere talking shop with little real power, the same is widely alleged of many national parliaments, including Westminster (see Chapter 13). Indeed, recent reforms have given the European Parliament more involvement in legislation and the budget. The Commission has become more accountable to the European Parliament following the corruption scandal in 1999. In some respects MEPs arguably now have more influence over the Commission than backbench MPs at Westminster have over the British Cabinet (Nugent, 2010 pp.205–6).

The real problem for the European Parliament is the hybrid nature of the European Union and the power of intergovernmental bodies such as the Council of Ministers and the European Council. In so far as the governments of member states, accountable to national parliaments, often seem to take the crucial decisions, the influence of the European Parliament is likely to remain peripheral. Nor is it likely in these circumstances that voters will perceive European Parliament elections as important or meaningful. Yet there is an element of hypocrisy in some of the criticisms. Thus Eurosceptics routinely condemn the 'democratic deficit' at Strasbourg and Brussels but generally resist proposals to give the European Parliament more powers, because this would encroach on the sovereignty of nation states and national parliaments.

## Bureaucracy in the European Union

The European Union is also widely criticized for its bureaucracy. If bureaucracy implies regulation and 'red tape', that is the essence of modern government and organization. If bureaucracy is taken to mean officialdom, there are obvious reasons why the bureaucracy of the European Union should appear cumbersome. The institutional complexity of the EU requires a similarly complicated bureaucracy. Besides the bureaucracy serving the Commission (which is small by the standards of that of member states), there are the officials of COREPER on whom the Council of Ministers and European Council are dependent, and the administrative support services for the European

Parliament and other EU organizations. Operating in three main sites hardly helps. While MEPs attend plenary sessions of the European Parliament at Strasbourg and committee meetings in Brussels, their officials are based in Luxembourg. More important still, the number of languages now spoken in the European Union requires an army of translators and interpreters. Procedures for approving new legislation or the annual budget are undoubtedly complex. Some of this complexity arises from the necessity of consulting and winning the approval of member states, key institutions and major interests within the EU.

## The impact of the European Union on the British state and government

The impact of membership of the European Union on the British state and system of government can be considered at various levels: firstly, its effect on the British constitution and long-established constitutional principles, secondly, its effect on the machinery of government, and thirdly, its impact on the day-to-day process of governing.

The impact of EU membership on the British constitution remains a highly contentious issue. For Eurosceptics, the European Union presents a continuing and increasing threat to British national sovereignty and the sovereignty of the Westminster parliament. Those better-disposed toward the EU emphasize the gains resulting from pooled sovereignty (e.g. Cope in Savage and Atkinson, 2001). Indeed, it can be argued that even if the UK was outside the EU, the British government's freedom of action would be constrained by the EU and its influence on world trade and investment, without it being able to influence EU policy. The European treaties signed by British governments are not so very different from other treaties; benefits are secured in exchange for undertakings that constrain future freedom of action.

Yet obligations arising from membership of the European Union do differ from the obligations imposed and freely accepted in other treaties and international associations both in scope and kind, particularly because of their major implications for a wide range of domestic policies. More specifically,

the British government and the Westminster parliament have had to accept the supremacy of EU law over UK law. It is true that the British government can influence the framing of EU law, and that there are procedures for consultation with the parliaments of member states, but it is difficult to deny that parliamentary sovereignty has been affected. Moreover, the use of referendums, the devolution Acts and the incorporation of the European Convention on Human Rights (incidentally unconnected with the European Union) all have damaging implications for parliamentary sovereignty (see Bogdanor in Seldon, 2001, and the discussion in Chapters 10, 14 and 16 of this book). Moreover some modern critics of the British constitution would deny that parliamentary sovereignty is a principle worth defending anyway (Mount, 1992, Hutton, 1995, 1997).

Membership of the European Union has had an impact on other aspects of the British system of government. The referendum was first introduced into Britain for a vote on whether the country should remain in the European Community, and has since become an accepted if irregular mechanism for settling controversial issues of a constitutional nature (such as devolution). Although pressures for electoral reform existed prior to EU membership, they were strengthened by European precedents. Thus in 1999 the regional list system was used for British elections to the European Parliament, while the system of election used for the Scottish Parliament and Welsh Assembly (the additional member system) followed another model familiar in Germany. Much the same could be said of demands for devolution and regional government, which predated membership of the European Community, but were reinforced by the parallel pressures for more national and regional autonomy in other member states, and by the development of European regional policy and the establishment of the Committee of the Regions. European legal principles and procedures have also begun to influence British law.

The machinery of government has been less affected than might have been expected by EU membership; the British state has adjusted its institutions and procedures incrementally rather than radically (Bulmer and Burch in Rhodes, 2000). Departmental organization has been scarcely affected. There is no separate department for Europe nor a Secretary of State for Europe in the Cabinet. As a consequence, there is also no Departmental Select Committee for Europe in the House of Commons, although there is a European Legislation Committee to examine (mainly) proposals for European legislation. There is now a European section of the Cabinet Secretariat, which signals the importance of Europe at the heart of British government. Even so, any one studying the changing formal structures of the Cabinet, Departments and Parliament over the last thirty years or so would hardly conclude that they had been much affected by EU membership.

Yet if the formal structure of British government appears little altered, the change in the working practices of ministers and civil servants, and in the business content of British government has been marked, reflecting the extensive consequences of EU membership for many areas of policy. 'On an administrative level, most senior British ministers and many senior civil servants spend many days each month commuting to Brussels for EU meetings. Much of the rest of their time back in Westminster and Whitehall is spent tackling questions relating to the EU agenda.' (Hix, in Dunleavy *et al.*, 2002, p. 48)

## The impact of European Union membership on British parties

Membership of the European Union has had considerable implications for British parties and the party system. Both the major parties have been split over Europe. The European issue was a major factor in the 1981 SDP split from Labour, which helped ensure Conservative dominance for 18 years. Conservative divisions over Europe date back at least as far as Labour's, but were initially less disastrous for the party, although Powell's break from the Conservatives in 1974, perhaps tipped a close election in Wilson's favour. Conflicting attitudes towards Europe caused tension within Thatcher's last administration, but became far more damaging under John Major, threatening the survival of his government and undermining any immediate prospects of a Conservative party recovery after the landslide defeat of 1997. If they appear

**Table 15.2** Party representation in the European Parliament following 2009 elections

| Party | Seats | UK MEPs |
|---|---|---|
| European People's Party (EPP) | 265 | |
| Progressive Alliance of Socialists and Democrats (S&D) | 184 | 13 Labour |
| Alliance of Liberals and Democrats for Europe | 84 | 11 Liberal Democrats |
| Greens/ European Free Alliance (Greens/EFA) | 55 | 2 Green, 2 SNP, 1 PC |
| European Conservatives and Reformists (ECR) | 54 | 25 Conservatives |
| European United Left/ Nordic Green Left | 35 | |
| Europe of Freedom and Democracy (EFD) | 32 | 13 UKIP |
| Non-aligned | 27 | 2 BNP |

*Sources*: European Parliament website and Nugent (2010, p. 196).

less marked today it is because the bulk of the Conservative party is now eurosceptic.

The Liberals and their Liberal Democrat successors profited from the divisions among their opponents, but otherwise their more consistent and united support for Europe has hardly profited them electorally. In elections for the European Parliament, the old single member plurality voting system gave them negligible representation until the introduction of a regional party list system in 1999 (see Table 15.3). The Green Party, whose best share of the vote in a UK-wide election ever, 15 per cent in 1989, gave them no seats, have also now secured better representation at Strasbourg. The natural concentration of nationalist party votes in Scotland and Wales has also given the SNP and Plaid Cymru seats in the European Parliament.

The European issue has also spawned new parties with some impact on the British political scene. Thus UKIP managed to pick up three seats on the new voting system introduced for European Parliament elections in 1999, and dramatically

**Table 15.3**   Votes and seats for UK parties in European Parliament elections, 1989–2009

| Party | 1989 Votes % | Seats | 1994 Votes % | Seats | 1999 Votes % | Seats | 2004 Votes % | Seats | 2009 Votes % | Seats |
|---|---|---|---|---|---|---|---|---|---|---|
| Con | 33 | 32 | 27 | 18 | 36 | 36 | 27 | 27 | 28 | 25 |
| Lab | 39 | 45 | 43 | 62 | 28 | 29 | 23 | 19 | 16 | 13 |
| Lib/LD | 6 | 0 | 16 | 2 | 13 | 10 | 15 | 12 | 14 | 11 |
| SNP | 3 | 1 | 3 | 2 | 3 | 2 | 1 | 2 | 2 | 2 |
| Plaid C | 1 | 0 | 1 | 0 | 2 | 2 | 1 | 1 | 1 | 1 |
| UKIP | | | | | 7 | 3 | 16 | 12 | 17 | 13 |
| Greens | 15 | 0 | 3 | 0 | 6 | 2 | 6 | 2 | 9 | 2 |
| BNP | | | | | | | | | 6 | 2 |

*Notes*: Elections up to 1994 under single member plurality system; from 1999 by regional party list system. Northern Ireland elects three MEPs by single transferable vote system.

*Sources*: various, including 2009 election statistics.

secured 12 seats in 2004, and 13 in 2009. However, UKIP is widely regarded as a single-issue party, and its strong performance in European elections has not yet been replicated in other British elections, where membership of the European Union has not been a major concern for most voters. The success of the British National Party in winning two seats at Strasbourg in 2009 attracted more notice, as the first significant breakthrough for this far-right party in a nationwide election.

The need to organize for European elections, and subsequently the need to become part of European parties in the European Parliament, has had some knock-on effects for the major British parties. For Labour this was perhaps less of a problem as the party was a member of the Socialist International, and leading Labour politicians were used to fraternizing with European socialists and social democrats. Thus they have been consistent members of the European socialist party (now the Progressive Alliance of Socialists and Democrats). The Conservatives found the search for acceptable ideologically sympathetic partners in Europe rather more difficult. The ideas of Christian Democracy which were influential on the centre-right on the continent involved too much state intervention and social partnership for a Thatcherite Conservative Party convinced of the virtues of the free market, while Christian Democrats found British Conservatives rather too right-wing. Thus for a time the Conservative MEPs were linked with a few

Spanish and Danish MPs in the European Democratic Group, then joined the main centre-right European People's Party. Following Cameron's leadership election pledge and the 2009 European elections they are now part of the small European Conservatives and Reformists group, whose ranks include some MPs accused of anti-semitism and homophobia, causing some embarrassment for the Conservatives' new progressive credentials.

How far closer involvement with other parties in Europe has influenced the political thinking of British parties is perhaps less clear. German and Swedish social democracy, and to a lesser extent perhaps French socialism, certainly helped influence the transformation of the Labour Party in the 1980s and 1990s. Labour's red rose symbol was borrowed from Francois Mitterrand's French socialists. Germany's Gerhard Schroeder was for a time closely linked with Tony Blair over the Third Way. British Conservatism seems to have been rather less susceptible to influence from its continental neighbours, although this may be changing as the party desperately seeks new ideas for running public services.

## The impact of the European Union on pressure group politics

As the impact of the European Union on UK public policy has grown, Brussels has become increasingly a natural target for pressure group activity (Mazey and Richardson, 1993). Some of this has simply involved British groups like the CBI or the NFU or British-based firms extending their range, acquiring their own offices in Brussels or employing professional lobbyists. However, many groups have sought to combine with comparable interests in other member states to establish Europe-wide groups, with potentially more muscle to influence EU policy. It is estimated that there are some 700 of these Europe-wide groups, of which over 65 per cent represent business, 20 per cent public interest groups, 10 per cent the professions and 6 per cent trade unions, consumers, environmentalists and other interests (Nugent, 2003, p. 281–2).

The European Commission is the main target of most groups, partly because of its powers and its readiness to consult with interests, especially 'eurogroups'. It is more difficult to lobby directly either the European Council or the Council of Ministers, so groups tend to seek to influence these bodies indirectly through national governments (Grant in Mazey and Richardson, 1993). The increasing influence of the European Parliament on the legislative process and the EU budget has led to more intensive lobbying at Strasbourg. There is also the Economic and Social Committee, the EU's own institution for representing group interests – yet most groups prefer to target more influential bodies directly (Nugent, 2010, p. 230).

---

### BOX 15.2

## Examples of Europe-wide interest groups

| Organization | Acronym |
| --- | --- |
| Committee of Agricultural Organisations in the EU | COPA |
| Union of Industrial and Employers' Confederation of Europe | UNICE |
| European Trade Union Confederation | ETUC |
| Association of European Automobile Constructors | ACEA |
| European Chemical Industry Council | CEFIC |
| European Association of Manufacturers of Business Machines and Information Technology | EUROBIT |
| Council of European Municipalities and Regions | CEMR |
| The European Citizen Action Service (represents and lobbies for the voluntary and community sector) | ECAS |

---

## The impact of the European Union on the British public

It has proved much more difficult to persuade the British people to engage with Europe. There is continued evidence of widespread ignorance and confusion about the EU and over specific institutions and issues. Although the only referendum held on Europe resulted in a substantial majority in favour of remaining in the European Community in 1975, opinion surveys since then have indicated a pervasive if ill-informed euroscepticism, and more recently opposition to the single currency (Hix in Dunleavy et al., 2002, pp. 53–8).

Curiously, however, major parties that have aligned themselves with eurosceptic public opinion have signally failed to profit electorally. Labour in 1983 and the Conservatives in 2001 both campaigned on a manifesto hostile or unsympathetic to Europe, and both managed to lose disastrously, indicating that it was not a priority issue for voters. However, while Labour has proved it can win general elections despite being out of step with voters on Europe, the problems of winning a referendum on the single issue of joining the Euro proved too daunting to risk.

## The impact of the European Union on UK policies

The actual impact of the EC/EU on UK policy has been increasingly significant but highly variable, depending on the policy area concerned. Fiscal policy has clearly been affected. UK entry to the EC involved the introduction of Value Added Tax, and there are EU rules that constrain taxation and expenditure, yet pressures to harmonize taxation have been generally resisted. Factors that favour greater convergence on, for example, duties on alcohol have more to do with the loss of revenue from smuggling than EU regulations.

Yet Simon Hix (in Dunleavy *et al.*, 2002, p. 48) claimed that while 'The British Government is still sovereign in deciding most of the main areas of public expenditure…this is only one aspect of policy making. In the area of *regulation,* over 80% of rules governing the production, distribution and exchange of goods, services and capital in the British market are decided by the EU.' Hix argued that this severely constrained British economic policy, preventing the adoption of either neo-Keynesian demand management and pump priming or a Thatcherite deregulatory supply-side policy.

Agriculture and fisheries policy has been dramatically affected, as EC entry required a shift from farm income support policies (with low prices) towards price support policies. Both systems involved agricultural subsidy, although the Common Agricultural Policy (CAP) notoriously led to periodic over-production, with 'butter mountains' and 'wine lakes'. Britain, with its relatively small agricultural sector, was always likely to be a net loser from the CAP. British farmers have, however, benefited substantially from EU subsidies. Persistent efforts to reform the CAP have been partly frustrated by the strength of farming interests in some member states. However, some British criticism of continental agriculture seems exaggerated or misplaced. The BSE and foot-and-mouth crises were substantially the consequence of British policy and farming practices, and cannot be attributed to the EU.

The UK has gained rather more from the EC/EU regional and social policy. The net benefits to deprived regions have sometimes been less than they might have been, as British governments have sometimes seen EU funding as an alternative rather than addition to UK spending on economic regeneration, contrary to the intentions and sometimes the regulations of the European Commission.

Many other policy areas have been much less affected. The management and funding of health services differs markedly between the member states of the EU. Educational policy and social security payments and social services have been only relatively marginally affected, although member states increasingly face common problems (e.g. over funding pensions) which may ultimately lead to increased convergence. Foreign and defence policy was until recently also only marginally affected. Early attempts by the original six members to develop a European Defence Community foundered in the 1950s, and UK defence and foreign policy has been shaped by the requirements of NATO, and more specifically the 'special relationship' with the USA. Attempts to develop a common foreign policy more recently have not been conspicuously successful. It remains to be seen whether the new European foreign minister will be able to preside over a coherent European foreign policy, but early indications suggest otherwise.

## A new crisis for the European Union?

The relatively smooth introduction of the single European currency in 2002 followed by the substantial enlargement of the EU in 2004 and 2007 appeared a triumphant culmination of the original European vision of the founding fathers. Closer European integration had taken a decisive step forward. Many of the countries of eastern Europe, long divided from the west by the Iron Curtain, became full members of the European club, with further enlargement in prospect. European unity had triumphed over old national rivalries and ideological divisions.

Yet the European project had been driven forward by potent fears, threats and challenges, and inspired by ideals of peace and reconciliation. These included the need to transcend the damaging mutual enmity of Germany and France, to rebuild the shattered economies of western Europe after the war, and to face the new economic and political threat from Soviet-dominated eastern Europe. Once European unity was realized, the threat of war between major European states virtually vanished.

The unexpected rejection of the proposed new European constitution in 2005 by voters in two original member states, France and the Netherlands, not only caused an immediate crisis for the institutions and processes of the European Union, but threw a long shadow over the earlier triumphs. The voters seemed to have rejected not only a constitution which few seem to have read or understood, but more widely, the whole recent direction of the EU. Thus some voters seemed to be opposed to EU enlargement (both recent and proposed), while others were registering their objection to the single currency. Behind these grievances lay more fundamental economic concerns over growth and living standards, unemployment and prospects. The old European Community was popular with the original member states because it had apparently delivered economic prosperity and steadily rising living standards. These countries have experienced low growth and increased economic difficulties in the new larger European Union, in which they are proportionally less politically influential.

The 'no' vote may also be attributed to the impact of globalization, and the EU's response to it. While the British government has pressed for market reforms to make the EU more competitive, many French critics seek to maintain protection for European producers and labour regulation to look after the interests of workers. The European constitution which British Eurosceptics condemned for being too federalist and interventionist was attacked in France for being too neo-liberal, pro-market and British.

The European project already appeared to have stalled even before the credit crunch, economic recession and the currency crisis affecting particularly Greece but also other countries, including Ireland and Portugal and ultimately the Euro. The current crisis may for the first time threaten the whole future of the European Union. A rescue package for Greece was only slowly and reluctantly agreed. The Germans, long the paymasters of the European Union, contributing substantially more to the EU budget than they gain from it, are now notably reluctant to bail out less provident fellow EU members. The bail-out of Greece followed by similar bail-outs for Ireland and Portugal has caused a crisis for the Eurozone and the whole future of the single currency. Other

major issues (further enlargement, global warming and the environment, increased co-operation on foreign policy) have been marginalized by the all-consuming economic crisis. Enlargement is now seen by some of the older member states as part of the problem rather than the solution. The initial enthusiasm of the new member states that joined in 2004 and 2007 has already turned to disillusion for some, as the hoped-for economic and political benefits failed to materialize. The financial crisis and economic recession has damaged both states that once conspicuously prospered from the EU membership, such as Ireland, and those new and poorer member states, such as Latvia, Estonia, Romania and Bulgaria. Yet it can be argued that the problems now facing Europe are still better addressed by the co-operation of European states than a retreat to the pursuit of national self-interest. The problems transcend national boundaries, and so, ultimately, must the solutions.

The British role in Europe has long appeared problematic. Many Britons seem to lack or positively reject a European identity, and may feel a closer affinity with the USA, because of a common language and a substantially shared culture. Yet the sometimes canvassed possibility of the UK exchanging EU membership for membership of the North American Free Trade Agreement (NAFTA), even if feasible, would substitute an unequal dependent relationship with a superpower inevitably preoccupied first and foremost with the interests of the Americas for a partnership between equals. Isolation appears dangerous in an era of intensifying globalization, and there seems little realistic alternative to continued if troubled engagement with the rest of Europe.

## The Cameron coalition and the European Union

A Conservative majority government would almost certainly have intensified tensions between the United Kingdom and the European Union over powers, the budget and policies. The formation of a coalition between the now predominantly eurosceptic Conservative party and the Liberal Democrats, long the most consistently pro-European mainstream party, poses considerable problems for maintaining coalition unity, but reduces the prospect of an immediate crisis in UK–EU relations. Foreign Secretary William Hague has made conciliatory noises, and it seems the repatriation of powers from Brussels to London will be placed on the back burner. To an extent the eurosceptic tone of Hague when party leader, and more recently David Cameron, was perhaps designed to appease parts of the parliamentary party and the party in the country, and head off the perceived threat from UKIP. This threat was not imaginary; although UKIP secured less support than they hoped and others feared in 2010, it was still arguably sufficient to deny the Conservatives victory in enough constituencies to prevent them securing an overall majority.

For the present, both Cameron and Hague may be secretly relieved to be freed by the need to conciliate the pro-Europe Liberal Democrats from embarrassing pre-election pledges that might have proved difficult to fulfil, and would certainly have led to difficult relations with their EU partners. Meanwhile the crisis affecting the Eurozone in 2010 has reduced Liberal Democrat enthusiasm for the single European currency. The appointment of a moderate Conservative, David Lidington, to the sensitive post of Europe Minister instead of the committed Eurosceptic, Mark Francois, who had earlier shadowed the post, suggests Cameron is keen to conciliate other European leaders and his own coalition partners. However, the inherent tensions between the two parties on such a central area of policy remains a potential source of crisis for the coalition.

## SUMMARY

- Britain initially failed to engage with the movement for European integration because of the continuing illusion of world power status, the special relationship with the USA and continuing ties with the Commonwealth.

- Britain eventually joined in 1973, too late to help shape early institutions and policies, and did not seem to secure the same economic benefits as founder members and some later members enjoyed.

- UK membership of the EC/EU has long been a divisive issue in British politics, leading to splits in old parties and the establishment of new ones. While enthusiasts have welcomed Britain's closer engagement with Europe, Eurosceptics have been critical of the impact on national independence and parliamentary sovereignty.

- UK membership has had a major impact on the process of government and on key areas of policy but implications for the British constitution and the principle of parliamentary sovereignty are contested. .

- The European Union is a complex organization. Some institutions represent the EU as a whole (European Commission, European Parliament, European Court of Justice) while others represent the interests of member states (European Council, Council of Ministers, COREPER).

- There has been some tension between the further integration of policies within the EU (deepening) and enlargement of the EU to include new members (widening). Recent and proposed further enlargements cause some problems for EU institutions and policies, and raise questions over the nature of Europe itself.

- Britain's role in Europe remains an important issue in British politics. Following the Iraq war, a key question is how far Britain can engage fully with Europe and maintain its 'special relationship' with the USA.

- Both public opinion and the Conservative party have become increasingly eurosceptic, raising the prospect of a partial or total disengagement from the European Union.

- However, the formation of a Conservative–Liberal Democrat coalition government considerably reduces the immediate threat of a crisis in UK–EU relations.

# QUESTIONS FOR DISCUSSION

- Why did European statesmen seek to promote European integration? Were the motives economic or political?

- Why did the UK government not seek to join the European Coal and Steel Community and the European Economic Community from the beginning?

- Account for the generally lukewarm or hostile attitude to the EU shown by much of the British public compared with the apparent enthusiasm of the citizens of other member states.

- How far has Britain been a significantly more 'awkward partner' than other EU member states?

- Is the European Union a federal superstate or an inter-governmental association of sovereign states? How far do specific EU institutions meet either description?

- Where does real power lie today within the European Union, with the governments of member states or with European Commission and other pan-European institutions?

- How far is there a 'democratic deficit' within the European Union?

- How far is there a tension between further enlargement and closer integration of the European Union?

- Is there still a case for Britain joining the Euro?

- How far has membership of the European Union transformed British government and politics?

- How far does Britain's future lie in Europe? Are there realistic alternatives?

- What impact will the formation of the coalition government have on UK relations with the EU?

# FURTHER READING

Pinder (2001) provides a useful introduction to *The European Union*. Nugent (2010) *The Government and Politics of the European Union*, remains the best guide to European institutions and procedures. See also McCormick (2008), *Understanding the European Union*. For analysis of developments in the European Union see Cowles and Dinan (2004). On enlargement see Nugent (2004). Detailed up-to-date information on all current developments can be obtained from the EU website www.europa.eu.int.

On the troubled history of the UK's relationship with the European Union, Young (1998), *This Blessed Plot* provides a full if now dated account from the perspective of a Euro-enthusiast. See also George (1998), *An Awkward Partner: Britain in the European Community*. Other slightly more recent interpretations include Geddes (2003). Gamble (2003) provides a stimulating analysis of the impact of these conflicting pulls on British politics. The accounts of key protagonists such as Heath, Thatcher and Major can be consulted in their memoirs. There is a useful chapter on Blair's early approach to Europe in Rentoul's (2001) biography. For Blair's views on subsequent EU developments and problems, see Blair (2010) especially pp. 530–40. Bulmer and Burch examine 'The Europeanisation of British Central Government' in Rhodes (2000). Simon Hix reviews the impact of the EU and the Euro on British politics in Dunleavy et al. (2002), while Ben Rosamond has a chapter on 'The Europeanization of British Politics' in Dunleavy et al. (2003). See also Smith in Dunleavy et al. (2006). Some of the constitutional issues arising from Britain's membership of the EU are discussed by Paul Craig in Jowell and Oliver (2007).

# CHAPTER 16

# Devolution: A Disunited Kingdom?

The British state appears to be under pressure from both above and below. While some fear British national sovereignty is threatened by the growth of a European superstate, others suggest that it could disintegrate into smaller component parts in response to demands from separatist nationalists in Scotland, Wales and Northern Ireland. At the heart of the problem are confused and conflicting national identities and interests within the United Kingdom. We explore briefly the implications of the ideology of nationalism for British government and politics. We examine the growth and possible decline of British nationalism, as well as the variously expressed nationalist pressures in Northern Ireland, Scotland and Wales. We go on to discuss the political background to the development of different forms of devolved government within the United Kingdom, and some of the unresolved problems remaining, including the substantial problem of England, and the now stalled prospects for English regional devolution. We conclude with a brief analysis of alternative scenarios, particularly following the installation of a Conservative–Liberal Democrat coalition in Westminster.

## Nationalism and the British state

For a long time it appeared that nationalism and the doctrine of national self-determination (see Chapter 7) had little immediate relevance to Britain. It was a principle to be applied to others – to Greeks, Belgians, Italians, and Poles – whose demands for national freedom were regarded sympathetically by many British politicians in the nineteenth century. It was assumed that Britain was already a kind of nation state, although a 'British' state only really emerged after the Act of Union between England and Scotland in 1707 (following the 'union of crowns' from 1603). A new sense of British national identity was substantially forged in the eighteenth and early nineteenth centuries, symbolized by the figure of Britannia on coins and in the anthem *Rule Britannia*. Pride and loyalty in Britain were strengthened by successful industrial development, imperial expansion and the visible evidence of great power status (Colley, 2003).

Mainstream accounts of British history imply that the growth of the British state was a beneficial and largely voluntary process from which all Britain's peoples ultimately benefited. Thus, it could be claimed, Wales and Scotland prospered from being partners with England in a profitable commercial and imperial enterprise. There is something in the claim, particularly as far as Scotland is concerned. Scottish and Welsh nationalists of course tend to interpret history rather differently, arguing that their culture, and perhaps their economy, suffered as a consequence of English dominance.

Indeed, British nationalism overlaid rather than replaced older Scottish and Welsh identities, while in Ireland the incompatible claims of Irish and British nationalism led ultimately to the establishment of an independent Irish Republic in the south of the island. The now reduced United Kingdom of Great Britain and Northern Ireland was a more awkward and less satisfactory focus for national loyalty. The historian Norman Davies (2000, p. 870) has asserted categorically, 'The United Kingdom is not, and never has been, a nation state.' The Scottish nationalist Tom Nairn (2001) has coined the term 'Ukania' to describe what he regards as an outdated and artificial multi-national state (like the old Austro-Hungarian empire), ripe for disintegration into its separate nations.

The establishment of the Irish Free State (later the Irish Republic) was one stimulus to some revived stirrings of separatist nationalism in Scotland and Wales. Plaid Cymru, the Welsh nationalist party, was founded in 1925, while the Scottish National Party dates back to 1928. Yet these did not initially achieve much political impact. Sir Ivor Jennings still felt able to claim in 1941, in the midst of the Second World War: 'Great Britain is a small island with a very homogeneous population. Few think of themselves as primarily English, Scots or Welsh' (Jennings, [1941] 1966, p. 8).

Today the population of Britain appears less homogeneous, and the cultural identities and political allegiances of the varied peoples living within the borders of the UK state have become particularly complex and confused. Most of the Catholic community in Northern Ireland has long continued to regard itself as Irish rather than British, owing political allegiance to the Irish Republic, although the Unionist majority passionately insist on their British identity. Opinion polls indicate that an increasing proportion of those living in Scotland and Wales regard themselves as Scots or Welsh rather than British (see Chapter 3), one factor which helps to explain rising support for the Scottish and Welsh nationalist parties from the early 1970s onwards. England remains by far the largest part of this complex mosaic of nations and communities. Many of its inhabitants still refer to themselves as interchangeably 'English' or 'British', although there has been some debate over 'Englishness' and its potential political implications (see, for example, Paxman, 1998).

Post-war immigration has intensified and complicated ethnic divisions that cut across these old national communities and identities. Some of the ethnic minorities in many of Britain's large cities maintain a complex pattern of allegiances, often retaining strong cultural or religious links with other countries and communities, alongside a sometimes strong sense of British identity, unless they have become alienated by rejection and discrimination. In some respects it seems easier to be 'Black and British' than to be Black and English, Scottish, Welsh or European.

Conflicting cultural influences resulting from the pressures of globalization have added additional dimensions to these confusions over identity and allegiance. Membership of the European Union, along with the growth of package tour holidays to European destinations and increased sporting and cultural ties, should have helped to reinforce a sense of a common European cultural heritage. Yet the media reflect more the influence of the American and English-speaking world, and weaken a sense of a pan-European identity. Not all citizens of the UK would, however, freely identify with Anglo-American, or western, or liberal capitalism, as the anti-globalization movement indicates (see Chapter 8). Nor, clearly, would they all any longer identify with Christian values and civilization. A multi-faith and multicultural Britain has created new tensions and divisions within the state.

For the future much depends on how far these various identities are felt to be exclusive and overriding. Norman Davies (2000, p. 874) argues 'multiple identities are a natural feature of the human condition' as 'everyone feels a sense of belonging to a complex network of communities, and there is no necessary tension between them'.

Indeed, multiple identities fit comfortably with the notion of multi-level governance, suggesting that it is unnecessary to choose between being Glaswegian, Scottish, British or European. Yet many nationalists remain unwilling to settle for anything less than independence and full national sovereignty. In the end the British state is likely to last as long as the various peoples who live within its borders want it to, and this will depend on issues of political identity and allegiance.

## Northern Ireland and Irish nationalism

If Britain does break up as a political unit, 'John Bull's other island' – Ireland – began the process. It was the demand for Irish Home Rule in the nineteenth century which provided the stimulus for the policy which the Gladstonian Liberal Party adopted of 'Home Rule all round' – the forerunner of devolution. Irish nationalism and Irish separatism subsequently provided a precedent for Scottish and Welsh nationalism.

Ireland was always the least integrated part of the United Kingdom. Its people had remained predominantly and obstinately Catholic while most inhabitants of Great Britain were converted to varieties of Protestantism. What has come to be called the 'Irish problem' was really an 'Ulster' or 'British problem' resulting from 'the English, and their self-serving strategies of plantation and subordination begun in the seventeenth century' (Judd, 1996, p. 49). Protestants were deliberately settled in Northern Ireland. Hatreds stirred then remain alive today. Union with Ireland only came about in 1801 following the crushing of the revolt of the United Irishmen in 1798, and was never a success. The growth of British power and prosperity hardly impacted on the bulk of the Irish, who earned a bare subsistence from land rented from absentee landlords. The 1845 Irish potato famine and the failure of land reform fed a growing nationalist movement which eventually convinced the Liberal leader, William Gladstone, that Home Rule was the only solution to the 'Irish problem'. This led to a crisis in British politics, split the Liberal Party and resulted in a 20-year period of dominance by the Conservatives who supported the Union. The

failure to concede Home Rule to moderate nationalists before the First World War led to the Easter Rising of 1916 and its bitter aftermath, with the dominance of a new breed of nationalist who demanded full independence and were prepared to fight for it. The failure of repression led to the Irish Treaty of 1921 and the emergence of the 26-county Irish Free State, leaving the remaining six counties as a Northern Ireland statelet within the United Kingdom.

It is often said that Northern Ireland is 'a place apart'. The people of Northern Ireland live in a distinctive political culture, support different political parties (see Table 16.1), and face a unique constitutional problem yet to be resolved. The partition of Ireland in 1922 did not solve the 'Irish problem', since a sizable Catholic and substantially Republican minority, now amounting to 40 per cent of the population, still lived in the North. In a sense, two minorities live side by side in Northern Ireland; the Catholic minority in Northern Ireland that feels threatened by the Protestant majority, and the Protestant minority in the island as a whole that feels threatened by Irish nationalism and Catholicism. The troubles in Northern Ireland arise from centuries of divisive historical experiences that have embittered relations between the communities to an extent that it is difficult to comprehend outside the province. Rulers and politicians long forgotten in Britain are celebrated in exotic murals. Quaint ceremonies, ritual marches, rival flags and symbols have become central to Northern Irish politics. Anyone seeking a solution to the Irish problem would prefer 'not to start from here'.

## The troubles in Northern Ireland

However, although the roots of the Irish troubles lie in the distant past it was only comparatively recently that they re-erupted. The years following the end of the Second World War were relatively peaceful. It appeared that differences between the two communities might be progressively eroded by their shared interest in increasing affluence. Although Catholics remained discriminated against in terms of employment, welfare and political rights, they appeared better off economically than their counterparts in the South. The Irish

**Image 16.1    Loyalist mural in Northern Ireland**

Both loyalists and republicans covered walls and the gable ends of houses with elaborate painted celebrations of their respective heroes and martyrs. This example from the Protestant Shankill Road area of Belfast commemorates a fallen member of the loyalist Red Hand Commandos, a paramilitary group formed in 1972, loosely linked with the Ulster Volunteer Force (UVF). Such murals have become tourist attractions, drawing coach parties to view these reminders of Ulster's recent bloody past.

Republican Army (IRA) waged an unsuccessful campaign in the late 1950s and this too was taken as evidence that most Catholics now accepted the political status quo in return for improved living standards.

The emergence of moderate Unionists, such as Terence O'Neill, who became Northern Ireland's Prime Minister in 1963, offered the prospect of further improvements in community relations. However, O'Neill's brand of progressive Unionism was opposed by many Ulster loyalists determined to resist change, and he was forced out of office. Serious rioting led to British troops being sent to restore order. Initially Catholics welcomed these troops, but inevitably their strong-arm role became identified with supporting the Protestant state rather than defending the Catholic minority. The political condition of Northern Ireland moved close to a state of revolution. Violence against Catholics led many to accept the more militant provisional wing of the IRA as their defenders. This support was strengthened by the policy of internment, the imprisonment of suspected terrorists without trial, sometimes described as the 'recruiting officer for the IRA'. The troubles intensified after Bloody Sunday (30 January 1972) when British paratroopers appeared to overreact on the

streets and killed 13 unarmed individuals participating in a civil rights march. Prime Minister Edward Heath announced that the parliament at Stormont was suspended. From April 1972 Northern Ireland came under direct rule from Westminster.

Northern Ireland experienced a grim cycle of violence. Discrimination and repression won more recruits into the Provisional IRA who regarded British soldiers and members of the (largely Protestant) Royal Ulster Constabulary as representatives of an alien occupying power and thus legitimate targets. Loyalist paramilitaries attacked Catholics, particularly those suspected of IRA sympathies, and there were well-founded nationalist suspicions of collusion between loyalist paramilitaries and the security forces. Much of the killing seemed more random: sometimes just the religious affiliation of the victim appeared sufficient excuse for murder. The escalation of violence led to a rising cumulative total of death and serious injury in the province, besides the economic damage caused by the destruction of businesses and the deterrent to new investment. Social segregation was intensified as Catholics living in mainly Protestant areas and Protestants in mainly Catholic areas were forced out of their homes. In some parts of Belfast

## The roots of conflict in Northern Ireland: different perspectives

*Religious struggle?* Some see religion as central rather than incidental to the conflict. The struggle between Protestantism and Roman Catholicism, which began in sixteenth-century Europe as a life-and-death contest between rival ideologies, has survived in Ulster when antagonism has long softened elsewhere. Religious differences still keep the two communities apart. Church attendance remains high (contrary to trends in mainland Britain). Other institutions preserve a link between religion and politics, including the Orange Order, a semi-secret fraternal organization having the support of around two-thirds of Protestant males, and segregated schooling, which provides the children of the Catholic community with an Irish identity.

*Internal colonial struggle?* Alternatively, the conflict in Northern Ireland might be understood as an internal colonial struggle between periphery and core, similar to the struggle of Algeria for independence from France in the 1950s. The argument runs as follows. Although the native populations enjoyed rising living standards under minority colonial rule, they still demanded full equality with the more privileged settlers (in the case of Northern Ireland, the descendants of the Scots Presbyterians settled in Ulster from the seventeenth century). The beleaguered settler population includes fundamentalists ('loyalists' in

Ulster terminology) unwilling to compromise. There is a struggle, often bloody, between the native majority who have discovered nationalism and want independence and a settler minority who want to maintain the power and privileges enjoyed under the colonial system of exploitation.

*Class struggle?* Finally, the conflict may be viewed as essentially a class struggle distorted by the labels of Ulster Protestantism and Irish Catholicism. This perspective suggests the dominant class has maintained its position of power by pursuing a policy of 'divide and rule', manipulating members of the working class into fighting each other. According to this analysis the Protestant working class 'have been duped into thinking they enjoy (economic) advantage' over Catholics (Bruce, 1986, p. 254). The advantage may be more illusory than real: the economic gap between members of the Protestant and Catholic working class in employment has diminished, and a common culture of poverty afflicts Protestants and Catholics alike many of whom are without work and rely on welfare. However, because they believed that they were better off than Catholics, the Protestant working class remained loyal to the state and were unwilling to unite with the Catholic working class in order to advance their common class interests.

and Derry (or Londonderry to Unionists) virtual no-go areas were established, 'policed' by paramilitaries using punishment beatings and shootings to maintain internal discipline.

Periodically, violence was exported to the British mainland. In 1984 Margaret Thatcher narrowly escaped when an IRA bomb exploded at the Conservative Party Conference, killing five people and seriously injuring two senior ministers, Norman Tebbit and John Wakeham. John Major's Cabinet survived a mortar attack on Downing Street in 1991. There were other more random victims of IRA violence following pub bombings in Guildford and Birmingham. To the British government and the bulk of British public opinion the perpetrators were despicable terrorists and murder-

ers. However, IRA volunteers who died in the course of the 'armed struggle' were treated as heroes and martyrs within their own community. Such divergent perspectives are not uncommon in similar conflicts where particular communities totally reject the legitimacy of the state and its agents (examples include the Basque extremists in Spain, or Kashmir separatists in India). However, it became increasingly clear over time that neither side could win by the use of force. The British government could not defeat the IRA, and the IRA could not achieve their goal of a united Republican Ireland through the armed struggle.

Whatever the root cause of the conflict between the two communities (see Box 16.1), further divisions have developed within both, leading to a

**Table 16.1**   Main political parties in Northern Ireland

| Party | Support and aims | Politicians |
|---|---|---|
| Ulster Unionist Party (UUP) | Protestant, supports union with Britain, supported the peace process, but became divided and outflanked by DUP | David Trimble, Sir Reg Empey |
| Democratic Unionist Party (DUP) | Protestant, supports union with Britain, opposed power sharing in 1998, but shared power with Sinn Fein since 2007 | Ian Paisley, Peter Robinson, Arlene Foster |
| Social Democratic and Labour Party (SDLP) | Catholic, republican and nationalist, but committed to constitutional methods. Supports peace process. | Seamus Mallon, John Hume, Mark Durkhan |
| Sinn Fein (SF) | Catholic, republican and nationalist, linked with IRA and 'armed struggle' but signed up to peace process in 1998 and shared power with DUP in 2007 | Gerry Adams, Martin McGuinness |
| Alliance Party of Northern Ireland (APNI) | Non-sectarian, seeks to bridge gap between two communities | John Alderdice, Sean Neeson, David Ford |

complex and confused party system. Northern Ireland parties were always distinctive. The main British parties refrained from contesting Northern Ireland elections. In the old Stormont parliament and in representation at Westminster until the 1970s the dominant (almost the only) party was Ulster Unionist, then linked with the Conservatives. Republican Sinn Fein commonly won a couple of mainly Catholic constituencies, but the victors refused to take their seats. The troubles from the late 1960s onwards led to a split in Unionism. Ian Paisley was elected as an independent Unionist against the official Unionist in 1970 and founded the Democratic Unionist Party (DUP) in 1971. In 2003 the DUP finally overtook their Ulster Unionist rivals, who suffered from periodic splits over the 'peace process'. On the Catholic or nationalist side the most obvious division is between the peaceful constitutional nationalism of the Social Democratic and Labour Party (SDLP) and the more uncompromising Sinn Fein (linked with the IRA and the 'armed struggle'). However, the peace process has also opened up fissures in the republican ranks between the main Provisional IRA and splinter movements such as 'Continuity IRA' and the 'Real IRA' opposed to the Republican cease fire.

Attempting to bridge the community divide is the small Alliance Party.

## The search for peace in Northern Ireland

A series of attempts to find a peaceful settlement were made in the 1970s and 1980s, although in all these attempts Sinn Fein was regarded as beyond the pale, while Paisley's DUP was effectively excluded also, for it regarded every new initiative as a sell-out. Instead, British governments tried to secure agreement on a new devolved government for Northern Ireland between the moderate nationalist SDLP and moderate Unionists through the Sunningdale Agreement (1973–4), the Prior plan (1981–5) and the Anglo-Irish Agreement (1985).

What differentiated a new peace process begun by Major's government in 1993 from earlier initiatives was that for the first time Sinn Fein (and effectively the IRA also) was party to the negotiations. The SDLP could support successive plans for peace but could not end the violence. Only the IRA and Sinn Fein could do that. After 20 years of armed struggle it was clear that the IRA could neither be defeated nor achieve victory by force. A series of both public and secret communications broke the deadlock. Talks between the SDLP's John Hume and the Sinn Fein leader Gerry Adams, secret messages from the Republican leadership to the British government and, finally, talks between British Prime Minister John Major and Albert Reynolds (the Irish Taoiseach) led to the Downing Street Declaration (1993). This renounced any long-term British strategic interest in Northern Ireland and accepted the right of the peoples of North and South to unite at some time in the future. Sinn Fein would be able to join negotiations for a settlement if they renounced violence.

The Ulster Unionists responded to the Declaration cautiously but positively, while the DUP condemned it as a 'sell-out'. Dramatic progress was made in August 1994 when the IRA announced a 'complete cessation of military operations'. This led in turn to agreement on Joint Framework Documents by the British and Irish governments in 1995, which foreshadowed most of the details of the later Belfast Agreement of 1998. However, further progress in the peace process was put on hold by Unionist demands for prior IRA decommissioning of its weapons. John Major opted for elections to a Northern Ireland forum, which Sinn Fein and the IRA regarded as a delaying tactic, and in February 1996 the IRA ended its ceasefire. In April 1996 elections went ahead, but negotiations between the parties could make little progress before the UK general election of 1997.

## The peace process after 1997

The Labour election victory in 1997 restarted the Northern Ireland peace process. The IRA announced a restoration of its ceasefire in July 1997, and after six weeks of non-violence the new Northern Ireland Secretary, Mo Mowlam, invited Sinn Fein to join the peace talks on the long-term future of Northern Ireland. Ian Paisley's Democratic Unionists had already pulled out, but David Trimble's Ulster Unionists continued to participate. After a period of intense negotiations in which Mowlam wooed the Republicans while Tony Blair reassured the Unionists, a formal agreement was eventually reached on Good Friday, 1998. Most of the ideas in the Belfast Agreement 'were articulated

or prefigured before Labour took office' (O'Leary, in Seldon, 2000, p. 449.) Key elements included:

- Parallel referendums to be held on the Agreement in both parts of Ireland.
- A devolved assembly in Northern Ireland, elected by the Single Transferable Vote system of proportional representation, with legislative and executive functions.
- A First Minister and Deputy First Minister to be elected together by parallel consent of parties representing a majority of unionists and of nationalists.
- An executive consisting of ten ministers to be allocated by the D'Hondt procedures (to ensure proportionate power sharing).
- A North–South Ministerial Council.
- An inter-governmental 'British–Irish Council' (providing an East–West forum to balance the North–South body).

The Good Friday Agreement was popularly endorsed in May in by a referendum majority of 94 per cent in the Republic of Ireland and 71 per cent in the North, where nearly all Catholics and a narrower majority of Unionists voted in favour. There was also important backing not only from the UK and Irish governments but also from the US government, and the terms were incorporated in an international treaty, the British-Irish Agreement. However, the key issue of arms decommissioning remained unresolved. Here Blair gave assurances to Trimble which were to be a source of trouble later.

Implementation of the Agreement was predictably difficult. While the nationalists were broadly supportive of the peace process, the unionists remained deeply divided. The first elections to the new Northern Ireland Assembly in June 1998 produced a delicate balance on both the nationalist and unionist side. Sinn Fein came closer to parity with the more constitutional and peaceful SDLP among the nationalists, while the Ulster Unionists and their pro-agreement unionist allies only just won more seats (and fewer first preference votes) than Paisley's DUP and other anti-agreement parties. This led to the election of Ulster Unionist David Trimble and the SDLP's Seamus Mallon as First and Deputy First Ministers in July. However, in August 1998 the worst atrocity of the troubles, a massive bomb killing 29 people in Omagh by dissident Republicans, threatened a return to violence but was condemned by Sinn Fein and in the end perhaps strengthened the mood for peace and reconciliation.

Unionists feared they were making all the concessions without any guarantee that violence was over. Yet in November 1999 Trimble secured 58 per cent support from his party's Ulster Unionist Council for entry into government, promising to resign if there was no progress on arms decommissioning. In December the Republic of Ireland modified its constitutional claim to Northern Ireland to reassure Northern Ireland's Unionists, and in the same month the first meetings of the North–South Ministerial Council and the British–Irish Council were held.

It appeared that the main elements in the agreement were all in place, but arms decommissioning remained a ticking time-bomb under the peace process. Although the IRA promised to eventually 'place its arms beyond use' in May 2000, the future of the agreement remained precarious. In autumn 2002 Trimble and the Unionists withdrew from the Executive, and devolved institutions were suspended for a fourth time. Further attempts were made to restore the Assembly in autumn 2003, but progress on arms decommissioning by the IRA failed to satisfy the Unionists, and fresh elections eventually went ahead while the devolved institutions remained suspended.

The results of the elections in November 2003 intensified the deadlock between the nationalists and unionists, and prevented any early restoration of the Assembly and Executive. The DUP, opposed to the 1998 Agreement, emerged as the largest party, while Trimble's Ulster Unionists were weakened further when three of their elected members defected to the DUP. On the nationalist side Sinn Fein similarly overtook the more constitutional SDLP. The growing strength of the more extreme nationalist and unionist parties was confirmed by the 2005 general election in which only one Ulster Unionist MP was elected and Trimble lost his own seat, resigning immediately as party leader. Paisley's DUP won nine Westminster seats.

These election results seemed most unlikely to assist any early resumption of the peace process

**Table 16.2**   Results of the March 2011 elections (2007 figures in brackets)

| Party | % first preference votes | Number of seats |
|---|---|---|
| Democratic Unionist Party | 30.0 (30.1) | 38 (36) |
| Ulster Unionist Party | 13.2 (14.9) | 16 (18) |
| Sinn Fein | 26.9 (26.2) | 29 (28 |
| Social Democratic and Labour Party | 14.2 (15.2) | 14 (16) |
| Alliance Party of Northern Ireland | 7.7 (5.2) | 8 (7) |
| Traditional Unionist Party | 2.5 (NA) | 1 (NA) |
| Green Party in Northern Ireland | 0.9 (1.7) | 1 |

A variety of other parties secured 2% of first preference votes between them, and no seats/One independent was elected.

*Sources:* www.electoralcommission.org.uk; www.ark.ac.uk/elections; wikipedia; the BBC and various newspapers.

and the return of devolved government. Yet on 28 July 2005 the IRA issued a statement in which they 'formally ordered an end to the armed campaign'. This was followed by the decommissioning of the IRA's entire arsenal of weapons, witnessed by the head of the international decommissioning body, John de Chastelain, and two clergymen (one Catholic, one Protestant) on 26 September. Although the initial reaction of Unionists was suspicious and cautious, ongoing talks involving the two major parties and the British and Irish governments laid the foundations for fresh Assembly elections in March 2007 (see Table 16.2) and a remarkable power-sharing administration involving the DUP and Sinn Fein., headed by the once intransigent Ian Paisley as First Minister and former IRA brigade commander Martin McGuinness as his deputy. This unlikely combination proved sufficiently warm for them to be disrespectfully described as the 'chuckle brothers'. The relationship became more formal when Paisley resigned as First Minister a year later to be succeeded by Peter Robinson.

So the peace process was back on the road. As earlier, there were both problems and advances. While some loyalist paramilitaries finally gave up their weapons, attacks by new Republican splinter groups such as the Real IRA and Continuity IRA intensified. One response was the Sinn Fein demand for the promised devolution of policing to Northern Ireland. While Sinn Fein wanted a cross-community force that more Catholics could join, Unionists feared the recruitment of former IRA members.

Difficult talks were interrupted by a bizarre scandal involving the First Minister's wife, also a DUP MP, involving an affair with a much younger man. Peter Robinson received more sympathy than censure, and after stepping down temporarily as First Minister resumed his post a month later when a lawyer declared he had not breached the ministerial code of conduct. Shortly afterwards the devolution of justice and policing was finally agreed after protracted negotiations, and the Alliance Party's David Ford joined the Northern Ireland Executive as Justice Minister. The only dissenting party was the Ulster Unionists, with whom Conservative leader David Cameron had signed a new alliance in 2009, reviving the close union between the two parties that had lasted until the troubles. The 2010 General Election saw the return of five Sinn Fein members (who decline to take their seats at Westminster), eight DUP, three SDLP and one Alliance, remarkably defeating the DUP's leader (and First Minister) Peter Robinson.

Before the 2011 elections in Northern Ireland there were Unionist fears that Sinn Fein might even overtake the DUP to make Martin McGuinness First Secretary. In the event, the results substantially confirmed the balance of power in the Assembly and Executive, with the DUP making further gains and Sinn Fein consolidating its position as the second largest party. The continued progress of the cross-sectarian Alliance party was another hopeful sign for the future.

Thus peace of a kind survives in Northern Ireland. It may be flawed but it has already brought economic and political benefits to both communities. While a small minority of dissident nationalists remain committed to violence, the murder of a young Catholic policeman in 2011 united north and south, unionists and republicans, in their horrified condemnation. The vast majority of nationalists now appear fully committed to 'exclusively peaceful means' to achieve their long-term objectives of a united Ireland, but for the present

**Table 16.3** The Northern Ireland Executive (2011)*

| Post | Holder | Party |
| --- | --- | --- |
| First Minister | Peter Robinson | DUP |
| Deputy First Minister | Martin McGuinness | Sinn Fein |
| Enterprise, Trade and Investment | Arlene Foster | DUP |
| Finance and Personnel | Sammy Wilson | DUP |
| Regional Development | Danny Kennedy | Ulster Unionist |
| Education | John O'Dowd | Sinn Fein |
| Employment and Learning | Stephen Farry | Alliance |
| Environment | Alex Attwood | SDLP |
| Culture, Arts and Leisure | Caral Ni Chuilin | Sinn Fein |
| Health, Social Services and Public Safety | Edwin Poots | DUP |
| Agriculture | Michelle O'Neill | Sinn Fein |
| Social Development | Nelson McCausland | DUP |
| Justice | David Ford | Alliance |

* Elected 16 May 2011 by full Northern Ireland Assembly.

are content to share power with the once intransigent unionist opponents.

In time demographic trends may produce a nationalist majority in Northern Ireland and Irish unification, although this prospect is distant and uncertain. Meanwhile the Irish Republic appears less threatening to unionists. It constitution has been changed. The Catholic church has lost some of its former dominance. Thus the two Irelands may draw closer together over time. Altogether it seems unlikely that Northern Ireland will remain part of the United Kingdom indefinitely, although there could be interim arrangements for joint sovereignty, or at least continuing co-operation on matters of mutual interest.

## Scottish nationalism and devolution

It is possible that Scotland could become independent ahead of any significant changes to the status of Northern Ireland. Once this had seemed unlikely. Scotland had been an independent state for centuries when its King, James VI, succeeded to the English throne in 1603 as James I. This union of crowns became a full union of the two states and parliaments in 1707, but the inequalities in population, wealth and power ensured that England dominated. However, Scotland retained much of its distinctive national identity which, in the twentieth century, was reflected in a separate legal system, education system and established church. Scottish affairs were handled by the Scottish Office, with a 'mini-parliament' of Scottish MPs meeting in the form of the Scottish Grand Committee.

Many Scots once fully supported the Union. Scots peopled the empire, including the settlement of Scottish Presbyterians in Northern Ireland in the early years of the seventeenth century. Even as late as the 1945 general election, separatist nationalist sentiment was weakly expressed, with the Scottish National Party (SNP) winning only 1.3 per cent of the Scottish vote. The decline of Britain's empire and world role, along with industrial decline that adversely affected the Scottish mining, shipbuilding and textile industries gave renewed significance to Scottish nationalism. The SNP began to win significant votes and seats in the 1970s. These successes worried the Labour Party which had come to dominate Scottish politics and helped commit the 1974–9 Labour government to devolve some power to a new Scottish Parliament.

The 1979 devolution referendum was lost because of a requirement of support from at least 40 per cent of the Scottish electorate (not just those who voted). In the event, although 32.5 per cent of the Scottish electorate voted 'yes', compared with 30.7 per cent who voted 'no', the largest proportion of the electorate (37 per cent) abstained. The failure of the referendum effectively brought down Callaghan's Labour government and ushered in 18 years of Conservative rule, ending any immediate prospects for devolution. The SNP initially lost votes and seats, although nationalist feelings were re-aroused by Margaret Thatcher's strident expression of English nationalism, and by policies such as the poll tax (introduced in 1989 in Scotland, a year earlier than in England). One consequence was that

---

● **Devolution** involves the transfer of power to nations or regions within the state from the central government and parliament, although the latter retains sovereignty or supreme power.

the number of Conservative MPs returned for Scottish seats declined with each successive election until none at all were elected in 1997.

Labour became strongly recommitted to devolution in the 1980s, and from 1988 to 1995 joined with the Liberal Democrats, Scottish trade unions, local authorities and other organizations in a Scottish Constitutional Convention. This hammered out an agreed programme for devolution, which was to provide the basis for the 1998 Scotland Act. The SNP, committed to full independence, declined to join the Convention, while the Conservative government under John Major and the Conservative Party in Scotland maintained its opposition to devolution and its support for the Union. After the Labour landslide in the general election of 1997 a referendum in September 1997 gave overwhelming backing to a Scottish parliament (74.3 per cent) with a smaller majority (63.5 per cent) for tax-varying powers. This conclusively settled the issue, rendering further Conservative opposition to the parliament fruitless. The party of the union was obliged to accept a major constitutional change that they had previously argued would lead to the break-up of Britain.

## The Scottish Parliament and Government

In the first elections for the new Scottish Parliament (May 1999). Labour comfortably maintained its position as the largest party in Scotland but under the Additional Member voting system failed to secure an overall majority. This system benefited both the nationalists and (ironically) the Conservatives, who had always opposed both devolution and proportional representation. Labour moved immediately towards a coalition administration with the Liberal Democrats, with whom they had worked closely in the Constitutional Convention, with Donald Dewar as First Minister. Dewar, the 'father of the nation', did not live long to enjoy his new position. He died on 11 October 2000, to be succeeded by Henry MacLeish, and later, Jack McConnell.

A second round of elections in 2003 left the Conservatives and Liberal Democrats with the same number of seats as before. Both Labour

**Table 16.4** Elections for the Scottish Parliament, May 2011 (2007 in brackets)

| Party | % constituency votes | Constituency seats | % regional list votes | List seats | Total seats |
|---|---|---|---|---|---|
| SNP | 46.4 (32.9) | 53 (21) | 44.0 (31.0) | 16 (26) | 69 (47) |
| Labour | 31.7 (32.2) | 15 (37) | 26.3 (29.2) | 22 (9) | 37 (46) |
| Conservative | 13.9 (16.6) | 3 (4) | 2.4 (13.9) | 12 (13) | 15 (17) |
| Lib Dem | 7.9 (16.2) | 2 (11) | 5.2 (11.3) | 3 (5) | 5 (16) |
| Scottish Green | 0 (0.2) | 0 (0) | 4.4 (4.0) | 2 (2) | 2 (2) |

*Note:* One Independent, Margo MacDonald, was elected.

*Sources: The Guardian, The Daily Telegraph* (7/5/2011), Wikipedia, and Electoral Commision.

(down from 56 to 50) and the SNP (down from 35 to 27) lost ground to various minority political groups, including the Greens (7 seats) and the Scottish Socialist Party (6). However, the Labour–Liberal Democrat coalition headed by Jack McConnell survived, despite early intra-coalition differences over student fees and proportional representation in local elections, and public outcry over the escalating cost of the new Scottish Parliament.

Following fresh elections in 2007 the SNP narrowly overtook Labour in both seats and votes, while the fringe parties that had done well in 2003 lost support, restoring the four-party system of 1999–2003. The SNP, now the largest party, formed a minority nationalist administration with the canny Alex Salmond as the First Minister. Without sufficient votes in Parliament or the country to press for an immediate referendum on independence, their ultimate goal, the SNP was content to run devolved institutions and wait.

The SNP administration took over shortly before Brown succeeded Blair as UK Prime Minister. With an indubitably Scottish premier and a Scottish Chancellor, it might have been expected that the SNP independence option would appear less attractive. Indeed, despite the growing unpopularity of Brown's government south of the border, support for Labour in Scotland held substantially. Moreover, some observers concluded that the 2008 financial crisis that particularly affected Scottish banks weakened the case for independence. Until then Salmond and the SNP had held up the example of apparently prosperous small independent nations like Iceland or Ireland as confirmation that an independent Scotland could successfully 'go

it alone'. Yet the SNP put out a White Paper on three future options for Scotland, including independence, and more devolved powers while the opposition parties set up the Calman Commission , which reported in June 2009, recommending further devolution of powers short of independence. Some observers saw signs of increased convergence cross-party convergence around what was described as 'devolution max' or 'unionist nationalism', involving a union of crowns, a common currency but increased fiscal autonomy (Jeffery, 2010).

The SNP fell far short of its own expectations in the 2010 UK general election, and early in the new Parliament it appeared that Labour would profit in Scotland from the unpopularity of the new coalition government. Instead elections for the Scottish Parliament in 2011 saw dramatic massive gains for the SNP at the expense of all the other parties, but particularly the Liberal Democrats, most of whose votes were transferred to the nationalists. The SNP emerged with a clear overall majority that had previously eluded Labour, winning 53 constituency seats compared with just 21 in 2007, with a further 16 regional list seats making 69 in all. Labour's vote was not much down on 2007, but the SNP nationalists benefited from the collapse of the Liberal Democrat vote, most of which seems to have gone to the nationalists.

Salmond can now hold a referendum on independence when he chooses. Past polls have shown only around a third of Scots favour ending the union, but Salmond is in strong position to build support for the independence option over the course of a parliament, as he demands more powers from the UK government. Scottish inde-

# The independence option

The nationalist Tom Nairn (1981, 2000, 2001) has glee-fully described the break-up of Britain as virtually accomplished, assuming it is only a question of time before Scotland becomes an independent state. Iain McLean (in Seldon, 2001, pp. 444–6) has suggested two alternative future scenarios, based on comparisons with Quebec and Slovakia. Quebec is a French-speaking province of Canada where there has been persistent pressure from nationalists for an independent Quebec state. Yet voters, perhaps fearful of adverse economic consequences, have narrowly rejected the independ-ence option in referendums. Thus Quebec, for now, remains part of Canada, in contrast with Slovakia, which having threatened separation from the former Czechoslovakia, suddenly found itself 'unexpectedly independent, to its short run disadvantage' (McLean in Seldon, 2001, p. 444). Both the Czech Republic and Slovakia however went on to join the European Union in 2004. Will Scotland's future resemble the Quebec scenario (substantial home rule within a federal state) or the Slovak scenario of independence? Either seems possible.

pendence now looks a real possibility, perhaps sooner rather than later. The United Kingdom that lost most of Ireland in 1922 could lose Scotland as well, with all kinds of consequences for the rest of the truncated state that remains.

## Devolution in Wales

Early support for Welsh nationalism had more to do with preserving the Welsh culture and language from extinction rather than Welsh self-government. By the early twentieth century, English was taught as the language of advancement, and the use of Welsh was discouraged. Support for Plaid Cymru, the Welsh nationalist party, remained negligible until the late 1960s, and, even after that, was substantially confined to the Welsh-speaking areas of north and central Wales. In the 1979 devolution referendum only 12 per cent of the Welsh electorate voted 'yes' to devolution, heavily crushed by the 46 per cent who voted 'no' and the complacent 42 per cent who did not bother to vote one way or the other. An even lower turnout marked the 1997 devolution referendum, and although the percent-age voting 'yes' more than doubled and secured a wafer-thin majority for devolution, it still only represented one in four of the Welsh electorate. Welsh devolution was the by-product of the demand for Scottish devolution rather than the result of Welsh pressure. The limited demands from the Welsh for autonomy were reflected in the relatively weak powers of the proposed new Welsh *Assembly*, with no tax-raising powers, and no right to pass primary legislation, especially when compared with those of the Scottish *Parliament*.

However, the bare majority for devolution on a low poll was enough to trigger the introduction of a Government of Wales bill in November 1997, which became an Act in July 1998. The executive powers of the Welsh Office were transferred to the Assembly, which however had only secondary legislative powers. The first elections (under the Additional Member System, as in Scotland) took place in May 1999, and surprised expectations by failing to produce an overall Labour majority (only 28 seats out of 60). Labour formed a minority government, firstly under Alun Michael, then after a successful opposition vote of no confidence in Michael, the more popular Rhodri Morgan. Morgan governed firstly with an informal under-standing with Plaid Cymru, and subsequently in a full coalition with the Liberal Democrats. In fresh elections in May 2003 Rhodri Morgan's Labour Party won half the seats and went on to form a single party administration.

Despite an uncertain start, support for devolu-tion in Wales has strengthened. The Richard Commission (2004) found increased support for a

Table 16.5  Welsh National Assembly election results, May 2011 (2007 results in brackets)

| Party | % constituency vote | Constituency seats | % regional list vote | no. list seats | Total seats |
|---|---|---|---|---|---|
| Labour | 42.3 (32.2) | 28 (24) | 39.6 (29.6) | 2 (2) | 30 (26) |
| Plaid Cymru | 19.3 (22.4) | 5 (7) | 17.9 (21.0)) | 6 (8) | 11 (15) |
| Conservative | 25.0 (22.4) | 6 (5) | 22.5 (21.4) | 8 (7) | 14 (12) |
| Lib Dem | 10.6 (14.8) | 1 (3) | 8.0 (11.7) | 4 (3) | 5 (6) |

Sources: *The Guardian*, *The Daily Telegraph* (7/5/2011), Wikipedia, and Electoral Commission.

Welsh parliament, on the Scottish model, while the number wanting no elected body at all had dropped from 40 to 21 per cent. There was a widespread view that the Assembly had been given too few powers to be effective. The Government of Wales Act (2006) conferred limited legislative powers on the Assembly, and separated the executive, the Welsh Assembly government, more clearly from the Assembly. Plaid Cymru attacked the Act for its failure to deliver a full Welsh parliament, similar to the Scottish Parliament.

In fresh elections for the Welsh Assembly in 2007, Labour lost seats, but Rhodri Morgan continued to headed a minority Labour administration as First Minister before negotiating a coalition government with Plaid Cymru. In 2009 Morgan was replace by Carwyn Jones as First Minister. In March 2011 with the support of all parties, a referendum was held in Wales on extending full law-making powers over the devolved functions of the assembly: 63 per cent voted 'yes' on a turnout of 35 per cent. Thus the Welsh Assembly can now legislate on devolved function, like the Scottish Parliament. In elections in 2011 both Labour and the Conservatives made gains at the expense of the nationalists and Liberal Democrats, with Labour winning half the seats, enabling the party once more to govern alone (see Table 16.5).

## Asymmetrical devolution

Although the devolution process in Wales, Scotland and Northern Ireland has run in parallel, with new assemblies and devolved governments established in each within a few months, what is striking is how different the pattern of devolution in each country has been. 'One's overall impression of Labour's constitutional design is its incoherence' to the extent that it must be 'incomprehensible to most citizens' (Ward in Jowell and Oliver, 2000, p.135). 'Each of the assemblies has a different size and composition, a different system of government, and a very different set of powers.' (Hazell, 2000, p. 3) The divergence is more striking still if the new London government (see Chapter 17) is included in the overall assessment of devolution, as it sometimes is (Hazell, 2000, chapters 5 and 9).

Does this administrative untidiness matter? On the one hand it provides supporting evidence for the view that Labour's constitutional reforms lack any coherent overall vision; each initiative has been seemingly pursued in isolation, and some of the differences appear arbitrary. On the other hand it could be argued that most of the more obvious differences reflect very different histories, cultures and political problems. The legacy of inter-communal strife and hatred in Northern Ireland and whole history of the British engagement with Ireland as a whole and its contentious partition marks off the province from the generally peaceful nationalist politics of Scotland and Wales. Thus an awkward collection of unique institutions with clumsy checks and balances designed to protect minorities and assuage the fears and suspicions of the majority were the minimum requirement for progress.

Scotland and Wales are more superficially similar. Yet whereas Wales was effectively colonized by England, the political union of England and Scotland (whatever Scottish nationalists may now claim) began as a more equal partnership with the

● **Asymmetrical devolution** suggests that there is no common pattern to the devolution of powers within the UK state. Different nations or regions within the state involve very different size ranges, and involve different institutions, powers and processes.

willing assent and even some enthusiasm from much of the Scottish establishment. Scotland retained its own distinctive church, and legal and education systems, and substantially separate administration, which could be readily transferred to the new Scottish government. Moreover, the demand for a Scottish Parliament was based on a distant historical precedent and a more recently established but fairly clear consensus in favour of devolution. Detailed plans had been drawn up in the Scottish Constitutional Convention, backed by a broad swathe of Scottish opinion, and only required implementation.

The situation was very different in Wales, where devolution had been decisively rejected only 20 years before, and where popular backing remained in doubt until the last minute. It is often argued that Welsh nationalism is more commonly expressed in terms of culture and language rather than political institutions. Welsh law and administration were closely integrated with that of England, there were fewer functions that could be readily transferred, and the case for legislative devolution appeared more questionable. It could be claimed that the Welsh voted uncertainly for devolution first, and only then began to consider what powers their new devolved institutions should have. The Welsh Assembly and government have acquired rather more powers following the 2006 Government of Wales Act, including law-making after the 2011 referendum. Even so they still lag somewhat behind their Scottish equivalents, and the gap could become larger if proposals to devolve more powers to Scotland are implemented.

Most federal systems involve a considerable range in state populations, reflecting specific historical and cultural factors. Other countries that have pursued devolved government, such as Spain, have, like the UK, tackled the process incrementally, with considerable variations in powers and levels of autonomy for different areas. Yet it seems likely in such situations that nations and regions with fewer powers will, over time, demand functions and resources comparable to those where devolution has been extended further.

For all these reasons, devolution, in its current form, does not appear a final settlement. Ron Davies, the Welsh politician and former Secretary of State for Wales, who led the devolution campaign until his abrupt political demise in October 1998, has declared that devolution was 'a process not an event'. This was particularly true in Wales where the case for and extent of devolution continues to be debated, but it is also manifestly the case for the UK as a whole. The referendums of 1997 and 1998, the Acts establishing devolved parliaments and assemblies in 1998 and 1999, and the elections for those devolved bodies in 1999, 2003, 2007 and 2011 have not marked the achievement of devolution, but stages in the devolution process which remains unfinished. Where it will eventually lead is unclear, and may not be so for decades.

## The English Question

An obvious problem with devolution to date is that it is asymmetrical in another sense. Devolution to Scotland, Wales and Northern Ireland together only involves a small minority of the population of the United Kingdom. Of the 'four nations in one', England is much the largest in area and even more in population. The growth of nationalist politics and changing national identities and allegiances pose questions for members of the majority nation. Some fear a narrow and racist English nationalist backlash, while others more optimistically believe that devolution, and perhaps the ultimate break-up of Britain could help the English rediscover their own national culture and identity. There has been a spate of books on what it means to be English (e.g. Paxman, 1998).

There are more pressing political and constitutional concerns arising out of devolution. One issue concerns the number and role of Scottish MPs in the Commons following devolution. Scotland was over-represented at Westminster, and this, always difficult to justify, became more anomalous once Scotland had its own parliament. The implementation of the Scottish Boundary Commission recommendations has largely removed this over-representation. Scottish and English constituencies now have a similar average electorate. This does not, however, resolve the issue of the post-devolution role of Scottish MPs at Westminster (see Box 16.2).

One apparently logical solution is the creation of a separate English parliament in addition to the

## BOX 16.2

# The West Lothian Question

The so-called 'West Lothian question', named after the old constituency of the dissident Labour MP, Tam Dalyell, who asked it, has yet to be answered (Dorey, 2002). As Dalyell pointed out, Scottish MPs cannot vote on, for example, Scottish education because that has been devolved to the Scottish Parliament, yet they can vote on education in England. This seems illogical. Thus Dalyell himself declared that he would not vote on English matters. Former Conservative leader William Hague demanded 'English votes on English laws' restricting involvement on legislation affecting only England, or England and Wales to those MPs representing English or English and Welsh constituencies. This could involve the development of a two-tier House of Commons, with some MPs with considerably restricted responsibilities. It could also profoundly affect executive–legislature relations. A future UK government with an overall Commons majority could find itself in a minority on English matters, which might constitute the bulk of its work, particularly if further powers are devolved in Wales as well as Scotland.

Westminster parliament representing the whole of the United Kingdom. If the Scots, Welsh and Northern Irish are entitled to Home Rule, why not the English also? Thus each 'nation' within the union would acquire its own devolved assembly (which could also provide the basis for the development of a federal Britain). This solution, however, has not yet attracted much support. One problem is the sheer preponderance of the population of England within the UK. An English parliament would represent 84 per cent of the UK population. There would be damaging scope for duplication and conflict between the UK and English parliaments.

## English regional government

Another solution is the development of English regional government, particularly if the main aim of devolution is seen as bringing government closer to people, decentralizing power and promoting regional economic development rather than satisfying nationalist aspirations. This would match initiatives in several other member states of the European Union, which itself established a Committee of the Regions as part of the Maastricht Treaty.

Under John Major's Conservative government some efforts were made to rationalize the untidy pattern of existing regional administration, bringing together previously separate regional offices of central Departments into new integrated Government Offices for the Regions (GOs). The Labour government went further with the introduction of appointed Regional Development Agencies with very limited budgets and powers. Labour also promised referendums on elected regional assemblies, a promise not implemented in its first term but reaffirmed in a White Paper published by the Department of Transport, Local Government and the Regions in May 2002 (Cabinet Office/DTLR, 2002). However, referendums were initially planned in just three northern regions, subsequently reduced to one, the North-east, considered the most likely region to support devolution. Yet the outcome in 2004 was a massive vote against a regional assembly, which has virtually ended any prospects for more regional devolution for the foreseeable future (Rathbone, 2005a), particularly after the fall of the Labour government in 2010. The Conservative–Liberal Democrat coalition has since announced the scrapping of Regional Development Agencies.

## Devolution, federalism or separation?

Some alternative future scenarios have already been touched upon. One possibility is that the process will not go much further. The present pattern of sub-UK national devolution will more or less continue within the current complex system of multi-level governance. Extensive further powers may not be conceded to existing devolved bodies, and the sovereignty of the Westminster parliament may appear unaffected. However, for different reasons it seems unlikely that the present arrangements for governing Scotland, Wales and Northern Ireland can persist for long in their current form.

Inter-governmental relations ultimately may have to be more formalized. It is possible that the devolution process will be extended to create, over time, a quasi-federal or fully federal Britain (with or, more probably, without Northern Ireland). This would end the unitary status of the United Kingdom and the sovereignty of the Westminster parliament. The Scottish and Welsh levels of government would no longer appear conditional and subordinate, but sovereign in their own sphere. This would almost certainly require a written constitution, if only to regulate the functions and inter-relationships of the various levels of government. How far the British system of government has already progressed in this direction is contentious. Bogdanor (in Seldon, 2001, pp. 148–51) argues that parliamentary sovereignty has already been virtually destroyed and a quasi-federal system established.

A third possibility is that Northern Ireland could eventually unite with the South, and Scotland and perhaps Wales also could become independent sovereign states within the European Union. These areas of the present United Kingdom would cease to send representatives to the Westminster parliament, which would become an English rather than a UK or British parliament. The 'break-up of Britain' predicted and advocated by nationalists like Tom Nairn would become an accomplished fact. From 2007, nationalists shared power in Northern Ireland, ran a minority government in Scotland (a majority was gained in 2011), and were junior partners in a coalition government in Wales. Few would have predicted such developments 50 years ago when nationalists were a tiny minority.

● **Federalism** is a system of government in which sovereignty is divided between two or more levels, with each level supreme in its own sphere.

The eventual separation of Northern Ireland from Britain seems quite likely. Political circumstances leading to Scotland's separation are certainly a highly plausible, although certainly not the only future scenario (see Comparative Politics 16:1 on Quebec and Slovakia). A sizeable minority of Scots (from a quarter to a third in recent years – see Curtis and Seyd, 2009, p.122) support independence, but it would need the settled support of a majority to succeed. Religious differences are a major factor inhibiting further nationalist advance, as the large Catholic minority which has been the bedrock of the Scottish Labour vote has shown little interest to date in the SNP. Support for independence in Wales remains much lower than in Scotland.

## Coalition government and the future of the Union

The installation of a Conservative–Liberal Democrat coalition after the 2010 election may increase the tensions within the component parts of the United Kingdom, even though both governing parties remain committed to the Union. For most of the post-war period Scots and Welsh have been prominent in the Westminster parliament and government, and in all the mainstream political parties. Thus the Liberals had a Welsh leader, Clement Davies, and later two Scottish leaders, Jo Grimond and David Steel, while their Liberal Democrat successors had the Scots Charles Kennedy and (briefly) Menzies Campbell as leaders. Labour's champion of the left, Nye Bevan, was Welsh as was its later leader Neil Kinnock, while Scots have recently been particularly prominent – leaders John Smith, Tony Blair (more questionably) and Gordon Brown were Scots, and other Scots were also strongly represented in Labour Cabinets from 1997 to 2010. Scottish Conservatives included Prime Minister Sir Alec Douglas Home, and more recently the former Foreign Secretary Malcolm Rifkind and other Scottish ministers such as former Lord Chancellor Lord Mackay, Ian Lang and Michael Forsyth. Until the parliamentary expenses crisis another Scot, Michael Martin, was Speaker of the House of Commons, some time after a Welshman, George Thomas, had held the same position.

The 2010 election, and the coalition government that has emerged from it, has established more of a gulf between England and the other parts of the United Kingdom (Runciman, 2010). Scotland retains only one Conservative MP. Although the Welsh Conservatives did much better, they still have only eight out of 40 seats. In Northern Ireland the restored links between the Conservatives and the Ulster Unionists failed to bear fruit, as the latter won no seats. Thus Cameron's parliamentary Conservative party remains almost entirely English, as is his Cabinet. Moreover Scots are not prominent among Cameron's new Liberal Democrat partners.

The result is a UK government and parliament that will appear alien to Scots in particular. They did not vote for it, returning 41 Labour MPs. With the departure from Downing Street of Gordon Brown and Alistair Darling, Scots are no longer directing the fortunes of the United Kingdom. Scotland did return 11 Liberal Democrats, but many Scots are far from happy that these are helping to support a Conservative government. In the Scottish Parliament the Liberal Democrats were coalition partners with Labour from 1999 until 2007, and previously the two parties had worked together to establish devolution, then opposed by the Conservatives. Today Scots are much less prominent not only among Nick Clegg's Liberal Democrats, but in the post-Brown Labour Party. Alex Salmond will exploit the increasing gulf between the Scottish and UK government and parliament. It will strengthen the demand for the devolution of more powers. It may make it easier for the SNP to win a referendum on Scottish independence.

Cameron's Conservatives remain committed to the Union by their past history and ideology. Yet they may begin to question the value of a union with an increasingly awkward Scotland, particularly as, without it, they would have a comfortable overall majority at Westminster. If, in pursuit of reductions in the budget deficit, the coalition seeks cuts that affect Scotland, and particularly if they seek to revise the rather generous Barnet formula that helps finance Scottish spending, then a division of interest would be sharpened, and the SNP case for independence strengthened. The Liberal Democrats, who retained 11 Scottish Westminster seats in 2010, would seek to avoid such an outcome, and as coalition partners strive to prevent it, while obviously Labour, dependent on Scottish seats for any realistic prospects of a UK majority, would oppose it. Yet whether this would be enough to forestall what might appear to be in the mutual interest of both the Conservatives and the SNP remains to be seen.

The coalition government cuts provoked an early show of unity among the leading personnel and parties of the devolved governments of the UK in 2010. The then SNP minority government of Scotland, the former Labour/Plaid Cymru coalition in Wales and Northern Ireland's First Minister Peter Robinson and his deputy Martin McGuinness signed a joint statement of concern over the UK government's programme of spending cuts. The devolved governments increasingly appeared to be on a collision course with the Westminster coalition.

The divisions became sharper still following elections to devolved bodies in 2011. Neither of the two parties in the UK coalition have much of a stake in the various governments of the non-English territories. Indeed the Liberal Democrat vote collapsed in Scotland and declined in Wales. While the Conservatives did sufficiently well in Wales to become the main opposition to Labour, they lost votes and seats in Scotland, and in Northern Ireland the Ulster Unionists, now again affiliated to the Conservatives, also declined, and only retain one ministry in the five-party power-sharing executive.

The SNP majority in the Scottish Parliament means that there is now nothing to stop Alex Salmond introducing a referendum on independence for Scotland. Indications are that he will not seek to do this immediately, aware that there is still no majority for independence according to polls, and a referendum defeat would close the issue for a decade or more. Instead he will pursue further devolution of powers to Scotland, particularly over taxation, with a measure of support from other parties at Edinburgh. If the SNP proposals for more fiscal autonomy are refused or delayed, Salmond will have an issue on which to put the independence option to voters, perhaps towards the end of this Scottish parliament in 2015, with possibly more chances of success. Alternatively the

Scottish Parliament and government will acquire considerably more powers than they currently exercise, and the divisions between Scotland's and England's levels of taxation and spending, and over key area of policies will grow wider still.

The divisions between England and the other non-English territories of the United Kingdom may be less pronounced. Yet the Welsh Assembly, following the referendum in March 2011, now has legislative powers on devolved matters, and they too are likely to seek further devolution, following the example of Scotland. Indeed, the Labour government in Wales will seek to protect services in Wales from further cuts by the coalition government at Westminster. In Northern Ireland policing has recently been devolved, and both the executive and assembly will seek further powers. Thus The government and politics of England and the other nations that make up the United Kingdom will grow further apart.

Thus the disintegration of the United Kingdom is not unthinkable. Whatever eventually happens will no doubt appear in retrospect 'inevitable'. Yet at present the future seems uncertain, to be influenced by events, the successes and failures of governments and politicians, but ultimately the decisions of peoples. States in a democratic era require popular legitimacy. The British state will survive as long as enough people in its constituent parts want it to survive. It will break up if and when national communities seek independence. Ultimately what matters is the political consciousness and identities of peoples rather than institutional machinery, although of course the perceived performance of governments and parties may influence political attitudes.

## SUMMARY

- To many Britons in the nineteenth century, nationalism was a doctrine to be applied in other countries, as it was widely assumed that there was a British nation, and Britain was therefore a nation state.

- Yet British nationalism confronted Irish nationalism in Ireland, and never fully replaced older Welsh, Scottish and English identities and allegiances.

- Independence for 26 Irish counties, and divided allegiances in Northern Ireland, coupled with the rise of Scottish and Welsh nationalism, have contributed to the erosion of a sense of British national identity and posed problems for the long-term survival of the British state.

- In Northern Ireland following 30 years of bitter conflict between republicans on the one hand and the British state and 'loyalists' on the other, the Anglo-Irish agreement (1998) led to new devolved institutions with power sharing. Despite periodic crises the peace process survives. Arms have been decommissioned and justice and policing devolved to the Northern Ireland Assembly and Executive.

- The growth of nationalism in Scotland and Wales converted the Labour Party to a policy of devolving some powers to representative bodies in those countries. After the first attempt at devolution failed in 1979, Blair's Labour government established the Scottish Parliament and Welsh Assembly (with fewer powers).

- While Liberal Democrats were consistent supporters of devolution, the Conservatives opposed it, until referendums in favour obliged acceptance. Nationalists were at best lukewarm over devolution, but were prepared to accept it as a stage towards independence.

- Devolution is asymmetrical in that it involves different institutions, functions and electoral systems in Northern Ireland, Scotland and Wales, and it does not cover England (with 86 per cent of the UK population).

- One possible solution, a separate English parliament, would involve too much duplication with Westminster. Another, devolution to the English regions, is only weakly supported: an elected regional assembly was decisively rejected in the North-east.

- Outside England devolution is unlikely to be reversed. It is more likely that more powers will be devolved over time. Possible future scenarios could be a fully federal Britain, or the break-up of Britain into separate nation states.

- A Conservative-led coalition government may lead to increased tensions with Scotland in particular, and increase prospects for Scottish independence.

## QUESTIONS FOR DISCUSSION

- In what sense does a British nation exist? Why are national identities in Britain confused?

- What is the real problem in Northern Ireland? Why has a solution appeared so difficult?

- Account for the growth of Scottish nationalism. How far has devolution satisfied the demands of Scots for more control over the government of their country?

- Why was Welsh support for an elected assembly initially lukewarm? How does Welsh nationalism differ from Scottish nationalism?

- How does devolution differ from federalism?

- Account for the apparent lack of support for elected assemblies in the English regions.

- Should England have its own parliament?

- What political conflicts have arisen and could arise between the Westminster government and devolved governments, particularly following the 2010 general election?

- Is devolution likely to satisfy demands in Scotland, Wales and Northern Ireland for more say in their own affairs? How far might devolution be a stage on the road to federal Britain or the break-up of Britain?

# FURTHER READING

There is an extensive literature on nationalism in general (see Chapter 6), rather less on nationalism in Britain, which is, however, discussed in Leach (2009). Davies (2000) *The Isles* provides a stimulating history of the British Isles, which is a corrective to Anglo-centric accounts. Marr (1992) and Harvie (1994) both offer readable accounts of modern Scottish politics and the growth of nationalism, while Nairn (1981, 2000, 2001) provides a provocative nationalist perspective. Tonge (2004) is good on Northern Ireland politics, but needs updating. A more recent book is McGrattan (2010). Hall (2004) provides a brief general survey of nationalism in the UK. Paxman (1998) provides an engaging perspective on *The English*. See also Bechhofer and McCrone (2009).

On devolution Jeffery (2003) wrote a handy overview 'Devolution: What's it all for?' and has since published another brief article (2010) reviewing the current state of Scottish devolution (2010). There is a useful edited volume by Curtice and Seyd (2009). For up-to-date information consult the websites of the Scottish Parliament, Welsh Assembly and Northern Ireland Assembly. David Runciman (2010) has written a provocative short article entitled 'Is this the end of the UK?' following the results of the 2010 election.

# Local Government and Politics

Government is often seen as remote from the governed. Certainly the government discussed in earlier chapters is remote from most of Britain. Brussels and Westminster, even Edinburgh, Cardiff and Belfast seem a long way away from the majority of those affected by their decisions. Yet there is one level of government that appears reasonably close to the people: local government. To many, and particularly perhaps the young, local government by definition is parochial and rather dull. It does not have the appeal of the great political questions of war and peace, world poverty, global warming and the environment, that drive people onto the street to demonstrate. Nor is local government much concerned with some of those issues that apparently most exercise voters, such as the management of the economy, taxation, immigration, the National Health Service, security and civil liberties.

However, local government matters. Public services, delivered locally, and key local decisions critically affect the quality of lives of those inhabiting Britain's cities, towns and villages. Moreover, local councils, like Parliament, are representative bodies, accountable to local communities. Councillors, like MPs, are elected. The same parties that fight general elections also contest local elections. Some who make reputations locally go on to become MPs and play a role in national government. Moreover, while local government is legally subordinate to, and financially dependent on, central government,

local initiatives can sometimes influence national policy. Thus national and local politics are inter-related.

This chapter will examine both the case for local democratic institutions, and problems in realizing the ideal. It explores the practice of local politics, and the role of parties and community interests in local decision-making. It describes the extensive reforms to local government services, structure, management and finance over the last half-century. It reviews the growth of non-elected local public agencies, and the shift from old-style local government to local governance, and the concept of the enabling authority, with increased emphasis on networks and partnerships with other organizations and the private and voluntary sectors. A concluding section looks at local government in the wake of the financial crisis and public spending cuts and the implications of coalition politics, nationally and locally.

## Democratic local government?

Representative local government is often seen as the corollary of representative democracy nationally. Indeed, some saw local democratic institutions as crucial to the theory and practice of democracy generally. In his great work *Democracy in America* ([1835, 1840] 2003) the nineteenth-century French writer, Alexis de Tocqueville, declared that without local self-government people lacked the spirit of liberty. John Stuart Mill considered local representative bodies provided a crucial education in democracy in *Considerations on Representative Government* ([1861] 1972). In the course of the nineteenth century in Britain the reform and growth of local representative institutions parallelled the extension of representative democracy nationally, leading to a network of elected multipurpose local authorities that eventually covered the whole country. This system of democratic local government has been much reformed, amended and in some respects eroded in the second half of the twentieth century, yet survives. Indeed the arguments for local democratic institutions remain strong:

- **Choice** – elected local authorities offer local communities a degree of choice over local decisions and service levels, allowing them to satisfy different needs and preferences within a diverse United Kingdom.
- **Experimentation and variety** – a degree of autonomy for elected local authorities allows experimentation and the development of policies, which may be copied elsewhere or become national policy.
- **Public participation** – elected local authorities provide more opportunities for citizen participation in the political process.
- **A training ground for national politicians** – many MPs and leading national politicians gained their first political and government experience on local councils.
- **Dispersal of power** – local councils help to avoid central government wielding too much power.

However, it should be acknowledged that not all is well with what remains of democratic local government in Britain:

- Turnout in local elections is very low, 30 to 40 per cent on average, but much lower in some inner-city areas.
- The 'first past the post' system, still used in English and Welsh local elections as in Westminster elections, distorts the representation of parties and interests in the community, and creates many virtually one-party councils,

where there is no effective opposition and no prospect of a change in control.
- Those who do vote in local elections vote overwhelming on national trends and issues, almost regardless of the record of the local council, thus undermining effective accountability.
- Very few participate in local government in any way beyond voting. Surveys reveal low public interest in, and extensive public ignorance of, the functions, personnel and issues of local government (which goes some way to explaining some points above).
- Elected members (predominantly elderly, white, male and middle-class) are not socially representative of those they serve. There has been some criticism of the calibre of councillors, and the reluctance of people with relevant experience and expertise to stand for election to the council.
- Scandals have sometimes undermined public trust in local government.

Some of these points may be exaggerated. Thus scandals and corrupt practices are rare. There are elements of contradiction in other criticisms. Higher calibre councillors would almost certainly mean councillors who were less socially representative. Thus although it is sometimes lamented that not enough businessmen become councillors, businessmen (and they are usually men) are commonly over-represented compared with their numbers in the community. Moreover, it is still the case that elected multi-purpose bodies remain the simplest and most effective means of representing local communities, and providing a channel of contact and influence for citizens on local issues and services that affect them. If local democratic institutions are not working as well as they might, this suggests a need for reform rather than their further erosion.

## Local government, local politics and community power

Some of the issues already discussed in relation to central government have parallels in local government. Thus the once-influential thesis that civil servants were the real rulers of Britain (brilliantly illustrated in the television comedy series *Yes, Minister*) was matched by a widespread assumption that senior local government officers rather than elected councillors dominated town hall decision-making. Indeed there were more differences between local politicians and bureaucrats than their national equivalents (who often came from similar educational and social backgrounds). Unpaid (until comparatively recently), predominantly elderly and often lacking relevant knowledge and skills, elected members were sometimes only too ready to defer to the judgement of professionally qualified lawyers, accountants, engineers or town planners who headed local government departments.

Yet elected members of councils always had formal responsibility and could exercise real power if they were sufficiently determined. Here, the role of party politics was a significant factor. Even in the nineteenth century party politics was significant in the government of major cities. Thus Joseph Chamberlain established his political reputation as a radical Liberal mayor and leader of Birmingham Council, where his energy and drive transformed the city, before entering Parliament and pursuing a dazzling and controversial career in first Liberal and later Unionist governments. In the course of the twentieth century, local elections were increasingly fought on party labels.

Some regret this, arguing that party should have no role in local government. Yet many of the key issues in national politics are replicated at local level – particularly the balance between taxation and spending, public services or private provision. Labour, nationally and locally, have tended to support higher spending on public services while the Conservatives emphasize the need for economy and lower taxes. Moreover party politics has increased the number of contested elections and raised turnout levels. Perhaps most important of all, disciplined party groups on the council provide political leadership and make it more likely that elected members rather than appointed officers will have the final say.

Traditionally, Labour dominates in the cities, particularly in the inner urban areas, while the Conservatives have controlled the more rural and suburban authorities. Liberal Democrats, like lightning, can strike anywhere, including northern cities such as Liverpool, Sheffield or Newcastle, prosper-

ous commuter territory (e.g. some of the outer London boroughs, or Harrogate in Yorkshire), or the Celtic fringe – the south-west of England, rural Wales and Scotland. By and large, Labour-controlled authorities are more likely to favour spending on core public services, while Conservatives are keener to keep council tax low, although there are some important differences within both parties as well as between them. The Liberal Democrats in particular may be associated with different interests in different areas, championing inner-city interests sometimes taken for granted by Labour, and competing with the Conservatives for suburban and rural votes elsewhere. The relatively recent success of first Liberals and now Liberal Democrats in local government has led to more 'hung' or 'balanced' councils where no single party has overall control. This has led in many cases to informal and often formal coalitions, sometimes between Labour and the Liberal Democrats (as in the Scottish Parliament), but also between Conservatives and Liberal Democrats (e.g. Birmingham, Leeds). Such coalition politics would undoubtedly increase further were proportional representation ever to be introduced into English local elections, as has already happened in Scotland.

The evidence of recent years suggests that it certainly does matter which party or parties controls local councils. In the 1980s some Conservative-controlled councils such as Wandsworth or Westminster provided a testing ground for Thatcherite policies, while Liverpool, the Greater London Council, and the county and districts of what was described as the 'Socialist Republic of South Yorkshire' defiantly challenged the policies of a Conservative government. Today it is Conservative councils like Barnet or Suffolk (see p. 324) who energetically pursue cost saving and outsourcing, while many Labour councils still manage extensive council housing, control their own refuse collection and other council services, and subsidize public transport. Meanwhile, Liberal Democrats have used local politics to raise their own political profile and build support by articulating grassroots issues and concerns. Their readiness to work with other parties in local government provided a precedent for the 2010 coalition at Westminster.

## Academic controversy 17.1
# The Community Power debate

There has been a long academic debate among scholars in Britain, to an extent echoing similar debates in other countries such as the United States and France, over power in the local community. Pluralists who argue that power is widely distributed have often used urban politics to demonstrate this. They have cited evidence from urban decision-making to demonstrate that there is no single local elite dominating the town and its policy processes (Dahl, 1961). Others have cited different kinds of evidence to demonstrate the existence of urban elites. American radicals (e.g Crenson, 1971) and French Marxists (e.g Castells, 1977) have argued that urban decision-making systematically favours business interests. Much of this community power debate was replicated in Britain, and was similarly inconclusive. Particular case studies sometimes appeared to confirm the initial perspective of authors, finding evidence for a quasi-pluralist policy process in Birmingham (Newton, 1976), elite decision-making in Kensington and Chelsea (Dearlove, 1973), and strong business influence in Lambeth (Cockburn, 1977) and Croydon (Saunders, 1980). Perhaps this simply confirms that case studies cannot prove anything. However, at the very least the existing literature copiously illustrates the complexity of the conflicting interests involved in the governance of urban areas, and dramatizes some of the issues involved in the distribution of power, locally as well as nationally.

---

Local authorities are also influenced by a wide range of local interests (see Chapter 8). These include groups of local residents or council tenants, parent-teacher associations (PTAs), leisure groups (e.g. allotment associations, sports clubs), senior citizens, groups representing ethnic minorities and local producer interests (e.g. Chambers of Commerce representing business interests and Trades Federations representing workers and trade unions). These engage in the political process to protect their interests and secure benefits for their members – policy decisions in their favour, new equipment or facilities, often financial support of some kind. Some groups however, have something to offer local public bodies – information, expertise, even voluntary labour in the case of some established third sector groups. Gerry Stoker (1991) concluded that the willingness of councils to respond to various types of pressure groups depended closely on their prevailing politics. Labour councils may be more prepared to listen to trade unions, tenants' groups, women's groups and ethnic minority associations, while Conservative councils may pay more attention to the local Chamber of Commerce and business interests generally, as well as professional interests and local residents' associations. Other groups may be relatively ignored.

Just as it is often alleged that power in Britain is really exercised by interests outside government, it is also suggested that real power in cities and local communities is not held by the elected members or appointed officers of the council, but by outside interests. Indeed, many celebrated attempts by political scientists in the United States, France and Britain to assess the distribution of political power have focused on case studies of decision-making in towns and cities rather than nationally (see Academic Controversy 17.1).

Interest in community power studies has declined, partly perhaps because of their inconclusive (or sometimes contradictory) findings. However, another reason in Britain is the transfer of functions away from local government, and power from local communities. Local councils are still big business, and in many cases remain the largest single employer in their area. Yet they have lost effective control of key services and decisions, to central government, to other public agencies, and to the private and voluntary sectors (see below). Moreover, the private firms (and even some of the voluntary agencies) with which the council has to deal are no longer necessarily locally managed and controlled but branches of national and in some cases multi-national organizations. Thus the key players in urban development and planning may not be closely involved with the city whose future they affect. It is to the changing environment of local government and politics that we must now turn

## Changing local government

Local government in Britain has been substantially transformed, particularly in the last half- century. It has lost some functions completely, and operational control of many others. Its structure has been repeatedly overhauled. Its internal management has been extensively reformed. Its finance has been subject to some politically controversial transformations. It would take much more than a single chapter to explain all this fully. Here only an outline of the principal changes is attempted.

### Services – towards the 'enabling authority'

In the first half of the twentieth century, elected local authorities in the UK were directly responsible for an extensive range of services delivered locally. These included education, libraries and leisure services, social services and social welfare, police and fire services, environmental health and community health services, housing, highways, planning and urban development. Some authorities were also responsible for major public utilities such as water, gas, electricity and public transport. Some developed and ran their own airports. Birmingham had its own bank, Hull its own telephone service (Wilson and Game, 2006, p.55).

Some of these services were transferred because developments in technology required a scale of investment that local authorities individually or collectively could not provide. Thus municipal gas, electricity and, later, water undertakings were nationalized and subsequently privatized. Major trunk roads became a national responsibility. Social security was effectively taken over by central

government, partly to ensure that all those in the same circumstances were treated similarly, regardless of where they lived. For these and other reasons local authority hospitals and later community health service were transferred from local government to the National Health Service. By the mid-1960s William Robson (1966) was lamenting that local government was in crisis.

Since then, local government has lost all responsibility for many more services and operational control of others. Thus some of the once extensive education services of local councils have been substantially transferred (further education, vocational training, academy schools) or delegated downwards to school governing bodies and head teachers. Voluntary Housing Associations rather than the council provide much remaining public or social housing. Residential care for the old and infirm has been substantially privatized, although councils have regulatory responsibilities and have to finance the costs of those with insufficient income or assets to pay for their own care. Local public transport is operated by private bus and train companies, although partly regulated and often subsidized by local councils. Police services are controlled by essentially independent Police Authorities, although these still contain some indirectly elected local authority members (Wilson and Game, 2006, chapter 7).

Critics complain of the erosion of local autonomy by central government and the bypassing of elected local authorities by appointed agencies, sometimes described as the 'new magistracy' or 'local quangocracy' (Cochrane, 1993, Skelcher, 1998, Wilson and Game, 2006). There is, it is argued, a 'democratic deficit' in the running of local services. All the major parties, particularly when they are opposition, lament the decline in local democracy and promise to restore power to local communities. Yet both Labour and Conservative governments have contributed to the erosion or bypassing of democratic local government, and it remains to be seen whether the 2010 Conservative–Liberal Democrat coalition will do anything to reverse this trend.

Even where elected local authorities retain statutory responsibility for a service, it may be actually provided by another organization – by a voluntary body, largely funded by the council, by a private company under contract, or by another public agency. Working with voluntary bodies, such as the Women's Royal Voluntary Service (WRVS) goes back a long way, and is generally cheaper and often more effective than direct public provision. The voluntary or third sector is popular across the political spectrum, with all parties keen to encourage more citizen participation in welfare services. Partnership with the private sector has also long flourished, particularly in urban redevelopment schemes and other major capital building projects. The more recent involvement of the private sector in local public service provision is rather more contentious. Thus the Thatcher government first encouraged and then required health authorities and local authorities to put certain services out to tender (compulsory competitive tendering – CCT). As a consequence, some refuse collection, cleaning, ground maintenance, catering and leisure services are now provided by private firms under contract. The Blair government removed the element of compulsion, but by this time the delivery of many of these services had been effectively privatized.

The consequence of all this is that elected local authorities are no longer *the* local government for their area. As Blair (1998, p. 10) observed 'There are all sorts of players on the local pitch jostling for position where previously the local council was the main game in town'. Local authorities in Britain have thus been persuaded to assume more of an enabling role (Clarke and Stewart, 1988, Brooke, 1989). While local councils may retain ultimate responsibility for key local decisions and services, they should enable others, including local business, voluntary organizations and other public agencies and community groups, to participate in decisions and provide services rather than seeking to control everything. In reality local authorities, short of powers and resources, had little choice over co-operating with other agencies, the voluntary and private sector.

This reflects much of the fashionable **governance** literature. Governance emphasizes the *process* of governing rather than the *machinery* of

government. **Local governance** involves not just the formal *institutions* of **local government** but the whole *process* of delivering local services and governing local communities through complex partnerships or networks of public, private and voluntary bodies, and all manner of local interests (Leach and Percy Smith, 2002).

The new enabling role requires new skills, in drawing up and monitoring contracts, in inspecting and regulating. Where local councils are working with other agencies and the private and voluntary sectors in partnerships and networks, diplomatic co-operation is required, rather than the line management local government officials were used to in large hierarchical organizations. This is sometimes referred to as 'third way management'. Instead of the command and control management of old large and hierarchically structured public sector organizations or the competition and profit maximization which drives the private sector, third way management emphasized leadership, diplomacy and collaborative joint working.

However, local councils retain some advantages in this fragmented jumble of local agencies and networks. They still have extensive statutory powers, control many key resources, remain multipurpose bodies, and crucially are the only directly elected bodies which can claim to represent their local community. This gives them a legitimacy lacking in other public agencies, and in the business and voluntary sector, however public-spirited they may claim to be. As the only bodies with some claim to represent the whole of their local communities, they remain well-placed to take the lead on major local issues and projects which concern the community.

## Territory and community: the reorganization of local government

Local government, by definition, is about locality, but what kind of locality? How are the areas for the

---

● **Government** and **governance**. 'Governance is the process by which we collectively solve our problems and meet our society's needs. Government is the instrument we use.' (*Reinventing Government*, Osborne and Gaebler 1992)

● **Local government** is conventionally understood to mean the government provided by elected local authorities (or local councils). **Local governance** includes appointed agencies and other local governing bodies besides elected local authorities but also emphasizes the *process* of *governing*, rather than the *institutions* of *government*, and relations between local authorities, other agencies, voluntary bodies, local business and community groups.

**Image 17.1  Manchester Town Hall**

Many town and city halls built in the nineteenth century were impressive monuments to Victorian civic pride and power, built in the neo-gothic style as here, or in the neo-classical style of Leeds. Today most local government services are commonly administered from more functional and cramped modern buildings, symbolizing the decline in local government's prestige and resources.

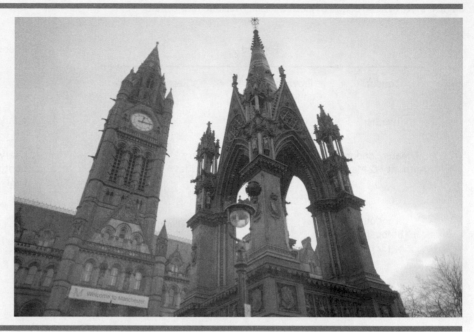

local governmental bodies drawn up? How large can they be (in area or population) and still be termed local? How small can they be and still fulfil their functions effectively? How far do they match the pattern of life and work in modern Britain, and how far do they match the local communities with which people actually identify? The changing structure of local government and governance reflects a continuing obsession with these question for 50 years or more, and they are no nearer a resolution than at the start. Behind theoretical discussions over efficiency and community there are often more covert concerns over power and influence. New boundaries may transform the balance between parties and interests. Most debate has taken place over the structure of Britain's elected local authorities, but there has also been a long-running argument over the optimum areas for administering health, and, more recently, on bodies concerned with specific functions such as police, or vocational training. Needless to say, different areas and boundaries for different agencies increase the problems of collaboration between them.

A common perception was that many of the ills of local government stemmed from a defective structure (Robson, 1966). Thus from the early 1960s onwards there have been a series of real and projected reorganizations of the size, boundaries and functions of elected authorities. Some of these reorganizations have been widespread, covering all or most of the country, such as the major upheavals of 1972–4, and the more recent reorganizations of Scottish and Welsh local authorities (1996) and English shire counties and districts (1992–6) under John Major's government. There have also been other changes restricted to particular parts of the country. Thus a London-wide strategic authority was established by one Conservative government (Macmillan's) in 1963, abolished by another (Thatcher's) in 1986, to be reestablished in rather different form by Blair's Labour government in 2000 (see Box 17.1, p. 318).

In retrospect, many of these structural reforms reflected prevailing fashion or current academic and political wisdom. In the 1960s it was argued that larger local authorities would result in economies of scale and improve efficiency. In the 1980s and 1990s there was a subsequent reaction against 'big government' in favour of more flexible units 'closer to the people'. Particular models drifted in and out of fashion – the notion of 'city regions', based on cities and their hinterland, (which partially inspired Scottish reorganization in 1974) or 'estuarine authorities', straddling both

**Figure 17.1**   The structure of elected local government in Britain

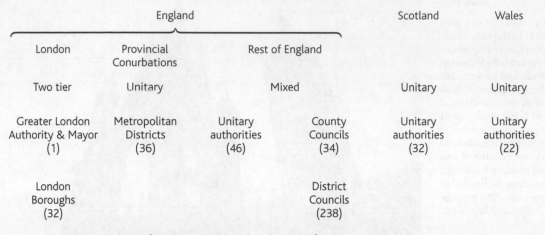

| England | | | | Scotland | Wales |
|---|---|---|---|---|---|
| London | Provincial Conurbations | Rest of England | | | |
| Two tier | Unitary | Mixed | | Unitary | Unitary |
| Greater London Authority & Mayor (1) | Metropolitan Districts (36) | Unitary authorities (46) | County Councils (34) | Unitary authorities (32) | Unitary authorities (22) |
| London Boroughs (32) | | | District Councils (238) | | |

(Parish or Neighbourhood Councils)

banks of river estuaries (Humberside, Teeside). Reorganization commonly stirred up a hornet's nest. Although relatively few people know much about local government or can be sufficiently bothered to vote in local elections, a minority seem to care passionately about particular names, areas and boundaries – for example, fervently campaigning to save or restore the tiny county of Rutland, abolish Humberside or reinstitute the Yorkshire Ridings.

One theme has dominated much of the recurrent debate over local government reorganization and remains influential – the principle of unitary local authorities, involving one level of local government for all local government services. Such unitary authorities, it is argued, make it easier for the public to understand who does what, and improve the co-ordination of services. Cities and larger towns in the old pre-1974 system were substantially all-purpose unitary authorities, and this ideal was the inspiration behind the abortive Redcliffe-Maud Report of 1969. These recommendations were largely endorsed by the then Labour government but rejected by the incoming Conservatives in favour of a revised and two-tier system of counties and districts, implemented in 1974.

However, a subsequent Conservative government under Thatcher removed a tier of elected government in London and other major conurba-

tions. In 1986 Major's government proceeded to impose unitary authorities in a fresh reorganization of Scottish and Welsh local government, and gave a strong steer in favour of unitary authorities to a Local Government Commission appointed to make recommendations for England. In the event, the outcome of the Banham Commission's proceedings was an unsatisfactory modification of the two-tier status quo (Leach. S., 1998). New Labour restored a London-wide elected authority, with a directly elected mayor (see Box 17.1). They also sought further amalgamations to create more unitary authorities, initially as part of their plans (later dropped) for elected regional assemblies but later simply on grounds of cost savings and greater efficiency, provoking some fierce local opposition. (The coalition government has since scrapped this further reorganization.) Overall, the resulting structure of elected local authorities in Britain is more complicated and confusing (see Figure 17.1). Much of local government now appears more remote than ever from those it is supposed to serve. It is at best questionable whether it has led to increased efficiency. The view of many of those who have followed the twists and turns of the whole local government reorganization saga, is that future governments would be well advised to think twice before embarking on another attempt (see, for example, Leach, R. 1998).

**Table 17.1** Who does what? English county and district councils (principal functions)

| County council | District council |
| --- | --- |
| **Education** (most of budget now delegated to schools) | |
| **Social services** (largely community social workers – but councils regulate privately provided institutional care) | |
| | **Housing** (regulation and some provision – but much former council housing sold to tenants and transferred to other landlords, especially housing associations) |
| **Planning** (structure plans, environment and conservation, economic and tourism development) | **Planning** (local plans, development control, environment and conservation, economic development) |
| **Highways and transport** (transport planning, county road building & maintenance) | **Street cleaning and lighting** |
| **Public protection** (waste disposal, trading standards, fire services | **Public protection** (refuse collection, food safety, pollution control) |
| **Leisure and amenities** (libraries, country parks, grants to village and community projects) | **Leisure and amenities** (allotments, museums, local parks, playing fields, swimming pools, sports centres) |

The division of the main functions between English county and district councils is shown in Table 17.1. By and large, the most important and expensive services are run by the counties. As we have seen, London also now has two elected tiers (London boroughs and the Greater London Authority), but here it is the boroughs that have most effective control of the delivery of local services. Unitary authorities (all those in Scotland and Wales, and in the metropolitan areas of England, plus a few new unitaries established by the 1992–6 reorganization in England) combine county and district functions. To complicate matters further, some areas (mainly more rural areas) have flourishing small parish councils with few powers, and others have introduced largely consultative lower-tier neighbourhood or community councils.

It should be added that what is sometimes termed 'other local government' – largely appointed local agencies supplying other local services – has also been periodically reorganized, but on rather different criteria. Thus the areas for administering local health services have been generally determined by the perceived functional requirements of the service rather than notions of community. Their boundaries rarely coincide with those of elected local authorities. The same is true of local agencies providing vocational training (Training and Enterprise Councils or TECs under Thatcher and Major governments, rather larger Learning and Skills Councils under New Labour). Police authorities have become increasingly autonomous from elected councils, and the operational requirements of the police force are often held to require larger areas than a single local council. While economic regeneration remains a major concern of elected local authorities, a plethora of initiatives from central government have involved the establishment of some more specialist agencies. Some of these have covered relatively limited inner-city areas (such as the now defunct Urban Development Corporations), while others focus on regions (such as Labour's Regional Development Agencies, now facing the scrapheap). This plethora of single-purpose agencies, all with their own distinctive boundaries, management structures and institutional cultures, makes effective co-operation between them in the interests of 'joined-up government' far more difficult. Yet on many issues – caring for the elderly, preventing child abuse, deterring crime and anti-social behaviour, promoting equal opportunities, assisting local

**BOX 17.1**

## The government of London: the London Mayor and Greater London Authority

Because of both its sheer size and its status as the capital city of the United Kingdom, the government of London has long appeared distinctive, and somewhat set apart from the rest of UK local government. The earlier London County Council (LCC) was replaced by the larger Greater London Council (GLC) in 1963, and subsequently abolished in 1986 by the Thatcher government, which detested its left-wing Labour council and leader, Ken Livingstone (dubbed 'Red Ken'). The 1997 Labour government was pledged to restore a strategic authority for London, and proposed a new Greater London Authority (GLA) with a directly elected mayor and a 25-member assembly, elected by the Additional Member System (AMS). These proposals were endorsed by 72 per cent of voters (on a turnout of 34 per cent) in a referendum of Londoners in 1998. The GLA (now housed close to Tower Bridge in the new building designed by Lord Foster) was given strategic (but not operational) responsibilities for transport, policing, fire and emergency planning, economic development, and planning.

The outcome of the first London mayoral election was a severe embarrassment for the Labour leadership, determined to block the candidature of the left-wing MP Ken Livingstone, the former leader of the GLC. Livingstone won anyway as an independent, defeating the Conservative candidate Steve Norris under the supplementary vote system with the official Labour candidate a distant and eliminated third. The first elections for the 25-strong assembly (under AMS) resulted in 9 Labour members, 9 Conservatives, 4 Liberal Democrats and 3 Greens.

The London Mayor combines a high public profile with relatively weak powers. Livingstone soon became engaged in a long-running battle with the Labour government over its Public–Private Partnership for the modernization of the London Underground, which did little to heal his rift with the party. A bold but controversial initiative was the introduction of congestion charges to alleviate London's

traffic jams. This has generally been regarded as successful, and is being studied by other cities although few have followed London's example.

Livingstone was subsequently readmitted to the Labour party and chosen as the official party candidate in time for the second mayoral election in 2004, which he won fairly comfortably under Labour colours. In the elections for the London Assembly Labour did less well, losing two seats to win just seven. The Conservatives retained nine seats, with five for the Liberal Democrats and two each for the UK Independence Party and the Greens.

In a third round of elections in 2008 Boris Johnson (Conservative) beat Livingstone in a closely fought contest for mayor. In the Assembly elections the Conservatives won 11 seats, Labour eight, the Liberal Democrats just three, the Greens two and the British National Party one (UKIP lost their seats). Johnson (see photo) was soon involved in a clash with the then Labour government over control of the Metropolitan Police, and retains a high public profile as London Mayor, although critics allege he has done little for the city. All the signs are that future elections will continue to be fiercely contested. Ken Livingstone has been chosen again by Labour to contest the 2012 election.

economic development – such co-operation is crucial.

Effective local governance, in its wider sense, faces many obstacles. Many of the reforms and developments described above take local governance further away from the local communities with which people identify, but which are generally deemed too small for the efficient delivery of some local services. This tension between community self-government and functional efficiency has been a key theme of the debate over areas and structures for 50 years or more. The debate is no nearer resolution, although the general trend is still towards larger areas, despite the reaction against 'big government' (see above).

## The changing management of local government

The internal decision-making processes of local councils aroused much criticism in the past, particularly the delays involved in the traditional and often very complex committee system. Moreover, this system obscured the realities of power in many councils, for the real debates and decisions took place behind closed doors in prior meetings of officers and party groups. Thus the all-party committee meetings, which were open to press and public, commonly involved little more than the formal registering of officers' recommendations or decisions already taken by the ruling party group. All this, it was argued, was confusing to the public and hardly helped the cause of increased accountability, democratic governance and local participation.

In the 1960s and 1970s there was a strong impetus to develop a more corporate approach to the management of local services, breaking down the specialization and fragmentation associated with the narrow professional and departmental loyalties among officers, mirrored by the specialist committees on which elected members served. Thus new Chief Executives and corporate management teams provided stronger leadership on the official side, while new beefed-up centralized Policy and Resources Committees performed a similar function for elected members.

Yet it may be questioned whether any of the reforms associated with the new corporate management made much impact with the wider public, for whom the processes of local government decision-making remained opaque. Faced with a bewildering array of changing departments and committees, local citizens could still not easily determine who did what. The very few who occasionally exercised their right to attend council or committee meetings were often bewildered by proceedings where major issues were apparently decided without discussion. Power and decision-making were not transparent.

One fashionable remedy, strongly advocated by the Conservative politician Michael Heseltine, among others, in the 1990s, and subsequently adopted by Labour, was directly elected mayors with real power, an idea borrowed from local government in France and some US cities (see Comparative Politics 17.1). In Britain the traditional role of mayor had become purely ceremonial, with no political power, a post usually held for one year by a respected long-serving councillor, regardless of party. In 1998 the Blair government issued a consultation paper *Modernising Local Government*, which argued for a stronger executive. This was followed by a White Paper in the same year, with a strong steer towards elected mayors, although a local Cabinet system was another recommended option. Legislation followed in 2000, which obliged every council to consult the local community on plans for reform.

It was hoped that prominent local figures outside conventional local party politics might be tempted to stand in mayoral elections. From a New Labour perspective, the promotion of elected mayors got off to a bad start with the voters' choice of Ken Livingstone (then standing as an independent) as Mayor of London (see Box 17.1) over the Conservative and official Labour candidates. Subsequently, most local referendums rejected elected mayors. Moreover, there have been some surprising results in the few local authorities where mayoral elections have already taken place. Thus 'H'Angus the Monkey' (Stuart Drummond) was elected as Mayor of Hartlepool on an independent platform which included free bananas for school children,(a pledge which was unfulfilled). The record of elected mayors to date is mixed, although they have proved 'an entertaining diversion' for local government scholars. Most councils have

## COMPARATIVE POLITICS 17.1
# Running US cities: mayors and city managers

American city government has provided some of the models for proposed reforms of UK local government, and particularly the introduction of elected mayors. There are four principal systems used in the USA:

- *Strong mayor and council* – there is a directly elected mayor who is the most powerful person in the city and appoints all departmental heads, although an elected council debates and endorses local policy.
- *Weak mayor and council* – the mayor is directly elected but so are many departmental heads, so the power of the mayor is less (although

may be strengthened by a disciplined party organization).

- *City commission* – a small number of commissioners are elected to run the city on a city-wide ballot. (This system was introduced in the early twentieth century to counteract corruption in city politics.)
- *Council manager systems* – councillors (or commissioners) are elected by the city, but appoint a city manager to execute their policy. The city manager appoints heads of department and other employees. Although city managers effectively run cities, they are not elected, but employees of the council and can be (and often are) sacked.

---

preferred a leader/local cabinet system (Wilson and Game, 2006, pp. 103–10).

## Reforming the finance of local government

Perhaps more politically controversial than any of the above has been reforming local government finance. Commonly, the local council is the largest single employer in its area, and local authorities are responsible for more than a quarter of all public spending. Unsurprisingly, local government expenditure is politically controversial. Those opposed to big government and high taxation are critical of council spending and efficiency, and seek to reduce the size and scope of local government. In contrast there are strong pressures from public sector unions, client groups and other specialist interests to improve service levels and raise spending.

Money has to be raised somehow to meet this spending, ultimately through national or local taxation. At times, controversy over local government taxation has led to tax strikes and violent demonstrations. One abortive reform, the ill-fated poll tax, substantially contributed to the downfall of a once dominant Prime Minister, Margaret Thatcher, in 1990.

An initial distinction should be drawn between the finance of local capital spending and current (or revenue) spending. Capital spending includes long-term projects like schools, or very expensive equipment expected to have a long life. Current or revenue spending includes money needed for wages and salaries of staff, fuel, materials, interest payments on borrowing, and so on. Local authorities usually finance their capital spending by borrowing (similarly to the way most individuals finance their purchase of houses and cars). Formerly, most of this money came from the issuing of government or local authority bonds. As this was part of public sector borrowing which successive governments have tried to keep under control to comply with dictates of prudence and international rules, public services have often been starved of capital investment.

As a consequence, both the Major Conservative government and the Blair/Brown Labour governments sought new sources of capital investment from the private sector under the Private Finance Initiative (PFI). The private sector provides the up-front capital finance, supposedly bears the risk, and undertakes responsibility for completion of projects on time (with penalties for underperformance). The cost to the public sector is transferred to the revenue budget. Generally, critics argue, this is a more expensive way of raising capital investment in the long run. The advantage for government is that the investment does not show up as part of public sector borrowing, while hospital trusts and local authorities may obtain new purpose-built hospitals and schools sooner rather than later.

However, local authority current expenditure (on salaries, materials, rent, debt servicing and so on) is supposed to be met from current revenue. Substantially this has to be raised from taxation. Local authorities have long had powers to raise their own local taxes, once in the form of property rates, briefly by the Community Charge, and more recently through the Council Tax (see below). Local voters often assume that the bulk of local spending is paid for by such local taxes. In truth, they meet only a diminishing proportion of local government expenditure. The rest comes in one form or another out of national taxes.

It might appear preferable in terms of local decision-making and accountability if local government had to meet all its spending out of local taxation. Yet some local communities are far better off than others. If the quality of local services depended largely or exclusively on the money which could be raised locally, the poorest areas with the greatest needs would have the least income for spending on public services. One purpose of central grants is to redistribute resources to help poorer areas with substantial problems and demands on spending. Thus, almost inevitably, local government is substantially dependent on central funding in some form or other, and the old adage 'he who pays the piper calls the tune' applies. Central governments of all parties employ the rhetoric of decentralization – devolving more autonomy to those responsible for the actual delivery of services. Yet all governments are aware that they will be judged on the effectiveness of their spending and service delivery, so money is given with strings attached – including an increasing number of centrally-determined targets which have to be met. Otherwise, it is feared, increased spending might disappear into a 'black hole', with no perceptible improvement in public services. Ultimately there is no easy answer to this tension between central direction and local autonomy, which is

particularly evident over spending, because local authorities rely substantially on income which they do not raise themselves.

For most of its history the main local taxation involved domestic and business rates. Householders and business owners paid rates annually based on the value of their property, with the actual payment varying with the rate in the pound levied by each local authority. Thus a householder would have to pay £400 if the council levied a rate of 40p in the pound on a property with a rateable value of £1000. As this example suggests, rateable value bore little relationship to a property's capital value. It was based on a notional rental value, but even this became quickly out of date with property inflation. Domestic rates were a highly visible tax, paid for out of current income, and widely hated, particularly by those with highly valued properties, although they were cheap to collect, difficult to avoid and broadly progressive, particularly after the introduction of rate rebates for those on low incomes.

Thus the Thatcher government decided to replace domestic rates with a new Community Charge or poll tax. (Business rates were retained but effectively nationalized, as National Non-domestic Rate, and turned into an inflexible form of central grant over which local authorities had no control.) The official name, Community Charge, was significant. It was deemed a *charge* on *consumers* for local government services, rather than a *tax* on local *citizens*. Yet it became universally known as the 'poll tax', a tax per head (similar to the poll tax which provoked the Peasants' Revolt back in 1381!). Almost all adult residents rather than just householders would pay, restoring the link between taxation and representation. The government hoped that this would deter high spending by local councils, who would be punished by voters through the ballot box for their higher poll tax.

It never worked as the government hoped. Although the new tax was popular with most Conservative party members, many of whom, living in highly-rated properties, stood to gain from the change, critics argued the new tax was regressive and unfair because it was not linked to ability to pay. Most local voters found they were paying more, sometimes much more. It proved a bureaucratic nightmare, three times as expensive to collect as the old rates and subject to widespread evasion. (Many councils were still chasing up defaulters years after the tax was abolished.) It was also widely seen as a tax on voting. Those seeking to evade the new tax (including many students) avoided registering to vote. This also affected population figures used as a basis for government grant calculations. Poorer councils thus suffered twice over – from loss of revenue from defaulters, and loss of income from grants based on an assessment of needs from low population estimates.

Public reaction was very hostile. The tax provoked serious riots and led to major reverses for the Conservatives in parliamentary by-elections and local elections, and contributed significantly to Margaret Thatcher's departure from Number Ten in 1990. The new Conservative government, under John Major, moved to scrap the poll tax, which had only lasted for three years in England (1990–3), although four in Scotland (where it had been introduced a year earlier in 1989). It was replaced with a new Council Tax in 1993, a tax on the capital values of domestic properties divided into eight bands, with a 25 per cent rebate for one-person households. The actual tax levied depends not only on the property band (and whether or not a rebate applies) but on the money needed by each local authority for its expenditure after all other receipts are taken into account. Thus levels of Council Tax depend on the spending of local councils where householders live, the value of their property and the number of adults in the household.

The proportion of total revenue which councils derive from the Council Tax can vary considerably between authority and authority, as well as over time, but the average council in recent years has met only around a quarter of its spending needs from the tax. Because income from other sources can fluctuate considerably from year to year, it does not necessarily follow that an above inflation increase in Council Tax is the result of some commensurate increase in a council's spending, nor does a reduction in tax necessarily mean spending cuts. Because changes in Council Tax levels often bear little relation to changes in spending, effective accountability to the local electorate is reduced. It is difficult even for the tolerably well-informed local taxpayer to know who to blame (or to reward) for his Council Tax bill.

Local government taxation remains acutely controversial. The Council Tax initially provoked surprisingly little criticism, largely because many were happy to see the poll tax abolished, while across the political spectrum there was little appetite for further change after recent upheavals. However, considerable opposition has grown, particularly in those parts of the country where large numbers of retired people live, often in highly-rated properties (e.g. Cornwall). The Liberal Democrats have long advocated a local income tax, and their pledge to abolish the Council Tax has played well in local elections, and was an issue in the 2005 general election (less so in 2010). Local income tax however would pose considerable administrative problems, and would inevitably create losers as well as winners. Even the Liberal Democrats are reported to be having second thoughts about the proposal. Local government tax remains a political hot potato.

## From central–local relations to 'multi-level governance'

There has been a long academic debate over what used to be called 'central–local relations', perceived as the relationship between the government at Westminster and elected local authorities. Central–local relations implies that there are only two levels of government which matter, and is now a rather inadequate term to describe the still developing system of multi-level governance in Britain.

Among the various levels of government to which English local authorities have to relate, the most important by far remains the government at Westminster, but it is no longer the only level which counts. Thus the European Union has a large and growing impact on British local governance, both as a source of additional funding, chiefly through the European Regional Development Fund and the Social Fund, and as specific funding for problems such as the decline of coal mining. EU legislation also affects local responsibilities for the environment, waste management, transport and planning. Local councils are now amongst the most vigorous lobbyists in Brussels. Similarly, local authorities in Scotland, Wales and Northern Ireland now have devolved national as well as the more remote UK government and the European Union to cope with. Even in England there is still a (now substantially threatened) tier of regional administration with which local councils have to deal.

Moreover, as we have seen, local authorities have to co-operate with neighbouring councils, and with a range of appointed local agencies, the local private and voluntary sectors and numerous community groups of all kinds in their own areas. The concept of the enabling authority has involved a shift to a more diplomatic rather than hierarchical relationship with partners in new complex networks. Moreover, councils have had to delegate some of their former educational functions to schools, and also often have to deal with parish councils which have some statutory rights to consultation (as well as powers to raise and spend a small part of council tax).

Central–local relations have been commonly illustrated in terms of various analogies or models. Thus some saw local government as the 'partner' of central government, which implies a degree of equality, while others perceived local government in a position of impotent dependence as the 'agent' of the centre. A third view uses the term 'steward', which emphasizes the subordinate position of local government but suggests rather more discretion than the agent model. Finally, the 'power dependence' model suggests that both central and local government have resources that they can use in relationship with each other (Rhodes, 1981, 1988). These models can be adapted (if somewhat awkwardly) to meet the more complex relationships arising within multi-level and inter-authority governance. If elected local authorities are too dependent on central government for their powers and finance to be regarded as 'partners', the same is even more true of other public agencies which do not have the legitimacy of election, or their own taxes. Yet knowledge of local conditions and responsibility for implementation of central policies can give local agencies of all kinds considerable leverage over decisions locally and policy outcomes. In practice, there are significant differences in policies and service levels between local authorities, and some similar differences between appointed local agencies. If such bodies were simply agents implementing national policy, these substantial differences would not exist.

It is the 'power dependence' model which can be most usefully adapted to inter-authority relations, and relations between the public, private and voluntary sectors (Rhodes, 1997). In partnerships and policy networks, for example, each participating organization may bring in certain strengths or resources which will help to determine their influence in decision-making. Thus in a public–private partnership, a local council may contribute significant statutory powers, finance, information, and legitimacy arising from its election, while a private firm may offer additional finance, commercial enterprise and experience and specific expertise. In a collaborative relationship between public agencies, such as between a local authority and health authorities over care in the community, each participant brings something which is useful to the other, and both may benefit from a fruitful co-operation (in a positive-sum rather than zero-sum game).

Optimists see the new world of local governance as offering many opportunities for the development of co-operative policy networks in which organizations from the public, private and voluntary sectors work together, drawing on a wide range of resources, and encouraging the inclusion and participation of people from across the whole local community. Both the command and control relationships typical of old-fashioned public bureaucracies, and the competitive zero-sum relationships of the free market are rejected. Instead, a true 'third way' of managing and delivering services to people is envisaged, involving collaborative networks of organizations and individuals working together as equals, employing more diplomatic and less authoritative forms of leadership (Rhodes, 1997).

Pessimists, by contrast, emphasize the fragmentation of government, the potential waste, duplication and inefficiency resulting from too many agencies with overlapping responsibilities. They are more cynical over the prospects for mutual co-operation between organizations in policy networks, assuming that each will follow their own institutional interests, guided by their own organizational culture. Some formal partners will be only token participants and will offer few if any useful resources. The bulk of the local community will be bemused by the more complex and fast-changing institutional environment, and will become apathetic and alienated rather than engaged participants. No-one will be effectively in charge and accountability will be weaker. Decisions will take longer and less will be achieved.

## Local government in hard times: from enabling authority to 'easyCouncil'?

Even before the change of government at Number Ten, local government faced hard times as a consequence of the financial and economic crisis from 2008 onwards, and the prospects of cuts in central grants and local spending, whoever was in power nationally. In the new political and economic climate more councils were coming under Conservative control, and many of these sought to be proactive in cutting their own costs, either by closing or outsourcing services.

Thus Barnet Council tried to reinvent itself as an 'easyCouncil' by cutting out the frills in local service provision on the lines of a budget airline (cf. Easyjet cutting out airline meals and other services not fundamental to the central purpose of transporting passengers from A to B): they proposed selling off libraries, and ending the provision of 24-hour wardens in sheltered housing. Another Conservative-controlled council, Suffolk, sought to go further and become Britain's first 'virtual council' by extending outsourcing (long familiar from the time of the Thatcher government for a few services under compulsory competitive tendering) to all services. Its workforce of 27,000 would be reduced to a few hundred supervising contracts with the private and voluntary sector. Local services would still be provided, but not by the council. Many of the same workers might end up still supplying them, but not employed by the council (perhaps with reduced pay and conditions). This would take the model of an 'enabling authority' to hitherto unimagined limits.

How far other councils will imitate these examples remains to be seen. Already there is considerable diversity between authorities in levels and modes of services. While some councils have sold off or transferred all their social housing, others, particularly in the North of England and Scotland, are still major landlords controlling thousands of properties. While some long ago outsourced refuse collection, cleaning, catering and ground maintenance to private firms, others retain a substantial council workforce to deliver these functions. While some councils have already lost any control over a rising number of the state schools in their area, some retain supervision over almost all local state schools. There are major variations in other council provision, including social services, libraries and leisure services. Some, but not all, of this reflects differences in party political control.

## Prospects for local government under the Conservative–Liberal Democrat coalition

While the coalition government's spending cuts will inevitably have a severe impact on local government, it seems unlikely that new approaches to local service provision will be centrally imposed, at least initially. Both former opposition parties have in the past criticized Labour government centralization, and advocated increased local autonomy. Some new MPs and new ministers (such as Eric Pickles, a former Conservative leader of Bradford Council, who became Secretary of State for Communities and Local Government in 2010) have a prior background in local government. Some optimists even hope for a new era for local government. They may be disappointed. Indeed, parties often champion local government when in opposition but impose more central control when in power. This is partly because they have policies to implement, want results and grow impatient with local government obstruction and delays over cherished programmes. Conflict is exacerbated when central government face councils predominantly held by opposition parties with different priorities. This is often the case, as voters use local elections to punish unpopular UK governments, even on issues that have nothing to do with local government. Good, bad and indifferent local councils are thrown out for the perceived deficiencies of UK governments of the same party or parties.

The Cameron coalition might have expected an easy ride initially, when, after thirteen years of Labour control of Downing Street, much of local government was in the hands of Conservatives and/or Liberal Democrats. Indeed, over the last two decades the Liberal Democrats had made considerable advances in local government, winning seats from both major parties, but particularly Labour, and establishing a significant power bases in many cities and towns across the country, including Liverpool, Sheffield, Newcastle, Birmingham and Bristol. Three-party politics and power-sharing in many local councils prefigured the hung parliament and Conservative–Liberal Democrat coalition following the 2010 election. By then Labour controlled few councils, having lost many of their old strongholds in the north. In the local elections in 2011 they recovered some ground, winning 26 more councils when voters punished hundreds of (largely) Liberal Democrat councillors for the decisions on tuition fees and spending cuts taken by the coalition government. Thus the Liberal Democrats lost control of Newcastle, Hull and Sheffield (where Clegg is an MP) to Labour, and lost seats in the south to their coalition partners in central government. The Conservatives emerged relatively unscathed from the carnage, making a net gain of three councils, and strengthening their hold on southern Britain.

Some Liberal Democrats blamed their coalition ministers and Clegg in particular for their council losses. While Conservative and Labour councillors are used to being punished in local elections for the real or presumed sins of their party nationally, it is a relatively novel experience for Liberal Democrats.

Although too much should not be read into a single year's local election results, the trend may continue while the 2010 Parliament lasts, with Labour making further gains in many of the towns and cities where the Liberal Democrats have established such a strong presence in recent years. The growing tensions between the coalition partners in Cabinet may be increasingly replicated in town halls up and down the country where the same parties share power.

Changes in council control are likely to lead to more clashes between central and local government, particularly over responsibility for painful cuts in services and council tax rises. In the current financial climate the government is bound to cut grants to councils, and then castigate them for introducing higher council taxes. Critics have already noted that, while local referendums may be introduced on council tax rises, there are no plans to introduce similar referendums on council spending cuts. Some left-wing councils will almost certainly seek to maintain levels of services where central government wants to make economics. Moreover, the coalition government plans for many more academy schools and 'free schools' (see Chapter 21) may take another large slice of education services out of local authority control. Further conflict between local and central government seems almost inevitable, sooner rather than later, whatever current rhetoric suggests.

## SUMMARY

- While there is a strong case for democratic local institutions, there are problems with the practice of local democracy including public ignorance and apathy and relatively weak local accountability.

- Elected local authorities have lost some important functions since 1945, and no longer necessarily provide all the services themselves for which they retain responsibility. They are increasingly expected to work with (or 'enable') others, including appointed public agencies, to provide local services rather than provide those services directly themselves.

- Local governance is a term widely used to cover all local community decision-making and the delivery of local public services.

- Repeated reorganizations of authorities, boundaries and functions over half a century have failed to produce a structure which satisfactorily reflects community identities and ensures efficient and effective local service provision. Local government remains varied and confusing, particularly in England.

- Attempts to make local authority decision-making and accountability more transparent, through (for example) elected mayors and local cabinets have as yet had little impact.

- Local government only finances a minority of its own spending from locally determined taxes (now the Council Tax), receiving the bulk of its money from central government grants. Local government taxation has long been controversial. Liberal Democrats seek to replace the Council Tax with a local income tax.

- Local public bodies of all kinds now work within a framework of multi-level governance. They have to work with other public bodies, the private and voluntary sectors within their own area, but also need to relate upwards not only to UK central government, but also to the European Union, devolved national government and regional adminsitration, and downwards to particular institutions, community and parish councils.

- The coalition government promise to decentralize power may not significantly increase local autonomy, particularly as local authorities will lose responsibilities for many schools under current plans.

# QUESTIONS FOR DISCUSSION

- Why is public knowledge and interest in local government apparently so low?

- Why are there 'all sorts of many players on the local pitch'? Should all local public services be run by elected local councils? Why are there so many appointed local bodies?

- How far are modern elected local authorities more enablers than providers? What are the implications in practice?

- In what ways are the private and voluntary sectors involved in the provision of local services? What advantages and disadvantages might there be in their involvement?

- Should local authorities be headed by directly elected mayors?

- Why has it proved so difficult to reorganize local government so as to provide for both local democratic accountability and efficient and cost-effective local services?

- Should the present council tax be replaced by a local income tax?

- Who holds real power in local communities, local politicians, officials or business interests? Is power concentrated in the hands of the few (elitism) or relatively widely dispersed (pluralism)? What evidence could be cited in support of either view?

- What are the obstacles to devolving more power to local councils?

# FURTHER READING

The relevant chapters (mainly 5, 6 and 7) of Greenwood *et al.* (2001), *New Public Administration in Britain* offers a very useful introduction. Wilson and Game (2006), *Local Government in the United Kingdom* provides a more thorough account of contemporary local government which focuses largely on elected local authorities, although it provides some coverage of non-elected local government. The most recent edition of an older textbook, Byrne (2000), *Local Government in Britain* can also still be recommended. Leach and Percy-Smith (2001), *Local Governance in Britain* (Palgrave) focuses on governance (including other public bodies, the private and voluntary sector) as well as traditional local government, although some of the local agencies and initiatives described have already been superseded. Stoker (2003) analyzes the changes that have taken place. Rhodes (1997), *Understanding Governance* does not focus exclusively on local governance but his analysis of policy networks remains useful for understanding

much of the governance literature. Stoker and Wilson (2004) have edited an excellent survey of recent developments in local governance and services.

Books covering more specific aspects of local governance include Gyford (1991), *Citizens, Consumers and Councils: Local Government and the Public* ; Stoker (1991), *The Politics of Local Government* ; and Skelcher (1998), *The Appointed State*. Butler *et al.* (1994), *Failure in British Government: the Politics of the Poll Tax* provides a detailed analysis of the poll tax story. Travers (2003) can be consulted on the government of London.

As always, websites provide important sources on recent and current developments, e.g. www.local.gov.uk and the Local Government Association's website www.lga.gov.uk. Most local authorities have their own websites. Newspapers and specialist academic journals (e.g. *Local Government Studies*) and professional journals are other useful sources.

In this chapter we seek to bring together some of the strands identified in previous chapters, as well as much additional material, in an attempt to characterize the newly emerging British state. Some of this involves re-examining the British constitution. How far does the traditional Westminster model still provide an accurate short-hand description of the British system of government? If the Westminster model is defunct, what has replaced it? Yet there are other questions surrounding British government and politics that are not so much linked with constitutional institutions and principles as with the whole role and functions of the state. What sort of things should government be doing, and how should it be doing it? Is the state larger or smaller than it was? Is it different in character? There is a growing literature that uses terms such as the enabling state, the regulatory state, partnership and networks. Increasingly the emphasis appears to be on the process of governance rather than the institutions of government. The state has become more complex and multi-layered, whether one considers constitutional change or other political developments. Thus multi-level governance appears to be the new reality.

## The end of the Westminster model?

Features of the Westminster model have long been criticized by constitutional reformers advocating devolution and decentralization, a clearer separation of powers, a proportional electoral system, and popular rather than parliamentary sovereignty, involving more direct or participatory democracy. These criticisms of the values and ideas implicit in the Westminster model were and are essentially normative. Yet they have helped inspire constitutional changes which, allied with some developments in political practice, have transformed British government to such an extent that it is questionable whether the Westminster model remains an accurate description of British government today (Dunleavy in Dunleavy *et al.,* 2006).

Thus devolution to Scotland, Wales and Northern Ireland suggests that Britain is no longer a unitary state. The transfer of the old judicial functions of the House of Lords to the new UK Supreme Court involves a clearer separation of judicial powers (although executive and legislative powers remain interdependent, with legislation largely an executive function). EU membership, devolution, and the Human Rights Act all imply some restrictions on parliamentary sovereignty,

## BOX 18.1

# The Westminster model

The Westminster model is a shorthand description of the traditional British system of government, derived ultimately from the analysis of Bagehot ([1867] 1963). The centre and focus of British government is Westminster and Whitehall. Constitutional principles associated with the Westminster model include the unitary state, parliamentary sovereignty, and strong government derived from the virtual fusion of executive and legislative functions, rather than a separation of powers. It is also taken to involve some features of relatively recent political practice including the two-party system and single-party majority government, both facilitated (but not necessarily produced) by a disproportionate electoral system, the single member plurality system. (For discussion of the Westminster model see chapters by Flinders, Jeffery and Dunleavy in Dunleavy *et al.*, 2006. See also Moran, 2005, p. 2, on the 'Westminster system'.)

which has been further eroded by the fall-out from the 2009 parliamentary expenses scandal. New, more proportional, electoral systems have been introduced for European parliamentary elections and devolved assemblies, and these have assisted wider party representation. Already the non-English territories of the United Kingdom have been familiar with coalition or minority government for some years, and following the 2010 election, coalition politics is the new reality at Westminster. Indeed recent general elections have seen a progressive decline of the two-party vote and an increasingly multi-party system.

However, the constitutional reforms and political changes that have taken place have been grafted onto the traditional British system of government rather than replacing it. Formally, the United Kingdom remains a unitary rather than a federal state, and the parliamentary sovereignty of Westminster is unaffected. Moreover, the media continue to focus on the old familiar confrontation between the government and opposition. Although the government is now a coalition of two parties, Conservative and Liberal Democrat ministers increasingly sing from the same hymn sheet. To many casual observers it may appear that nothing has fundamentally changed.

Yet there are now significant tensions, even contradictions, in the new British system of government. Some constitutional reforms have had unforeseen consequences. Mark Evans (in Beech and Lee, 2008), talks of 'spill-backs' and 'spill-overs'.

These tensions and spill-overs may be resolved in various ways. Reformers continue to urge the need for a written constitution that would lay down the principles and institutional framework for a modernized system of government. If this was a constitution like most others, the constitution rather than parliament would be sovereign, and the various powers of the state would be classified and defined. This could involve a fully federal system of government, although it would be difficult to accommodate England easily within a federal state, with 84 per cent of the UK population.

Additionally or alternatively, separatist nationalists in Scotland, Wales and Northern Ireland may ultimately achieve their objectives, and the unity of the United Kingdom would be formally dissolved. One possibility is that a separate English state, freed from its quasi-federal elements in non-English territories, could maintain or reassert the principles and practices of the traditional Westminster model, including the unitary state, parliamentary sovereignty and the two-party system with single-party majority government. The latter would be facilitated by the disappearance of separatist nationalist parties at Westminster, the weakening of the Liberal Democrats (who would lose seats in Scotland and Wales) and probable dominance by a Conservative party never keen on constitutional reform. Indeed, some Conservatives have criticized New Labour's constitutional changes as ill-conceived and dangerous tinkering with a fundamentally sound system (Norton, 2003).

Yet it is also possible the British system of government will continue to muddle along, with all its current tensions and contradictions. Indeed, similar tensions and contradictions are a feature of many states with written constitutions. (Consider the tensions between the federal government and state rights in the US constitution, or over the respective powers of President and Prime Minister in the Fifth French Republic.) Ambiguity can help to contain awkward differences over principle. Constitutional myths may have some value. Bagehot, considered the original source of the Westminster model, famously distinguished between the dignified and efficient elements of what he called the *English* constitution. However, he did not conclude that the dignified elements, such as the monarchy, were useless, but assisted confidence and legitimacy. Some analysts consider the Westminster model still shapes the behaviour of ministers and civil servants (Richards and Smith, 2004, p. 777). Although key parts of the Westminster model now appear to some more dignified than efficient, if many inside and outside government continue to accept its validity, it will continue to influence the way British politics is practised.

## The state and the market

Over and beyond these controversies around the principles and practice of the British system of government there is a continuing ideological debate over the nature and extent of the British state. A major theme in political theory, and perhaps the most significant divide between (and sometimes within) mainstream political ideologies, is over the respective roles of the state and the market. Classical liberalism involved leaving as much as possible to free market forces, with only a residual role for the state. Yet from the Second World War until the 1970s there was a prevailing cross-party consensus in favour of state intervention and planning. It was widely assumed that the British economy was a mixed economy in which the state had a major role not only in influencing the macro-economy along Keynesian lines, but in managing extensive welfare provision and major nationalized industries, particularly fuel and transport, and shaping income and employment poli-

cies. From the later 1970s onwards, this consensus supporting state intervention gave place to a new consensus favouring the free market which eventually included New Labour as well as the New Right. This new consensus involved the abandonment of Keynesianism, state planning and incomes policies, the privatization of former state-owned industries and the introduction of market competition into the management of public services. A presumption in favour of state intervention was replaced by a presumption in favour of the private sector and free market forces.

The Thatcher and Major governments certainly saw a significant transfer of assets and activities from the public sector to the private sector. Most significant here was the privatization of nearly all the former nationalized industries which the 1945–51 Labour government had transferred to state control (although some had previously been municipally owned and run). After a few relatively minor privatizations, gas, steel, telecommunications, water, electricity, coal and railways were sold off between 1984 and 1995.

One of the interesting aspects of privatization is that the transfer of assets from the public to the private sector has not removed these industries from the sphere of public policy, or even significantly reduced pressures on government to remedy perceived problems. Thus government is still held to account for the problems and deficiencies of rail transport despite the removal of the industry from state ownership and control. This is hardly surprising, as whether state-owned, privatized or controlled by a not-for-profit organization, the rail network still requires massive injections of public money which ultimately come from taxpayers. Rail users continue to agitate over prices, punctuality and reliability. Rail crashes provoke legitimate public concerns over rail safety, and demands for government action and tougher safety regimes. The state may divest itself of the ownership of troublesome industries, but not, it seems, of their problems.

Besides such massive transfers of assets, the Conservative governments from 1979–97 also attempted to introduce more competition into the provision of public services. One mechanism was the introduction of compulsory competitive tendering into parts of the National Health Service and local government. The deregulation of bus transport also led to a substantial shift from publicly owned and controlled bus companies into the hands of private operators. Thus many services previously provided almost exclusively by public organizations were now undertaken by private firms for profit, although they remained the statutory responsibility of local or health authorities who laid down the terms of contracts and monitored their implementation (Walsh, 1995).

In addition, further competition was introduced through internal markets (or quasi-markets) in health and, to a lesser extent, education. State grants were based on patients treated and pupils enrolled. As a consequence, hospitals were competing for patients, and schools for pupils. This was part of an attempt to inject more competition and private sector values into the public sector, through New Public Management. This involved not only a substantial change in culture for public servants, but major developments in administrative institutions, affecting not only the civil service, but the health service and local government.

## Restructuring the state

Although much New Right rhetoric was anti-government, and appeared to involve a 'rolling back' or 'hollowing out' of the state (Rhodes, 1997, 2000), it did not involve a significant shrinking of the size of the state as measured by public spending as a percentage of GDP. Indeed, for some commentators, Thatcherism involved a strong state rather than the minimal state lauded by neo-liberals (Gamble, 1988), and centralization rather than the decentralization to consumers and service users claimed in some government rhetoric. The apparent contradiction was sometimes explained by the suggestion that the government was seeking 'more control over less' (Rhodes, 2000, p. 156).

In practice, the state was substantially restructured rather than reduced, although this restructuring involved significant implications for the traditional British system of government, or Westminster model, as well as for the functions and scope of the state. In terms of administrative machinery, restructuring meant increased reliance on quangos, executive agencies, new single purpose bodies and state-aided voluntary bodies rather than government departments and elected local authorities.

One aspect of this restructuring was the growth in the number of **quangos**, appointed public bodies not directly controlled by elected politicians. Quangos were not new. There were always persuasive reasons for putting some government-sponsored or funded activities in the hands of an appointed body rather than party politicians and civil servants. In some cases it was particularly important that certain bodies were seen to be impartial and independent of the government of the day. Older examples include the BBC or ITA, the Equal Opportunities Commission or the Commission for Racial Equality (the last two now combined in the Equality and Human Rights Commission). In other cases a key motive was to attract the services of relevant experts as advisers. While some quangos have important executive responsibilities, employ numerous staff and manage multi-million pound budgets, many others are purely advisory, and experts provide part-time services for little or nothing. Indeed, it may often be much cheaper to establish a quango than run an activity as part of a government department.

Thus there can be good reasons for establishing independent public bodies. However, the main criticisms of quangos are over the issues of patronage and accountability. Many positions on non-departmental public bodies are effectively in the gift of ministers, and there has been considerable criticism of the criteria by which appointments are made. In the past, Labour governments appointed leading

---

● **Quango** is an acronym for (originally) quasi-autonomous non-governmental organization. Quangos are, however, normally funded, appointed and ultimately controlled by the state (so are part of government). They are appointed rather than elected, and not directly accountable to elected politicians. National quangos are officially described as '**non-departmental public bodies**' (NDPBs) and are thus distinguished from **Executive agencies** which have some managerial autonomy but are attached to departments.

---

● **Executive Agencies** are still part of the civil service, subject to civil service conditions and codes of practice. They are organized within government departments, and are subject to ministerially imposed policy objectives, budgets and performance targets. Yet they are headed by Chief Executives and operate within framework documents that give them considerable operational autonomy. Examples include the Child Support Agency and the UK Passports Agency.

trade unionists to many quangos, partly because some organizations needed representatives of 'labour' to balance business representatives. Conservative governments were sometimes accused of stuffing health authorities and urban development corporations with businessmen (often Conservative supporters), although they too could respond that such people brought essential management expertise to running these organizations. It is difficult to evade accusations of political partisanship in appointments, particularly where an organization may be seen as inherently party political.

Even more clearly, many quangos are not very accountable to the public (Plummer, 1994). Not only are they unelected, their proceedings are often held in secret, and even if reports and accounts are published, they receive little effective public scrutiny (although the Freedom of Information Act has recently had some impact here).

Parties in opposition often criticize quangos, but establish their own in government. Thus Mrs Thatcher promised a bonfire of quangos, and some indeed were abolished as the result of a report into 'non-departmental bodies' (Pliatzky Report, 1980). However, her governments proceeded to establish a wide range of new appointed bodies (although they generally refused to accept that these were 'quangos' because of the term's pejorative associations). Many new quangos were created as a result of the Thatcher government's determination to 'hive off' activities from the civil service and traditional local government. Indeed, some argued that the proliferation of quangos was part of a deliberate strategy to make the centre appear smaller – a somewhat cosmetic attack on 'big government'. Other new quangos were established to provide some regulation of pricing and investment of the privatized bodies running the former nationalized industries, for example the Office of Water Services (OFWAT) and the Office of Gas and Electricity Markets (OFGEM).

In government, Labour in turn created a range of new quangos to meet its own policy objectives, or meet specific problems. Thus the Food Standards Agency was established in the wake of the BSE and foot and mouth crises. Labour also set up a number of cross-cutting agencies designed to improve the co-ordination of government services

**Table 18.1**  Types and examples of quangos

| Type | Examples |
| --- | --- |
| Executive | Arts Council, Regional Development Agencies |
| Advisory | White Fish Authority, Advisory Committee on Hazardous Substances |
| Quasi-judicial | Pensions Tribunal, Employment Tribunal, Disability Appeal Tribunals |
| Regulatory | Audit Commission, National Audit Office, OFCOM, OFWAT, OFGEM, OFSTED, QAA, Food Standards Agency, |
| Cross-cutting | Social Exclusion Unit, Better Regulation Taskforce, New Deal Taskforce |

and secure better policy delivery, such as the Social Exclusion Unit, Better Regulation Taskforce and New Deal Taskforce. They renamed and partially reconstituted some independent public bodies and controversially amalgamated others.

In the 1980s more financial delegation and commercial disciplines were also introduced into the civil service. From 1988 the introduction of Executive Agencies involved more managerial autonomy but also obliged civil servants to reach prescribed targets and operate in a more commercial manner. One consequence was that ministerial responsibility and civil service anonymity were both eroded. Increasingly, heads of Executive Agencies were named and blamed for perceived shortcomings.

The transformation of most of the old unified civil service into a diverse collection of Executive Agencies with substantial managerial autonomy has also made British government more complex and confusing. Although distinctions can be drawn between older non-departmental public bodies (or quangos) and the new Executive Agencies, variations within both types of organization seem rather more significant than the differences between them. Indeed, even some leading participants appear confused over the formal status of their own organization. In effect, the Next Steps

## BOX 18.2

# A bonfire of quangos – again! The coalition's plans

As part of its programme to cut the budget deficit, the coalition government conducted an extensive review of quangos. In October 2010 Francis Maude, the Cabinet Office Minister, announced that 901 quangos would be reduced to 648 with another 40 still under review. Some major decisions, such as the scrapping of the Audit Commission, the UK Film Council, the 10 Strategic Health Authorities and 152 Primary Care Trusts, had been made earlier. Other quangos abolished included British Nuclear Fuels Ltd., the Youth Justice Board, Consumer Focus, the Renewable Fuels Agency and Cycling England. Some others are being merged (Competition Commission and Office of Fair Trading), converted into charities (British Waterways) or taken over by government departments, or in some cases the private sector. In many cases the functions will be carried on in another way, and there will be few savings, particularly when payment of pensions, redundancies and contractual liabilities are taken into account. Some advisory quangos cost very little, and their abolition will save next to nothing. Other quangos (e.g. the Equality and Human Rights Commission, the World Service, the British Council and the British Library) have been reprieved, although some are facing a substantial cut in funding. Maude argued that the changes would 'restore accountability and responsibility' to public life. Critics fear some of the functions of the axed quangos will be performed less effectively or not at all. A (January 2011) report by the Commons Public Administration Select Committee, chaired by Conservative MP Bernard Jenkin, suggested the 'Bonfire of the Quangos' had been botched and would lead to neither significant savings nor improved accountability.

programme has created many more public bodies with variable autonomy from direct ministerial control.

Similarly, successive reforms of the health service, education and the police service increased managerial delegation and reduced local democratic control. Local councils lost much of their control over schools formally to school governing bodies, but in practice to head teachers and senior management teams. For a time it was possible for schools to seek grant-maintained status (financed directly by central government) and opt out of local authority control completely.

Whether quangos, Executive Agencies and a range of other new public bodies involve more or less government and central control, they remain an area of legitimate concern. Once the only government bodies which seemed to count in the UK were government departments, headed by ministers and staffed by civil servants, and (a long way behind), elected local authorities. Lines of responsibility and accountability were fairly clear, and ultimately elected politicians were responsible for policy, accountable to Parliament or a local council, and they carried the can for failure. When things go wrong, it is now more often agency managers or officers who are blamed rather than politicians. Both old central departments and local councils have increasingly lost out to these other public bodies. Indeed, some have argued that the proliferation of appointed bodies reflected a purposeful bypassing of democratic institutions, particularly elected local government, in favour of a 'new magistracy' (so termed after the appointed local magistrates who administered much of county government until 1888). Whatever judgement is made, government certainly become more complex and less subject to direct control by elected politicians.

## Partnership with the private and voluntary sector

Both the Conservative governments of Thatcher and Major and the Labour governments of Blair and Brown emphasized the need for partnership with the private and voluntary sector. While Labour in opposition strenuously opposed most of the Conservative privatization programme, opposed compulsory competitive tendering and many of the changes introduced into the health

BOX 18.3

# From Railtrack to Network Rail

The Labour government took a politically controversial decision in 2001 to put Railtrack into receivership and introduce a new not-for-profit body, Network Rail, to administer Britain's rail infrastructure. Critics in the Conservative opposition and the City accused the government of back-door renationalization. They argued that the decision to pull the plug on Railtrack would undermine private sector investors' faith in public–private partnerships and make it far more expensive for the government to borrow, because of the extra element of risk and uncertainty. By contrast the government argued that Railtrack was a failed and effectively bankrupt company which required huge additional public funds to bail it out. It was unreasonable to expect taxpayers to foot the bill. Shareholders should realise that shares can go down as well as up. In the event a compromise deal was reached which involved some compensation for shareholders, although this did not prevent legal proceedings by angry former Railtrack shareholders. While Network Rail has performed more satisfactorily there have been continuing tensions with the train operating companies.

and education services, including internal markets, in government it generally proved unable or unwilling to put the clock back. The major Conservative privatizations were not reversed (with the partial exception of the collapse of Railtrack in the autumn of 2001; see Box 18.3), and Labour itself proceeded with the part privatization of air traffic control. Although CCT was replaced by the more flexible 'best value' regime, the provision of key local government services was still subject to competition, and many remain privately provided. Labour effectively endorsed greater managerial delegation and autonomy by continuing Next Steps Agencies and proceeding to further significant decentralization and delegation within the National Health Service.

New Labour also enthusiastically embraced partnership with the private sector, through **Public–Private Partnerships** (PPPs), under which government departments, local authorities and other public bodies enter into partnership agreements with private firms on key developments and initiatives. Perhaps the most politically controversial of these schemes were the partnership agreements funding an extensive programme of new investment in the London Underground railway system, despite the strong opposition of the then London Mayor, Ken Livingstone.

Increased private sector investment in the public sector is provided through a particular form of public–private partnership, the **Private Finance Initiative** (PFI). Many new PFI hospitals, schools and prisons have already been built, using the money and expertise of the private sector, paid for by the relevant public authority over a period, commonly 25 years. While PFIs were introduced by Major's Conservative government, they were endorsed and extensively utilized by Blair's Labour government. Under a PFI the ownership and maintenance of the building (e.g. school or hospital) commonly remains the responsibility of the private consortium, while the relevant public authority retains responsibility for running the service, employing and paying for professional staff, and meeting other day-to-day service costs. Some PFI prisons, however, were both built and run by the private sector.

The main attraction for government of PFIs is that they increase the funds available for public

● **Public–private partnerships** (PPPs) involve formal partnership between government bodies (such as local councils), private firms and sometimes voluntary organizations to manage a specific initiative or deliver a policy.

● **The Private Finance Initiative** (PFI) is a specific and controversial form of partnership, under which the private sector funds, builds and maintains public sector investment in, for example, hospitals, schools, prisons and roads. The relevant sponsoring public authority (e.g. a local council or hospital trust) makes annual payments, typically for a period of 25 years, after which the assets become its property.

sector capital investment (chronically underfunded in the past) without requiring public sector borrowing. Some argue that there are also efficiency gains arising from private sector involvement. Critics contend that PFIs are more expensive than traditional public sector borrowing, because of the pursuit of profit and the need to provide a return to shareholders. They also argue that there is little effective transfer of risk to the private sector, as the state cannot afford to allow the projects to fail. The long record of PFI hospitals, schools and prisons remains contentious, and includes some claimed successes and failures. Perhaps a more balanced verdict on the costs and benefits of PFIs will only be obtainable as projects reach the end of their 25-year agreements, and the ownership and maintenance of building reverts to the public sector.

Although much of the ideological debate has been over the relative merits of public provision on the one hand, and private provision for profit on the other, there has been some focus also on a third way – provision by mutually owned or voluntary organizations. The most important example of 'mutuals' used to be the building societies, which were owned by the members and not run for profit. However, after banking deregulation, most of the largest building societies became public limited companies with shareholders instead of members, who were generally happy to vote for the legal transfer of assets and pocket (often substantial) sums in recompense. Some of these staid and respectable former building societies became highly speculative banks that contributed significantly to the financial crisis from 2007 onwards.

The most significant example of voluntary provision of public services is now the housing associations which were favoured as a 'third force' in the supply of rented accommodation by the Thatcher Conservative government (the other two being the council and private landlords). While most Labour councils opposed the sale of council houses in the 1980s, many voluntarily co-operated in the transfer of much of their remaining housing stock to housing associations which over time have become major providers of rented 'social housing'.

Voluntary provision of public services is far from new in the UK. Indeed in the nineteenth century it was generally the preferred method of provision. Thus schools were provided by voluntary religious organizations, with increasing state subsidy, and many hospitals were initially established on a voluntary basis. This suited Victorian opinion which was suspicious of state intervention, and it remains more ideologically acceptable today to both free market advocates hostile to direct state provision and to many within the Labour party who retain an aversion to private provision of public services for profit.

'Voluntary organizations' conjures up images of small-scale operations by well-meaning but inexpert amateurs. However, many voluntary associations today are big businesses, employing substantial numbers of well-paid professional staff. Although they are 'not for profit' they are run on commercial lines, and while they are not part of government, they rely substantially on state financial support. They thus inhabit a grey area between the public and private sectors. However, while they lack some of the disadvantages of each, they may also lack some of their advantages. They may be less susceptible to the private sector discipline of market competition and less publicly accountable than mainstream government organizations. Nevertheless, they remain attractive to those seeking a third or middle way between the state and the market.

Overall, New Labour did not challenge the trend towards the proliferation of agencies and fragmentation of government. It continued Next Steps agencies, and replaced some older quangos with newer quangos of its own, although it cut or amalgamated others. However, it placed rather more emphasis on collaboration and co-operation between agencies and sectors. To counteract some of the problems of co-ordination arising from increased institutional fragmentation it established a number of cross-cutting units or task forces in the interests of 'joined-up government', such as the Social Exclusion Unit.

## 'Steering, not rowing': networks, enabling and governance

The cumulative impact of all these changes has transformed the character of the British state. While many services are still publicly funded, they

**Table 18.2**  From old government to new governance: the shifting focus

| Old government | New governance |
|---|---|
| The state | The state and civil society |
| The public sector | Public, private and voluntary (or third) sectors |
| Institutions of government | Processes of governing |
| Organizational structures | Policies, outputs, outcomes |
| Providing ('rowing') | Enabling ('steering') |
| Commanding, controlling, directing | Leading, facilitating, collaborating, bargaining |
| Hierarchy and authority | Partnerships and networks |

*Source*: Adapted from Leach and Percy-Smith (2001, p. 5).

are often no longer controlled and provided by government departments and local authorities but by all kinds and combinations of organizations, including private firms, the voluntary bodies or decentralized quasi-autonomous public sector bodies. This has been described as a 'hollowing out' of the state. Yet it also suggests the state is performing an essentially different role – an enabling role, to borrow a term first used in Britain to describe the new role of local government, but which can also be applied to the role of the state as a whole. The key point is that the state is no longer necessarily providing services directly but 'enabling' others to do so – business, public–private partnerships, the voluntary sector, the community itself. An analogous term employed by the Americans Osborne and Gaebler (1992) is the notion of the state 'steering' rather 'rowing'. Governments should facilitate and co-ordinate rather than attempt to do everything themselves.

Thus instead of the old 'command and control' state, involving formal hierarchies and highly centralized decision-making, policy and decisions emerge today from complex partnerships or less formal networks of public, private and voluntary and hybrid organizations, working co-operatively together with relevant community groups and interests.

The fashionable term 'governance' emphasizes the process of governing rather than the institutions of government, and blurs the distinction between government and governed. Governance does not just include those who as ministers, civil servants or elected councillors are part of 'government', but business and the voluntary sector, as well as parties and pressure groups in so far as they contribute to the process of governance and the delivery of services to the community. No-one is 'in charge'. Governance necessarily involves collaboration between agencies and sectors, and partnership working rather than the clear lines of authority and responsibility found in more traditional management hierarchies (Rhodes, 1997, Pierre and Stoker in Dunleavy *et al.*, 2002, Bevir and Rhodes, 2003). It draws on the agenda of Osborne and Gaebler in *Reinventing Government* (1992), some of the ideas of New Public Management (see chapter 12), together with strands of New Labour and Third Way thinking (Giddens, 1998, Newman, 2001).

Networks almost by definition require co-operation and collaboration, needing patience and diplomacy. Governance through networks involving a range of organizations and interests resembles a pluralist vision of widely dispersed power and influence. Yet while a large number of organizations may be formally associated with the process of decision-making, some are commonly far more closely involved and count far more than others. In practice those who bring useful resources to the table, such as money, land, expertise and legal authority are more likely to 'call the shots'. Politics is still about power, and some inevitably have more effective influence than others.

Some organizations may indeed be only token participants in networks. Perhaps this is as well, for a very large number of partners in any enterprise can be a recipe for procrastination. Yet decisions that emerge through networks raise other problems of responsibility and accountability. Formal partnerships may clearly determine respective responsibilities, commonly in legal documents. More complex and informal networks may not locate who is responsible and accountable, and real decision-makers may be able to hide behind the cloak of collective responsibility if things go wrong.

Table 18.3  Some important regulatory bodies

| | |
|---|---|
| Office of Fair Trading (OFT) – now to be merged with Competition Commission | Regulator charged with making markets work for consumers |
| Competition Commission (formerly Monopolies and Mergers Commission) | Promotes competition in the private sector, may declare that mergers are not in the public interest |
| Health and Safety Executive | Responsible for whole range of health and safety |
| Audit Commission (to be abolished) | Audits local authorities and health authorities |
| National Audit Office (NAO) | Audits central government |
| Office of Water Services (OFWAT) | Regulates privatized water industry |
| Office for Standards in Education (OFSTED) | Responsible for inspecting and raising standards in schools |
| The Financial Services Authority (FSA) (abolished by coalition government – and regulatory functions returned to Bank of England and other bodies) | Regulated banks, building societies, insurance companies, stock exchange, etc., absorbed functions of nine former regulatory bodies |
| Food Standards Agency | Independent regulator to monitor the food production and supply industry – set up by Blair government in wake of BSE scandal |
| Office of Gas and Electricity Markets (OFGEM) (formerly OFGAS and OFFER) | Regulates gas and electricity industry |
| Office of the Rail Regulator (ORR) | Regulation of train operators and rail network (prices, services, etc.) |
| The Strategic Rail Authority | Responsible for longer-term rail investment |

## The regulatory state

There is nothing essentially new in regulation. Governments have long been in the business of regulating, although the extent of regulatory activity and regulatory bodies seems to have increased dramatically over the last 30 years or so, sufficiently to justify the term 'regulatory state'. Professor Michael Moran (2000, 2001, 2003, 2005) has been particularly associated with the concept of the regulatory state involving a substantial shift in emphasis from state provision and control to state regulation.

Providers, public, private and voluntary, cannot be relied upon to regulate themselves. External regulation of services provided by the state appears necessary to measure performance and ensure

value for money. Voluntary bodies entrusted with taxpayers' money to provide public services need monitoring. Where former state-run enterprises or services have been privatized there is a continuing need to regulate quality, prices, safety and efficiency in the wider public interest, particularly where there are monopoly elements or continuing state subsidies. Parts of the private sector, such as banks and the financial sector generally, require state regulation and support to maintain public confidence in the banking system. Beyond all this the state is increasingly called upon to regulate all kinds of aspects of our lives in the wider public interest, including heath and safety, hygiene, drugs and alcohol consumption, childcare, care of the elderly, food standards, labelling and advertising

## COMPARATIVE POLITICS  18.1
# Regulatory capture in the USA

'Regulatory capture' is a term long used by observers of regulatory agencies in the United States. A particular agency established to regulate a profession or industry may become effectively captured by the interests it is supposed to regulate, instead of looking after the interests of consumers or the wider public. A notorious early example was the Interstate Commerce Commission established in the USA to prevent rail companies from collaborating to fix prices and exploit their customers, which instead became the protector and advocate of the railroad interests. Regulatory capture can arise from the practice of appointing regulators with relevant knowledge and expertise, most easily found among those employed by the industry being regulated. Thus

the Environmental Protection Agency was staffed by officials who had worked previously for known polluting firms, leading to a scandal and resignations when Congress investigated its ineffective enforcement of anti-pollution policy (Denenberg, 1996, pp. 159–60). Critics would argue that some British regulatory bodies have similarly 'gone native', adopting the perspective of those whose activities they were expected to police. Moran points out that the Financial Services Authority (see Box 18.4) is not a public body, but is effectively owned by the private interests that it is designed to regulate, and thus especially vulnerable to 'regulatory capture' (Moran, 2005, pp. 158–9).

and much else besides. The state may be providing less, but certainly appears to be regulating more. Thus there are a huge number of regulatory bodies of all kinds looking after us, some now facing abolition or merger following the coalition government's review.

Regulation implies a less positive and constructive role for the state than the notion of enabling. An enabling state may initiate, encourage, sponsor or stimulate others (in the public, private or voluntary sectors) to work together to achieve some positive outcome. Moreover the state is an active partner. Regulation suggests a more negative control function. The provision of goods and services is left to others. Managers in the public, private and voluntary sectors are given substantial discretion, autonomy and 'freedom to manage', but the state establishes appropriate regulatory authorities to inspect and measure their performance and police their activities. Rather more positively, governments can pursue policy objective by rewarding success and punishing failure in meeting performance targets.

Moran (2005, pp 158–9), however, argues that the regulatory state has created some serious problems. He notes problems for traditional ministerial

and parliamentary accountability, particularly because of what he calls the 'ambiguous legal status' of some regulatory bodies. He also questions the effectiveness of some regulation, alluding to the danger of regulatory capture and pointing out: 'in the case of the Financial Services Authority…the regulated actually "own" the regulator'. These comments appear prophetic in the light of the failure of 'light touch' regulation of the banks by the FSA, contributing to the banking crisis of 2007–8. Yet if some regulation appears weak and ineffective, critics suggest other regulation is damaging and counter-productive, particularly the extensive monitoring of the health and education services through targets (see Chapter 21). Thus the new 'regulatory state' may be no more successful in achieving policy objectives than the old 'welfare' or 'control' state. While the media seize on ludicrous examples of over-regulation, particularly on grounds of health and safety, they are quick to seize on failures of regulation, when relevant regulators have not picked up serious problems in hospitals, schools or social services. If much regulation is either heavy-handed or ineffective, the whole concept of a regulatory state seems suspect.

# A failure of regulation? The Financial Services Authority

The Labour government introduced what was supposed to be a new 'super-regulator', the Financial Services Authority (FSA) for banking and financial services, replacing nine separate regulatory agencies, including the Bank of England, which until then had responsibility for regulating the commercial banks. The FSA promised more co-ordinated and effective government scrutiny of the banking industry. Yet the FSA was never a public body, but a company limited by guarantee, dependent on money raised from the financial sector, and thus hardly independent. Moreover, the Labour government was so fearful of upsetting the banks, apparently the main engine of the British economy, that they endorsed 'light touch' regulation. Thus the FSA did little to prevent the complex new financial instruments banks devised to support questionable lending, involving self-certification of creditworthiness; one hundred and twenty per cent mortgages; and the 'buy to let' boom. In consequence the new regulatory machinery for the banking industry proved inadequate, contributing to the credit crunch and leading to Conservative proposals to wind up the FSA and restore the Bank of England's former regulatory role.

## From the secret state to open government?

While democracy has long been linked with more open government, the British state in the past often appeared highly secretive. Secrecy appeared to be one of the trademarks of the traditional practice of government in the United Kingdom. While the term 'secret state' is perhaps more commonly associated with the clandestine activities of British intelligence and security services, it is sometimes used more widely to describe British government. The more recent commitment to 'open government' indeed reflects a recognition that government has been less than open in the past.

To begin with the narrower but important issue of the British intelligence and security services, it would perhaps be generally conceded that all states may have to resort to clandestine operations in the interests of defence and internal security. Intelligence gathering on potential threats may save lives and prevent or deter serious threats. Some serious plots have been effectively forestalled, even if better intelligence might have detected and prevented the London bombing of 7 July 2005. When the stakes are high, particularly in time of war, it would also be conceded that secret operations, including 'dirty tricks' to destabilize the enemy, are to be commended, particularly if they are shown to materially affect the outcome. Thus Churchill established the Special Operations Executive in the Second World War, and British agents who operated behind enemy lines are celebrated as heroes (although of course enemy agents performing a similar role in the UK are commonly considered despicable). There is a continuing fascination with and some admiration for the whole world of espionage. Yet there are also important civil liberties issues surrounding the activities of the security services. There is a delicate balance to be struck between protecting British citizens against internal and external threats to their well-being and safety, and violations of the fundamental human rights and freedoms of those same citizens.

However, although the British secret services are often viewed as glamorous, some hard questions may be asked about their record, overall effectiveness and value for money.

- The discovery in the 1950s and 1960s that some high-ranking members of the security services (Burgess, Maclean, Philby, Blunt) were double agents working for the Soviet Union undermined faith in the reliability of the services, and their recruitment and internal vetting. Doubts resurfaced in the 1970s and 1980s with further prosecutions and damaging (but unproved) allegations against senior figures.
- Ostensibly far-fetched allegations that elements of MI5 were plotting against Prime Minister Harold Wilson appeared to have an element of truth and raised questions about the judgement, loyalty and political bias of the security services (Hennessy, 2000, pp. 372–5, but see also Andrew, 2009).
- The alleged use of the security services for partisan purposes, including intelligence gathering on trade unions and industrial disputes in the 1980s, renewed allegations of inappropriate targeting of those with left-wing politics. Ironically, some senior members of Blair's government were themselves earlier subjects of surveillance by the security services (Jack Straw, Harriet Harman and Peter Mandelson, according to former MI5 officer, David Shayler).
- The failure of western intelligence services generally, including the British intelligence services, to anticipate and prevent the events of 11 September 2001 and of 7 July 2005 suggests that they are ill-equipped to counter the new global terrorism, and may be too much locked into activities of the Cold War.

- The additional powers acquired by the government to counter terrorism and the detention without trial of suspects has provoked concerns over civil liberties in general and Islamophobia in particular.
- The serious deficiencies in the evidence gathered by the intelligence services on Saddam Hussein's 'weapons of mass destruction' used to justify the Iraq war in 2003 raised further questions over the effectiveness of these services.

By their very nature there are bound to be problems with the accountability and control of secret services. Full accountability would require detailed publicity for activities that would no longer be secret. Information on the activities of the security services is thus confined to as few politicians as possible, on a 'need to know basis' and overall responsibility lies with the Prime Minister alone. The most delicate secret operations have to be cleared with the Prime Minister personally

**Table 18.4**   Britain's security services

| Security and intelligence agencies | Functions |
| --- | --- |
| MI5 (Security Service) | Concerned with domestic security – primarily with internal threats to British state and countering 'serious crime' |
| Special Branch (2005 proposal that this should become part of a larger national force to counter terrorism, etc.) | Internal security arm of police – works with MI5 to counter terrorism, protect VIPs, conduct surveillance, etc. |
| MI6 (Secret Intelligence Service) | Gathering political, military and economic intelligence in foreign countries – combating serious crime (e.g. money laundering, drug smuggling, illicit arms deals, illegal immigration, etc.) |
| Government Communications Headquarters (GCHQ) | Intercepting and decoding of international communications |

(Hennesy, 2000, p. 83). Even so, the secret services have not been immune from the trend towards more open government. Stella Rimington, whose appointment to take charge of MI5 was announced by the Major government, has since published her own (rather unrevealing) memoirs. MI5 and GCHQ now have their own websites. Remarkably, an 'official history' of MI5 has appeared (Andrew, 2009), although critics understandably retain some scepticism over how fully this can be trusted (see, for example, Porter, 2009). Yet all present and former employees of the security services are still bound by the Official Secrets Act, which they are obliged to sign, and can be prosecuted for breaches. One former MI5 officer, David Shayler, was given a prison sentence in 2002 for interviews he had given five years earlier.

Beyond the fascinating world of the secret services proper there are however much wider questions about secrecy in British government. It is sometimes argued that the lack of open government and fuller accountability to Parliament and the public is the consequence of particular features of the unwritten British constitution. Thus British ministers and public servants formally serve the crown rather than 'the people' or 'the public interest'. In practice civil servants, and public officials generally, are expected to serve the government of the day. Advice to ministers is confidential. Civil servants are obliged to sign the Official Secrets Act and can be prosecuted for unauthorised disclosure of classified information. No public interest defence is allowable.

Once our knowledge of the internal workings of British government depended substantially on gossip, leaks and politicians' memoirs, rather than more authoritative sources. Some progress towards greater openness was made under recent governments. The comprehensive system of Departmental Select Committees set up under the Thatcher government led to some more effective parliamentary scrutiny of the executive. The Major government published details of Cabinet committees, their membership and terms of reference, provided a legal right of access to non-computerized personal files, and published a new 'Open Government' code of practice on information to be provided by government departments and agencies. The Citizen's Charter initiative led to the publica-

tion of much useful information on standards of service the public could expect, with procedures for complaint and redress. Yet despite this apparent commitment to greater openness, the veil of secrecy on government decision-making is commonly only lifted when something has gone badly wrong, leading to an independent investigation and report. Examples include the Scott Report (on arms to Iraq), 1996, the Phillips Inquiry on BSE, 2000, and the Hutton, Butler (2004) and Chilcot Reports (2010–11) on the Iraq war.

Two pressure groups, the Campaign for Freedom of Information and Charter 88, led to demands for more open government, including a Freedom of Information Act. Blair as opposition leader in 1996 proclaimed, 'We want to end the obsessive and unnecessary secrecy which surrounds government activity and make government information available to the public unless there are good reasons not to do so.' His government eventually honoured its manifesto pledge to pass a Freedom of Information Act in 2000, although critics argued that the initial proposals had been substantially watered down. Thus Austin (in Jowell and Oliver, 2000, p. 371) claimed that the Act involved such an 'extraordinary list of exemptions' that it was 'a regime for open government only by consent of government ministers' and 'a denial of democracy' (see also Rathbone, 2001).

The Act contributed to the changing of attitudes and procedures within government even before it finally became operative in 2005. Since then a mass of information has been made available (some of it for partisan political purposes in the run-up to the election). As anticipated, some other requests for information have been refused. However, the media and private citizens have learned to use the Act to obtain relevant information. Ultimately it was the Freedom of Information Act that led to the parliamentary expenses scandal of 2009 and a series of revelations that have embarrassed ministers. It is far more difficult now for government and officialdom in general to cover up damaging mistakes

Meanwhile, some questions remain over how far openness is practical or desirable. All governments retain an interest in maintaining some confidentiality for their internal deliberations (even if this can sometimes be compromised by the activities of WikiLeaks). Many ideas which are tentatively floated by ministers or their advisers never come to fruition, and some are abandoned at an early stage, but the knowledge that they had even been contemplated, however briefly, could have damaging political repercussions. If all deliberations and all advice to ministers were made public, this might inhibit the range of debate. Ministers would no longer dare to 'think the unthinkable' or come up with unpopular but perhaps necessary policy proposals because of the potential political damage. Governments might even become wary of making contingency plans to cope with threats or disasters, for fear of creating public alarm and perhaps panic. Blair (2010, pp. 516–17) later concluded that freedom of information had been a mistake. His government had 'strayed far beyond what it was sensible to disclose'.

## The surveillance state and civil liberties

Some critics have become increasingly concerned over the erosion of civil liberties and the increase in controls and surveillance of citizens. Partly this has arisen from the 'war on terror'. Clearly the British state and people do face real threats from within, as the attacks on London (2005) and Glasgow airport (2007) as well as some apparently foiled plots demonstrate. However, the threat has led to the suspension of some ancient liberties (through detention without trial and control orders) and to increased surveillance (phone tapping, security cameras, undercover police operations ) and was an argument behind the Labour government's plans for identity cards. The more long-standing 'war on crime' was a further argument for more security cameras (both closed circuit television, CCTV, and the more recent body-worn video cameras, BWC, increasingly used by police) and new restrictions, such as the contentious Anti-Social Behaviour Orders (ASBOs). While some felt safer as a result of increased surveillance, others were angered by the intrusion on their privacy.

The perceived erosion of civil liberties aroused concerns across the political spectrum. The established pressure group Liberty has been in the forefront of the criticism. On the right the former Conservative leadership candidate David Davis

quixotically (and against the advice of Conservative colleagues) resigned his seat in Parliament to fight and win a parliamentary by-election on a civil liberties platform in July 2008. The Conservative leadership has continued (without Davis) to proclaim their commitment to civil liberties, as have the Liberal Democrats and many Labour critics of the New Labour government. The coalition government has already scrapped Labour's planned introduction of identity cards, and is committed to abolishing other intrusions on privacy and civil liberties by cutting surveillance. However, early signs are that the coalition is to modify rather than abolish control orders for terrorist suspects, removing some of the more draconian restrictions that amount to a form of house arrest.

Table 18.5   The new multi-level governance, as applied to Britain

| Level | Institutions |
| --- | --- |
| Global | United Nations, IMF, WTO, G8, G20, multi-national organizations and companies, NGOs |
| Transatlantic | North Atlantic Treaty Organization |
| European | European Union, European Commission, European Parliament, European Court of Justice, Council of Europe, European Court of Human Rights |
| UK | Cabinet and core executive, Westminster parliament |
| Devolved national | Scottish Parliament and Government, Welsh Assembly and Executive, Northern Ireland Assembly and Executive |
| Regional | Government offices, Regional Development Agencies, Regional Chambers (both facing abolition) |
| Local | County, district, unitary and parish councils, non-elected local government |
| Institutional | Hospital trusts, universities and colleges, academy schools, 'free schools', etc. |

# The disintegration of the British state – or towards multi-level governance?

Although writers may not fully agree over exactly how and why the British state has changed, there is widespread agreement that it has changed, and profoundly. Instead of a unified, highly centralized state with its traditional core institutions in Westminster and Whitehall, there is a complex, fragmented and multi-layered system of government and politics that is still evolving. This more complex pattern of governance operates at an increasing range of levels – international, European, UK, devolved national, regional, local and institutional (see Table 18.5). While some levels remain more important than others, the balance is clearly shifting over time. Key decisions affecting the lives of British citizens are not just made in London but in Brussels or Edinburgh, or within local authorities, hospital trusts, Learning and Skills Councils, and within a range of other devolved agencies, units and networks. The unitary state associated with the old 'Westminster model' of British government has been replaced by a 'differentiated polity' in which a variety of agencies and interests are involved in the framing and delivery of policy at a number of different but interdependent levels.

For some, this trend towards multi-level governance is natural and inevitable in the modern world. It is the old nation state that is obsolete (Giddens, 1998, Pierre and Peters, 2000, Pierre and Stoker in Dunleavy *et al.*, 2002). For others, who cherish the traditional British state, British national independence and the sovereignty of the UK Westminster parliament, the changes are deeply unsettling. From their perspective the growing importance of the European Union on the one hand , and the devolution of power to nation to sub-UK nations and regions on the other, represents a danger to the British state which could prove terminal.

Partly the issue is what is the most appropriate level of government for functional efficiency and effectiveness. It might seem appropriate to decentralize some decision-making down from the UK government level to local communities or even institutions in the interest of improved delivery of

**Table 18.6** From the old Westminster model to the new British governance

| The Westminster model | The new British governance |
| --- | --- |
| The unitary state | The 'differentiated polity' |
| Parliamentary sovereignty | The devolution of power |
| Ministerial responsibility | Delegation of management |
| Central–local relations | Multi-level governance |
| Homogeneity, uniformity, 'Fordism' | Diversity, fragmentation, 'post-Fordism' |

*Source*: Adapted from Leach and Percy-Smith (2001, p. 7).

(for example) education and health services. There are other issues, such as international trade, disarmament, global pollution and conservation, which can only be effectively tackled at a supranational and global level. Yet for many services and functions there are many levels at which decisions may be appropriately taken, and multi-level governance appears almost inescapable.

However, issues of functional efficiency are bound up closely with the politics of identity and allegiance. The demands for closer European union, for a Scottish parliament, and even for successive UK local government reorganizations were not just driven by expectations of more efficient government and service provision, but by political ideals and loyalties. Much of the debate over Europe, or devolution, or local authority boundaries is ultimately about how people feel about who they are, and the communities they identify with. Do they feel part of Europe or the English-speaking world? Are they Scots or British? Do they identify with their city or county? Other identities – ethnic, religious, class – may cut across spatial boundaries. Some are comfortable with multiple overlapping identities and allegiances, but to others a particular identity may appear exclusive and all-important. For them we are either British or European, either Scots or British; we have to choose between UK national sovereignty or a European superstate, between allegiance to the United Kingdom or an independent Scotland. The whole notion of multi-level governance is hardly compatible with more exclusive identities and allegiances.

There is much which seems confusing and contradictory about this emerging system of multi-level governance, which explains some of the range of competing terms that have been employed to describe it (see Table 18.6). Is the new British politics all about devolution and decentralization, or does it more plausibly involve a new concentration of power by a bunch of control freaks? Has the state been 'hollowed out' or 'joined up'? Has the welfare state been replaced by a regulatory state?

Has representative democracy effectively been replaced by a new magistracy or quangocracy? Does the rhetoric about open government merely conceal the maintenance of secrecy? In part different answers reflect different assumptions and partisan viewpoints, yet they also reflect genuine uncertainty. Clearer answers to such questions may be subsequently available to historians with the benefit of hindsight but it is difficult to spot the truly significant trends in an era of extensive political and institutional upheaval.

## SUMMARY

- British government is still in the process of extensive transformation. It is not yet clear how the newly emerging British state should be characterized.

- The boundaries of the state have become blurred. In academic literature there has been some switch in emphasis from considering the institutions of government to the process of governing (or 'governance'), which can involve the private and voluntary sectors.

- Under Conservative governments from 1979–97 the rhetoric was about reining back the state. Some state assets and activities were privatized and others subjected to competition either from the private sector or through the introduction of internal markets.

- New Labour has emphasized partnership with the private and voluntary sectors and 'joined-up government'. Much new capital investment for the public sector has been financed through the controversial Private Finance Initiative (PFI).

- Under all governments there has been a growth in importance of appointed public bodies (quangos), for a variety of reasons.

- Under both recent Conservative and Labour governments the state's role has changed from providing to 'enabling'. A centralized and largely uniform welfare state has been replaced by more diversity of provision, and supervised by what has been described as a regulatory state.

- Despite moves towards more open government, culminating in the passage and implementation of the Freedom of Information Act, critics argue that British government is still too secretive.

- The old British state centred on Westminster and Whitehall has ceded some authority upwards to the European Union and other international bodies and devolved some power downwards. Multi-level governance has replaced the old centralized unitary state, with uncertain implications for the future.

# QUESTIONS FOR DISCUSSION

- What are the strengths and weaknesses of the Westminster model? Does the model still describe the British system of government with reasonable accuracy?

- In what ways has the state been 'hollowed out'?

- How far does the growth of appointed public bodies threaten the principle and practice of representative democracy?

- How far and how successfully have the free market principles of competition and choice been introduced into the running of public services?

- Has the old welfare state been replaced by a new regulatory state? Why has regulation grown? What are the difficulties associated with regulation?

- Has the Freedom of Information Act created a new climate of open government in Britain?

- What continuing threats are there to civil liberties in Britain?

- How far has multi-level governance replaced parliamentary sovereignty and the unitary state?

# FURTHER READING

On the Westminster model and its critics, see Dunleavy in Dunleavy *et al.* (2006). On the attack on the post-war consensus and 'big government' see Kavanagh (1990). On quangos and the 'democratic deficit' see Weir and Hall (1994), Weir (1995), Skelcher (1998), Weir and Beetham (1999). On privatization and marketization see Ascher (1987), Self (1993) and Walsh (1995).

On governance, see Rhodes (1997, 2000), Bevir and Rhodes (2003), Pierre and Peters (2000), Pierre and Stoker in Dunleavy *et al.*, (2002), *Developments in British Politics 6*, Leach and Percy-Smith (2001) and Flinders (2002, 2008). On regulation and the regulatory state see Moran (2000, 2001, 2003, 2005).

On freedom of information see Rodney Austin in Jowell and Oliver (2000), *The Changing Constitution*, and Rathbone (2001). The Freedom of Information Act was the responsibility of the Home Office (www.homeoffice.uk). The Campaign for Freedom of Information's website can be consulted at www.cfoi.org.uk. On the secret state see Hennessy (2010). On the security services it is possible to access the official MI5 website (www.mi5.gov.uk ) and read the official history (Andrew, 2009) and visit the GCHQ website (www.gchq.gov.uk). The Butler Report (2004) can be consulted on the uses (and misuses) of secret intelligence leading up to the Iraq war.

# Issues, Problems and the Policy Process

So far this book has focused on political and governmental institutions and processes, and only incidentally on issues, problems, policies and outcomes. In this chapter we examine how issues and problems get onto the political agenda, how they are analyzed, decided and approved, how policies are implemented (or in some cases not implemented), monitored and reviewed. We will see that issues and problems are regularly addressed, but seldom solved. While the chapter draws on the analysis in earlier chapters of key political and governmental institutions and processes, it also serves as an introduction to subsequent chapters on particular issues and policies. These chapters are not purely illustrative. On the contrary, they focus on problems that are at the very heart of British politics. In considering the outcomes of the policy process, they address the crucial questions asked by Lasswell, 'Who gets what, when, how?' (see Chapter 1).

## Policy-making and decision-taking

Governments at all levels make policy and take decisions. Policy is about aims, objectives or ends, while decisions are means to an end. Policy provides a framework within which particular decisions can be taken. Thus a transport policy should provide a framework for decisions on particular

road proposals. In practice the distinction between policy and decision-making is not clear cut, but one of interpretation and degree.

Both governing and opposition parties are expected to have a range of policies on, for example, taxation, health, education, transport, the environment, defence and foreign affairs, and often on more specific issues such as the Euro, local government finance or student fees. Yet there is an obvious difference between the policies declared by governing parties and by opposition parties. Government policies are designed to be implemented. Indeed, any problems in the policy may soon be apparent as it is implemented, and any inconsistency between particular decisions and the broad policy will also be noticed. Yet governments can hardly avoid having policies (declared or inferred) for virtually all the functions and services for which they are responsible.

Opposition policies involve pledges that will only have to be implemented should the party gain

---

● **Policy-making** involves taking up a clear position on a function, service or issue that will prove a framework for decision making (e.g. an integrated transport policy or an ethical foreign policy).

---

● **Decision-taking** involves making particular decisions, often within an overall policy framework. Thus an ethical foreign policy may provide a framework for decisions on arms exports to particular countries. Decisions often involve selecting from a range of options (the site of a new hospital, the route of a bypass).

power. They may never have to find the money to implement them, nor discover the potential snags. Moreover, opposition parties lack the resources of government for a full investigation of possible costs and consequences. Thus many opposition policies may be a 'wish list' of hopeful aspirations. Yet if their policy proposals are not costed and potential difficulties not considered, the governing party will happily do it for them. Policies are hostages to fortune. Thus oppositions may prefer to play it safe with as few policy pledges as possible, but there are dangers here also. If a party does not have a declared policy on an issue that is deemed important, their opponents will soon invent a damaging one for them, and challenge them to deny it!

## The policy cycle

Policies may be declared in a speech, government document or party election manifesto, but they commonly emerge over a period. Policy making is best thought of a process or cycle, involving a number of stages (see Figure 19.1). This may suggest a more rational process than often occurs in reality. Governments facing a sudden unexpected crisis (e.g. the 2008 credit crunch) may have to respond quickly and make up policy as they go along. Some of the stages in the policy process may be brief or perfunctory. There may not be time to appraise all the options. Implementation can be problematic, and on occasion may not even happen. Monitoring and review may be thorough, superficial or almost non-existent. Even so, the

stages of the policy cycle provide a useful conceptual framework for examining policy making both in theory and reality. It may help to identify shortcomings. Above all, it serves to emphasize that policy making is an iterative process. Problems are rarely solved. The 'end' of one policy cycle is commonly the beginning of the next, as difficulties in implementation, revealed by monitoring and review, or exposed by critics, lead to attempts to modify or transform established policy.

## Issues, problems and the political agenda

At any one time there appears to be a limited number of issues that the political system can address. A useful analogy is with the agenda for any formal meeting. The agenda consists of a list of items to be considered. The agenda determines not only what is to be discussed but the order in which they will be discussed. A common experience is that very long agendas result in some items being discussed very briefly or not all. Often only the items that are high on the agenda are really considered. Some other items might be hastily approved without discussion, and the rest postponed for consideration at a subsequent meeting, if at all.

While there is a formal agenda for meetings of particular political institutions such as the Cabinet or Parliament, and their numerous committees, there is not literally an agenda for the whole British political process. Yet at any moment there are a number of issues on that political agenda that seem to have a high profile with politicians, the media and the wider public.

This is particularly obvious at elections. Take the British general election of 2010. The issues that seemed to dominate political debate between the parties included the economy and dealing with the deficit, taxation, public services, particularly health and education, and reforming Parliament and the political system. Immigration, initially emphasized less by the Conservatives than in 2005, was raised by many voters. The three major parties talked less about the European Union, perhaps because it was in different ways a problem for them all. However, past general elections had shown that it was not a major concern for voters, despite the efforts of

**Figure 19.1**    The policy cycle

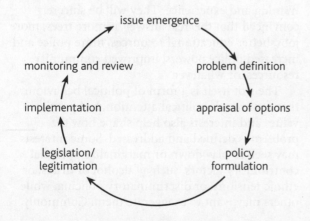

UKIP, for whom it was of course central. The environment and climate change also scarcely featured, despite or perhaps because of the Copenhagen summit only a few months earlier, but perhaps also because the leaders of the three main parties were substantially in agreement. Items that were relatively ignored include the Euro and the pound, transport, agriculture and the environment (key issues in 2001) or devolution and the minimum wage, important issues in 1997. Some big issues from previous decades have disappeared almost completely from the electoral radar screen – inflation, the balance of payments, trade union power, nationalization and privatization, food safety, nuclear disarmament. Some no longer seem to matter. In other cases the problem still exists, but the media and public have lost interest. They are low on the political agenda, until something happens to make them news again.

Of course, one reason why an item may be high on the political agenda is that leading politicians have put it there, in manifestos, speeches and photo-opportunities. Competing parties seek to emphasize those issues that they feel are to their advantage, and try to ignore other more awkward issues that might be potential vote losers. They may be successful in shaping the agenda, although sometimes they find that the media and the public are not particularly interested in the issues they want to focus on, but are concerned about something else. Events such as the fuel protests of 2000, the foot and mouth outbreak of 2001, or the race riots in northern towns in the same year can take politicians by surprise and force new issues onto the agenda (or, more commonly, old issues back onto the agenda). It may take a food scare or a rail crash to push food or rail safety up the agenda. An issue long neglected suddenly seems to strike a chord with the public. The mass media may reflect public concerns, but often may effectively stimulate them (see Chapter 9).

At any one time there are many issues and interests competing for the attention of politicians and other decision-makers. Getting an issue onto the agenda is the crucial first step. Maintaining it there may be more difficult. After a time it is no longer news. The problem may appear more difficult than first realized. It may be too expensive to make an appreciable impact. There may be conflicting interests to take into account. Proposed remedies may even seem worse than the disease. (see Anthony Downs' five-stage model for environmental issues, Chapter 23).

## Defining the problem

An issue may be raised by a particular event, but it is often far from self-evident what the problem really is. A major riot takes place in a British city. People are seriously injured or killed. Property worth billions of pounds is destroyed. It is an issue that must be addressed, but what really is the problem? Why did the riot take place? Only if the causes are understood can the real problem be addressed. Yet there are often competing explanations, implying very different remedies. Was it essentially a 'race riot' arising from ethnic tensions? Was it more the consequence of urban deprivation and unemployment? Was the physical environment a contributory factor? Did it reflect a breakdown in community, or the collapse of family life? Was it provoked by outside agitators or political extremists? Was it simply the consequence of poor or inadequate policing, or too lenient sentencing? Upon the definition of the problem depends the policy response.

Different interests may try to 'capture' the problem, defining it in such a way as to suggest more resources for the police, urban planners, inner city schools, social services or housing. They are not necessarily cynically pushing their own interests. Different professionals – police officers, economists, planners, teachers, social workers – naturally view the world through the prism of the assumptions involved in their own professional training and experience. They will be sincerely convinced that the 'real answer' is more trees, more jobs, better educational resources, more police and increased police powers, improved community resources, or whatever.

The riot itself is a form of political behaviour that commands political attention, but political values and interests also help shape how the problem is defined and addressed. Some interests may seek to play down or marginalize potential contributory factors, such as alcohol or drugs, or ethnic tensions, or discriminatory policing, while others may want to exaggerate them. Commonly,

## BOX 19.1

# Government by Commission?

Faced with a particular problem, a government may decide to appoint an independent commission or committee of experts to examine the issues, collect opinions, commission research, and make recommendations in a final report. Most of this can be done anyway, using the normal resources and contacts of government, but there may be political advantages to an independent Royal Commission or Committee of Inquiry.

- The government may be genuinely undecided, or internally divided, on a particular issue, and a commission may be a useful way of trying to resolve the issue.
- On controversial issues likely to cause political trouble, the conclusions of a prestigious Royal Commission, backed by extensive research, may add authority and legitimacy to a difficult decision that the government needs to make.
- Although the Commission may be independent, the government can influence or substantially determine the outcome by the choice of chair and members, and by setting the terms of reference. Thus the final report may come up with what the government thinks is the 'right' answer.
- Alternatively, the government is not obliged to accept the recommendations (particularly if they lead to a political outcry). They can 'pick and mix', accepting some recommendations and rejecting others. Critics of the report may be relieved if the government decides not to implement all its proposals.
- Appointing a commission may sometimes be a way of avoiding the need to declare a policy. Thus the government can fairly say they are awaiting the outcome of a report that it would be unreasonable to prejudge.
- Finally, appointing a commission may be a way of burying a difficult or politically damaging issue. With any luck, media and public attention will be transferred elsewhere when it finally reports.

Even so, it can be embarrassing if an independent commission or committee comes up with the 'wrong' or politically unacceptable answer. There are numerous examples of recommendations by high-profile commissions or committees being rejected, including the Roskill Commission on the site of the third London airport, the Layfield Committee on local government finance, and the Jenkins Commission on electoral reform. The conclusions of Roskill and Layfield were ignored, while the Jenkins Report was effectively 'kicked into the long grass' by the Blair government.

---

there will be an investigation, involving the collection of evidence, the publication of a report with recommendations for action, some of which may lead to a response. The report may be thorough and its analysis sensible, but it is not holy writ, and can never be the whole truth. Different interests will emphasize different parts of the report and put their own interpretation on the conclusions. Then the riot and its possible causes may be largely forgotten until another riot happens, perhaps somewhere else in rather different circumstances, and the whole anguished debate will start up again.

A similar process will follow any significant political crisis – a foot and mouth outbreak as in 2001, the attack on Glasgow airport or the run on the Northern Rock bank (both 2007), the shootings in Cumbria in 2010. The 'real issue' will be defined according to underlying ideological assumptions and political interests. There is no objective interpretation, and normally no single ideal solution.

## Appraising options

Nevertheless, attempts may be made to analyze a range of options more thoroughly, at least when governments enjoy the luxury of time, for sometimes an immediate decision is required. In such circumstances governments have to act fast and work out some rational justification for their actions afterwards. On other occasions governments may be able to explore a range of options or appoint a commission to do it for them (see Box 19.1).

A variety of techniques may be used in an ostensibly rational appraisal of options. Economists have sometimes used cost–benefit analysis (CBA) to assess particular projects or alternative possibilities. This involves putting a monetary value on all the identifiable costs and benefits to the community (not just the direct financial costs and benefits) to decide whether a project should go ahead, or which of several options is the best buy. Accountants have argued in favour of more overtly rational techniques for managing and controlling the budgetary process, such as planned programmed budgetary systems (PPBS), very fashionable in the 1970s, or, zero-base budgeting. (ZBB), influential in the 1980s. These rational systems have been advocated, however, precisely because much policy making in practice has not always appeared particularly rational, but commonly involves relatively small shifts (or increments) from past policy, without any real analysis of how far various options meet clear aims and objectives. Yet some argue that what has come to be called 'incrementalism' is not just the way in which most policy is made in practice, but is actually preferable to more ostensibly rational approaches (see Academic Controversy 19.1).

It has been claimed that the budgetary process is almost inevitably incremental. Commenting on the UK budgetary process, observers suggest that the next budget can only involve a shift of around two and a half per cent at most from the previous budget. The Chancellor of the Exchequer does not start with a blank sheet, but with past revenue and expenditure involving continuing programmes, with commitments and expectations that can only be ignored at considerable political costs. Yet understandably, successive governments have sought to make the process more rational, by linking spending to clear objectives, and planning spending over a longer period than the budgetary year. However, inevitably plans are blown off course by unanticipated developments and political pressures. Spending and taxation were central to the 2010 election campaign, even more than in previous campaigns. Yet the differences in planned expenditure and taxation between the major parties were relatively minor, as commentators observed. The post-election cuts in public spending may be more brutal and extensive than the incremental model suggests, yet past spending commitments will remain a significant constraint on planned future spending.

Many other areas of policy are inevitably substantially incremental. Health policy and education policy depend on past decisions on training and investment. Staffing, buildings and equipment cannot be transformed overnight. Yet radical shifts can and do take place in British government. Whatever might be said about the privatization programme of the Thatcher government or New Labour's devolution programme, neither could be characterized as incremental.

## Policy formulation

Sooner or later a policy emerges or a key decision is taken. Once a policy has been declared it is difficult to retreat, at least until the policy has been tried and perhaps found wanting. It is, however, not always easy to determine exactly when a new policy is established. It may be announced in a speech, or a government circular or sometimes a White Paper. This provides a convenient firm date, although of course a decision will normally have been made inside government, sometimes well ahead of any public announcement. Although the policy will be associated with the appropriate departmental minister and, under the assumption of collective Cabinet responsibility, with the government as a whole, its real instigator may be someone else, perhaps the Prime Minister or Chancellor, possibly a civil servant, or a special adviser. More commonly, many prominent and less prominent individuals may have contributed, over time, to a new policy.

Some policies, however, emerge almost by default, as other options are rejected or become discredited, and it gradually becomes clear that there is no realistic alternative. There may be no formal announcement, and indeed the policy may only become clear in retrospect. Thus after a long debate over the location of London's proposed third airport from the 1970s onwards, a number of proposed sites were rejected. As a consequence Stansted, an initially small airport rejected at any early stage by the official Roskill Commission, gradually grew to become in effect London's third airport as a result of the failure of successive governments to reach a decision. Luton has since developed as a fourth airport, while both Heathrow and Gatwick have expanded to cope with increased

## Academic controversy 19.1
# Rationalism and incrementalism

*Rationalism.* One common version of the rational model emphasizes the importance of first determining the *ends or objectives* of policy and then exploring all possible means to securing those ends, and choosing the best (the *ends–means model*).

Herbert Simon (1947), the leading theorist of rationalism, has argued that, ideally, the decision-maker should start from the *situation*, trace through all possible courses of action and their consequences, and choose the one with the greatest net benefits. However he recognized that in practice administrators are limited by time, information and skills, so that they cannot find the optimum solution, and search until they find a tolerably satisfactory solution. Thus they '*satisfice*' rather than *optimize*. This approach was described by Simon as involving '*bounded rationality*'.

*Incrementalism.* Charles Lindblom (1959) argued that in practice policy makers choose between relatively few options. Most policy making involves small scale extensions of past policy. It does not commonly involve a single decision-maker impartially sifting options, but requires accommodation and compromise between different interests, a process Lindblom described as '*partisan mutual adjustment*'. He also argued that much policy making does not follow any coherent plan, but proceeds rather disjointedly ('*disjointed incrementalism*'). Lindblom argued not only that his model better fitted the reality of policy making, so was the better descriptive model, but also that it led to better results than attempts at rationalism. Incremental policy making, building on the past, was more likely to be successful than radical shifts. It was also more likely to be acceptable because it was based on consultation and compromise. It was thus also a prescriptive model. Provocatively, Lindblom (1959) referred to his model as the '*science of muddling through*'.

The debate begun by Simon and Lindblom continues. Critics of Lindblom argue we should aspire to more than 'muddling through'. They also argue that there is an in-built conservative bias in incrementalism. Sometimes radical change is necessary. Lindblom has responded that a series of incremental shifts can achieve a radical change in policy over a period, although he has conceded the case for some forward planning and 'strategic analysis' in later versions of his model. There have also been attempts to construct a model incorporating elements of rationalism and incrementalism, such as Etzioni's (1967) 'mixed scanning'.

---

traffic. Faced with strong local political opposition to any new airport in the Home Counties, governments have tended to prevaricate, and in practice have preferred the rather less politically contentious expansion of existing airports. (However, the proposed new runway for Heathrow encountered strenuous objections, and has been scrapped by the coalition government.)

After an issue has aroused strong public emotions and demands for action, a government may eventually decide to take no action, because of the economic or political costs. Some analysts suggest that non-decision-making may tell us more about the exercise of power in western society than decision-making (see Academic Controversy 19.2).

## Legislation and legitimation

Government may decide what it wants to do, the policy may have been determined, but policy generally requires some form of official ratification if it is to be widely accepted as legitimate. This may involve legislation. Government policy may have been announced in a speech or White Paper, but it still may need to become the law of the land for it to be accepted by courts, media and public. Thus the transfer of the judicial functions of the House

## Academic controversy 19.2
# The politics of non-decision-making

Much of the debate on power and decision-making has been conducted by American academics using US examples, although the analysis has also been applied to British politics. Robert Dahl (1961) concluded from his own studies of decision-making in New Haven, Connecticut, that power was dispersed rather than concentrated in the hands of the few. Bachrach and Baratz (1970) argued that there were 'two faces of power'. One involved overt conflicts of interest on key political issues, of the kind analyzed by Dahl. Yet a second face of power involved the suppression of conflict and the effective prevention of decisions through 'the mobilization of bias' against interests effectively excluded from the decision-making process (such as black people in many American cities).

Steven Lukes (1974) argued that there was a 'third dimension of power' involving the shaping of people's preferences so that neither overt nor covert conflicts of interests exist. People are so conditioned by the prevail-

ing economic and social system that they cannot imagine alternatives. Thus potential political issues do not even get onto the political agenda. Lukes drew particularly on the work of Crenson (1971), who had shown that the issue of pollution control had not even come up for debate in some American cities whose economies were dominated by a major industry with a pollution problem. This was not because of the use of direct power and influence by employers, but because the bulk of the community had become conditioned to think that pollution was a natural and inescapable by-product of the employment and prosperity created by the industry.

There are some obvious problems in analyzing 'non-decisions'. Moreover, Lukes and others assume that people's 'real' interests may differ markedly from their 'felt' interests. While this is plausible, it does conflict with the assumption of liberal democracy that individuals are the best judge of their own self-interest.

---

of Lords to a new supreme court was established as government policy in 2003, but it took until 2005 for it to become law (and 2009 for the policy to be implemented). A policy of that importance clearly required legislation, and indeed there is always the possibility that a policy may be substantially modified or even abandoned as a bill proceeds through Parliament.

Other forms of legitimation may effectively derail a policy. Thus the Labour government instituted what has been described as a rolling programme of devolution for the English regions, involving directly elected regional assemblies, but gave voters an effective veto with the commitment to referendums in the regions concerned. Referendums initially announced for three regions were reduced to one, the North-east, where there was a well-established lobby for regional government. The overwhelming rejection of an assembly by voters in the North-east has seemingly buried

the policy for the foreseeable future. The commitment to a referendum before Britain joins the Euro, a referendum that polls indicate would be difficult to win, was a strong factor deterring Blair's government from pursuing entry to the Eurozone.

By no means all important government decisions require legislation, and only major constitutional issues are thought to require a referendum. Other decisions do normally depend on some kind of formal authorization or ratification, perhaps in the form of a Cabinet minute or a circular, order or regulation issued by a departmental minister under delegated authority. Important decisions in local government require formal council approval. On planning decisions there is normally a right of appeal, followed by a public inquiry (see Chapter 14). This can be a very important part of the legitimation process, although some argue that the whole inquiry system is weighted against objectors.

**BOX 19.2**

## Some examples of failed or imperfect policy implementation in Britain

- The 1970 Chronically Sick and Disabled Persons Act, an ambitious policy imperfectly administered because of lack of resources.
- Heath's industrial relations policy, effectively destroyed by the 1974 miners' strike.
- The incomes policy of Callaghan's government that eventually broke down in the 'winter of discontent' because of opposition from trade unions and some employers.
- The introduction of identity cards for football supporters, enacted by the Thatcher government, but never implemented, partly because of administrative problems.
- The poll tax introduced by the Thatcher government in 1989 and 1990 was evaded by a substantial minority, and eventually abandoned after riots in the streets and the replacement of Margaret Thatcher by John Major.
- The ban on hunting with dogs, that became law in 2005, with only marginal changes to hunting in practice, partly because of the determination of influential people to defy the law, partly because of alleged difficulties in policing the Act.

Constitutionally, some of the most important powers of government, including making war, are part of the prerogative powers of the crown, and strictly speaking do not require special authorization. Yet a Prime Minister who took a country to war without the support of Cabinet and Parliament would not survive. On Iraq the Cabinet did back Blair (with initially one and eventually two dissenters), and so did Parliament. The legality of the war was later challenged, partly because it was alleged that Blair had misled Parliament, but rather more because it seemed questionable under international law. Much hinged on the advice given by the Attorney General, who ultimately declared it legal.

## Implementation

Implementation is perhaps the most under-regarded part of the policy-making process but the most important. The passing of a law in Parliament or a policy pronouncement by a minister is often regarded as the end of the policy process when it may be just the beginning. Cabinet decisions may be taken, laws may be passed, but the policy is not necessarily implemented as intended. There is often a considerable 'implementation gap' when it comes

to applying policy (Hogwood and Gunn, 1984, ch. 11). Why?

A policy may break down because of significant strong opposition from the public or a section of the public (as some examples in Box 19.2 indicate). Yet the explanation for imperfect implementation can often be rather less dramatic. One reason is that ministers often rely on individuals or organizations outside central government to implement policy. Much government policy is implemented not by civil servants, but by local authorities, hospital trusts and a range of quangos. In health and education successive governments have made a virtue of devolving control to local professionals and to the community. Competition and choice require some autonomy for local producers and consumers. Local councils in particular are elected bodies, retaining some significant discretion over priorities and spending. They are often controlled by different parties with different priorities from the government's. Even where the law seems clear, councils may 'drag their feet' on policies to which they or local communities are opposed.

Public officials may often have significant discretion in administering policies. Terms such as 'street level bureaucracy' (see extracts from Lipsky and Hudson, in Hill, 1997b) or 'street level policy making' suggest that quite low-level staff who deal with the public at the sharp end of policy may have significant discretion over decisions. Such people may be 'gatekeepers', effectively controlling access to resources.

The problem is clearer still in areas where central government is reliant on organizations and interests outside government altogether for implementation. This was one of the difficulties with incomes policy, sometimes backed by the authority of the law, pursued by both Labour and Conservative governments in the 1960s and 1970s. Yet whether the policy was 'voluntary' or 'statutory', it still depended on the co-operation of employers and unions for implementation, and this was not always forthcoming. Much industrial, agricultural and environmental policy relies on private sector firms if it is to succeed. Much social policy depends heavily on the local community and the voluntary sector. While much can be done by central government through the stick of regulation and the carrot of grants, ultimately the implementation of policy is often in the hands of people who are outside the line management control of central departments.

However, the biggest obstacle to effective policy implementation is generally resources. Governments will the ends, but do not always provide adequate means. There may be lack of finance, lack of skilled staff, lack of usable land, lack of sufficient powers. Even where government is prepared to provide additional resources, it takes time for these to be converted into usable resources on the ground. It takes many years to train new teachers, doctors, nurses or police officers, often longer still to plan, build and equip new hospitals and schools. There is no tap that can be turned to provide an instant supply of additional resources.

Over and above all this there are problems with co-ordination. Many programmes require co-operation between different levels of government, between different agencies and departments, between the public, private and voluntary sectors. Issues such as drugs, vandalism, school truancy and drink-fuelled violent disturbances require co-operation between the police, schools, social workers and community organizations. Frequently there are difficulties in achieving co-ordination, arising from the different organization, processes and cultures of the services and agencies involved. The problem of coordination is not new. In the 1960s and 1970s there was an extensive literature on corporate management in local government, which was essentially about overcoming narrow service, departmental and professional attitudes. Today the concerns are much the same although the jargon is slightly different. A New Labour mantra was 'joined-up government'. It proved easier to proclaim than achieve.

Yet without effective implementation, or 'delivery' in the language of New Labour, policy will fail to achieve its goals. The Labour government discovered, like its predecessors, that there was no shortage of policy advice inside and outside government. What they required of their civil servants, and others involved at different levels and across sectors, was the effective delivery of policy. Thus a special Delivery Unit was established inside the Cabinet Office to monitor the implementation of government policy. Whether this made much difference in practice is questionable.

Finally, it is important to acknowledge that policy can have unintended as well as intended effects. A distinction can be drawn between policy *outputs*, the direct and intended result of inputs of resources, and policy *outcomes*, including the unintended consequences of policy. Thus some welfare payments intended to help the low-paid and unemployed involved a perverse disincentive against seeking work or higher-paid employment, in so far as it would entail the loss of means-tested benefits, and in some cases even leave them worse off. Thus the tax and benefit system created a 'poverty trap' from which it was difficult to escape, although the politicians and civil servants who had designed the policy had certainly neither expected nor intended this outcome. Iain Duncan Smith is far from being the first minister grappling with the problems of social welfare and the poverty trap, and almost certainly he will not be the last.

## Monitoring and review

To judge whether a particular policy is working, its implementation must be thoroughly monitored and reviewed. This appears common sense, but it

**BOX 19.3**

## The three Es – economy, efficiency and effectiveness

**Economy** – minimizing the cost of resources, or inputs (e.g. land, labour, capital) involved in producing a certain level of service (e.g. reducing the cost of providing a hospital bed for a patient).

**Efficiency** – securing maximum quantity and quality of outputs for a given quantity of inputs (e.g. treating more patients in the NHS without an increase in resources).

**Effectiveness** – securing effective outcomes, (e.g. improved health in the community).

While economy is about reducing costs, and efficiency about increased productivity, effectiveness is about realizing objectives – but this is the most difficult to measure. If a school teaches more pupils without any increases in resources, this implies increased economy (reduced costs per pupil) and increased efficiency, if results appear unaffected. Yet both teachers and parents assume that larger classes in some way involves less effective education, which is plausible but difficult to measure and prove. Similarly the quantity of patients treated in the NHS may increase, perhaps at the expense of quality of care.

has not always happened in the past, not is it necessarily practised effectively today.

Many organizations ostensibly build internal monitoring and review into their own processes, to check that they are meeting their own aims and targets. Thus many local councils established performance review committees to monitor their own policies. Other public sector organizations formally review their own performance. This is very much in their own interest as there are all kinds of external reviews that will draw attention to problems, and it is better to identify weaknesses internally and seek to remedy them to forestall more damaging criticism.

From the nineteenth century onwards various inspectorates were established by central government to measure performance. More recently, central government's performance review has been reformed and extended (for some of the regulatory bodies involved, see Chapter 18). The auditing of public spending used to be concerned primarily with the legality of expenditure – was money being spent as voted by Parliament? It is now much more concerned with achieving value for money, and the 'three Es' – economy, efficiency and effectiveness (see Box 19.3). The National Audit Office reviews performance in government departments and associated quangos, while the (now to be abolished) Audit Commission reviews the performance of local authorities and health authorities.

In addition, government may set up inquiries or commissions to review a particular service and recommend reforms. Parliament now has its own comprehensive system for monitoring the performance of all government departments and services through the Departmental Select Committees, as well as the Public Accounts Committee (PAC). Professional bodies such as the Chartered Institute of Public Finance and Accountancy (CIPFA) have also long published their own performance statistics.

There is no doubt that all this performance review has had a massive impact on government at every level. There are sanctions on poor performance. Pay, prospects and sometimes jobs are on the line. Comparative performance indicators can throw up some substantial variations in costs and standards, the money spent on school meals for example, or death rates arising from particular medical conditions in different hospitals or areas of the country. Poor performance can be addressed and remedied. Good practice can be analyzed and copied. Some object that the publication of comparative league tables can distort priorities, concentrating on the easily measurable at the expense of more important but less easily quantified outcomes. While there is some truth in the argument, the answer lies not in less performance review but better and more sensitive performance review. Government, service users and voters can hardly assess whether the large sums devoted to public services are efficient and effective without it. Finally, performance review can throw up evidence that existing policy is not working, and new think-ing is required. Thus the end of one policy cycle can provide the stimulus for the beginning of the next.

## SUMMARY

- Policy making may be analyzed as a cycle involving a number of stages, including issue emergence, problem definition, option appraisal, policy formulation, legislation and legitimation, implementation, monitoring and review.

- The crucial first stage is for an issue to get onto the political agenda, and to be identified as a priority.

- Once an issue is on the agenda, it is not necessarily self-evident what the 'real problem' is. Some familiar and recurring problems have been defined very differently. The problem may be 'captured' and defined by a particular interest in their own terms.

- Various options or proposed solutions may be appraised using a variety of ostensibly rational techniques. However, much policy making in practice appears incremental rather than rational, and some argue that the incremental approach may be preferable.

- A policy may be clearly announced, or emerge over time. Some analysts suggest that non-decision-making explains more about the nature and distribution of power than decision-making.

- A policy is normally decided well in advance of legislation or some other form of formal legitimation. However, legitimation is crucial for public acceptance and democratic accountability. Sometimes prob-lems with legitimation may effectively derail a policy.

- Policies may not always be effectively implemented for a variety of reasons, including inherent problems, lack of resources, dependence on other agencies or interests for implementation, and political difficulties.

- There is extensive machinery for the monitoring and review of policy. This may not always work as well as it might and can be counter-productive, but is essential in measuring efficiency and effectiveness. It can reveal that existing policies are not working, and thus inaugurate a new policy cycle.

## QUESTIONS FOR DISCUSSION

- How and why do issues get onto the policy agenda? What kind of issues might be relatively neglected?

- Why are some familiar issues, such as crime or inner city poverty, so variously defined and explained? How important are the different definitions for policy?

- Why does it often appear that past policy is the most important factor influencing future policy? What radical shifts in policy have occurred in recent years and why?

- Do the issues that are not debated tell us more about power in Britain than those issues that are debated?

- In what ways are policies legitimated? How might problems in legitimation derail a policy?

- Why are some policies not implemented effectively (and sometimes not implemented at all)? How might governments secure fuller implementation?

- Why has the monitoring and review of policy become politically controversial?

# FURTHER READING

There is an extensive literature on policy making and policy analysis. Hill (1997a) provides a good overview of the policy process, while the same author (1997b) has edited an excellent reader, which contains extracts from some of the sources referred to here, and many others besides. Wayne Parsons (1995) provides more extensive and detailed analysis of specific aspects.

Some of this chapter refers back to analysis in earlier

chapters, most notably the discussion of power and democracy in Chapter 1, the chapters on pressure group politics and the media, and chapters on particular institutions and processes. There are a few illustrative examples of policy making in this chapter, and some in earlier chapters. Many of the examples of particular policy areas and services examined in the following chapters also illustrate specific points about the policy process.

# Managing the Economy

Few chapters of this book require more substantive revision than 'Managing the Economy'. The 2006 edition recorded that New Labour had 'captured the record of economic competence previously enjoyed by the Conservatives, with a record of low inflation and relatively low unemployment'. However, the next paragraph struck a more cautionary note:

> Yet critics allege that the real structural weaknesses of the economy have not been addressed. Productivity . . . remains poor compared with Britain's main competitors. Manufacturing industry continues to decline. British economic prosperity seems to depend on a consumer boom, fuelled by mounting debt. (Leach *et al.*, 2006, p. 366)

This reservation now appears more than justified, following a major financial crisis and economic recession in 2008–9. The Brown government reasonably maintained that the crisis was global. Yet Labour had claimed the credit for presiding over economic prosperity, and could hardly escape responsibility for the subsequent collapse, particularly as Prime Minister Brown had earlier incautiously boasted, as Chancellor, that he had 'ended boom and bust'. In so far as the rash lending of banks created the crisis, this could in part be attributed to the failure of the new regulatory machinery Brown introduced and the 'light touch' regulation he endorsed. Moreover, the British economy was already in poor shape to ride the downturn, with high levels of private and rising public debt. Government support for the banks coupled with the cost of the recession and tax and spending measures to stimulate demand in the wider economy incurred massive deficits that will take years to reduce. However, the coalition government's plans to cut the deficit in four years have been widely criticized, both for their immediate effect on public services, welfare benefits, unemployment and living standards, and for their potential impact on economic recovery.

This chapter will review the causes of the financial crisis and economic recession, and the measures taken by both the Brown government and then the Cameron coalition government to deal with them. However, first we examine the making of economic policy in broader terms, exploring who makes it, the instruments they use, and the theoretical assumptions that influence decision-making, before discussing the record of successive British governments on the economy. While policy choices may throw some further light on the distribution of power and influence in Britain, they also illustrate some of the international constraints on British economic policy making.

# Who makes and shapes economic policy in Britain?

Within government the Chancellor of the Exchequer and the Treasury are more important today than ever in the framing of economic policy. From time to time there have been attempts to separate longer-term economic policy from immediate decisions on budgets and public finance (e.g. Wilson's creation of a separate Department of Economic Affairs in 1964). Other departments, such as Trade and Industry or more recently Business, have sometimes briefly appeared to have a major proactive role in various aspects of economic policy. Some Prime Ministers, particularly those with some claim to economic expertise (Wilson), strongly-held economic assumptions (Heath, Thatcher), or who have previously served as Chancellor (Churchill, Macmillan, Callaghan, Major and Brown) have taken a particular interest in economic policy. Some Chancellors have been effectively subservient to dominant Prime Ministers (Lloyd to Macmillan, Barber to Heath) while others have been forced out because their economic policies diverged from those of Number Ten (e.g. Thorneycroft, Lawson). Among post-war premiers only Attlee, Eden, Home and, most recently, Blair have been content to leave economic management substantially to their Chancellors. In the case of Blair, this self-denying ordinance allegedly went back to a deal in 1994, under which Brown agreed not to challenge for the Labour leadership in return for a free hand in economic policy and related areas.

The Treasury's power has sometimes been perceived as largely negative, responsible for cutting down the creative policies and spending plans of other departments. This has particularly been the case during recurrent periods of economic crisis in Britain. Brown's role as Chancellor was much more proactive, extending over welfare, labour and industrial policy, Europe and international development. Indeed, critics complained that 'the Treasury had become the Department of Social Policy' (Sampson, 2005, p. 130). Thus Brown dominated much of the Labour government's domestic policy making, and increasingly appeared co-equal with Blair, before he succeeded him as Prime Minister.

Within the Treasury Chancellors have sometimes appeared the mouthpiece for their officials, the formidable 'Treasury mandarins'. Yet others such as Roy Jenkins, Denis Healey, Geoffrey Howe, Nigel Lawson, Ken Clarke and Gordon Brown, have dominated the Treasury from the start, and put their personal stamp on government economic policy. Thus following Labour's election victory in 1997 Treasury officials discovered that their new Chancellor Gordon Brown 'had already taken the decisions that would set the new government's economic course' (Stephens, in Seldon, 2001, pp. 187–8). Much the same could be said of George Osborne in 2010.

Among other institutions the Bank of England, formally nationalized by Labour in 1946, but operating as an independent body, has long loomed large in economic policy. Brown's decision to hand over decisions on interest rates to the Bank's Monetary Policy Committee in 1997 was balanced by the transfer of most of the Bank's former regulatory power over the financial sector to the new Financial Services Authority (FSA). Osborne has since decided to phase out the FSA and restore regulatory authority to the Bank of England, which now appears more powerful than ever.

Government economy policy making, although dominated by the Chancellor, is still strongly influenced and constrained by forces outside government. Influence is sometimes attributed to important or colourful entrepreneurs such as Richard Branson, Alan Sugar or Rupert Murdoch, although rather more significant are impersonal institutions, interests and markets, many of which transcend national boundaries. Among these are business interests in general and financial interests in particular. Recently, financial services have appeared the engine of Britain's economic growth, and both Brown and Conservative Shadow Chancellors endorsed a 'light touch' regulatory regime over the bankers. The influence of the banks on policy has remained strong even after banking profits were replaced by massive losses, as the government could not allow them to fail without undermining confidence.

Other major business firms, including multinational corporations, may exert a direct influence on government, and various sectors of the economy are represented by their own organizations (such as the Society of Motor Manufacturers and Traders). Powerful groups such as the Confederation of British Industry (CBI) and the Institute of Directors have a high public profile and also exert influence behind the scenes. Prestigious think tanks, professional associations and some academic institutions are also listened to. Of course economists weigh in with their own analysis and prescription, and this often underpins policy (for example the influence of monetarism and public choice theory on the Thatcher government's economic management). Yet divisions among economists have perhaps limited their influence more recently. There are powerful health and education lobbies to which any government would be advised to pay some attention.

Trade unions recovered some of their former influence with a Labour government from 1997 to 2010, but they remained much less powerful than in the immediate post-war decades. 'One of the things that struck most visitors to 11 Downing Street during the first Blair parliament was that they were as likely to meet a departing venture capitalist as a trade unionist' (Stephens in Seldon, 2001, p. 198). Trade union influence on the economic policies of the Cameron coalition government already appears vestigial. Whether public sector unions retain sufficient industrial muscle to mount a serious challenge against projected public spending cuts remains to be seen.

Beyond the ranks of organized business and labour, the influence of more specialist interests can be amplified considerably if they secure significant media publicity and public support, as was the case with truckers' protest in the fuel crisis of September 2000, which led to some modification of fuel taxation. Behind these particular institutions and interests are the wider public as voters, taxpayers and consumers of goods and services, including public services. Governments that ultimately must seek re-election ignore wider public concerns at their peril.

International obligations as represented through such bodies as G7/G8 (and also more recently G20), the World Trade Organization (WTO), the International Monetary Fund (IMF) and of course the European Union inevitably constrain British economic policy and effectively rule out some options. Credit ratings agencies can downgrade the ratings of sovereign states, making it more expen-

sive for them to borrow money. Beyond all this, impersonal global markets can have a massive impact on national economies, particularly the British economy that is so locked in to the global economy. Wyn Grant (2002, pp. 8–9) recalls a seminar of international economic decision-makers. Someone asked, 'Who calls the shots?' 'Not us,' say the international financial institutions, 'it's the G7 finance ministers.' 'Not us,' say the finance ministers, 'It's really the markets.' Indeed, governments often appear helpless in the face of market forces. Yet markets are not quite as impersonal as they sometimes appear. While some markets consist of countless virtually powerless price-takers, others comprise a few very powerful price-makers.

## The tools of economic management: direct intervention, fiscal policy and monetary policy

Political fortunes rest substantially on successful economic management. How, then, do governments try to manage the economy? They can intervene directly to control key aspects of the economy. They can use fiscal policy (taxation and government spending). They can use monetary policy (control of the money supply and interest rates). Generally, governments have employed a mix of these economic management tools, although the balance has varied over time, and more recently government rhetoric has generally emphasized the need for less state intervention and regulation, and more encouragement for free market forces and business enterprise

### Direct intervention

Governments can manage the economy through direct controls and intervention. In Britain such direct control of the economy has been most evident in wartime. In directing the wartime economy, the coalition government led by Winston Churchill assumed massive powers of intervention in controlling the labour force, deciding on the location of industry, requisitioning economic assets, rationing the supply of raw materials to factories, and so on. Some of these controls were briefly retained in the immediate aftermath of war,

## BOX 20.1

# Incomes policies in the 1960s and 1970s

In 1961 a Conservative Chancellor, Selwyn Lloyd, introduced the 'pay pause', a nine-month-long incomes policy designed to hold down pay awards. It was hoped that this direct attack on wage increases would help restrain price inflation. Between 1965 and 1969 Labour pursued a prices and incomes policy, and the Conservative government which followed converted an informal incomes policy into a statutory policy which controlled all incomes between 1972 and 1974. Labour, returned to office in 1974, developed a voluntary incomes policy – known as the 'social contract' – under which trade unions accepted wage restraint in return for welfare benefits (the 'social wage').

Yet neither voluntary nor statutory incomes policy proved effective in holding down wages for long. The social contract finally broke down in the 'winter of discontent' of 1978–9. This was an important factor in the 1979 Conservative election victory that saw Margaret Thatcher enter Number Ten promising economic management which would rely much more on market forces and far less on government intervention. Since then governments of both parties have avoided any formal incomes policy (either statutory or voluntary). Labour however introduced a statutory minimum wage in 1997.

but largely disappeared during the 1950s. Nevertheless peacetime governments have since attempted to control aspects of the economy through direct intervention.

A contentious example was the 1945–51 Labour government policy of nationalization, involving the compulsory acquisition by the state of a number of key industries. Had Labour pursued a policy of wholesale nationalization of industry, as implied in Clause Four of its constitution (see Chapter 6) this might have involved the kind of direct state management of the economy long advocated by many socialists. Yet in practice Labour only nationalized what they described as 'the commanding heights of the economy', and industries which were either already substantially municipally owned (gas, electricity, water) or that appeared to be declining or in trouble (coal, gas again, railways, iron and steel). Moreover the government did not seek to manage these industries directly, nor were they owned and run by workers, as some socialists had demanded. Instead they were placed in the hands of 'arm's length' Public Corporations. While governments could and sometimes did lean on the chairs of boards to influence decisions on pricing or investment, they never sought to use state-owned industries to manage the economy.

With the exception of steel, the maintenance of a mixed economy with a substantial state sector remained a bipartisan policy from the 1950s through to the 1970s, when governments of both parties were prepared to take failing industries into public ownership. This policy was sharply reversed by the Thatcher and Major governments. New Labour not only failed to reverse privatization, but marginally extended it. Part nationalization of the banks in the wake of the financial crisis was presented as a necessary but strictly temporary expedient.

Both major parties pursued other policies involving direct intervention in the economy. For example, in the fight against inflation Labour and Conservative governments implemented prices and incomes policies (see Box 20.1). Both Labour and Conservative governments also from 1945 through to 1979 pursued an industrial policy involving incentives to encourage investment and growth. Impressed by the success of economic planning in France, in 1962 a Conservative government set up the National Economic Development Council (NEDC) – familiarly known as 'Neddy' – as a forum in which governments and both sides of industry discussed plans to improve Britain's industrial efficiency and international competitiveness. Later Labour governments set up other interventionist bodies – the Industrial Reorganisation Corporation (IRC) in 1966 and the National Enterprise Board (NEB) in 1975 – with a view to restructuring and strengthening Britain's industrial base. Labour and Conservative governments also strove to help economically depressed areas of Britain with an interventionist regional policy to attract new investment through grants and other financial incentives. During Thatcher's years in office her governments pursued a more free market and less interventionist approach to the problems of the British economy, privatizing the former state industries, abandoning incomes policy, cutting regional aid, scrapping interventionist bodies and allowing unemployment to rise, and manufacturing industry to contract. (Urban policy however remained interventionist.)

From 1997 onwards New Labour's direct economic intervention, if it can be so called, involved incentives for investment and training, the micro-management of the delivery of public services (see Chapter 21) and tax and welfare policies designed to increase incentives to work and reduce child poverty (see Chapter 22).

## Fiscal policy

Governments have to raise taxes to pay for their expenditure. Gladstonian public finance (named after William Gladstone, the great nineteenth-century Liberal Chancellor and Prime Minister) involved 'balancing the books' in the annual budget, ensuring that planned government expenditure over the coming year was met by planned government revenue from taxation and other sources. The budgetary process has always involved awkward choices between the calls on the public purse from different departments with spending needs, and between different ways of raising taxation, with varying implications for individual taxpayers and businesses.

Government spending, commonly over two-fifths of national income since the war and rising to over a half in the recent recession, inevitably has a major influence on the wider national economy, while taxation can have a major impact on the economic behaviour of individuals and firms. Thus changes in taxation may encourage or discourage saving, investing, and spending by households or firms, and may increase or decrease incentives for work and enterprise. Tax changes may be used for more specific purposes – for example, to discourage consumption of harmful goods (alcohol and tobacco) or encourage 'green' energy saving.

More broadly, **fiscal policy** may be used to stimulate or deflate the national economy. From the 1940s through to the 1970s governments of both parties used fiscal policy as a key tool of Keynesian demand management policies. Keynes himself was never a socialist, but a progressive liberal who believed in capitalism and free enterprise. He sought not direct state intervention and detailed control of the economy but a system of managed capitalism. His theories involved a crucial distinction between **micro-economics** and **macro-economics**. The government would leave micro-economics, the behaviour of individual households and firms, substantially to free market forces. It would seek instead to influence and control macro-economics and aggregate demand in the economy through fiscal and monetary policy to secure full employment, stable prices and steady growth.

Keynes argued that economic depressions are caused by a lack of sufficient demand in the economy to purchase all goods and services when all economic resources (and particularly labour) are fully utilized. Falls in output and employment result in lower government revenue, higher welfare cost and budget deficits. In such circumstances raising taxes and cutting public spending to reduce the deficit will cut demand still further and worsen

● **Fiscal policy** is about the management of public finances and the economy through taxation and government spending. Thus all governments use fiscal policy to finance their spending plans. Governments may also use fiscal policy to achieve other objectives, to influence the behaviour of individuals and businesses by providing financial incentives or disincentives, and/or influence aggregate (or total) demand in the economy. Sometimes fiscal policy is also used purposely to redistribute income and wealth.

● **Micro-economics** involves theories about the behaviour of individual consumers, households and firms in the economy. Basic micro-economic theory assumes free markets, although it goes on to examine the effects of imperfect competition and government intervention on market forces.

● **Macro-economics** is concerned mainly with the performance of the national economy, including levels of inflation, employment, growth and the balance of payments, and techniques for influencing or controlling these. It focuses on aggregate (or total) demand and supply in the economy and assumes that governments have considerable potential influence on inflation, employment, foreign trade and growth.

the depression. Nor will cuts in wage rates help to raise demand for labour, as lower wages will reduce purchasing power and demand for goods and services and thus labour. The Keynesian remedy is to stimulate demand using both fiscal policy (if necessary incurring a temporary budget deficit) and monetary policy (lower interest rates and easier credit). Inflation, on the other hand, is caused by excessive demand in the economy – too much money chasing too few goods. If the economy is already operating at full employment it is not possible to increase supply to meet excess demand, and the consequence will be higher prices. Here, the Keynesian remedy is to reduce aggregate demand by taking purchasing power out of the economy through fiscal policy (a budgetary surplus) and monetary policy (higher interest rates and credit restrictions).

Although Keynes' theory was developed in a period of depression for both the British and wider world economy, with policy implications for achieving economic recovery, it also involved remedies for inflation. Deficit finance, a deliberate surplus of government expenditure over income, was only supposed to be applied for a specific purpose for a limited period. However, the ideas of Keynes have sometimes been misinterpreted to justify government borrowing in general. Moreover, haunted by the memories of depression in the 1930s, governments of both parties in the early post-war period tended to respond to any rise in unemployment with measures to increase demand. They also were tempted to use Keynesian remedies for political purposes, to engineer a boom before an election, which commonly required deflation afterwards, with cuts in spending, and higher taxation and interest rates and the familiar 'stop–go' economic cycle. When Keynesian remedies appeared in the 1970s to lead to both steeply rising inflation *and* unemployment (termed 'stagflation'), as well as a mounting deficit in public finances, a Labour government, under James Callaghan, effectively abandoned Keynes.

Keynesianism was to remain out of fashion until the credit crunch and recession of 2007–9 led to a revival of arguments for deficit finance to encourage recovery (Skidelsky, 2010). Indeed many countries, including Britain, initially sought to kick-start the economy by cutting taxes and main-taining spending. However, financial markets, credit ratings agencies and central banks together provided strong pressures for a rapid reduction in deficits almost everywhere. In Britain it was soon clear that the 'hawks', led by Chancellor George Osborne, dominated the Cameron coalition's economic policies, apparently marginalizing Keynesian economics once more, although the argument is by no means over. Indeed, the coalition's Business Secretary Vince Cable (2011) has argued that 'Keynes would be on our side.'

## Monetary policy

Just as all governments inevitably use fiscal policy, they also can hardly avoid having a **monetary policy**. The issue and control of money has long been a government function, with substantial implications for the economy. In the early sixteenth century King Henry VIII expanded the money supply by debasing the coinage, with serious inflationary consequences. In 1923 the German government provoked hyper-inflation by issuing too many banknotes, which were ultimately not worth the paper they were printed on. Today it is rather more difficult to define, let alone control, the money supply, but it is still the case that a failure in monetary policy can have dire consequences.

British governments in the immediate post-war period often tried to restrict the availability of credit, for example, requiring a substantial down-payment as a condition of a bank loan or 'hire purchase'. More generally, governments have sought to influence the cost of borrowing by influencing or determining interest rates. Higher interest rates may deter borrowing and encourage saving, thus damping down demand in the economy, while lower interest rates may encourage spending and investment, stimulating an economy in recession.

---

● **Monetary policy** is about influencing the money supply and the cost and/or availability of credit. Other things being equal, high interest rates may deter individuals from buying houses, cars and consumer goods, and businesses from new investment. Low interest rates may encourage both consumption and investment. Thus monetary policy, like fiscal policy, can also be used to reduce or stimulate aggregate demand in the economy, although it was subsequently advocated as an *alternative* to Keynesian demand management. Some economists argued that effective control of the money supply was the key to the control of inflation.

British governments have also sometimes felt obliged to increase interest rates to encourage foreigners to hold sterling when there is pressure on the currency in international money markets. Yet governments can only normally alter interest rates within fairly narrow limits set by market forces. Moreover, as a major borrower, government is not above the market but part of it. If the government seeks to increase its own borrowing by issuing more bonds, it will normally have to offer higher rates of interest to attract savers.

Overall, however, there are limits to the effect of changes in interest rates on behaviour. Very low interest rates will not encourage consumption and investment if households and businesses remain pessimistic about the future. Very high interest rates may similarly be ineffective. Thus 15 per cent interest rates did not discourage the selling of sterling on 'Black Wednesday' in 1992 (see below), and indeed it had almost the opposite effect. Currency speculators saw it as a panic measure, confirming that the depreciation of sterling was inevitable, and sold pounds in the expectation of being able to buy them back later at a lower price.

The discrediting of Keynesianism, deficit finance and 'tax and spend' policies led to more emphasis on monetary policy as a means to manage the economy, and in particular to restrain inflation, which had appeared out of control in the early and mid-1970s. The economic policy of the Thatcher government was described as 'monetarism'. In narrow terms, monetarism meant controlling the money supply as the means to control inflation. Yet it also entailed a return to Gladstonian public finance, and the need to 'balance the books', in part because persistent government borrowing to finance current spending leads to inflationary pressures. The Thatcher government saw the control of inflation rather than prevention of unemployment as the paramount aim of economic policy. To control the money supply, interest rates were kept high, which pushed up the value of the pound against other currencies. High interest rates and a high pound depressed investment and exports, with disastrous consequences for British manufacturing industry. Moreover, monetarism in the narrow sense proved unsuccessful. Whatever definition of the money supply was used, it did not seem to have much

direct impact on inflation and the overall performance of the economy. If the Thatcher government achieved any success in the economic sphere it was in spite of its failure to control the money supply or secure significant cuts in overall public spending.

Interest rates began to come down after 'Black Wednesday', in the latter years of Major's government, and have remained historically low since. The Labour government appeared to abandon any control of monetary policy with its surprise decision to hand over control of the minimum lending rate (MLR) to the Monetary Policy Committee of the Bank of England. This was a clever political move that gained the all-important confidence of business and the markets. Yet the government retained influence over monetary policy through its appointments, and more importantly through its broader economic policy that provided the background to the decisions of the Monetary Policy Committee.

## Encouraging market forces

Behind the debates over Keynesianism and monetarism lies an older and wider argument over the whole role of government and the state in the economy. In the immediate post-war decades there was a presumption in favour of state intervention to provide work, welfare 'from the cradle to the grave' and more equality. This presumption was shared by 'one nation' Conservatives, as well as Labour. Yet from the 1970s it was increasingly challenged by many on the New Right who argued that the state had grown too big, that high taxation destroyed incentives and enterprise, that state welfare encouraged a 'dependency culture'. A radical remedy was needed which went beyond tinkering with fiscal and monetary policy. The state must be 'reined back' and market forces allowed to work.

Advocacy of the free market by the Thatcher government never involved a wholesale rejection of state intervention, public spending and public services. To this extent her economic policies disappointed the more enthusiastic apostles of the free market in the Institute of Economic Affairs. However, three key policy areas involved a shift towards the free market.

1 A reduction in the power and influence of trade unions led to a freer labour market.
2 The privatization of state-owned assets promoted wider share ownership, home ownership and 'popular capitalism'.
3 Elements of competition and 'quasi-markets' were introduced into the management of public services, particularly health and education (see Chapter 21).

The intellectual climate was transformed. A presumption in favour of state intervention and state provision that had dominated the politics of the post-war decades was replaced by a presumption in favour of the free market and private enterprise. Even the Labour Party leadership was largely converted. Although Labour had opposed the Thatcher government's trade union reforms, the privatization of public utilities, the sale of council houses and the marketization of public services, they did not subsequently seek to reverse them and indeed embraced the language of competition and choice. New Labour first in opposition and then in government courted business, and was no longer seen as hostile to business interests.

## The under-performing economy: economic management 1945–97

There have long been some fundamental questions over the health of the British economy. Britain was the first country to industrialize, and was once the world's leading economic power. Yet although the British economy has continued to grow over the last century or more, other countries have grown faster, and Britain has thus suffered a relative economic decline. This relative economic decline began in the late nineteenth century, was manifest between the two world wars, and became the subject of heated economic and political argument in the post-war period (see pp. 23–6, 39–40). Productivity, growth and living standards were higher not only in North America but in Japan and among Britain's main competitors in Europe. Successive governments sought to diagnose and address Britain's economic problems, but largely failed. Economic failure was perhaps the main explanation for the defeat of Attlee's Labour

government in 1951, of the Conservative government in 1964, of Wilson's defeat in 1970, Heath's in 1974, Callaghan's in 1979, and Major's in 1997. No government had managed to achieve steady economic growth, and none had ultimately been able to escape from the 'stop–go' boom and bust cycle of the post-war years (see Figure 2.1, p. 25).

Admirers credit the Thatcher government (1979–90) with addressing long-standing problems with the British economy: poor industrial relations partly reflecting trade union power, inflation, escalating public spending, lack of incentives for enterprise and over-reliance on subsidies. Critics argue that the economic, social and political costs of Conservative remedies were worse than the disease. High interest rates led to two recessions that further reduced British manufacturing industry, and led to over three million unemployed. Boom and bust in the housing market led to repossessions and ruin for many. The defeat of union power, symbolized by the bitter miners' strike of 1984–5, coupled with divisive tax and welfare policies, split the country and intensified social and political opposition to Thatcherism. Although Major's more emollient style enabled him to win a narrow election victory in 1992, continuing economic problems culminated in Britain's forced exit from the ERM and a consequent devaluation of the pound. The latter, however, assisted exports and economic recovery, so that by 1997, under the Chancellorship of Kenneth Clarke, inflation, growth, exports and unemployment were all moving in a favourable direction, but too late to restore the Conservatives' reputation for economic competence.

## Economic management under New Labour 1997–2007

Thus Labour, for once, inherited a sound economy which they maintained for a decade. As Chancellor, Gordon Brown prudently kept Labour's pre-election pledge to stay within Conservative taxing and spending plans for two years. He immediately and unexpectedly announced the transfer of decisions on interest rates to the Monetary Policy Committee of the Bank of England. He also signalled his determination to keep inflation low by announcing a 2.5 per cent target rate, and announced his 'golden rule' of only borrowing to finance investment, and keeping public debt at a stable and prudent proportion of national income over the economic cycle. Labour honoured two further Labour pre-election pledges, to sign up to the Social Chapter of the Maastricht Treaty (from which Major had secured an opt-out) and to introduce a national minimum wage. Neither proved as damaging to business as critics had feared. Indeed they had little if any measurable impact on inflation and unemployment. One very important issue was, however, ducked. All parties pledged a referendum before Britain joined the Euro. While Blair appeared keen, Brown was more cautious, supporting entry only if five economic tests could be met. However, the main problem was perhaps political – winning a referendum in the face of a largely hostile British public.

The commitment to keep within Conservative spending plans constrained Labour's policies in the first two years. However, Brown did raise some additional revenue from a windfall tax on the privatized utilities, raising national insurance contributions, and removing some forms of tax relief. These 'stealth taxes', as the opposition called them, enabled him to pursue some (very limited) redistribution of income, inject some (initially fairly modest) additional money into public services, and finance his New Deal to move the young unemployed 'from welfare to work'. Investment was encouraged through the establishment of Regional Development Agencies (with limited budgets, however) and, more controversially, enthusiastic encouragement of the Private Finance Initiative (PFI), developed under the previous government. A major attraction was that PFIs enabled substantial additional investment in new hospitals, schools and prisons without increasing public sector borrowing, although critics objected that the long-term costs would be higher.

Subsequently, the self-imposed shackles on public spending were partially removed, and substantial new money was made available for public services, particularly health and education . Critics argued that Brown was abandoning prudence and returning to Labour's traditional 'tax and spend' policies. Increased spending was achieved partly through economic growth (resulting in a higher tax take) and expectation of further growth, although some extra revenue was raised through more 'stealth taxes' with a less immediately visible impact. Thus while the standard rate of income tax was actually reduced, along with some business taxes, national insurance contributions and indirect taxes were increased. Yet although the Conservative opposition criticized the 'stealth taxes', they promised to match Labour's increased spending on health and education. At the 2005 election they could only promise minor cuts in taxation, financed largely by claimed 'efficiency savings'. While Labour had earlier been accused of adopting Conservative policies, the Conservatives were now increasingly following Labour's agenda.

Thus Labour captured the record for economic competence previously enjoyed by the Conservatives. Chancellor Gordon Brown claimed he had broken the cycle of boom and bust of earlier years, achieving steady economic growth for 40 consecutive quarters (Lee, in Beech and Lee, 2008, p. 33). In marked contrast to earlier decades, Britain's economic performance appeared rather better than most of its leading competitors. By the time Brown moved from Number Eleven to Number Ten Downing Street in 2007, some admirers were hailing him as Britain's most successful Chancellor for a century or more. Through his long period at the Treasury the British economy experienced low inflation, low interest rates, relatively high employment and continuous economic growth higher than most of Britain's major competitors, a combination many previous Chancellors of any party would have longed for. Moreover, Brown had also appealed to progressive opinion by achieving some modest redistribution to benefit mothers and poor families (e.g. through higher Child Benefit and Child Tax Credits), and by taking a lead in cancelling third world debt and supporting international trade and development.

Yet Brown always had his critics. Ken Clarke, his Conservative predecessor at the Treasury, claimed that Brown's 'success' was attributable largely to the favourable economic conditions he inherited, an inheritance that Clarke alleges Brown largely wasted. 'I left Gordon Brown a strong economy. He squandered it' (The Guardian, 26 April 2005). Business interests had become increasingly critical of the rise in public spending and the economic consequences in terms of higher taxation, although others suggested that Labour had not raised taxation sufficiently to cover necessary increases in spending on health and education. Left-of-centre critics argued that Labour had not significantly reduced inequality in general, and had only tinkered with the substantial inequality among pensioners. Green critics deplored Labour's uncritical pursuit of economic growth, its concessions to the road lobby on fuel taxes, and its refusal to make the aircraft industry bear the full cost of its fuel consumption and environmental pollution.

Indeed, many of the old problems in the British economy remained. There was still a substantial balance of payments deficit, a lack of skills and lack of investment in manufacturing industry and a persistent productivity gap compared with Britain's main competitors (Lee, in Beech and Lee, 2008). A more immediate concern was the alleged developing 'black hole' in Britain's public finances. Many independent critics suggested that the government's economic forecasts were over-optimistic, and that further tax increases or spending cuts were required to maintain Brown's 'golden rule' of balancing taxation and expenditure over the economic cycle and only borrowing to fund new investment. Thus Britain was not ideally placed to face the economic storms ahead.

## Managing the global financial crisis and recession 2007–10

Soon after Brown became Prime Minister his government faced mounting problems with first banks and then the economy as a whole. The financial crisis, which few had anticipated, substantially originated in the United States, where a housing boom collapsed with increasing defaults on mortgages, particularly on 'sub-prime' mortgages given to high-risk borrowers sometimes described by the acronym NINJA (no income, no job or assets). This led to serious cash flow problems for the financial institutions involved, both in the United States and elsewhere (Lanchester, 2010). The crisis rapidly became global. Countries that were particularly badly affected included Iceland, Ireland, Greece, Spain and Portugal.

The root causes of the financial crisis have been much analyzed. It has been blamed on a combination of a property boom (or more specifically a housing boom), easy credit and reckless lending by financial institutions, combined with weak and inadequate government regulation of the financial system (Lanchester, 2010, Skidelsky, 2010). The crisis was dramatically illustrated by a series of failures or near failures of major banks, with bail-outs by governments (and ultimately taxpayers) to prevent a collapse in confidence in the whole banking system. Yet the financial crisis and the measures taken to cope with it precipitated recession in the global economy. Although interest rates were historically low, bank lending was reduced and loans called in, house prices and consumer spending dropped, businesses failed, and output and employment fell. All this inevitably meant lower government revenue from taxes, and higher public spending on unemployment and other benefits. Coupled with other measures taken by governments to boost the economy and take countries out of recession this led to mounting government deficits, to an extent that disturbed international financial institutions (Skidelsky, 2010, chapter 1).

The Labour government could, not unreasonably, blame Britain's financial crisis and recession on global forces outside its control. Moreover, Brown acted energetically to deal with the crisis and save the banking system in 2008. With his long experience and extensive contacts around the world, he took a lead role in securing concerted international action, dominating the deliberations of the G20 London emergency summit in 2009. Rawnsley (2010, pp. 633–4), no admirer of Brown, comments that the British Prime Minister successfully assumed the role of global Chancellor which 'played to his strengths … garnered approving headlines and won the applause of his international peer group'. However, he adds, 'The missing ingredient was making it relevant to voters.'

Brown may have helped avert catastrophe, but he was hardly blameless for the problems Britain faced. He and the regulatory system he put in place had done nothing to curb the rise in credit card debt and over-generous 120 per cent mortgage loans (which in some cases relied on self-certified declarations of borrowers' income), practices comparable to the disastrous sub-prime mortgages offered in the United States. By October 2007 there

## BOX 20.2

# Northern Rock

Northern Rock had been a respectable building society based in Newcastle, offering mortgages financed by the savings deposited by its members, like other mutual societies. In common with many other mutuals it took advantage of Conservative government legislation allowing building societies to convert into banks, a process that gave windfall profits to members in the form of shares, often sold on. The new demutualized bank expanded rapidly with mergers and acquisitions, and pursued new business vigorously, more than tripling its share of the UK mortgage market from 6 to 19 per cent, sometimes by offering up to 120 per cent of a house's value (compared with 75 or 80 per cent traditionally offered by building societies). Its funding was no longer dependent on savers in the region; instead 80 per cent came from wholesale money markets. However, its cash reserves were soon insufficient to meet potential demands arising from its very liquid liabilities, and highly illiquid assets (in the shape of bricks and mortar). Faced with a funding crisis, the bank was forced to seek help from the lender of last resort, the Bank of England, in September 2007. This failed to restore confidence, and long queues formed outside branches by savers anxious to withdraw their money, the first major run on a British bank for more than a century. The immediate crisis only ended when the Chancellor, Alistair Darling, guaranteed all Northern Rock deposits. The government then sought and failed to find a suitable buyer for the bank, and was virtually forced to nationalize it in February 2008. This may have been the least bad option, but it was a bitter pill for New Labour, which had repudiated the party's previous commitment to public ownership (Elliott and Atkinson, 2009, pp.42–72).

was £1200 billion outstanding on mortgage debt and £222 billion on unsecured consumer credit. In seven years personal debt had risen by 115 per cent while over the same period earnings had risen by less than 30 per cent (Elliott and Atkinson, 2009, p. 176). Many had incurred levels of debt that they were in no position to repay, particularly if faced with a drop in income. That meant that financial institutions were left holding assets (mortgages and loans) on their balance sheets that were over-valued and could not be realized if their customers defaulted. Many of these 'toxic' mortgages and loans were packaged up and sold on to other financial institutions in a process misleadingly described as 'securitization', thus affecting the whole financial sector and not just those banks responsible for the initial unsound loans.

Meanwhile, the government's own finances had become more suspect, as Brown abandoned his earlier prudence in his latter years as Chancellor, and relied on optimistic forecasts of growth and government revenue to meet dramatic increases in public spending. He only avoided breaking his own 'golden rule' to finance new investment out of revenue by changing the accounting period. Thus the government was not ideally placed to deal with the crisis it soon faced. As David Cameron observed, in a metaphor that resonated with voters, the government had failed to fix the roof when the sun was shining. An early harbinger of the troubles to come was the run on the Northern Rock bank in September 2007, not long after Brown himself became Prime Minister (see Box 20.2).

Northern Rock provided an early warning of problems in the banking system in Britain and many other countries. Financial institutions in the USA, France, Belgium, Iceland, Ireland and elsewhere faced similar liquidity crises. Some were rescued by mergers and takeovers, others by state bail-outs, while a few like the massive US investment bank Lehman Brothers were allowed to fail. Bank regulation in the United States and other countries besides Britain appeared to be ineffective.

In September 2008 HBOS (formed from a merger of another former building society, the Halifax, and the Bank of Scotland) was taken over by Lloyds TSB, a marriage arranged and supported by the government. Another former building society, the Bradford and Bingley, was virtually nationalized after it had expanded rashly into providing mortgages in the buy-to-let market. In October the government took a controlling stake in the Royal Bank of Scotland (which also owns the NatWest), and a 40 per cent share in Lloyds TSB and HBOS. Among the major British banks only Barclays and HSBC avoided part-nationalization.

While there was all-party agreement that state support was necessary to preserve public confidence in the banking system and the economy generally, there was criticism of the failure of the regulatory system, with the Conservatives pledging to return regulation from the FSA to the Bank of England. The wider public was incensed that some of the leading bankers largely responsible for the crisis could walk away with huge pensions. There was also anger at the 'bonus culture' in the city that provided an incentive for the aggressive marketing of risky loans, the more so when it appeared the government was unable to curb extravagant bonuses, even in banks which they virtually owned.

There was more disagreement over coping with the ensuing economic recession. A recession technically involves two consecutive quarters of negative economic growth; Britain was to suffer a year and a half of negative growth. The Labour government reverted to quasi-Keynesian remedies, declining to cut public spending immediately to meet the deficit, but on the contrary increasing spending by bringing forward new investment, assisting employment, and introducing a car scrappage scheme and cutting VAT in an attempt to boost consumer spending. The Conservatives attacked the VAT cut, and called for a clear and specific timetable on reducing the deficit. Yet as the 2010 election approached they pledged few specific spending cuts of their own, while remaining committed to maintaining and even increasing spending on health.

Labour's strategy for dealing with the recession was similar to that of governments in many other leading economies. There was initially broad agreement that cutting public spending and increasing taxation to reduce mounting deficits too early would only make the recession worse and delay recovery. Although the deficits would eventually have to be tackled, this would have to wait until the return of growth. This was one lesson learned from the 'Great Crash' of 1929 (see Box 20.3). However, some countries, like Ireland, introduced a tougher regime of public spending cuts and tax increases to reduce their deficits. It is too early to judge the success or failure of the various strategies.

Brown and Darling argued that the British recession would have been far worse without the measures they took to deal with it. Yet, as opposition parties pointed out, recovery in Britain was slower than in many other countries. However, this may be partly due to Britain's over-dependence on its troubled financial sector, and the relative weakness of manufacturing, although exports were given a potential boost by the depreciation of sterling against other currencies, including the Euro. Indeed, some claimed that Brown's earlier reluctance to join the Euro was retrospectively justified, as troubled economies in the Eurozone (Greece, Ireland, Spain and Portugal) could not improve their competitiveness by devaluing their currencies. Labour's improved opinion poll rating in 2010 suggested that some voters were prepared to give the government the benefit of the doubt over its economic management. While the economic recovery may have been sufficient to deny the Conservatives an overall majority, it could not prevent Labour's defeat and the emergence of a Conservative–Liberal Democrat coalition government.

## BOX 20.3

# The 2009 recession compared with the Great Depression of 1929

The severity of the recession of 2008–9 has been compared with the depression of 1929. There are some obvious similarities. Both started in the United States with rash speculation in property and shares leading to a stock market crash and a banking crisis. However, the 1929 recession was deeper and longer. Skidelsky (2010, p,15) points out that the Great Depression saw twelve successive quarters of economic contraction (1929–32) compared with five in 2008–9. In 1929 unemployment rose much faster and higher, remaining high for most of the 1930s, with massive enduring social consequences. There were more major bank failures in the USA and around the world, triggering a huge crisis in confidence. World GDP fell by 12 per cent from 1929–30 but only by 1.37 per cent in 2008–9 (although some countries were worse affected than others).

It can be argued that the recession was less damaging in 2008–9 because policy makers had learned from the mistakes made in 1929. Thus central banks slashed inter-est rates, governments propped up the banks with public money and G20 leaders agreed to stimulate national economies and avoid economic protection of the kind that led to a major contraction of world trade in the 1930s. However, it can also be argued that the later crisis happened because one of the lessons of 1929 had been forgotten – the need for tight regulation of financial services and controls over the growth of credit.

One curious similarity is that while both involved crises of capitalism and market failure, the political beneficiaries were largely parties of the right (and in some cases, particularly in the earlier Great Depression, the extreme right) rather than the left. In Britain both crises led to the emergence of Conservative-dominated coalitions – the national government of 1931 and the Conservative–Liberal Democrat coalition of 2010 (see Galbraith [1955] 1992, for an account of *The Great Crash* in the USA and Skidelsky, 1970, for analysis of the 1929 slump from a British perspective).

## Coalition economic management

There appeared considerable potential for inter-party tension in the economic policies of the coalition government formed after the election in May 2010. Prior to the election the Liberal Democrats seemed closer to Labour than the Conservatives in their approach to managing the British economy. Then Vincent Cable, the party's economic spokesman, agreed with Chancellor Darling in opposing early massive spending cuts to reduce the budget deficit, for fear that these could halt the fragile economic recovery and lead to a double-dip recession. His party proposed some spending cuts, on identity cards and Trident replacement, but balanced these with pledges of more money to help poorer pupils and students, and to phase out university tuition fees. Their tax proposals were radically redistributive, advocating raising personal allowances on income tax to £10,000, and taking many on low pay out of income tax altogether. This was to be paid for by raising capital gains tax, restricting pension tax relief for the higher paid, reducing tax avoidance and introducing a new 'mansion tax' on properties worth over £2 million.

Meanwhile the Conservatives, who had earlier pledged to match Labour's spending plans, demanded immediate substantial cuts, and attacked Labour's planned increase in National Insurance as a 'jobs tax' that would threaten recovery. The Liberal Democrats warned that the Conservatives would raise VAT, despite Cameron's assurance that his party had no plans to do so. Thus the two parties appeared far apart on their fiscal policy. However, the coalition deal hammered out between the two parties in the days after the election involved compromises over some of these differences, and soon Conservative and Liberal Democrat ministers were working together in surprising harmony.

George Osborne, the new Chancellor, moved swiftly to make institutional changes which were

## BOX 20.4

# The Office for Budget Responsibility

This was set up by Chancellor George Osborne in May 2010, ostensibly to provide economic forecasting independent of government, although initially it was staffed largely by a team seconded from the Treasury. This initiative of the new Chancellor has been compared with the earlier decision of Gordon Brown in 1997 to transfer responsibility for setting interest rates to the Monetary Policy Committee of the Bank of England. Both moves were well received by the markets and commentators, and were politically astute. Osborne argued that earlier Treasury forecasts were often over-optimistic, influenced by government hopes and aspirations, although it remains to be seen whether the OBR's forecasts are more accurate. Critics have argued that the OBR is not truly independent, as it is not responsible to Parliament like the Office for National Statistics (ONS) and the National Audit Office (NAO).

foreshadowed before the election, including an independent Office for Budget Responsibility (see Box 20.4) and a new financial regulatory system to replace the FSA established by Labour.

A commitment to wind up the FSA had been made by Cameron a year earlier. The details of the new regulatory machinery were unveiled in June 2010. Overall responsibility for regulating banks and financial services was handed back to the Bank of England. A new Financial Policy Committee was established within the Bank of England to oversee the whole financial sector. An independent commission under the chairmanship of Sir John Vickers was appointed to look into the possible break-up of large banks. A new Prudential Regulatory Authority (headed by the current boss of the FSA, Hector Sants), also within the Bank, is responsible for regulating specific capital requirements and credit controls of financial institutions. In addition there is an independent Consumer Protection and Markets Authority, and it is proposed that a new single agency be established to tackle economic crime.

## Reducing the deficit

These institutional reforms were soon overshadowed by the main thrust of the coalition government's economic policy, set out in the emergency budget of 22 June 2010. This followed the outgoing Labour Chancellor's budget of March 2010, that had raised national insurance contributions (denounced by the Conservatives as a 'job tax'), announced £11 billion pounds of spending cuts, and conceded the need for substantial future spending cuts, without specifying details. Previous Labour budgets had introduced a new 50 per cent tax rate and reduced tax relief on pension contributions for high earners. None of this, apart from the increased employer's national insurance contributions, was substantially altered by Osborne, although his tax changes and proposed cuts went much further, amounting to a significant change in direction for British economic policy.

Osborne promised a programme of spending cuts and tax rises that would transform the massive deficit to a surplus within the life of a parliament. One issue was how far this larger and faster programme of cuts might endanger the fragile economic recovery, and threaten a double-dip recession. Osborne seems to have convinced his coalition partners, including the previously sceptical Cable, that a more rapid reduction of the deficit was necessary to reassure markets and the all-important credit ratings agencies to avoid increases in interest on government debt.

Even more controversial was the balance between planned spending cuts (77 per cent) and tax increases (23 per cent) to achieve the deficit reduction. The size of the additional proposed cuts, on top of Labour's, implied an average cut in the budgets of all departments not ringfenced of 25 per cent. Extensive changes in taxes and benefits were spelt out. Key measures included:

**Figure 20.1** The new system for managing the economy and regulating financial services

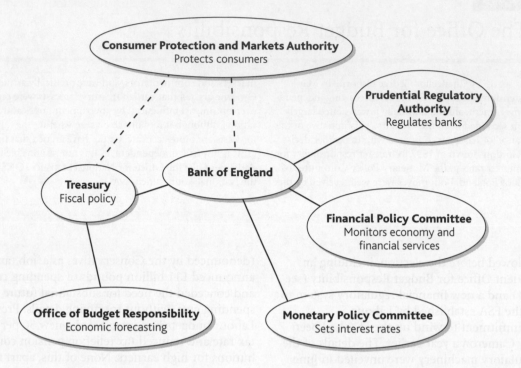

- Raising VAT from 17.5 to 20 per cent from 2011
- Raising capital gains tax for higher-rate taxpayers to 28 per cent
- Increasing personal income tax allowances by £1,000 to £7, 475
- Cutting corporation tax by one per cent for four years successively from 28 to 24 per cent
- A new levy on banks to raise £2 billion
- Freezing child benefit for three years
- Freezing public sector pay for two years, except for those earning less than £21,000
- Restoring the link between the basic state pension and earnings rather than prices
- Reducing tax credits for families earning more than £40,000
- Restricting housing benefits to £400 a week
- Reviewing disability allowances
- Reviewing public sector pensions.

The government described the budget as 'tough but fair'. The toughness was undisputed, although the claim to fairness was more contentious. Liberal Democrats hailed the higher personal tax

allowances as the first stage in a programme to take all those earning under £10,000 out of income tax, a key plank in their election manifesto. They also argued that the major tax changes would affect mostly high earners. However, the Institute for Fiscal Studies pointed out that much of this (the new 50 per cent top rate for income tax, and the reductions in tax allowances for pension contributions of high earners) was the responsibility of the outgoing Labour government. The cuts in public spending and reductions in welfare benefits, particularly housing benefits, would clearly impact mostly on poor families and poor regions. Moreover the increase in VAT (for which Cameron claimed there were 'no plans' before the election), while affecting everyone, impacts more on those who have little choice but to spend all their income (although food and children's clothes remain exempt).

Details of government cuts were announced in the Comprehensive Spending Review on 20 October 2010, although some were revealed rather earlier. In total the cuts over a four-year period amount to £81 billion, involving an estimated loss of 490,000 public sector jobs, and additional job losses in the private sector as a result of reduced public sector contracts. As pre-announced, the NHS and International Development were ring-fenced, and Education also came reasonably well out of the exercise with just a 3.4 per cent cut in the overall budget and some additional money for schools. Yet this increased pressure on other departments. Defence stood to lose 7 per cent of its budget, Transport 21 per cent, Justice 23 per cent, the Home Office 23 per cent, Business, Innovation and Skills 25 per cent, Local Government 27 per cent and the Environment, Food and Rural Affairs 29 per cent.

As far as the impact on people is concerned, a total of £18 billion is being cut from the welfare budget, covering pensions, child benefit, housing benefit and a range of incapacity and disability benefits. Among the obvious losers are the poor and particularly perhaps poor children, and women, who will lose benefits and services and see their retirement age rise rapidly to 66, (the same as for men) by 2020. Employee contributions to public sector pensions will rise also. The elderly emerge from the review comparatively unscathed – their free bus passes, winter fuel allowances and free television licenses all survive the cuts while the earnings link of the state pension is restored. However, the elderly and infirm may suffer from cuts in social services.

The impact of the cuts on the nations and regions of Britain is similarly variable. The budgets for Scotland, Wales and Northern Ireland are each reduced by about seven per cent. This is likely to intensify demands for further devolution of power, and for nationalists, independence. The devolved governments have signed a joint protest on the effect of cuts on their economies. Those regions of England substantially dependent on public sector spending and employment (such as the North-east or Yorkshire) may suffer disproportionately, although the coalition government has tried to maintain investment projects in these areas.

According to the opinion polls, a majority of the public supported the scale of the government cuts although there was more disagreement on some specific measures. As always the devil lies in the detail, and it will take time for the impact of the review to be felt on services, communities and sections of the population. Expert opinion still

appears divided, particularly on the broader economic impact of the programme.

One issue is how far the scale of the cuts will be realized. It is one thing to announce cuts, another to achieve them. Efficiency savings are notoriously difficult. Unanticipated events or developments, such as increased terrorist threat or another war, may affect some planned reductions in spending. Other projected savings may be upset by unexpected changes in people's behaviour. Thus it was initially announced that cutting child benefit for higher-rate taxpayers would save a billion pounds. Some two weeks later the saving had grown to two and a half billion, as the number likely to be affected was recalculated. However, the Office for Budgetary Responsibility sounded a warning note, suggesting that those who only just qualified for the higher rate might reduce their pay and/or increase their pension contributions to retain their child benefit. As those with several children stand to lose thousands, that seems highly plausible.

Some continue to question whether the size and speed of the programme to reduce the deficit is necessary. Osborne argues that this programme was crucial to preserve the UK's triple-A credit rating, maintain low interest rates and keep down the costs of servicing government debt. He claims to have ended a decade of debt and prevented national bankruptcy. His critics suggest he has exaggerated the scale of the UK's economic plight. The UK current account deficit in relation to GDP is slightly higher than most other advanced western states, although its public debt is relatively smaller. A slower, slightly smaller and more balanced programme of deficit reduction, as proposed by Labour in government and in opposition, might be enough to satisfy the markets with less risk to Britain's economic recovery.

Osborne's critics argue his programme to reduce the deficit recklessly endangers economic recovery and risks a double-dip recession. One of the key issues here is how far the private sector can expand economic activity and employment to make up for the cuts in public spending and public sector jobs (and linked job losses in the private sector). The government and some of its advisers suggest it can. The low pound may boost exports. However the sluggishness of the global economy

## *Academic controversy 20.1*
## Disagreements among economists on the economic crisis and the coalition's economic strategy for dealing with it

Very few economists predicted the banking crisis and ensuing economic recession. Lanchester (2010, p. 167) quotes an American university provost lamenting that not a single one of his entire economics department saw it coming. According to Skidelsky (2010, pp. 29–44), macro-economists are currently divided into two contending schools, New Classicals and New Keynesians. Neither of these explained the crisis, and each offered contrasting policy remedies. To beat the recession New Keynesians argued for a fiscal stimulus based on government spending, which New Classical economists claimed would do more harm than good (Skidelsky, 2010, pp. 44–51).

The USA and many other countries initially opted for such a fiscal stimulus. Thus the UK Brown government cut VAT to boost consumer spending, although Chancellor Darling also planned to reduce the growing government deficit through spending cuts and tax increases. Subsequently the 2010 coalition government's plans to eliminate the deficit in four years, largely through spending cuts, divided economists.

*The Observer* newspaper (24 October 2010) sought the views of a number of Nobel prize-winning economists on the UK coalition government's programme. In support, Robert Mundell considered it the right approach while Edward Prescott observed that no country ever spent its way to prosperity. By contrast both Daniel McFadden and Paul Krugman considered that the UK government risked deflation and a repetition of the 1931 depression. Eric Maskin thought massive spending cuts at a time of relatively low economic activity were a mistake. Robert Engel criticized the policy but doubted whether the cuts would be fully implemented, as they would be too painful. When leading economists disagree to such an extent it is difficult for non-specialists to know who to believe.

---

and protectionist measures by other countries may reduce the potential for export growth, while reduced income and confidence could dampen domestic demand. Only time will tell whether the UK economy emerges leaner and fitter or suffers a double-dip recession, as Keynesian economists suggest. If the latter, reduced tax revenues and an increased welfare bill could threaten deficit reduction. Economists, as often, are divided over the coalition's economic strategy (see Academic Controversy 20.1).

These are the most immediate economic issues around the June budget and October spending review neither of which were affected significantly by the subsequent March 2011 budget, which was intended to be neutral on the overall balance between spending and taxation. However, there are two other linked debates around the coalition government's economic management. One is about its underlying motivation. Critics on the left argue that the real objective of Cameron, Osborne, and perhaps also their *Orange Book* Liberal Democrat partners, is an ideological project to shrink the state and dramatically reduce the scope and scale of Britain's public services. The size of the budget deficit provides a plausible excuse for doing what they want to do anyway. There is some justification for perceiving the cuts as ideologically driven, and comparisons have been made with Thatcherism. Yet both Cameron and Osborne have lamented the need for cuts and described themselves as progressive One Nation Conservatives, (although such protestations might be cynically interpreted as just good public relations). There has been an even more vociferous argument about the fairness or otherwise of the programme (however fairness is defined). This takes us somewhat beyond economics. Economists tend to leave such arguments to moral philosophers and politicians. Although economists are interested in the distributional impact of economic policy (or who gets what, who wins and who loses), many are disinclined to make moral judgements on outcomes. Others (including both Adam Smith and Keynes) have been rather more concerned with ethics. For politicians the arguments over fairness appear critical. Cameron, Osborne and Clegg have sold their programme as 'tough but fair'. Voters may agree it is tough. Whether they also ultimately accept it is fair may determine the outcome of the next election. We will return to questions of fairness, social justice and equality in Chapter 22.

# SUMMARY

- The Treasury and the Chancellor of the Exchequer remain at the heart of British economic policy making, along with a few other ministers, and their advisers.

- Yet governments have limited powers to influence economies shaped by market forces. The British economy is part of an increasingly globalized economy, affected by global trends.

- The main tools of government economic policy are direct intervention, fiscal policy and monetary policy. The balance between them has changed over the years with less direct intervention, and less reliance on fiscal policy to manage the economy, and rather more emphasis on monetary policy, with interest rates determined by the Monetary Policy Committee of the Bank of England.

- The economic policies of successive governments in the post-war period have had to tackle deep-seated problems in a British economy that has suffered relative decline.

- Although both the Thatcher governments and more recently the Blair governments have been credited with halting and reversing Britain's relative economic decline, the record of both is now contentious.

- New Labour's economy policy was characterized initially by prudence and a restraint on public spending and taxation, subsequently by substantial increased spending and investment, particularly on health and education.

- Although New Labour presided for a decade over low inflation, low interest rates, and (until the credit crunch) relatively high employment and steady growth, deep-seated problems in the British economy (under-investment, poor training, low productivity) were not resolved..

- The financial crisis followed by recession faced by Brown's government was global in scope and also severely affected other leading western countries. Yet over-dependence on financial services and the growth of personal and government debt rendered the British economy particularly vulnerable.

- The crisis led to some revival of Keynesian ideas, with government action to stimulate demand to assist recovery from recession. However the bond markets and credit rating agencies have provided strong pressures for speedy deficit reduction.

- The coalition government plans to cut the deficit faster than Labour intended, largely through public spending cuts, to the general approval of markets and bankers, but with some controversy over the possible impact on economic recovery, and on poorer communities and regions in Britain.

# QUESTIONS FOR DISCUSSION

- Why has the British economy suffered relative decline? What are the enduring problems of the British economy and how might they be remedied?

- Who 'calls the shots' on decisions over the British economy?

- Why did Labour abandon its past commitment to nationalization? Why did Brown's government take some banks into public ownership?

- Why did Keynesian demand management become less fashionable, and why has it made an apparent return to favour?

- How far was the monetarism pursued by the Thatcher government a failure?

- How far and with what success did new Labour embrace markets, competition and choice?

- Who or what is to blame for the banking crisis and ensuing recession? Why did few see it coming? How successful were the measures taken to deal with it? Could it happen again?

- Is the scale and speed of the coalition's programme to reduce the deficit necessary? How far may it endanger economic recovery? Is there a credible alternative?

- Does anyone really manage the economy?

# FURTHER READING

Inevitably the pre-recession literature requires updating but some sources are still useful. Grant, (2002), Economic Policy in Britain examines economic policy and policy making in the post-war years. The economic management of earlier Labour governments is usefully discussed by Thomas (1992). Gamble (1994) examines the political context of Thatcherism. There is useful analysis of New Labour's economic management by Stevens in Seldon (2001), Smith in Seldon and Kavanagh (2005), Coates (2005) and both Lee and Mullard and Swarey in Beech and Lee (2008).

There are already numerous sources on the global banking crisis and economic recession, although some of these focus principally on the United States. For the impact on Britain see among others Gamble (2009),

Cable (2009), Elliot and Atkinson (2009), Lanchester (2010) and a symposium in *Political Studies Review* (January 2010). Brown (2010) has now given his own insider account. Skidelsky (2010, Chapter 1) provides a useful brief 'anatomy of the crisis', and discusses who (or what) is to blame for it.

Useful official websites on economic policy include the Treasury www.hm-treasury.gov.uk, Downing Street www.number-10.gov.uk, the Cabinet Office www.cabinet-office.gov.uk, and the Bank of England www.bankofengland.co.uk. Further analysis can be derived from the websites of think tanks (such as the Institute of Fiscal Studies) the financial press, business and trade unions.

# CHAPTER 21

# Government Spending: Delivering Public Services

What services the state should provide and how it should provide them are key issues. The cost and efficiency of public services has become central to political debate in Britain. Conservative governments from 1979 to 1997 sought to improve the efficiency of public services by exposing them to increased competition and market forces. This controversially involved more private sector involvement in public service provision. Labour governments after 1997 maintained much of this reform agenda, while increasing substantially spending on health and education in particular. To show extra cash, paid for by taxpayers, involved real improvements in services, Labour imposed tough performance targets, and published comprehensive league tables of the record of all schools and hospitals. However, targets and league tables became politically controversial. Some argued that the whole process involved increased central control and diminished discretion for front-line workers. Others suggested that targets distorted priorities and provided perverse incentives that were counter-productive. Thus the coalition government elected in 2010 moved quickly to reduce targets, ostensibly to increase local and professional autonomy. However, the new government also sought massive cuts in the social care and welfare bill to reduce the huge budget deficit.

The financial crisis and recession led to a surge in public expenditure relative to GDP in Britain as elsewhere, intensifying the political debate over the relative size of the public and private sectors, and the role of the state and the market. Those on the right of the political spectrum argue that government has grown too large, involving too much control over its citizens, and too much interference with free market forces. Others, on the left, maintain that a high level of state spending remains crucial to provide those services vital for the well-being of all its citizens.

While the Conservative Chancellor George Osborne claimed there was no alternative to massive cuts in public spending, Labour critics argued he was ideologically committed to shrinking the state. Yet while there are real political choices to be made, now and for the near future, it is also clear that demographic trends will intensify longer-term pressures for increased public spending.

## The welfare state: consensus and controversy

The welfare state was very much part of the post-war consensus (see Chapter 2). Labour, One Nation Conservatives and Liberals would have had no qualms in supporting the 'positive rights' laid down in the United Nations Universal Declaration of Human Rights (1948). These included rights to 'housing, medical care and necessary social services, and the right to security in the event of unemployment, sickness, disability, widowhood, old age…' as well as maternity benefits (Article 25). Article 26 specified a right to free elementary education, and the availability of technical, professional and higher education.

Some of the foundations of the British welfare state were laid by the coalition wartime government (1942 Beveridge Report, 1944 Education Act, 1945 Family Allowances), although the post-war 1945–51 Labour government was responsible for the establishment of the National Health Service (1948) and the implementation of education and welfare reforms.

The financial cost of extending public services was under-estimated. For example, it was assumed that NHS costs would fall in the long run as a consequence of the nation's improved health, after an initial backlog of untreated conditions had been cleared. In reality an ageing population (in part the consequence of improved health care) coupled with medical advances and rising public expectations increased demand for health services. Demographic change, particularly increasing longevity, fuelled an ever-expanding demand for pensions, welfare and medical services for the elderly. While school-age children were a declining proportion of the UK population, increased demand for nursery education, post-16 and (particularly) university education led to substantial increases in education spending also.

As the rising cost of public services became increasingly burdensome to taxpayers, it was increasingly questioned whether particular services were really delivering the anticipated benefits. In the 1960s and early 1970s problems such as child poverty, inner city deprivation, homelessness and failing schools indicated that the welfare state was not providing effective security 'from the cradle to the grave'. Many did not question the need for public health and social services, but raised issues over their finance, organization and delivery. Could not the administration of public services be more efficient? Yet some critics went on to claim that some welfare provision actually made social problems worse, by encouraging a 'culture of dependency' and stifling initiative. Neo-liberal economists argued services free at the point of use were bound to stimulate an excess of demand, while what they termed 'bureaucratic over-supply' was in the interests of the pay and careers of public service workers. Thus an alliance of welfare-dependent service and benefit claimants and public service professionals would provoke an ever-expanding growth of public spending and taxation.

## Conservative reforms to public services 1979–97

The Conservative response was to restructure rather than abolish the welfare state. Some public services (notably housing) were cut. Over a million council houses (with subsidized rents) were sold at a discount to their tenants. Other municipal housing stock was transferred to the preferred new suppliers, voluntary housing associations. Those who could not afford market rents claimed housing benefit. The management of other services was reformed through the introduction of more competition and increased private provision. Thus the provision of residential care for the elderly was substantially privatized, with local authorities providing regulation and much of the funding. Ancillary services in health and education (e.g. cleaning, catering, laundry, ground maintenance) were subjected to compulsory competitive tendering (CCT), leading to increased private sector provision, at lower cost, but with poorer conditions of service for the workers involved. For core teaching and medical services 'internal markets' or 'quasi-markets' were introduced to provide more consumer choice (in theory at least) and promote more efficiency and drive down costs through the stimulus of competition between rival contractors or providers. This involved a new and more private sector approach to the management of public services, termed 'New Public Management' in place of traditional public administration (see Box 21.1).

Market reforms reduced some costs and arguably improved efficiency. However, competition between service providers inevitably also involved some reduction in effective co-operation. Moreover, the introduction of financial costs and benefit calculations by accountants and business managers into decisions on health care and education conflicted with the notion of the provision of public services on the basis of need, almost irrespective of cost, particularly in the health service. While it could be argued that escalating demands on public services compel some form of rationing in the public sector, doctors and teachers feared

**BOX 21.1**

## Contrasting administrative cultures in provision of public services

| Traditional public administration | New Public Management |
|---|---|
| • Informed by a 'public service ethos' | • Informed by private sector management principles |
| • Services delivered according to written rules, minimum managerial discretion | • Services delivered more flexibly with more managerial autonomy, and competition between providers. |
| • All citizens in the same circumstances receive the same service – equity and uniformity | • Services tailored more to the requirements of consumers and local circumstances – variations in services. |
| • Service delivery audited to ensure strict legality – the spending of money as authorized | • Service delivery audited to measure economy, efficiency and effectiveness (the 3 Es) |

their professional judgement was eroded by such financial decision-making.

Yet the impact of such reforms on spending should not be exaggerated. The overall cost of the NHS and spending on education per pupil continued to rise, although at a slower rate. Margaret Thatcher famously declared the National Health Service was safe in her hands. Her successor, John Major, maintained competition within public services, but also introduced the Citizen's Charter. Specific charters for particular services published standards for provision and clear complaints procedures where performance fell short of what was promised. More positively, Charter Mark awards were given for those demonstrating 'excellence and innovation in delivering services in line with Charter principles' (Chandler, 1996, p. 4).

## Labour and the public services – a third way?

The Labour party, returned to office in 1997, had long seen itself as the champion of the welfare state and public service provision. Health and education were seen as key Labour issues and priorities for the new government. Yet Labour struggled to

satisfy the sometimes conflicting demands of voters, taxpayers, service users and, particularly, public service workers, who looked to Labour to reverse the market-oriented reforms introduced by the Conservatives and to improve substantially public service pay and conditions. In practice, New Labour both provided substantial additional resources for some public services, and also maintained much of the thrust of Conservative management reforms.

Thus Labour's White Paper *The New NHS* declared, 'There will be no return to the old centralised command and control system of the 1970s … But nor will there be continuation of the divisive internal markets of the 1990s.' New Labour promised a 'third way of running the NHS based on partnership and driven by performance' (Department of Health, 1997). The new buzzwords were 'partnership', 'co-operation' and 'networks', implying collaboration rather than competition. Yet the Labour government wanted to maintain elements of competition between providers both as a spur to efficiency, and to provide more choice for consumers.

So although Labour claimed that it had scrapped the Conservatives' internal market in the health service, this was 'more superseded than abolished' (Denham in Dunleavy, 2003, p. 288). The hospital trusts established by the Conservatives continued, and subsequently the best performers were allowed to apply for Foundation Hospital status. The Conservatives had also encouraged groups of doctors in general practice to apply for fundholder status, to control their own budgets. Labour abolished GP fundholders, and made all GPs and other 'primary care' health workers (such as community nurses, midwives and chiropodists) join new Primary Care Trusts (PCTs) with control of their own budgets as both suppliers and purchasers of health care. These Primary Care Trusts contracted with hospitals of their choice for the supply of further health care, although some work previously performed in hospitals, including some simple operations, could now be performed in PCT clinics. A new central body, the National Institute for Clinical Excellence (NICE), was established to advise on common standards of health treatment and best medical practice. Another body, the Commission for Health Improvement, advised on the quality of local services. These new arrangements were designed to reduce some of the differences and inequalities in health care provision, although inevitably they also reduced somewhat the autonomy of the medical profession.

## Partnership with the private sector

It was over the delivery of public services that New Labour parted company from its union allies and 'old Labour' critics, for whom public services have to be delivered by the public sector. For New Labour (including Brown as well as Blair), 'a sharp distinction is drawn between how services are funded and how they are delivered' (Denham, in Dunleavy et al., 2003, p. 282). They particularly sought funding from the private sector through the Private Finance Initiative (PFI) for a massive programme of public sector investment to remedy decades of under-investment (see also Chapter 18). Between 1997 and 2004 over 600 PFI deals were signed and, by 2003, 451 had been completed (Driver in Beech and Lee, 2008, p. 58).

While still committed to state funding of public services, delivered free at the point of use, New Labour also sought more private sector involvement in the delivery of public services,

breaking up the old public sector monopoly. In part this was simple pragmatism – 'what matters is what works'. If there was unsatisfied demand for health services – for example for the removal of cataracts from eyes or for hip replacements – and this demand could not be met within the public sector, it made sense to buy in resources from the private sector to meet demand and reduce waiting times. NHS patients wanted free and effective treatment as soon as possible, and it hardly mattered to them who provided it. Much the same went for the provision of state education. School pupils and their parents wanted good facilities and good teaching, without having to pay for private education, but precisely how this was provided was a secondary consideration. Thus businesses and voluntary organizations were encouraged to sponsor new city academies in poor areas. For New Labour, private sector involvement in the delivery of public services stimulated competition and choice, but also exemplified the principle of partnership between the public and private sectors.

To critics, private sector involvement in the provision of state services was a Trojan horse, threatening the future of the welfare state through the creation of a two-tier system. Public service providers feared that the private sector would 'cream off' the most potentially profitable parts of the system, leaving them with the most difficult and expensive patients, pupils and consumers. Thus the private sector would perform routine uncomplicated surgery, leaving NHS staff and facilities to cope with the more problematic cases, incidentally involving a much lower potential 'success rate'. Similarly, it was feared the new city academies would not take their share of pupils with special needs or with marked behaviour problems, who would be left in 'bog-standard comprehensives'. Those who defended Labour's reforms pointed out there had always been a 'two-tier' or indeed a 'multi-tier' NHS and state education system, with marked differences in performance between schools and health treatments across the country, the quality of service depending on a 'postcode lottery'. Additional resources, wherever they come from, public, private or voluntary sector, could only raise standards of provision.

BOX 21.2

## Student protests against higher fees for university education

Funding higher education has raised acute political controversy both for Labour and the 2010 coalition government. Spending on higher education has failed to match the substantial growth in student numbers, from which those from poorer backgrounds have largely not benefited. Labour initially ended free university education by introducing flat-rate tuition fees, (covering only a quarter of course costs), following the 1997 Dearing Report. However, elite universities, disturbed at their increasing difficulty in competing internationally, wanted to be able to charge more for their degrees. As part of a package of reforms, Labour later allowed variable fees, with interest-free loans, repayable by students after graduation, and reintroduced non-repayable maintenance grants for students

from poorer families. Labour's U-turn on top-up fees, which it had promised not to introduce in 2001, caused huge political difficulties for the party. In 2004 its majority was reduced to just five on the issue. In the 2005 general election there were substantial anti-Labour swings in parliamentary constituencies with a large student population. The Liberal Democrats, who opposed tuition fees both in 2005 and 2010, were the main beneficiaries.

The coalition government accepted the recommendations of the 2010 Browne report on university finance, and proposed trebling tuition fees, although providing some more help for poorer students, and deferring loan repayments for low-paid graduates. The plans provoked a storm of student protest. On 10 November 2010 a minority among a largely peaceful demonstration hurled missiles at the police and attacked and damaged the Millbank building housing Conservative HQ (pictured above). However, the Liberal Democrats bore the brunt of student outrage, as their ministers voted for a huge fee increase that they were pledged to oppose. To the accompaniment of another student demonstration, involving further clashes with the police and damage to property in and around Parliament Square in December, the Liberal Democrats split three ways in a crucial Commons vote that saw the government majority reduced to 21.

## Spending on public services

In the Labour government's early years there was little extra money for public services. Labour's first priority was to establish its credentials for sound management of the national economy, by honouring its commitments not to raise personal taxation and to keep within Conservative spending limits for the first two years. The government rather exaggerated the relatively small increases in health and

education spending they did manage to introduce, and there was some over-claiming and double-counting. Later, very substantial additional sums were promised and delivered, for health and education.

Britain's health expenditure had lagged well below the European average, following decades of under-funding and under-investment, and Blair pledged to raise health spending from 6.8 per cent of GDP to the EU average (then 8 per cent) by 2006. This target was reached, and Gordon Brown's three-year spending plan for 2005 involved a further rise to 9 per cent of GDP. Indeed, 'Public expenditure on health, education and social security increased more rapidly under New Labour than under previous Conservative and Labour governments' (Mullard and Swaray, in Beech and Lee, 2008, p. 48).

Yet major problems in funding other public services persisted. Thus social care for the growing numbers of elderly and infirm remained chronically underfunded, NHS dentistry remained a national scandal, while successive governments had not succeeded in adequately financing the huge growth in university education (see Box 21.3). Meanwhile the cost of a range of supplementary benefits, including housing, incapacity and unemployment continued to escalate, trapping many recipients in poverty.

## Targets and league tables

As always, however, it is debatable how far additional spending secured value for money.

Increased spending simply involves additional inputs into a service. It does not guarantee a commensurate improvement in outputs and outcomes (see Chapter 19). Indeed, critics of high public spending had long argued that problems cannot be solved by simply throwing money at them. Thus it was politically necessary for Labour to demonstrate additional money involved real improvements in public services, rather than additional waste and bureaucracy. This meant that the government had to publish clear targets, and measures for achieving those targets.

Moreover, a government committed to consumer choice had to provide more evidence to enable service users to make informed decisions. Thus 'league tables' of hospital and school performance were published. Those that met government targets were given star rating, those that did not were 'named and shamed'. However, some measures, it was suggested, were misleading and unfair. Some hospitals appeared to have poorer success rates in surgical operations because they were treating patients with more difficult conditions. Some schools had poorer exam results

because their pupils came from disadvantaged backgrounds, with fewer skills on entry. The government tried to respond to these criticisms by providing more sophisticated measures of performance, for example providing measures for 'added value' in school league tables.

For public sector managers and staff the stakes could be high. Failure to meet government targets and performance indicators could lead to dismissal for individuals deemed responsible, and sometimes even the takeover or closure of failing institutions. By contrast, success might be rewarded not only with additional resources, but also with more discretion over their use. Labour promoted the notion of 'earned autonomy' through the introduction of new Foundation Hospitals for successful 'three-star' hospital trusts. Foundation Hospitals were freed from detailed control by the Department of Health, and could manage their own assets and raise private funds for investment purposes (Coates, 2005, p. 125). In education more power was devolved to successful schools, particularly 'trust schools' and the new private sector-backed city academies (Driver, in Beech and Lee, 2008, p. 61). Yet there was always some tension at the heart of Labour's management of the public services. While they emphasized the need for greater flexibility, choice and the delegation of more discretion to institutions and front-line staff, it was also politically essential to be able to demonstrate improved service delivery and performance, which meant they could not afford to give up detailed regulation and control.

Did Labour deliver improved public services? Toynbee and Walker (2005, 2010) deliver a mixed verdict. Labour certainly increased capital and current spending on health and education, evident in the huge school and hospital building programme, remedying decades of under-investment. By 2010 only a fifth of hospitals dated from before 1948. They reduced waiting times in the NHS and improved performance in schools. They also presided over an expansion of nursery education and university education. However, there remain questions over value for money. Toynbee and Walker suggest that the NHS probably got too much extra too fast, and it was not always spent wisely. Some of the extra cash for the NHS ended up in the pockets of doctors and consultants.

## BOX 21.3

# Reducing waiting times in the NHS

A major target in the NHS was reducing the waiting time from ordinary GP appointments to the diagnosis and treatment of serious medical conditions. Delays in seeing GPs and consultants prolong patient anxieties and can often cause real pain, suffering and avoidable extra risk. Yet resource constraints in the past compelled rationing by queuing. To escape queues and avoidable suffering those who could afford to 'went private' to obtain an immediate operation. The Labour government introduced targets that reduced waiting times for an operation from up to 18 months under the previous government to 18 weeks, from the first GP referral to the day of operation by 2008 (Toynbee and Walker, 2005, pp. 12–13, 45–6). There were also new targets for waiting times for primary care, with access to a nurse promised within 24 hours and to a GP within 48 hours. Some of these targets were later criticized for distorting priorities. Thus seeing all patients who asked for an appointment within a fixed time limit failed to discriminate between urgent and routine cases. The 2010 coalition government has since scrapped some targets (e.g. waiting time targets for seeing a GP).

Productivity stagnated. Many criticized the government's micro-management through targets and its repeated reorganizations. Yet health and education improved. The record is more mixed elsewhere. 'Welfare to work' had a limited impact, and Labour ducked a comprehensive reform of welfare benefits. There were more policemen and (not necessarily as a result) lower crime (although the public never quite believed it). Yet many more criminals were locked up, requiring a substantial expansion of prisons and the prison service, a rather dubious achievement.

## Public services in a cold climate – coalition spending cuts

Mounting budget deficits resulting from the financial crisis and recession, and pressure for massive cuts in public spending from central banks and the markets, have created a cold economic climate for public services. Many countries, like Britain, have sought massive cuts in public spending (most notably Canada and Ireland). Before the 2010 election all parties agreed on the need to reduce the deficit over time, but without specifying details. While the Conservatives emphasized the need for early cuts, but promised to ring-fence health spending, Brown apparently found it difficult to utter the word 'cuts', while the Liberal Democrats largely agreed with Labour that although the deficit was serious and must be reduced, premature spending cuts could endanger economic recovery.

The mood changed rapidly after the election, with veiled threats to the UK's credit rating and warnings from business leaders and bankers. The coalition government swiftly agreed a massive programme of cuts, involving average reductions in departmental budgets of 25 per cent, with the continued commitment not to cut health or international development. Although a small real increase in spending on the NHS (1.3 per cent per annum) is pledged, because of steadily rising demand arising from increasing longevity and new treatments, coupled with the costs of yet another major reorganization of the service (involving scrapping Primary Care Trusts), many observers doubt whether this will be enough to maintain current service levels and avoid job losses. Education has also fared relatively well, with only a predicted 3.4 per cent per annum cut in spending. Schools have been ring-fenced, but there are doubts as to whether a miniscule real increase in spending (0.1 per cent per annum) will be sufficient to cover increased numbers of primary schoolchildren. There is additional funding for the poorest children in the form of a pupil premium, the cost of which will rise to £2.5 billion in 2014. Yet there are significant cuts elsewhere in the education budget, including major cuts in capital spending, cuts in

## COMPARATIVE POLITICS 21.1
# Welfare provision

Most modern western states developed welfare services (including health and unemployment insurance, pensions and family allowances) in the course of the twentieth century, although the type and extent of welfare provision varies considerably. Esping-Anderson (1990, 1999) distinguishes between three welfare models: liberal, conservative and social democratic. The liberal model (e.g. United States) assumes citizens insure themselves, privately or through company schemes against ill-health, accident, unemployment and the costs of old age. The state provides only means-tested and basic support for those who are uninsured. The conservative model (e.g. Germany) involves occupational insurance schemes to which employers and employees contribute. The social democratic model involves universal state welfare provision funded out of taxation, and free at the point of use. Sweden is considered the archetypal example (although some aspects of the Swedish system have been eroded). Britain largely falls within the social democratic model – although charges are made for prescriptions, glasses, dentistry, and much care of the elderly, while state pensions are inadequate, and in practice are topped up by occupational and private pensions, or means-tested supplementary benefits. The advantages of different schemes are contested, and the subject of fierce political debate. Thus in the United States 40 per cent of the population have no health insurance. President Clinton attempted and failed to introduce a federal insurance scheme. President Obama made it a central plank of his election campaign, but legislation ran into strong opposition in Congress and the country. Britain's National Health Service has become a football in the debate. Critics describe it as 'socialized medicine' and criticize its alleged shortcomings. (See e.g. Bale. 2008, ch. 8; Judt, 2010.)

---

16–19 education, in school sports and extra-curricular activities and in education services provided by local authorities. However, the biggest cuts are in university teaching budgets: state spending on higher education is to fall from £7.1to £4.2 billion, with arts and humanities hardest hit, but science, technology, engineering and mathematics protected.

Among other services there are major cuts in policing (a 20 per cent cut in central funding over four years) and the prison service. The government proposed to reduce by a massive 60 per cent the budget for building affordable houses, with new tenants facing rents of 80 per cent of market value. As most social housing tenants (65 per cent) are on benefits they will be heavily dependent on housing benefits that are also being squeezed (see below). Overall, local government is facing a major cut in central funding (27 per cent over four years). The budget for local authority social care looks particularly vulnerable, despite the government providing an extra £2 billion for care of the elderly, which may not be enough to meet rising demand. Other local authorities services, such as libraries, face cuts and closures.

## Protecting front-line services?

The coalition has stressed its intention to protect, as far as possible, front-line services supplied by doctors, nurses, teachers, police and others, by cutting 'back-office staff', sometimes described, more derogatively, as 'pen pushers'. Yet the scope for such savings may prove limited. Most clerical workers are relatively low-paid, and, moreover, provide valuable resources for better-paid professionals who are freed to concentrate on the work that only they are qualified to do. Record keeping and record sharing is not a luxury, as is shown by periodic scandals indicating that serial rapists and other offenders could and should have been caught earlier had reports been properly collated and interpreted. Similar points can be made about local authority social services, and scandals involving the

## Coalition plans for more academies and free schools

The coalition government's Secretary of State for Education, Michael Gove, is committed to a massive expansion of academies and the introduction of new 'free schools', based on Swedish and US models. The Labour government introduced city academies, as charitable trusts with business sponsors, outside local authority control, largely to turn round failing schools in poor areas. Additional resources and new management led to some high-profile success stories, although the general record of performance was more contentious. The coalition government has allowed successful primary and secondary schools (rather than failing schools in deprived areas) to secure academy status. They argue that this will give more autonomy to schools and teachers removed from local authority control. Critics fear that the consequence will be fewer resources for remaining local authority schools and a divisive two-tier system. The impact could be similar to the earlier Conservative government's grant-maintained schools, encouraged to opt out of local authority control to receive more generous central funding.

Under Gove's plans parents, teachers or voluntary groups could also apply to run their own 'free schools' (based on precedents in Sweden and the USA), receiving government funding for each pupil recruited equivalent to spending in state schools. Much of the early publicity has been around the proposals of parents dissatisfied with existing state school provision in their area to set up and run their own schools, although Gove has suggested some teachers also may jump at the chance to run their own school, free from council control. Critics suggest 'pushy' middle-class parents and their children are the most likely beneficiaries, with poorer children left in worse-resourced local authority schools the potential losers. The evidence of improved performance in Swedish 'free schools' has been challenged, and government now places more emphasis on the US record of free schools.

---

severe maltreatment and sometimes death of children, where danger signs were ignored or not shared between workers and agencies. The efficiency of all parts of the NHS also clearly depend on easy access to accurate patient records. Cuts to 'back-office staff.' are likely to lead to specialist professionals wasting more of their valuable time not on the work they have been expensively trained to perform, but on routine administration and clerical work, to the detriment of efficiency and effectiveness.

## New ways of providing services

Before the election David Cameron argued for a 'big society' rather than 'big government', implying that many services could be delivered by voluntary groups, community self-help, and user or producer co-operatives. Co-operation is an ideal commonly linked with Labour. Indeed for many years the Co-operative Party has been affiliated to Labour, with some candidates standing as 'Labour and Co-op'. More recently Labour has sought to re-emphasize the centrality of co-operation and mutualism to its philosophy. Yet in the run-up to the 2010 election David Cameron attempted to steal Labour's clothes by advocating co-operatives in the delivery of Britain's public services. He argued this would empower front-line staff, give them a real sense of ownership of their own schools and hospitals, raise morale and productivity, and thus improve the quality of services for consumers and service users. Michael Gove's 'free schools' are one example (see Box 21.4).

Devolving or decentralizing power is appealing, but should power be devolved to local communities, to service providers, or service consumers? Devolving power to local communities might suggest handing back more decision-making to elected local councils, and indeed some ministers in the coalition such as Secretary of State for Communities and Local Government Eric Pickles have talked in these terms. Yet the proposed education reforms will further reduce local authority responsibilities. Many state-funded schools will be removed from the supervision of any intermediate public authority below the Department for Education, which raises some questions over effective accountability. Devolving more power to 'front-line staff' or professionally qualified service providers (doctors, teachers) through 'producer cooperatives' may conceivably improve decision-making, but it leaves questions over public accountability and the interests of consumers and taxpayers. Moreover, in education especially, Education Secretary Michael Gove is effectively imposing new central controls on the curriculum through the 'English baccalaureate' without much in the way of preparation or consultation.

Health Secretary Andrew Lansley seems determined to give more power in the NHS to general practioners, although it is far from clear that most GPs want this. The NHS has experienced frequent reorganizations since it was established in 1948, particularly since the 1974 reorganization (Ham, 2009, Chapters 1–3). The uncertainty of constant change carries its own costs, and yet the coalition government is in the process of replacing Primary Care Trusts, responsible for healthcare in the community with a system of consortiums of GP commissioning services for patients. A representative survey of doctors conducted for the King's Fund suggests that only one in four doctors agree with the proposals. GPs are rather more sceptical than other doctors of a major restructuring that will give them responsibilities for which most of them are not trained (*The Guardian* 25 October, 2010).

Opposition grew when Lansley published his bill in January, not only from professionals in the NHS and BMA, but from Labour, many Liberal Democrats, and even some Conservatives. These included the veteran Lord Tebbit, a leading minister under Mrs Thatcher, and former Conservative Health Secretary Stephen Dorrell, who now chairs the Commons Health Committee, that proposed significant changes to Lansley's plans. On 4 April, 2011, Lansley announced in the Commons that the government would table amendments to the bill to meet some of the concerns, but insisted the government remained committed to the main thrust of GP commissioning, while accepting that others might be involved in the process. It is clear that the government has a problem in selling its health reforms. Justice Secretary Kenneth Clarke has encountered most criticism from some in his own party for his reforms to the prison service, which his expanded considerably recently. Clarke has criticized the hardline 'bang 'em up' approach to crime adopted by previous Conservative and Labour Home Secretaries. While he concedes that prison is necessary for many offenders, he argues that the prison population has grown far faster than crime (much of which has actually fallen) and prison fails to rehabilitate, but commonly produces tougher criminals. Clarke favours greater use of alternative sentences, including fines and community service. Normally this is not a line of argument that appeals to many Conservatives, but in the current economic climate it chimes with the need for cost savings in public services. Thus the cost of Britain's criminal justice system is projected to shrink by 24 per cent over four years in the Comprehensive Spending Review (October 2010). Clarke's department loses 14,000 of its 75,000 jobs with cuts in front-line prison, probation and court staff. Some prisons may close. It remains to be seen whether this significant shift in policy will succeed.

## Reforming welfare benefits

However, the biggest projected cuts are in welfare benefits (£18 billion in four years). There will ultimately be major savings in the pensions bill as a result of the rise in pension age for both men and women to 66, but these will only be fully realized in 2020 at the end of the next parliament. Higher contributions to their pensions by public sector workers (excepting the very low-paid and members of the armed forces) are expected to save the government £1.8 billion by 2014–15. However, the cut which has resulted in some of the loudest protests has been the removal of child benefit from households where there is a higher tax payer. This is now estimated to affect 1.5 million families, and save £2.5 billion, but will particularly hurt families with one earner and several children. While a single parent earning £44,000 will be up to £1, 750 worse off, a couple who earn £43,000 each will retain child benefit. Moreover, as this previously universal benefit is paid to the mother, it is women who will be the losers, as they are also the main losers from pension changes.

While the removal of child benefit from higher tax payers will hit some of the relatively well-to-do middle classes, it is more particularly the poor and needy who will be affected by cuts in housing benefits, incapacity benefits, disability allowances , working tax credits and child tax credits. The longer-term aim of the Work and Pensions Secretary, Iain Duncan Smith, is to replace the range of existing benefits with a single universal credit, costing £2 billion, which he hopes will end the 'poverty trap' and ensure that those securing work are better off.

It is true that some of these benefits have grown out of proportion The total spent on housing benefit has expanded massively initially partly as a consequence of the end of highly subsidized council house rents, once enjoyed by a third of UK householders. To a degree it made sense to subsidize all those with incomes too low to afford the market rate for a basic standard of housing, rather than just council house tenants. Yet public expenditure on housing benefit rose inexorably with the house price boom, particularly in London. Incapacity and disability benefits also made sense for those physically or mentally incapable of working. Yet it was potentially open to abuse from claimants capable but disinclined to work, and also from governments keen to reduce unemployment figures by shifting some of the longer-term unemployed onto incapacity benefit (when they no long counted as part of the potential labour force). The effect of these benefits and other cash benefits contributed to a 'poverty trap' in which for some, getting a job promised little or no extra money because of the withdrawal of benefits and liability for taxation. Thus on some 'sink estates' there remains a culture of unemployment, in which there are few adults in paid work to provide role models for children. Thus a cycle of deprivation, and living on benefit, is perpetuated, with little hope of escape.

It is hardly a new problem. Both the 'poverty trap' and the 'cycle of deprivation' were identified by writers on social policy from the 1960s, and successive governments have tried to address them. Gordon Brown's New Deal sought to shift people from welfare to work (which he claimed was the best form of welfare), with only limited success (Coates, 2005, pp.72–6, 168–9). Frank Field was appointed by Blair as Minister for Welfare Reform, but only lasted a year in the post, complaining of Treasury domination. Significantly, the coalition government has since enlisted Field to advise on welfare reform.

Duncan Smith has identified subsidized housing as a significant impediment to the unemployed moving to look for work in areas where jobs are more plentiful. Indeed a large part of the problem is that there are few jobs available in some regions of the country, and those regions are heavily dependent on public sector jobs that are under threat from major public spending cuts. (While slightly over 21 per cent of UK employment is in the public sector, in some parts of the country the figure is well over 40 per cent.) In the last decade three-quarters of the new jobs created in the north of England were in the public sector (partly aided by the further decentralization of the civil service). However, moving to areas of higher employment is not an easy answer, even if the housing issue is disregarded. Families may be temporarily or even permanently divided. If a whole family is uprooted they lose their extended network of local support. For some children, moving away from home, friends and relations, school and neighbourhood may cause enduring traumas.

Yet however mobile or immobile the labour market, any significant shift from welfare to work depends on the creation of millions of new jobs, and it is difficult to see where these are going to come from. If the new jobs are not created, the removal or reduction of welfare benefits can only lead to increased poverty, and other associated social problems.

## Shrinking the state?

While George Osborne has protested that there is no realistic alternative to the programme of substantial budget cuts he has indicated, others have claimed that there is an alternative, and that Osborne is simply implementing his own radical neo-liberal ideology to 'shrink the state'. Osborne maintains that a public sector share of half or more of GDP is 'unsustainable', involving potentially dire economic consequences. Yet as Table 21.1 indicates, recent public spending in Britain is not out of line with other countries in the European Union. As a

**Table 21.1**   Government expenditure as a percentage of GDP in selected EU countries

| Country | 2006 | 2007 | 2008 | 2009 |
|---|---|---|---|---|
| United Kingdom | 44.1 | 44.2 | 47.3 | 51.7 |
| Belgium | 48.6 | 48.4 | 50.0 | 54.2 |
| France | 52.7 | 52.3 | 52.8 | 55.6 |
| Germany | 45.4 | 43.7 | 43.7 | 47.6 |
| Greece | 43.2 | 45.0 | 45.8 | 50.4 |
| Ireland | 34.4 | 36.6 | 42.0 | 48.4 |
| Italy | 48.7 | 47.8 | 48.8 | 51.9 |
| Netherlands | 45.5 | 45.5 | 45.9 | 51.8 |
| Portugal | 46.3 | 45.8 | 46,1 | 51.0 |
| Spain | 38.4 | 39.2 | 41.1 | 45.9 |
| Sweden | 53.5 | 52.0 | 52.5 | 55.8 |
| 27 EU states average | 46.3 | 45.7 | 46.8 | 50.7 |

*Source*: Eurostat (2010) (compare with table 9.2 in Bale, 2008, p. 283).

proportion of GDP it is lower than in Sweden, France and Belgium, comparable with the Netherlands, Italy and Portugal, and only appreciably higher than Germany and Spain.

By contrast, the USA has kept government spending between 30 and 36 per cent of GDP over the last 50 years or so (Bale, 2008, pp. 275–83, and table 9.2).

So clearly there is a choice, for governments, parties and ultimately voters. Yet while polls indicate that voters want good public services, they are reluctant to pay the price in higher taxes. Thus Labour managed to sell their case for higher spending on health and education, but never dared make the case for higher taxes, preferring to rely on increased tax receipts from sometimes over-optimistic forecasts of economic growth and various 'stealth taxes'. The Liberal Democrats boldly suggested an extra penny on income tax to pay for extra money on education in 1997and 2001, which allowed voters to give them credit for their greater integrity, without any risk that the proposal would have to be implemented. The Conservatives until recently tried to 'detoxify' their party's brand by promising to match Labour's spending, but claimed they would find (largely unspecified) 'efficiency savings' to enable them to maintain or reduce taxation levels. Even in the lead-up to the 2010 election, while Osborne spoke

of the need to reduce the deficit faster and further than Labour, Cameron denied that cuts would be draconian.

The post-election reality soon proved otherwise. While the initial public reaction to the June emergency coalition budget and the October Comprehensive Spending Review was perhaps more muted than the coalition had feared, they became louder and angrier as the cuts began to bite and affected jobs and living standards. How far the short- and medium-term outlook involves a real shrinking of the British state remains to be seen. Public spending might be cut from above half of GDP down to the mid-forty per cent level of the Thatcher and early Blair years. There are certainly neo-liberal economists, think tanks and some politicians who would favour further reductions to around 35 per cent, comparable with US levels, with commensurate cuts in taxes. However, such a drastic reduction of the welfare state is perhaps not politically feasible. Not only would it be strongly resisted by the parliamentary opposition, by public service unions, and the large proportion of the public with some dependence on public provision of health, education and welfare. It would also face opposition from the Conservatives' coalition partners, and probably from some 'progressive' Conservatives and those with more pragmatic concerns about the electoral consequences. Thus the 'shrinking of the state' may be largely confined to reversing the recent surge in public spending and government deficit following the banking crisis and recession. Indeed there are continuing pressures for increased state spending, particularly on the health and social care needs of an ageing population.

Yet the debate over the role and proper functions of the state will continue. Tony Judt's recent book (2010) laments the decline of the public realm and the retreat of the social democratic consensus (described in his earlier *Post War*, 2007) over a period of 30 years or more. While there are many who would agree, the political tide seems to be flowing the other way. In the agonized internal debate within the Labour party following its election defeat there are some who question whether the party has become too closely associated with big government and high public spending. Thus former Labour MP Tony Wright (*The*

*Guardian*, 30 June 2010) argues that if his party 'stands only for spending public money and for a bigger state they will be out of the game. A real argument is opening up about the size, shape and role of the state, and Labour has to engage with it.'

It is a debate in which the other parties are already involved, with Cameron's call for a 'big society' rather than 'big government' and the dialogue between social and economic liberals within the Liberal Democrats.

## SUMMARY

- A consensus over Britain's welfare state in the post-war decades gave way to increased questioning of the efficiency of public services, and attempts to introduce more competition and private sector methods into their management.

- New Labour continued much of the reform process, including internal markets and partnership with the private sector, while increasing substantially spending on public services such as health and education.

- Labour set numerous targets for public services, and extensively monitored performance, publishing 'league tables' on the records of schools and hospitals and other institutions. Some argued that targets and league tables were dysfunctional and distorted priorities.

- There is a continuing tension between politicians' rhetoric on decentralization and delegation and (both Conservative and Labour) government intervention in specific areas of public service management.

- Although there have been substantial increases in spending on health and education especially, there remain doubts whether value for money has always been achieved.

- The recession and mounting government debt have led to substantial cuts in public spending, and an ongoing debate over the size, shape and role of the state. Some in the coalition government have been accused of following an ideological agenda to 'shrink the state'.

- Coalition spending cuts have particularly hit welfare benefits, local government services and higher education.

- Yet there remain continuing long-term pressures to extend and expand public expenditure.

## QUESTIONS FOR DISCUSSION

- How far does Britain still have a welfare state providing security 'from the cradle to the grave'?

- How far are there significant differences between the parties in the delivery and management of public services?

- What are the objections to the proliferation of targets and league tables in health and education? Can targets and league tables serve any useful purpose?

- Why is it apparently so difficult for governments to devolve the management of services to local communities, service users and/or front-line staff?

- How should higher education be funded?

- Overall, did New Labour deliver improved public services?

- How far does the coalition government offer alternative ideas for delivering public services?

- Is it possible or desirable to 'shrink the state'? What kind of pressures may drive up public spending?

## FURTHER READING

It is difficult to keep up with this fast-changing subject. For the performance of the Labour government in delivering services see the chapters by Glennester (on social policy) and Smithers (on education) in Seldon (2001) and Seldon and Kavanagh (2005), the chapters by Driver in Dunleavy *et al.* (2006) and in Beech and Lee (2008), the critical but balanced assessment of Coates (2005), and the useful audit of Labour's record by Toynbee and Walker (2005, 2010). On health policy the standard work is Ham (2009), which is particularly useful on the policies of the Blair and Brown governments, but this of course does not cover the coalition government's reorganization.

There is not yet (at the time of writing) an extensive academic literature on post-recession public services and the policies of the coalition government, so recourse has to be made to newspapers, journals and websites. However, Chapter 9 of Bale (2008) looks at the debate within Europe over the size and functions of the state, while Bale (2010) provides some discussion of recent Conservative ideas. Judt (2007) provides European historical background, while Judt (2010) involves a provocative analysis of the decline of both the public realm and the social democratic consensus in favour of public services.

# Rights, Equality and Social Justice

Chapter 20 focused on the management of the economy, and Chapter 21 on delivering public services. This chapter is concerned with issues of distribution, or 'Who gets what, when, how' in Lasswell's terse definition of politics (see Chapter 1). Thus the study of politics may entail measuring 'who gets what, when, how' in particular societies, and perhaps drawing some inferences about the distribution of political power. Yet for political philosophers, and many politicians, this is also a moral question, who *should* get what, when, how. While some substantially defend the existing distribution of income and property, others seek radical redistribution. Essentially, moral concepts are central to this argument, notions of rights, social justice and fairness. All three major British parties proclaim their commitment to universal human rights, although they may have different views on how these rights should be interpreted and implemented. All three also freely employ the language of social justice and fairness, although here there is rather more scope for disagreement over what these terms entail. Thus Conservatives emphasize the right to property and defend its unequal distribution, partly as a just reward for effort and initiative, partly for the broader social

and economic benefits derived from individual enterprise and risk taking. On the left, social justice and fairness have been traditionally linked with the pursuit of greater equality, and the improvement of the material circumstances of the working classes. However, the Human Rights Act (1998) and the Equality Act (2006) introduced by the last Labour government reflects a long-term shift towards reversing injustices and inequalities suffered by people because of their gender, ethnicity, faith, disability, age or sexual orientation. Thus the Equality and Human Rights Commission has no overt responsibilities to promote greater economic equality, nor deal with class differences, and the widening gap in Britain between the rich and poor. However, it has been persuasively argued that economic inequality has grown significantly and has exacerbated a range of social problems. Thus an older conception of social justice, implying some redistribution of wealth and income, is back on the political agenda.

## Rights

One approach to the issue of the distribution of the good things of life is to insist that everyone (or at least all men or all citizens) has a right to them. Thus John Locke (1632–1704) assumed natural rights to life, liberty and property. The American Declaration of Independence (1776) asserted the 'self-evident' truths 'that all men are created equal, and that they are endowed by their creator with certain inalienable rights, that among these are life, liberty and the pursuit of happiness'. The French revolutionaries proclaimed 'liberty, equality, fraternity'. In Britain Tom Paine (1737–1809) explored and defended the rights of man, while Mary Wollstonecraft (1759–97) extended these rights to women. Some rights were enumerated in authoritative documents, such as the French *Declaration of the Rights of Man and Citizen* or the US *Bill of Rights* (both 1789). More recent and more extensive statements of rights are the *United Nations Universal Declaration of Human Rights* (1948) and the *European Convention on Human Rights*. The last-named was ratified by the UK in 1951 and incorporated into British law through the Human Rights Act in 1998 (see Chapter 14). Some of the rights listed are essentially negative, freedom *from* oppression or discrimination, others more positive, such as the right *to* health care, education, work, etc. Positive rights pose more awkward questions over sufficiency and quality – what sort of work, how much health care, what standard of education?

Rights often suggest a minimum entitlement below which no-one should fall, but do not necessarily imply that everyone should have the same. Indeed some rights, the right to property advanced by Locke and defended by Burke and modern conservative thinkers and philosophers, and contained in some declarations of rights, implies the acceptance of substantial inequality in the distribution of property. Some have rejected this, advocating the abolition of private property, so that all goods are enjoyed in common by all, although such pure communism has rarely been practised. Socialists have demanded equality, in practice much greater equality rather than absolute equality, and have advocated a radical redistribution of income and wealth in favour of the poor.

## Equality and inequality in Britain: tackling poverty

Although only a minority in Britain advocated an immediate radical redistribution of wealth and income, post-war Labour and Conservative governments up until the 1970s largely agreed that redistribution to eliminate poverty should be a key principle of social policy. (In practice this meant reducing **relative poverty** rather than the **absolute poverty** suffered by many in the wider world.) Taxation was progressive, with the better-off paying much greater percentages of their incomes in tax than the less well-off. Tax revenues were used by governments to provide a 'social wage' – including free education, free healthcare, pensions and other benefits for all, but particularly benefiting the poor. Thus from 1945 to 1979 wealth and income became significantly more equally distributed (Mullard and Swaray in Beech and Lee, 2008, pp. 36–8).

Yet from the 1970s the rising costs of welfare benefits and services led to a more targeted approach by governments. There was rather less emphasis on promoting greater equality through general redistribution, more on dealing with specific problems. Concerns were expressed over the poverty or exclusion of particular sections of the population, articulated by pressure groups such as the Child Poverty Action Group, Help the Homeless or Age Concern. Labour and Conservative governments sought to tackle child or pensioner poverty, homelessness, inner city decline and deprivation, and the social exclusion of the long-term unemployed and disaffected teenagers.

---

● A distinction is commonly made between **absolute** and **relative poverty**.

**Absolute poverty** involves the lack of basic necessities of life: food, clothing, shelter, etc. While many millions around the world experience absolute poverty, very few do in advanced western economies like Britain. Yet many experience **relative poverty**, which means they cannot afford things that most people in Britain take for granted. Relative poverty changes over time. In the early 1950s most Britons did not own a car, television, refrigerator or telephone, but were not therefore considered poor, although they would be today. Some critics on the right argue that relative poverty is a term invented by the left to describe inequality, which they claim is inevitable and essentially desirable as an incentive to labour and enterprise.

## Increasing inequality

From the 1970s onwards the New Right challenged the former progressive consensus that increased equality was good in principle, arguing that high taxation reduced incentives to work and enterprise, while state welfare produced a 'dependency culture'. Cutting taxes and reducing welfare would release enterprise and energy that would result in the creation of more wealth. The fear of poverty, no longer cushioned by generous welfare benefits, would encourage many poor people to 'get on their bikes' in search of work. The poor would benefit from the 'trickle down' of prosperity from the rich. Creating new wealth would assist the poor more than redistributing existing wealth.

This change in attitudes to economic and social inequality underpinned changes in public policy under Conservative administrations from 1979. Inequalities in income and wealth that had been declining in the post-war decades increased sharply in the 1980s and 1990s. Income differences in the UK grew 40 per cent from the mid-1970s until the early 1990s (Wilkinson and Pickett, 2010, pp. 239–41). Partly the widening gap between rich and poor was the consequence of deliberate changes in the tax and benefit system, including a shift from direct to indirect taxation and cuts in the higher rates of income tax. It also reflected other developments, including rising unemployment, the decline of mining and manufacturing, and the reduced membership and power of trade unions.

## Combating discrimination and disadvantage

Yet if the gap between rich and poor was wider, this did not mean that governments or the public were unconcerned about inequalities and rights in Britain. However, there appeared to be a gradual shift in emphasis away from the class politics of the first half of the century towards identity politics, the groups or communities with which individuals subjectively identified. There was a parallel shift away from a general redistribution of wealth and income towards remedying the disadvantage suffered by particular categories, such as women, ethnic minorities, the disabled, gays and others. This reflected extensive evidence of discrimination

on these grounds in Britain, clearly visible in official statistics, but illustrated further by the evidence of campaigning groups and commissioned reports.

Thus particularly from the 1960s and 1970s onwards there were strenuous efforts to reverse the discrimination and disadvantage that some suffered, by reason of their gender, race or disability. Some of this involved equal opportunities legislation, assisted by the creation of new official bodies such as the Race Relations Board, the Equal Opportunities Commission and the Disability Rights Commission. However this also provoked some political backlash, with criticism of 'politically correct' ('PC') values and attitudes.

Tackling discrimination and prejudice suffered by some parts of the general population provided a precedent for other disadvantaged groups. While the early focus was on rights for women, ethnic minorities and the disabled, the agenda has progressively broadened to cover inequality and discrimination on grounds of age, sexual orientation and religion (see sections below). Freedom from discrimination on most of these grounds was covered by the European Convention on Human Rights. All are now the explicit concern of the Equality and Human Rights Commission (see Box 22.1). Both the Human Rights Act (which the Conservatives in opposition wished to replace with a new British Bill of Rights), and the new Equality Commission remain controversial. Issues around the equality and rights of specific groups will be explored in subsequent sections.

## Women's rights: towards more equality between the sexes?

Despite the formal recognition of equality between the sexes, symbolically affirmed in the right to vote and in various declarations of human rights, the condition of women in post-war Britain remained profoundly unequal. They had far fewer opportunities in education and employment, particularly in the professions and business. Even where they were doing the same work as men, they were commonly paid much less. Most married women were financially dependent on their husbands. They were widely expected to be responsible for all the domestic chores and child-rearing, even if they

BOX 22.1

# The Equality and Human Rights Commission

This Commission was set up by the Equality Act (2006) and formally inaugurated in 2007. It takes over the responsibilities previously exercised by the Commission for Racial Equality (CRE), the Equal Opportunities Commission (EOC) and the Disability Rights Commission, but it also has new responsibilities for other equality and rights issues, including religion, age and sexual orientation. The bundling together of equalities and rights previously treated separately aroused some opposition. Some feared that the rights of women, ethnic minorities and the disabled would be less effectively served by an all-embracing, less focused commission. Yet inequality and discrimination can not only be cumulative (for example, disabled women, or gay Muslims), but also involve conflicting interests (thus minority rights may potentially limit some individual human rights).

The new commission has been dogged with controversy. Replacing three major quangos with one did not save money. The Public Accounts Committee found that it had cost the taxpayer £39 million (*The Guardian*, 4 March 2010). The chair of the new commission, Trevor Phillips, (formerly chair of the CRE) has attracted criticism. There has been a series of resignations among the 16 commissioners. Yet it is perhaps unfair to judge the commission on its relatively short life to date. In 2010 the EHRC produced a massive report *How Fair is Britain?* extensively documenting the extent of inequality in Britain.

were also undertaking paid work outside the home. Despite the right to vote, women remained grossly under-represented at every level of British politics. The House of Commons long remained an overwhelmingly male-dominated chamber, while the House of Lords was all-male until the 1960s (see Chapters 3 and 13).

Women are now more equal than they were, although feminists maintain that there is still a long way to go to achieve justice for women. Some improvements have been formally registered in government policy and law. There has also been some change in public attitudes, not always reflected in specific sub-cultures, however. The reasons for changes in policy and attitudes are complex, reflecting economic and social factors, grassroots pressure from women themselves, as well as influences within the political and governmental system.

Some changes were the product of the 'permissive sixties', although these were never quite as permissive as legend suggests. The widespread availability of new forms of contraception (principally the Pill), controlled by women rather than men, made it easier for both married and unmarried women to avoid pregnancy. Many 'career women' sought to delay motherhood, and some chose to avoid it altogether. The legalization of

abortion and the reform of divorce laws in the late 1960s both reflected changes in social attitudes and assisted further change (see Box 22.2). Women did not always gain from the new social and legal climate. Men were arguably the main beneficiaries of sexual liberation and increased marital breakdown. Yet most women did have more choice and control in relationships and sexual behaviour.

There were also changes in the world of work, particularly as traditional male employment in mining and heavy manufacturing declined and opportunities for employment for women grew in the services and professions. Opportunities in higher education expanded markedly for both sexes. From being a tiny minority of university graduates, women over time achieved near equality. Many more women entered, and advanced in, the traditionally male-dominated professions of law, medicine, accounting and education, and to some degree in banking, business and the media, even if a 'glass ceiling' often seemed to prevent them from rising to the highest levels.

Many of the advances in the 1960s and 1970s can be attributed to the pressure of the women's movement, the archetypal new social movement. It lacked formal organization, identifiable leaders or even members. It involved, at most, a very loose network of groups (some well-established and

## TIMELINE 22.1

### The law and women: some measures affecting women in the UK

**1945**  The introduction of family allowances, paid to mothers.

**1967**  The Abortion Act legalized abortion.

**1969**  The Divorce Reform Act made divorce simpler and cheaper, allowing divorce by mutual consent.

**1970**  The Equal Pay Act required equal pay for equal work and outlawed explicit discrimination against women.

**1975**  The Sex Discrimination Act banned sexual discrimination against women and established the Equal Opportunities Commission to monitor implementation.

**1976**  The Child Benefit Act merged child tax allowances (paid to men) with family allowances to create a more substantial child benefit (paid to mothers).

national, others more ephemeral and local) and individual sympathisers and supporters. It contained many different shades of opinion and attitude. Its broad aim has been not unfairly described as women's liberation (or, more dismissively 'women's lib'). This aim implicitly acknowledged that women's formal legal and political equality had not secured their liberation. The women's movement involved other implicit premises; that only women could really understand the problems of women, and they would have to rely substantially on themselves for their liberation.

The women's movement was perhaps more about securing changes in attitude and behaviour (both of men and women) than changes in the law, institutions and public policy. Yet it did provide substantial pressure for further reforms in these areas. Thus an Equal Pay Act was passed in 1970 and an Equal Opportunities Act in 1975 (see Timeline 22.1), the latter also establishing the Equal Opportunities Commission to monitor the implementation of both Acts (since absorbed by the Equality and Human Rights Commission; see Box 22.1).

The woman's movement also agitated for better childcare and nursery provision, with some eventual success. It became a major plank in New Labour's attempt to move women and poor families from welfare into work. While one motivation was clearly to reduce the social security bill, the increased provision of childcare and nursery education, coupled with changes in the tax system has enlarged choice for many relatively poor women, and enabled them to escape the poverty trap.

The women's movement also drew attention to a long-standing evil that had long been virtually ignored, the evidence of persistent violence against women, and the sexual abuse of women. This has led to rather more serious and sympathetic police investigations into allegations of violence and rape, and some change in public attitudes, although it remains very difficult to persuade women to pursue prosecutions and even more difficult to prove them. Women's groups have also established refuges and other forms of support for abused women.

Most of all, perhaps, the women's movement has helped achieve a substantial change in the portrayal of women, in both the visual images and the language used by the mass media and people in public life. While sexist attitudes undoubtedly remain, sexist vocabulary and sexist advertisements

## BOX 22.2

# Women in UK politics

- **Voting.** Women outnumber men in the population, and women voters outnumber male voters. This is the only level at which women predominate in the political process.
- **MPs at Westminster.** Less than 5 per cent of MPs were women for the whole period from 1945 to 1987, when 41 women MPs were elected (6 per cent). 60 women were elected in 1992 (9 per cent) and 121 in 1997 (18 per cent), of whom 101 were Labour. The number slightly declined in 2001, but rose again to 128 in 2005 (20 per cent) and to 142 (22 per cent) in 2010.
- **Lords and Ladies.** Until the introduction of life peers there were no women in the Upper House, and even after that very few. In the semi-reformed House of Lords following the 1999 House of Lords Act, 16 per cent of all peers are women.
- **Women in the Cabinet.** For most of the post-war period there was rarely more than one woman Cabinet minister and sometimes not that. Mrs

Thatcher, Britain's first woman Prime Minister, was generally the only woman in her Cabinet (although those who admired her 'macho' style claimed she was the only *man* in the Cabinet!). John Major's first Cabinet was all-male. Blair's Cabinet has included up to seven women, although few have occupied the most senior posts. Cameron's 2010 coalition Cabinet included just four women (all Conservative): Teresa May (Home Secretary), Caroline Spelman (Environment), Cheryl Gillan (Wales) and Lady Warsi (Minister without portfolio and party chair).

- **Women in local government.** Although the proportion of women councillors has doubled over the last 30 years they still constitute only 27 per cent of all councillors in England and Wales.
- **Women in devolved assemblies.** Here women have fared rather better. Thus following the 2003 elections exactly half the representatives in the Welsh Assembly (30 out of 60) were women.

are much less in evidence. Indeed some television commercials have gone almost to the opposite extreme, portraying powerful women bosses or househusbands in mini soap operas, implying a greater reversal of traditional gender roles than is the reality. Even so, this was a symbolic improvement on previous media depiction of women in subordinate roles.

Not all feminists were interested in conventional politics, but specific women's pressure groups drew attention to the continuing under-representation of women in Parliament and local councils, and pressed for changes. The Labour party in particular responded, by the introduction of all-women shortlists in winnable parliamentary seats. Although this increased the number of women candidates and MPs, it was initially declared illegal, ironically under the Equal Opportunities Act, as it denied the rights of aspiring male candidates in the constituencies involved (the law has since been modified). There is a continuing debate on the rights and wrongs of positive discrimination to reverse inequality. Other parties have not resorted

to all-women shortlists, but have sought to increase the number of women candidates contesting winnable seats. However, despite the relatively recent increase in the representation of women in Parliament and the Cabinet, women remain substantially under-represented in politics at almost every level (see Box 22.2).

Overall, while there have been advances for women, veteran feminists remain disappointed with the achievements. Women in the UK are still paid 12 per cent less than men, despite the Equal Pay Act. There are only four female chief executives in the FTSE 100 leading companies. The vast majority of top company executives, surgeons, judges and civil servants are still men, while an estimated 30,000 women a year lose their jobs for becoming pregnant, despite the work of the EOC. Indeed, its more recent successor the EHRC reports that women aged 40 earn on average 27 per cent less than men of the same age (EHRC, *How fair is Britain?* 2010). Moreover, violence against women remains a shocking and largely unpunished feature of British society. Only 7 out of every 100 rapes

## BOX 22.3

# Lesbian and gay rights

The lesbian and gay lobby, Stonewall, has been prominent in campaigning for gay and lesbian rights, which are increasingly recognized not only in law but by public opinion.

● The Law Lords ruled that a homosexual couple living in a stable relationship could be defined as a family. This conferred new legal rights for gays and lesbians, such as the right of one partner to claim damages if dependent on the other partner who died through a third party's negligence. Also, one partner now has the right to inherit a tenancy in the name of a dead partner.

● The Children's Society has lifted its ban on gay and lesbian couples adopting children.
● The European Court of Human Rights ruled that the Ministry of Defence's policy of sacking gay members of the armed forces was 'inhuman and degrading'.
● A voluntary code on sexual orientation and discrimination in the workplace has been agreed.
● Section 28 of the Local Government Act (1988), which banned the 'promotion' of homosexuality in schools and colleges, has been repealed.
● The age of consent is now the same (16) as in different-sex relationships.

reported to the police lead to a conviction. Within the home women remain responsible for most of the housework and childcare. While, in theory, men too may gain from the end of gender stereotyping, to find fulfilment in parenting and homemaking, in practice they still leave most of this work to women. Thus far from 'having it all' (fulfilling sexual relationships, careers and motherhood), many women are left trying to juggle conflicting demands on their time and energy.

## Gay and lesbian rights

Once homosexual relations, even between consenting adults, were a criminal offence. Gay men who were caught in homosexual acts were charged and sent to prison. Police sometimes hid in public toilets to catch offenders and even dressed up in what they regarded as appropriate clothes to act as *agents provocateurs*, to lure unsuspecting gays to make advances, before arresting them. Homosexual relations between consenting adults were only decriminalized in 1967, although it is taking much longer for public attitudes to change. Many homosexuals long feared to 'come out' and some suffered blackmail as a consequence.

To anyone brought up in the 1950s and 1960s the changes since then have been massive. Increasingly, people in the public eye including

actors, artists, sports personalities, leading politicians (including Cabinet ministers) and even some police, have 'come out' without apparent damage to their reputation or careers. Thousands parade on gay marches. The Equality and Human Rights Commission campaigns to secure equality of sexual orientation, and from 2009 has also championed the rights of transsexuals (see Box 22.3).

However, the change in attitudes towards homosexuality has not extended to all communities. Homosexuals can still suffer 'gay bashing' that has even extended to murder. A third of gay pupils report they have been bullied at school. Some religious groups have problems with same-sex relationships, particularly Protestants in Northern Ireland, Roman Catholics and evangelicals in the Church of England (even though homosexuality is common among the clergy). Catholic adoption agencies are unwilling to consider adoption by same-sex couples. Some ethnic minorities and non-Christian faiths remain particularly intolerant of same-sex relationships. Yet overall, compared with a half a century ago, homosexuals today face far less discrimination and prejudice.

## Disability and age discrimination

Until relatively recently disabled people had no rights that could be enforced in courts and suffered extensive discrimination. Those considered mentally disabled were often shut away in remote 'lunatic asylums'. The physically disabled fared little better. There were few jobs available, as employers were not obliged to provide facilities for the disabled, nor to employ them at all. There were severe problems of access to shops and services as there was no obligation to provide ramps, lifts, or even doors sufficiently wide to take wheelchairs. Both physically and mentally disabled people suffered from discrimination and prejudice and were often treated as if they were invisible.

Their position has improved somewhat as a result of government legislation and some changes in public attitudes. Thus the Disability Discrimination Act (1995) made it illegal to discriminate against the disabled in employment, the provision of goods and services, education and transport. From 2004 service providers were supposed to provide improved physical access to facilities. There have been further Acts (2005) and amending legislation to extend rights and services to disabled people. In 2000 the Disability Rights Commission was established, replacing the former National Disability Council (since replaced by the Equality and Human Rights Commission in 2007).

Campaigners have helped to change public attitudes, although this has been further assisted by the growth of the numbers of elderly disabled. As life expectancy has increased, many more people inevitably experience physical and mental disabilities as they age. Some of the cost of care is born by the state, but much by families. Commonly, the family house has to be sold to meet the cost of institutional care. Care at home is often provided by (largely female) relatives, some already elderly themselves.

One partial answer to an ageing population that governments around the world have edged towards involves raising the retiring age. This makes sense in so far as people in their sixties now appear healthier and more active than was the case previously. Moreover, many of pensionable age want to carry on working, yet are often obliged to retire by employers. Indeed, age discrimination not only faces those of pensionable age, but often those in their fifties or even younger who seek work. Employers may fear that it is more difficult to teach old dogs new tricks.

Some pensioners who rely largely on state benefits suffer considerable poverty and find it difficult to finance basic necessities, particularly heating. Yet others are more fortunate, especially those with relatively generous final salary pension schemes enabling them to retire on half or even two-thirds pay, and enjoy state pensions as well. Homeowners also gained substantially from house price rises well above inflation. Those who remain relatively fit are able to continue to enjoy a range of leisure activities and sometimes several holidays abroad a year.

Indeed, the 'baby boomers' (those born soon after the war when birth rates rose) were a fortunate generation. They escaped the war but benefited from free healthcare, free university education, rising house prices, employment and living standards, as well as retirement benefits that will not be received by later generations. Indeed, the latter are paying, through their taxes, for the relatively comfortable life of the 'baby boomers'. New graduates today have fewer employment opportunities and often cannot afford to climb onto the housing ladder, particularly if they remain saddled with student debts. Thus it has been persuasively argued that in so far as there is inter-generational conflict, it is the young who face disadvantage as compared with their elders (Willetts, 2010).

## Race and ethnicity

Sixty years ago British society appeared relatively homogeneous, with social class being the only politically significant division. With the partial exception of the Jewish and Irish communities, ethnic minorities were too small to be politically significant. In sharp contrast, contemporary Britain is characterized by ethnic diversity, particularly in most major cities, largely as a result of relatively recent immigration from former British colonies, from Europe, and to some degree the rest of the world. Britain's new multicultural society arguably offers a rich variety of experience and opportunity to the general benefit, although it has also brought some tension within and between communities that place complex demands on the system of governance and politics. Many ethnic minorities have unhappily suffered from discrimination and prejudice. Racial prejudice can be shown by whites against blacks, blacks against whites or, indeed,

## BOX 22.4

# Ethnic minorities and political representation

- **Parties.** Although blacks and Asians overwhelmingly supported Labour, their voice was formerly marginalized within the party, leading to strong demands that were not conceded for separate black sections. More recently Labour has selected more ethnic minority candidates for both local and national elections, and other parties have begun to follow suit.
- **Representation at Westminster.** There has been some increase recently in the number of MPs from ethnic minorities. In 2001, 12 black or Asian MPs were

elected. In the 2010 election 27 MPs including 9 Conservatives (4 per cent of all MPs) were elected from ethnic minorities.
- **Government.** Ethnic minorities have been conspicuous by their absence at the higher levels of British government, at least until recently. Paul Boateng became the first black Cabinet minister in 2001, soon followed by Baroness Amos, the first black Leader of the Lords, and in 2010 by Lady Warsi.

between other ethnic groups, as in the case of Asian prejudice against West Indians (Mohapatra, 1999, p.79). Clearly, however, the most politically significant prejudice in Britain is that expressed by the white majority against the black and Asian minorities.

Earlier governments were only forced to act when racial prejudice and conflict involved civil disorder. In the late 1950s Britain experienced its first major 'race riots' which were an unexpected shock. In response successive governments introduced increasingly tough restrictions on immigration. These restrictions appeared racist, as effectively they targeted non-whites, but they were not tough enough to satisfy the far right and even some mainstream politicians who sought a virtual halt to black immigration and the 'repatriation' of those already in Britain.

Restrictive immigration policies have generally been accompanied by more liberal policies towards ethnic minorities already resident within Britain. The Race Relations Acts of 1965, 1968 and 1976 outlawed direct and indirect discrimination in widening areas of public life and provision such as housing, employment and education. What is sometimes called the 'race relations industry' was established, with complaints taken to the Race Relations Board (later replaced by the Commission for Racial Equality, and later still by the Equality and Human Rights Commission). Yet anti-discrimination legislation has not ensured the equal treatment of ethnic minorities, who continue to be

under-represented in many occupations and professions as well as in the political arena (see Box 22.4). Similarly, most black and Asian minorities are much more likely to be unemployed or employed in low-paid work with poor conditions than their white counterparts. Non-white ethnic minorities are still conspicuous by their absence from most company boardrooms, and in the higher ranks of the civil service, judiciary and police.

A more radical approach to equal opportunities involves a fair distribution of resources and not simply fair procedures. Employers may proclaim their equal opportunities credentials, and establish procedures to eliminate bias, yet still not employ many (or even any) blacks and Asians. Discrimination is difficult to prove, even where it may be suspected. Moreover, anecdotal evidence of discrimination, coupled with a virtual absence of positive role models, may deter members of ethnic minorities from applying for certain jobs. Thus it is unlikely that a young Asian will consider joining the police force, if he has never seen an Asian policeman in his own area.

One option is to establish targets or quotas for the recruitment and promotion of those from ethnic minorities to ensure they obtain a proportion of posts similar to their numbers in the local community. Such a policy has been pursued for a time in the United States where it is called 'affirmative action'. In the United Kingdom it is more usually described as 'positive discrimination' but is currently illegal under equal opportunities legislation. Even if the law could be changed it might worsen rather than improve race relations. There is already a persistent myth that local councils unduly favour ethnic minorities and asylum seekers (against much available evidence to the contrary) and the open adoption of positive discrimination might only serve to inflame racist sentiments. Yet it is important that employers monitor the ethnic composition of their workforce, because the under-representation of certain minorities may suggest there could be something wrong with the way posts are advertised, or there may be some hidden bias in selection procedures.

Allegations of **institutional racism** in the police persist. Blacks and Asians are still far more likely than whites to be stopped on suspicion and searched. While some police forces have made strenuous efforts to counter racism and recruit more officers from ethnic minorities, these have sometimes found it difficult to secure acceptance from colleagues and promotion within the force. Institutional racism has also sometimes been blamed for the under-performance of black pupils in schools. Young black males are still much more likely to be excluded from schools than their white counterparts. Predominantly white teachers may unconsciously have low expectations of black pupils, which contribute to low self-esteem and poor behaviour among the students themselves, who lack positive role models to inspire them. Yet this does not seem to affect all ethnic minorities equally: Indian and Chinese children perform better, indicating that the causes of poor perform-ance among some groups may be more complex.

Thus institutional racism suggests that racist assumptions are so embedded in organizations and society generally that discrimination can persist,

---

• **Institutional racism**. The 1999 Macpherson Inquiry into the murder of the black teenager, Stephen Lawrence, concluded that the Metropolitan Police Service was 'institutionally racist' according to the Inquiry's own definition:

> The collective failure of an organisation to provide an appropriate and professional service to people because of their colour, culture, or ethnic origin. It can be seen or detected in processes, attitudes and behaviour which amount to discrimination through unwitting prejudice, ignorance, thoughtlessness and racist stereotyping which disadvantage minority ethnic people. (Macpherson, 1999, p. 28)

even in the absence of conscious racist intentions and behaviour. The concept was developed in the United States, where it is suggested that racism was deeply ingrained as a consequence of the historical experience of slavery and racial segregation. Thus the dominant white community continue to unconsciously exclude and disadvantage blacks.

Altogether, some ethnic minorities remain significantly disadvantaged in Britain. According to the EHRC 2010 report, nearly three-quarters of Bangladeshi children and half of Black African children grow up in poverty. Unemployment remains significantly higher among all non-whites. David Cameron has cited recent research showing 'almost half of young black people are unem-ployed, well over twice the rate for young white people' (article in *The Guardian*, 17 March 2010). There are other telling indications that many among the ethnic minorities remain second-class citizens. Black students are far more likely to be excluded from school. One in four people in prison come from an ethnic minority background, while Muslims make up 12 per cent of the prison population in England and Wales (EHRC report, 2010). Equality for non-white ethnic minorities still seems a long way off.

## Discrimination and prejudice on grounds of religion

Religious discrimination and prejudice was common in Britain in earlier centuries, targeting Jews, Protestant dissenters and Catholics. Indeed, religious conflict was a significant element of British politics into the early twentieth century, particularly over education. However, by the time of the Second World War Sir Ivor Jennings ([1941] 1966, p. 8) claimed, 'The sting has long been taken out of religious controversy.' Few would make the same point today. Ethnic tensions and racial preju-dice in Britain have been complicated and rein-forced by religious prejudice. While blacks of Caribbean origin are overwhelmingly Christian, Asian communities have built Islamic, Hindu and Sikh temples in British cities. The religious obser-vances, dress codes and diet of these new faith communities caused some problems over school uniform requirements and school and hospital meals, but these have been accommodated without too much difficulty.

Rather more serious conflict arose from the publication in 1989 of Salman Rushdie's *The Satanic Verses*, a book that Muslims regarded as offensive to their faith, leading to death threats against the author, who was obliged to go into hiding with police protection. For western liberals the principle of freedom of speech was at stake. For many Muslims the Rushdie affair symbolized a wider lack of respect for their religion and culture. It has sharpened other issues over Muslim dress and religious observance. However, such issues remain less divisive in Britain than in France, where Muslim girls are forbidden to wear the veil (or *hijab*) in state schools (see Parekh, 2000b, pp. 249–54.)

The attack on the Twin Towers of 9/11, followed by the 'war on terror' and the London bombings of July 2005, drove a potentially far more dangerous wedge between British Muslims and the rest of the population. To some in the west these terrorist atrocities chillingly confirmed the predictions of Samuel Huntington (1996), who had argued that the old Cold War ideological conflict between two superpowers would be replaced by broader struggles between rival cultures, such as between Islam and the West. While Bush and Blair insisted that the invasion of Afghanistan and Iraq involved a 'war against terrorism', not 'a war against Islam', many Muslims believed that Britain and America were indeed involved in such a war.

Inevitably, the conflict provoked divided loyalties for British Muslims and, for some, further weakened their British allegiance and identity. At the same time, fears aroused by Al-Qaeda atrocities inflamed popular prejudice and suspicion against British Muslims, even though leading British Muslim organizations had roundly condemned the terrorists. Extremist groups and parties exploited popular fears, suggesting that Muslims were a potential 'enemy within'. There were some 'revenge attacks' against Muslims and their mosques, and even attacks on some non-Muslim Asians. This indiscriminate Islamophobia has seriously damaged inter-community relations.

Compared with the problems associated with Islamophobia, other religious controversy appears less serious. Even so, some other minority faiths, such as Hindus and Sikhs, have concerns over issues of dress and diet, while some Jews detect a revival of anti-Semitism. Even some Christian groups have issues around aspects of gender equality (such as women priests and bishops) and gay rights (for example the rights of same-sex couples to adopt children). Meanwhile, secular humanists continue to criticize what they consider to be the unreasonable privileges of faith groups (e.g. subsidies for faith schools) and the established church in particular.

## Multiculturalism and rights

Overall, ethnic minorities and different faith communities have contributed hugely to the British economy and many would argue that they have also enormously enriched British culture. The arts, the media, sport, fashion and cuisine would be immeasurably poorer without the variety and vitality of the contributions of Britain's ethnic minorities. Thus Britain has become a multi-ethnic, multi-faith and multicultural country. Yet this is far from being universally welcomed. Some see it as threat to the traditional British way of life and national identity. Norman Tebbit, the Conservative politician, claimed 'most people in Britain did not want to live in a multi-cultural, multi-racial society, but it has been foisted on them' (quoted in Solomos, 2003, p. 218). Moreover, although there are areas where different communities freely intermingle in a genuinely multicultural society, residential segregation and mutual misunderstanding and suspicion is rather more common.

The fresh outbreak of race riots in 2001 in a number of northern towns, including Bradford, Burnley and Oldham, dramatized inter-community tensions. Subsequent inquiries, such as the Cantle (2001) and Denham (2002) Reports confirmed much that was already evident to many observers. The populations of these towns (and several others where riots had not occurred) appeared to be fragmented and polarized in terms of ethnicity. People from different ethnic backgrounds were effectively segregated in terms of housing and schooling and were leading 'parallel lives' with little interaction between the communities. In these towns multiculturalism was little more than a 'consenting form of apartheid'. The lack of contact between different

## COMPARATIVE POLITICS 22.1
# Multiculturalism and indigenous minorities

Although multiculturalism is commonly discussed in terms of acceptance of non-white ethnic minority cultures and non-Christian religious faiths, the concept can clearly also embrace other sub-cultures, including distinctive indigenous national and faith communities. The Canadian philosopher Will Kymlicka has powerfully advocated the rights of indigenous minorities, such as the Inuit Indians in Canada, the Aborigines in Australia or the Maori in New Zealand who inhabited these countries before white settlers of European origin and thus have a special right to consideration. What could be described as indigenous minorities in Britain were once discouraged from preserving their distinctive cultures. Minority languages, such as Welsh, Gaelic or Cornish, were discouraged. Yet policy has progressively changed. Thus the Welsh language is part of the curriculum in every Welsh school and has equal status with English in official documents and in Welsh political institutions.

---

groups fuelled mutual fear and suspicion, which was then exploited by extremist political groups like the BNP. What was needed, the reports advocated, was the development of more 'cohesive communities'.

Thus there is a continuing debate over the extent to which Britain has become a multicultural society in reality. There is also another debate over multiculturalism both as a principle and in its practical implications for policy (see Comparative Politics 22.1 and Academic Controversy 22.1). A common assumption in many modern nation states is the existence of a national culture that all citizens should share. Thus the USA in the past welcomed immigrants but insisted they should be formally instructed and thoroughly assimilated into the American way of life and become loyal American citizens. The British approach was less formal but still assumed a process of naturalization and assimilation. The ideal was integration.

Multiculturalism, both in the USA and Britain, involved an alternative approach to assimilation and integration. Rather, it was argued that differences between communities should be accepted and respected. Children from minority ethnic communities should have pride in their own language, religion and culture, which should be part not only of their own school curriculum, but also that of the wider community, to promote mutual understanding. Such an approach provoked something of a backlash from those who claimed that British culture and Christian values were being sacrificed on the altar of 'political correctness'.

Others argued that the new multicultural education involved the neglect of vital skills which young blacks and Asians needed if they were to prosper in the British labour market and British society. 'Unfortunately the right to be different can all too readily be conceded without allowing for equality of opportunity and perhaps positively reinforcing inequality of opportunity' (Rex, 1986, p. 120). Others again have claimed that multiculturalism has encouraged the development of separate faith schools and separate community facilities for ethnic groups that have impeded the development of cohesive communities in which minorities might interact with each other.

## Social justice, equality and rights: New Labour's record

The Labour party has long proclaimed a commitment to **social justice** (see Academic Controversy 22.2), equality and rights; some of the policies described in previous sections have taken place under Labour governments, and others have been pursued by Labour councils. Yet some commentators have argued that New Labour involved a significant shift of emphasis away from the pursuit of greater equality. Although Labour's new Clause Four, adopted in 1995, (see Box 7.5 p. 129) still aspired to

## Academic controversy 22.1
# Multiculturalism, minority rights and human rights

The political theorist **Bhikhu Parekh** (2000b) argued that western liberals wrongly assumed their ideas had universal validity. Thus western liberal values embodied in declarations of rights conflicted with other communities' cultures, which involved other values, such as 'social harmony, respect for authority, orderly society, a united and extended family and a sense of filial piety' (Parekh, 2000b. p. 137). Human beings are not the same everywhere, but 'culturally embedded in the sense that they are born into, raised in and deeply shaped by their cultural communities'. The distinctive cultures of minority communities should be respected by the majority, even where they appear to conflict with universal human rights.

The British political philosopher **Brian Barry** (2001, p. 58) argued that respecting minority rights 'is liable to be harmful to women and children in minority communities and to those within them who deviate from prevailing norms'. Respecting the values of other

cultures might entail accepting discrimination on grounds of gender or caste, and legitimating prejudices against different sexual orientations. The appeal to universal principles and rights helped to abolish slavery and transform the status of women, while hitherto prevailing cultural norms had justified discrimination on grounds of race and gender. The cultural values of minority communities may even involve restricting rights to free speech (see the Rushdie affair).

Parekh (2000b, p. 196), however, acknowledged inevitable tensions between the norms of majority and minority communities. Any society 'should foster a strong sense of unity and common belonging among its citizens'. The problem is how to reconcile unity with diversity. Parekh went on to discuss sensitively several controversial issues, including female circumcision, polygamy, Muslim and Jewish methods of slaughtering animals, arranged marriages, initiation ceremonies, and exemption from legal or school requirements on dress.

---

create 'a community in which power, wealth and opportunity are in the hands of the many not the few', the key word here is perhaps 'opportunity'. Coates (2005, pp. 39–40) argues. 'New Labour came to power preferring policies that privileged equality of opportunity over equality of outcome.'

Labour's Commission on Social Justice (1994), established by John Smith as party leader, declared 'the gap between the earnings of the highest-paid and those of the lowest-paid worker is greater than at any time since record were first kept in 1886' (p. 28). Yet for New Labour an open commitment to redistribution was a potential vote loser. Some concluded that it was Shadow Chancellor John Smith's very mildly redistributive 'alternative budget' that had cost Labour the election in 1992. Labour could not win by appealing to the have-nots, who were no longer in the majority (and were also less inclined to vote). They had to win over a substantial proportion of 'middle England', who would be

frightened off by the prospect of tax rises to help the poor. Also, both Blair and Brown were substantially convinced by the economic arguments of the New Right, that wealth creation was more important than wealth distribution. Labour governments in the past had failed to deliver the economic modernization and prosperity that was the condition for effective social reform. Improved economic performance would provide new resources for better public services, and a better life for the most vulnerable in society, including the young and the elderly.

However, the difference between 'old' and 'new' Labour approaches to equality and social justice can be exaggerated. New Labour's rhetoric was markedly similar to the classless appeal of an earlier Labour modernizer, Harold Wilson, who also hoped to finance social reform from economic growth (Coates, 2005, pp. 30–1). Moreover, as Denham has observed (in Dunleavy *et al.*, 2003, pp. 285–6), much of New Labour's 'approach to social policy was anticipated by

## *Academic controversy 22.2*
# Social justice – Rawls and his critics

The concept **social justice** implies that the distribution of goods should be morally justified. John Rawls (1921–2002) elaborated a theory of justice as fairness, involving limits to inequality (*A Theory of Justice*, 1971). He assumed a hypothetical situation in which people are ignorant of their own social situation and their own talents and abilities, but aware that certain 'primary goods' are valuable and want as many as they can. Rawls argues that people in such a state of ignorance would be prepared to accept two moral principles. One principle is that everyone should enjoy as much liberty as possible as long as this does not interfere with the liberty of others. The second is that any economic inequalities should be to the benefit of the least advantaged, so that even the least well-off (which could be them) would have sufficient resources to enjoy a reasonable life. Rawls' theory was championed by the British political philosopher Brian Barry (1936–2009) and enthusiastically taken up by many social democrats and liberals, because it appeared to justified the promotion of equality of opportunity and greater equality of outcome, but not absolute equality. It was criticized by Robert Nozick (1938–2002) for its interference with property rights, and by communitarian thinkers such as Michael Sandel (1953– ), who disagreed with its individualist assumptions.

---

the analysis of the Commission on Social Justice'. This explicitly rejected 'a strategy for social justice based on redistribution of wealth and incomes', involving 'a kinder, poorer Britain'(Commission on Social Justice, 1994, Chapter 3). Instead, it emphasized investment through a market economy, arguing that 'the extension of economic opportunity is not only the source of economic prosperity but also the source of social justice'.

In place of an overt commitment to a general redistribution of income and wealth in pursuit of social justice, New Labour instead promised to tackle social exclusion and made more specific commitments to reduce 'child poverty' and 'pensioner poverty'. There were political advantages in explicitly targeting children and the elderly who appeared 'deserving' and less responsible for their own deprivation. However, helping children out of poverty meant in practice helping their families, including not just the 'hard-working families' favoured by politicians of all parties, but some who might appear less deserving. Brown's targeted tax and welfare reforms were, however, designed to provide positive incentives for work as a way out of poverty and dependence on welfare.

At the heart of New Labour's thinking was the belief that paid employment was crucial in combating poverty and social exclusion. A key part of Labour's strategy (following US precedents) was to move people off welfare and into work, which involved both the provision of training for skills to improve employability and tax and welfare changes to make work pay. Gordon Brown's 'welfare to work' programme was initially funded by a £5.2 billion windfall tax on the profits of the privatized utilities. Key elements of Labour's policy included:

- The national minimum wage, designed to reduce the extent and impact of low pay, and increase the incentive to work. Although fixed at a level substantially below that sought by the TUC, it is estimated that it has increased the wages of around 1.5 million low-paid workers, the majority of whom were women.
- The New Deal, which allocated £3 billion to get the unemployed into training or work. (It is not clear how far the subsequent reduction in unemployment was due specifically to the New Deal, rather than the general improvement of the economy.)
- More money for adult learning, focused particularly on developing basic literacy and numeracy to help those held back by low skills.

## BOX 22.5

# Social exclusion

Social exclusion may be defined as the experience of people who suffer from a combination of connected problems such as unemployment, poor education and poor skills, low incomes, poor housing in high crime areas, bad health and family breakdown. In opposition, Blair talked of 'a new "underclass", cut off and alienated from society. Part of our job is to ensure that the people frozen out of Tory Britain are brought in from the cold, their talents used, their potential developed' (quoted in Coates, 2005 p. 143). In government a Social Exclusion Unit was established in Number Ten. This identified 1,400 poor housing estates, with high unemployment, poor housing, high mortality and morbidity, low educational performance, excessive underage pregnancies and high crime rates. Prospects of escape from such blighted areas were poor. The government introduced its New Deals for Communities programme, the latest in a long string of initiatives by successive governments to tackle 'depressed urban areas' or break 'the cycle of deprivation'. Social exclusion was thus a new label for an old and familiar problem. Over time, New Labour's response to the problems of those living in deprived communities became more punitive than supportive, as drugs, drink, crime, vandalism and anti-social behaviour of all kinds were targeted, and the 'work-shy' pressurized into jobs or training. Increasingly, many of the people living in run-down neighbourhoods were not seen as victims of deep-seated inequality in British society, and of lack of facilities and opportunities.

- A national child care strategy to provide a massive increase in subsidized child care.
- Increased child benefit, and a new Working Families Tax Credit (later consolidated and replaced by Child Tax Credit ) to guarantee a tax-free minimum income for those raising children on low pay.

All this aspired to erode the 'poverty trap' or 'benefit trap' under which the poor were often better off on benefits than in work. It also particularly helped women who wanted paid work to enter the labour market. Coates (2005, p. 76) remarks that Brown as Chancellor was 'sensitive to the problems of combining child care and paid work, and ... raising children on low and inadequate pay'. He was also aware of the problems 'faced by working women in a society that was still deeply patriarchal in its private division of labour'.

Child poverty, a concern since the 1960s, had grown to such an extent that by 1997 the proportion of British children classified as poor by the EU had trebled and Britain had the highest rates of child poverty among the (then) 15 member states of the European Union.

Labour pledged to halve child poverty by 2010 and abolish it by 2020. Labour also aspired to end pensioner poverty (with no date attached).

Increased longevity has dramatically increased the scale of the problem not just in Britain but in many other western countries. Yet the problem in Britain has been aggravated by additional factors. The value of the basic state pension has been eroded over time. Many private sector pension schemes linked to final salary have ended. Some pension funds have collapsed. Increasingly the houses of pensioners too ill or disabled to live alone have to be sold to meet the high costs of care in residential homes.

As the increasing elderly are more inclined to use their votes than the young, politicians are bound to take some notice of 'grey power'. Labour was made painfully aware of 'grey power' when Brown put up the basic state pension by just 75p (in line with inflation figures) in 2000. The political backlash obliged rather more generosity in future budgets, so that the basic state pension increased by 7 per cent in real terms from 2000 to 2004. Yet it is universally recognized that the basic state pension alone remains totally inadequate for survival. Brown argued that more could be done for poor pensioners through targeted benefits rather than raising the universal state pension. The Pension Credit, its value linked with earnings, supplements the state pension for the poorest third of pensioners. Yet the Pension Credit does not reach all who

**Image 22.1  Pensioner sitting by a fire**

Pensioners now receive winter fuel payments, but these nowhere near compensate for the rising costs of heating. Pensioner poverty remains a real problem especially for those dependent on the inadequate state pension and means-tested additional benefites. However, some of those with relatively generous occupational pensions linked to final salary are comparatively well-off.

need it, a familiar problem with selective means-tested benefits. Labour also gave pensioners a mix of other benefits, including winter fuel payments, free local public transport off-peak, free television licences for the over 75s, and help with council tax bills. All these were useful, but hardly compensated for inadequate pensions.

More recent post-recession changes in the tax system targeting the higher-paid may have helped to reduce the income gap. Thus the Institute for Fiscal Studies (IFS) concludes that after 13 years of Labour rule from 1997 to 2010, the poorest 10 per cent gained 13 per cent, as a percentage of net income, while the richest 10 per cent were 5 per cent worse off. Even so, according to United Nations figures, the richest 20 per cent were seven times better off than the poorest 20 per cent (*The Guardian*, 26 March 2010). Top salaries and associated perks continued to rise much faster than average wages, sometimes, it appears, regardless of success or failure.

The financial crisis and recession helped publicize the huge salaries and bonuses of bankers but also other businessmen, local authority chief executives and highly paid BBC employees, among others, fuelling renewed debates over fairness. This emboldened Labour to pursue some very modest redistribution, through a tax on bankers' bonuses, a new 50p in the pound tax for higher earners, coupled with some relief for the poor and unemployed. Yet radical critics point out that while national income and profits (particularly bank profits) have increased since July 2009 as a result of the (very minor) economic recovery, wages have scarcely risen at all.

Toynbee and Walker (2010) conclude that although Labour stopped inequality getting worse they did not make Britain more equal. They cut child poverty significantly, but by a quarter, rather than the half promised. The employment rate among lone parents rose from 45 to 57 per cent, a modest but significant shift from welfare to work. Moreover, there was some further progress towards reducing the discrimination and disadvantage suffered by women, ethnic minorities, the disabled and gays. Yet 'the inequality that hardly dared speak its name was social class', an inequality 'manifest in everyday ill-health, obesity, drunkenness, truancy, school failure, teenage motherhood and childhood unhappiness'.

Wilkinson and Pickett's analysis of the relationship between inequality and social problems naturally appeals to those on the left and centre committed to a more equal society (see, for

## COMPARATIVE POLITICS  22.2
# Inequality and social problems

Wilkinson and Pickett (2010, pp. 15–19) review the distribution of income in 23 rich countries with a population over three million, using UN figures to compare the gap between the richest and poorest 20 per cent. The UK is the fourth most unequal society, behind Singapore, the USA and Portugal. The most equal societies in this survey were Japan followed by the Scandinavian countries, Finland, Norway, Sweden and Denmark. Wilkinson and Pickett go on to correlate inequality with a wide range of health and social problems, showing that the most unequal countries have lower levels of trust, and lower life expectancy with high infant mortality. They also have more mental illness (including drug and alcohol addiction), more obesity, teenage births, homicides and people in prison, and lower children's educational achievement and social mobility. Thus the most unequal societies are worse off in other respects. UK policies, targeted to reduce health or educational inequality, have largely failed because they are tackling symptoms rather than accepting 'the glaringly obvious fact that these problems have common roots in inequality and relative deprivation' (Wilkinson and Pickett, 2010, pp. 238–9).

example, Judt, 2010, Hutton, 2010), although it has been much criticized by interests on the other side, particularly the Taxpayers' Alliance. Yet any significant redistribution of income and wealth will not be easy. One 'elephant in the room' is corporate power that transcends state boundaries and limits the scope of democratic politics (Wilkinson and Pickett, 2010, pp. 249–53). This chimes with conservative and neo-liberal objections to redistribution through high and progressive taxes, and increased state welfare spending, which they argue will provoke an exodus of enterprise and talent.

## Social justice and fairness: the coalition approach

Social justice and fairness has been a traditional Labour theme. Thus Gordon Brown used the words 'fair' and 'fairness' 40 times in his 2008 Labour conference speech. Yet today both the Liberal Democrats and the Conservatives proclaim their own commitment to the same objective. Iain Duncan Smith, Conservative leader from 2001–3, set up the Centre for Social Justice after a mind-changing visit to a deprived Glasgow housing estate led him to advocate a return to the values of One Nation Conservatism. His enthusiasm was endorsed by David Cameron, eager to 'detoxify' the Conservative brand and preach compassionate conservatism. Following the 2010 election, Duncan Smith was appointed Secretary for Work and Pensions in the coalition government, and made chair of the Cabinet Committee on Social Justice.

Yet Cameron's compassionate Conservatism does not involve redistribution through government. Indeed, Cameron's earlier pledge to slash death duties and his criticism of the 50p income tax paid by the highest-paid, hardly suggests an interest in redistributing income and wealth in favour of the poor. The Conservative commitment to social justice and helping the poor seems to depend on a mixture of self-help and voluntary work (Derbyshire, 2010). Other more robust right-wing Conservatives like Simon Heffer reject the whole social justice and fairness agenda. Life is not fair, he argues, and government attempts to promote fairness through redistribution can only make things worse (*The Daily Telegraph*, 24 February 2010).

The Liberal Democrats have expressed a commitment to social justice over a longer period. They have generally shown more consistent support for a progressive tax system, supporting higher income tax to support increased educational expenditure, a higher rate of tax on higher incomes, and local income tax to finance local services. Yet more recently some Liberal Democrats have flirted with flat-rate taxes, and even a re-emphasis of the old values of old free market liberalism (see Chapter 7).

In government together the two parties continue to stress their commitment to social justice, but particularly to fairness. The new coalition government cited fairness as the motive for their commitment to reduce high salaries and perks in the public sector, with proposals that no executives or managers of any public agency should receive more than 20 times the remuneration of its lowest-paid employee. The June emergency budget was presented as fair, because it was claimed it hit the better-off more than the poor. The Liberal Democrats made much of the budget's progressive elements, particularly the higher personal allowances that will take 850,000 out of paying income tax, and increases in capital gains tax (both derived in part from their own manifesto pledges). George Osborne used the word fairness no fewer than 24 times during his speech presenting the coalition government's Comprehensive Spending Review to the Commons on 20 October 2010.

However, these claims have not been accepted uncritically. The IFS pointed out that the new government's tax increases and spending announced in the June budget were regressive in effect, affecting the poor disproportionately. It was only the retention of past Labour budgetary measures (such as the 50p top rate for tax) that made the whole package appear fairer. Similarly the IFS claimed that the poor would be hardest hit by the government cuts announced in the Comprehensive Spending Review. The cuts reinforced the point that that 'the tax and benefit changes are regressive rather than progressive across most of the income distribution'. Deputy Prime Minister Nick Clegg fundamentally disagreed with the IFS conclusion: 'It goes back to a culture of how you measure fairness that took root under Gordon Brown's time, where fairness was seen through one prism only which was the tax and benefit system.' (*The Guardian* 22 October 2010)

Clegg's objection to the IFS analysis illustrates a problem with the whole concept of fairness. Unlike equality, which presents some problems but can be

measured with tolerable accuracy, fairness cannot be measured at all, unless it is further defined. 'Fairness' is highly subjective. Like beauty, fairness lies in the eye of the beholder. The failed banker Fred Goodwin considered his pension fair. Yet the imprecision of the term is one of its attractions to politicians – you can make the term mean whatever you want it to mean. Thus it is perfectly possible to argue that cutting benefits is fair, fair to the hard-working taxpayers who have to fund them, and ultimately even fair to claimants, who will be obliged to seek work, and may end up better off and no longer reliant on the state. Neo-liberals commonly assume that interfering with market forces is counter-productive and inefficent, will lead to worse outcomes, and thus may be deemed unfair, although they are generally reluctant to use such moral judgements

Social justice carries rather more intellectual baggage, as it has long been a concern of moral philosophers and political theorists. It has appealed to modern socialists, social democrats and liberals who feel there should be a moral dimension to the distribution of the good things in life. Thus 'sympathy for social justice ... usually goes hand-in-hand with support for government intervention in economic and social life' although Heywood (2000, p. 136) goes on to point out that while the socialist interpretation assumes support for more social equality, liberals emphasize individual liberty and meritocracy. The more recent Conservative interest in social justice seems to reflect, in part, a similar concern with meritocracy and just deserts on the one hand, but notions of community and voluntary service (big society rather than big government) on the other. Thus it clearly does not entail more government intervention, although there is a hope and expectation that the lot of the poor can be improved, if partly by self-help.

Thus how far the coalition can deliver more social justice depends on how social justice is interpreted. It seems unlikely that current policies will do much to redistribute income and wealth and reduce the gap between rich and poor, but that does not seem to be what Conservative ministers, and perhaps some of their Liberal Democrat partners, mean by fairness. However, it will be politically embarrassing if the gap between rich and poor widens. Whether they succeed in the more limited goal of improving the condition of the poor and deprived depends substantially on what happens to the UK economy, and whether or not the private sector creates enough new employment to compensate for job losses following the cuts in the public sector. The jury is out on this, but many economists seem sceptical (see Chapter 20). Gordon Brown only had modest success in encouraging a shift from welfare to work in a period of economic growth, and it may prove difficult for the coalition to do better in less propitious UK and global economic circumstances.

## SUMMARY

- After the end of the Second World War a cross-party consensus accepted that government had a responsibility to reduce poverty and inequality.

- This progressive consensus was increasingly challenged by New Right (or neo-liberal) analysis that suggested that welfare benefits encouraged a dependency culture that reduced incentives and harmed the poor they were supposed to help.

- Under Conservative governments after 1979 top rate taxes were reduced and unemployment increased, leading to significantly wider inequality in income and wealth.

- New Labour from 1997 sought to reduce poverty by encouraging a shift from welfare to work. It significantly reduced child poverty through a package of reforms and somewhat alleviated pensioner poverty, without tackling the growing pensions crisis. Overall it stemmed the increase in inequality but failed to reverse it significantly.

- There has been less focus recently on reducing economic inequality, and more on remedying the discrimination and disadvantage suffered by particular categories or groups of people – women, gays, the disabled, ethnic and faith minorities. Monitoring and remedying their disadvantages is now the responsibility of the Equality and Human Rights Commission (EHRC).

- There is continuing controversy around the theory and practice of multiculturalism.

- Evidence of the social problems associated with a wider gulf between rich and poor has helped revive the case for more economic equality. However the post-recession economic climate may not help to reduce income inequality.

## QUESTIONS FOR DISCUSSION

- Why was there an apparent reduction in inequality from the Second World War onwards and an increase in inequality after 1979?

- How far should it be the business of government to reduce inequality and promote greater social justice?

- How far is the UK substantially more unequal than other leading western countries? Does this matter?

- Why are women still unequal and under-represented in business, the professions and politics? How far does this matter? How might it be remedied? How far are women interested in a different kind of politics?

- How far and why are ethnic minorities under-represented in British society and politics?

- What is multiculturalism? How far do ethnic minorities and the population as a whole benefit from multiculturalism? Is Britain now a multicultural society? Is multiculturalism a threat to British identity? Might it adversely affect individual rights?

- How far has the Human Rights Act and the Equality and Human Rights Commission been a success? Should either be scrapped or reformed?

- What do you understand by the term 'social justice', and how far are major British political parties committed to it?

- Why may a wide gap between rich and poor be harmful? How might a more equal society be created or encouraged?

# FURTHER READING

Some of the concepts, ideas and ideologies referred to in this chapter are discussed in earlier chapters, notably chapter seven. For more on particular thinkers and terms see introductory handbooks (e.g. Heywood, 2000, 2007, Leach 2008, 2009) and specialist dictionaries (e.g. Robertson, 1993, McLean and McMillan, 2003, Scruton, 2007). Good accounts of women in politics and the women's movement are provided by Randall (1987), and Lovenduski and Randall (1993). Two more recent books are Sarah Childs (2004), *New Labour's Women MPs*, and Wendy Stokes (2005), *Women in Contemporary Politics*. On ageism and inter-generational conflict see Willetts (2010). Celebrated reports on racism in Britain include Scarman (1981), Macpherson (1999), Parekh (2000a), Cantle (2001) and Denham (2002). Saggar (1992), Skellington (1996) and Solomos (2003) provide broad surveys of race and

politics in Britain. Parekh (2000b) is responsible for an extended discussion of multiculturalism. His work has been subjected to criticism by Brian Barry (2001).

On inequality and redistribution Coates (2005) is useful on New Labour's record (particularly his last chapter). See also Mullard and Swaray in Beech and Lee (2008) and Toynbee and Walker (2005, 2010). Wilkinson and Pickett (2010) has already become required reading on the case for equality. See also Judt (2010) and Hutton (2010). For criticism see the publications and website of the Taxpayers' Alliance.

Relevant statistics can be found in recent editions of *Social Trends* and the publications of the Equality and Human Rights Commission (especially the 2010 report *How Fair is Britain?*) and the Office for National Statistics.

# Politics and the Environment

This chapter examines the impact of green thinking on British politics. It evaluates the contributions of pressure groups, mainstream political parties and the Green Party to the debate on the environment in Britain. It considers the response of UK governments to environmental problems and concerns, and continuing controversy over energy supply in general and nuclear power in particular as well as ongoing issues over agriculture (such as GM food) and transport. At another level, it examines the ongoing debate over the contribution of humanity to climate change, and the reasons for the apparent failure of the Copenhagen summit. It concludes with a brief assessment of prospects for environmental policy under the UK coalition government that took office in 2010.

## The rise of green politics in Britain

Much of the post-war consensus in British politics was built on the assumption common to both Labour and Conservatives that economic growth would provide the extra resources for higher living standards and an expanding welfare state, without the need for higher taxation. Maximizing growth and promoting affluence was seen as the key to economic and political success. Yet growth was based substantially on the exploitation of non-renewable resources and commonly involved more environmental pollution.

The modern environmental debate began with the publication of Rachel Carson's book *Silent Spring* in 1962, which drew attention to the deadly impact of pollution on the natural environment. In 1972 the Club of Rome report *The Limits to Growth* argued that current rates of economic growth were unsustainable (Meadows *et al.*, 1972). Their projections suggested that non-renewable resource depletion, population growth and environmental pollution would lead to a collapse of the world system. The new concerns over the environment spurred by these and other warnings led to the establishment of the major international radical pressure groups Friends of the Earth in the USA in 1969 and Greenpeace in Canada in 1972. Membership expanded rapidly in Britain, where the new groups became part of a growing environmental lobby. This included some traditional well-established organizations such as the National Trust, the Council for the Protection of Rural England and the Royal Society for the Protection of Birds, and some newer, more radical groups such as Transport 2000 and the Centre for Alternative Technology. These groups over the years helped draw the attention of the British

BOX 23.1

# Some important environmental issues in British politics

**Nuclear energy.** In the 1960s nuclear power ('atoms for peace') was seen as a clean solution to Britain's energy needs, although some felt the technology was indissolubly linked with nuclear weapons. However other concerns grew over the storage of nuclear waste, and the risks of leaks or more serious disasters, dramatized by the Chernobyl disaster in 1986. The costs and risks of nuclear energy led to the halting of the construction of new nuclear power stations in Britain. However, the depletion and high cost of alternative energy sources has led to contentious (Labour and coalition) government plans to build new nuclear power plants (still opposed by most Greens but supported by James Lovelock and others).

**Acid rain.** Meanwhile, pollution from coal-fired power stations endangers plant and animal life both in Britain and in neighbouring countries. It has been a factor leading to the running down and replacement of coal-fired power stations. Those remaining attract hostile demonstrations.

**Food scares.** A succession of food scares has raised public concerns over farming practices and food safety (e.g. salmonella in eggs, BSE and contaminated beef, pesticides on fruit and vegetables, foods with genetically modified (GM) ingredients). Such concerns led to the establishment of the Food

Standards Agency and the Department for Environment, Food and Rural Affairs (DEFRA). More recently there have been concerns over the impact of 'junk food' on obesity and health in general, particularly for children.

**The environmental costs of transport.** Pressure groups (e.g. Transport 2000 and Plane Stupid) have highlighted the serious resource depletion and pollution consequences arising from the growth of road and air transport in particular. Yet although new roads and airports arouse furious protests from local residents (combining with environmentalists), restrictions on car use and cheap air flights are seen as unpopular and electorally damaging. Planned increases in petrol tax to deter car use were scrapped following the fuel protests of September 2000. Further fuel price increases in 2010–11 have put pressure on the coalition government to cut duty.

**Global warming, climate change and floods.** Freak weather and flooding in Britain (for example, in Cumbria in 2009) have been widely blamed on climate change, leading to more pressure on government to address the perceived cause by cutting greenhouse gas emissions, and the perceived consequences, through, for example, flood control measures.

public and politicians to a number of important environmental issues in British politics (see Box 23.1).

However, as some of these issues indicate, it is easier to raise the alarm than find politically acceptable remedies. Anthony Downs (1973) argued that political concern about the environment would pass through a five-stage process (Box 23.2). Downs' model has often proved to be broadly accurate in terms of a range of environmental issues (e.g. oil pollution, $CO_2$ emissions, nuclear waste), although some clear progress has been made on others (e.g. lead in petrol, salmonella, BSE). Part of the problem is that there are often marked conflicts of interest between sections of the public on environmental issues (e.g. bypasses, wind farms, flood management).

## Making environmental policy in Britain

Only recently have British governments accepted an explicit responsibility for the environment. In 1970 Peter Walker became the first Secretary of State for the Environment in Heath's Conservative government. A number of other senior politicians, including Crosland, Heseltine and Chris Patten, later held the post in subsequent Labour and Conservative Cabinets. In 1997 Labour's Deputy Prime Minister John Prescott was given responsibility for a new Department of the Environment, Transport and the Regions (DETR). While there was some logic in the combination of these functions, they were perhaps too extensive for any single minister or department. In 2001 environment was joined with agriculture in the new Department for Environment, Food and

## BOX 23.2

# Downs' five-stage model for environmental issues

**Stage 1: The pre-problem stage.** The problem exists and is recognized by experts, but the public is unaware, the media are uninterested and only interest groups are alarmed.

**Stage 2: Alarmed discovery and euphoric enthusiasm.** The public are alerted to the issue, often by a dramatic event (e.g. the Chernobyl disaster). The public demand solutions and politicians promise action.

**Stage 3: Realizing the cost of significant progress.** Over time public and politicians come to realize that the cost of proposed solutions is likely to be high and involve sacrifices.

**Stage 4: Gradual decline of public interest.** Public and media interest declines, either from boredom or from a realization of the scale of changes necessary and costs involved.

**Stage 5: Post-problem stage.** The issue has lost its previously high position and receives only spasmodic attention. (Derived from Downs, 1973, Richardson and Jordan, 1979, Savage and Robins, 1990.)

---

Rural Affairs (DEFRA), while transport became for a year part of the Department of Transport, Local Government and the Regions, and then in 2002, the Department of Transport.

Yet other departments, such as agriculture, trade (or trade and industry, or more recently business), and energy, whether they were formally linked with the environment or not, always had major implications for the environment. The crucial importance of energy policy for the environment was explicitly recognized when Gordon Brown in 2008 made Ed Miliband the Secretary of State for Energy and Climate Change, and in effect the lead minister on environmental policy, despite the survival of DEFRA. The 2010 coalition government changed some departmental titles and responsibilities but retained both DEFRA and the Department for Energy and Climate Change (the latter headed by the Liberal Democrat Chris Huhne who had been narrowly defeated for the party leadership in 2007).

To some degree all ministers and civil servants now feel obliged to consider the environmental implications of departmental decisions, even if this sometimes appears token. Government policy towards the environment is also substantially influenced by a range of interests, including not only green and other environmental pressure groups but other interests, which may not be actuated mainly or at all by environmental concerns. These include major energy suppliers, manufacturers, builders and retailers (including the major supermarkets) as well as agriculture, fishing, the aviation industry and the road transport lobby. All of these have routine contact with ministers and civil servants, and far more financial and other resources to influence government, parliamentary and public opinion than the green pressure groups.

As issues such as poverty, energy and climate change have become globalized, governments have to respond to international pressure and public opinion as well as their own domestic electorate. Moreover, because much environmental policy inevitably transcends state boundaries, the UK government seeks to influence, and is also influenced by, the governments of other states, multinational business corporations and all kinds of international organizations, both governmental and non-governmental. The European Union is one key player, and EU decisions and laws have often had significant implications for the UK environment (see Box 23.3).

The government also has to co-ordinate its environment policies with other lower levels of government and administration. Within the UK much environmental policy is the responsibility of devolved government in Scotland, Wales and Northern Ireland. Also, local authorities have extensive environmental responsibilities for regu-

## The European Union, the UK and the environment

It has been estimated that 'over 80% of British environment policy originates in the EU' (Jordan, in Dunleavy *et al.*,2002, p. 262). Of course, the British government has also often played a proactive role in the shaping of EU environmental policy, notably over Kyoto and emission targets. However, while past governments were prepared to set ambitious targets for recycling waste they frequently seemed unable to deal with the detailed problems of implementing EU directives which should contribute to meeting those broad targets. As a consequence of this failure, crises have arisen (for example over indiscriminate

car, fridge and freezer dumping, and fly tipping generally) which the UK media often blame on the EU directives rather than the UK government (Humphrey, in Dunleavy *et al.,* 2003, pp. 314–16).

While the green lobby generally approve of the EU approach to recycling, there are other aspects of EU policy that appear less environmentally friendly, including much of the Common Agricultural Policy (protection, over-production, intensive farming, draining of wetlands) and some environmentally damaging major civil engineering schemes.

---

lating pollution and for waste collection and disposal. In some cases the actions of councils may reflect pressure from the British government or EU directives. In others, local action may be innovative, providing examples to be followed elsewhere, and perhaps adopted as national policy. Environmental policy necessarily involves multi-level governance.

## The greening of British political parties?

As environmental concerns rose up the issue agenda, mainstream parties sought to address them. Each party developed its own green organizations – Labour the Socialist Environment and Resources Association (SERA), the Liberal Democrats the Green Democrats (replacing the old Liberal Ecology Group), and the Conservatives the Tory Green Initiative. Such groups tried to push green issues higher up each party's policy agenda, although with rather limited success. The most apparently dramatic conversion was of Margaret Thatcher, who startled the 1988 Conservative Party Conference with a speech in which she proclaimed:

We Conservatives are not merely friends of the Earth – we are its guardians and trustees for generations to come. The core of Tory philosophy and the case for protecting the environment

are the same. No generation has a freehold on this Earth. All we have is a life tenancy – with a full repairing lease. And this Government intends to meet the terms of the lease in full.

Margaret Thatcher was a science graduate, and appears to have been convinced of the scientific arguments on the dangers of population growth, global warming and environmental pollution. Her conversion helped bring environmental concerns into the British political mainstream. More recently David Cameron initially put the environment at the forefront of his efforts to transform the image of his party. Thus he changed the party logo from the old 'freedom torch' to a green tree, adopted the slogan, 'Think Green, vote Blue', and appointed the environmentalist Zac Goldsmith as an adviser. He also pursued a personal green lifestyle, fixing a wind turbine on his house, and cycling to work (albeit with a car following to carry his papers). Meanwhile, a succession of Labour politicians, including Ed Miliband, pushed the environment up their party's agenda, while the Liberal Democrats continued to proclaim their own long-standing green commitments.

Yet, while all mainstream parties began to show more concern for environmental issues, there were conflicts of interest and ideas within each of them that prevented a wholehearted commitment to a green philosophy. For example, while it was true

## COMPARATIVE POLITICS 23.1
# The German Greens (Die Grünen)

The green movement developed in Germany in the late 1970s. Green candidates won election to state parliaments and in 1983 the Green Party won 5.6 per cent of the vote and 28 seats in the German federal parliament (the Bundestag). The new Green representatives caused a stir by turning up in jeans and T-shirts and placing potted plants on their desks in the chamber. Their best-known early leader, Petra Kelly, proclaimed they were an 'anti-party party'. However, the Greens were soon split between *realos* (realists, who were prepared to make compromises and form alliances with other parties) and *fundis* (fundamentalists), who were not. Some Greens joined the Social Democrats in 'red–green' coalitions in state parliaments. Party fortunes subsequently fluctu-

ated at national level, until in 1998 they won 6.7 per cent of the vote and joined in a coalition government with the Social Democrats under Gerhard Schroeder. The Green leader Joschka Fisher became foreign minister, and three other Greens entered the Cabinet. Defying predictions, the red–green coalition remained in power after fresh elections in 2002, but lost office in 2005.

The German Greens show what the British Green Party could achieve, particularly if a more proportional electoral system was introduced at Westminster. However, the internal tensions and splits among German Greens also indicate the problems in moving from an anti-party of protest to a party of government.

---

that Conservatism involved conservation, and within the party there were strong interests committed to the preservation of the countryside, Thatcherism had also strongly emphasized the free market and deregulation, whereas many environmental issues appeared to require more regulation. In practice, in Britain as elsewhere, Greens are more likely to be found on the left than the right, and Labour contains some radical environmentalists. Yet Labour was historically committed to economic expansion, high growth and full employment. Both Labour and its trade union allies were more concerned to defend jobs than the environment. The Liberal Democrats have often appeared more sensitive to environmental issues than the other major parties, but even they have felt obliged to make concessions to conflicting interests, for example concerns in rural areas over rising fuel costs. All mainstream parties are wary of offending motorists by advocating higher car taxes or restrictions on car use.

The problem is that mainstream parties have generally competed by promising to make people better off, whereas a more thorough green philosophy might entail making them materially worse off, at least in public perception, and this is an intrinsi-

cally difficult message to sell to voters. Thus the major parties prefer to express a generalized concern for the environment, particularly the global environment, and only emphasize some relatively easy, voter-friendly environmental issues (such as recycling and energy conservation) that will not cost too much nor upset significant vested interests

## The Green Party

The Green Party would claim that it is the only party wholeheartedly committed to a green agenda. So far it has not made the same progress as some green parties in other countries (notably Germany; see Comparative Politics 23.1 ), although the British Green Party can trace its origins back further than the more successful German Greens. The party began as the People Party in 1973, changed its name to the Ecology Party in 1975, and finally to the Green Party in 1985. In the early years it only secured between 1 and 1.5 per cent of the vote in general elections, although rather more in local elections. Then in 1989 it appeared to make a decisive breakthrough in electoral politics, winning 15 per cent of the vote in the elections for the

European Parliament, although no seats under the single member plurality system then used in Britain for European elections. It proved a false dawn. The circumstances in 1989 were unusual. The centre was in disarray as the old Liberal Party and its recent electoral partner the SDP had proceeded to a clumsy and hotly contested merger after the 1987 election, and the Greens attracted protest votes from those who did not want to support either of the two main parties.

They have never approached their 1989 performance in any subsequent election. However, they have benefited modestly from the introduction of more proportional representation into elections for Europe and devolved assemblies. Thus in 1999 and again in 2004 and 2009 they won two seats in the European Parliament on 6 per cent of the vote (a much smaller share than in 1989). They won seven seats in the Scottish Parliament in 2003 (on 6.9 per cent of the regional list vote), but only retained two of these in 2007. They retained two seats in the London Assembly in 2004 and 2008 (down one on 2000). This representation has given the Green Party a rather higher profile, but they came nowhere near winning a seat at Westminster under 'first past the post' until 2010. They are penalized not only by the electoral system, but also by a lack of financial resources and media publicity.

The Greens have perhaps not in the past helped their cause by refusing to behave like a normal political party, reflecting some ambivalence towards conventional parliamentary politics. Thus until recently they declined to choose a single party leader, preferring to nominate several spokespersons. All this is reminiscent of the behaviour of the early German Greens as an 'anti-party party'. Yet it is worth noting that their level of support (over 6 per cent) in recent elections held under proportional representation is very close to that of the German Greens who were in the German government from 1998 to 2005. Even so, the Green Party remains marginal to British politics, and still less influential than the major pressure groups, Greenpeace and Friends of the Earth. However, Caroline Lucas, now the sole leader of the Green party, has raised its profile as well as her own in regular mainstream media appearances, and by her success in becoming the first elected Green MP in 2010.

## New Labour and the environment

Blair and New Labour came to power in 1997 committed to placing the environment at the heart of its policy making. Labour embraced sustainability and announced a number of targets: to meet 10 per cent of UK energy needs from renewable resources by 2010, to cut the 1990 level of greenhouse gas emissions by 23 per cent by 2010, to recycle 35 per cent of all household waste by 2015.

### Energy

The Labour government took over at a time when the decline of coal-fired power stations and the 'dash for gas' to replace them was already far advanced. Labour sought to arrest the decline in the coal industry and maintain competition in energy supply. Even so, the energy White Paper published in 1998 predicted that on current trends coal would meet just 10 per cent of the electricity industry's needs by 2003 (compared with 70 per cent in 1990) while gas would supply 50–60 per cent. The switch might help the UK to meet its emission targets, but at the cost of making the country dangerously dependent on gas, and increasingly imported gas, as Britain's own supply of gas from the North Sea was rapidly declining. The UK's ageing nuclear power stations were also providing a declining contribution to electricity generation. Initially, the Labour government were reluctant to build new or replacement nuclear power stations, because of the high cost of nuclear power, the problems and cost of disposing of nuclear waste, and fears on security and safety grounds.

The Labour government sought on the one hand to cut energy consumption, by the encouragement of more efficient use of energy both by industry and households, and on the other hand to seek new renewable energy resources. Neither made an appreciable impact. It was hoped that wind farms would help the government reach its target of meeting 10 per cent of energy needs from renewable resources. Yet electricity produced by wind farms is irregular and expensive. Moreover, the location of large numbers of giant windmills on attractive countryside aroused increasing opposition from local pressure groups, leading to more

## BOX 23.4

# The politics of energy: wind farms split the green lobby

A public inquiry began in April 2005 on proposals by Chalmerston Wind Power (CWP) to build 27 wind turbines at Whinash, on the edge of the Lake District. Wind power was seen as the green answer to Britain's energy needs – a renewable, clean, non-polluting source of electricity. Yet turbines have to be sited where there will be sufficient wind to drive them, normally on hilltops, where they can ruin familiar landscapes and local beauty spots. The projected Whinash wind farm was just outside the Lake District National Park and close to the borders of the Yorkshire Dales National Park. It was opposed by the Council for National Parks, the Council for the Protection of Rural England and the Countryside Agency, as well as local residents' groups, but supported by the Friends of the Earth and Greenpeace. All these organizations are part of the green lobby, which remains deeply split on the issue of inland wind farms. One well-known environmentalist, David Bellamy, threatened to chain himself to a turbine if the wind farm was built. The CWP project manager argued that they had to find sites where the wind blew and Whinash was the most appropriate site in the North-west: 'A quarter of England is covered by national parks or Areas of Outstanding National Beauty. We have to pick up the scraps that are left.'

Opponents of inland wind farms argue that offshore wind farms are viable alternatives. Indeed, several large offshore wind farms are now fully operational. However, while these benefit from more reliable wind, they are more expensive to build and run. They may not arouse strong local opposition, but there are some problems with shipping and fishing interests.

---

emphasis on more expensive off shore wind farms (see Box 23.4).

Other bold schemes to generate electricity through the use of wave power (e.g. the proposed Morecambe Bay barrage) have yet to get off the ground. In the circumstances, the Labour government began to 'think the unthinkable' and recommit to nuclear power, previously ruled out on cost and security grounds. Despite the massive problems of nuclear waste disposal and eventual plant decommissioning, atomic power stations are relatively 'greenhouse-friendly' (Jordan, in Dunleavy *et al.,* 2002, p.283). Thus as dependence on imported gas and oil rose, the Labour government actively sought to construct a new generation of nuclear power stations. Even some prominent Greens such as James Lovelock (2007, pp. 116–34) support nuclear power as the only way to meet Britain's (and the world's) energy needs without destroying the planet. Others have become reluctant converts, although many still remain implacably opposed.

## Transport

Not only is transport of course a major consumer of energy, but its infrastructure – roads, airports, railways – has a major impact on the physical environment, and almost all new developments are politically contentious. Noise pollution, with massive effects on the quality of life and both physical and mental health, is an important factor here, but there are also invariably concerns over the impact on the landscape and flora and fauna. So transport and the environment have become closely linked.

In 1997 it was hoped that the large and high-profile Department of the Environment, Transport and the Regions under John Prescott would place environmental concerns at the centre of government, and build an integrated transport system in which public transport would no longer suffer neglect and under-investment. However, the new Department proved too large for effective control. After the 2001 election, it was broken up, and the environment was combined with food and rural affairs in a new ministry (DEFRA) to replace the old Ministry of Agriculture Fisheries and Food, while transport re-emerged as a separate department.

Labour's planned integrated transport policy soon ran into trouble, compelling a U-turn. John Prescott had boldly announced in 1997, 'I will have failed if, in five years' time, there are not many more people using public transport and far fewer journeys by car.' Yet it was clear that Labour was reluctant to upset motorists for electoral reasons. After the September 2000 fuel protests, the government abandoned regular increases in fuel duty as a policy instrument to deter car use, and Brown fought shy of increasing petrol taxes substantially. Moreover, it was not central government that was responsible for the only significant curb on car use. Congestion charges, introduced in London in 2003 by the London Mayor Ken Livingstone, proved reasonably successful in reducing congestion and raising revenue, and led to interest in other cities, (although residents in Edinburgh and elsewhere later voted against following London's example). Meanwhile, Labour's hopes of boosting rail transport were dealt a major blow by the emergence of serious problems in the rail management system they had inherited. The Hatfield crash forced a rethinking of priorities, led to substantial delays because of new safety restrictions, and contributed to the collapse of Railtrack. Labour effectively abandoned any prospect of reducing car use, which has continued to increase.

More recently, and tardily, all parties have expressed support for new high-speed rail links between Britain's major cities. Even if these lines are eventually built (and there is strong local opposition), Britain remains well behind other European countries such as France and Spain in the development of high-speed rail. Meanwhile, Labour did nothing to deter the expansion of air transport and backed proposals for a third runway at Heathrow, opposed not only (and predictably) by local residents and Greens, but also by the Conservatives and Liberal Democrats, (who have since scrapped them following the 2010 election).

## Food, agriculture and the countryside

Agriculture and food production in Britain has become big business. Small farms have become increasingly uneconomic as farming has become more mechanized and capital-intensive. An already small agricultural workforce has shrunk – only around 1 per cent of the working population. Although the countryside has increasingly attracted refugees from the pressures of urban life, most of those who now live in the more rural parts of Britain no longer work there. While farmers and landowners claim to be the custodians of the natural environment, they are, like those engaged in other kinds of business, also, and primarily, intent on securing the maximum return on their investment, regardless of the environmental consequences. Major supermarkets increasingly dominate food production, because of their purchasing power and marketing. Thus most British agricultural produce is not consumed locally but transported, sometimes hundreds of miles, to be processed, packaged, and promoted. Consumers predominantly want cheap and convenient food, and most are not concerned where it comes from, although there are periodic food scares that cause alarm and lead to consumer boycotts.

British governments have not generally sought radical change in food policy. Cheap food helps keep inflation low. Beyond that, much of the regulation of British agriculture now lies primarily with the European Union, whose subsidies largely reward the big 'agri-businesses', for all their proclaimed interest in small farms, although more recently some financial assistance has been directed towards environmental conservation and organic farming. The 1997–2010 Labour governments sought to give rather more priority to these areas, although like their predecessors, they necessarily became involved with periodic food scares and crisis management, particularly over GM foods (see Box 23.5) and the foot and mouth outbreak in 2001.

In 2004–5 concerns over obesity, particularly child obesity, linked with concerns over diets and 'junk food' with high sugar and salt content, and numerous additives for colour and flavouring, increased pressure for more regulation of the food industry and healthier school meals. However, EU proposals to require bolder warnings on foods, with a traffic light system (red for high calories, yellow for medium and green for low), were dropped in 2010 after intense lobbying by food manufacturers.

Labour had a troubled relationship with rural interests, who accused the party of urban bias. The government's most significant achievement involved opening up the countryside to walkers under the Countryside and Rights of Way Act. This

## BOX 23.5

# Frankenstein foods? The controversy over genetically modified (GM) crops

Genetically modified (GM) crops became a familiar feature of American agriculture throughout the late 1980s and 1990s, and it was anticipated they would become equally familiar in Europe. The Labour government were initially strong supporters of the biotechnology industry, as Britain was a world leader in GM research. GM foods appeared to offer the prospect of increased agricultural productivity – more food for all. But in 1998 the British public became aware of alleged risks from GM food, while environmental groups were particularly concerned about the threat to wildlife. In 1998, a decision by the multinational corporation, Monsanto, sparked public concern in Britain over GM food. Monsanto planned to cease separating GM and non-GM soya beans, meaning the consumer could no longer choose between the two in food products that used Monsanto beans. Environmental groups such as Greenpeace helped alert public opinion, turning it against GM crops and the companies that created and sold them. Major supermarkets capitalized on the public concern and offered GM-free products.

The events of 1998 forced the government to backtrack on their full support of GM food and rather than rely on original, mainly favourable, scientific research the government opted for a neutral position claiming more research was needed. The biotechnology industry announced a moratorium on the introduction of commercial crops until 2002. This did not ease public concern, as the trials of new GM crops across the British countryside led to fears that GM crops could cross-pollinate to other species of plant. Greenpeace activists participated in the destruction of GM crops around Britain claiming they had a moral duty to do so. The hysteria over what were described as 'Frankenstein foods' scarcely helped any rational scientific assessment of the costs and benefits of genetically modified seeds, although the outcome of trials suggests that both the claimed advantages and the dangers have been exaggerated. Some continue to argue that growing world food shortages can only be met through GM crops.

had the support not only of the Ramblers Association but of the green lobby, whose environmental concerns were largely met, although the measure was resisted by most farmers and landowners. Increased access to the countryside largely serves the leisure needs of urban dwellers, although it can be argued that it is they who pay through their taxes for substantial subsidies to agriculture, and the countryside should be for the benefit of all.

It was, however, the hunting issue that stoked up rural resentment against the Labour government and led to the creation of the Countryside Alliance, covering a number of rural grievances (although hunting always remained the chief motivating force). The Countryside Alliance was defending traditional rights and a traditional way of life, and. they argued, the countryside itself. Yet most of the environmental lobby was on the other side. Hunting itself is a highly emotive but essentially peripheral concern to environmental conser-

vation. The real political issues are: why and how to preserve the countryside, and for whom?

Yet for all its difficulties with environmental issues, in its last years the Labour government reasserted its green credentials, and Ed Miliband, then Secretary of State for Energy and Climate Change, maintained a high profile, working to build cross-national coalitions to secure international co-operation on measures to control climate change, particularly in the period leading up to and during the Copenhagen conference. It was hardly his or his government's fault that the outcome proved so underwhelming (see below).

## Coalition politics and the environment

Environmental policy was not a significant problem in the formation of the Conservative–Liberal Democrat coalition in 2010. David

Cameron had placed the environment at the very centre of his own rebranding of the Conservative party and had sought to maintain his own and his party's commitment to green issues. The Liberal Democrats under Nick Clegg had continued their own identification with environmental concerns, and in the inter-party bargaining following the election secured the key environmental Cabinet post, Secretary of State for Energy and Climate Change, for Chris Huhne. Whatever rumblings of discontent there were over global warming in the Conservative ranks (in which the former Chancellor Lord Lawson was prominent), these were clearly not shared by Cameron and the Conservative front bench.

However, despite general agreement on the environmental agenda there was one important issue on which the two parties appeared divided. While the Conservatives broadly sided with the outgoing Labour government on the need for nuclear power as part of Britain's energy mix, the Liberal Democrats were strongly opposed. This was not an issue that was resolved by the talks leading up to the formation of the new government. There was effectively an agreement to disagree. Some observers thought that this could be a breaking point for the coalition. However, early developments increasingly suggest otherwise. The outgoing Labour government had chosen eleven sites for new nuclear power stations (almost all close to existing nuclear stations, where it was expected there would be less opposition). In October 2010 Chris Huhne rejected three of these sites on environmental grounds but identified eight others as potential sites for new nuclear power stations (all already producing nuclear energy). Huhne declared he was 'fed up with the stand-off between advocates of renewables and of nuclear which means we have neither. I am making it clear that new nuclear will be free to contribute as much as possible with the onus on developers to pay for the clean-up.' How far Huhne's apparent conversion is accepted by Liberal Democrat MPs and the party in the country remains to be seen. Yet it no longer appears that the issue of nuclear energy is likely to destroy the coalition. However, the key environmental group Greenpeace remains implacably opposed to nuclear power, although a few prominent Greens, including James Lovelock

and George Monbiot, are now advocates of nuclear power. However, the impact of the Japanese earthquake and tsunami of March 2011 on the nuclear power plant at Fukushima and the serious radioactive contamination of the surrounding environment and food and water supplies has reawakened concerns over the safety of nuclear power, particularly in Japan, but also elsewhere. It may strengthen opposition to the renewed nuclear power programme in Britain.

Meanwhile, the Department of Energy and Climate Change has suffered significant cuts in the coalition government's spending review, but has fared rather better than most. The government still appears committed to investment in renewables and carbon capture and storage, and is establishing a new green investment bank, which it is hoped will attract substantial private sector finance, although the size of the government contribution (reported to be £1 billion) remains somewhat unclear and controversial.

Elsewhere the coalition government has approved a number of expensive transport capital investment plans around the country, including the cross-rail project in London, high-speed rail links between London, the Midlands and North, a new Mersey bridge, and a revamp for the Tyne-Wear metro. While the green lobby may be encouraged by the commitment to investment in rail transport, they and passenger groups are much less happy with projected substantial increases in rail and bus fares. These will do nothing to encourage the use of public transport, ease road congestion or reduce carbon emissions.

## Climate change and international action to combat it: from Kyoto to Copenhagen and Cancun

The issue that has come to dominate UK, EU and now international environmental policy is global warming (or climate change) and, more specifically, both humanity's contribution to climate change and efforts to halt or slow it by reducing emissions of carbon dioxide and other 'greenhouse gases'. Yet it has proved difficult to secure full co-operation from all national governments, including some allegedly contributing most to climate change.

## BOX 23.6

# 'Climategate' 2009

Climate change sceptics claimed that scientists at the Climatic Research Unit at the University of East Anglia (UEA) had colluded to withhold scientific information and had manipulated data to exaggerate the extent of global warming, following hacking into UEA emails and documents in November 2009. The accusations were widely circulated and reproduced in the world's media, and considerably damaged public confidence in the scientific evidence supporting climate change. They led to the establishment of three independent reviews of aspects of the whole affair. While these reviews were critical of some aspects of the practices of the UEA, including a 'culture of withholding information', the more serious allegations of

deliberately selecting and distorting evidence were rejected. Indeed, it was reaffirmed that the huge weight of scientific evidence, including that collected and analyzed by the UEA as well as numerous studies elsewhere, demonstrated that global warming was happening and was caused or substantially exacerbated by human activity. Yet by the time the reviews were published the damage had been largely done. 'Climategate' as the media dubbed the affair (after 'Watergate' the scandal that eventually brought down US President Nixon) substantially increased scepticism over the reality of global warming in Britain and elsewhere and may have contributed to lack of progress on the issue at Copenhagen and subsequently.

Negotiated in 1997, the Kyoto Agreement set targets for 186 states (including 38 developed states) to bind them to reduce their emissions of carbon dioxide and other greenhouse gases by 2012. The European Union committed all member states to keep to their targets by law. However, the United States unilaterally withdrew from the Kyoto Agreement. While President Clinton was supportive, the Senate rejected the agreement. The election of George W. Bush in 2000 destroyed any prospect of US participation in international co-operation to stem climate change.

In December 2009 the United Nations Climate Change Conference met at Copenhagen, amidst high hopes of securing new binding targets on reducing greenhouse gas emissions and checking global warming, particularly as the United States government, now headed by President Barack Obama, was an active participant. Yet the outcome was widely reckoned a failure. Delegates only agreed to 'take note of the Copenhagen Accord'. Thus while the scientific arguments for keeping global temperature rises below 2 per cent were acknowledged, there were no legally binding commitments. Some blamed the richer nations for not offering more assistance to developing nations in reducing emissions. Others blamed the reluctance of major developing powers such as China

and India to commit to restrictions on emissions that might adversely affect their own rapid growth, based substantially on coal.

One possible contributory factor to the failure of the Copenhagen conference was public, and to some extent governmental, scepticism over the reality and implications of climate change. This is despite the apparently almost unanimous consensus of the international scientific community that significant global warming is occurring, that human activity significantly contributes to global warming, and that action is urgently required now to prevent potentially calamitous effects. In part, this public scepticism reflects difficulty in accepting the reality of long-term climate trends against direct experience of short-term climate fluctuations. Thus the British public that experienced the relatively cold and rainy summers of 2008 and 2009 and cold winter of 2010–11 are hardly convinced that the world is dangerously heating up. This is one reason why the terminology of debate has subtly altered from 'global warming' to 'climate change'. It may be easier to convince British (and US) opinion that we are now experiencing more extreme variations in climate (including violent storms and floods) at the same time as a long-term trend towards global warming, the thawing of the polar ice caps and rises in sea levels However, public opinion has also been affected by 'climate change deniers' on the one hand, and allegations on the other hand that some scientists have used and publicized evidence selectively to demonstrate the reality of climate change (see Box 23.6).

It appears that only a very small minority of scientists are climate change deniers, but there are some, and they have some high-profile political supporters. One problem here is that the media thrive on controversy, and tend to present the argument in terms of a balanced thesis and antithesis, regardless of the gross disparity in numbers of those who affirm and deny climate change and the weight and quality of the evidence on each side. The case was damaged further by the apparent failure of some scientists to present their evidence fairly.

A further UN climate summit at Cancun, Mexico in December 2010 led to a deal to curb climate change that included an agreement on a fund to help developing countries, which had been a significant sticking point at Copenhagen. Pledges by rich countries to cut greenhouse emissions by 2020 have now been formally recognized by the UN. Yet the cuts are not legally binding, and critics argue they are inadequate. Moreover, while developing countries have agreed to consider how they might cut emissions in future, they have not made specific pledges. Thus Prime Minister David Cameron cautiously observed that the world must deliver on its promises and that there was more hard work to be done ahead of the climate change conference in South Africa in 2011. Even so, the mood is rather more positive than after Copenhagen.

## Obstacles facing environmental policy in the UK and elsewhere.

Environmental policy frequently conflicts with other policy objectives. This is true of all policy making. Different departments and the policy areas for which they are responsible are frequently in competition with each other for government prior-ity and resources. Yet environmental policy particularly cuts across any government's broad economic objectives for growth, high employment and low inflation, and the aim of business to maximize profits in a free market, with minimum regulation. Thus the now substantial environmental lobby frequently comes up against a well-organized, influential and highly resourced business lobby, which can often argue that particular restrictions and regulations will damage their competitiveness in world markets. This is an argument that can be highly persuasive with politicians and governments, and also with workers and ultimately consumers and voters. Politicians may be quite sincere in the concerns they express for the environment, but in the real world they have to balance these concerns against other desirable objectives relating to jobs, services and living standards.

There is another particular problem with environmental issues and policies. Their impact is frequently long-term and sometimes contentious, while politicians deal primarily with the short term and the immediate impact on the economy and political prospects. Many of the presumed beneficiaries of environmental conservation are not current voters and have little weight in the political marketplace. There often appears to be an urgent need to satisfy present demands. The horizons of us all, not just politicians, tend to be short-term. It is often difficult to persuade people, in their own interests, to forgo current consumption for some benefit, such as a comfortable retirement. It is much more difficult to persuade them to forgo current consumption for the benefit of unknown peoples in distant continents, still less for future generations yet unborn. Thus the green lobby has its work cut out. The political process, not just in Britain but more generally, has an inbuilt bias against their concerns. In the wake of the immediate problems caused by the financial crisis and economic recession of 2008–9, longer-term but more fundamental environmental issues have slipped down the national and global political agenda.

# SUMMARY

- It is only relatively recently that environmental issues and policies have become a central concern of British politics and government.

- The main impact on British politics has been through green pressure groups rather than mainstream parties, although all these have increasingly sought to address environmental concerns.

- The British Green Party has had negligible political influence until very recently, partly because it has been under-represented through the British electoral system. The introduction of more proportional voting systems has led to representation in the European Parliament, Scottish Parliament and London Assembly.

- New Labour claimed that the environment was central to its programme, yet its record on energy, transport and agriculture was mixed and contentious, reflecting other political pressures.

- Both parties in the 2010 coalition government ostensibly share a commitment to the environmental. Nuclear power remains a divisive issue, but no longer appears a potential coalition breaker.

- The issue that now dominates UK and international environmental policy is climate change, although progress towards binding agreement has been slow.

- Longer-term green issues and problems are not well served in a democratic political system that (inevitably?) reflects the immediate concerns and demands of current voters

# QUESTIONS FOR DISCUSSION

- How far is sustainability compatible with a real increase in living standards in countries like Britain?

- How far should Greens engage in traditional politics? What else can they do?

- Why is it difficult for mainstream British parties to pursue environmental policies wholeheartedly?

- Why has the German Green Party apparently been so much more successful than the British Green Party?

- How might Britain's dependence on imported fossil fuels be reduced? Is renewable energy a convincing answer to Britain's energy needs? Should Britain build a new generation of nuclear power stations? Can the nuclear option be safe?

- What might a green transport policy look like, and what would be the problems in achieving it?

- Is there a case for further trials of GM crops?

- Who or what is the British countryside for? Who can be best trusted to look after it?

- How far is the democratic political process ill-equipped for addressing environmental concerns?

# FURTHER READING

Green 'classics' include Carson (1962), *The Silent Spring*, the Club of Rome's *The Limits to Growth* (Meadows *et al.*, 1972) Schumacher (1973), *Small is Beautiful*, O'Riordan (1976), *Environmentalism* and Lovelock (1979), *Gaia; A New Look at Life on Earth*. The latter may be compared with Lovelock's more recent *The Revenge of Gaia* (2007). There are useful short chapters on green ideas and policies in several general books on contemporary ideologies, including Eccleshall *et al.* (2003 ), Heywood (2007) and Leach (2009). Green thinking is explored further in Goodin (1992), Eckersley (1993) and Dobson (2007). Some older accounts are still useful for the growth of green politics in Britain and more generally, including Porritt and Winner (1988), McCormick (1991), Robinson (1992) and Garner (2000). Accounts of the early environmental policy of the Blair government are provided by Jordan in Dunleavy *et al.* (2002) and by Humphrey in Dunleavy *et al.* (2003). Foster in Seldon (2001) discusses the Blair government's transport policy. Bale (2010) is useful on Conservative environmental policy.

# CHAPTER 24

# Britain and the World: Making Foreign Policy

Foreign policy often seems part of a closed, secretive world, substantially insulated from the routine political pressures affecting other parts of government, yet with potentially massive consequences for both Britain and, sometimes, the wider world. British foreign policy since 1945 has had to adapt painfully to the loss of empire and world power status. It was shaped by the Cold War between the two superpowers, the USA and USSR and their allies in NATO and the Warsaw Pact, until the fall of the Berlin Wall in 1989 and the implosion of the Soviet empire. The end of the Cold War failed to produce the hoped-for 'peace dividend', but instead posed new threats from revived ethnic and religious conflicts around the globe.

Both in the Cold War period and subsequently, Britain has claimed a 'special relationship' with the United States. Membership of the European Community (later Union) from 1973 provided another focus for British policy. British governments hoped to preserve both the special relationship with America and ties with Europe. However, particularly since 9/11 and the growth of the terrorist threat, they have drawn closer to the USA as junior partners in contentious wars in Afghanistan and Iraq that have had significant implications for domestic British politics, and especially for the significant Muslim minority. This chapter examines the making of British foreign policy in the context of international relations in which independent sovereign states are no longer the main or even necessarily the most important players. It explores the tensions between the pursuit of national interest and the acknowledgement of wider obligations to the international community and international law. It concludes with an examination of New Labour's contentious foreign policy, and a discussion of coalition policy following the 2010 election.

## Making foreign policy

Foreign policy differs from domestic policy in three important respects. Firstly, foreign policy tends to be *reactive* rather than *proactive*. The government has far greater control over areas such as education or health, where it can direct policy through legislation and financial support. Foreign policy by contrast commonly involves reacting to the behaviour of other governments and international organizations. Secondly, public opinion tends to divide less on foreign policy than on domestic policy. Government economic policy, education policy or health policy tends to create 'winners' and 'losers', where some gain at the direct expense of others. This is rarely the case when government faces a foreign crisis or perceived external threat, when it can usually (but not always) count on widespread cross-party public support. Thirdly, foreign policy has generally tended to interest only a relatively small minority of the population. It receives very

**Figure 24.1**   The British foreign policy process

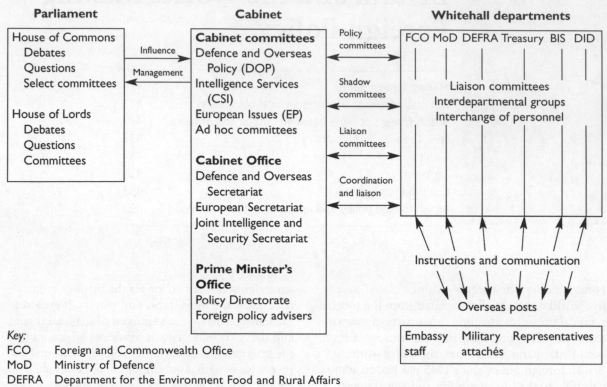

Key:
FCO      Foreign and Commonwealth Office
MoD      Ministry of Defence
DEFRA    Department for the Environment Food and Rural Affairs
BIS      Business, Innovation and Skills
DID      Department for International Development

little coverage in the media, and is particularly ignored by the popular press. It is seldom a major election issue (but see next paragraph). Partly as a consequence, pressure groups, parties and the media play a lesser role compared with their influence in shaping domestic policy. Indeed, much foreign policy seems to be made not through any pluralist process but by a small specialist elite.

Even so, foreign and defence policy has on occasion been acutely divisive, spawning massive popular demonstrations. Examples include the 'Ban the bomb' marches from the late 1950s, the anti-Vietnam war demonstrations of the 1960s and 1970s, and most recently, the huge protests against the Iraq war. Public opinion may not always appear decisive (as these examples demonstrate), although it can constrain foreign policy. Thus although popular opposition to the Vietnam war in Britain did not lead to any official condemnation of US

policy by the British government, it was perhaps one reason why Wilson's Labour government declined to send any troops in support. While Blair committed Britain to war on Iraq despite considerable public opposition, the decision appreciably weakened his position, and was a major factor in Labour's reduced electoral support in 2005, and perhaps Blair's subsequent resignation in 2007. The prospect of further public and party opposition may inhibit any similar initiatives in the future. War in the absence of broad public support is a very risky undertaking.

In constitutional terms, responsibility for foreign policy lies with the Secretary of State for Foreign Affairs, and is implemented both directly by the Foreign and Commonwealth Office (FCO), and through British embassies and missions abroad. Defence, trade and aid (the responsibilities of the Ministry of Defence, the Department for

Business, Innovation and Skills, and the Department for International Development) are closely linked with foreign policy and require careful co-ordination. Other departments, such as the Department for Environment, Food and Rural Affairs (DEFRA), whose responsibilities are primarily domestic, may be frequently involved in international or European Union negotiations.

Most Prime Ministers have had a major role in foreign policy, and some have overshadowed their Foreign Secretaries. A few Prime Ministers, such as Churchill, Eden or Macmillan, could claim some special prior experience or expertise to justify their dominant role in foreign policy. However, neither Margaret Thatcher nor Tony Blair, who both substantially controlled Britain's foreign policy from 10 Downing Street, had any special preparation for that role. Yet it is difficult for Prime Ministers to avoid involvement in foreign affairs. In the modern world any head of government is expected to represent his or her country abroad. The relationships that they can establish with other national leaders may be crucial in shaping informal alliances and agreements, as well as more formal treaties.

At times a Prime Minister with strong convictions on foreign affairs may be in conflict with the prevailing view among senior officials and career diplomats in the Foreign Office. As Prime Minister, Margaret Thatcher was noted for her long-running hostility towards the FCO and occasional bitter battles with her own Foreign Secretary. There were complex reasons for this antagonism, but of central importance amongst them was the clash between Thatcher's *Atlanticist* foreign policy outlook and the *Europeanism* of the FCO. Similarly, Blair's foreign policy, particularly his close alliance with George W. Bush, did not always have the full support of senior officials in the Foreign Office and the Ministry of Defence, as became clear from some of the evidence to the Hutton and Chilcot Inquiries.

The influence of the Chancellor of the Exchequer on foreign and defence policy should not be underestimated. Part of this influence is essentially negative. It is the Treasury that has to fund foreign policy as well as domestic policy. Thus the implicit support of the Chancellor is essential for international commitments, defence spending and above all, war. Financial constraints have played a key role in shaping and limiting Britain's diplomatic and defence commitments, for example leading to the closure of bases 'east of Suez' and the abandonment of specific weapons programmes. Moreover, the strength or weakness of the British economy substantially determines the extent of British influence in Europe and the world. The responsibility of the Chancellor for the health of the national economy, coupled with his role in European and international economic decision-making, necessarily involves him in foreign policy at the highest level. Gordon Brown as Chancellor effectively vetoed any moves to early UK membership of the Euro, played a leading role in advocating more competitive labour markets within the EU, and took the lead in cancelling third world debt and promoting international development to help the African continent. All these policies were maintained when he became Prime Minister.

## National interests and international obligations

There has long appeared an inherent conflict in foreign policy between the pursuit of national interest and the honouring of international obligations. A realist interpretation of international relations (see Academic Controversy 24.1) suggests that state power and state interests determine foreign policy. From this perspective, international obligations are only accepted when they appear to be in the national interest, and are freely broken when this no longer seems to be the case. Might is right, a concept sometimes illustrated by the German words *machtpolitik* (power politics) or *realpolitik* (the politics of the real, of the world as it is, as opposed to the world as one might prefer it to be). Alliances should depend on advantages to the national interest rather than ethical considerations or ideological sympathies. Such an approach has often seemed to guide the foreign policies of states. Thus republican France forged an alliance with Tsarist Russia in the lead-up to the First World War, while Nazi Germany signed a non-aggression pact with the communist Soviet Union in 1939. Both the Nazi–Soviet pact and its subsequent violation with the German invasion of Russia appeared to validate *realpolitik*.

*Academic controversy 24.1*
# Liberal and realist theories of international relations

Anarchy and recurrent war has long appeared the condition of international relations compared to order and (generally) the rule of law in state politics. The slaughter of the First World War provided a catalyst for a more liberal (or idealist) theory of international relations, associated with the US President Woodrow Wilson. Collective security and international law would replace anarchy and war. However, the failure to prevent aggression, culminating in the Second World War, led to some disillusion with the liberal approach to international relations (Carr, 1939). Hans Morgenthau (1948) promoted an alternative realist theory of international relations involving 'states pursuing interests in terms of power'. Peace and security could not be preserved by diplomacy and international institutions but only by the realistic threat of force, backed by strong military capability. This realist perspective on international relations underpinned foreign and defence policy for the Cold War period. Kenneth Waltz (1979) developed a neo-realist theory

that perceived a fairly stable bipolar balance of power between the USA and USSR with their respective allies, rather than a more volatile anarchy. Similarly, the so-called English school postulates a 'society of states' that accepts norms of behaviour (Bull, [1977] 2002) despite the apparent anarchy of international relations. The sudden end of the Cold War (not predicted by international relations theorists) has spawned other approaches, including constructivism (Wendt, 1999 which emphasizes social factors, and particularly identity, in international relations. A revived liberal approach recognizes the increasing importance of international governmental and non-governmental organizations. Those responsible for acts of genocide or illegal war should be punished in international courts according to international law. Radical liberals argue that states are obsolete in a world of globalized communications and markets, and argue for a new international order accountable to the world community rather than states.

National interest, however, is a rather nebulous concept. It appears to suggest that nations or states have a single exclusive objective interest that can be determined. This national interest is not the same as the public interest. It cannot be simply identified with the expressed interests of the majority of the population of a state. It may indeed be the case that among the citizens that belong to a state there are diametrically opposed views over what is in the national interest. As far as Britain is concerned, some are convinced that it is in Britain's national interest to engage fully with the European Union, while others argue that it is in Britain's interest to disengage from Europe and pursue a close alliance with the United States (see Chapter 15). In practice, the national interest is what leading politicians and officials with responsibility for foreign policy declare it to be. Whatever foreign policy is pursued by ministers or their civil servants, it will inevitably be accompanied by

claims that this decision or that treaty is 'in the national interest'.

Others argue that the recognition of international law and obligations is in the interests of states and peoples, in the same way as acceptance of the rule of law and freely entered agreements is in the interests of individuals within states. Just as rational individual self-interest and the wider public interest may coincide within communities, so state interests and international interests may coincide in the global community. A rising number of multi-national and international institutions has arisen to regulate inter-state relations. They include the International Court of Justice, the United Nations, the International Monetary Fund (IMF), the World Bank, the World Trade Organization (WTO), the International Criminal Court, G8 (the Group of Eight advanced industrial states), and more recently G20. The jurisdiction of these international institutions has been recognized by

# International organizations

**The International Court of Justice** was established (1946) under the auspices of the United Nations as the successor body to the Permanent Court of International Justice, established at The Hague (Netherlands) in 1922. Using international law, it adjudicates on disputes between states.

**The United Nations (UN)** is a voluntary association of states who have signed the UN Charter (1945), committed to the maintenance of international peace and security, the solution of problems through international co-operation, and the promotion of human rights. Based in New York, it is headed by a Secretary General, with a Security Council of five permanent members (each of whom can use a veto on decisions) and ten further members elected by the General Assembly representing all states. UN peacekeeping is dependent on troops and finance from member states. Its reputation for effective peacekeeping was blighted by the failure of UN troops to prevent the massacre in Srebrenica, Bosnia in July 1995. The US government has become critical of the UN.

**The International Monetary Fund (IMF)** was set up following the Bretton Woods agreement (1944) to oversee currency exchange rates and the international payments system. Governments could borrow from the IMF to defend their currencies, but often with onerous conditions attached on state finance and economic policy (e.g. the UK loan from the IMF in 1976). As a promoter of sound finance and economic liberalization (often with harsh consequences for particular economies), the IMF has attracted criticism and protest.

**The World Bank** (strictly speaking the International Bank for Reconstruction and Development, IBRD, along with affiliated organizations) was established in 1945. It is owned by the governments of members states, and makes loans to developing countries, although the conditions have made the bank a target for anti-globalization protestors.

**The World Trade Organization (WTO)** emerged from the former **General Agreement on Tariffs and Trade** (GATT, established 1947). WTO regulates world trade, promoting free trade and adjudicating on disputes between countries involving restrictions on trade, and over 'dumping' surplus goods on world markets. Anti-globalization protestors argue that free trade does not always benefit developing countries.

**The G8** consists of a group of eight advanced industrialized states that meet every year to discuss important economic and political issues. The present G8 began in 1975 as a group of five states (USA, UK, Germany, France and Japan), joined by Italy and Canada to make the G7, and subsequently Russia, to make G8 in 1998. It has attracted criticism from anti-globalization protestors as a rich man's club. At Gleneagles in 2005 representatives of African states attended the meeting of G8 that discussed aid, trade and debt cancellation in Africa.

**G20** is a wider group, including some developing nations, that is becoming increasingly important.

**The International Criminal Court** was created following an agreement in Rome in 1998, and formally established in 2002 in The Hague, Netherlands. Whereas the International Court of Justice is concerned with disputes between states, the International Criminal Court is able to bring to justice individuals, including former heads of state, accused of war crimes or atrocities. The government of the United States has not recognized it.

increasing numbers of states including the United Kingdom, although not always by their peoples. Thus the World Bank, the World Trade Organization and G8 have been increasingly targeted by demonstrators opposed to global capitalism (see Box 24.1).

Such international institutions may offer opportunities to national governments to wield influence in the wider world on issues of concern, such as security, trade, development and the global environment, but also may limit or control their relations with other states and even aspects of their domestic policy. The British government, as a permanent member of the United Nations Security Council, and a founder member of G8, has some influence on the decisions of these bodies. Yet these and other international institutions such as the WTO and IMF have also from time to time acted as significant constraints on British policy.

Nation states pursuing national interests are not the only, nor perhaps even the main, actors in the global economy and the international political system. Powerful **multi-national corporations** operating across state boundaries can move capital across frontiers and manipulate transfer prices and costs between their subsidiaries, minimizing the effects of particular countries' business taxation and regulation. Indeed, they can be far more powerful than the states that have the theoretical authority to control them. The turnover of some of these multi-nationals exceeds the national income of many of the supposedly independent sovereign states represented at the United Nations, and has far more influence on the operation of global capitalism.

Alongside the multi-national corporations there is the growing influence of **non-governmental organizations** (NGOs), global pressure groups representing a range of interests and causes that also transcend national boundaries. Non-governmental organizations are defined by the United Nations as 'any international organization which is not established by a government entity or international agreement'. The UN already recognizes around 2,000 NGOs, many of which have also established relationships with other international governance institutions, such as the WTO and IMF. Although there are inevitably some problems with the democratic accountability and legitimacy of NGOs, they can put pressure on states, multi-national corporations and international institutions to consider the moral and humanitarian implications of their behaviour.

Besides these recognized international organizations there are today many more amorphous and loosely organized interests and causes. Some of these freely indulge in the politics of protest, while generally avoiding violence (such as most of the campaigners against global capitalism). Other more clandestine organizations pursue violence and terrorism as a means to often ill-defined ends which allow no compromise. The most infamous of these is al-Qaeda, responsible for a string of atrocities across the world in New York, Bali, Istanbul, Madrid and (almost certainly) London. States, individually and collectively, increasingly have to take into account the threats such terrorist organizations with a global reach represent to their own peoples, as much as or more than the potential threats from hostile states. Global terrorism provides a new and potent challenge to the conduct of foreign policy.

In the context of a more complex and interdependent world involving layers of governance and a variety of non-governmental organizations transcending national boundaries, the pursuit of national interest, even if it can be discerned, inevitably involves compromise and negotiation. This is particularly the case when the 'national interest' of any state, such as the UK, runs counter to the interest of other states, or major multi-national corporations, or the wider international community. There are, moreover, political costs if the authority of international bodies is flouted or the views of influential non-governmental organizations are ignored. A state, or a multi-national, or even an international institution loses moral and political credibility when it appears to reject the consensus of the global community. Thus a more 'ethical' foreign policy may be in the national interest.

## British foreign policy – between Europe and America?

In the past, British national interest often appeared to require a balance of power in Europe to prevent the emergence of a dominant continental state that might threaten Britain's commerce and industry. Thus British governments sought allies to resist French dominance of Europe in the eighteenth and early nineteenth centuries, German dominance in the first half of the twentieth century, and Soviet Russia's dominance after the Second World War. The relative decline of Britain's economic and military strength in the post-war era obliged Britain (as well as other western

---

● **Multi-national corporations** (MNCs) are business firms that operate in many countries, and across national boundaries. They can shift their operations between countries to maximize profits.

---

● **Non-governmental organizations** (NGOs) are international organizations or pressure groups not established by governments or international agreements.

## BOX 24.2

# Britain's 'special relationship' with the United States

Britain's 'special relationship' with the United States involved the leaders of both countries working together closely. It developed out of the close co-operation between the two states during the Second World War. Subsequently, Labour Foreign Secretary Ernest Bevin helped draw the USA into a post-war European defence commitment with the establishment of the North Atlantic Treaty Organisation (NATO). America continued to contribute directly to Britain's defence when, after the failure of Britain's own nuclear weapons programme, the USA provided Britain with the most modern systems in the shape of Polaris and Trident, advanced submarine-launched inter-continental ballistic missiles. This underlines the point that the relationship was always unequal, reflecting the unequal military and economic strength of the two countries, and meant more to the British as the weaker, dependent partner. Indeed, the former German Chancellor Helmut Schmidt once drily observed that the relationship was 'so special that only one side knows it exists' (quoted by Ash, 2005, p. 199).

Yet the special relationship was never altogether a myth. It was facilitated by a common language and the notion of an 'English-speaking union'. The ideological and party affinities of particular national leaders and the development of close personal ties, between Thatcher and Reagan, Blair and Clinton, and more surprisingly, Blair and George W. Bush, sometimes further strengthened it. While Blair hoped to provide a 'bridge' between Europe and America, in practice he chose the American alliance over working more closely with Britain's European partners, notably over Iraq. Brown had a less warm partnership with Bush, but was keen to establish close links with President Obama, as also has been Prime Minister Cameron. Thus the 'special relationship' survives with continuing implications for British foreign policy.

European states) to accept US leadership in NATO (North Atlantic Treaty Organization), an alliance founded to contain the perceived threat of Soviet expansion.

The Soviet threat appeared to require the development and retention of nuclear weapons to deter aggression through the prospect of **mutually assured destruction** (MAD). It could be argued that this 'balance of terror' worked, and kept the two great powers out of direct military conflict with each other. Although Russia armed and encouraged resistance to the United States in Korea and Vietnam, while the United States similarly armed and financed opposition to the Soviet Union in Afghanistan, both superpowers avoided steps which might have engaged them directly with each other in a war neither could win.

For those responsible for Britain's foreign policy there initially appeared to be no realistic alternative to the American alliance – certainly not the new Commonwealth, replacing the fast vanishing British empire, which was little more than a loose association of independent states with different interests. Nor did closer European co-operation offer a viable substitute, at least in the post-war decades. Early attempts to build a European Defence Community had failed. Not just Britain but Western Europe generally depended on American arms and NATO for its defence. The one occasion when Britain and France risked independent military action in defiance of American opinion, over Suez in 1956, ended in a humiliating withdrawal. British membership of the European Community, when it was sought and eventually obtained in 1973, was not perceived as an alternative to Britain's 'special relationship' with the United States, which then welcomed closer European integration as another bulwark against Communism.

● **MAD**, the acronym for **Mutually Assured Destruction**, was the basis of nuclear deterrence throughout the Cold War. It rested on the premise that if both the USA and USSR had nuclear parity (i.e. each posed an identical risk to the other) then neither would risk a first strike as this would guarantee destruction of the attacking side. MAD demanded a second-strike capacity, which accounted for the thousands of warheads stockpiled by the superpowers during the Cold War.

## Academic controversy 24.2
# Three influential US views on the end of the Cold War

**Francis Fukuyama** (1989, 1992) provocatively announced the 'end of history'. The end of the Cold War, he argued, marked the decisive victory of economic and political liberalism over its ideological rivals, and the end of the contests which had dominated the history of the twentieth century.

**Samuel Huntington** (1996) maintained in *The Clash of Civilisations* that ideological conflicts between superpowers would be replaced by broader struggles between cultures, such as between Islam and the West. His analysis acquired greater resonance with the growth of the threat of Islamic fundamentalism and al-Qaeda terror.

**Robert Kagan** (2004) asserts in *Paradise and Power* that 'on major strategic and international questions today, Americans are from Mars and Europeans are from Venus'. Europeans prefer to rely on international law and diplomacy to deal with crises because of their military weakness, while Americans are prepared to use force, if necessary unilaterally, because they have the military resources. Yet, Kagan argues, European peace and security continues to depend on America's readiness to use force to defend western values and democracy from real threats.

---

The abrupt end of the Cold War following the destruction of the Berlin Wall, the reunification of Germany and the re-establishment of independence for states in eastern Europe removed the perceived Soviet threat that had dominated British and western European foreign policy for more than three decades. There was no longer a single clear enemy, a single obvious threat to prepare against. The democratic revolutions that swept through Eastern Europe ended the ideological division of the continent that had existed since end of the Second World War. The old bipolar certainties of the Cold War disappeared very rapidly; Germany reunited, the communist Warsaw Treaty dissolved, and President Yeltsin announced that he wanted Russia to join NATO. Some optimistically predicted a 'peace dividend' as defence spending was diverted to more productive purposes. In practice, the Cold War was replaced by a series of more localized but brutal conflicts in outlying parts of the former communist bloc, the Middle East and Africa. This increasingly looked not so much like the 'end of history' celebrated by Fukuyama (1992) but a return to the petty nationalist and ethnic conflicts of the era before the First World War in place of the ideological conflict between liberal capitalism and communism.

The end of the Cold War also increased the potential for conflict between the USA and an enlarged European Union pursuing closer European integration in economic and monetary policy and reviving aspirations for a distinctive European foreign and defence policy. The old European Community had appeared to some as the economic underpinning for NATO. The new European Union seemed to aspire to become an alternative to NATO, whose whole role and purpose appeared problematic following the end of the Cold War (see Box 24.3). During the 1990s the European Union itself sought to develop more effective common foreign and defence policies. Part of the rationale for the capacity for EU military action was the inability of the EU to deal with crises on its own doorstep, such as Bosnia and Kosovo. To an extent it reflected a realization that the United States could not be expected to sort out all Europe's problems, and a fear, prior to 9/11, that the United States might retreat into isolationism, as it had done previously between the two world wars. Thus the Maastricht Treaty incorporated the objective of a common foreign policy. The Treaties of Amsterdam and Nice involved the development of a Common Foreign and Security Policy (CFSP) and European Security and Defence Policy (ESDP).

## BOX 24.3

# A new role for NATO?

The North Atlantic Treaty Organization was founded in 1949. The original member states included the USA, Canada and twelve European countries, including the UK. Greece and Turkey also joined in 1952. Members of the alliance were obliged to assist each other if attacked. NATO was established in the face of what appeared to be a threat from the Soviet Union and its allies or satellites, which in 1955 established the rival Warsaw Pact. Following the end of the Cold War and the dissolution of the Warsaw Pact in 1991, it was not immediately clear whether NATO still had a role. Post-communist Russia was no longer perceived as the enemy. Yet NATO has grown. The former communist states of Poland, Hungary and the Czech Republic joined in 1999, five years before they joined the European Union. Since then seven other former communist states have joined, bringing the total membership to 26 states. NATO today is a US-led coalition of countries prepared to intervene if deemed necessary in troublespots around

the world. Thus the war on Serbia in 1999 to assist the Muslim majority in Kosovo was a NATO operation. NATO countries also supplied most of the coalition military force in the First Gulf War in 1991, and, since 2001, the Afghanistan war.

The Lisbon Treaty, finally ratified in 2009, involved the appointment of an EU foreign minister, a post for which Blair was once widely tipped, but which was eventually secured by the relatively unknown Lady Ashton.

However, it has to be said that the EU has never played a large role in British foreign and defence policy. This is perhaps because Britain, along with most other EU members, belongs to NATO. Many strategic thinkers do not believe that the EU structures have the potential to be the basis of Britain's foreign or defence policy. The EU has been described as an 'economic giant but a military worm' (Kegley and Wittkopf, 1999, p.168). The massive spending gap between the USA and its Western European NATO allies sets the two apart. Others have commented that a common security and defence policy to include Britain remains

impractical for the EU because it is too diverse an organization, unable to take on a robust defensive military role for the foreseeable future. Thus Britain's foreign and defence policies continue to be developed within an Atlanticist framework. Even so, most leading British politicians have never wanted or expected to make a choice between Europe and America, believing that they could and should preserve the special relationship with the United States along with involvement in Europe (Gamble, 2003).

## New Labour's foreign policy

Labour's return to power in 1997 might have been expected to herald a marked change of direction in the conduct of foreign affairs. Indeed, Labour's new Foreign Secretary, Robin Cook, proclaimed in a mission statement that Britain would 'once again be a force for good in the world'. No longer 'could the national interest be defined by realpolitik'. Instead there would be a new 'ethical dimension' to Britain's foreign policy (Rawnsley, 2001, p. 169). The centrepiece of this approach was the promise not to sell arms to repressive regimes that might use them to suppress their own civilian population or aggressively against neighbouring countries. Thus Britain signed and ratified the 1998 Ottawa Convention that banned the use, production, stockpiling and export of anti-personnel landmines (APLs). However, the wider arms trade remained big business for Britain, the second largest supplier of arms in the world behind the USA. Export earnings and jobs were at stake. The international arms industry was highly competitive, with, arguably, little room for ethics. Thus arms continued to be exported to Indonesia, then engaged in the brutal suppression of a revolt in East Timor. Indeed Buller (in Ludlam and Smith, 2001, p. 231) concluded that Labour's record showed 'a rather depressing continuity with the activities of previous governments'.

Neither Robin Cook nor his successors at the Foreign Office, Jack Straw, Margaret Beckett or even David Miliband, proved able to put their own personal stamp on their government's foreign policy, which was substantially dominated by Blair and subsequently Brown. Labour Prime Ministers were as committed to the American alliance as their Conservative predecessors, developing a strong relationship with American Presidents Clinton, Bush and Obama. Yet Blair also initially appeared to be the most enthusiastically pro-European premier since Heath. To Blair this involved no contradiction, for in a favourite metaphor he saw Britain as a bridge between Europe and America.

## Blair's wars

The enduring close alliance with the United States surprised many, not least inside the Labour Party. The early good relationship between Blair and Clinton was not so surprising. New Labour had copied some of the campaigning techniques of Clinton's Democrats, with whom they shared some ideological inspiration. The Republican Party of George W. Bush, however, was never a natural ally

of the British Labour Party. Yet Blair, apparently encouraged by Clinton, sought to establish good relations with Bush, and these were cemented by the events of 9/11 that led to British forces joining the American-led invasions of Afghanistan in 2001 and Iraq in 2003. One argument advanced for the strong support Blair gave to the government of George W. Bush was that it gave Britain a restraining influence on American policy. Thus Blair was able to persuade his ally to seek a second UN Resolution (unsuccessfully as it turned out) before invading Iraq. Critics, however, have suggested there is little other evidence that Blair had much influence on the Bush administration (e.g. on the Palestinian question or the issue of global warming).

Even before 9/11, however, Blair's Labour government had been prepared to resort to arms. In December 1998 it had supported US airstrikes against Iraq (Operation Desert Fox). From March 1999 British planes had joined with the USA and other NATO allies in bombing Serbia in response to their treatment of Albanian Muslims in Kosovo. Finally, after a prolonged civil war in Sierra Leone, the British government took unilateral action in 2000, sending a small force, initially to protect British citizens, but ultimately to support the elected government against rebel forces. While the latter two wars could both be criticized as involving unwarranted outside interference in the internal affairs of independent sovereign states, they were substantially justified both in Britain and the wider world in terms of humanitarian intervention to prevent further atrocities and 'ethnic cleansing'. As a consequence, the Kosovan refugees were able to return home and the Serbian leader Milosevic toppled and put on trial for war crimes, while an elected government and a measure of peace was restored in Sierra Leone. Many would argue that in these two cases, the ends justified the means.

The attack by al-Qaeda terrorists on New York's Twin Towers on 11 September 2001 had a dramatic impact on the foreign and defence policy of both the United States and Britain, its closest ally. It led directly to the invasion of Afghanistan in the same year, and the overthrow of the Taliban government that was providing shelter and training facilities for Osama bin Laden's terrorists. Less directly, it led to

## TIMELINE 24.1

### Blair's wars

**1998**  US/UK airstrikes against Iraq after Saddam Hussein withdrew co-operation with UN weapons inspectors.

**1999**  US/UK bombing of Serbia secures withdrawal of Serbian forces from Kosovo and eventually the fall of Serb leader Milosevic and his trial for war crimes and genocide.

**2000**  UK troops sent to Sierra Leone initially to release UN hostages and evacuate expatriates caught up in civil war, and then assist the elected government to defeat rebellion.

**2001**  UK joined US-led attack on Afghanistan following 9/11. After an apparently easy defeat of the Taliban, the latter launched increasingly effective guerrilla war against the occupiers.

**2003**  US and UK forces invaded Iraq and overthrew Saddam Hussein's regime, but faced a long and bloody insurgency.

(See Kampfner, 2004.)

the far more controversial invasion of Iraq in 2003, and the removal from power of Saddam Hussein's regime. While British involvement in the Afghanistan war had substantial cross-party and public support, the subsequent Iraq war divided Parliament and public. The former Foreign Secretary, Robin Cook, resigned from the government immediately, along with two junior ministers, while Clare Short, the Secretary of State for International Development, resigned subsequently. 139 Labour MPs broke ranks and rebelled on an anti-war motion in the Commons. They were joined by the Liberal Democrats and a small number of Conservatives, including Kenneth Clarke. (The main body of the official opposition sided with the government.) A majority of the public was initially against war (although this briefly changed once British troops were in action) and the Stop the War coalition organized another massive demonstration in London. Perhaps the most damaging consequence was the impact that the two wars had on some of Britain's Muslim population, many of whom saw them as an attack on Islam. The controversy over British involvement in Iraq has persisted, kept alive by the continued bloody insurgency there. It was a significant issue

in the 2005 election, and some were quick to link the terrorist attacks on London in July 2005 with the Iraq war.

It is difficult to summarize briefly and dispassionately events and policies that have proved so divisive. Few would have anticipated that a Labour government would have involved Britain in a series of wars (five, if the airstrikes on Iraq and the intervention in Sierra Leone are included). Some have argued that the Iraq war, and perhaps others, were illegal under international law. According to the United Nations Charter the use of force against another sovereign state is illegal, except in self-defence. The Clinton administration argued that some rogue states justified pre-emptive action as they were developing weapons of mass destruction which threatened their neighbours and the wider international community. Both before and increasingly after 9/11 it was maintained that these states were also harbouring and exporting terrorism. The case for pre-emptive self-defence could be argued more convincingly in the case of Afghanistan, where the link with al-Qaeda terrorism was clear. In the case of Iraq there was no evidence of a link with al-Qaeda. There were, however, reasonable grounds for suspecting that Saddam Hussein had

## BOX 24.4

# The case for humanitarian intervention: Blair's Chicago speech, 1999

Blair maintained that intervention over Kosovo (Kampfner, 2004, pp.36–61) was 'a just war, based not on any territorial ambition but on values. We cannot let the evil of ethnic cleansing stand.' While Blair conceded that non-interference in another country's internal affairs was an 'important principle of international order' which 'we would not want to jettison too readily', he argued that 'the principle of non-intervention must be qualified . . . Acts of genocide can never be a purely internal matter.' The 'international community' should be prepared to act. He was later to use similar arguments to justify intervention in Sierra Leone, and the wars in both Afghanistan and Iraq. Thus the Taliban government had breached human rights, most notably in their denial of the rights of women, while Saddam Hussein had massacred many thousands of opponents of his regime, particularly Kurds and Shia Muslims. However the humanitarian argument for regime change (passionately argued by the Labour left-winger Ann Clwyd in the case of Iraq) remains highly contentious. It could justify further intervention against numerous other repressive governments around the world, yet in practice western governments have not rushed to intervene to protect human rights in Burma, China and North Korea (Hill in Seldon and Kavanagh, 2005, Cox and Oliver in Dunleavy *et al.*, 2006, Plant in Beech and Lee, 2008).

dangerous weapons: some had been earlier sold to him by the west, and he had used them both against neighbouring Iran and Kuwait and against his own people. Moreover, the Iraqi government's failure to co-operate with the United Nations weapons inspectors gave grounds for suspicion that there were continuing programmes to develop weapons of mass destruction. The threat posed by these weapons was the main justification for war. Yet after Saddam Hussein's regime was overthrown no such weapons were discovered.

While the case for armed intervention and even for 'regime change' was partly advanced on grounds of a real or potential threat to peace, it was also argued on humanitarian grounds. In the 1990s the failure of the international community to prevent a series of massacres, sometimes amounting to systematic ethnic cleansing, in Rwanda, Bosnia, the Congo and Chechnya, had led to much agonized soul-searching, not least in Britain and elsewhere in Europe. Thus most Europeans subsequently supported the NATO attack on Serbia over Kosovo in 1999. 'They believed Europe in particular had a moral responsibility to avert another genocide on the European continent.' (Kagan, 2004, p. 124). Blair had been a passionate advocate of war over Kosovo, and during that war advanced the case for

humanitarian (or liberal) intervention (see Box 24.4).

## Terrorism

The British and American governments interpret these recent conflicts in the context of an ongoing war against terrorism. The global reach of the new terrorism, threatening states and peoples across continents, is a new phenomenon (see Timeline 24.2) requiring new kinds of responses by governments. Some critics have argued that the United States and Britain have exaggerated the threat of terrorism to justify repressive measures at home and aggressive action abroad. Yet the history of terrorist atrocities over four continents credibly linked to al-Qaeda suggests the threat is only too real. The terrorists appear to regard anyone who does not adhere to their own extreme and fanatical version of Islam as a legitimate target, regardless of ethnicity or religion (indeed, many of their victims have been Muslims). The terrorist threat is more potent because of its indiscriminate nature and the abundance of 'soft' targets that are difficult to protect. The knowledge and technology to kill hundreds is now relatively widespread and fairly simple. The terrorists are as careless of their own

## TIMELINE 24.2

# Terrorist attacks across four continents

| | |
|---|---|
| **26 February 1993** | **New York**. Bomb at the World Trade Centre. Six killed, more than 1,000 injured. |
| **7 August 1998** | **East Africa**. Bombs at three US embassies kill 224 and injure 5,000 (largely Africans). |
| **11 September 2001** | **New York**. Planes flown into the Twin Towers kill 2948 and injure thousands more. |
| **12 October 2002** | **Bali**. Bombs in beach resort kill 202 and injure many others. |
| **28 November 2002** | **Mombasa**. Bomb in Israeli-owned hotel kills 16. |
| **12 May 2003** | **Riyadh**. Suicide bombers kill 34 in attack on housing compounds for expatriates. |
| **15 and 20 November 2003** | **Istanbul**. Bombs outside synagogue and at bank and British Consulate kill 55. |
| **11 March 2004** | **Madrid**. Bomb attacks at stations kill 191 and leave 1,463 injured. |
| **7 July 2005** | **London**. Bombs on three underground trains and a bus kill over 50 and injure hundreds. (A second similar attack on 21 July caused further disruption but no deaths when bombs failed to explode.) |
| **23 July 2005** | **Sharm el-Sheikh, Egypt**. Three car bombs in holiday resort kill over 60 . |
| **11 July 2006** | **Mumbai, India**. Train bombings kill 209. |

*Note*: Also numerous bombings and other attacks in Iraq, Afghanistan and Pakistan. Many other planned attacks were foiled, such as that on Glasgow Airport in 2007.

lives as those of their victims, willingly embracing what they see as martyrdom. While some states like Afghanistan may have given active assistance to terrorists, they are quite capable of acting without such help.

However, critics suggest that western actions have intensified rather than diminished the threat of terrorism, not least because many Muslims perceive the wars with Afghanistan and Iraq as part of a western war against Islam. This perception is questionable. In Kosovo the US-led NATO intervention was in support of Muslims.

Afghanistan was attacked not because it was Muslim but because it was harbouring terrorists, while Saddam Hussein's regime was essentially a secular dictatorship opposed by many Muslims. Even so, the long-running saga of Palestine, coupled with American support for repressive regimes in the Middle East, lends support to the grievances of Muslims against the west. These and other grievances have been fed by the continuing insurgency against the western occupation of Iraq (although most of the victims of this insurgency have been other Muslims). The American raid on

Pakistan that killed Osama bin Laden in May 2011, hailed as a triumph by US opinion, may not mark the end of the terrorism he inspired, and could in the short run increase the risk of revenge attacks, but new upheavals in the Arab and Muslim world (see below) suggest tha al-Qaeda is now less relevant.

## Coalition foreign policy

Although there was some ideological convergence on economic policy between the Conservative party and the *Orange Book* liberals who now dominate the leadership of the Liberal Democrats, there still appeared a yawning gulf between the coalition partners on foreign policy. While the Conservative front bench and most of its backbenchers had supported the Iraq war, the Liberal Democrats were united in opposition to it. While the Conservatives sought increased defence spending, and the replacement of Trident, the Liberal Democrats were attacked as soft on both issues. While the Conservatives had become more Eurosceptic than Labour, the Liberal Democrats were solidly committed to the European Union. There were thus clear differences on foreign and defence policy that could severely test the coalition.

Yet there were few early signs of intra-coalition difficulties over foreign policy. It helped that British troops had already left Iraq, although Clegg caused some embarrassment with his reference to Iraq as an illegal war at Prime Minister's Questions. For the present the new government seems as committed as the old to the Afghanistan war, and all that flows from it. It also helped that the Lisbon Treaty had been ratified, enabling Cameron to escape from his commitment to a referendum. If that issue had still been unresolved, then it would have been embarrassing had the two parties to the coalition taken diametrically opposite sides on a referendum central to UK–EU relations. Instead, Cameron and Hague were free to pursue a more conciliatory line on the European Union. Apart from anything else, British economic recovery depends substantially on demand from its main trading partners in Europe, and British industry and agriculture is closely bound up with that of the European Union. The financial health of European banks and other European states remains of vital importance to the British economy, almost as much as British banks and the British government deficit.

Although Britain's pretensions to world power status have been routinely reaffirmed by the government, there is also a tacit acceptance of a diminished British role in global politics. American Presidents may continue to humour British politicians by referring to the 'special relationship' between the two countries, but the reality suggests otherwise. The relationship was always unequal and will become more so. US Presidents will always put domestic political considerations ahead of appeasing a lightweight ally. While British military and diplomatic support is useful, the United States has always in the last resort been prepared to act alone. Other countries such as China, Japan, India, Germany, Russia and (even or particularly) Israel are more likely than Britain to affect US interests and policy.

Britain's defence spending has steadily declined as a proportion of total public expenditure, and arguably limited the country's military capacity to wage two major wars in Afghanistan and Iraq. Blair's controversial foreign policy arguably overstretched Britain's limited armed forces. Thus there appeared little appetite in government, Parliament or the country for any new foreign adventures. This was particularly the case with the junior partners in the coalition, the Liberal Democrats, a party with a strong commitment to international institutions and international law and who opposed the Iraq war. By contrast, many Conservatives emphasize instead the paramount need to pursue British national interests, and strongly support Britain's independent nuclear capability and increased spending on Britain's armed forces. In other times this marked difference in attitude between the parties might spell trouble for the coalition. Yet the scale of the budget deficit has rather reduced the scope for disagreement over defence spending and policy.

Thus following the government's spending review and the Strategic Defence and Security Review, and despite the robust public opposition of defence secretary Liam Fox, which secured some concessions, the defence budget has been cut further. The RAF and Navy will both lose 5,000 jobs, the Army 7,000 and the Ministry of Defence 25,000 civilian staff. The aircraft carrier HMS Ark Royal is decommissioned and its Harrier jump jet aircraft are to be withdrawn. The contract for two new aircraft carriers is too expensive to cancel, but with no British jet planes capable of using it, the first of these will initially serve as a helicopter carrier. (French and US planes will be able to use it for joint military operations however.) Britain will not have a carrier strike capacity for ten years. Meanwhile, a decision over the replacement of the Trident nuclear deterrent has been delayed until after the next election, which means that new nuclear submarines will not be ready until 2028 at the earliest, and the lives of Vanguard submarines will be extended.

All this means that Britain scarcely has the capacity to undertake military operations on its own (as it did in the Falklands), and will have reduced capability on joint operations, and may be seen as a less valuable ally. In these circumstances, British foreign policy may become more oriented to multi-lateral initiatives on climate change, international trade and development, world poverty and disarmament, working through the United Nations, the Commonwealth and the European Union. Such a lower, but perhaps more effective, profile may also help to alleviate continuing concerns over terrorism and security. International development has been ring-fenced by the coalition from the consequences of draconian government spending cuts elsewhere, and it seems that the broad commitments of the previous Labour government will be maintained, although the efficiency of specific programmes will be re-examined. The perennial question is how far the government can ensure that aid goes to those who most need it, rather than being wasted through corruption and poor implementation.

## British foreign policy and upheavals in the Arab World

As mentioned at the beginning of this chapter, foreign policy tends to be reactive rather than proactive, and often has to react to the unexpected. Few predicted the dramatic upheavals that spread through the Arab world in the first months of 2011, that led to regime change in Tunisia and Egypt, followed by rebellion in Libya, and challenges to the regimes in Yemen and Syria. These upheavals caught Britain and its coalition govern-

ment unprepared, and reawakened the debate over foreign policy, with further implications for theories of international relations (discussed above, p. 428).

Although British foreign policy in theory favoured democracy and human rights, it had often supported (and armed) dictators who abused the human rights of their own people. This was compatible with the realist approach to international relations, involving the pursuit of national interest and accepting the world as it is, and not as one would like it to be, refraining from interfering with the internal affairs of other states. By contrast. Blair justified humanitarian intervention to prevent genocide and crimes against humanity (Box 24.4, p. 436). Yet the controversy over Blair's wars provoked a reaction in favour of a less interventionist approach. Blair himself sought to bring Libya's dictator Gaddafi into the international fold, to secure the abandonment of his nuclear ambitions and support for international terrorism, as well as trade benefits. The coalition government initially appeared to favour a more cautious and realist approach to foreign policy, which seemed to accord more closely with the national interest.

Yet the popular Arab uprisings against repressive governments forced a rapid reappraisal. Doing business with dictators no longer appears in the national interest when revolution leads to regime change. Indeed, British interests are now arguably better served by support for democracy and human rights. Thus Cameron, along with the French government, ultimately secured US and Arab League backing for a UN resolution which authorized a no-fly zone over Libya, to protect the civilian population from Gadaffi's forces. This new humanitarian intervention has had overwhelming cross-party support in Britain. However, some sceptics have raised pertinent questions about longer-term objectives. Thus, inevitably, the allied attacks on Gaddafi's military forces have appeared to support the Libyan rebels, suggesting a covert aim of regime change. Some question why Britain is intervening here and not elsewhere (e.g. in Syria or Yemen). Others query the impact on Britain's over-stretched and now reduced armed forces. Much will depend on the length of the operation and its final outcome.

# SUMMARY

● Although foreign policy is often perceived as a relatively specialist and elitist field, it can have massive consequences for the wider public, with considerable potential implications for British politics.

● British Prime Ministers have often appeared more important in shaping foreign policy than their Foreign Secretaries. Under Blair in particular the influence of the Chancellor of the Exchequer has also been significant. This is even more likely with coalition foreign and defence policy in the light of spending cuts.

● There is persistent tension in foreign policy between the pursuit of national interests and the acceptance of international obligations and international law. This reflects the continuing disagreement between realist and liberal (or idealist) theories of international relations.

● Increasingly, international institutions, multi-national corporations and non-governmental organizations have become influential players alongside state governments in global politics.

● In the period of the Cold War between the two superpowers of the USA and USSR, British foreign policy was shaped by NATO and the special relationship with the United States. The European Community was perceived as complementary with (rather than competing against) the American alliance.

● The end of the Cold War posed new and different threats, with implications for the role of an enlarged NATO and European Union, with some potential tensions between the two, and for British foreign policy, caught 'between Europe and America'.

● International terrorism, particularly after 9/11, strengthened the Atlanticist tendencies in the Labour government's foreign policy, as America's closest ally in the invasions of Afghanistan and Iraq, with potentially far-reaching consequences for British politics and British society.

● The continuing divisions over Iraq (and to a lesser extent Afghanistan), coupled with the impact of the recession and public spending cuts, make it unlikely that British governments of any party will lightly contemplate armed intervention for the foreseeable future.

● In this and other respects the replacement of the Labour government by the Conservative–Liberal Democrat coalition has not involved a sharp change of direction for Britain's foreign, defence and international development policies.

# QUESTIONS FOR DISCUSSION

● Is foreign policy inherently more elitist and less subject to effective democratic control than other areas of policy?

● Why is it that Prime Ministers often appear more important in making and shaping British foreign policy than Foreign Secretaries?

● How far do international institutions and a body of accepted international law effectively restrain state governments from pursuing their national interest? Are international relations essentially determined by *realpolitik*?

- Consider the perspectives of Fukuyama, Huntington and Kagan on the end of the Cold War and the post-Cold War world. Which, if any, is the most persuasive and illuminating?

- For what purposes is there still a role for NATO following the end of the Cold War?

- Why does there appear to be a growing rift between Europe and America, particularly following the end of the Cold War? How far can Britain be a 'bridge' between the two?

- How far has Britain's 'special relationship' with the United States imposed obligations on both sides?

- Account for the growth of international terrorism, particularly that associated with al-Qaeda. Why has it proved so difficult to combat? How far have British and American policies contributed to a diminution or increase of the terrorist threat?

- How far is there a case for humanitarian intervention, involving armed intervention if necessary, to prevent atrocities or genocide?

- Does Britain still need an independent nuclear deterrent?

# FURTHER READING

A thought-provoking overview that is illuminating on the foreign policy dilemmas facing Britain (although it covers far more than foreign policy) is Andrew Gamble's *Between Europe and America*. Useful surveys of the foreign policy of the Blair government are provided by Caroline Kennedy-Pipe and Rhiannon Vickers in Dunleavy *et al.* (2003), Jim Buller in Ludlam and Smith (2004) and Plant in Beech and Lee (2008). A more detailed critical account of *Blair's Wars* is provided by John Kampfner (2004). Events in foreign policy and the war on terrorism are however so fast-moving that even the most recent book sources may appear dated. Analysis of more recent developments can be found in newspapers and their websites, and from a variety of perspectives on the internet (some useful websites are indicated below).

Some of the wider issues of international relations are rather beyond the scope of a book on British politics, although some might wish to consult some of the texts that have been influential and widely quoted, such as Francis Fukuyama, *The End of History and the Last Man* (Penguin, 1992), Samuel P Huntington, *The Clash of Civilizations and the Remaking of World Order* (Simon and Schuster, 1996) and Robert Kagan, *Paradise and Power* (Atlantic Books, 2004). Timothy Garton Ash, *Free World* (Penguin, 2005) is a thought-provoking British contribution to the debate on modern global politics and Britain's role within it.

Useful websites include the government departments the Foreign and Commonwealth Office (www.fco.gov.uk), the Ministry of Defence (www.mod.gov.uk) and the Department for International Development (www.dfid.gov.uk), and various international organizations such as NATO (www.nato.int), the European Union (www.europa.eu.int) and the United Nations (www.un.int).

# Bibliography

Adams, I. (1998) *Ideology and Politics in Britain Today* (Manchester: Manchester University Press).

Adonis, A. (1993) *Parliament Today*, 2nd edn (Manchester: Manchester University Press).

Adonis, A. and Pollard, S. (1997) *A Class Act: The Myth of Britain's Classless Society* (London: Hamish Hamilton).

Alder, J. (2009) *Constitutional and Administrative Law*, 7th edn (Basingstoke: Palgrave Macmillan).

Allison, G.T. (1971) *Essence of Decision* (Boston: Little, Brown).

Almond, G. and Verba, S. (1965) *The Civic Culture* (Boston and Toronto: Little, Brown).

Almond, G. and Verba, S. (eds) (1980) *The Civic Culture Revisited* (Boston: Little, Brown).

Anderson, A. (1997) *Media, Culture and Environment* (London: UCL Press).

Anderson, B. (1991) *Imagined Communities* (London: Verso).

Andrew, C. (2009) *The Defence of the Realm: The Authorised History of MI5* (London, Allen Lane).

Arblaster, A. (1987) *Democracy* (Buckingham: Open University Press).

Ascher, K. (1987) *The Politics of Privatisation* (London: Macmillan).

Atkinson, R. and Durden, P. (1990) 'Housing Policy in the Thatcher Years', in S. Savage and L. Robins (eds), *Public Policy under Thatcher* (London: Macmillan).

Bachrach, P. and Baratz, M. (1970) *Power and Poverty: Theory and Practice* (New York: Oxford University Press).

Back, L. and Solomos, J. (2000) *Theories of Race and Racism: A Reader* (London: Routledge).

Bagehot ([1867]1963) *The English Constitution* (London: Fontana).

Baggott, R. (1995) *Pressure Groups Today* (Manchester: Manchester University Press).

Baker, A. (2000) 'Globalization and the British "Residual State"', in R. Stubbs and G. Underhill (eds), *Political Economy and the Changing Global Order* (Oxford: OUP).

Bale, T. (2008) *European Politics*, 2nd edn (Basingstoke: Palgrave Macmillan).

Bale, T. (2010) *The Conservative Party from Thatcher to Cameron* (Cambridge: Polity).

Barberis, P. (ed.) (1996) *The Whitehall Reader* (Buckingham: Open University Press).

Barker, A. and Wilson, G.K. (1997) 'Whitehall's Disobedient Servants? Senior Officials' Potential Resistance to Ministers in British Government Departments', *British Journal of Political Science*, 27:2, April.

Barker, M. (1981) *The New Racism* (London: Junction Books).

Barker, R. (1997) *Political Ideas in Modern Britain* 2nd edn (London: Routledge).

Barnett, A. (1997) *This Time: Our Constitutional Revolution* (London: Vintage).

Barnett, A., Eltis, C. and Hirst, P. (eds) (1993) *Debating the Constitution* (Oxford: Polity Press).

Barnett, H. (2002) *Britain Unwrapped: Government and Constitution Explained* (Harmondsworth: Penguin).

Barnett, H. (2009) *Constitutional and Administrative Law*, 7th edn (Abingdon: Routledge-Cavendish).

Barry, B. (2001) 'Multicultural Muddles', *New Left Review*, March/April.

Beauvoir, S. de ([1949] 1972) *The Second Sex* (Harmondsworth: Penguin).

Bechhofer, F. and McCrone, D. (eds) (2009) *National Identity, Nationalism and Constitutional Change* (Basingstoke: Palgrave Macmillan)

Beech, M. and Lee, S. (eds) (2008) *Ten Years of New Labour* (Basingstoke: Palgrave Macmillan).

Beech, M. and Lee, S. (eds) (2009) *The Conservatives under David Cameron: Built to Last?* (Basingstoke: Palgrave Macmillan).

Beer, S. (1982a) *Modern British Politics* (London: Faber & Faber).

Beer, S. (1982b) *Britain Against Itself: The Political Contradictions of Collectivism* (London: Faber & Faber).

Beetham, D. and Boyle, K. (1995) *Introducing Democracy 80 Questions and Answers* (London and Paris: Polity Press and Unesco Publishing).

Bell, A. (1991) *The Language of News Media* (Oxford: Blackwell).

Bell, D. (1960) *The End of Ideology* (New York: Free Press).

Berridge, G.R. (1992) *International Politics: States, Power and Conflict since 1945* (London: Harvester Wheatsheaf).

Beveridge, W.H. (1942) *Social Insurance and Allied Services*, Cmnd 6404 (London: HMSO).

Bevir, M and Rhodes, R.A.W. (2003) *Interpreting British Governance* (London: Routledge).

Bilton, T. Bonnett, K., Jones, P., Lawson, T., Skinner, D., Stanworth, M. and Webster, A.. (2002) *Introductory Sociology*, 4th edn (Basingstoke: Palgrave Macmillan).

Bingham, T. (2010) *The Rule of Law* (London: Allen Lane).

Birch, A.H. (1979) *Political Integration and Disintegration in the British Isles* (London: Allen & Unwin).

Birch, A.H. (1993) *The Concepts and Theories of Modern Democracy* (London: Routledge).

Birkinshaw, P. (1991) *Reforming the Secret State* (Milton Keynes: Open University Press).

Birkinshaw, P. (1996) *Freedom of Information,* 2nd edn (London: Butterworth).

Birkinshaw, P. (1997) 'Freedom of Information', *Parliamentary Affairs,* 50:1, January.

Blackburn, R. and Plant, R. (eds) (1999) *Constitutional Reform* (London, Longman).

Blair, T. (1996) *New Britain: My Vision of a Young Country* (London: Fourth Estate).

Blair, T. (1998) *Leading the Way: A New Vision for Local Government* (London: Institute for Public Policy Research).

Blair, T. (2010) *A Journey* (London: Hutchinson).

Blakeley, G. and Bryson, V. (eds) (2002) *Contemporary Political Concepts* (London: Pluto Press).

Blond, P. (2010) *Red Tory: How Left and Right Have Broken Britain and How We Can Fix It* (London: Faber).

Blumler, J.G. and McQuail, D. (1967) *Television in Politics* (London: Faber & Faber).

Bogdanor, V. (1984) *What is Proportional Representation?* (Oxford: Martin Robertson).

Bogdanor, V. (ed.) (1988) *Constitutions in Democratic Politics* (Aldershot: Gower).

Bogdanor, V. (2009) *The New British Constitution* (Oxford: Hart).

Bolton, R. (1990) *Death on the Rock and Other Stories* (London: W.H. Allen).

Borthwick, R.L. (1997) 'Changes in the House of Commons', *Politics Review,* 6:3, February.

Bottomore, T. (1991) *A Dictionary of Marxist Thought* (Oxford: Blackwell).

Boucek, F. (2010) 'The Least Worst Option? The Pros and Cons of Coalition Government', *Political Insight,* 1(2).

Bradbeer, J. (1990) 'Environmental Policy', in S. Savage and L. Robins (eds), *Public Policy under Thatcher* (London: Macmillan).

Bradbury, J. (2003) '2003 Scottish Parliament Elections: Labour Reclaims Power', *Politics Review,* November .

Braybrooke, D. and Lindblom, C. (1963) *A Strategy of Decision* (New York: Free Press).

Brazier, R. (1988) *Constitutional Practice* (Oxford: Clarendon).

Brazier, R. (1991) *Constitutional Reform* (Oxford: Clarendon).

Breuilly, J, (1993) *Nationalism and the State,* 2nd edn (Manchester: Manchester University Press).

Briscoe, S. (2005) *Britain in Numbers: The Essential Statistics* (London: Politicos).

Brittan, S. (1968) *Left or Right: The Bogus Dilemma* (London: Secker & Warburg).

Brooke, R. (1989) *Managing the Enabling Authority* (Harlow: Longman/LGTB).

Brown, G. (2010) *Beyond the Crash: Overcoming the First Crisis of Globalisation* (London: Simon & Schuster).

Bruce, S. (1986) *God Save Ulster: The Religion and Politics of Paisleyism* (Oxford: Oxford University Press).

Bryson, V. (1999) *Feminist Debates: Issues of Theory and Political Practice* (London: Macmillan).

Bryson, V. (2000) 'Men and Sex Equality' *Politics,* 20 (1).

Bryson, V. (2003) *Feminist Political Theory* (Basingstoke: Palgrave Macmillan).

Bull, H. ([1977] 2002) *The Anarchical Society* (Basingstoke: Palgrave Macmillan).

Bulmer, M. and Solomos, J. (eds.) (1999) *Racism* (Oxford: Oxford University Press).

Bulpitt, J. (1983) *Territory and Power in the United Kingdom. An Interpretation* (Manchester: Manchester University Press).

Burch, M. (1995a) 'Prime Minister and Whitehall', in D. Shell and R. Hodder-Williams (eds), *Churchill to Major: The British Prime Ministership since 1945* (London: Hurst).

Burch, M. (1995b) ' Prime Minister and Cabinet: An Executive in Transition?', in R. Pyper and L. Robins (eds), *Governing the UK in the 1990s* (London: Macmillan).

Burch, M. and Holliday, I. (1996) *The British Cabinet System* (London: Harvester Wheatsheaf).

Burch, M. and Wood, B. (1997) 'From Provider to "Enabler": The Changing Role of the State', in L. Robins and B. Jones (eds), *Half a Century of British Politics* (Manchester: Manchester University Press).

Burke, Edmund (ed. Hill. B.W. 1975) *Government, Politics and Society* (including *Reflections on the Revolution in France* [1790] and other writings) (London: Fontana/Harvester Press).

Butcher, T. (1995) 'A New Civil Service. The Next Steps Agencies', in R. Pyper and L. Robins (eds), *Governing the UK in the 1990s* (London: Macmillan).

Butcher, T. (2004) 'The Civil Service under the Blair Government', in S. Lancaster (ed.) *Developments in Politics, volume 15.*

Butler, D. and Butler, G. (2000) *Twentieth Century British Political Facts 1900-2000* (Basingstoke: Palgrave Macmillan).

Butler, D. and Butler, G. (2006) *British Political Facts Since 1979* (Basingstoke: Palgrave Macmillan).

Butler, D. and Kavanagh, D. (1992) *The British General Election of 1992* (London: Macmillan).

Butler, D. and Kavanagh, D. (1997) *The British General Election of 1997* (London: Macmillan).

Butler, D. and Kavanagh, D. (2001) *The British General Election of 2001* (Basingstoke: Palgrave Macmillan).

Butler, D. and Kavanagh, D. (2005) *The British General Election of 2005* (Basingstoke: Palgrave Macmillan).

Butler, D. and Stokes, D (1969) *Political Change in Britain* (London: Macmillan).

Butler, D., Adonis, A. and Travers, T. (1994) *Failure in British Government: The Politics of the Poll Tax* (Oxford: Oxford University Press).

Butler, R. (2004) *Review of Intelligence on Weapons of Mass Destruction: Report of a Committee of Privy Counsellors* (London: The Stationery Office HC898).

Byrne, P. (1997) *Social Movements in Britain* (London: Routledge).

Byrne, T. (2000) *Local Government in Britain* (Harmondsworth: Penguin).

Cable, V. (2009) *The Storm: The World Economic Crisis and What it Means* (London: Atlantic Books).

Cable, V. (2011) 'Keynes Would Be on Our Side' *New Statesman* 17 January, 2011

Cairncross, A. (1981) 'The Post War Years 1945–1977', in R. Floud and D. McCloskey (eds) *The Economic History of Britain since 1700*, vol. 2 (Cambridge: Cambridge University Press).

Cairncross, A.K. (1992) *The British Economy since 1945* (Oxford: Blackwell).

Callaghan, J. (1987) *Time and Chance* (London: Collins).

Campbell, J. (1993) *Edward Heath: A Biography* (London: Jonathan Cape).

Cantle, T. (2001) *Community Cohesion: A Report of the Independent Review Team* (London: Home Office).

Carr, E.H, ([1939] ed. Cox, 2001) *The Twenty Years Crisis, 1919-1939* (London: Macmillan).

Carroll, A. (2009) *Constitutional and Administrative Law*, 5th edn (Harlow: Pearson Longman).

Carson, R. (1962, Penguin edition 1965) *Silent Spring* (Harmondsworth: Penguin).

Carter, A. (1988) *The Politics of Women's Rights* (Harlow: Longman).

Castells, M. (1977) *The Urban Question* (Cambridge, MA: MIT Press).

Castle, B. (1980) *The Castle Diaries, 1974–1976* (London: Weidenfeld & Nicolson).

Cerny, P. (1996) 'What next for the state?', in E. Kofman and G. Youngs (eds), *Globalizaion: Theory and Practice* (London: Pinter).

Chadwick, A. and Hefferman, R. (2003) *The New Labour Reader* (Cambridge: Polity).

Chandler, J. (ed) (1996) *The Citizen's Charter* (Aldershot: Dartmouth).

Chang, Ha-Joon (2010) *23 Things They Don't Tell You About Capitalism* (London: Allen Lane).

Chester, Sir N. (1979) 'Fringe Bodies, Quangos and All That', *Public Administration*, 57(1).

Childs, S. (2002) 'Parliament, Women and Representation' *Talking Politics* 14(3).

Childs, S. (2004) *New Labour's Women MPs: Women Representing Women* (London: Taylor & Francis).

Clarke, M. and Stewart, J. (1988) *The Enabling Council* (Luton: Local Government Training Board).

Coates, D. (1984) *The Context of British Politics* (London: Hutchinson).

Coates, D. (2005) *Prolonged Labour* (Basingstoke: Palgrave Macmillan).

Coates, D. (2009) 'Chickens Coming Home to Roost? New Labour at the eleventh hour', *British Politics*, 4 (4): 421–33.

Cochrane, A. (1993) *Whatever Happened to Local Government?* (Buckingham: Open University Press).

Cockburn, C. (1977) *The Local State* (London: Pluto).

Coleman, S. (2001) 'Online Campaigning', *Parliamentary Affairs*, 54.

Colley, L. (2003) *Britons: Forging the Nation 1707–1837* (London: Pimlico).

Commission on Social Justice (1994) *Social Justice: Strategies for National Renewal* (London: Vintage).

Commoner, B. (1971) *The Closing Circle* (London: Jonathan Cape).

Cooper, M.-P. (1995) 'Understanding Subsidiarity as a Political Issue in the European Community', *Talking Politics*, 7(3), spring.

Cowles, M.G. and Dinan, D. (eds) (2004) *Developments in the European Union 2* (Basingstoke: Palgrave Macmillan).

Cowley, P. (1996–7) 'Men (and Women) Behaving Badly? The Conservative Party since 1992', *Talking Politics*, 9(2), winter.

Cowley, P. (2005) 'Whips and Rebels' *Politics Review*, 14(3).

Cowley, P. and Stuart, M. (2003) 'Shifting the Balance: "Modernising" the House of Commons', *Politics Review* 12(4).

Cowling, D. (1997) 'A Landslide Without Illusions', *New Statesman*, May Special Edition.

Coxall, B. (2001) *Pressure Groups in British Politics* (Harlow: Pearson Longman).

Coxall, B. and Robins, L. (1998) *British Politics since the War* (London: Macmillan).

Crafts, N. (1997) *Britain's Relative Economic Decline* (London: Social Market Foundation).

Cram, L, Dinan, D. and Nugent, N. (eds) (1999) *Developments in the European Union* (Basingstoke: Macmillan).

Crenson, M.A. (1971) *The Un-politics of Air Pollution: A Study of Non-decision Making in the Cities,* (Baltimore: Johns Hopkins Press).

Crewe, I. and King, A. (1995) *SDP: The Birth, Life and Death of the Social Democratic Party* (Oxford: Oxford University Press).

Crick, B. (ed.) (1991) *National Identity* (Oxford: Blackwell).

Crick, B. (1993) *In Defence of Politics,* 4th edn (Harmondsworth: Penguin).

Crosland, C.A.R. (1956) *The Future of Socialism* (London: Jonathan Cape).

Crossman, R. (1963) 'Introduction' to W. Bagehot: The *English Constitution* (London: Fontana).

Crossman, R. (1975, 1976, 1977) *Diaries of a Cabinet Minister, three volumes,* (London: Hamish Hamilton and Jonathan Cape).

Curran, J. and Seaton, J. (2003*) Power without Responsibility: The Press, Broadcasting, and New Media in Britain* (London: Routledge*).*

Curtice, J. (2010) 'The New Politics? 2010 General Election in retrospect' *Political Insight,* 1(2), September.

Curtice, J. and Jowell, R. (1995) 'The Sceptical Electorate', in R. Jowell, J. Curtice, A. Park, L. Brook and D. Curtice, J. and Seyd, B. (2009) *Has Devolution Worked?* (Manchester: Manchester University Press).

Curtice, J. and Jowell, R. (1997) 'Trust in the Political System', in R. Jowell, J. Curtice, A. Park, L. Brook, K. Thomson and C. Bryson (eds), *British Social Attitudes: The 14th Report* (Aldershot: Ashgate).

Dahl, R.A. (1961) *Who Governs?* (New Haven: Yale University Press).

Davies, A.J. (1996a) *To Build a New Jerusalem: The British Labour Party from Keir Hardie to Tony Blair* (London; Abacus)

Davies, A.J. (1996b) *We The Nation: The Conservative Party and the Pursuit of Power* (London: Abacus)

Davies, N. (1996) *Europe: A History* (Oxford: Oxford University Press).

Davies, N. (2000) *The Isles* (Baingstoke: Palgrave Macmillan).

Dearlove, J. (1973) *The Politics of Policy in English Local Government* (Cambridge: Cambridge University Press).

Denham, J. (2002) *Building Cohesive Communities: A Report of the Ministerial Group on Public Order and Community Cohesion* (London; Home Office).

Denver, D. (2006*) Elections and Voters in Britain* (Basingstoke: Palgrave Macmillan).

Denver, D. (2003) '2003 Scottish Parliament Elections: Messages for unpopular parties', *Politics Review,* November.

Derbyshire, J. (2010) 'Fingers on Buzzwords', *New Statesman* 10 May 2010.

De Smith, S.A. and Brazier, R. (1994) *Constitutional and Administrative Law,* 7th edn (Harmondsworth: Penguin).

De Smith, S.A. and Brazier, R. (1998) *Constitutional and Administrative Law,* 8th edn (Harmondsworth: Penguin).

Dicey, A.V. ([1885] 1959) *An Introduction to the Study of the Law of the Constitution* (London: Macmillan).

Digby, A. (1989) *British Welfare Policy* (London: Faber & Faber).

Dobson, A. (ed.) (1991) *The Green Reader* (London: Andre Deutsch).

Dobson, A. (1993) 'Ecologism', in R. Eatwell and A. Wright (eds), *Contemporary Political Ideologies* (London: Pinter).

Dobson, A. (2007) *Green Political Thought,* 4th edn (London: Routledge).

Donoughue, B. (1987) *Prime Minister* (London: Jonathan Cape).

Dorey, P. (1995) *British Politics since 1945* (Oxford: Blackwell).

Dorey, P. (2002) 'The West Lothian question in British politics', *Talking Politics,* September.

Dorey, P. (2004) 'The Conservative Party under Iain Duncan Smith', in S. Lancaster (ed.), *Developments in Politics,* volume 15, (Ormskirk: Causeway Press).

Dorril, S. (1992) *The Silent Conspiracy Inside the Intelligence Services in the 1990s* (London: Heinemann).

Dowding, K. (1995) *The Civil Service* (London: Routledge).

Dowds, L. and Young, K. (1996) 'National Identity', in R. Jowell, J. Curtice, A. Park, L. Brook, and K. Thomson (eds), *British Social Attitudes: The 13th Report* (Aldershot: Dartmouth).

Downs, A. (1957) *An Economic Theory of Democracy* (New York: Harper & Row).

Downs, A. (1973) 'Up and Down with Ecology', in J. Bains *Environmental Decay* (Boston: Little, Brown).

Drake, R.F. (2002) 'Disabled people, Voluntary Organisations and Participation in Policy Making', *Policy and Politics,* 30(3).

Drewry, G. and Butcher, T. (1991) *The Civil Service Today,* 2nd edn (Oxford: Blackwell).

Driver, S. and Martell, L. (1998) *New Labour: Politics after Thatcherism* (Cambridge: Polity Press).

Driver, S. and Martell, L. (2002) *Blair's Britain* (Cambridge: Polity Press).

Dunleavy, P. (1991) *Democracy, Bureaucracy and Public Choice* (London: Harvester Wheatsheaf).

Dunleavy, P. and O'Leary, B. (1987) *Theories of the State* (London: Macmillan).

Dunleavy, P. and Jones, G.W. (1993) 'Leaders, Politics and Institutional Change: The Decline of Prime Ministerial Accountability to the House of Commons, 1868–1990', *British Journal of Political Science,* 23.

Dunleavy, P. and Margetts, H. (1997) 'The Electoral System', *Parliamentary Affairs,* 50(4), October.

Dunleavy, P. and Weir, S. (1995) 'Media, Opinion and the Constitution', in F.F. Ridley and A. Doig (eds), *Sleaze: Politicians, Private Interests and Public Reaction* (Oxford: Oxford University Press).

Dunleavy, P., Jones, G.W. and O'Leary, B. (1990) 'Prime Ministers and the Commons: Patterns of Behaviour, 1868–1967', *Public Administration,* 68, spring.

Dunleavy, P., Gamble, A., Heffernan, R., Holliday, I. and Peele, G. (2002) *Developments in British Politics 6* (revised edition) (Basingstoke: Palgrave Macmillan).

Dunleavy, P., Gamble, A., Heffernan, R. and Peele, G. (eds) (2003) *Developments in Politics 7* (Basingstoke: Palgrave Macmillan).

Dunleavy, P., Heffernan, R., Cowley, P. and Hay, C. (eds) (2006) *Developments in British Politics 8* (Basingstoke: Palgrave Macmillan).

Dunn, J. (ed.) (1992) *Democracy: The Unfinished Journey 508 BC to AD 1993* (Oxford: Oxford University Press).

Dutton, D. (1997) *British Politics since 1945: The Rise and Fall of Consensus* (Oxford: Blackwell).

Duverger, M. (1964) *Political Parties* (London: Methuen).

Duverger, M. (tr. Wagoner, 1972) *The Study of Politics* (Sunbury on Thames: Nelson).

Eatwell, R. (1997) 'Britain', in R. Eatwell (ed.), *European Political Culture* (London: Routledge).

Eccleshall, R. (1986) *British Liberalism: Liberal Thought from the 1640s to the 1980s* (London: Longman).

Eccleshall, R. (1990) *English Conservatism since the Reformation: An Introduction and Anthology* (London: Unwin Hyman).

Eccleshall, R., Geoghegan, V., Jay, R., Kenny, M., MacKenzie, I. and Wilford, R. (2003) *Political Ideologies*, 3rd edn (London: Routledge).

Eckersley, R. (1993) *Environmentalism and Political Theory: Towards an Ecocentric Approach* (London: UCL Press).

Economist, The (1997) *Election Briefing, 1997* (Economist Publications).

Elliott, L. and Atkinson, D. (2009) *The Gods That Failed* (London: Vintage Books).

Ellison, N. and Pearson, C. (2003) *Developments in British Social Policy*, 2nd edn (Basingstoke: Palgrave Macmillan).

English, R. and Kenny, M. (eds.) (2000) *Rethinking British Decline* (Basingstoke: Palgrave Macmillan).

Etzioni, A. (1967) 'Mixed Scanning: A "Third" Approach to Decision-Making', *Public Administration Review, 27*.

Etzioni, A. (1995) *The Spirit of Community* (London: Fontana).

Evans, M. (1997) 'Political Participation', in P. Dunleavy, A. Gamble, I. Holliday and G. Peele (eds), *Developments in British Politics 5* (London: Macmillan).

Eysenck, H. J. (1957) *Sense and Nonsense in Psychology* (Harmondsworth: Penguin).

Farrell, D. (1997) *Comparing Electoral Systems* (London: Macmillan).

Fielding, S. (2003) *The Labour Party* (Basingstoke: Palgrave Macmillan).

Figes, E. (1978) *Patriarchal Attitudes* (London: Virago).

Finer, C.J. (1997) 'Social Policy' in P. Dunleavy, A. Gamble, I. Holliday and G. Peele (eds), *Developments in British Politics 5* (London: Macmillan).

Finer, S.E. (1979) *Five Constitutions* (Harmondsworth: Penguin).

Finer, S.E., Bogdanor, V. and Rudden, B. (1995) *Comparing Constitutions* (Oxford: Clarendon).

Fisher, J. (1996) *British Political Parties* (Hemel Hempstead: Prentice-Hall/Harvester Wheatsheaf).

Flinders, M. (2002) 'Governance in Whitehall', *Public Administration* 80 (1).

Flinders, M. (2008) *Delegated Governance and the British State:Walking without Order* (Oxford: Oxford University Press).

Flude, M. and Hammer, M. (eds) (1990) *The Education Reform Act, 1988. Its Origins and Implications* (London: Falmer Press).

Foley, M. (1993, 2000) *The Rise of the British Presidency* (Manchester: Manchester University Press).

Foote, G. (1996) *The Labour Party's Political Thought* (London: Croom Helm).

Ford, R, and Goodwin, M. (2010) 'Angry White Men: Individual and Contextual Predictors of Support for the British National Party.' *Political Studies* 58(1).

Frankel, J. (1970) *National Interest* (London: Pall Mall).

Franklin, B. (1994) *Packaging Politics* (London: Edward Arnold).

Franklin, B. (2004) *Packaging Politics*, 2nd edn (London: Edward Arnold).

Franklin, M. (1985) *The Decline of Class Voting* (Oxford: Oxford University Press).

Freeden, M. (1996) *Ideology and Political Theory* (Oxford: Clarendon Press).

Freeden, M. (1999) 'The Ideology of New Labour', *The Political Quarterly, 70(1)*.

Freedman, L. (1994) 'Defence Policy', in A. Seldon and D. Kavanagh (eds), *The Major Effect* (London: Macmillan).

Freely, M. (1995) *What About Us? An Open Letter to the Mothers Feminism Forgot* (London: Bloomsbury).

Freeman, M. (1997) 'Why Rights Matter', *Politics Review, 7(1)*, September.

Fukuyama, F. (1989) 'The End of History?' *National Interest,* 16, Summer.

Fukuyama, F. (1992) *The End of History and the Last Man* (London: Hamish Hamilton).

Galbraith, J.K. ([1955] 1992) *The Great Crash* (Harmondsworth: Penguin).

Gamble, A. (1981) *Britain in Decline* (London: Macmillan).

Gamble, A. (1988) *The Free Economy and the Strong State: The Politics of Thatcherism* (London: Macmillan).

Gamble, A. (1994) *The Free Economy and the Strong State,* 2nd edn (London: Macmillan).

Gamble, A. (2003) *Between Europe and America* (Basingstoke: Palgrave Macmillan).

Gamble, A. (2009) *The Spectre at the Feast: Capitalist Crisis and the Politics of Recession* (London: Palgrave Macmillan).

Gamble, A. (2009) 'British politics and the financial crisis', *British Politics,* 4 (4): 421–33.

Gamble, A. (2010) 'The Political Consequences of the Crash' *Political Studies Review,* 8(1):3–14

Game, C. (2001) 'The Changing Ways We Vote', in Lancaster, S. (ed.), *Developments in Politics,* volume 12 (Ormskirk: Causeway Press).

Game, C. (2004) 'Direct Democracy in 2003: Referendums, Initiatives and Recall', in Lancaster, S.(ed.), *Developments in Politics,* volume 12 (Ormskirk: Causeway Press).

Garner, R. (2000) *Environmental Politics: Britain, Europe and the Global Environment* (Basingstoke: Palgrave Macmillan).

Garner, R. and Kelly, R. (1998) *British Political Parties Today,* 2nd edn (Manchester: Manchester University Press).

Garnett, M. (1996) *Principles and Policies in Modern Britain* (London: Longman).

Garnett, M, (2004) 'Judges versus Politicians', *Politics Review,* 14(1).

Garnett, M. (2005) 'First Among Equals', *Politics Review,* 14(4).

Garton Ash, T. (2005) *Free World* (Harmondsworth: Penguin).

Gavin, N. and Sanders, D. (1997) 'The Economy and Voting', *Parliamentary Affairs,* 50(4), October.

Geddes, A. (2003) *The European Union and British Politics* (Basingstoke: Palgrave Macmillan).

Geddes, A. and Tonge, J. (2005) *Britain Decides: The UK General Election 2005* (Basingstoke: Palgrave Macmillan).

Gellner, E. (1983) *Nations and Nationalism* (Oxford: Basil Blackwell).

George, S. (1998) *An Awkward Partner: Britain in the European Community* (Oxford: Oxford University Press).

Giddens, A. (1998) *The Third Way: The Renewal of Social Democracy* (Cambridge: Polity).

Giddens, A. (2000) *The Third Way and its Critics* (Cambridge: Polity).

Giddens, A. (2002) *Where Now for New Labour?* (Cambridge: Polity).

Giddens, A. (2007) *Over to you, Mr Brown: How Labour Can Win Again* (Cambridge: Polity Press).

Gilmour, I. (1978) *Inside Right* (London: Quartet Books).

Gilmour, I. (1992) *Dancing with Dogma* (London: Simon & Schuster).

Gilmour, I. and Garnett, M. (1997) *Whatever Happened to the Tories? The Conservatives since 1945* (London: Fourth Estate).

Glasgow Media Group (1980) *More Bad News* (London: Routledge).

Glennerster, H., Power, A. and Travers, T. (1991) 'A New Era for Social Policy: A New Enlightenment or a New Leviathan?', *Journal of Social Policy,* 20(3).

Glennerster, H. (1995) *British Social Policy since 1945* (Oxford: Blackwell).

Golding, P. (1974) *The Mass Media* (London: Longman).

Goodin, R. (1992) *Green Political Theory* (Cambridge: Polity).

Goodlad, G.D. (2005) 'Devolution in the United Kingdom: Where are We Now?', *Talking Politics,* 18(1).

Graber, D. (1997) *Mass Media and American Politics* (Washington, DC: CQ/Press).

Grant, M. (1994) 'The Rule of Law – Theory and Practice', *Talking Politics,* 7(1), autumn.

Grant, W. (1995) *Pressure Groups, Politics and Democracy,* 2nd edn (Hemel Hempstead: Prentice-Hall/Harvester Wheatsheaf).

Grant, W. (2000) *Pressure Groups and British Politics* (Basingstoke: Palgrave Macmillan).

Grant, W. (2001) 'Pressure Politics: From "Insider" Politics to Direct Action?' *Parliamentary Affairs,* 54: 337–48.

Grant, W. (2002) *Economic Policy in Britain* (Basingstoke: Palgrave Macmillan).

Gray, J. (1986) *Liberalism* (Buckingham: Open University Press).

Gray, J. (2010a) 'Thatcher, Thatcher, Thatcher', *London Review of Books,* 32(8), 22 April.

Gray, J. (2010b) 'Progressive, Like the 1980s', *London Review of Books,* 32(20), 21 October.

Greenaway, J.R., Smith, S. and Street, J. (1992) *Deciding Factors in British Politics: A Case-Studies Approach* (London: Routledge).

Greenleaf, W.H. (1973) 'The Character of Modern British Conservatism', in Benewick, R., Berkhi, R.N. and Parekh, B. (eds), *Knowledge and Belief in Politics* (London: Allen & Unwin).

Greenleaf, W.H. (1983) *The British Political Tradition, vol. 2: The Ideological Heritage* (London: Methuen).

Greenwood, J. (2007) *Interest Representation in the European Union* (Basingstoke: Palgrave Macmillan).

Greenwood, J., Pyper, R. and Wilson, D. (2001) *New Public Administration in Britain* (London: Routledge).

Greenwood, J. and Robins, L. (2002) 'Citizenship Tests and Education: Embedding a Concept', *Parliamentary Affairs,* 55(3): 505–22.

Greer, G. (1970) *The Female Eunuch* (London: MacGibbon & Kee).

Griffith, J.A.G. (1989) 'The Official Secrets Act 1989', *Journal of Law and Society,* 16(2), autumn.

Griffith, J.A.G. (1997) *The Politics of the Judiciary* (London: Fontana).

Griffith, J.A.G. and Ryle, M. (1989*) Parliament* (London: Sweet & Maxwell).

Gyford, J. (1991) *Citizens, Consumers and Councils: Local Government and the Public* (London: Macmillan).

HMSO *Annual Abstract of Statistics* (London: HMSO).

Hague, R. and Harrop, M. (2007) *Comparative Government and Politics,* 7th edn (Basingstoke: Palgrave Macmillan).

Hague, R and Harrop, M (2010) *Comparative Government and Politics,* 8th edn (Basingstoke: Palgrave Macmillan).

Hall, M. (2004) 'Nationalism in the UK', *Talking Politics,* April.

Hall, W. and Weir, S. (1996) *The Untouchables: Power and Accountability in the Quango State* (London: The Democratic Audit/Scarman Trust).

Hamlin, A. (2010) 'Fixed-Term Parliaments; Electing the Opposition', *Politics,* 30 (1).

Halsey, A.H. (ed.) (1988) *Trends in British Society Since 1900* (London: Macmillan).

Ham, C. (2009) *Health Policy in Britain,* 6th edn (Basingstoke: Palgrave Macmillan).

Harrison, M. (1985) *TV News: Whose Bias?* (Hermitage: Policy Journals).

Harvie, C. (1994) *Scotland and Nationalism* (London: Routledge).

Hay, C. (2007) *Why We Hate Politics* (Cambridge: Polity Press).

Hayek, F. A. von (1944) *The Road to Serfdom* (London: Routledge & Kegan Paul).

Hazell, R. (ed.) (1999) *Constitutional Futures: A History of the Next Ten Years* (Oxford: Oxford University Press).

Hazell, R. (ed.) (2000*) The State and the Nations* (Thorverton: Imprint Academic).

Hazell, R. (2001) 'Reforming the Constitution' *Political Quarterly ,* 72(1).

Hazell, R. (ed.) (2003) *The State of the Nations 2003: The Third Year of Devolution in the United Kingdom* (Thorverton: Academic Imprint).

Heath, A. and Park, A. (1997) 'Thatcher's Children', in R. Jowell, J. Curtice, A. Park, L. Brook, K. Thomson and L. Bryson (eds), *British Social Attitudes: The 14th Report* (Aldershot: Ashgate).

Heath, A. and Topf, R. (1987) 'Political Culture', in R. Jowell, S. Witherspoon and L. Brook (eds), *British Social Attitudes: The 5th Report* (Aldershot: Gower).

Heath, A., Jowell, R. and Curtice, J. (1985) *How Britain Votes* (Oxford: Pergamon).

Hechter, M. (1975) *Internal Colonialism: The Celtic Fringe in British Colonial Development, 1536–1966* (London: Routledge & Kegan Paul).

Heclo, H. and Wildavsky, A. (1974) *The Private Government of Public Money* (London: Macmillan).

Hefferman, R. (2002) 'The Possible as the Art of Politics: Understanding Consensus Politics', *Political Studies* 50.

Held, D. (1996) *Models of Democracy* (Cambridge: Polity Press).

Held, D., McGrew, A., Goldblatt, D. and Perraton, J. (1999) *Global Transformations: Politics, Economics and Culture* (Cambridge: Polity Press).

Henn, M., Weinstein, M. and Forrest, S. (2005) 'Uninterested Youth? Young People's Attitudes towards Party Politics in Britain', *Political Studies,* 53 (3): 556–78.

Hennessy, P. (1987) *Cabinet* (Oxford: Blackwell).

Hennessy, P. (1990) *Whitehall*, 2nd edn (London: Fontana).

Hennessy, P. (1993) *Never Again: Britain 1945–51* (London: Vintage).

Hennessy, P. (1995) *The Hidden Wiring Unearthing the British Constitution* (London: Gollancz).

Hennessy, P. (1998) 'The Blair Style of Government: An Historical Perspective and an Interim Audit', *Government and Opposition*, 33(1), winter.

Hennessy, P. (2000) *The Prime Minister: The Office and its Holders since 1945* (Harmondsworth: Allen Lane).

Hennessy, P. (2010) *The Secret State: Preparing for the Worst 1945-2010* (Harmondsworth: Penguin Books).

Heywood, A. (2000) *Key Concepts in Politics* (Basingstoke: Palgrave Macmillan).

Heywood, A. (2007 *Political Ideologies: An Introduction*, 4th edn (Basingstoke: Palgrave Macmillan).

Heywood, A. (2007) *Politics*, 3rd edn (Basingstoke: Palgrave Macmillan).

Hill, M. (1997a) *The Policy Process in the Modern State* (London: Harvester Wheatsheaf).

Hill, M. (1997b) *The Policy Process: A Reader* (Hemel Hempstead: Hall).

Himmelweit, H., Humphries, P. and Jaeger, M. (1984) *How Voters Decide* (Milton Keynes: Open University Press).

Hirschman, A. (1970) *Exit, Voice and Loyalty*, (Cambridge, MA: Harvard University Press).

Hobsbawm, E. (1984) *Worlds of Labour: Further Studies in the History of Labour* (London: Weidenfeld & Nicolson).

Hogwood, B.W. and Gunn, L. (1984) *Policy Analysis for the Real World* (Oxford: Oxford University Press).

Holland, R. (1991) *The Pursuit of Greatness: Britain and the World Role, 1900–1970* (London: Fontana).

Hollingsworth, M. and Fielding, N. (2003) *Defending the Realm: Inside MI5 and The War on Terrorism* (London: Andre Deutsch).

Holme, R. and Elliot, M. (1988) *1688-1988 Time for a New Constitution* (London: Macmillan).

Holsti, K.J. (1967) *International Politics* (Englewood Cliffs, NJ: Prentice-Hall).

Hood, C. and James, D. (1997) 'The Core Executive', in P. Dunleavy, A. Gamble, I. Holliday and G. Peele (eds), *Developments in British Politics 5* (London: Macmillan).

Hood-Phillips, O., Jackson, P. and Leopard, P. (2001) *Constitutional and Administrative Law* (London: Sweet & Maxwell).

Huntington, S.P. (1996) *The Clash of Civilizations and the Remaking of World Order* (New York: Simon & Schuster).

Hutchinson, J. (1994) *Modern Nationalism* (London: Fontana).

Hutton, B. (2004) *Report of the Inquiry into the Circumstances Surrounding the Death of Dr David Kelly* (London: The Stationery Office, HC 247).

Hutton, W. (1995 *The State We're In*, new and revised edn (London: Jonathan Cape).

Hutton, W. (1997) *The State to Come* (London: Vintage).

Hutton, W. (2010) *Them and Us: Politics, Greed and Inequality – Why We Need a Fair Society* (Boston, MA: Little, Brown).

Ingle, S. (2000) *The British Party System* (London: Pinter).

Jackson, N. (2004) 'Marketing Man', *Politics Review*, 13(4).

James, S. (1992) *British Cabinet Government* (London: Routledge).

James, S. (1995) 'Relations between Prime Minister and Cabinet: From Wilson to Thatcher', in R.A.W. Rhodes and P. Dunleavy (eds), *Prime Minister, Cabinet and Core Executive* (London: Macmillan).

Jeffery, C. (2003) 'Devolution: What's it all for?' *Politics Review*, 13(2).

Jeffery, C. (2010) 'An Outbreak of Consensus: Scottish Politics after Devolution', *Political Insight*, 1(1).

Jeffries, L. (2003) 'The Judiciary', *Talking Politics*, 15(2).

Jenkins, J. and Klandermans, B. (eds) (1995) *The Politics of Social Protest* (London: University College, London Press).

Jenkins, R. (1991) *A Life at the Centre* (London: Macmillan).

Jenkins, R. (2001) *Churchill* (Basingstoke: Palgrave Macmillan).

Jennings, I. ([1941]1966) *The British Constitution*, 5th edn (Cambridge: University Press).

John, P. (1997) 'Local Governance', in P. Dunleavy, A. Gamble, I. Holliday and G. Peele (eds), *Developments in British Politics 5* (London: Macmillan).

Johnson, P. (ed.) (1994) *Twentieth Century Britain* (London: Longman).

Jones, B. (ed.) (1999) *Political Issues in Britain Today,* 5th edn (Manchester: Manchester University Press).

Jones, B. (2003) 'Apathy: Why don't people want to vote?' *Politics Review,* April.

Jones, B. (2004) *Dictionary of British Politics* (Manchester; Manchester University Press).

Jones, H. and Kandiah M. (eds) (1996) *The Myth of Consensus: New Views on British History, 1945–64* (London: Macmillan).

Jones, B. and Robins, L. (eds) (1992) *Two Decades in British Politics* (Manchester: Manchester University Press).

Jones, G.W. (1965) 'The Prime Minister's Power', *Parliamentary Affairs* xviii (Spring).

Jones, G.W. (1990) 'Mrs Thatcher and the Power of the Prime Minister', *Contemporary Record,* 3(4).

Jones, G.W. (1995) 'The Downfall of Margaret Thatcher', in R.A.W. Rhodes and P. Dunleavy (eds) *Prime Minister, Cabinet and Core Executive* (London: Macmillan).

Jones, N. (1996) *Soundbites and Spin Doctors* (London: Indigo).

Jones, N. (1999) *Sultans of Spin* (London: Gollancz),

Jones, P. (1997) *America and the British Labour Party: The Special Relationship at Work* (London: Tauris Academic Studies).

Jordan, G. (2001) *Shell, Greenpeace and Brent Spar* (Basingstoke: Palgrave Macmillan).

Jordan, G. (2004) 'Groups and Democracy', *Politics Review,* 13(3).

Jordan, G. and Mahoney, W. (1997) *The Protest Business* (Manchester: Manchester University Press).

Jordan, G. and Richardson, J.J. (1987) *Government and Pressure Groups in Britain* (Oxford: Clarendon)

Jowell, J. and Oliver, D. (2007) *The Changing Constitution,* 7th edn (Oxford: Oxford University Press).

Jowell, R., Curtice, J., Park, A., Brook, L. and Thomson, K. (eds) (1996) *British Social Attitudes: The 13th Report* (Aldershot: Dartmouth).

Jowell, R., Curtice, J., Park, A., Brook, L., Thomson, K. and Bryson, C. (eds) (1997) *British Social Attitudes: The 14th Report* (Aldershot: Ashgate).

Judd, D. (1996) *Empire: The British Imperial Experience from 1765 to the Present* (London: Fontana).

Judge, D. (1993) *The Parliamentary State* (London: Sage).

Judt, T. (2005) *Postwar: A History of Europe since 1945* (London: William Heinemann).

Judt, T. (2010) *Ill Fares the Land* (London: Allen Lane).

Kagan, R. (2004) *Paradise and Power* (London: Atlantic Books).

Kampfner, J. (2004) *Blair's Wars* (London: Free Press).

Katz, R. and Mair, P. (1995) 'Changing Models of Party Organisation and Party Democracy: The Emergence of the Cartel Party', *Party Politics,* I:5–28.

Kavanagh, D. (1980) 'Political Culture in Great Britain: The Decline of the Civic Culture', in G. Almond and S. Verba (eds), *The Civic Culture Revisited* (Boston: Little, Brown).

Kavanagh, D. (1990) *Thatcherism and British Politics*, 2nd edn (Oxford: Oxford University Press).

Kavanagh, D. (1991) 'Prime Ministerial Power Revisited', *Social Studies Review*, 6(4), March.

Kavanagh, D. (1995) *Election Campaigning: The New Marketing of Politics* (Oxford: Blackwell).

Kavanagh, D. (1997) 'The Labour Campaign', *Parliamentary Affairs,* 50(4), October.

Kavanagh, D. and Cowley, P. (2010) *The British General Election of 2010* (Basingstoke: Palgrave Macmillan).

Kavanagh, D. and Morris, P. (1994) *Consensus Politics from Attlee to Thatcher,* 2nd edn (Oxford: Blackwell).

Kavanagh, D. and Seldon, A. (eds) (1994) *The Major Effect* (London: Macmillan).

Kegley, C. and Wiitkopf, E. (1999) *World Politics* (New York: Worth).

Kemp, P. (1996) 'Handling the Machine: A Memo to Labour', *Political Quarterly*, 67(14), October–December.

King, A. (ed.) ([1969] 1985) *The British Prime Minister: A Reader*, 2nd edn (London: Macmillan).

Kingdom, J. (1995) 'The European Context', in M. Mullard (ed.) *Policy-Making in Britain* (London: Routledge).

Kirchheimer, O. (1966) 'The transformation of Western European Party Systems', in J. LaPolambara and M. Weiner (eds), *Political Parties and Political Development* (Princeton, NJ: Princeton University Press).

Klein, R. (1989) *The Politics of the NHS* (London: Longman).

Klug, F., Starmer, K. and Weir, S. (1996) *The Three Pillars of Liberty* (London: Routledge).

Krugman, P (2008) *The Return of Depression Economics and the Crisis of 2008* (London: Allen Lane).

Kuhn, R. (2007) *Politics and the Media in Britain* (Basingstoke: Palgrave Macmillan).

Laffan, B. (1992) *Integration and Cooperation in Europe* (London: Routledge).

Lanchester, J. (2010) *Whoops! Why Everyone Owes Everyone and No One Can Pay* (London: Allen Lane).

Lasswell, H. (1936) *Politics: Who gets What, When, How?* (New York: McGraw-Hill).

Layton-Henry, Z. (1992) *Immigration and 'Race' Politics in Post-War Britain* (Oxford: Blackwell).

Leach, R. (1998) 'Local Government Reorganisation RIP? *Political Quarterly,* 69(1).

Leach, R. (2004) 'Democracy and Elections', in S. Lancaster (ed.), *Developments in Politics* (Ormskirk: Causeway Press).

Leach, R. (2008) *The Politics Companion* (Basingstoke: Palgrave Macmillan).

Leach, R. (2009) *Political Ideology in Britain,* 2nd edn (Basingstoke: Palgrave Macmillan).

Leach, R. and Percy-Smith, J. (2001) *Local Governance in Britain* (Basingstoke: Palgrave Macmillan).

Leach, S. (ed.) (1998) *Local Government Reorganisation* (London: Frank Cass).

Leftwich, A. (ed.) (2004*) What is Politics?* (Oxford: Polity).

Lilleker, D., Negrine, R. and Stanyer, J. (2003) 'Media Malaise: Britain's Political Communication Problems', *Politics Review*, 12(3).

Lindblom, C. (1959) 'The Science of Muddling Through', *Public Administration Review,* 19.

Lloyd, J. (2004) *What the Media are Doing to Our Democracy* (London: Constable).

Loughlin, M. and Scott, C. (1997) 'The Regulatory State', in P. Dunleavy, A. Gamble, I. Holliday and G. Peele (eds), *Developments in British Politics 5* (London: Macmillan).

Loveland, I. (1997) 'The War Against the Judges', *Political Quarterly,* April–June.

Lovelock, J. (1979) *Gaia: A New Look at Life on Earth* (Oxford: Oxford University Press).

Lovelock, J. (2007) *The Revenge of Gaia* (Harmondsworth: Penguin).

Lovenduski, J. (1997) 'Gender Politics: A Breakthrough for Women?', *Parliamentary Affairs,* 50(4), October.

Lovenduski, J. and Randall, V. (1993) *Contemporary Feminist Politics* (Oxford: Oxford University Press).

Lowe, R. (1993) *The Welfare State in Britain since 1945* (London: Macmillan).

Lucas, J.R. (1985) *The Principles of Politics* (Oxford: Oxford University Press).

Ludlam, S. (1996) 'The Spectre Haunting Conservatism: Europe and Backbench Rebellion', in S. Ludlam and M.J. Smith (eds), *Contemporary British Conservatism* (London: Macmillan).

Ludlam, S. and Smith, M.J. (eds) (1996) *Contemporary British Conservatism* (London: Macmillan).

Ludlam, S. and Smith, M. (eds) (2001) *New Labour in Government* (Basingstoke: Palgrave Macmillan).

Ludlam, S. and Smith, M. (eds) (2004) *Governing as New Labour* (Basingstoke: Palgrave Macmillan).

Lukes, S. (1974) *Power: A Radical View* (London: Macmillan).

Lupton, C. and Russell, D. (1990) 'Equal Opportunities in a Cold Climate', in S. Savage and L. Robins (eds), *Public Policy under Thatcher* (London: Macmillan).

Lustgarten, L. and Leigh, I. (1994) *National Security and Parliamentary Democracy* (Oxford: Clarendon).

Lynch, P. (1996) 'Labour, Devolution and the West Lothian Question', *Talking Politics,* 9 (1), autumn.

Lynch, P. (2002) 'Goodbye Ballot Box, Hello Post Box', *Talking Politics,* 15(1).

McAllister, I. (1997) 'Regional Voting', *Parliamentary Affairs,* 50(4), October.

Mac an Ghaill, M. (1999) *Contemporary Racisms and Ethnicities* (Buckingham: Open University Press).

McCartney, M. (2005) 'Mayor Livingstone: An Assessment', *Talking Politics,* 18 (1).

McCormick, J. (1991) *British Politics and the Environment* (London: Earthscan Publications).

McCormick, J. (2008) *Understanding the European Union: A Concise introduction,* 4th edn (Basingstoke: Palgrave Macmillan).

McCulloch, A. (1988) 'Politics and the Environment', *Talking Politics,* 1(1), autumn.

McDowell, L. Sarre, P. and Hamnett, C. (eds) (1989) *Divided Nation: Social and Cultural Change in Britain* (London: Hodder & Stoughton).

McGrattan, C. (2010) *Northern Ireland 1968-2008: The Politics of Retrenchment* (Basingstoke: Palgrave Macmillan).

McGrew, A. and Wilson, M. (eds) (1982) *Decision-Making: Approaches and Analysis* (Manchester: Manchester University Press).

McIlroy, J. (1989) 'The Politics of Racism', in B. Jones (ed.), *Political Issues in Britain Today* (Manchester: Manchester University Press).

Mackintosh J. (1962) *The British Cabinet* (London: Stevens).

McKee, V. (1996) 'Factions and Tendencies in the Conservative Party since 1945', *Politics Review,* 5(4), April.

McKenzie, R.T. (1955) *British Political Parties* (London: Heineman).

McLean, I. and McMillan, A. (eds) (2003) *The Concise Oxford Dictionary of Politics* (Oxford: Oxford University Press).

McLellan, D. (1980) *The Political Thought of Karl Marx* (London: Macmillan).

McLellan, D. (1995) *Ideology,* 2nd edn (Buckingham: Open University Press).

McNair, B. (2003) *An Introduction to Political Communication* (London: Routledge).

Macpherson, C.B. (1977) *The Life and Times of Liberal Democracy* (Oxford: Oxford University Press).

Macpherson, Sir W. (1999) *The Stephen Lawrence Inquiry* (Cm 4262) (London: The Stationery Office).

McQuail, D. (1987) *Mass Communications Theory* (Beverly Hills: Sage).

Madgwick, P. (1991) *British Government: The Central Executive Territory* (London: Philip Allan).

Madgwick, P. and Rawkins, P. (1982) 'The Welsh Language in the Policy Process', in Madgwick. P. and Rose, R (eds), *The Territorial Dimension in United Kingdom Politics* (London: Macmillan).

Madgwick, P. and Woodhouse, D. (1995) *The Law and Politics of the Constitution* (Hemel Hempstead: Harvester Wheatsheaf).

Magee, E. and Lynch, P. (2003) 'The Changing British Constitution', *Politics Review* 13(2).

Mair, P. (1994) 'Party Organizations: From Civil Society to State', in Katz and Mair (eds), *How Parties Organize: Change and Adaptation in Party Organizations in Western Democracies* (London: Sage).

Major, J. (1999) *The Autobiography* (London: HarperCollins).

Mandelson, P. (2010) *The Third Man: Life at the Heart of New Labour* (London: HarperCollins).

Marr, A. (1992) *The Battle for Scotland* (Harmondsworth: Penguin).

Marr, A. (1996) *Ruling Britannia: The Failure and Future of British Democracy* (Harmondsworth: Penguin).

Marr, A. (2007) *A History of Modern Britain* (Basingstoke: Palgrave Macmillan).

Marsh, D. (1995) 'The Convergence between Theories of the State', in D. Marsh and G. Stoker (eds), *Theory and Methods in Political Science* (London: Macmillan).

Marsh, D. and Rhodes, R.A.W. (eds) (1992) *Policy Networks in British Government* (Oxford: Oxford University Press).

Marsh, D. and Stoker, G.(eds) (1995) *Theory and Methods in Political Science* (London: Macmillan).

Marshall, G. (ed.) (1989) *Ministerial Responsibility* (Oxford: Oxford University Press).

Marshall, P. and Laws, D. (eds) (2004) *The Orange Book: Reclaiming Liberalism* (London: Profile Books).

Marshall, T.H. (1950) *Citizenship and Social Class and Other Essays* (Cambridge: Cambridge University Press).

Mason, P. (2009) *Meltdown: The End of the Age of Greed* (London: Verso).

Maynard, G. (1988) *The Economy under Mrs Thatcher* (Oxford: Blackwell).

Mazey, S. and Richardson, J.J. (eds) (1993) *Lobbying in the European Community* (Oxford: Oxford University Press).

Meadows, D.H., Meadows, D.L., Randers, D. L. and Behrens III, W. (1972, Pan edition 1974) *The Limits to Growth* (London: Pan).

Michels, R. ([1915] 1965) *Political Parties* (New York: The Free Press).

Milbrath, L. (1965) *Political Participation: How and Why People Get Involved in Politics* (Chicago: Rand McNally).

Miles, R. (1989) *Racism* (London: Routledge).

Miles, R. (1993) *Racism after Race Relations* (London: Routledge).

Miliband, R. (1972) *Parliamentary Socialism*, 2nd edn (London: Merlin Press).

Miliband, R. (1973) *The State in Capitalist Society* (London: Quartet).

Miliband, R. (1984) *Capitalist Democracy in Britain* (Oxford: Oxford University Press).

Miliband, R. (1994) *Socialism for a Sceptical Age* (Cambridge: Polity).

Miliband, D. (ed.) (1994) *Reinventing the Left* (Cambridge: Polity).

Mill, J.S. (1859, ed. Acton, H.B. 1972) *On Liberty* (London: Dent).

Mill, J.S. (1861, ed. Acton, H.B. 1972) *Considerations on Representative Government* (London: Dent).

Mill, J.S. (1869, ed. Okin, S. 1988) *The Subjection of Women* (Indianapolis: Hackett Publishing Company).

Miller, C. (2000) *Politicos Guide to Political Lobbying* (London: Politicos Publishing).

Miller, D. (1991) *The Blackwell Encyclopaedia of Political Thought* (Oxford: Blackwell)

Miller, W. et al. (1990) *How Voters Change* (Oxford: Clarendon).

Millett, K. (1977) *Sexual Politics* (London; Virago).

Mills, C. Wright (1956) *The Power Elite* (New York: Oxford University Press).

Minkin, L. (1992) *The Contentious Alliance: Trade Unions and the Labour Party* (Edinburgh: Edinburgh University Press).

Minogue, K. (1995) *Politics: A Very Short Introduction* (Oxford: Oxford University Press).

Mohapatra, U. (1999) *With Love, From Britain. A Mother Writes to her Children: Observations on Changing Overseas Indian Culture* (Mumbai: Bhavans Book University).

Moran, M. (2000) 'From command state to regulatory state', *Public Policy and Administration*, 15(4).

Moran, M. (2001) 'Not steering but drowning: policy catastrophes and the regulatory state', *Political Quarterly* 72 (4).

Moran, M. (2003) *The British Regulatory State: High Modernism and Hyper-innovation* (Oxford: Oxford University Press)

Moran, M. (2005) *Politics and Governance in the UK* (Basingstoke: Palgrave Macmillan).

Morgan, K. (1990) *The People's Peace: British History, 1945–1989* (Oxford: Oxford University Press).

Morgan, K. and Owen, K. (2001) *Britain Since 1945* (Oxford: Oxford University Press).

Morgenthau, H.J. ([1948] 1978) *Politics Among Nations: The Struggle for Power and Peace,* 5th edn (New York: Kopf).

Morozov, E. (2011) *The Net Delusion: How Not to Liberate the World* (London: Allen Lane).

Mount, F. (1992) *The British Constitution Now* (London: Heinemann).

Mowlam, M. (2002) *Momentum: The Struggle for Peace, Politics and People* (London: Hodder & Stoughton).

Mudde, C. (2007) *The Populist Radical Right in Europe* (Cambridge: Cambridge University Press).

Mulhall, S. and Swift, A. (1996) *Liberals and Communitarians* (Oxford: Blackwell).

Mullin, C. (2009) *A View from the Foothills* (London: Profile Books).

Nairn, T. (1981) *The Break-up of Britain* (London: NLB and Verso).

Nairn, T. (2000) *After Britain* (London: Granta Books).

Nairn, T. (2001) 'Post Ukania', *New Left Review,* Jan–Feb.

Neunreither, K. (1993) 'Subsidiarity as a Guiding Principle for European Community', *Government and Opposition,* 28(2).

Newman, J. (2001) *Modernising Governance: New Labour, Policy and Society* (London: Sage).

Newton, K. (1976) *Second City Politics* (Oxford: Oxford University Press).

Niskanen, W.A. (1971) *Bureaucracy and Representative Government* (Chicago: Aldine-Atherton).

Niskanen, W.A. (1973) *Bureaucracy: Servant or Master?* (London: Institute of Economic Affairs).

Norris, P. (1991) 'Gender Differences in Political Participation in Britain: Traditional, Radical and Revisionist Models', *Government and Opposition,* 26(1).

Norris, P. (1997) 'Anatomy of a Landslide', *Parliamentary Affairs,* 50(4), October.

Norris, P. (ed.) (2001) *Britain Votes, 2001* (Oxford: Oxford University Press).

Norris, P. and Lovenduski, J. (1995) *Political Recruitment: Gender, Race and Class in the British Parliament* (Cambridge: Cambridge University Press).

Norton, P. (1990) 'Public Legislation', in M. Rush (ed.), *Parliament and Pressure Politics* (Oxford: Oxford University Press).

Norton, P. (1997) 'The United Kingdom: Restoring Confidence?', *Parliamentary Affairs,* 50(3), July.

Norton, P. (2003) 'Governing alone', *Parliamentary Affairs,* 56(4).

Norton, P. (2004) 'The Power of Parliament', *Politics Review,* 14(2).

Norton, P. (2005) *Parliament in British Politics* (Basingstoke: Palgrave Macmillan).

Nugent, N. (2010) *The Government and Politics of the European Union,* 7th edn (Basingstoke: Palgrave Macmillan).

Nugent, N. (ed.) (2004) *European Union Enlargement* (Basingstoke: Palgrave Macmillan).

Oakeshott, M. (1962) *Rationalism in Politics and other essays* (London: Methuen).

O'Gorman, F. (1986) *British Conservatism* (London: Longman).

Oliver, D. (1993) 'Citizenship in the 1990s', *Politics Review,* 3(1), September.

O'Neill, M. (ed.) (2004) *Devolution and British Politics* (Harlow: Pearson Longman).

Oppenheim, C. (1990) *Poverty: The Facts* (London: CPAG).

O'Riordan, T. (1976) *Environmentalism* (London: Pion).

Orwell, G. and Angus, I. (1968) *The Collected Essays, Journalism and Letters of George Orwell, vol. II* (London: Secker & Warburg).

Outhwaite, D. (2004) 'How Should Parties be Funded?' *Politics Review,* 14(2).

Osborne, D. and Gaebler, T. (1992) *Reinventing Government* (Reading, MA: Addison-Wesley).

Panebianco, A. (1988) *Political Parties: Organization and Power* (Cambridge: Cambridge University Press).

Parekh, B. (2000a) *The Future of Multi-Ethnic Britain: Report of the Commission on Multi-Ethnic Britain* (London: Profile Books in association with Runnymede Trust).

Parekh, B. (2000b) *Rethinking Multiculturalism: Cultural Diversity and Political Theory* (Basingstoke: Palgrave Macmillan).

Parry, G. and Moyser, G. (1990) 'A Map of Political Participation in Britain', *Government and Opposition,* 25(2).

Parry, G., Moyser, G. and Day, N. (1992) *Political Participation and Democracy in Britain* (Cambridge: Cambridge University Press).

Parsons, W. (1995) *Public Policy: Introduction to the Theory and Practice of Policy Analysis* (Aldershot: Edward Elgar).

Pateman, C. (1970) *Participation and Democratic Theory* (Cambridge: Cambridge University Press).

Paxman, J. (1998) *The English* (London: Michael Joseph).

Payne, G. (ed.) (2000) *Social Divisions* (Basingstoke: Palgrave Macmillan).

Peston, R. (2005) *Brown's Britain: How Gordon Brown Runs the Show* (London: Short).

Peston, R. (2008) *Who Runs Britain… and Who's to Blame for the Economic Mess We're In?* (London: Hodder & Stoughton).

Peterson, J. (1997) 'Britain, Europe and the World', in P. Dunleavy, A. Gamble, I. Holliday and G. Peele (eds), *Developments in British Politics 5* (London: Macmillan).

Pierre, J. and Peters, B.G. (2000) *Politics, Governance and the State* (Basingstoke: Palgrave Macmillan).

Pimlott, B. (1992) *Harold Wilson* (London: HarperCollins).

Pimlott, B. (1994) 'The Myth of Consensus', in B. Pimlott, *Frustrate Their Knavish Tricks* (London: HarperCollins).

Pinder, J. (2001) *The European Union* (Oxford: Oxford University Press).

Pliatzky, L. (1980) *Report on Non-Departmental Bodies,* Cmnd 7797 (London: HMSO).

Pliatzky, L. (1982) *Getting and Spending* (Oxford: Blackwell).

Plummer, J. (1994) *The Governance Gap: Quangos and Accountability* (London: Demos/Joseph Rowntree Foundation).

Porritt, J. and Winner, D. (1988) *The Coming of the Greens* (London: Fontana).

Porter, B. (2009) 'Other People's Mail', *London Review of Books,* 31(22).

Prabakar, R. (2004) 'New Labour and Education', *Politics Review,* 14(1).

Price, L. (2010) *Where Power Lies: Prime Ministers v The Media* (London: Simon & Schuster).

Pugh, M. (1994) *State and Society: British Political and Social History 1870–1992* (London: Edward Arnold).

Pulzer, P. (1967) *Representation and Elections in Britain* (London: Allen & Unwin).

Putnam, R. (1995) 'Bowling Alone: America's Declining Social Capital', *Journal of Democracy,* 6: 75–8.

Putnam, R. (2000) *Bowling Alone: the Collapse and Revival of American Community* (New York: Simon & Schuster).

Pyper, R. (1994) 'Individual Ministerial Responsibility: Dissecting the Doctrine', *Politics Review,* 4(1), September.

Pyper, R. (1995) *The British Civil Service* (London: Harvester Wheatsheaf).

Pyper, R. and Robins, L. (1995) (eds) *Governing the UK in the 1990s* (London: Macmillan).

Quinton, A, (1978) *The Politics of Imperfection* (London: Faber & Faber).

Raban, J. (2010) 'Crankish', *London Review of Books,* 32(8), 22 April.

Ramsden, J. (ed.) (2005) *The Oxford Companion to Twentieth Century Politics* (Oxford: Oxford University Press).

Randall, V. (1987) *Women and Politics,* 2nd edn (London: Macmillan).

Rathbone, M. (2001) 'The Freedom of Information Act', *Talking Politics,* 13(3).

Rathbone, M. (2002) 'Labour and the Liberal Democrats', *Talking Politic,* 14(3).

Rathbone, M. (2005a) 'The November 2004 Referendum in the North East', *Talking Politics,*17(2).

Rathbone, M. (2005b) 'The Future of the Liberal Democrats', *Talking Politics,* 18(1).

Rawnsley, A. (2001) *Servants of the People: The Inside Story of New Labour* (Harmondsworth: Penguin).

Rawnsely, A. (2010) *The End of the Party* (Harmondsworth: Penguin).

Rentoul, J. (2001) *Tony Blair: Prime Minister* (London: Little, Brown).

Rex, J. (1986) *Race and Ethnicity* (Buckingham: Open University Press).

Reynolds, D. (1991) *Britannia Overruled: British Policy and World Power in the Twentieth Century* (London: Longman).

Rhodes, R.A.W. (1981) *Control and Power in Central-Local Government Relations* (Farnborough: Gower).

Rhodes, R.A.W. (1988) *Beyond Westminster and Whitehall: The Sub-Central Governments of Britain* (London: Allen & Unwin).

Rhodes, R.A.W. (1997) *Understanding Governance* (Buckingham: Open University Press).

Rhodes, R.A.W. (ed.) (2000) *Transforming British Government Volume 1: Changing Institutions* (London: Macmillan).

Rhodes, R.A.W. and Dunleavy, P. (eds) (1995) *Prime Minister, Cabinet and the Core Executive* (London: Macmillan).

Richard, Lord (2004) *Report of the Richard Commission* (Cardiff: National Assembly for Wales).

Richards, D. and Smith, M.J. (2002) *Governance and Public Policy in the United Kingdom* (Oxford: Oxford University Press).

Richards, D. and Smith, M.J. (2004) 'Interpreting the World of Political Elites', *Public Administration*, 82(4).

Richards, S. (2010) *Whatever it Takes: The Real Story of Gordon Brown and New Labour* (London: Fourth Estate).

Richardson, J.J. (ed.) (1993) *Pressure Groups* (Oxford: Oxford University Press).

Richardson, J.J. and Jordan, G. (1979) *Governing Under Pressure* (Oxford: Martin Robertson).

Ridley, F.F. and Rush, M. (eds) (1995) *British Government and Politics since 1945* (Oxford: Oxford University Press).

Ridley, F.F. and Wilson, D. (1995) *The Quango Debate* (Oxford: Oxford University Press).

Ridsdill-Smith, C. (2003) 'Protest and the Environment', *Politics Review*, 12(3).

Roberts, H. (2004) 'The Last Lord Chancellor', *Politics Review*, 13(4).

Robertson, D. (1993) *Dictionary of Politics* (Harmondsworth: Penguin).

Robinson, M. (1992) *The Greening of British Party Politics* (Manchester: Manchester University Press).

Robson, W. (1966) *Local Government in Crisis* (London: Allen & Unwin).

Rose, R. (2001) *The Prime Minister in a Shrinking World*, (London: Polity).

Runciman, D. (2010) 'Is This The End of the UK?', *London Review of Books*, 32(10), 27 May.

Rush, M. (ed.) (1990) *Parliament and Pressure Politics* (Oxford: Clarendon).

Ryan, M. (2004) 'A Supreme Court for the United Kingdom?', *Talking Politics*, 17(1).

Saggar, S. (1992) *Race and Politics in Britain* (London: Harvester Wheatsheaf).

Saggar, S. (1997) 'Racial Politics', *Parliamentary Affairs*, 50 (4), October.

Sampson, A. (2005) *Who Runs This Place?* (London: John Murray).

Sanders, D. (1990) *Losing an Empire, Finding a Role* (London: Macmillan).

Sanders, D. (1995) '"It's the Economy, Stupid": The Economy and Support for the Conservative Party, 1979–1994', *Talking Politics*, 7(3), spring.

Sanderson, M. (1994) 'Education and Social Mobility', in P. Johnson (ed.) *Twentieth Century Britain* (London: Longman).

Saunders, P. (1980) *Urban Politics: A Sociological Interpretation* (Harmondsworth: Penguin).

Savage, S. and Robins, L. (eds) (1990) *Public Policy under Thatcher* (London: Macmillan).

Savage, S. and Atkinson, R. (eds) (2001) *Public Policy under Blair* (Basingstoke: Palgrave Macmillan).

Saville, J. (1988) *The Labour Movement in Britain* (London: Faber & Faber).

Scarman, Lord (1981) *The Brixton Disorders 10–12 April, 1981: Special Report* (London: HMSO).

Schumacher, E.F. (1973) *Small is Beautiful* (London: Sphere Books).

Schumpeter, J. (1943) *Capitalism, Socialism and Democracy*, (London: Allen & Unwin).

Scruton, R. (2007) *Dictionary of Political Thought*, 3rd edn (Basingstoke: Palgrave Macmillan).

Sedgemore, B. (1980) *The Secret Constitution* (London: Hodder & Stoughton).

Sedley, S. (2009) 'On the Move', *London Review of Books*, 13(19), 8 October.

Seldon, A. (1994) 'Policy Making and Cabinet', in D. Kavanagh and A. Seldon (eds), *The Major Effect* (London: Macmillan).

Seldon, A. (ed.) (1996) *How Tory Governments Fall* (London: HarperCollins).

Seldon, A. (ed.) (2001) *The Blair Effect* (London: Little, Brown).

Seldon. A. (2004) *Blair* (London: The Free Press).

Seldon, A. and Kavanagh, D. (2005) *The Blair Effect 2001–5* (Cambridge: Cambridge University Press).

Self, P. (1993) *Governing by the Market* (London: Macmillan).

Seliger, M. (1976) *Ideology and Politics* (London: Allen & Unwin).

Semetko, H.A., Scammell, M. and Goddard, P. (1997) 'Television', *Parliamentary Affairs*, 50(4), October.

Seyd, P. and Whiteley, P. (2002) *New Labour's Grass Roots: The Transformation of the Labour Party Membership* (Basingstoke: Palgrave Macmillan).

Seymour-Ure, C. (1974) *The Political Impact of the Mass Media* (London: Constable).

Seymour-Ure, C. (1995) 'Prime Minister and the Public: Managing Media Relations', in D. Shell and R. Hodder-Williams (eds), *Churchill to Major: The British Prime Ministership since 1945* (London: Hurst).

Seymour-Ure, C. (1997) 'Editorial Opinion in the National Press', *Parliamentary Affairs*, 50(4), October.

Shaw, E. (1996) *The Labour Party since 1945* (Oxford: Blackwell).

Simon, H. (1947) Administrative Behaviour (Glencoe, Ill: Free Press).

Sked, A. and Cook, C. (1979) *Post-War Britain: A Political History* (Harmondsworth: Penguin).

Skelcher, C. (1998) *The Appointed State* (Buckingham: Open University Press).

Skellington, R. (1996) *'Race' in Britain Today* (London: Sage).

Skidelsky, R. (1967) *Politicians and the Slump* (Harmondsworth: Penguin).

Skidelsky, R. (2010) *Keynes: The Return of the Master* (Harmondsworth: Penguin).

Skocpol, T. (1996) 'Unravelling From Above'. *The American Prospect,* March/April.

Smith, A.D. (1979) *Nationalism in the Twentieth Century* (Oxford: Martin Robertson).

Smith, A.D. (1991) *National Identity* (Harmondsworth: Penguin).

Smith, D. (1994) *North and South: Britain's Economic, Social and Political Divide,* 2nd edn (Harmondsworth: Penguin).

Smith, M.J. (1995*) Pressure Politics* (Manchester: Baseline Books).

Smith, M.J. (1999) *The Core Executive in Britain* (London: Macmillan).

Smith, M.J. and Ludlam, S. (eds) (1996) *Contemporary British Conservatism* (London: Macmillan).

Smith, M.J., Marsh, D. and Richards, D. (1995) 'Central Government Departments and the Policy Process', in R.A.W. Rhodes and P. Dunleavy (eds), *Prime Minister, Cabinet and Core Executive* (London: Macmillan).

Snowdon, P. (2010) *Back from the Brink: The Inside Story of the Tory Resurrection* (London: Harper Press).

Snyder, R.C., Bruck, H.W. and Sapin, B. (1960) 'Decision-Making as an Approach to the Study of International Politics', in S. Hoffman (ed.), *Contemporary Theory in International Relations (*Englewood Cliffs, NJ: Prentice-Hall).

Solomos, J. (2003) *Race and Racism in Britain*, 3rd edn (Basingstoke: Palgrave Macmillan)

Solomos, J. and Back, L. (1996) *Racism and Society* (London: Macmillan).

Souza, C. (1998) *So You Want to be a Lobbyist?* (London: Politicos Publishing).

Stanworth, P. and Giddens, A. (1974) *Elites and Power in British Society* (Cambridge: Cambridge University Press).

Stanyer, J. (2000) 'A Loss of Political Appetite' *Parliamentary Affairs*, 55.

Steed, M. (1986) 'The Core-Periphery Dimension of British Politics', *Political Geography Quarterly,* supplement to 5(4), October.

Stoker, G. (1991) *The Politics of Local Government* (London: Macmillan).

Stoker, G. (2003) *Transforming Local Governance* (Basingstoke: Palgrave Macmillan).

Stoker, G. (2006) *Why Politics Matters: Making Democracy Work* (Basingstoke: Palgrave Macmillan)

Stoker, G. and Wilson, D. (eds) (2004) *British Local Government into the 21st Century* (Basingstoke: Palgrave Macmillan).

Stokes, J. and Reading, A. (eds) (1999) *The Media in Britain: Current Debates and Developments* (London: Macmillan).

Stokes, W. (2005) *Women in Contemporary Politics* (Cambridge: Polity).

Street, J. (2001) *Mass Media, Politics and Democracy* (Basingstoke: Palgrave Macmillan).

Sutherland, K. (ed.) (2000) *The Rape of the Constitution* (Thorverton: Academic Imprint).

Taylor, A. (2000) 'Hollowing out or Filling in? Task Forces and the Management of Cross-cutting Issues in British Government', *British Journal of Politics and International Relations,* 2(1).

Thain, C. (2009) 'A Very Peculiar British Crisis? Institutions, Ideas and Policy Responses to the Credit Crunch', *British Politics,* 4(4): 434–49.

Theakston, K. (1995a) 'Ministers and Civil Servants', in R. Pyper and L. Robins (eds), *Governing the UK in the 1990s* (London: Macmillan).

Theakston, K. (1995b) *The Civil Service since 1945 (*Oxford: Blackwell).

Theakston, K. (1999) *Leadership in Whitehall* (London: Macmillan).

Thomas, G.P. (1992), *Government and the Economy Today* (Manchester University Press).

Thompson, E. P. (1963) *The Making of the English Working Class* (London: Gollancz).

Thucydides ([5th century BCE] tr.Warner, R., 1972) *History of the Peloponnesian War* (Harmondsworth: Penguin).

Tocqueville, A. de ([1835, 1840] 2003) *Democracy in America* (Harmondsworth: Penguin Books).

Tomkins, A. (1997) 'Intelligence and Government', *Parliamentary Affairs*, 50(1), January.

Tonge, J. (2004) *The New Northern Ireland Politics* (Basingstoke: Palgrave Macmillan).

Tonge, J. and Geddes, A. (1997) 'Labour's Landslide? The British General Election of 1997', *ECPRN News*, 8(3).

Topf, R. (1989) 'Political Change and Political Culture in Britain, 1959–1987', in J.R. Giddens (ed.), *Contemporary Political Culture* (London: Sage Publications).

Townsend, P., Davidson, N. and Whitehead, M. (1990) *The Health Divide* (Harmondsworth: Penguin).

Toynbee, P. and Walker, D, (2005) *Better or Worse? Has Labour Delivered?* (London: Bloomsbury).

Toynbee, P. and Walker, D. (2010) *The Verdict: Did Labour Change Britain?* (Cambridge: Granta).

Travers, T. (2003) *The Politics of London* (Basingstoke: Palgrave Macmillan).

Trenaman, J. and McQuail, D. (1961) *Television and the Political Image* (London: Methuen).

Trench, A. (ed.) (2009) *The State of the Nations 2008* (Thorverton: Imprint Academic).

Tunstall, J. and Maching, D. (1999) *The Anglo-American Media Connection* (Oxford: Oxford University Press).

Wade, H.W.R. (1988) *Administrative Law,* 6th edn (Oxford: Clarendon).

Wadham, J. and Mountfield, H. (2000) *Human Rights Act, 1998,* 2nd edn (London: Blackstone Press).

Waldegrave, W. (1993) *The Reality of Reform and Accountability in Today's Public Service* (London: Public Finance Foundation).

Wallace, M. and Jenkins, J.C. (1995) 'The New Class, Post-Industrialism and Neo-Corporatism: Three Images of Social Protest in the Western Democracies', in J. Jenkins and B. Klandermans (eds), *The Politics of Social Protest* (London: University College London Press).

Wallas, G. (1908, 3rd edn, 1920) *Human Nature in Politics* (London: Constable).

Waller, R. and Criddle, B. (2002) *The Almanac of British Politics* (London: Routledge).

Walter, N. (1999) *The New Feminism* (London: Virago).

Walsh, K. (1995) *Public Services and Market Mechanisms* (London: Macmillan).

Waltz, K. (1979) *Theory of International Politics* (Reading, MA: Addison-Wesley).

Watts, D. (1997) *Political Communication Today* (Manchester: Manchester University Press).

Watts, D. (2004) 'The Politics of the Environment' in S. Lancaster (ed.), *Developments in Politics* (Ormskirk: Causeway Press).

Webb, P. (2000) *The Modern British Party System* (London: Sage).

Weir, S. (1995) 'Quangos: Questions of Democratic Accountability', in F.F. Ridley and D. Wilson (eds), *The Quango Debate* (Oxford: Oxford University Press).

Weir, S. and Beetham, D. (1999) *Political Power and Democratic Control in Britain: The Democratic Audit of Great Britain* (London: Routledge).

Weir, S. and Hall, W. (eds) (1994) *Ego Trip: Extra Governmental Organisations in the UK and their Accountability* (University of Essex: Human Rights Centre).

Welfare, D. (1992) 'An Anachronism with Relevance: The Revival of the House of Lords in the 1980s and its Defence of Local Government', *Parliamentary Affairs,* April.

Wendt, A (1999) *Social Theory of International Politics* (Cambridge: Cambridge University Press).

Whale, J. (1977) *The Politics of the Media* (London: Fontana).

Whiteley, P. and Winyard, S. (1987) *Pressure for the Poor* (London: Methuen).

Whiteley, P., Seyd, P. and Richardson, J. (1994) *True Blues: The Politics of Conservative Party Membership* (Oxford: Clarendon).

Widdicombe Report (1986) *The Conduct of Local Authority Business: Report of the Committee of Inquiry into the Conduct of Local Authority Business,* Cmnd 9797 (London: HMSO).

Willetts, D. (2010) *The Pinch: How the Baby Boomers Stole Their Children's Future – And How They Can Give It Back* (London: Atlantic).

Wilkinson, R. and Pickett, K. (2010) *The Spirit Level* (Harmondsworth: Penguin Books).

Williams, R. (1976) *Keywords: A Vocabulary of Culture and Society* (London: Fontana).

Williamson, A. (2010) '2010: The Internet Election that wasn't', *Political Insight,* 1(2).

Wilson, D. (1996) 'Quangos in British Politics', *Politics Review,* 6(1), September.

Wilson, D. and Game, C. (2006) *Local Government in the United Kingdom,* 4th edn (Basingstoke: Palgrave Macmillan).

Wilson, G.K. (1991) 'Prospects for the Public Service in Britain: Major to the Rescue?', *International Review of Administrative Sciences,* 57.

Wilson, H. (1976) *The Governance of Britain* (London: Weidenfeld & Nicolson and Michael Joseph).

Wollstonecraft, M. (1792, edn Tauchert 1995) *Vindication of the Rights of Woman,* (London: Dent).

Wood, B. (1992) *The Politics of Health* (Manchester: Politics Association).

Woodhouse, D. (1994) *Ministers and Parliament: Accountability in Theory and Practice* (Oxford: Clarendon).

Woodhouse, D. (1997) 'Judicial/Executive Relations in the 1990s', *Talking Politics,* 10(1), autumn.

Wright, A. (1983) *British Socialism* (London: Longman).

Young, H. (1990) *One of Us,* expanded edition with new epilogue (London: Pan in association with Macmillan).

Young, H. (1998) *This Blessed Plot: Britain and Europe, from Churchill to Blair* (London: Macmillan).

# Index